BEACHAM'S GUIDE
to the
ENDANGERED SPECIES
of NORTH AMERICA

BEACHAM'S GUIDE
to the
ENDANGERED SPECIES
of NORTH AMERICA

Volume 3
Arachnids and Crustaceans,
Insects, Lichens, Fern Allies, True Ferns, Conifers, Dicots

Edited By
Walton Beacham
Frank V. Castronova
Suzanne Sessine

GALE GROUP

Detroit
New York
San Francisco
London
Boston
Woodbridge, CT

Library of Congress Cataloging-in-Publication Data

Beacham's guide to the endangered species of North America / edited by Walton Beacham, Frank V. Castronova, Suzanne Sessine.
    p. cm.
    Includes bibliographical references.
    ISBN 0-7876-5028-5 (set: hardcover)—ISBN 0-7876-5029-3 (vol. 1)—ISBN 0-7876-5030-7 (vol. 2)—ISBN 0-7876-5031-5 (vol. 3)—ISBN 0-7876-5032-3 (vol. 4) —ISBN 0-7876-5033-1 (vol. 5)—ISBN 0-7876-5034-X (vol. 6)
    1. Endangered species—North America. 2. Nature conservation—North America. I. Beacham, Walton, 1943- . II. Castronova, Frank V. (Frank Vincent), 1971- . III. Sessine, Suzanne, 1976- .
QH77.N56 B43 2000
578.68'0973—dc21
                                      00-062297

10 9 8 7 6 5 4 3 2 1
Printed in Canada

Contents

Introduction

Scope

Beacham's Guide to the Endangered Species of North America describes more than 1,200 animals and plants that occur in North America both within and outside the boundaries of the United States of America. These volumes cover species that were identified before April 2000 by the U. S. Fish and Wildlife Service (FWS) as either Endangered or Threatened. This set of books supercedes and updates *The Official World Wildlife Fund Guide to the Endangered Species of North America,* which was published by Beacham Publishing, Inc., in 1990-94.

The species described herein have been identified as Endangered or Threatened by the FWS. Inclusion on the federal list prohibits any governmental agency from initiating or funding activities that might have adverse impacts on an endangered or threatened species (such as activities that cause habitat degradation). Also, the importation and sale of these endangered species or any derived products is restricted within the boundaries of the United States.

How to Use This Set of Books

The species are arranged taxonomically. Volume 1 includes mammals, birds, and reptiles; amphibians, fishes, snails, and mussels and clams are in volume 2; in volume 3 are arachnids and crustaceans, insects, lichens, fern allies, true ferns, and conifers; dicots can be found at the end of volume 3 and in volumes 4, 5, and 6; monocots are in volume 6. Each species account begins with the species' common and scientific names. Most entries will also include one or more full-color images of the species described. Following this, the user will find a **Summary** section, which outlines the key information found within the species account. Within this section is found: the species' status as determined by the FWS; the date listed by the FWS; the family to which the species belongs; and brief descriptions of the following (if applicable or known): physical description, habitat, food, reproduction, threats, and the range of states, countries, or geographical regions in which the species occurs.

The main body of each species account begins with the **Description** section, which provides a general description of the plant's or animal's physical characteristics.

Behavior describes reproductive information, social organization and behavior, and dietary preferences and requirements.

Habitat describes the species' preferred habitat.

Distribution describes where the species can be currently found and where the species may have been found in the past.

Threats describes the natural or human-made events which have led to the decline of the species' population, and potential threats.

Conservation and Recovery describes conservation efforts and the survival outlook for the species.

Contacts lists street addresses, telephone and facsimile numbers, and web addresses for organizations which can be of assistance to the researcher.

In the **References** section are sources that the user can use to gain more information on the species.

In volume 6 the following appendices and indexes are found:

The **Glossary** provides definitions of specialized terms used throughout the text of the book.

The **Organizations** appendix lists agencies that focus on environmental and wildlife issues.

The **Geographic Index** is organized by country, body of water, or other geographical area, and arranges species alphabetically within each geographical division.

The **Master Index** lists the species alphabetically by common name and by scientific name, with references to its nominal counterpart, and also includes variant common and scientific names.

Acknowledgment

Special thanks are due to Dr. Bill Freedman, Professor of Biology at Dalhousie University, Halifax, Nova Scotia, Canada, for his editorial and research efforts related to this project.

Comments and Suggestions are Welcome

The editors invite comments and suggestions from users of *Beacham's Guide to the Endangered Species of North America.* You may contact us by mail at: The Editors, *Beacham's Guide to the Endangered Species of North America,* Gale Group, Inc., 27500 Drake Rd., Farmington Hills, MI 48331-3535; by telephone at (248) 699-4253 or (800) 347-4253; or by facsimile at (248) 699-8065. Our web site is http://www.galegroup.com.

Photo Acknowledgments

These photos are on the covers of all six volumes of *Beacham's Guide to the Endangered Species of North America* (clockwise from upper left): Mitchell's Satyr Butterfly, Larry West, U. S. Fish and Wildlife Service; Cactus Ferruginous Pygmy-owl, George Andrejko; Pitkin Marsh Lily, Robert J. Gustafson; Louisiana Black Bear, Louisiana Department of Wildlife and Fish.

These photos appear on the spines of each volume: volume 1, Tipton Kangaroo Rat, B. "Moose" Peterson/WRP; volume 2, Puerto Rican Crested Toad, David M. Dennis; volume 3, Silvery Blue Butterfly *(Glaucopsyche lygdamus),* George Proctor; volume 4, Stebbins' Morning-glory, Rich York; volume 5, Hoffman's Slender-flowered Gilia, Steve Junak; volume 6, Thread-leaved Brodiaea, B. "Moose" Peterson/WRP.

Arachnids and Crustaceans

Spruce-fir Moss Spider

Microhexura montivaga

Status	Endangered
Listed	February 6, 1995
Family	Dipluridae
Description	Light brown to darker reddish brown mygalomorph spider. Has yellowish brown carpace, long spinnerets. Chelicerae project forward.
Habitat	Damp, well-drained moss and liverwort mats growing on thoroughly shaded rocks or boulders in mature, high-elevation Fraser fir and red spruce forests.
Food	Unknown.
Reproduction	Egg sack may contain seven to nine eggs. Spiderlings emerge in September.
Threats	Rapid deterioration of the forest habitat.
Range	North Carolina, Tennessee

Description

The spruce-fir moss spider, *Microhexura montivaga*, was originally described in 1925 from collections made two years earlier in the mountains of western North Carolina. Only a few specimens were taken, and little was known about the species until its rediscovery approximately 50 years later. *M. montivaga* is one of only two species belonging to the genus *Microhexura*, the northernmost representative of the family Dipluridae. *M. idahoana*, the other species in the genus, occurs only in the Pacific Northwest. Diplurids belong in the primitive suborder Mygalomorphae, which are often popularly referred to as "tarantulas."

The genus *Microhexura* is one of the smallest of the mygalomorph spiders, with adults measuring only 0.10-0.15 in (0.25-0.38 cm). Coloration of the spruce-fir moss spider ranges from light brown to a darker reddish brown, and there are no markings on the abdomen. The carapace is generally yellowish brown. The most reliable field identification characteristics for the spruce-fir moss spider are chelicerae that project forward well beyond the anterior edge of the carapace, a pair of very long posterior spinnerets, and the presence of a second pair of book lungs, which appear as light patches posterior to the genital furrow.

Behavior

There is no record of prey having been found in the webs of the spruce-fir moss spider, and so its food sources are unknown.

The egg sac, thin-walled and nearly transparent, may contain seven to nine eggs, laid in June. The female remains with the egg sac and, if disturbed, will carry the egg sac with her fangs. Spiderlings emerge in September. The means of dispersal of the spiderlings from the parental moss mat is not known. Ballooning, a process by which the spiders use a sheet of silk played out into the wind to carry them into the air, has been suggested as a possible means of long-range dispersal, but this species's high sensitivity to desiccation would likely preclude this dispersal method. The life span of the species is also unknown, although experts in the field have esti-

Joel Harp

mated that it may take three years for the species to reach maturity.

Habitat

The typical habitat of the spruce-fir moss spider is found in damp but well-drained moss and liverwort mats growing on thoroughly shaded rocks or boulders in mature, high-elevation Fraser fir (*Abies fraseri*) and red spruce (*Picea rubens*) forests. The forest stands at the sites where the species has been observed are composed primarily of Fraser fir intermingled with only scattered spruce. The moss mats found to contain the spider have all been found under fir trees. The spider cannot tolerate extremes of moisture; although very sensitive to desiccation, it can also be harmed by large drops of water. This is why the damp moss mats the spider inhabits can be neither too dry nor too wet. The spider constructs its tube-shaped webs in the interface between the moss mat and rock surface, although occasionally the web extends into the inte-

rior of the moss mat. The tubes are thin-walled and typically broad and flattened with short side branches.

Distribution

Status surveys conducted from 1989 through 1992 for the spruce-fir moss spider at its five historic locations and in other seemingly suitable habitat found the spider at only three sites in western North Carolina and one in eastern Tennessee. The historic North Carolina occurrence in Yancy County appears to have been extirpated, and only the population located along the Avery County and Caldwell County line in North Carolina seems relatively stable. The two other North Carolina populations are located in Swain County.

Both of the Swain County populations are extremely small with only one spruce-fir moss spider having been found at each of these two sites in recent years, probably because the forests at these locations are rapidly declining. The Tennessee population is located in Sevier County.

This population was considered relatively healthy at the time of the 1989 survey; however, revisits to this site in 1992 found dwindling spider numbers, apparently in conjunction with a rapid decline of Fraser fir at the site and associated desiccation of moss-mat habitat.

The most recent monitoring of this occurrence in 1994 indicates that it will likely be extirpated within the next several years.

Threats

The primary threat to the survival of the spruce-fir moss spider is the rapid deterioration of its damp, high-elevation forest habitat. This habitat alteration and loss has been primarily brought about by the infestation of an exotic insect, air pollution precipitated out as acid rain, and past land use history. The spider is also threatened by factors that have not yet been fully identified, as well as by its very small population base that increases its vulnerability to stochastic extinction.

The spruce-fir moss spider, very sensitive to lack of moisture, requires situations of high and constant humidity, a microclimate which is regulated and preserved by the forest canopy. The dominant canopy species in the forest stands where the spider lives is the Fraser fir, and the decline and death of Fraser firs begins a cycle inimical to this species. As the canopy dwindles more unfiltered light reaches the forest floor, promoting evaporation in previously shaded damp areas and the eventual desiccation of the moss mats often found there without which this spider cannot survive. Dr. Frederick Coyle, a leading expert on the spruce-fir moss spider, provides some anecdotal commentary on this problem in a 1991 letter sent to Keith Langdon. Dr. Coyle writes that the spider, common at one of the Swain County sites as late as 1983, had become extremely rare only five years later. He states that many of the moss mats at this site had become dry and loose, due largely, in his opinion, to deterioration of the forest canopy at the site.

Fraser fir at all four extant spider occurrences have suffered extensive mortality, believed to be primarily due to infestation by the balsam wooly adelgid (*Adelges piceae*), an alien insect pest believed to have been introduced around 1900 into the United States from Europe. The adelgid was first detected in North Carolina on Mount Mitchell in 1957, although it was likely established at that site as early as 1940, and from Mount Mitchell it spread to Fraser fir communities throughout the southern Appalachians. Most mature Fraser fir are easily killed by the adelgid, with death occurring within two to seven years of the initial infestation.

While the loss of the Fraser fir appears to be the most significant threat to the remaining spruce-fir moss spider populations, the combined effects of several other factors seem to be highly taxing to its forest habitats and have contributed to the decline of the high-elevation spruce-fir forest stands. In 1988 it was estimated that trees 45-85 years of age at the summit of Mount Mitchell, the site in Yancy County where the species appears to be extirpated, showed an average defoliation of 75%-90%, and that all the trees exhibited some form of growth reduction. He hypothesized that atmospheric pollution was a possible factor in the decline. Regional scale air pollution in combination with other stress factors is believed to have played a significant role in the deterioration of the health of high-elevation red spruce in the East. The past land-use history in the southern Appalachians, especially former logging and burning practices, may well have contributed to present spider-site deteriorations. Winter tree injury has also been identified as a possible contributing factor to these declines. The death and thinning of the canopy trees within these stands also cause the remaining trees to be more susceptible to wind and related storm damage, which has become a major concern at the site in Sevier County, Tennessee.

The spruce-fir forest at the Avery County/Caldwell County location has not experienced the degree of decline that has occurred and is still occurring at the other sites known to support or to have supported populations of the spider. This habitat and spider occurrence is, nonetheless, also threatened by the same factors that are believed to have resulted in the decline of the spruce-fir forest and the associated loss of suitable moss-mat habitat at these other locations.

The spruce-fir moss spider is not currently known to be commercially valuable; however, because of its extreme rarity and uniqueness, it is conceivable that it could be sought by collectors. This spider is one of only two members of the genus *Microhexura*, is the only representative of the primitive family Dipluridae in eastern North America, and is one of the smallest of the world's "tarantulas." While collecting or other intentional take is not presently identified as a factor contributing to the decline of this species, the low numbers, slow reproductive rate, and extremely restricted range of the spruce-fir moss spider make it unlikely that the species could withstand even moderate collecting pressure.

It is presently unknown whether disease and predation have played roles in the decline of the spruce-fir moss spider, and further research is much needed in this area. While predation is not thought to be a significant threat to a healthy population of the spruce-fir moss spider, it could limit the recovery of the species or contribute to the local extirpation of populations already depleted by other factors. Possible predators of the spruce-fir moss spider include pseudoscorpions, centipedes, and other spiders.

In summary, the spruce-fir moss spider has been greatly reduced in number throughout its historic range; survives in only four locations, two of which have only one individual each; and has only one occurrence that might be described as currently stable, although this population is also threatened by many of the same factors that are believed to have resulted in the extirpation or decline of the other historically known populations. The four remaining populations are geographically isolated from one another, and three of them are so small as to have very little genetic variability left. All these circumstances make the spruce fir-moss spider endangered.

Conservation and Recovery

The U.S. Fish and Wildlife Service (FWS) believes that a detailed characterization of the spruce-fir moss spider's habitat, better knowledge of threats to this habitat, and additional information concerning its biology will be necessary in order to properly manage and implement protection and recovery measures. These, as well as other research needs and activities necessary to ensure the long-term survival of the species, will be addressed by the FWS in the development and implementation of a recovery plan for the spruce-fir moss spider.

Contacts

U.S. Fish and Wildlife Service
Regional Office, Division of Endangered Species
1875 Century Blvd., Suite 200
Atlanta, Georgia 30345
http://southeast.fws.gov/

U.S. Fish and Wildlife Service
Asheville Field Office
330 Ridgefield Court
Asheville, North Carolina 28806
(704) 665-1195 ext. 225

References

Coyle, F. A. 1985. Observations on the Mating Behavior of the Tiny Mygalomorph Spider, *Microhexura montivaga* Crosby & Bishop (Araneae, Dipluridae). *Bulletin. British Arachnological Society* 6 (8): 328-330.

Eagar, C. 1984. "Review of the Biology and Ecology of the Balsam Woolly Aphid in Southern Appalachian Spruce-fir Forests." In: P. S. White (ed.), *The Southern Appalachian Spruce-fir Ecosystem: Its Biology and Threats.* Research/Resources Management Report SER-71. U.S. Dept. of Interior, National Park Service.

Harp, J. M. 1991. "Status of the Spruce-fir Moss Spider, *Microhexura montivaga* Crosby and Bishop, in the Great Smoky Mountains National Park." Unpubl. report to the National Park Service, U.S. Department of the Interior. 12 pp. plus appendix.

Harp, J. M. 1992. "A Status Survey of the Spruce-fir Moss Spider, *Microhexura montivaga* Crosby and Bishop (Araneae, Dipluridae)." Unpubl. report to the North Carolina Wildlife Resources Commission, Nongame and Endangered Wildlife Program, and the U.S. Fish and Wildlife Service, Asheville, North Carolina. 30 pp.

U.S. Fish and Wildlife Service. February 6, 1995. "Spruce-Fir Moss Spider Determined To Be Endangered." *Federal Register* 60 (24): 6968-6974.

Tooth Cave Spider

Neoleptoneta myopica

Status	Endangered
Listed	September 16, 1988
Family	Leptonetidae (Cave spider)
Description	Tiny, pale-colored arachnid with long legs and reduced eyes.
Habitat	Cave dwelling.
Food	Insects.
Reproduction	Not widely studied.
Threats	Habitat degradation from residential development.
Range	Texas

Tooth Cave Spider, photograph. U. S. Fish and Wildlife Service. Reproduced by permission.

Description

The Tooth Cave spider, *Neoleptoneta myopica*, has a very small, pale-colored body up to 0.1 in (0.5 cm) in length with relatively long legs. Although it lives in near-total darkness, reduced eyes are present. The spider's body consists of two main parts, the prosoma and the abdomen, which are connected by a narrow stalk, the pedicel. The prosoma provide locomotion and food intake while the abdomen provides digestion, circulation, respiration, excretion, reproduction, and silk production. Attached to the carapace is one pair of biting chelicerae and one pair of leg-like pedipalps situated in front of four pairs of walking legs. In mature males the pedipalps are modified into copulatory organs.

Behavior

This arachnid is highly sedentary, spinning webs from the ceiling and walls of Tooth Cave. It feeds on insects that inhabit the cave or happen to enter it. The victims are subdued by the spider's venom, then crushed with the chelicerae while being bathed with quantities of digestive fluid from the maxillary glands. The softer parts of the prey are broken down and predigested in a liquid state, and this liquid is sucked into the stomach. As the prey is rolled and chewed, it becomes smaller and smaller until only a small ball of indigestible material remains.

The spider's reproductive biology has not been well studied. It is nonmigratory, remaining sedentary over its lifetime.

Habitat

The Tooth Cave spider occurs in a single population in one small, dry cave. It depends on the infiltration of groundwater, which makes it vulnerable to chemicals that may seep into the groundwater supply.

Distribution

The Tooth Cave spider is endemic to Tooth Cave, which is located northwest of Four Corners in Travis County near the city of Austin, Texas.

The number of Tooth Cave spiders is unknown. While only a few specimens have ever been collected, this may reflect the limited size of the habitat rather than a declining population. Tooth Cave is the sole known habitat for this arachnid.

Threats

The Tooth Cave spider depends on some infiltration of groundwater, and a disruption of flow due to development, such as construction for a proposed pipeline, would pose an immediate threat. Likewise, the seepage of urban runoff into the ground is likely to degrade water quality.

Conservation and Recovery

At time of the Karst Invertebrates Recovery Plan publication, the Tooth Cave spider had a U.S. Fish and Wildlife Service (FWS) recovery priority of 2C, indicating a species with a high degree of threats, high potential for recovery, and in conflict with construction or development projects of other forms of economic activity.

Contact

U.S. Fish and Wildlife Service
Regional Office, Division of Endangered Species
P.O. Box 1306
Albuquerque, New Mexico 87103-1306
Telephone: (505) 248-6911
Fax: (505) 248-6915
http://southwest.fws.gov/

References

Gretsch, W. J. 1974. "The Spider Family Leptonetidae in North America." *The Journal of Arachnology* 1: 145-203.

Reddell, J. R. 1984. "Report on the Caves and Cave Fauna of the Parke, Travis County, Texas." Unpublished Report to the Texas System of Natural Laboratories.

U. S . Fish and Wildlife Service. 16 September 1988. "Determination of Five Texas Cave Invertebrates to Be Endangered Species." *Federal Register* 53 (180): 36029-36033.

U. S. Fish and Wildlife Service. 1994. "Recovery Plan for Endangered Karst Invertebrates in Travis and William Counties, Texas." U.S. Fish and Wildlife Service, Albuquerque.

Kauai Cave Wolf Spider

Adelocosa anops

Status	Endangered
Listed	January 14, 2000
Family	Lycosidae
Description	Cave-dwelling blind spider; has light brown or orange cephalothorax, no eyes, long, translucent, orange bristly legs, and a dull white abdomen.
Habitat	Requires a permanent moisture source, constant 100% relative humidity, and stagnant air.
Food	Invertebrates.
Reproduction	Clutch of 15-30 eggs.
Threats	Withdrawal and pollution of groundwater, alterations on the surface for tourist facilities and urbanization, elimination of plant roots by destruction of the surface vegetation, human visitors.
Range	Hawaii

Description

Known in Hawaii as *pe'e pe'e maka'ole*, this cave-dwelling blind spider has a body length of 0.39-0.78 in (10-20 mm). The cephalothorax (fused head and thorax) is light brown or orange, with no eyes and long, translucent, orange bristly legs; the abdomen is dull white. All other members of this family have large, well-developed eyes, thus their common name.

Behavior

The no-eyed big-eyed wolf spider does not spin webs but actively stalks and overwhelms other invertebrates.

The species has a low reproductive capacity, laying only 15-30 eggs per clutch. The adult lifespan is at least six months.

Habitat

In its extremely limited cave ecosystem, the spider requires a permanent moisture source, constant 100% relative humidity, and stagnant air; temperatures between 75-80°F (24-27°C) are its preferred conditions.

Distribution

The no-eyed big-eyed wolf spider is known only from the deep zone of Koloa Cave, from where the type specimen was described, and from smaller populations in nearby segments of the same cave some 1.5 mi (2.4 km) away on the southeast coast of Kauai Island, in the Hawaiian group. These caves are lava tubes resulting from a single eruption of the Koloa volcanic series. This spider inhabits small cavities impenetrable to humans, as well as the caves themselves, but its distribution is limited to a single series of lava flows.

Threats

The greatest threats to this species are the withdrawal and pollution of groundwater and alterations on the surface for tourist facilities and urbanization. Water is already scarce, and natural water sources have been disrupted; some moisture in the caves now comes from surface irrigation of sugar cane. The spider and other cave invertebrates are extremely sensitive to desiccation, and a failure in water supply could be disastrous. Runoff from developments and urban areas can pollute the groundwater with pesticides and toxic chemicals. Agriculture has already ruined the largest lava cave in the area: it became covered with waste residue from sugar cane production. The introduction and spread of invertebrate disease organisms for biological control of soil pests may decimate the endemic cave fauna. The elimination of plant roots by destruction of the surface vegetation removes an important food source from the habitat. Human visitors may affect cave habitats by trampling, littering, smoking, vandalizing, destroying tree roots, or altering the microclimate. Until recently, the two Koloa caves were Civil Defense shelters and are well-known to local people. Although the spiders would probably survive in remote crevices, human interference could destroy those spiders accessible to scientists and the public.

Conservation and Recovery

Some beneficial cooperation has been obtained from landowners in the area, and limited funds have been acquired, which have permitted intermittent surveys and research. Of the many small caves in the area, only four segments in two areas have suitable moisture and microclimates and harbor small populations of the spider. Plans have been initiated to establish reserves for these caves; two are slated for protection within a golf course development, and the Koloa caves are to be protected within a new housing development. Another cave segment has been protected and efforts made to attract the spider.

The largest and most stable populations of the spider occur in Koloa Cave No. 2, and formal reserve status for all of this cave should be established. Long-term monitoring of the populations within the two reserve caves on resort property is necessary to ensure that the size of these reserves is adequate for the survival of the species. Management regulations need to be developed and should include provisions for limiting access to the caves and restrictions on the type of modifications allowed on the surface near and above the caves.

Contact

U. S. Fish and Wildlife Service
Regional Office, Division of Endangered Species
Eastside Federal Complex
911 N. E. 11th Ave.
Portland, Oregon 97232-4181
Telephone: (503) 231-6121
http://pacific.fws.gov/

Reference

U. S. Fish and Wildlife Service. 14 January 2000. "Endangered and Threatened Wildlife and Plants; Final Rule To List Two Cave Animals From Kauai, Hawaii, as Endangered." *Federal Register* 65(10): 2348-2357.

Bee Creek Cave Harvestman

Texella reddelli

Status	Endangered
Listed	September 16, 1988
Family	Phalangodidae (Harvestman)
Description	Pale yellow-brown, eyeless arachnid.
Habitat	Dry caves.
Food	Probably insects.
Reproduction	Unknown.
Threats	Urbanization.
Range	Texas

Description

Harvestmen are anatomically and evolutionarily quite distinct from spiders. The eyeless Bee Creek Cave harvestman, *Texella reddelli*, has a pale yellow-brown body, barely 0.13 in (0.33 cm) in length, with relatively long legs. It has well-developed eyes set in broadly conical eye mounds. Juveniles are white to yellowish-white. It is similar in appearance to the common daddy long-legs. It uses its two front legs, which are longer than the others, to feel its way through its lightless habitat. *T. reddelli* can be distinguished in the field from its closest relative, *T. reyesi* by its shorter legs, its well developed eyes, and its color, which is more orange.

Behavior

Little is known of this cave dweller's behavior and reproductive activity. It is probably predatory, feeding on other insects.

Habitat

The Bee Creek Cave harvestman is restricted to five, dry limestone caves.

Distribution

This harvestman is an example of a localized cave fauna found in Travis and Williamson Counties, Texas. It has been collected from five caves in the region and is suspected to occupy a sixth.

The size of the Bee Creek Cave harvestman population has not been estimated, but the U. S. Fish and Wildlife Service (FWS) biologists believe that the species may be more limited in numbers than previously thought. This spider has been collected from Tooth, Bee Creek, McDonald, Weldon, and Bone Caves. In 1984, it was reported from Root Cave in Travis County, but its presence there has not been confirmed.

Threats

In recent years, the suburbs of the city of Austin have expanded into Travis and Williamson Counties, causing the loss of many caves and natural sinkholes. Land-clearing, digging, and blasting have caused collapsed caves or buried the entrances. Weldon Cave—site of a past biological survey—lay along the path of a recent road expansion and may no longer exist. Coffin Cave also appears to have succumbed to bulldozing in 1988. New roads in the area have stimulated construction of subdivisions closer to the main caves of the system—Tooth, McDonald, and Root Caves. The subdivisions and other construction projects, such as a proposed pipeline, are expected to alter drainage patterns and degrade the quality of the groundwater on which the cave species depends.

Bee Creek Cave Harvestman, photograph. U. S. Fish and Wildlife Service. Reproduced by permission.

Conservation and Recovery

Protection of the harvestman requires the creation of sufficient easements around the caves to prevent physical disturbance or pollution of groundwater. Human intrusion and habitat disturbance also must be discouraged. Endemic cave species are also covered in the 1991 FWS Recovery Plan for the black-capped vireo (*Vireo atricapillus*), which nests in the area.

Contact

Regional Office of Endangered Species
U.S. Fish and Wildlife Service
P. O. Box 1306
Albuquerque, New Mexico 87103
http://southwest.fws.gov/

References

Goodnight, C. J., and M. L. Goodnight. 1967. "Opilionids from Texas Caves (Opiliones Phalangodidae)," *American Museum Novitates* 2301.

Reddell, J. R. 1984. "Report on the Caves and Cave Fauna of the Parke, Travis County, Texas." Unpublished Report to the Texas System of Natural Laboratories.

U.S. Fish and Wildlife Service. 1988. "Determination of Five Texas Cave Invertebrates to Be Endangered Species." *Federal Register* 53:36029-36033.

U.S. Fish and Wildlife Service. 1994. "Recovery Plan for Endangered Karst Invertebrates in Travis and William Counties, Texas." U.S. Fish and Wildlife Service, Albuquerque.

Bone Cave Harvestman

Texella reyesi

Status	Endangered
Listed	September 16, 1988
Family	Phalangodidae (Harvestman)
Description	Long-legged, blind, pale orange harvestman.
Habitat	Limestone caves, sinkholes, and other subterranean voids.
Food	Eggs, feces, nymphs, and dead body parts.
Reproduction	Unknown.
Threats	Land development, pollution, vandalism, and fire ants.
Range	Texas

Bone Cave Harvestman, photograph. U. S. Fish and Wildlife Service. Reproduced by permission.

Description

The Bone Cave harvestman is a troglobite, which is a species which spends its entire life in openings underground usually with small or absent eyes, attenuated appendages, and other adaptations to its subsurface dwelling.

This species is a long-legged, blind, pale orange harvestman. It measures 0.06-0.11 in (1.41- 2.67 mm) in body length. Scute length is 0.05-0.07 in (1.26-1.69 mm). The leg II length is 0.24- 0.46 in (6.1-11.79 mm). The leg II to scute length is 0.17-0.34 (4.3-8.68 mm). The exoskeleton is rough. A few small tubercles can be observed on the eye mound, which is broadly conical; the retina is absent; the cornea variable. The penis possesses a ventral plate prong and is round apically. There are two dorsal, 17 lateral, and four ventral setae. The apical spine of this species is bent and apically pointed; its length is 0.002 in (0.05 mm). The glans have a basal knob which appears narrow and conical in shape. The middle lobe is long and the parastylar lobes are claw-shaped. The stylus of the Bone Cave harvestman is long, curved and ventrally carinate; apically spatulate. The basal fold is well-developed.

Juveniles are white to yellow in color, while adults are pale orange. This species displays geographical polymorphism. Northern populations have longer legs, a smoother exoskeleton, and reduced or absent corneas.

Behavior

This species spends its entire life underground. It is endemic to the karst (limestone) formations. These formations include caves, sinkholes, and other subterranean voids.

The Bone Cave harvestman is sensitive to less-than-saturated humidities. Most individuals are found only under large rocks, but are occasionally seen walking on moist floors. In Temples of Thor Cave, individuals are typically found on a rough slope about 32.8 yds (30 m) from the entrance in absolute darkness. Humidity is high in this particular area.

Habitat

This species is dependent on outside moisture and nutrient inputs generated from the subsurface. This species inhabits areas of the cave where temperature and humidity are constant. The surface vegetation ranges from pasture land to mature oak-juniper woodland.

Karst is formed by the slow dissolution of calcium carbonate from limestone bedrock by mildly acidic ground water. This process results in subterranean voids resembling a honeycomb. The water enters the subsurface through cracks, crevices, and other openings, dissolving soluble beds of rock.

Nutrients to this ecosystem are provided from the outside surface washed in. These nutritional sources include plant material, feces, eggs, and carrion. Cave crickets are believed to provide an important component to the nutritional balance of this cave ecosystem. These crickets introduce nutrients through eggs, feces, nymphs, and dead body parts on which many invertebrates are known to feed.

Raccoon feces provide a rich medium for fungi growth which, in turn, is a haven for collembolans (small insects).

Distribution

The Bone Cave harvestman was originally discovered in 1989 in Bone Cave, Williamson County, Texas.

As this species has only been distinguished as a separate species of *Texella* recently, past distribution is difficult to ascertain. This species currently inhabits 54 caves, 46 known occurrences, and eight possible locations from northern Travis to northern Williamson Counties, Texas.

Threats

This species and seven other invertebrates of the karst (limestone) formations are threatened by land development, pollution, vandalism, and/or fire ants.

The primary threat to Bone Cave harvestman is habitat loss due to urban development activities. Continued urban expansion such as residential subdivisions, schools, golf courses, roads, commercial and industrial facilities, etc. poses a threat in the form of cave filling or collapse, water diversion, vegetation/fauna alteration, and increased pollution.

Some caves have already been filled as a result of road construction and building site preparation. Development directly above caves could result in the collapse of cave ceilings.

Ranchers may have also filled some caves. Justification is placed in reducing hiding places for predators of cattle and goats as well as preventing these animals from falling into the formations.

Troglobites rely upon and in fact require a controlled environment of high humidity and constant temperature. If water drainage paths are altered, this balance is no longer on an even keel. Water diversion away from the caves could lead to the direct mortality of this species. Increased water infiltration could lead to flooding and loss of air space.

As the karst ecosystem relies on the infiltration of nutrients from the surface, a fluctuation in the vegetation or fauna would alter nutrient supplies. During development, native vegetation may be replaced with non-native species, as well as cause the introduction of exotic animal species, such as fire ants. An overall nutrient depletion would result. The removal of vegetation could also lead to temperature fluctuations, a change in moisture regime and potential for contamination and increased sedimentation from soil erosion.

Conservation and Recovery

A Recovery Plan was published for the Bone Cave harvestman in 1994. The conservation of this rare insect requires the strict protection of its cave habitats from disturbances and other changes associated with residential, agricultural, or commercial development. Other necessary actions include studies to monitor the abundance of the Bone Cave harvestman and research into its biology and habitat needs. There should also be a public education campaign to develop a broad base of support for the protection of rare cave habitats.

Contact

U.S. Fish and Wildlife Service
Regional Office
P. O. Box 1306
Albuquerque, New Mexico 87103
http://southwest.fws.gov/

References

U.S. Fish and Wildlife Service. 1993. "Endangered and Threatened Wildlife and Plants; Coffin Cave Mold Beetle (*Batrisodes texanus*) and the Bone Cave Harvestman (*Texella reyesi*) Determined to Be Endangered." *Federal Register* 58(158): 43818-43819.

U.S. Fish and Wildlife Service. 1994. Recovery Plan for Endangered Karst Invertebrates in Travis and Williamson Counties, Texas. Albuquerque, New Mexico.

Tooth Cave Pseudoscorpion

Tartarocreagris texana

Status	Endangered
Listed	September 16, 1988
Family	Neobisiidae (Pseudoscorpion)
Description	Tiny scorpion-like arachnid.
Habitat	Cave dwelling.
Food	Small insects and arthropods.
Reproduction	Male deposits sperm on the substratum, which the female picks up for fertilization.
Threats	Development, exotic predators.
Range	Texas

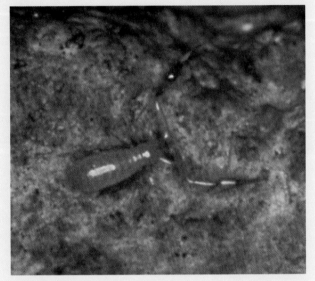

Tooth Cave Pseudoscorpion, photograph. U. S. Fish and Wildlife Service. Reproduced by permission.

Description

The Tooth Cave pseudoscorpion, *Tartarocreagris texana*, is a pale yellow to whitish arachnid that resembles a tiny scorpion, reaching about 0.2 in (4 mm) in length. It has the same enlarged pedipalpi terminating in pinching chelae, but the segmented abdomen is broadly rounded behind and lacks a whip or stinger and book lungs. It uses its pinchers to prey on small insects and other arthropods. The unpigmented pseudoscorpion is eyeless; the numerous sensory hairs take the place of eyes.

Behavior

The Tooth Cave pseudoscorpion preys on small insects and other cave-dwelling arthropods, which it captures with its pinchers and tears into pieces with its strong chelicerae. It is possible that it anesthetizes its victims with venom produced in tiny glands in the chelicerae.

Along with spiders and some mites, this pseudoscorpion produces a kind of silk that comes from the glands that in spiders is used to produce venom. During periods when the species is helpless, such as when the female is distended with eggs or when molting, it spins silk to enclose itself for protection.

To reproduce, the male deposits on the substratum a distinctive spermatophore consisting of a thin stalk whose tip contains a sperm. The female picks it up and fertilizes herself.

Habitat

This species is found in two dry, relatively small, limestone caves that have some infiltration of groundwater.

Distribution

The Tooth Cave pseudoscorpion is endemic to Tooth, Amber, and possibly McDonald Caves in

Travis and Williamson Counties near Austin, Texas. The pseudoscorpion is not known to exist elsewhere.

The number of Tooth Cave pseudoscorpions in Amber and Tooth Caves has not been estimated, but surveys have only uncovered a single specimen from each cave. Because of the size of the available habitat and the small size of the pseudoscorpion, these survey figures are not thought to indicate actual numbers, although the total population is certainly not large.

Threats

Located adjacent to a developing urban area, the caves inhabited by this pseudoscorpion are threatened by land clearing and residential construction. Tooth Cave lies along a proposed route for a water pipeline and, even if bypassed by construction equipment, could suffer from nearby blasting. Residential development of the area will also contribute to the degradation of groundwater.

Conservation and Recovery

Recovery options include acquiring, through purchase or donation, wide easements around caves to protect them from ground disturbance and water pollution. Cave entrances will probably be grated to prevent unauthorized entry and vandalism.

Because the black-capped vireo (*Vireo atricapillus*) nests in the region, the U. S. Fish and Wildlife Service (FWS) treated the pseudoscorpion in the vireo's

1991 Recovery Plan, affording additional protection and oversight.

Contact

U. S. Fish and Wildlife Service
Regional Office, Division of Endangered Species
P. O. Box 1306
Albuquerque, New Mexico 87103-1306
Telephone: (505) 248-6911
Fax: (505) 248-6915
http://southwest/fws.gov/

References

Muchmore, W. B. 1969. "New Species and Records of Cavernicolous Pseudoscorpions of the Genus *Microcreagris* (Arachnida Chelonethida, Neobisiidae, Ideobisiinae)." *American Museum Novitate* 2932:21.

Reddell, J. R. 1984. "Report on the Caves and Cave Fauna of the Parke, Travis County, Texas." Unpublished Report to the Texas System of Natural Laboratories.

U. S. Fish and Wildlife Service. 1988. "Determination of Five Texas Cave Invertebrates to Be Endangered Species." *Federal Register* 53: 36029-36033.

U. S. Fish and Wildlife Service. 1994. "Recovery Plan for Endangered Karst Invertebrates in Travis and William Counties, Texas." U. S. Fish and Wildlife Service, Albuquerque.

Conservancy Fairy Shrimp

Branchinecta conservatio

Status	Endangered
Listed	September 19, 1994
Family	Branchinectidae (Freshwater shrimp)
Description	Delicate elongate body, large stalked compound eyes, no carapace, and 11 pairs of swimming legs.
Habitat	Vernal pools with high turbidity and low alkalinity.
Food	Algae, bacteria, protozoa, rotifers, and bits of detritus.
Reproduction	Eggs are dropped to the pool bottom or remain in the brood sac until the female dies and sinks.
Threats	Loss of habitat.
Range	California

Larry Serpa

Description

Branchinecta conservatio (Conservancy fairy shrimp), a member of the family Branchinectidae, was first described from specimens collected at the Jepson Prairie Preserve, located in the Central Valley east of Travis Air Force Base in Solano County.

The earliest known collections of the Conservancy fairy shrimp were made in 1979. This shrimp ranges in size from 0.6-1.1 in (14-27 mm) long and is most similar in appearance to Lindahl's fairy shrimp (*B. lindahli*). However, the female brood pouch is fusiform and usually ends under abdominal segment eight in the Conservancy fairy shrimp, whereas the pouch is cylindrical and usually ends under segment four in Lindahl's fairy shrimp. The large, oval pulvillus at the proximal end of the basal segment of the male antenna appears similar in both species, however, the terminal end of the distal antennal segments of the Conservancy fairy shrimp are distinctive.

Behavior

The Conservancy fairy shrimp has been observed from November to early April. It is usually collected at cool temperatures and appears to be relatively long-lived.

Habitat

The Conservancy fairy shrimp inhabits vernal pools with highly turbid water. The pools at Jepson Prairie and Vina Plains inhabited by this animal have very low conductivity, total dissolved solids, and alkalinity.

Distribution

The species is known from six disjunct populations: Vina Plains, Tehama County; south of Chico, Tehama County; Jepson Prairie, Solano County; Sacramento National Wildlife Refuge, Glenn County; near Haystack Mountain northeast of Merced in Merced County; and the Lockewood Valley of northern Ventura County. The pools inhabited by the Conservancy fairy shrimp are large, such as the 89-acre (36-hectare) Olcott Lake at Jepson Prairie. Four of the six known populations of the Conservancy fairy shrimp are imperiled, and three of the six populations are comprised of single or less than five pools.

Threats

Proposed highway construction in Solano County could damage vernal pools inhabited by the Conservancy fairy shrimp. The State of California has proposed to extend State Highway 505 from Vacaville to Collinsville in Solano County; this project directly and/or indirectly would impact vernal pools inhabited by the Conservancy fairy shrimp. In Solano County, an off-road vehicle park adjacent to the Jepson Prairie Reserve owned by the Nature Conservancy (TNC) could adversely impact populations of the Conservancy fairy shrimp.

Conservation and Recovery

The Conservancy fairy shrimp is known from habitats in Jepson Prairie Preserve, owned by TNC (a private conservation organization), and on federally owned Sacramento National Wildlife Refuge and Travis Air Force Base. The federally owned habitats should be strictly protected against any threatening influences. Other non-federal habitats are threatened by various development activities. The largest of the privately owned habitats should be protected. This could be done by acquiring the land and establishing ecological reserves, or by negotiating conservation easements with the landowners. The known populations of the Conservancy fairy shrimp should be monitored, and research undertaken into its biology and habitat needs.

Contacts

U. S. Fish and Wildlife Service
Sacramento Fish and Wildlife Office
Federal Building
2800 Cottage Way, Room W-2605
Sacramento, California 95825-1846
Telephone: (916) 414-6600
Fax: (916) 460-4619

U. S. Fish and Wildlife Service
Regional Office, Division of Endangered Species
Eastside Federal Building
911 N. E. 11th Ave.
Portland, Oregon 97232-4181
Telephone: (503) 231-6121
http://pacific.fws.gov/

Reference

U.S. Fish and Wildlife Service. 19 Sept. 1994. "Endangered and Threatened Wildlife and Plants; Determination of Endangered Status for the Conservancy Fairy Shrimp, Longhorn Fairy Shrimp, and the Vernal Pool Tadpole Shrimp; and Threatened Status for the Vernal Pool Fairy Shrimp." *Federal Register* http://www.cdpr.ca.gov/docs/es/estext/fr091994.txt

Longhorn Fairy Shrimp

Branchinecta longiantenna

Status:	Endangered
Listed:	September 19, 1994
Family:	Branchinectidae (Freshwater shrimp)
Description:	Delicate elongate bodies, large stalked compound eyes, no carapace, and 11 pairs of swimming legs.
Habitat:	Clear to turbid grass-bottomed vernal pools in grasslands and clear-water pools in sandstone depressions.
Food:	Algae, bacteria, protozoa, rotifers, and bits of detritus.
Reproduction:	Eggs are dropped to the pool bottom or remain in the brood sac until the female dies and sinks.
Threats:	Loss of habitat.
Range:	California

Description

Branchinecta longiantenna (longhorn fairy shrimp), a member of the family Branchinectidae, was described from specimens collected at Souza Ranch in the Kellogg Creek watershed, about 22 mi (35 km) southeast of the city of Concord, Contra Costa County.

The earliest known collections of the longhorn fairy shrimp were made in 1937. It ranges in size from 0.5-0.8 in (12.1-20.8 mm). This species differs from other branchinectids in that a portion of the distal segment of its antennae is flattened in the antero-posterior plane rather than the latero-medial plane.

Behavior

The longhorn fairy shrimp has been observed from late December until late April.

Habitat

The longhorn fairy shrimp inhabits clear to turbid grass-bottomed vernal pools in grasslands and clear-water pools in sandstone depressions. All vernal pools inhabited by this species are filled by winter and spring rains and may remain inundated until June. The water in grassland pools inhabited by this species has very low conductivity, total dissolved solids, and alkalinity.

Distribution

This species is known only from four disjunct populations along the eastern margin of the central coast range from Concord, Contra Costa County south to Soda Lake in San Luis Obispo County: the Kellogg Creek watershed, the Altamont Pass area, the western and northern boundaries of Soda Lake on the Carrizo Plain, and Kesterson National Wildlife Refuge in the Central Valley.

Threats

Other vernal pools located in San Luis Obispo County, including most of the known populations of the longhorn fairy shrimp, are located in subdivided areas with constructed roads and lots for sale and development. To date, some of the sites have been cleared and continued habitat loss is ongoing or impending. The Coastal Branch Phase II (Coastal Aqueduct) of the State Water Project, proposed by the California Department of Water Resources, an-

Larry Serpa

nually would convey 70,000 acre-feet (86 billion l) of water from the Delta region of California to San Luis Obispo and Santa Barbara Counties. It is unclear if this source of water would allow urban development of the Soda Lake area, however, the longhorn fairy shrimp and the vernal pool fairy shrimp may be adversely affected by commercial development made possible by this project.

Conservation and Recovery

The longhorn fairy shrimp is known from habitats in Kesterson National Wildlife Refuge. This federally owned habitat should be strictly protected against any threatening influences. The longhorn fairy shrimp also occurs in habitat secured by the Nature Conservancy, a private conservation organization. Other critical habitats are on privately owned land and are severely threatened by various human activities, particularly residential development. The largest of the privately owned habitats should be protected. This could be done by acquiring the land and establishing ecological reserves, or

by negotiating conservation easements with the landowners. The known populations of the longhorn fairy shrimp should be monitored, and research undertaken into its biology and habitat needs.

Contacts

U. S. Fish and Wildlife Service
Sacramento Fish and Wildlife Office Federal Building
2800 Cottage Way, Room W-2605
Sacramento, California 95825-1846
Telephone: (916) 414-6600
Fax: (916) 460-4619

U. S. Fish and Wildlife Service Regional Office
Division of Endangered Species
Eastside Federal Building
911 N. E. 11th Ave.
Portland, Oregon 97232-4181
Telephone: (503) 231-6121
http://pacific.fws.gov/

Reference

U.S. Fish and Wildlife Service. 19 Sept. 1994. "Endangered and Threatened Wildlife and Plants; Determination of Endangered Status for the Conservancy Fairy Shrimp, Longhorn Fairy Shrimp, and the Vernal Pool Tadpole Shrimp; and Threatened Status for the Vernal Pool Fairy Shrimp." *Federal Register* http://www.cdpr.ca.gov/docs/es/estext/fr091994.txt

Vernal Pool Fairy Shrimp

Branchinecta lynchi

Status	Threatened
Listed	September 19, 1994
Family	Branchinectidae (Freshwater shrimp)
Description	An aquatic crustacean.
Habitat	Temporary (vernal) pools.
Food	Phytoplankton.
Reproduction	Lays externally fertilized eggs.
Threats	Habitat loss.
Range	California, Oregon

Description

The vernal pool fairy shrimp ranges in body length from 0.4-1.0 in (11-25 mm). It can be differentiated from related species by the ridge-like basal segment outgrowth below and posterior to the pulvillus of the antennae of the male, and by the relatively shorter, pyriform brood pouch of the female.

Behavior

The vernal pool fairy shrimp is typically active in adult form from about December to early May. The rest of the year it survives as persistent eggs. It matures and breeds quickly, allowing populations to persist in shallow, short-lived pools. If the pond is longer lasting, the vernal pool fairy shrimp can persist later into the spring or early summer.

Habitat

The vernal pool fairy shrimp inhabits vernal (or temporary) pools with fresh, clear to tea-colored water. It usually occurs in mud-bottomed swales of grassy vegetation, or in basalt-flow depression pools in grasslands. One population, however, is known from sandstone rock outcrops, and another from alkaline vernal pools. The water in pools inhabited by this species typically has low concentrations of dissolved solids, alkalinity, and chloride, and has low conductivity. It often has a sporadic distribution within local complexes of vernal pools, in that not all pools in a complex are inhabited by the species.

Distribution

Populations of the vernal pool fairy shrimp are known from California and Oregon, but are most numerous in central California. There are 32 known populations.

Threats

The habitat of the vernal pool fairy shrimp is imperiled by urban, commercial, and industrial development, the conversion of land from natural grassland into agricultural use, and activities to manage water supply and control flooding. Habitat loss is caused by destruction through changes in land-use, infilling, grading, and other activities, and by the modification of the watershed of the vernal pools. Overall, the most significant threats are associated with rapid urbanization and agricultural conversion. These human influences have already resulted in the loss of most of the original aquatic habitat of the vernal pool fairy shrimp. Moreover, 28 of the 32 known populations of the vernal pool fairy shrimp are considered by the U. S. Fish and Wildlife Service to be under threat.

Vernal Pool Fairy Shrimp, photograph by Larry Serpa. Reproduced by permission.

Conservation and Recovery

The vernal pool fairy shrimp is not a protected species, and its critical habitat is not being effectively conserved. Some development projects affecting critical habitat have been required to institute conservation-related mitigations as a result of findings from environmental impact assessments. However, this has not always proven to be an effective way of avoiding or repairing damage to the critical habitat of the vernal pool fairy shrimp. Moreover, the artificial creation of vernal pools as compensatory mitigation has not been proven to be successful in dealing with the effects on dependent species, including the vernal pool fairy shrimp. Portions of four populations of the vernal pool fairy shrimp are on lands under public ownership, and the Nature Conservancy also owns and conserves some sites. Management plans for some federal, state, local government, and all Conservancy properties include provisions to protect vernal pools, but the plans do not specifically address the needs of the vernal pool fairy shrimp.

Contacts

U. S. Fish and Wildlife Service
Regional Office, Division of Endangered Species
Eastside Federal Complex
911 N. E. 11th Ave.
Portland, Oregon 97232-4181
(503) 231-6121
http://pacific.fws.gov/

Sacramento Field Office, U. S. Fish and Wildlife Service
2800 Cottage Way, Room E-1823
Sacramento, California 95825-1846
(916) 978-4866

Reference

U. S. Fish and Wildlife Service. 1994. "Endangered and Threatened Wildlife and Plants; Determination of Endangered Status for the Conservancy Fairy Shrimp, Longhorn Fairy Shrimp, and the Vernal Pool Tadpole Shrimp; and Threatened Status for the Vernal Pool Fairy Shrimp." http://www.cdpr.ca.gov/docs/es/estext/fr091994.txt

San Diego Fairy Shrimp

Branchinecta sandiegonensis

Status	Endangered
Listed	February 3, 1997
Family	Branchinectidae (Freshwater shrimp)
Description	Male San Diego fairy shrimp can be distinguished from males of other *Branchinecta* species by the shape of the second antenna.
Habitat	Small, shallow vernal pools, which range in depth from 2-12 in (5-30 cm) and inwater temperature from 50-68°F (10-20°C).
Food	Algae, bacteria, protozoa, rotifers, and bits of detritus.
Reproduction	Hatches and matures within 7 days to 2 weeks depending on water temperature.
Threats	Loss of habitat, degradation of water quality.
Range	California

Description

Adult male San Diego fairy shrimp, *Branchinecta sandiegonensis*, range in length from 0.4-0.6 in (9-16 mm) and the females are 0.4-0.5 in (8-14 mm) long. Mature individuals have a delicate elongate body, large stalked compound eyes, no carapace covering the back, and 11 pairs of swimming legs. They swim or glide gracefully upside down by means of complex beating movements of the legs that pass in a wave-like front-to-back direction. Nearly all species of fairy shrimp feed on algae, bacteria, protozoa, rotifers, and bits of organic matter. The second pair of antennae in adult female San Diego fairy shrimp are cylindrical and elongate, but in the males they are greatly enlarged and specialized for clasping the females during copulation. The females carry their eggs in an oval or elongate ventral brood sac. Five other species of branchinectid fairy shrimp occur in southern California. The only other branchinectids in southern California that are similar in appearance to the San Diego fairy shrimp are Lindahl's fairy shrimp (*B. lindahli*) and the threatened vernal pool fairy shrimp (*B. lynchi*), which occurs in southwest-

ern Riverside County. Male San Diego fairy shrimp can be distinguished from males of other *Branchinecta* species by the shape of the second antenna. Female San Diego fairy shrimp are distinguishable from other members of the genus by the shape and length of the brood sac and by the presence of paired dorsolateral spines on five of the abdominal segments. The San Diego fairy shrimp, a member of the aquatic crustacean order Anostraca, was recognized as a distinct taxon by scientists in 1990, although it was not described taxonomically until 1993.

Behavior

Adult San Diego fairy shrimp are usually observed from January to March; however, in years with early or late rainfall, the hatching period may be extended. The species hatches and matures within 7 days to 2 weeks depending on water temperature. The San Diego fairy shrimp disappear after about a month, but shrimp will continue to hatch if subsequent rains result in additional water or refilling of the vernal pools. The eggs are either dropped to the pool bottom or remain in the brood sac until the female dies and sinks. The resting, or summer, eggs are capable of withstanding heat, cold, and prolonged drying. When the pools refill in the same or subsequent rainy seasons, some but not all of the eggs may hatch. Fairy shrimp egg banks in the soil may be comprised of the eggs from several years of breeding.

Habitat

The San Diego fairy shrimp is a habitat specialist occurring only in small, shallow vernal pools, which range in depth from 2-12 in (5-30 cm) and in water temperature from 50-68°F (10-20°C). Water chemistry is one of the most important factors in determining the distribution of fairy shrimp. The San Diego fairy shrimp appears to be sensitive to high water temperatures; present data indicates that pool temperatures below 41°F (5°C) and above 86°F (30°C) represent the natural limits for this species. This means that pools located in the inland mountains and in desert regions may be out of this range.

Distribution

The species was first collected in 1962 in San Diego County at Poway and Ramona; it was first described *B. sandiegonensis* based on collections made at Del Mar Mesa in San Diego County. The species is restricted to vernal pools in coastal southern California south to extreme northwestern Baja California, Mexico. No individuals have been found in riverine waters, marine waters, or other permanent bodies of water. All known localities are below 2,300 ft (700 m) in altitude and within 40 mi (65 km) of the Pacific Ocean, from Santa Barbara County south to northwestern Baja California.

Threats

The San Diego fairy shrimp is imperiled because its vernal pool habitat is being damaged, fragmented, and destroyed by a variety of human-caused activities: urban development and agricultural conversion, water development and flood control projects, highway and utility construction, modifications of surrounding uplands that alter vernal pool hydrology, off-road vehicle activity,

and livestock overgrazing. Urban development and agricultural conversion have been the primary causes of habitat destruction. Habitat loss occurs from destruction and modification of vernal pools due to filling, grading, discing, leveling, and other activities, as well as any activity that alters vernal pool watersheds. High livestock densities may result in excessive physical disturbances analogous to vehicle damage, such as trampling and rutting, resulting in altered pool water chemistry and degraded water quality. Trampling of pool margins and thinning of vegetation from overgrazing may increase pasture runoff, leading to erosion and increased siltation of vernal pool habitat.

The continuing rapid urbanization of areas containing vernal pools poses a significant threat to the San Diego fairy shrimp. Nearly all of the vernal pools that occurred throughout the range of the species from southern Santa Barbara County to extreme northwestern Baja California have been eliminated: 838 vernal pools comprising 698 acres (283 hectares) were eliminated by urban development between 1979 and 1986. San Diego County, where most of the remaining vernal pools are, is one of the fastest-growing counties in the nation, with a population increase of 349% between 1950 and 1990. The population growth rate that is predicted could further fragment and degrade the remaining vernal pool habitat of the San Diego fairy shrimp.

There remain only a modest number of very small and widely scattered vernal pools that are fit habitat for the San Diego fairy shrimp. The San Diego County locations are in Tijuana Slough National Wildlife Refuge, Proctor Valley, Otay Mesa, Otay Lakes, Sweetwater Reservoir, Mission Trails County Park, Kearney Mesa, Del Mar Mesa, Lopez Ridge, Mira Mesa, Carlsbad, Marine Corps Base Camp Pendleton, Poway, Ramona, and San Marcos. The largest remaining number of vernal pools and the largest block of contiguous habitat occurs on Miramar Naval Air Station.

Approximately 65 acres (26 hectares) of vernal pools are here, 70% of the extant total. These pools exhibit a wide variety of conditions from disturbed to pristine, and vary greatly in size, depth, type and number of cobbles, soil type, hydrological characteristics, and species composition. The San Diego fairy shrimp has been estimated to inhabit 80% of the vernal pools at the base. The Marine

Corps has proposed construction of additional helicopter landing fields, ammunition bunkers, and other facilities that may adversely affect areas containing habitat for the San Diego fairy shrimp. The vernal pools at Montgomery Field occur within the approach path of the airport in a heavily urbanized area. Three separate areas of airport land encompass the watershed containing 138 vernal pools

The construction of a sludge processing facility and mounding of excess dirt at the Miramar Landfill, as well as on-going landfill maintenance have eliminated vernal pools inhabited by the San Diego fairy shrimp. The proposed extension of Nobel Drive would damage or eliminate the vernal pools containing habitat for the species.

The San Diego fairy shrimp is especially vulnerable to alterations in hydrology. Its vernal pool habitat is also vulnerable to indirect destruction due to the alteration of supporting watersheds. Development projects adjacent to vernal pools are often responsible for adverse alterations in drainage. Hydrological alterations can result from urban or agricultural development or a combination of these activities. An increase in water due to urban runoff leads to increased inundation, making the pools vulnerable to invasion by marsh plant species that outcompete obligate (restricted to) vernal pool taxa, resulting in decreased abundance of obligate vernal pool taxa. At the other extreme, some pools have been drained or blocked from their source of water and have shown an increased domination by upland plant species. Alterations in vernal pool hydrology may adversely impact the San Diego fairy shrimp due to changes in the maximum and minimum water temperatures. At least three of these parties likely intended to alter the elevations of the site to eliminate one or more of the parameters used by the U. S. Army Corps of Engineers to define a wetland according to their 1987 jurisdictional manual. Similar deliberate activities that are damaging or destroying vernal pools are likely occurring throughout the range of the San Diego fairy shrimp.

The primary threat to the San Diego fairy shrimp of habitat loss due to human activities is reinforced by another factor: extraordinary increases in the human population and associated pressures from urban development have rendered existing regulatory mechanisms inadequate.

No state or local laws exist that adequately protect the San Diego fairy shrimp, and other regulations aimed at the conservation of its vernal pool habitat have also proven ineffective and insufficient.

Secondary impacts associated with urbanization also pose a very significant threat to the continued existence of this species. These include disposal of waste materials, trash, and toxic substances into habitat for the San Diego fairy shrimp. Solid waste can disrupt pool hydrology; and malathion, herbicides, laundry detergent, household plant fertilizer, and motor oil are known to be fatal to the San Diego fairy shrimp through outright poisoning or by the formation of an asphyxiating barrier to gas exchange on the vernal pool surfaces. Dust and other forms of air or water pollution from commercial development or agricultural projects may also be injurious to the shrimp. Off-road vehicles crush fairy shrimp eggs, cut deep ruts over dried pool beds, compact soil, destroy native vegetation, and alter pool hydrology.

Fire fighting activities, security patrols, military maneuvers, and recreational activities have cumulatively damaged vernal pool habitats in many areas within the range of the species. Livestock grazing can ultimately lead to pool siltation and trampled pool margins that compromise water quality.

Conservation and Recovery

The continued survival and recovery of the San Diego fairy shrimp can only be assured at this time by the preservation and enhancement of extant vernal pools and their associated watersheds.

Contacts

Regional Office of Endangered Species
U. S. Fish and Wildlife Service
Eastside Federal Center
911 N. E. 11th Ave.
Portland, Oregon 97232
http://pacific.fws.gov/

Carlsbad Fish and Wildlife Office
2730 Loker Ave. W.
Carlsbad, California 92008-6603
Telephone: (760) 431-9440
Fax: (760) 431-9624

References

U.S. Fish and Wildlife Service. 1997. "Determination of Endangered Status for the San Diego Fairy Shrimp." *Federal Register* 62(22):4925-4939.

Riverside Fairy Shrimp

Streptocephalus woottoni

Status:	Endangered
Listed:	August 3, 1993
Family:	Streptocephalidae (Freshwater crustacean)
Description:	Small freshwater crustacean with a red color on the ninth and eighth abdominal.
Habitat:	Vernal pools in areas with Mediterranean climates.
Food:	Plankton, algae, small crustaceans.
Reproduction:	Eggs are hatched into larvae.
Threats:	Habitat loss.
Range:	California

Description

The Riverside fairy shrimp is a small freshwater crustacean. Both males and females have a red color covering all of the ninth and 30-40% of the eighth abdominal segments. Mature males are 0.56-0.92 in (1.4-2.3 cm) in length. The frontal appendage is cylindrical, double-lobed at the tip, and extends only part way to the distal end of the basal segment of the antenna. The spur of the thumb is a simple blade-like process. The finger has two teeth; the proximal tooth is shorter than the distal tooth. The distal tooth has a lateral shoulder that is equal to about half the tooth's total length measured along the proximal edge. The brood pouch extends to abdominal segments seven, eight, or nine. The cercopods are as in the male. Both males and females have the red color of the cercopods covering all the ninth abdominal segment and some of the eighth abdominal segment.

Behavior

The species begins life from resting eggs from which they are hatched into a larvae stage after which there are dozens of molts before an individual reaches maturity. Even as adults, they continue to molt throughout their lives.

The species is for the most part a filter-feeder. They feed on plankton and algae. Yet, they also may eat particles ranging in size from algae to small crustaceans. Thus, the species is omnivorous.

This species most likely shows seasonal variations in activity related to reproduction and changes in temperature regime.

Habitat

The species occurs in deep, cool pools and occasionally in depressions, such as road ruts and ditches.

Distribution

The species is known from four vernal pools in a 37 sq mi (96 sq km) area in southwestern Riverside County, California, and from one population in Orange County, California. In San Diego County in the fall of 1989, the species was discovered within vernal pools on Miramar Naval Air Station and Otay Mesa. However, since the 1989 discovery of the species in San Diego County, numerous vernal pool complexes in the county have been surveyed without additional populations being found. The species was also found at two locations in Baja California, Mexico in the past.

Threats

The habitat and range of this species has been greatly reduced. Vernal pools, existing as slight de-

Riverside Fairy Shrimp, photograph by Larry Serpa. Reproduced by permission.

pressions on flat mesas, are found in locations that are especially vulnerable to one or more of the following habitat disturbances: urban and agricultural development, off-road vehicle use, cattle trampling, human trampling, road development, military activities, and water management activities. Many pool groups were entirely eliminated and replaced with urban or agricultural developments.

The vernal pool habitat upon which this species depends is also vulnerable to destruction due to alteration of the watershed. In some cases, an increase in pool water volume due to urban run-off has led to more prolonged periods of inundation, and at the other extreme, some pools have been drained or blocked from their source of water.

Pools have also been degraded due to the use of off-road vehicles, which have impacted the habitats of this species. These vehicles compact soils, crush plants when water is in the pools, cause turbidity, and leave deep ruts. The damage may alter the microhydrology of the pools. Dirt roads that go through or adjacent to pools are widened as motorists try to

avoid the inevitable mud puddles. Thus, pools are gradually destroyed by vehicles traveling on dirt roads. Vehicle access and damage has occurred on virtually all remaining vernal pool complexes.

Preliminary designs by the California Department of Transportation for a state route running near this species' habitat include alignments that sever the existing natural connection between two of the largest remaining vernal pool complexes on Otay Mesa. The construction of this new major highway access route into Otay Mesa would further facilitate its development.

An existing local airport is presently being evaluated as a potential site for an international airport servicing San Diego. This proposal includes alternative runway alignments that would destroy portions of one of the two largest remaining vernal pool complexes. A binational airport is also being considered for Otay Mesa, although these plans are too preliminary to allow assessment of potential impacts to vernal pools. An increase in the number of vehicle trips in this area would occur as a result of the airport, and this increased traffic would likely lead to a demand for more roads, which could directly impact the pools.

Habitat trampling, and in some cases trampling of the species itself, due to livestock grazing, occurs on Otay Mesa in areas where several vernal pool complexes collectively contain all four of the proposed species. Organisms within the pools may be trampled and killed by livestock prior to reproduction. Soil may become compacted or eroded, and water may be impacted with sediment.

Otay Mesa is a common area for travel from Mexico to the United States; hence, habitat and plants are threatened with trampling by humans. Also, the U.S. Immigration and Naturalization Service has proposed several projects at the international border, including border lighting, that could result in direct adverse impacts to vernal pools on Otay Mesa, due to construction activities.

The species has very narrow habitat requirements. It is only found in deep lowland pools that retain water through the warmer weather of late spring. It will not hatch in pools that receive cool waters from early winter rains, such as those pools on the Santa Rosa Plateau, nor will they hatch in shallow pools.

It is vulnerable to land use changes affecting the small number of pools that meet the species' strict habitat requirements. Of the four remaining pools supporting the species in Riverside County, only one is greater than one acre in size. This pool is within a planned development. Other sites supporting the species may lack some of the topical vegetation of vernal pools, but that condition probably reflects impacts from past agricultural activities. One pool is located within an approved tract for a housing development.

A third pool is on a parcel that is currently proposed for a housing development, adjacent to a golf course. This pool is in an agricultural field and was disced. The Environmental Impact Report prepared by a consultant for the developer of this project failed to acknowledge the existence of the species on the site. Representatives of the landowner expressed a willingness to offer some protection for this site. However, as discussed above, a currently proposed road project would impact the pool.

A fourth pool that contains this species is located partially on private land and partially on an Indian reservation. The portion on private land was culti-

vated during 1990. The region's drought conditions over the last two to three years may have rendered the pool dry enough to be plowed. A fifth pool was recently converted into a gravel pit. Only one documented population occurs in Orange County.

Other factors have greatly impacted the existence of this species, including introduction of non-native plant species, competition with invading species, trash dumping, fire, fire suppression activities, and drought. The low numbers of vernal pool habitats remaining and their scattered distributions make this species vulnerable to extinction due to future events that are unpredictable, human, or naturally caused.

Many vernal pools on Otay Mesa are dominated by non-native plants such as the common grass *Lolium perenne*. This species is tolerant of inundation and crowds out the native vernal pool species. Ranchers introduced non-native species into some areas to increase the amount of forage available to livestock. Excessive cover of weedy non-native grasses was noted in six of the pool groups and partially explained two extirpations of *P. nudruscula*.

Trash dumping also degrades vernal pools. Chunks of concrete, tires, refrigerators, sofas, and other pieces of garbage or debris were found in pools containing this species. This trash crushes or shades vernal pool plants, disrupts the hydrologic functions of the pool, and in some cases may release toxic substances.

Conservation and Recovery

A Recovery Plan has been released for the Riverside fairy shrimp. This crustacean is only known from habitats on privately owned land, all of which are severely threatened by various human activities. The largest of the privately owned habitats should be protected. This could be done by acquiring the land and establishing ecological reserves, or by negotiating conservation easements with the landowners. The known populations of the Riverside fairy shrimp should be monitored, and research undertaken into its biology and habitat needs.

Contacts

U. S. Fish and Wildlife Service
Sacramento Fish and Wildlife Office
Federal Building
2800 Cottage Way, Room W-2605
Sacramento, California 95825-1846
Telephone: (916) 414-6600
Fax: (916) 460-4619

U. S. Fish and Wildlife Service
Regional Office, Division of Endangered Species
Eastside Federal Building
911 N. E. 11th Ave.
Portland, Oregon 97232-4181
Telephone: (503) 231-6121
http://pacific.fws.gov/

References

Thorp, James H., and Alan P. Covich, eds. 1991. *Ecology and Classification of North American Freshwater Invertebrates.* New York: Academic Press. pp. 765-769.

U.S. Fish and Wildlife Service. 3 Aug. 1993. "Endangered and Threatened Wildlife and Plants; Endangered Status the Riverside Fairy Shrimp." *Federal Register* 58(147): 41384-41391.

U. S. Fish and Wildlife Service. 1998. "Recovery Plan for Vernal Pools of Southern California." U.S. Fish and Wildlife Service, Portland.

Madison Cave Isopod

Antrolana lira

Status	Threatened
Listed	October 4, 1982
Family	Cirolanidae (Cave isopod)
Description	White, blind, shrimplike crustacean.
Habitat	Subterranean freshwater pools.
Food	Detritus.
Reproduction	Unknown.
Threats	Habitat destruction, ground-water pollution.
Range	Virginia

Description

The only member of the genus *Antrolana*, the Madison Cave isopod, *A. lira*, is a white, shrimplike crustacean lacking eyes. This cave-adapted (troglobitic) isopod grows up to 0.4 in (1.02 cm) in length, making it among the longer, and the largest, subterranean isopods in the eastern United States. Females are slightly larger than males. The body is flattened, compact, and approximately three times longer than it is broad.

Behavior

The Madison Cave isopod consumes organic matter, such as leaf litter or dead insects, that is washed into its aquatic habitat by surface runoff. Females carrying eggs have never been found, but juveniles have been located, showing that reproduction is occurring. It is believed that females may hide in the leaf litter in the bottom of the fissures or in the inaccessible channels which feed the pools.

Habitat

The Madison Cave isopod inhabits freshwater, subterranean pools, which are fed primarily by an aquifer. Little is known of the physical and chemical conditions of its habitat. The temperature of the water ranges from 51.8-57.2°F (11-14°C), typical of groundwater for the latitude, and the water is sat-

urated with calcium carbonate, a condition also typical of groundwater in areas of limestone. The level of the karst aquifers can fluctuate for tens of meters at some sites. The extent of the recharge zone of the aquifer at any site is unknown.

Biologists have observed a slow seepage of water from Madison Cave pools into the nearby South River, a tributary of the South Fork Shenandoah River. Water levels in the cave vary somewhat with the river flow. For instance, two habitat pools found in Madison Cave have decidedly different depths: One is about 35 ft (11 m) deep, the other 75 ft (23 m) deep. Another habitat pool, in Stegers Fissure, is quite deep, at 100 ft (30.4 m).

Madison Cave—until 1990 thought to be the species' only habitat—was the first cave ever mapped in the United States, and the mapper was Thomas Jefferson (president of the United States, 1801-1809). George Washington (president of the United States, 1789-1797) also visited the cave and left his signature on the cave wall.

Distribution

The Madison Cave isopod is endemic to Madison Cave and the nearby Stegers Fissure (Augusta County), Virginia, as well as Front Royal Caverns and Linville Quarry Cave No. 3. This isopod is the only member of the Cirolanidae family in the eastern United States. Other members are found in Texas, Mexico, and the Caribbean.

Madision Cave Isopod, photograph by Russell Norton. Reproduced by permission.

Only a few of these isopods have ever been collected, and the size of the population is unknown. The isopod is difficult to study and collect, and is known only from areas where fissures descend to the groundwater table, thus allowing access to the surface of underground lakes, or deep karst aquifers.

Until 1990, the species was known only from two sites, Madison Cave and Stegers Fissure (near the cave); since June 1990, the isopod has been collected from five additional sites. Although specimens from all seven sites are morphologically identical, they probably represent more than one but less than seven genetic populations. Population size appears to be extremely small at five of the species' seven occurrence sites.

Threats

As early as 1812 deposits of bat guano in Madison Cave were mined for saltpeter (potassium nitrate) for use in the manufacture of gunpowder. Over the years visitors and spelunkers have left behind an accumulation of trash and contributed to siltation of the pools by trampling the steep clay talus banks. The entrance to the cave has now been secured against unauthorized entry, and the cave's private owner has developed a conservation plan, which is designed to satisfy parties interested in the cave's history, as well as those interested in the welfare of the Madison Cave isopod.

The aquatic resources of the isopod's habitat face the serious threat of mercury contamination. High levels of mercury have been measured in the South River, discharged by the now-defunct E. I. du Pont de Nemours and Company factory upstream at Waynesboro. Although no mercury has yet been found in the cave pools, it is feared that the groundwater could be contaminated during prolonged periods of high water. Even low levels of contamination would jeopardize the surviving population of the Madison Cave isopod.

Conservation and Recovery

Madison Saltpeter Cave is protected through co-operation between the property owner and cave conservation organizations. The cave entrance is protected by a steel gate, and all visits to the cave must be approved for scientific or educational purposes.

In 1995, a draft Recovery Plan was announced, developed to protect the isopod's population from potential threats to the quality of its deep karst aquifer habitat, thereby enabling the removal of the species from the federal list of endangered and threatened wildlife and plants. According to the plan, delisting may be considered when: (1) populations of Madison Cave isopod and groundwater quality at Front Royal Caverns, Linville Quarry Cave No. 3, and Madison Saltpeter Cave/Stegers Fissure are shown to be stable over a 10-year monitoring period; (2) the recharge zone of the deep karst aquifer at each of these population sites is protected from all significant contamination sources; and (3) sufficient population sites are protected to maintain the genetic diversity of the species.

Recovery activities designed to achieve these objectives include: (1) determining the number of genetic populations, (2) searching for additional populations, (3) identifying potential sources and entry points of contamination of the deep karst aquifer habitat, (4) protecting known populations and habitats from a watershed perspective, (5) collecting baseline ecological data for management and recovery, and (6) implementing a program to monitor recovery progress and future needs. Contingent on vigorous implementation of all recovery tasks, the plan reports that full recovery is anticipated by 2005.

Contact

Regional Office of Endangered Species
U.S. Fish and Wildlife Service
300 Westgate Center Dr.
Hadley, Massachusetts 01035
http://northeast.fws.gov/

References

Bowman, T. E. 1964. "*Antrolana lira*, A New Genus and Species of Troglobitic Cirolanid Isopod from Madison Cave, Virginia." *International Journal of Speleology* 1(1-2):229-236.

Holsinger, J. R. 1979. "Freshwater and Terrestrial Isopod Crustaceans (Order Isopoda)." *Proceedings of the Endangered and Threatened Plants and Animals of Virginia Conference 1978*. Virginia Department of Fish and Game, Richmond.

U.S. Fish and Wildlife Service. 1996. "Recovery Plan for the Madison Cave Isopod." USFWS, Newton, MA.

Lee County Cave Isopod

Lirceus usdagalun

Status	Endangered
Listed	November 20, 1992
Family	Cirolanidae (Cave Isopod)
Description	Eyeless, unpigmented crustacean-like isopod.
Habitat	Subterranean freshwater pools.
Food	Detritus.
Reproduction	Unknown.
Threats	Habitat disturbance, pollution.
Range	Virginia

Description

The *Lirceus usdagalun* (Lee County cave isopod) is an eyeless, unpigmented crustacean-like species measuring 0.2-0.3 in (5-7 mm) in length. The body is about 64% longer than wide, and the head is about one-third as long as wide, with deep incisions on its lateral margins.

Behavior

Unlike most other members of its genus, the Lee County cave isopod has adapted to a totally subterranean aquatic existence.

This isopod is undoubtedly a food item in the diet of certain natural predators, including cave salamanders and possibly cave crayfish.

Specific food items eaten by this isopod are unknown. However, it is believed that this species feeds on decaying organic matter consisting of deciduous leaf litter, twigs, and other wood particles. Parts from dead insects, presumably from decomposition of epigean insects that wash into the aquifer, are also eaten. It is also likely that this species feeds on bacteria, fungi, and other microorganisms associated with the organic matter.

Habitat

The area the Lee County cave isopod inhabits is riddled with caves, sinks and ravines in a water-soluble limestone substrate (karst). Such areas are particularly susceptible to contamination of groundwater from surface contaminants leaching through the porous substrate.

Distribution

This isopod was known historically from two cave systems, located approximately 6 mi (9 km) apart, in Lee County, Virginia.

The Lee County cave isopod is known to occur in only one cave in Lee County, Virginia. Since the discovery of *L. usdagalun* in 1971, biologists have conducted intensive searches of caves in Lee and surrounding counties with the specific goal of finding any additional populations of this species. Although these searches have revealed no additional populations of *L. usdagalun*, other isopod species of the genus *Lirceus* have been located in some other caves. When other species fill *L. usdagalun's* ecological niche in a closed cave ecosystem, there is virtually no chance of finding *L. usdagalun*.

Threats

This isopod was extirpated by groundwater pollution from one of the two cave systems it originally occupied. This pollution resulted when large quantities of sawdust, the by-product of a sawmill operation, were piled on the ground surface over the cave. Rainwater leached tannins and other toxins from the sawdust and transferred these through the porous substrate into the underlying groundwater, stripping

Lynda Richardson

oxygen from the water. Prior to its extirpation, a study comparing the populations in the two caves discovered that the populations differed in many ways. The unique characteristics of the extirpated population have been lost to the species forever.

The Lee County cave isopod could be adversely affected by an increase in human foot traffic through the cave, which could increase siltation in the streams it occupies. Presently, the location of the cave is not widely known, which led U.S Fish and Wildlife Service (FWS) to determine not to designate critical habitat.

Conservation and Recovery

The FWS published a Recovery Plan for the Lee County cave isopod in 1997. The only known critical habitats are privately owned and threatened by various human activities, especially those causing changes in hydrology or water pollution. These habitats must be protected by acquiring the land and designating ecological reserves, or by negotiat-

ing conservation easements with the owners. Nearby land-use must be managed to avoid threats to the underground habitat of the endangered crustacean. The populations of the Lee County cave isopod should be monitored, and research undertaken into its biology, habitat needs, and the development of beneficial management practices.

Contacts

U. S. Fish and Wildlife Service
Chesapeake Bay Ecological Services Office
177 Admiral Cochrane Drive
Annapolis, Maryland 21401-7307
Telephone: (410) 573-4500

U. S. Fish and Wildlife Service
Regional Office, Division of Endangered Species
300 Westgate Canter Dr.
Hadley, Massachusetts 01035-9589
Telephone: (413) 253-8200
Fax: (413) 253-8200
http://www.northeast.fws.gov/

References

Holsinger, J. R. 1979. *Freshwater and terrestrial arthropods freshwater and terrestrial isopod crustaceans (order Isopoda).* Proc. of symp. on endangered and threatened plants and animals in Virginia. Virginia Polytechnic Institute & State University, Blacksburg.

U.S. Fish and Wildlife Service. 1997. "Lee County Cave Isopod (*Lirceus usdagalun*) Recovery Plan." U. S. Fish and Wildlife Service, Hadley, Massachusetts.

Socorro Isopod

Thermosphaeroma thermophilus

Status	Endangered
Listed	March 27, 1978
Family	Sphaeromatidae (Isopod)
Description	Tiny crustacean with a flattened, oblong to egg-shaped body.
Habitat	Warm springs and algae-covered pools.
Food	Algae, detritus.
Reproduction	Three to 57 eggs laid every two months.
Threats	Restricted habitat.
Range	New Mexico

Socorro Isopod, photograph by Gerald L. Burton. Reproduced by permission.

Description

The Socorro isopod is a tiny aquatic crustacean with an average length of 0.32 in (8 mm). It has a flattened oblong to egg-shaped body with as many as eight mid-region (thoracic) segments. The abdomen is formed of two distinct segments. It has seven pairs of legs, antennae on the head, and oar-like extensions (uropods) on the last segment. The body is smooth and colored grayish-brown with small black spots and lines forming a band through each of the thoracic segments. Exposed edges of the body are tinged with bright orange. Various species of isopods are called pill bugs, sow bugs, or wood lice. The Socorro isopod was previously classified as *Exosphaeroma thermophilus*.

Behavior

Females produce broods every two months with April being the peak reproductive period. Brood sizes range from three to 57 eggs, and gestation is about 30 days. Isopods feed on algae, detritus, dragonfly larvae, and are occasionally cannibalistic.

Habitat

The Socorro isopod habitat consists of two small pools and two runs with relatively stable physical characteristics. Water temperatures range between 88 and 90°F (31 and 32°C). Algae covers most of the pool surfaces.

Distribution

The Socorro isopod is found naturally only in Socorro County, New Mexico, in three inter-connected warm springs.

The surviving population is confined to the water system of an abandoned bathhouse known as the Evergreen about 1.8 mi (3 km) west of the city of Socorro. This water system is supplied by thermal outflows from Cedillo Springs and consists of an animal watering tank, a smaller pool, and about

132 ft (40 m) of irrigation pipe. Captive populations have been established at the University of New Mexico in Albuquerque and at the Dexter National Fish Hatchery in Dexter, New Mexico. The wild population is relatively stable at about 2,500.

Threats

The Socorro isopod is threatened by the limited size of its existing habitat. Its native warm springs were long ago capped and the water diverted to the city of Socorro's municipal water supply. The amount of water in the isopod's present pool is so small that any interruption of flow jeopardizes its survival. In 1987 the plumbing broke down, the water system dried up, and the isopod ceased to exist in the wild. Captive isopod populations at the University of New Mexico and the Dexter National Fish Hatchery were used to restock the repaired pool, and population levels have nearly returned to normal.

Conservation and Recovery

In 1988 the state of New Mexico received a grant from the federal government to construct a larger, more natural, and more stable habitat for the Socorro isopod. This habitat consists of a series of connected pools supplied by a natural water flow. Cooperation among the state, the city of Socorro (which owns the water rights), the private landowner, and the U. S. Fish and Wildlife Service on behalf of the isopod has been exceptional. In fact, this little crustacean has attracted such favorable local attention that a nearby school's soccer team has been named the Socorro Isopods.

Contact

Regional Office of Endangered Species
U.S. Fish and Wildlife Service
P.O. Box 1306
Albuquerque, New Mexico 87103
http://southwest.fws.gov/

References

Cole, G. A., and C. A. Bane. 1978. "*Thermosphaeroma subequalum* (Crustacea: Isopoda) from Big Bend National Park, Texas." *Hydrobiologia* 59(3):23-28.

U.S. Fish and Wildlife Service. 1982. "Socorro Isopod (*Thermosphaeroma thermophilus*) Recovery Plan." U.S. Fish and Wildlife Service, Albuquerque.

Hay's Spring Amphipod

Stygobromus hayi

Hay's Spring Amphipod, photograph by C. Kenneth Dodd, Jr. Reproduced by permission.

Status	Endangered
Listed	February 5, 1982
Family	Crangonyctidae (Amphipod)
Description	White aquatic crustacean, 0.5 in (1.2 cm) long.
Habitat	Springs.
Food	Organic matter.
Reproduction	Eggs are carried on the female's belly until they hatch.
Threats	Flooding, construction, collection.
Range	District of Columbia

Description

The Hay's Spring amphipod, *Stygobromus hayi*, is a white, eyeless, shrimp-like crustacean only about 0.5 in (1.2 cm) in length.

Behavior

The Hay's Spring amphipod feeds on organic matter, such as leaf litter, decaying organic detritus, and dead insects. Individuals may live five to 10 years. Females carry eggs attached to their belly until they hatch.

Habitat

This species occurs in a small spring, possibly permanent but seeplike in appearance, within the National Zoological Park (in Washington, D. C.) in the heart of a densely populated urban area. The spring appears to issue forth from crevices in Precambrian rocks. The amphipods occur in decaying deciduous leaf litter and mud at the spring's exit. The spring water is cool, fresh, and not obviously polluted.

Distribution

This crustacean is endemic to Hay's Spring, a small outflow located within Rock Creek National Park in the District of Columbia. Only a small percentage of the population has been seen in the spring habitat itself. It likely inhabits cracks, crevices, and the bedrock area that form the recharge zone for the spring. The full range may extend to the limits of the groundwater aquifer.

The Hay's Spring amphipod is only known from Hay's Spring, on the grounds of the National Zoological Park in Washington, D. C. Although there are other springs within Rock Creek National Park, this species has not been found elsewhere since its discovery in 1940. No more than 10 individuals have ever been seen at the site at any one time. From what is known about similar species, such as *Stygobromus tenuis,* this amphipod probably evolved as a cave-adapted inhabitant of underground cracks and crevices. A second amphipod found in Rock Creek National Park is the undescribed *Stygobromus* sp., also a candidate for federal endangered status.

Threats

Flood waters from Rock Creek occasionally reach the level of the spring habitat, degrading water quality and disturbing the leaves and bottom sediments that form the amphipod's microhabitat. The site of the spring has been fenced, although protection is minimal, and no signs have been posted. Because the zoo attracts so many visitors, administrators fear that calling further attention to the small spring would cause greater harm than good.

Because of its location within major urban and commercial areas, there is always a possibility that Rock Creek, and the Hay's Spring, are vulnerable to sewage effluent and overflow during a flood. Urban runoff could threaten the aquifer. With such a small and limited population, even short-term changes to the water quality could result in stochastic extirpation.

Conservation and Recovery

The Smithsonian Institution's National Zoological Park has developed a memorandum of understanding with the U. S. Fish and Wildlife Service to protect the amphipod and the area adjacent to the spring. Some measures that have been undertaken in accordance with the agreement include limiting human access to the area, ensuring that park maintenance does not disturb the habitat, and monitoring water quality in the spring.

Contact

U. S. Fish and Wildlife Service
Regional Office, Division of Endangered Species
300 Westgate Center Dr.
Hadley, Massachusetts 01035-9589
Telephone: (413) 253-8200
Fax: (413) 253-8308
http://northeast.fws.gov/

References

Holsinger, J. R. 1977. "A Review of the Systematics of the Holarctic Amphipod Family Crangonyctidae." *Proceedings of the 3rd International Colloquium on* Gammarus *and* Niphargus, *Schlitz, West Germany: Crustaceans* 4: 244-281.

Holsinger, J. R. 1978. "Systematics of the Subterranean Amphipod Genus *Stygobromus* (Crangonyctidae), Part II: Species of the Eastern United States." *Smithsonian Contributions to Zoology,* no. 266.

U. S. Fish and Wildlife Service. 1982. "Determination of Hay's Spring Amphipod as an Endangered Species." *Federal Register* 47 (25): 5425-5426.

Peck's Cave Amphipod

Stygobromus pecki

Status	Endangered
Listed	December 18, 1997
Family	Crangonyctidae (Crustacean)
Description	Eyeless, unpigmented amphipod.
Habitat	Underground aquifer feeding the springs.
Food	Probably feeds on organic detritus.
Reproduction	Unknown.
Threats	Decrease in water quantity and quality; groundwater pollution.
Range	Texas

Description

Peck's cave amphipod is a subterranean, aquatic crustacean in the family Crangonyctidae. Like all members of the exclusively subterranean genus *Stygobromus*, this species is eyeless and unpigmented, indicating that its primary habitat is a zone of permanent darkness in the underground aquifer feeding the springs. In 1993, most specimens were collected in drift nets at spring orifices and were found less often downstream, supporting the notion that they are basically defenseless outside the aquifer and have little chance of survival much beyond its confines.

Peck collected the first known specimen of the amphipod later named *Stygobromus (=Stygonectes) pecki* in his honor at Comal Springs in June 1964. A second specimen was collected at the same place in May 1965. J. R. Holsinger named the species *Stygonectes pecki* in 1967, selecting the 1965 collection as the type specimen. He later included all the nominal *Stygonectes* species in the synonymy of the large genus *Stygobromus*. The U. S. Fish and Wildlife Service has used "cave amphipod" as a generic common name for members of this genus, and this name was simply transliterated as "Peck's cave amphipod" without reference to a particular cave.

Behavior

Little is known about the behavior of the Peck's cave amphipod. It occurs in a totally dark habitat, and avoids light. It probably feeds on organic detritus, such as dead biomass of plants, animals, and feces.

Habitat

Its primary habitat is a zone of permanent darkness in the underground aquifer feeding the springs. Individuals are easy prey for predators above ground, so they usually take shelter in crevices in rock and gravel, where they may succeed in reentering the spring orifice.

Distribution

Over 300 specimens of Peck's cave amphipod have been collected since its description. Most specimens were netted from crevices in rock and gravel near the three largest orifices of Comal Springs on the west side of Landa Park in Comal County, Texas. In 1993 one specimen was collected from a fourth Comal spring run on private property adjacent to Landa Park, and one specimen was collected from Hueco Springs, about 4 mi (6.4 km) north of Comal Springs. Despite extensive collecting efforts, no specimens have been found in other areas of the Edwards Aquifer.

Threats

The primary threat to Peck's cave amphipod is a decrease in water quantity and quality as a result of water withdrawal throughout the San Antonio segment of the Edwards Aquifer. Groundwater pollution from human activities also threatens to seriously degrade the water quality of its habitat.

Conservation and Recovery

The Peck's cave amphipod will only survive if its only critical habitat at Comal Springs is protected, and its essential hydrological and water-quality characteristics are conserved. Since the primary threat is associated with the withdrawal of water from the San Antonio segment of the Edwards Aquifer, it is crucial that this hydrological use be limited to an intensity that does not degrade the critical habitat at Comal Springs. The acceptable rate of water use by humans will have to be determined, and will have to account for the effects of periodic drought on groundwater recharge in the region. It will also be necessary to control the risks of local spills of pesticides, hydrocarbon fuels, fertilizers, and other chemicals, any of which could seriously degrade groundwater and damage habitat at Comal Springs. The populations of the Peck's cave amphipod will have to be monitored, and research undertaken into its basic biology and habitat needs.

Contacts

U. S. Fish and Wildlife Service
Regional Office, Division of Endangered Species
P.O. Box 1306
Albuquerque, New Mexico 87103-1306
Telephone: (505) 248-6911
Fax: (505) 248-6915
http://southwest.fws.gov/

U. S. Fish and Wildlife Service
Ecological Services Field Office
10711 Burnet Road, Suite 200,
Austin, Texas 78758
Telephone: (512) 490-0057
Fax: (512) 490-0974

Reference

U. S. Fish and Wildlife Service. 18 December 1997. "Endangered and Threatened Wildlife and Plants: Final Rule To List Three Aquatic Invertebrates in Comal and Hays Counties, TX, as Endangered." *Federal Register* 62 (243):66295-66304.

Illinois Cave Amphipod

Gammarus acherondytes

Illinois Natural History Survey

Status	Endangered
Listed	September 3, 1998
Family	Gammaridae
Description	Light gray-blue amphipod; first antenna is more than one-half the length of the body; primary flagellum has up to 40 segments.
Habitat	Dark zone of cave entrances.
Food	Dead animal and plant matter or the thin bacterial film.
Reproduction	Clutch size of up to 21 eggs.
Threats	Degradation of habitat through the contamination of groundwater.
Range	Illinois

Description

Sexually mature Illinois cave amphipod, *Gammarus acherondytes,* males are up to 0.8 in (2.0 cm) long; sexually mature females are 0.5-0.6 in (1.3-1.5 cm) long. The amphipod's color is light gray-blue, and the eyes are reniform (kidney-shaped), small, and degenerate with the pigment drawn away from the facets in an irregular black mass. The first antenna is long and slender, more than one-half the length of the body. The primary flagellum has up to 40 segments and the secondary flagellum has up to six segments. The second antenna is about three-fourths as long as the first antenna. The flagellum of the second antenna has up to 18 segments and lacks sensory organs in either sex.

Behavior

The clutch size is up to 21 eggs; egg-bearing females have been observed in summer and fall.

They are omnivorous scavengers, feeding on dead animal and plant matter or the thin bacterial film covering most submerged surfaces throughout their aquatic habitat.

This species is best differentiated from other amphipods in the field, especially from *Gammarus fasciatus,* which it resembles, by its color, small degenerate eyes, and a much longer first antenna. *G. acherondytes* is usually associated with the larger *G. troglophilus* but is much less common.

Habitat

This amphipod is a troglobitic (cave-dependent) species that lives in the dark zone of cave entrances. *G. acherondytes* inhabits the dark zone of cave streams. As a group, amphipods require cold water and are intolerant of wide ranges in temperature. They are strongly sensitive to touch and react negatively to light. High levels of dissolved oxygen appear to be an environmental necessity.

From an ecological perspective, an amphipod belongs to a group of species called detritivores that consume dead and decaying organic matter, recycling their nutrients back into the environment. Nutrient recycling is a critically important function in all ecosystems, especially nutrient-poor cave ecosystems. Amphipods can also be considered to be indicator species; that is, species especially sensitive to physical and chemical changes in their habitat, which can tell us when there is something critically wrong in the environment in general.

Distribution

The Illinois cave amphipod is endemic to the Illinois Sinkhole Plain of Monroe and St. Clair Counties and was historically known from six cave systems, which are all within a 10-mi (16.1-km) radius of Waterloo, Illinois. The main entrances to two of the caves, Illinois Caverns and Fogelpole Cave, are in public ownership and the other four are privately owned. The cave streams from which this species is historically known are each fed by a distinct watershed or recharge area; and there are no known interconnections between them, or with other cave systems. Two of the six caves may become hydrologically connected during extremely high rainfall over short periods of time. Thus, it is believed that there is virtually no opportunity for this species to become distributed to other cave systems via natural pathways.

There are few data or adequate survey techniques on which to base population, productivity, or trend estimates for this species. Sampling for cave fauna is difficult at best, and the challenges of surveying are compounded by the relatively small size of this species and the difficulty of researchers to distinguish it from other similar amphipods in the field. Thus, survey data are not sufficient to accurately record numbers of this small subterranean invertebrate; however, they do demonstrate a reduction in its range and the number of extant populations.

Since the initial collections in 1938 of unknown numbers from two caves, other collections were made. In 1965 at least 19 specimens were taken from the two caves sampled in 1938, plus a third cave. In 1972 unknown numbers were taken from two additional caves, and in 1974 six specimens were taken from one of the caves sampled in 1938. In 1986 there were two specimens taken from one of the caves sampled in 1938 and from a new, sixth cave. In 1992 a total of 20 specimens taken from one of the caves

sampled in 1938, and in 1993 there were 11 specimens taken from the two caves sampled in 1938.

A final twentieth-century sampling effort, and the most extensive, was in 1995 in which the Illinois Natural History Survey (INHS) investigated 25 caves in the Illinois Sinkhole Plain and confirmed the presence of the species in only three of the original six cave systems, all in Monroe County. The species was not found in any additional caves. In 1995, 56 specimens were taken from Illinois Caverns, 19 specimens from Fogelpole Cave, and two specimens from a third, privately owned cave. The species appears to be extirpated from the two caves where no specimens were collected in 1965 or 1986. Its status in a sixth cave remained uncertain because the cave entrance was closed by the landowner, and no surveys of the cave have taken place since 1965.

As a result of the extensive searches conducted by INHS, it is possible, but unlikely, that there are populations in other caves in the Illinois Sinkhole Plain. The INHS made an intensive effort to survey all the small side rivulets and drip pools in the 25 caves it sampled and believes that the collection results reasonably reflect the relative abundance of the species in cave streams of the Sinkhole Plain.

Threats

The degradation of habitat through the contamination of groundwater is believed to be the primary threat to the Illinois cave amphipod. Karst terrain, where this amphipod is found, is a geologic land formation typified by sinkholes and fissures that provide direct and rapid conduits for water and water-borne material from the surface to the groundwater, thereby avoiding the filtering and cleansing mechanisms normally provided by overlying soils. Water movement from the land surface to the water table in karst terrain often is nearly instantaneous, and flood pulses following a rainstorm may cause levels of contaminants to become up to 10,000 times higher than before the event.

There are several sources of groundwater contamination affecting the amphipod's habitat. The application of agricultural chemicals, evidence of which has been found in spring and well water samples in Monroe County, is one source. Also, bacterial contamination from human and animal wastes, which finds its way to subsurface water via septic systems, the direct discharge of sewage waste into sinkholes, or from livestock feedlots, is problematic.

Likewise the application of residential pesticides and fertilizers can cause contamination, as can accidental or intentional dumping of a toxic substance into a sinkhole.

This primary threat is believed to be caused by a reduction in the dissolved oxygen content of underground cave streams which, at times, may fall below life-sustaining levels. To a certain extent, this is a natural phenomenon that occurs during a rainstorm event. Storm water runoff is typically low in dissolved oxygen; when the runoff enters the groundwater, it depresses the ambient dissolved oxygen level in the cave stream. Under natural conditions, cave stream fauna can survive these short term, probably rare, depressions that may reach lethal levels.

However, human activities on the land surface have resulted in changes to this natural condition that make lethal levels of depressed ambient dissolved oxygen more common. With agricultural, residential, and municipal development, storm water now runs off the land more rapidly, reducing the time in which it reaches underground streams. Because of this more rapid runoff, the ambient dissolved oxygen in the cave stream will be depressed to a greater degree and can reach lethal levels faster. Furthermore, pesticides typically bind to soil particles; with the loss of vegetated buffers around sinkholes and fissures, more soil particles erode from the land surface and enter the groundwater carrying more pesticides with them. In addition, nitrogen-based fertilizers and organic wastes increase the demand for dissolved oxygen to accomplish biochemical breakdown. These factors exacerbate the natural depression of dissolved oxygen levels. Agricultural chemicals may either be lethal in themselves at certain concentrations, have chronic effects such as inhibiting reproduction, or can leave the amphipod in a weakened condition and less able to cope with short term depressions of dissolved oxygen.

Conservation and Recovery

Recovery can be achieved by protecting the quality of its habitat and by restoring stable and viable populations to the caves from which it has been extirpated. The U.S. Fish and Wildlife Service, the Illinois Speleological Society, and the Illinois Department of Natural Resources, are investigating the significance of cave visitation as a threat to the species.

The Illinois cave amphipod is listed as an endangered species under the Illinois Endangered Species Protection Act. As such, it is protected from direct taking (i.e., injury or mortality) regardless of whether it occurs on public or private land. However, state law does not protect species from indirect harm, such as habitat alteration. As long as the actions of private landowners are otherwise in compliance with the law, actions that destroy or degrade habitat for this species are allowed under Illinois law.

Contacts

U.S. Fish and Wildlife Service
Regional Office, Division of Endangered Species
1 Federal Drive
BHW Federal Building
Fort Snelling, Minnesota 55111
Telephone: (612) 713-5360
http://midwest.fws.gov/

Rock Island Field Office
U.S. Fish and Wildlife Service
4469 48th Avenue Ct.
Rock Island, Illinois 61201-9213
Telephone: (309) 793-5800
Fax: (309) 793-5804

Reference

U. S. Fish and Wildlife Service. 3 September 1998. "Endangered and Threatened Wildlife and Plants; Final Rule To List the Illinois Cave Amphipod as Endangered." *Federal Register* 63 (171): 46900-46910.

Kauai Cave Amphipod

Spelaeorchestia koloana

Status	Endangered
Listed	January 14, 2000
Family	Talitridae
Description	A cave-dwelling crustacean.
Habitat	Caves in limestone and calcareous rocks, and in lava tubes.
Food	Dead organic matter, especially plant biomass.
Reproduction	Lays externally fertilized eggs.
Threats	Destruction of the cave ecosystem by the influences of above-ground land use for various development activities, as well as poisoning by pesticides, and effects of predation and competition by introduced invertebrates.
Range	Hawaii

Description

The Kauai cave amphipod was first "discovered" in 1971. This unusual animal is placed within its own, unique genus (*Spelaeorchestia*). Among its unusual characteristics is a highly reduced, pincer-like condition of the first gnathopod appendage, while the second gnathopod is mitten-like in both sexes (these are attached to the cephalothorax, or the fused head and thorax in the middle region of the animal). This amphipod is also unusual because it lacks eye facets (lens-like divisions of a compound eye), is non-pigmented, and has extremely long and spiny post-cephalic appendages (located behind the head). Adult Kauai cave amphipods are 0.25-0.40 in (7-10 mm) long and slender-bodied, with a hyaline exoskeleton (a translucent outer cuticle). Its antenna is slender and elongate, with the flagellum (a thread-like structure used for movement) only slightly longer than the peduncle (a stalk-like structure). Its peraeopods (the abdominal walking legs) are very elongate, and tipped with slender, attenuated claws. All of the pleopods (swimming legs) are reduced, and their branches are vestigial (i.e., they are small and rudimentary, and probably non-functional) or lacking. The first and second uropods (tail-like appendages) have well-developed prepeduncles, and the brood plates are vestigial or absent in mature females.

Behavior

The Kauai cave amphipod is a detritivore, meaning it feeds on dead organic matter of decomposing plants, animals, and fecal material. Much of its food washes into its cave habitat, or is dead roots from trees growing above. It is not particularly gregarious. When disturbed, individuals typically move slowly away rather than jumping like most amphipods. Nothing is known of the reproductive biology of the Kauai cave amphipod, but the vestigial brood plates of the female suggest that they give birth to a small brood of relatively large offspring.

Habitat

The Kauai cave amphipod inhabits underground caves formed in limestone and calcareous sandstone, as well as lava tubes. It occurs in microhabitats that are dark and moist, and have organic debris of various kinds, including dead and living tree roots.

Distribution

The Kauai cave amphipod is a locally evolved (or endemic) species that is only known from five sites on the Hawaiian island of Kauai. Its populations occur in an area of only about 4 sq mi (10.5 sq km), in a coastal section of the Koloa lava flows that have not filled with erosional sediment.

Threats

The local area where the Kauai cave amphipod occurs is rapidly being developed, resulting in degradation or destruction of the cave habitat. The dominant land-uses are for agriculture, residential and tourism development, and golf courses; there is little natural habitat left. In fact, the Koloa cave systems are considered to among the ten most-endangered cave ecosystems in the world. The rare amphipods are also at risk from predation by and competition with introduced invertebrates, and the contamination of groundwater with pesticides and nutrients used in nearby residential areas and golf courses. Because of the small number of populations, each containing few individuals, the species is also at risk from such unpredictable catastrophes as hurricanes.

Conservation and Recovery

All of the known habitats of the Kauai cave amphipod are on privately owned land. The deliberate killing or collecting of the rare amphipod is illegal, but its critical habitat has not been conserved effectively. However, from the mid-1990s significant progress was made in the planning and implementation of conservation measures around three of the Koloa caves. In 1995, the U. S. Fish and Wildlife Service negotiated a cooperative agreement with a lo-

cal development company to implement conservation measures for two caves. The measures included gating of the cave entrances to restrict human access and reduce air-flow (to increase ambient humidity), and the planting of native trees over the caves to develop a root system that will serve as a food base for the cave animals. The private landowner also agreed to set aside an area above the two caves as either a limited-use park or reserve, and to not use any pesticides or dump refuse in this special-management zone. Negotiations are being undertaken with another landowner to conserve a third cave ecosystem beneath a golf course.

Contacts

U. S. Fish and Wildlife Service
Regional Office, Division of Endangered Species
Eastside Federal Complex
911 N. E. 11th Ave.
Portland, Oregon 97232-4181
(503) 231-6121
http://pacific.fws.gov/

U. S. Fish and Wildlife Service, Pacific Islands Ecoregion
300 Ala Moana Boulevard, Room 3-122
P.O. Box 50088
Honolulu, Hawaii 96850
Telephone: (808) 541-3441
Fax: (808) 541-3470

Reference

U. S. Fish and Wildlife Service. January 14, 2000. "Endangered and Threatened Wildlife and Plants; Final Rule To List Two Cave Animals From Kauai, Hawaii, as Endangered." *Federal Register* 65 (10): 2348-2357.

Alabama Cave Shrimp

Palaemonias alabamae

Status	Endangered
Listed	September 7, 1988
Family	Atyidae (Freshwater shrimp)
Description	Small decapod crustacean with a transparent shell.
Habitat	Cave pools.
Food	Detritus and plant matter.
Reproduction	Eggs possibly mature in autumn and hatch in winter.
Threats	Contamination of groundwater; collectors.
Range	Alabama

Description

Alabama cave shrimp (*Palaemonias alabamae*) is a small decapod crustacean that grows to 1.2 in (3 cm) in length. It is similar in outward form to a common ocean shrimp, but its carapace (outer shell) is colorless and largely transparent. It differs from the only other species of the genus, the endangered Kentucky cave shrimp (*P. ganteri*), by its smaller size, shorter rostrum (flattened frontal portion of the head), and fewer dorsal spines.

Behavior

Alabama cave shrimp feeds on detritus and plant matter that is washed into the caves. It is thought to have a low reproductive potential, bearing one-half to one-third fewer eggs than its closest relative, the Kentucky cave shrimp.

The species probably has a slow larval development. Throughout this period, many larvae die due to adult female death and genetic or embryonic developmental problems. As a result, the number of embryos emerging from the eggs are reduced by 50-66%. During the first summer, larval growth is rapid, but sexual maturity is not reached until the second summer.

In 1975 the first observation of gravid shrimp (females full of eggs) was made during every month between July and January. The number of eggs carried ranged from four to 30. It is believed that the eggs mature during the autumn months and are ready to hatch in the winter.

The sex ratios of Alabama cave shrimp seem to be equal. Longevity is unknown; however, results from aquaria studies on the closely related Kentucky cave shrimp indicated an estimated life span of 10-15 years.

Habitat

This albino shrimp is adapted to underground pools and streams eroded into the Warsaw Limestone formation of Alabama's Interior Low Plateau. Water levels in the five inhabited caves fluctuate seasonally; some portions of the caves dry out completely during the summer.

Shelta Cave, located in an urbanized area of Huntsville, consists of three large rooms with smaller alcoves. Water is present in all of the cave areas during wet periods; however, water levels fluctuate as much as 22 ft (6.7 m), leaving some areas of the cave seasonally dry. Miller Hall, the westernmost chamber, contains the only permanent body of water, West Lake, and the only permanent stream, West Creek. West Creek is shallow—6-8 in (15.2-20.3 cm) deep during low flow—has few riffles, flows to the southeast, and sinks 197 ft (60 m)

Alabama Cave Shrimp, photograph by Dave Dieter, Huntsville Times. Reproduced by permission.

from its source. High flows in the cave occur during winter and spring months of heavy precipitation. The recharge area (source of water) surrounding Shelta Cave encompasses approximately 34 sq mi (88.1 sq km) and is privately owned. Land use in the recharge area is urban or industrial/suburban.

Bobcat Cave is found on the Redstone Arsenal, a U. S. Army installation, and access is restricted. The cave consists of one large room with a low ceiling and several alcoves and passages. Water levels fluctuate dramatically throughout the year and at high levels may block the entrance passage. During summer and fall low water levels, the cave pool retreats through the cave floor to the aquifer below. Initial recharge surveys of Bobcat Cave have been completed. On the Redstone Arsenal, the land immediately surrounding the cave is in pasture and is leased for cattle grazing. Redstone Arsenal airfield is located about 1 mi (1.6 km) east of Bobcat Cave. Surrounding land is suburban, forested, pastured, or in agriculture. The suburban/urban areas are expanding and becoming more densely populated.

Hering Cave has a large tunnel-like stream passage and a large boulder-strewn outflow channel that exits from the cave entrance. Stream depth varies from about 3 in (7.6 cm) to approximately 8 ft (2.4 m) deep, with the cave flooding during rainstorms.

Glover Cave contains a tunnel stream passage with very few side passages and three standing pools of deep water. Water flowing from Hering Cave enters Glover Cave through an entrance and a sinkhole. Glover Cave can contain swiftly flowing water during the wet winter and spring seasons.

Brazelton Cave is a solution tunnel with numerous permanent pools of water and seasonal stream flow. This stream is hydrologically connected to the stream that flows in Glover Cave. Brazelton Cave floods completely during intense rainstorms and seasonally in the winter and spring.

Distribution

A search of more than 200 caves in northern Alabama has failed to locate Alabama cave shrimp anywhere but in the five aforementioned localities (Shelta, Bobcat, Hering, Glover, and Brazelton Caves) in Madison County, Alabama, in the Huntsville Spring Branch and Indian Creek drainages. Shelta Cave is within the northwest limits of Huntsville, Alabama. Bobcat Cave is located approximately 8 mi (12.9 km) southwest of Shelta Cave on Redstone Arsenal. Brazelton, Glover, and Hering caves are located approximately 12 mi (19.3 km) southeast of Huntsville and are privately owned. (These three caves are hydrologically connected and are considered one system.)

A sighting of three cave shrimp was reported in December 1993 from a cave in western Jackson County about 15 miles northeast of Hering Cave, but this sighting had not been verified as of September 1997.

The occurrence of Alabama cave shrimp in Shelta Cave is seasonal; no individuals have been observed during the months of March through June, and only a single specimen was observed during February. Typically, the winter and spring months receive more precipitation than other months. Difficulties in finding shrimp appear to coincide with high water levels as aquatic habitat expands and disperses the shrimp. During low water, the aquatic habitat shrinks and forces shrimp into the remaining available habitat, thereby increasing the chances of finding them. The greatest number of shrimp observed occurred in November (24 shrimp) and December (25 shrimp) 1968.

During December 1988, a six-day search of Shelta Cave failed to locate the Alabama cave shrimp, and shrimp surveys conducted there from 1990 to 1993 were also unsuccessful in relocating the species. No Alabama cave shrimp have been observed in Shelta Cave since 1973, and surveys indicate that the shrimp has apparently been extirpated. At least ten gravid females were observed in Bobcat Cave on the following dates: one in May 1992, an undetermined number in July 1991, three in August 1991, and four in October 1991. From a total of 128 shrimp observed in Bobcat Cave, only five gravid female cave shrimp were noted.

Not much information is available on the sparse populations of Alabama cave shrimp discovered in the hydrologically connected Glover, Hering, and Brazelton cave system.

Threats

The cave systems containing Alabama cave shrimp are found in karst formations. Karst is a lime-stone region characterized by solution features such as sinks, springs, underground streams, tunnels, and caverns. The susceptibility of karst to groundwater pollution has been well-documented. Surface pollutants can easily and rapidly enter the subsurface aquifer, particularly during storm events.

Urbanization of areas surrounding Shelta and Bobcat Caves and development in the recharge area of the Glover, Hering, Brazelton system may cause contamination of the aquifers containing Alabama cave shrimp. Groundwater contamination may result from sewage leakage, industrial contaminants, road and highway runoff, toxic spills, pesticides, and siltation. Urbanization has also increased water demand in Huntsville, Alabama. Huntsville experienced severe water shortages in the 1990s due to increased demand and drought. In response, the city drilled the Drake well, which is capable of pumping up to 2,000 gal per min (7,570.8 l per min). This well is located less than 0.5 mi (0.8 km) from Bobcat Cave. Increased water consumption has the potential to affect Bobcat and Shelta Cave aquifers by lowering groundwater levels and reducing the amount of available Alabama cave shrimp habitat.

Habitat degradation has occurred in Shelta Cave from unknown causes. Water samples taken in 1987 indicated that the aquifer had become contaminated by cadmium (almost five times the drinking water standards), heptachlor epoxide, and dieldrin.

Suburbanization is affecting areas near Glover, Hering, and Brazelton Caves. Forested land is being cleared for new homes on Keel Mountain. Septic tank systems are needed for each new home since no sewer system in place. The shrimp found in Glover, Hering, and Brazelton Caves will no doubt be in danger of surface water and groundwater contamination from sewage leakage, lawn fertilizers, pesticides, and increased surface runoff from residential development.

Predation may also have an impact on cave shrimp populations. Southern cavefish, (*Typhlichthys subterraneus*) is know to eat cave shrimp in Shelta Cave. Other potential predators in this cave include the Tennessee cave salamander and two troglobitic crayfishes. Potential predators that have been observed in Bobcat, Brazelton, Glover, and Hering Caves include bullfrogs, the southern cavefish, troglobitic crayfish, unidentified salamanders, and the Tennessee cave salamander. Predation by naturally occurring predators is a normal aspect of the population dynamics of a species. However, the effect of predation on a declining troglobitic species with an apparently low reproductive potential would be more significant than if the population were stable.

Conservation and Recovery

Until the early 1970s a maternity colony of the endangered gray bat (*Myotis grisescens*) provided energy in the form of guano (dung) to the aquatic system of Shelta Cave. The bat colony abandoned the site, possibly as a result of the installation of an entrance gate, development around the cave, or a combination of these and other factors. The entrance gate was modified in 1981 in an attempt to accommodate gray bats but based on more recent studies, additional modifications or a different style gate are needed to promote recolonization. Loss of the Shelta Cave gray bat colony caused a decrease in the organic input to the aquatic community of the cave, and may have resulted in, or contributed to, a corresponding decrease in the populations of other cave species. No bat colonies are known to have occurred in Bobcat, Brazelton, Glover, or Hering Caves, but individual bats have been seen hibernating or flying in Bobcat, Glover, and Hering Caves.

The entrances to Shelta Cave are owned by the National Speleological Society (NSS), which has erected gates to control unauthorized access to the caves. (Speleology is the scientific study of caves.) The NSS has also produced a management plan for Shelta Cave with the purpose of protecting and recovering the biological resources of the cave. The Environmental Protection Agency has restricted the use of heptachlor epoxide and has banned all uses of dieldrin. The Geological Survey of Alabama, Department of Army, and the U. S. Fish and Wildlife Service (FWS) have conducted hydrogeologic studies of Shelta and Bobcat Cave aquifers. A Huntsville schoolteacher and his students, along with members of the Huntsville Grotto, conducted water quality measurements and monitored cave species, including bats in Shelta Cave and fauna of caves in Madison, Marshall, Morgan, and Jackson Counties. The University of Alabama in Huntsville has completed

hydrologic modeling for Bobcat Cave and is developing a pollution model for the cave. Water quality and risk assessment studies of Bobcat Cave are also being developed. In a separate effort not directly related to the recovery of Alabama cave shrimp, the Alabama Department of Environmental Management initiated a groundwater protection education project for Madison County.

The FWS and the U. S. Army have developed a habitat management plan to protect Bobcat Cave against potentially damaging groundwater contamination. The FWS is also working closely with the NSS to develop regulation for recreational spelunkers (cave explorers) who use Shelta Cave. In the past there was evidence that spelunkers collected the cave shrimp, and, because of its low rate of reproduction, collection may have caused the shrimp's decline.

Contact

U. S. Fish and Wildlife Service
Regional Office, Division of Endangered Species
1875 Century Blvd., Suite 200
Atlanta, Georgia 30345
(404) 679-4000
http://southeast.fws.gov/

References

Bouchard, R. W. 1976. "Crayfishes and Shrimps." In H. Boschung, ed., *Endangered and Threatened Plants and Animals of Alabama*. Bulletin No. 2. Alabama Museum of Natural History, Birmingham.

Environmental Protection Agency. 1986. "Report on the Remedial Action to Isolate DDT from People and the Environment in the Huntsville Spring Branch-Indian Creek System, Wheeler Reservoir, Alabama." Environmental Protection Agency, Atlanta.

Smalley, A. E. 1961. "A New Cave Shrimp from Southeastern United States." *Crustaceana* 3 (2): 127-130.

U. S. Fish and Wildlife Service. 1997. "Recovery Plan for the Alabama Cave Shrimp." U. S. Fish and Wildlife Service, Atlanta.

Kentucky Cave Shrimp

Palaemonias ganteri

Status	Endangered
Listed	October 12, 1983
Family	Atyidae (Freshwater shrimp)
Description	Nearly transparent decapod crustacean with only rudimentary eyestalks.
Habitat	Cave streams and pools.
Food	Protozoans, insects, fungi, algae.
Reproduction	16-24 eggs.
Threats	Groundwater contamination; predators.
Range	Kentucky

Description

Kentucky cave shrimp (*Palaemonias ganteri*) is a small, nearly transparent decapod crustacean characterized by rudimentary eyestalks and bristlelike hairs on its unequally sized pincers. It is superficially similar to a common ocean shrimp, but the presence of reduced eyes and a lack of pigmentation indicate that this crustacean has survived underground for perhaps thousands of years.

Behavior

The cave shrimp is a nonselective grazer, feeding on sediments and detritus. Tiny protozoans and insects, fungi, and algae appear to make up the bulk of the diet. This species breeds year-round. Females produce 16-24 eggs.

Habitat

Kentucky cave shrimp inhabits the lowest passages of the Flint-Mammoth Cave System, the most extensive cave system ever discovered. In the absence of light, food sources must enter the cave in groundwater. The cave drainage comprises a complex network of still pools and flowing streams. The free-swimming Kentucky cave shrimp are concentrated in deeper pools where currents are minimal.

Distribution

Kentucky cave shrimp is endemic to the Flint-Mammoth Cave System, extending beneath Edmonson, Barren, and Hart counties, Kentucky. This broad system of passages and pools includes the Mystic, Echo, Styx, and Colossal rivers, Lake Lethe, and the Golden Triangle. In 1983 two crustaceans resembling the Kentucky cave shrimp were sighted in Blue Spring (Hart County), Kentucky. If confirmed, this sighting would extend the known range of the species outside of the caves proper. Surveys in the early 1980s examined 95 sites in 37 caves and produced a population estimate for the Kentucky cave shrimp of only 500 individuals.

Threats

The Flint-Mammoth Cave region has been extensively developed for tourism, and, although this shrimp has weathered many individual events, the cumulative effects of development on the quality of the groundwater may now be materializing. Surveys have shown a significant decline in the Mammoth Cave fauna since the mid-1980s due to pervasive groundwater pollution. The shrimp's small population makes it particularly vulnerable to extinction.

Kentucky Cave Shrimp, photograph. U. S. Fish and Wildlife Service. Reproduced by permission.

Because groundwater contamination recognizes no convenient boundaries, protecting the aquatic habitat of the caves is considered a regional problem. Several communities adjacent to the Mammoth Cave National Park are known to have inadequate sewage treatment facilities or lack facilities altogether. Untreated sewage could enter the cave system at numerous points and contribute to oxygen deficiencies or nutrient toxicity. Because the cave system is interconnected, the primary drainage runs directly through the caves, and harmful substances entering from the surface are immediately transported throughout the system. Additionally, contaminants from traffic accidents or roadside businesses have been introduced into the drainage. In 1980 a truck carrying toxic cyanide salts overturned on Interstate Highway 64 south of the park, and the resulting contamination killed thousands of aquatic cave organisms.

The McCoy Blue Spring, Suds Spring, and part of Groundwater Basins are located in oil fields where oil and gas are drilled. Brine from these wells is commonly washed into a sinkhole or into the Green River. It is also common for drillers to pull out casing, leading to the intrusion of oil, gas, and brine from the deeper strata that underlie the relatively shallow cave. In addition, agricultural development in the national park region has the potential of affecting cave fauna by contributing to the erosion of surface land that drains into the cave system. The introduction of rainbow trout into the watersheds of the Mammoth Cave National Park region may also contribute to the decline of the cave shrimp. Although the trout population seems to be relatively small, it may have successfully adapted to the cold subterranean waters, utilizing cave fauna as a food source. The trout has been observed eating the cave shrimp.

Conservation and Recovery

The U. S. Fish and Wildlife Service (FWS) and the Park Service hope to work closely with county and municipal governments to improve regional standards of sewage treatment and disposal. Additionally, a plan has been proposed to reroute vehicles carrying toxic chemicals, solvents, and fuels to provide a measure of security for the watershed of the Mammoth Cave National Park. It may be necessary to control the rainbow trout population as well. A section of habitat considered critical for the survival of this species has been designated to include 1 mi (1.6 km) of the Roaring River passage of Mammoth Cave. The FWS has stated that it may expand the size of critical habitat in the future, if groundwater contamination worsens.

Contacts

U. S. Fish and Wildlife Service
Regional Office, Division of Endangered Species
1875 Century Blvd., Suite 200
Atlanta, Georgia 30345
Telephone: (404) 679-4000
http://southeast.fws.gov/

U. S. Fish and Wildlife Service
Asheville Ecological Services Field Office
160 Zillicoa St.
Asheville, North Carolina 28801-1082
Telephone: (828) 258-3939
Fax: (828) 258-5330

References

Environmental Protection Agency. 1981. "Final Environmental Impact Statement, Mammoth Cave Area, Kentucky: Wastewater Facilities." Report No. EPA 904/9-81-076. Environmental Protection Agency, Atlanta.

Holsinger, J. R. and A. T. Leitheuser. 1983. "Ecological Analysis of the Kentucky Cave Shrimp, *Palaemonias ganteri* Hay, Mammoth Cave National Park (Phase III)." Report. National Park Service, Atlanta.

Leitheuser, A. T., and J. R. Holsinger. 1983. "Ecological Analysis of the Kentucky Cave Shrimp at Mammoth Cave National Park." *Central Kentucky Cave Survey Bulletin* 1: 72-80.

U. S. Fish and Wildlife Service. 1983. "Determination of Endangered Status and Designation of Critical Habitat for the Kentucky Cave Shrimp." *Federal Register* 48: 46337-46342.

U. S. Fish and Wildlife Service. 1988. "Recovery Plan for the Kentucky Cave Shrimp." U. S. Fish and Wildlife Service, Atlanta.

California Freshwater Shrimp

Syncaris pacifica

Status	Endangered
Listed	October 31, 1988
Family	Atyidae (Freshwater shrimp)
Description	Decapod crustacean; translucent when submerged; greenish gray with pale blue tail fins out of water.
Habitat	Freshwater streams with low gradients, slow currents, and overhanging vegetation.
Food	Fine particulate matter, including algae and zooplankton.
Reproduction	Lays 50-120 eggs.
Threats	Agricultural and residential development.
Range	California

Description

California freshwater shrimp (*Syncaris pacifica*) is a decapod crustacean similar overall in appearance to other North American freshwater (atyid) shrimp. Atyid shrimp can be separated from others based on the lengths of chelae (pincerlike claws) and presence of terminal setae (bristles) at the tips of the first and second chelae. The presence of a short supraorbital spine (above the eye) on the carapace (body) and the angled articulation of the second chelae with the carpus (wrist) separate the California freshwater shrimp from other shrimp found in California.

Adults are generally less than 2.2 in (5.6 cm) in postorbital length (from eye orbit to tip of tail). Females are generally larger than males. Females range from 1.3-1.8 in (3.3-4.6 cm) in length, whereas males range from 1.2-1.5 in (3-3.8 cm) in length.

Shrimp coloration is quite variable. Male shrimp are translucent to nearly transparent, with small surface and internal chromatophores (color-producing cells) clustered in a pattern to help disrupt their body outline and to maximize the illusion that they are submerged, decaying vegetation. Undis-turbed shrimp move slowly and are virtually invisible on submerged leaf and twig substrates and among the fine, exposed, live roots of trees along undercut stream banks. Both sexes may darken their bodies uniformly or gradually from top to bottom, but females have the striking ability to darken much more than males. The coloration of females ranges from a dark brown to a purple color. Two observed individuals in Lagunitas Creek were red. In some females, a broad tan dorsal band may also be present. Females may change rapidly from this very dark cryptic color to transparent with diffuse chromatophores, a distinctly different coloration. Neither juveniles nor males have the ability to change color to this degree.

Behavior

The reproductive ecology of the California freshwater shrimp has not been formally described. Reproduction seems to occur once a year. Based upon the reproductive physiology and behavior of other marine and freshwater shrimp, the male probably transfers and fixes the sperm sac to the female shrimp immediately after her last molt,

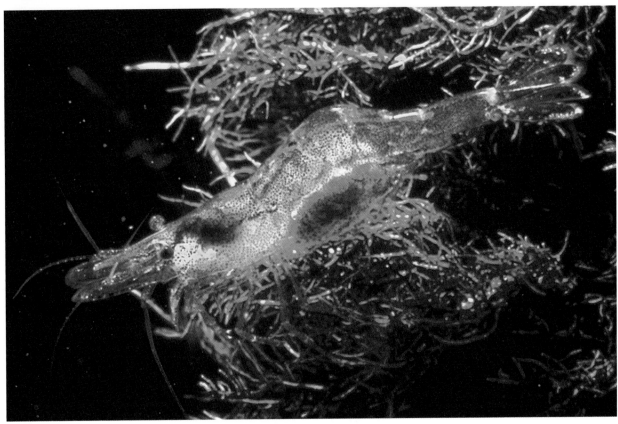

California Freshwater Shrimp, photograph by Larry Serpa. Reproduced by permission.

before autumn. It is typical for aquatic crustaceans to copulate during the female's molt just prior to the time of year she becomes egg bearing. The timing of mating was deduced from the presence of ovigerous (egg-bearing) females starting in September. Adult females produce relatively few eggs, generally 50-120. The eggs adhere to the pleopods (swimming legs on the abdomen), where they are protected and cared for during the winter incubation. Although not documented, fecundity (fertility) and egg size may vary based on the size of the female. In studies of other freshwater atyid shrimp, fecundity and egg size increased as the size of the female increased. Young are released in May or early June and are approximately 0.2 in (5.1 mm) in length.

Atyid shrimp (*Caridina* spp.) in tropical climates tend to breed throughout the year, while those in more temperate areas breed primarily in the summer. Apparently, California freshwater shrimp is one of the few atyid species that breeds during the winter period. The winter (December through March) incubation period is advantageous because the larvae are released during the favorable part of the hydrologic cycle in California, following winter and spring high flows.

Several aspects of the reproductive ecology of the shrimp are unknown. Courtship and mating behavior have not been described. No information is available on the percentage of larvae that reach reproductive maturity. In addition, there is no information as to whether aspects of reproduction are density dependent. The proportion of egg-bearing females of a tropical atyid shrimp has been shown to decline with increased population density.

Newly hatched young (postlarvae) grow rapidly and reach 0.8 in (2 cm) in length by early autumn. Growth slows through the fall, winter, and early spring and then increases through the second summer. A size difference between males and females becomes apparent around this time. Shrimp also reach sexual maturity by the end of their second summer of growth. California freshwater shrimp may live longer than three years; tropical atyid shrimp live only one year.

In aquariums, observed shrimp have remained motionless for long periods, clinging to plants and other objects. Cryptic coloration and limited movements probably reduce their risk of predation. Adults and young have been observed maintaining their positions in midwater through movements of their pleopods and telson (tail). In addition to being able to swim forward and backward, shrimp can "skip" over the water surface when disturbed.

California freshwater shrimp can be described as collectors. They feed upon fine particulate organic matter. Their food sources include 1) fecal material produced by shredders (a functional group that feeds on coarse particulate organic matter); 2) fine organic matter produced by physical abrasion and microbial maceration; 3) senescent periphytic (organisms attached to underwater surfaces) algae; 4) planktonic (free-floating) algae; 5) aquatic macrophyte (large underwater plants) fragments; 6) zooplankton (microscopic animals); 7) particles formed by the flocculation (formation of small loose clusters) of dissolved organic matter; and 8) aufwuchs (a matrix of bacteria, extracellular materials, fungi, algae, and protozoa). Shrimp observed on pool bottoms, submerged twigs, and vegetation seemed to feed on fine particulate matter. Atyid shrimp use their chelae to scrape and sweep detritus (loose organic debris) and small organisms from substrates. Captive shrimp have been observed frequently moving their maxillipeds (front legs) from substrate to mouth. Much of the material ingested is probably indigestible cellulose.

California freshwater shrimp may use visual, tactile, or chemical cues in foraging activities. Shrimp maintained in aquariums scavenge dead fish and shrimp. Captive shrimp have been able to detect and selectively consume commercial fish feeds. Commercially formulated feeds for prawns often incorporate chemoattractants such as glycine, proline, taurine, and trimethylammonium hydrochloride (imparts a fecal odor).

Presumably, shrimp diets change with food availability and age. For example, algae and plant matter increase in the stomachs of grass shrimp by the summer months. However, detritus and insects become more important in the winter. Younger grass shrimp typically had a higher percentage of detrital material in their stomachs than older, larger grass shrimp.

Habitat

Streams inhabited by California freshwater shrimp are part of the Coast Range, a geomorphic province that lies between the Pacific Ocean on the west and the Central Valley of California on the east. The Coast Ranges are composed of marine sedimentary rocks interspersed with metamorphic and igneous materials. Geologically recent erosion of surrounding mountains has resulted in the deposition of variable depths of alluvial materials along the floodplains and valleys of most of the shrimp-bearing streams. Shrimp have been found only in low elevation and low gradient streams. With the exception of Yulupa Creek, shrimp have not been found in stream reaches with boulder and bedrock bottoms. In fact, high velocities and turbulent flows in these streams may hinder upstream movement of shrimp.

The shrimp-bearing streams occur in counties with a Mediterranean climate. Such streams near the town of Sonoma experience average air temperatures of approximately 46°F (7.8°C) in the winter and 70°F (21.1°C) in the summer.

California freshwater shrimp has evolved to survive a broad range of stream and water temperature conditions characteristic of small, perennial coastal streams. The shrimp appears to be able to tolerate warm water temperatures (greater than 73°F [22.8°C]) and no-flow conditions that are detrimental or fatal to native salmonids. Under controlled conditions, juvenile and mature shrimp in an aquarium can tolerate standing water and water temperatures of about 80°F (26.7°C) for extended periods.

Although the laboratory studies indicate that the shrimp can tolerate brackish water conditions—at least for short periods of time—all records of the shrimp are from freshwater reaches in streams. Similarly, other atyid shrimp have demonstrated laboratory tolerance to brackish water but have not been found in similar salinities in nature. The current disjunct distribution of the shrimp and its suspected intolerance to ocean salinities make movement of adults among coastal streams and streams flowing into Tomales and San Pablo bays highly unlikely.

California freshwater shrimp are generally found in stream reaches where banks are structurally diverse, with undercut banks, exposed roots, overhanging woody debris, or overhanging vegetation.

Excellent habitat conditions for the shrimp involve streams 12-35 in (30.5-88.9 cm) in depth with exposed live roots (e.g., alder and willow trees) along undercut banks (greater than 6 in [15.2 cm]), with overhanging stream vegetation and vines.

During the winter, the shrimp is found beneath undercut banks with exposed fine root systems or dense, overhanging vegetation. These microhabitats may provide shelter from high water velocity as well as some protection from high suspended sediment concentrations typically associated with high stream flows.

Habitat preferences apparently change during late-spring and summer months. Shrimp are rarely found beneath undercut banks in the summer; submerged leafy branches were the preferred summer habitat. In Lagunitas Creek, Marin County, the shrimp was found in a wide variety of trailing, submerged vegetation. Highest concentrations of shrimp were in reaches with adjacent vegetation consisting of stinging nettles (*Urtica* sp.) and vine maple. None were caught from cattails (*Typha* sp.), cottonwood (*Populus fremontii*), or California laurel (*Umbellularia californica*). Populations of shrimp were proportionately correlated with the quality of summer habitat provided by trailing terrestrial vegetation. However, during summer low flows, shrimp have been found in apparently poor habitat such as isolated pools with minimal cover. In such streams, opaque waters may allow shrimp to escape predation and persist despite the lack of cover. Further research is needed to determine if both winter and summer habitat needs to be provided within the same location or if shrimp can move between areas containing either winter or summer habitat.

Although largely absent from existing streams, large, complex, organic debris dams may have been prevalent in streams supporting shrimp populations. These structures may have been important feeding and refugial (resting) sites for the shrimp because they tend to collect detrital material (shrimp food) as well as leaf litter, which can be broken down by microbial activity and invertebrates to finer, detrital material. In addition, debris dams may offer shelter during high flow events and reduce displacement of invertebrates.

Interestingly, atyid shrimp from other parts of the world display similar habitat preferences. Highest densities of *Caridina fernandoi* were found in areas underneath branched hairy roots of trees (tree roots afford protection from fish predation); only very low numbers were found on decaying leaves.

Distribution

Prior to human disturbances, California freshwater shrimp is assumed to have been common in low-elevation perennial freshwater streams within Marin, Sonoma, and Napa counties. By the late 1990s this shrimp was found in 16 stream segments within these counties. With the exception of Lagunitas Creek, stream reaches containing populations of shrimp flow through private lands. A substantial portion of Lagunitas Creek flows through the Samuel P. Taylor State Park, managed by the California Department of Parks and Recreation, and the Golden Gate National Recreation Area, managed by the National Park Service. A small segment of Salmon Creek flows through the Watson School historic site, managed by the Sonoma County Department of Parks and Recreation. On East Austin Creek, the Austin Creek State Recreation Area lies immediately upstream of shrimp populations. The most extensive surveys for the shrimp were conducted between 1982-85, when 146 locations were studied.

The distribution of the shrimp can be separated into four general drainage units: (1) tributary streams in the lower Russian River drainage, which flows westward into the Pacific Ocean, (2) coastal streams flowing westward directly into the Pacific Ocean, (3) streams draining into a small coastal embayment (Tomales Bay), and (4) streams flowing southward into northern San Pablo Bay. Many of these streams contain shrimp populations that are now isolated from each other.

Rising sea levels may also explain the presence of isolated populations in streams draining into Tomales Bay and the Pacific Ocean. Before the last sea level rise, the California coastline was 15-20 mi (24.1-32.2 km) westward from where it is situated today. During this period, Stemple, Walker and Lagunitas creeks were probably connected tributaries. The presence of shrimp in Walker Creek could have resulted in their movement to other streams draining into Tomales Bay at that time.

New information regarding the distribution of the California freshwater shrimp has been collected since its listing. The shrimp has been rediscovered in Stemple Creek, and new populations have been found in Keys, Redwood, and Garnett creeks (1994). In addition, U. S. Fish and Wildlife Service (FWS) biologists found a shrimp population in a new location on Austin Creek, upstream of its confluence with East Austin Creek. As evidenced by the recent discovery of shrimp within Keys, Garnett, and Redwood creeks, unsampled and inadequately sampled streams within Marin, Sonoma, and Napa counties could contain additional shrimp populations.

In instances where shrimp are present (historically or currently) in two connecting watercourses, the smaller tributaries generally support more abundant numbers of shrimp than the larger, receiving streams.

Threats

California freshwater shrimp's cryptic coloration and behavioral characteristics imply that predation played an important role in the evolution of the species. All life stages of the shrimp may be prey items for native fish. Other aquatic vertebrate predators may include western pond turtles, salamanders, and newts, which are probably present throughout many of the streams. Although western pond turtles are opportunistic generalists, their diet usually consists of small- to moderate-sized invertebrates. They are able to consume water-column invertebrates through a form of gape-and-suck feeding and may presumably use this technique to consume shrimp as well.

Several features of the shrimp's distribution and life history make it vulnerable to extinction. Existing shrimp distribution within streams is not continuous and is often along short distances. The few streams that historically supported the shrimp were permanent, low gradient streams in just three counties. Through geologic and climatic changes, shrimp populations in coastal streams (such as Salmon Creek, which may have been formerly connected to other streams) are now isolated by inhospitable reaches of sea water. As previously noted, adult shrimp are unable to effectively adjust internal body fluids at high salinities and presumably have lost the ability to persist in sea water. Therefore, local extinctions in streams draining to saline waters may prevent recolonization by natural means.

Furthermore, the shrimp does not have life-history characteristics that favor quick recovery following disturbances. The shrimp has relatively low fecundity, is believed to reproduce only once a year, and maturation requires over a year of growth.

The freshwater shrimp is threatened by several types of human activities, many of which operate synergistically and cumulatively with each other and with natural disturbances (e.g., floods and droughts). Factors associated with declining populations of shrimp include degradation and loss of its habitat through increased urbanization, instream gravel mining, overgrazing, agricultural development and activities, impoundments, water diversion, water pollution, and introduced predators. Shrimp populations in most streams are threatened by more than one factor. Although there have been no new threats to the shrimp since its listing, some of the factors that led to its listing have intensified.

Conservation and Recovery

The U. S. Army Corps of Engineers, which must issue permits for the construction of temporary dams, is now required to ascertain the impact of these dams on the habitat of the freshwater shrimp.

This species was listed as endangered by the State of California in 1980, and the California Department of Fish and Game has sponsored a significant amount of research on the ecology and the distribution of the freshwater shrimp. The Soil Conservation Service and the Coastal Conservancy are working with landowners along Salmon and Blucher creeks to develop conservation measures for the shrimp.

In the meantime, schoolchildren are getting into the act as well. One of the FWS's most unusual Partners for Wildlife projects evolved near the small town of Two Rock in a coastal dairy-producing region of Sonoma County in northern California. In 1993 the fourth grade class of Brookside School in the city of San Anselmo began discussing the plight of endangered species. The students' concern about the loss of wildlife led them to take action by "adopting" the California freshwater shrimp, forming a "Shrimp Club" and lobbying, raising money, and sending out information packets to educate the public, legislators, and area farmers about the importance of shrimp conservation.

Working with local dairy farmers, the students also rehabilitated portions of Stemple Creek by (1) fencing off parts of it, (2) planting native riparian trees, shrubs, and native perennial grasses on the banks, and (3) devising a system that allowed cattle to cross from one pasture to another without entering the creek. An estimated 4,000 ft (1,219.2 m) of Stemple Creek was enhanced by the school project, and the quality of shrimp habitat has improved markedly.

Contact

U. S. Fish and Wildlife Service
Regional Office, Division of Endangered Species
Eastside Federal Complex
911 N. E. 11th Ave.
Portland, Oregon 97232-4181
(503) 231-6121
http://pacific.fws.gov/

References

Eng, L. L. 1981. "Distribution, Life History, and Status of the California Freshwater Shrimp, *Syncaris pacifica.* " Endangered Species Special Publication 18-1, Sacramento.

Hedgpeth, J. W. 1975. "California Fresh and Brackish Water Shrimps, with Special Emphasis to the Present Status of *Syncaris pacifica*." Report. U. S. Fish and Wildlife Service, Portland.

Serpa, Larry. 1996. "The California Freshwater Shrimp." *Tideline* summer issue.

Strait, Daniel. 1996. "A Shrimp Spawns Partnership." *Endangered Species Bulletin* 21: 1.

U. S. Fish and Wildlife Service. 1977. "Draft: California Freshwater Shrimp Recovery Plan." U. S. Fish and Wildlife Service, Portland. 87 pp.

Squirrel Chimney Cave Shrimp

Palaemonetes cummingi

Status	Threatened
Listed	June 21, 1990
Family	Palaemonidae
Description	Transparent shrimp with reduced eyes.
Habitat	Flooded caves.
Food	Plant matter, insects, algae.
Reproduction	Females probably lay about 16-24 eggs.
Threats	Water pollution.
Range	Florida

Description

Squirrel Chimney cave shrimp (*Palaemonetes cummingi*) is transparent and measures about 1.2 in (3 cm) in length. The body and eyes are without pigment, and the eyes are smaller than surface-dwelling species. This species is also known by the common name Florida cave shrimp.

Behavior

Little is known of the reproductive cycle or diet of this species, although it is assumed to be similar to that of other cave-dwelling shrimp. The endangered Kentucky cave shrimp feeds on plant detritus, insects, algae, and fungi. It breeds year-round, with females producing 16-24 eggs.

Habitat

This cave shrimp inhabits a single sinkhole and flooded cave system near Gainesville, Florida. The 100-ft-deep (30.5-m-deep) system supports one of the richest cave invertebrate faunas in the United States, including McLane's cave crayfish (*Troglocambarus maclanei,*), the light-fleeing crayfish (*Procambarus lucifugus*), the pallid cave crayfish (*Procambarus pallidus*), and Hobbs' cave amphipod (*Crangonyx hobbsi*).

Distribution

Squirrel Chimney cave shrimp was described in 1954, after its discovery in Squirrel Chimney, a sinkhole in Alachua County, Florida, on the outskirts of Gainesville.

This cave shrimp has not been found in any other cave system. No population estimates are available.

Threats

Because of the limited range of Squirrel Chimney cave shrimp and the fragile nature of its habitat, any change in the sinkhole or the underlying aquifer could be devastating to the species and perhaps lead to its extinction.

The surrounding land consists of oak hammock and pine plantation. The area, situated on the outskirts of Gainesville, is undergoing residential development. The current owners have indicated a willingness to offer the Nature Conservancy the first option on the land surrounding the sinkhole if they decide to sell. However, this will not prevent the development of nearby areas. The increased erosion and pollution from septic tanks, pesticides, and herbicides resulting from such development could threaten the fragile cave fauna.

Construction of a proposed business/industrial park near the cave could pose a danger to this shrimp and other rare cave species. Alachua County has approved the development at a site about 6 mi (9.7 km) from Squirrel Chimney. Some scientists fear that the system of caves and underground streams that make up the aquifer could become contaminated by industrial pollution. The county development plan is awaiting state approval. Meanwhile, a local citizen's group has filed a complaint with the county government, the first step in trying to block the development in the courts.

Conservation and Recovery

In 1983 Squirrel Chimney was proposed for recognition as a National Natural Landmark. The National Park Service has not yet taken action on this proposal.

Contacts

U. S. Fish and Wildlife Service
Regional Office, Division of Endangered Species
1875 Century Blvd., Suite 200
Atlanta, Georgia 30345
(404) 679-4000
http://southeast.fws.gov/

U. S. Fish and Wildlife Service
Jacksonville Field Office
3100 University Blvd. South, Suite 120
Jacksonville, Florida 32216
(904) 791-2580

References

Chace, F. A., Jr. 1954. "Two New Subterranean Shrimp (Decapoda: Caridea) from Florida and the West Indies, with a Revised Key to the American Species." *Journal of the Washington Academy of Sciences* 44: 318-324.

Mohr, C. E., and T. L. Poulson. 1966. *Life of the Cave.* McGraw-Hill, New York.

Cave Crayfish

Cambarus aculabrum

Status	Endangered
Listed	April 27, 1993
Family	Cambaridae (Crayfish)
Description	Small, white obligate cave-dwelling crayfish with no pigment and reduced eyes.
Habitat	Along walls or edges of cave pools.
Food	Unknown, but probably roots, stems, and leaf fragments.
Reproduction	Egg laying likely occurs in late winter and early spring.
Threats	Depletion of oxygenated water.
Range	Arkansas

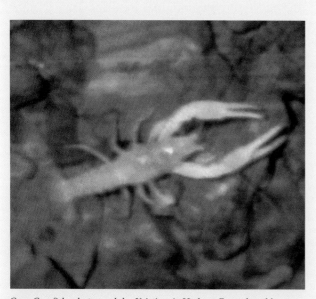

Cave Crayfish, photograph by Kristine A. Herbert. Reproduced by permission.

Description

The cave crayfish is a small, white obligate cave-dwelling crayfish. The body length of this species has been measured to reach up to 1.8 in (4.6 cm). This species has no pigment and has reduced eyes. It also has an acute or subacute apex of the antermomedian lobe of the epistome.

First form males are distinguished by a fully formed and hardened first pleopod (reproductive appendages). These males can be further distinguished from closely related *Cambarus setosus* and *C. tartarus* by the absence of a transverse groove separating the proximolateral lobe from the shaft on the first pleopod. It differs from *C. zophonastes* in that it possesses a longer central projection of the first pleopod that also has a shallow subapical notch.

Behavior

The reproductive habits of this species, as well as other sociobiological information, is not known at this time. This species, however, displays similar reproductive characteristics of other decopods. The males probably begin molting into the reproductive state in late summer with copulation occurring in late summer and fall. Egg laying likely occurs in late winter and early spring. Most males molt back to the nonreproductive form during April.

Habitat

Bear Hollow Cave contains a small stream approximately 660 ft (201.2 m) long and an undescribed pool that are habitat for *C. aculabrum*. The cave stream flow and depth varies. At times, parts of the stream may dry up leaving tiny pools of water or parts of the stream may completely disappear underground leaving no trace. After some rainfall events the cave may nearly fill up with water, as evidenced by trash found lodged up near the cave ceiling.

Water quality and clarity of Logan Cave Stream is generally high and many water parameters remain relatively constant for much of the year. Most changes in water properties occur when the cave's stream flow increases after a storm.

The cave crayfish is most commonly found along the walls of the pool, or along stream edges.

Distribution

The type locality of this species is Logan Cave as well as its associated stream and lake. The cave crayfish is also known from Bear Hollow Cave and its associated stream about 23 mi (37 km) from Logan Cave. Both of these areas are located in Benton County, Arkansas.

The numbers of crayfish observed in Logan and Bear Hollow Caves has varied dramatically between cave visits. The greatest number of crayfish observed in a single visit is nine in Bear Hollow Cave and 21 in Logan Cave. In 14 visits to Logan Cave, crayfish were observed on only three occasions. In a 1990 survey, three *C. aculabrum* were observed in Logan Cave, one of which was dead, and only a single crayfish in Bear Hollow Cave. Six crayfish were observed in Logan Cave during another cave visit in 1995 while four were observed in Bear Hollow Cave. From October 1994 through September 1995, between seven and 21 cave crayfish were observed in Logan Cave.

In an observation of other cave crayfish and troglobitic species, small population sizes have been a result of reduced food sources. As an adaptation to this it has also been observed that these species display a lower metabolic rate, increased longevity, delayed maturity and reproduction and decreased fecundity. The otherwise adaptive characteristic could make the cave crayfish highly vulnerable to environmental pollution and limit this species' ability to recover.

Threats

Cave crayfish are highly specialized for living in stable cave environments with low light and low temperatures and are unable to cope with changes in their habitats that may be induced by human activities. Water quality degradation represents a major threat to *C. aculabrum.* This species is also vulnerable due to its limited distribution, with only two known populations containing a small number of individuals; its limited reproductive potential; and the potential for take by humans.

Conservation and Recovery

In 1989 the U.S. Fish and Wildlife Service (FWS) purchased 123.9 acres (50.1 hectares) at Logan Cave (the cave crayfish's original locality). This attempt will facilitate preservation activities initiated by the FWS. The rest of the area, however, is privately owned.

A collecting permit is required for collecting for any species, except for fish bait under state regulations. Troglobites are protected from possession and sale by Arkansas state law.

Potential conservation measures and federal involvement are expected to include: (1) Environmental Protection Agency: Clean Water Act's provisions for pesticide registration and waste management actions. (2) Corps of Engineers: Inclusion of the cave crayfish in project planning and operation and during permit review. (3) Federal Highway Administration : Consideration of the cave crayfish in bridge and road construction in known areas of occupancy. (4) Farmers Home Administration: Consideration of impacts of the cave crayfish in loan processes. (5) Soil Conservation Service: Inclusion of the cave crayfish in farmer's assistance programs.

Contact

U.S. Fish and Wildlife Service
Regional Office
1875 Century Blvd., Suite 200
Atlanta, Georgia 30345
Phone: 404-679-4000
http://southeast.fws.gov/

References

U.S. Fish and Wildlife Service. 27 April 1993. "Endangered and Threatened Wildlife and Plants; Determination of Endangered Status Determined for the Cave Crayfish (*Cambarus Aculabrum*)." *Federal Register* 58(79): 25742-25746.

U. S. Fish and Wildlife Service. 30 October 1996. "Recovery Plan for the Cave Crafish (*Cambarus aculabrum*)." U.S. Fish and Wildlife Service, Atlanta, 37pp.

Cave Crayfish

Cambarus zophonastes

Status	Endangered
Listed	April 7, 1987
Family	Cambaridae (Crayfish)
Description	Translucent, cave-dwelling crayfish.
Habitat	Underground pools and streams.
Food	Organic matter and detritus.
Reproduction	Breeds at intervals of five years.
Threats	Restricted distribution, groundwater pollution.
Range	Arkansas

Description

The cave crayfish, *Cambarus zophonastes*, is a cave-adapted species that lacks pigment in the body and eyes. Its beaklike snout bears several spines. The overall body length reaches about 2.5 in (6.4 cm) at maturity. The carapace is translucent.

Behavior

This slow-moving crayfish, which appears lethargic because of its low metabolic rate, is an opportunistic omnivore, feeding on whatever organic matter washes into the cave system. It feeds on organic detritus, aquatic insects, and small crustaceans such as isopods, copepods, and amphipods. The crayfish reproduces very slowly; females deposit eggs perhaps only once in five years. In general, very little is known about the ecology and natural history of cave crayfish, and only limited observations have been made of this species.

Habitat

The cave crayfish is adapted to a constant, cool temperature and total absence of light. For food, deep cave organisms depend for the most part on organic matter imported in the groundwater. One of the primary sources of organic matter in caves is bat guano deposited by colonies of gray bats (*Myotis grisescens*), a federally Endangered mammal. When bat populations decline, the entire cave ecosystem suffers from the loss of guano as an energy source.

The cave crayfish is found in an Ozark Mountain cave that has been carved out of the Plattin Limestone formation. The cave is a "solution channel" or "tunnel" cave, most of which is wet and muddy year-round. Many of its passages are flooded during storms and wet seasons. The cave stream flows through 1,400 ft (426.7 m) of passage and emerges at three springs some 150 ft (45.7 m) from the cave entrance.

Distribution

The historic range of this species has not been clarified, but it could not have enjoyed a widespread distribution. More than 170 caves in north-central Arkansas and more than 430 caves in Missouri have been surveyed for this crayfish without success. The species may have never existed beyond the present distribution in Stone County, Arkansas.

The only known population of the cave crayfish is found in Hell Creek Cave in Stone County, Arkansas. Scuba divers located only 15 individuals in deep cave pools in 1983. In 1984 the total population was estimated at less than 50.

Threats

Probably the most significant cause of crayfish decline has been the decline of the (endangered)

Ken Smith, Arkansas Natural Heritage Commission

gray bat population. In the past a colony of over 16,000 gray bats used Hell Creek Cave, but few bats have been seen there in recent years. Though access to the cave is limited, it is feared that the presence of adventurous spelunkers may further reduce the bat species. Cavers also may have a direct, negative impact on the crayfish by forcing the often sedentary crayfish to become active, thus increasing their metabolic rate in a system where energy conservation is highly important.

The existing population is also threatened by water quality degradation from nearby highway traffic and its attendant hazards (such as a 4,000 gal, or 15,141.7 l, gasoline spill in March, 1985), siltation from industrial operations (concrete company and petroleum product storage) and real estate development (residential and commercial), sewage or effluents from septic systems, and transmission line right-of-way maintenance with herbicides. The species apparently has low reproductive rates, characteristic of obligate cave dwellers, and is also susceptible to collecting, a potential threat that looms in the future.

Conservation and Recovery

The Arkansas Natural Heritage Commission owns a 160-acre (65-hectare) tract that includes the entrance of Hell Creek Cave. The agency regulates access to the cave to prevent human disturbance, but much of the watershed surrounding the cave is privately owned. Protection of the habitat can only be assured by controlling the introduction of foreign substances into the groundwater. Monitoring of water quality and population levels will be conducted periodically. The recovery of the cave's gray bat population would aid in the recovery efforts for the cave crayfish as well.

Contact

Regional Office of Endangered Species
U.S. Fish and Wildlife Service
1875 Century Blvd., Suite 200
Atlanta, Georgia 30345
http://southeast.fws.gov/

References

Aley, T., and C. Aley. 1985. "Water Quality Protection Studies at Hell Creek Cave, Arkansas." Report. Arkansas Natural Heritage Commission and the Arkansas Nature Conservancy, Little Rock.

Harvey, M. J., *et al.* 1981. "Endangered Bats of Arkansas: Distribution, Status, Ecology, and Management." Report. Arkansas Game and Fish Commission, U.S. Forest Service, and National Park Service, Little Rock.

Smith, K. L. 1984. "The Status of *Cambarus zophonastes*, an Endemic Cave Crayfish from Arkansas." Report. U.S. Fish and Wildlife Service, Atlanta.

U.S. Fish and Wildlife Service. 1988. "A Recovery Plan for the Cave Crayfish, *Cambarus zophonastes*." U.S. Fish and Wildlife Service, Atlanta.

Nashville Crayfish

Orconectes shoupi

Status	Endangered
Listed	September 26, 1986
Family	Cambaridae (Crayfish)
Description	Green to dark brown body with a lighter region running along the mid-back to the head.
Habitat	Pools and flowing water.
Food	Animal and vegetable matter.
Reproduction	Copulation in late summer or fall; egg laying likely occurs in late winter and early spring.
Threats	Urbanization, degradation of water quality.
Range	Tennessee

Description

The Nashville crayfish, *Orconectes shoupi*, is a decapod crustacean that grows as large as 6 in (15 cm). Crayfish have four pairs of walking legs and two large claws in front, which are used to capture prey. The pinchers are elongated and the tips have a distinctive orange and black coloration. The hard shell terminates in a sharp point between the eyes. The general body coloration varies from green to dark brown. However, most specimens have displayed an area of lighter coloration on the mid-back region extending down along the sides toward the head.

Behavior

Very little is known about the biology of this species. It is an efficient bottom scavenger and feeds on plant and animal detritus, small invertebrates, and fish eggs. Males probably begin molting into the reproductive state in late summer with copulation in late summer or fall. Egg laying likely occurs in late winter and early spring. Most males molt back into the nonreproductive form during April. Parental care may occur as females with eggs and young have been observed in the spring.

Sex ratio and size of males and females appear to be about equal. Individuals appear to establish territories whose size is dependent upon the size of the individual and availability and size of cover, and the degree of crowding pressures exerted by such conditions as drought, lack of available habitat, and density. Densities have been reported from 0.6-11.9 individuals per square yard or square meter.

Habitat

The Nashville crayfish has been found in a wide range of aquatic habitats in Tennessee, including swift-flowing cobble runs and deep, still pools with mud bottoms. It often hides along the stream banks under limestone slabs. Crayfish require very high-quality water and have a low tolerance for pollution and siltation.

Distribution

The Nashville crayfish has been collected from four Tennessee localities—Mill Creek watershed (Davidson and Williamson counties), Big Creek in the Elk River system (Giles County), South Harpeth River (Davidson County), and Richland Creek, a Cumberland River tributary (Davidson County). Surveys conducted in 1985 suggest that the Nashville crayfish has been eliminated from all but the Mill Creek watershed.

Nashville Crayfish, photograph. U. S. Fish and Wildlife Service. Reproduced by permission.

The Nashville crayfish is currently found only in the Mill Creek basin in Davidson and Williamson counties, Tennessee. There are no current population estimates.

Threats

The Nashville crayfish has been eliminated from much of its former range by residential and urban development, which has contributed to a steep decline in water quality. Contaminants carried by rainwater runoff, silt from land clearing and residential construction, and diversion of groundwater have degraded many former portions of the crayfish's habitat. The lower Mill Creek basin lies within the Nashville metropolitan area, and it is estimated that more than 40% of the watershed has already been developed. Construction of a proposed wastewater management facility and a reservoir would seriously jeopardize the survival of this species. The upper Mill Creek basin has been degraded by silt and chemicals from agricultural runoff.

Crayfish are frequently used for bait by sports fishermen, and this rare species is often taken along with the more common crayfish. To counter this threat, personnel from the Tennessee Department of Conservation, Tennessee Wildlife Resources Agency, Army Corps of Engineers, and U. S. Fish and Wildlife Service (FWS) collaborated to develop a public awareness program to enable sports fishermen to identify the Nashville crayfish.

Conservation and Recovery

The FWS Nashville Crayfish Recovery Plan recommends that a second self-sustaining population be established outside of the immediate Mill Creek basin to guard against any accidental catastrophic event, such as a toxic chemical spill. If the Mill Creek population stabilizes and a second population proves stable for at least 10 years, the FWS would consider reclassifying this species as Threatened. Because of its low numbers and limited range, it is doubtful whether the Nashville crayfish could ever be completely removed from the protection of the Endangered Species Act.

Contact

Regional Office of Endangered Species
U.S. Fish and Wildlife Service
1875 Century Blvd., Suite 200
Atlanta, Georgia 30345
http://southeast.fws.gov/

References

Bouchard, R. W. 1984. "Distribution and Status of the Endangered Crayfish *Orconectes shoupi* (Decapoda: Cambaridae)." Tennessee Technical University, Cookeville.

Hobbs, H. H., Jr. 1948. "On the Crayfishes of the Limosus Section of the Genus *Orconectes* (Decapoda, Astycidae)." *Journal of the Washington Academy of Science* 38(1):14-21.

O'Bara, C. J. 1985. "Status Survey of the Nashville Crayfish (*Orconectes shoupi*)." Report. U.S. Fish and Wildlife Service, Asheville, North Carolina.

U.S. Fish and Wildlife Service. 1987. "The Nashville Crayfish Recovery Plan." U.S. Fish and Wildlife Service, Atlanta.

Shasta Crayfish

Pacifastacus fortis

Status	Endangered
Listed	September 30, 1998
Family	Cambaridae (Crayfish)
Description	Decapod crustacean with a dark green or dark brown back and bright orange underside.
Habitat	Spring-fed lakes, cool rivers and streams.
Food	Encrusting organisms, aquatic invertebrates, detritus, dead fish.
Reproduction	Mates in late September and October after the last molt of the year; females lay an average of 40 eggs in the fall.
Threats	Competition with non-native crayfish, degradation of water quality, stream diversion.
Range	California

Description

Also known as the placid crayfish, the Shasta crayfish is a small, decapod crustacean with a carapace length of 1-2 in (25-50 mm). Its color varies from dark green to greenish brown above, and the underside is bright orange or red, especially on the pincher-like claws. The often mottled coloration of the back provides excellent camouflage against stream and pool bottoms of volcanic rubble. Occasional individuals in isolated populations may be blue-green or blue on the top with a salmon-colored underside.

Adult Shasta crayfish are sexually dimorphic—males have narrower abdomens and larger pincers than females, and their first two pairs of swimming legs (swimmerets) are modified to transfer sperm to the female during mating.

Shasta crayfish are long-lived and slow-growing. Although age-class boundaries are often not very distinct, especially in older reproductive crayfish, the relative age of individual Shasta crayfish can be estimated from graphs based on data showing the relationship between age and size. It takes five years

for a Shasta crayfish to reach sexual maturity at 1.06 in (2.7 cm). The largest Shasta crayfish found to date was a male, probably 10-15 years old, with a length of 2.31 in (5.9 cm).

Behavior

No research has determined the food preferences and nutritional requirements of Shasta crayfish, but there have been a number of observations and hypotheses based on anatomy and observation in the field and laboratory. The failure to capture this species by using baited traps led to the premise that Shasta crayfish were either carnivores (meat eaters) or browsers (grazing on aquatic vegetation) rather than omnivorous scavengers (feeding on dead or decaying plants and animals) like signal crayfish, which are readily lured to baited traps. The structure of the mouthparts makes Shasta crayfish more efficient at scraping foods such as periphyton than the signal crayfish, which has a more generalized incisor surface. Shasta crayfish have been observed feeding on the small blackish-green snail, *Fluminicola* spp. In the field, Shasta

Shasta Crayfish, photograph by B. "Moose" Peterson/WRP. Reproduced by permission.

crayfish were observed apparently feeding on snails, a strand of dead aquatic vegetation that was probably a filamentous green algae, and organic debris.

During night dives, researchers have observed Shasta crayfish on rocks with their mouthparts moving; this behavior suggests the crayfish are eating organisms attached to rocks (periphyton) and possibly snails; however, crayfish can also move their mouthparts as a sensory behavior when they are not feeding. Shasta crayfish have been observed moving their first walking legs (pereiopods) to their mouths or moving their claws to suggest feeding; although the crayfish were apparently grazing, no specific food items could be identified. Other observations have been made under artificial or experimental settings that suggest that Shasta crayfish feed on freshwater limpets and tubifex worms.

The primary food of Shasta crayfish appears to be the periphyton and invertebrates that are abundant in their native environment. Other potential food resources include trout, sucker, and sculpin eggs, which are seasonally abundant. Although some of the items Shasta crayfish will consume are known, nothing is known about their actual nutritional requirements. Some understanding of the nutritional requirements of Shasta crayfish is necessary before initiating long-term captive breeding programs.

It is active mainly after dark, unlike other related crayfish species. The Shasta crayfish is a solitary creature, except during mating season. As it grows it undergoes several molts, during which it sheds its carapace. It mates in late September and October after the last molt of the year. Females lay an average of 40 eggs in the fall, which hatch the following spring. Crayfish reach sexual maturity after five years.

Habitat

The Shasta crayfish prefers clear, spring-fed lakes, streams, and rivers, and usually congregates near spring flows where the water remains cool throughout the summer. Most colonies are found in still or slow currents over a base composed of cobbles and pebbles or of clean sand.

The past and present distribution of the Shasta crayfish is integrally tied to the geologic history of the Modoc Plateau, an immense lava field covering most of northeastern California. Because volcanic rock is porous, most rainfall percolates through the lava into the groundwater. Surface water is minimal, so rainfall from more than 50 mi (80.5 km) away and snowmelt from Lassen Peak, Medicine Lake Highlands, and other lesser peaks feed the groundwater that comes to the surface at contact springs, formed where permeable lava flows overlie less-permeable material such as lakebed sediment, in the midsections of the Pit River drainage. The midsections of the Pit River drainage lie along the western margin of the Modoc Plateau geomorphic province.

The Lassen volcanic highlands are the source of water for springs where Shasta crayfish are found in the Hat Creek Basin. Precipitation on the Lassen volcanic highlands percolates through the lava into a large central aquifer system underlying Hat Creek Valley, which supplies water to Rising River and Crystal Lake springs.

Shasta crayfish are generally found in the cold, clear, spring-fed headwaters of the midsections of the Pit River drainage, particularly in the headwaters of the Fall River subdrainage. In general, Shasta crayfish habitat is defined by the availability of cover, or refugia (protected places), provided by clean lava cobbles and boulders on gravel or sand. Although potential food resources, temperature, and water chemistry, such as dissolved oxygen, calcium, and pH, may also limit the distribution of Shasta crayfish, the range of these conditions where Shasta crayfish are found is considerable.

The Bear Creek substrate is composed of silt, sand, Bear Creek gravel, lava gravel, lava cobbles, lava boulders, lava bedrock, diatomaceous earth/clay (earth composed of the shells of diatoms, a type of unicellular algae), or earthen clumps.

Shasta crayfish in the upper Tule River were found in two distinctly different habitat types that had only lava substrate in common. The spring areas were characterized by constant temperature, flow, and clarity, and the lava substrate in the immediate spring areas was clean, with relatively little silt. The headwater spring areas of the upper Tule River are much more turbulent.

Distribution

This species is endemic to a portion of the Pit River basin in extreme northern California. The Pit River arises in the mountains above the town of Alturus and flows south and west to empty into Shasta Lake. A population recorded from Sucker Spring Creek was extirpated before 1970. Populations documented from Lake Britton, Burney, Clark, Kosk, Goose, Lost, and Rock creeks disappeared some time before a 1974 census. Since 1978 the crayfish has disappeared from Baum Lake and Spring Creek.

The Shasta crayfish is currently found in the Pit River and in the watersheds of two of its tributaries—Hat Creek and Fall River (Modoc, Lassen, and Shasta counties), California. The largest concentrations of crayfish are found in the Fall River feeders—Big Lake and Tule River, Mallard, Squaw, and Lava creeks, and Crystal, Thousands, and Rainbow springs. Lesser densities occur in the Hat Creek feeders, Rising River Lake and Lost Creek. In 1980 the total population was estimated at less than 6,000 individuals, but had declined significantly by 1988.

As a result of construction of physical barriers and other disturbances that created large stretches of unsuitable habitat, Shasta crayfish became isolated into eight populations; however, only seven populations survive. The Fall River population, which was probably originally much more continuous than present, is now separated into four geographically isolated populations: (1) upper Fall River, (2) Spring Creek, (3) Lava Creek, and (4) upper Tule River, including Ja-She Creek, upper Tule River, and Big Lake. The (5) Fall River, Fall River Mills population is considered extirpated. The remaining populations include the (6) Pit River, (7) Hat Creek, Cassel, and (8) Rising River populations. The seven existing populations comprise several locations or subpopulations that may or may not have genetic exchange through interbreeding.

The largest population of Shasta crayfish, estimated at more than 4,000 individuals, is found in Spring Creek upstream of the four culverts at the Spring Creek Road crossing. Under normal flow conditions, the culverts at the Spring Creek Road crossing appear to create a barrier to the upstream invasion of signal crayfish.

Threats

Because the Shasta crayfish is slow to reach sexual maturity and has a low rate of reproduction, it is being displaced by two faster-breeding species of introduced crayfishes (*Pacifastacus leniusculus* and *Orconectes virilis*). These crayfishes reach sexual maturity within two years, and each female lays up to 150 eggs. Since 1978 more than half of the Shasta's historic range has been taken over by these aggressive species.

Human activities have also played a role in the Shasta crayfish's decline. Streams and springs have been impounded and diverted into artificial channels to support irrigation agriculture. Agricultural chemicals have washed into streams, degrading water quality, and excessive pumping of groundwater has lowered the water table.

Development of the Fall River and Hat Creek Valleys for hydroelectric production began in 1920. Major land reclamation and water diversion projects for agriculture and cattle grazing began even earlier in the Fall River Valley. These activities further divided the population of Shasta crayfish into isolated pockets. The introduction of normative species of fish and crayfish into the drainage has also had a significant negative impact on Shasta crayfish. Many species of fish introduced into the area are known to prey on crayfish, and the introduced crayfish can be predators and competitors of the Shasta crayfish as well. In addition, natural disturbances resulting from the eruptions of Lassen Peak, floods, and drought have likely had a significant negative impact on Shasta crayfish.

Hydroelectric development, including the operation of four powerhouses in the midsections of the Pit River, represented one of the first broad-scale disturbances to the Shasta crayfish population. The range of Shasta crayfish and other aquatic species was divided into at least five regions by 1922 due to habitat alterations, such as excavations, river impoundments, water diversions, inundations, and changes and reductions of flows. Some of the habitat alterations decreased the amount of available lava substrate.

Some secondary effects resulting from hydroelectric operations and management in the area include increased siltation and water temperature and decreased dissolved oxygen content in impounded sections. In 1964, California Department of Fish and Game constructed the Pit River Fish Hatchery.

Heavy machinery was used in the stream channel to remove boulders, and Shasta crayfish were most likely crushed. Almost all of the preferred substrate for Shasta crayfish, lava cobble and boulders, was removed. River gravel was placed in the channel to facilitate hatchery. A dam across the Sucker Springs Creek upstream has caused siltation and sedimentation, eliminating any remaining Shasta crayfish habitat upstream. The dam has also improved habitat for snails (*Fluminicola* spp.) that are the intermediate host for the gill fluke, a common parasite that causes hatchery fish mortality. Sucker Springs Creek was chemically treated on several occasions as either a treatment for, or prevention of, some trout diseases. In 1994, 2,400 lbs (1089.6 kg) of salt was added to the stream to exterminate snails. Salting is a nonspecific treatment that is harmful and even lethal to Shasta crayfish.

Six major activities associated with fisheries and fisheries management have affected Shasta crayfish: (1) the introduction of non-native crayfish species; (2) the introduction of non-native game fish species to provide sport fishing, with or without the sanction of California Department of Fish and Game and other agencies; (3) the introduction of potential crayfish pathogens by introduced species; (4) the management of hatcheries and hatchery trout; (5) the restoration and improvement of wild trout habitat; and (6) crayfishing. These activities have contributed to the observed decrease in the distribution and abundance of Shasta crayfish.

Within the last two decades, two species of non-native crayfish have been introduced into the midsections of the Pit River drainage. The Virile crayfish was introduced in the 1960s, and the signal crayfish was introduced in the 1970s. The introduction of both species probably resulted from angling and the use of crayfish as bait. Virile crayfish have since been replaced throughout most of their range by signal crayfish. The signal crayfish has rapidly expanded its range throughout most of the Pit River drainage and occurs with Shasta crayfish in at least a portion of five of the seven populations. The rapid expansion of signal crayfish has been linked to the diminished distribution of Shasta crayfish within their range.

Signal crayfish have all the characteristics of a classic invading species; they are larger, more aggressive, faster growing, earlier maturing, produce more offspring, and have a larger native range than Shasta crayfish. Signal crayfish also have a broader diet, greater physical tolerance to water temperature and quality, and a higher daytime activity rate than Shasta crayfish. In contrast, Shasta crayfish are slower growing, with a long generation time, a smaller native range, a more restricted diet, a narrower tolerance range of physical conditions, and a smaller body size at all ages than signal crayfish. Signal crayfish are aggressive and cannibalistic, and Shasta crayfish do not change their behavior to avoid signal crayfish, making Shasta crayfish vulnerable to competition and predation. Signal crayfish also carry several diseases, including those resulting from fungal (crayfish plague), protozoan, bacterial, and viral agents. Signal crayfish both carry and are resistant to the fungus that causes crayfish plague.

The introduction of exotic species of fish and crayfish, which are potential predators, competitors, and sources of new diseases and pathogens, is one of the biggest threats to the continued existence of the Shasta crayfish. Many species of game fish were intentionally introduced into the Pit River to provide sport fishing opportunities, including brown trout, largemouth bass, smallmouth bass, black crappie, green sunfish, black bullhead, brown bullhead, and channel catfish, all known to prey on crayfish. Common carp, which have also been introduced in the area, eat invertebrates living on river and lake bottoms.

Many native and introduced fish, amphibian, reptile, and mammal species in the midsections of the Pit River drainage are known to prey on crayfish. Other potential predators include bullfrogs, turtles, garter snakes, mammals, and a variety of birds. Bullfrogs, which are not native west of the Rockies, were introduced and are now common in Crystal Lake and Big Lake. Bullfrogs and garter snakes prey on crayfish.

Two of the three native aquatic mammals, river otters and mink, are known to prey on crayfish. Observations of a pair of river otters feeding on signal crayfish in the Pit River indicate that they are extremely effective and efficient crayfish predators. Most of the river otter scat found in the area is composed solely of pieces of crayfish shell. Muskrats, which prey on crayfish, were introduced into the drainage in the early 1930s. Racoons are also known to eat crayfish.

Conservation and Recovery

Between 1990 and 1995, three projects were initiated to study and/or manage Shasta crayfish, which included ecology and competition studies, competitor control and habitat improvement, and disease and fungus control studies. Habitat enhancement has been initiated in the Upper Fall River during the course of surveys for Shasta crayfish. Lava rocks covered by sediment were turned over and laid on top of the sediment to provide refugia for Shasta crayfish.

The invasion of non-native crayfish species, in particular signal crayfish, is the single largest threat to the continued existence of Shasta crayfish. The continued existence of Shasta crayfish will be ensured when the subpopulations of the seven remaining populations are protected from the invasion of non-native species, particularly signal crayfish, and from other disturbances. Spring Creek and Rising River are the only two populations where all subpopulations are currently free of non-native crayfish; all of the Hat Creek and Pit River subpopulations have been invaded.

The primary recovery goal is to protect and stabilize the known Shasta crayfish subpopulations, which will maintain the genetic diversity of the species. An important task is the designing, testing, and installing of efficient barriers that will prevent signal crayfish invasions. Other site-specific tasks include habitat restoration and enhancement, working with landowners, improving land use practices, eradicating signal crayfish, stabilizing river and stream banks with plantings, developing dredging alternatives, eliminating fish hatchery operations, and establishing fishing restrictions.

Contact

Regional Office of Endangered Species
U.S. Fish and Wildlife Service
Eastside Federal Complex
911 N. E. 11th Ave.
Portland, Oregon 97232
http://pacific.fws.gov/

References

Daniels, R. A. 1980. "Distribution and Status of Crayfishes in the Pit River Drainage, California." *Crustaceana* 38:131-138.

Eng, L. L., and R. A. Daniels. 1982. "Life History, Distribution, and Status of *Pacifastacus fortis*." *California Fish and Game* 68:197- 212.

Schwartz, F. J., R. Rubelmann, and J. Allison. 1963. "Ecological Population Expansion of the Introduced Crayfish *Orconectes virilis.*" *Ohio Journal of Science* 63:266-273.

U.S. Fish and Wildlife Service. 1988. "Determination of the Shasta Crayfish to Be an Endangered Species." *Federal Register* 53(190):38460-38464.

U.S. Fish and Wildlife Service. 1998. "Recovery Plan for the Shasta Crayfish." U. S. Fish and Wildlife Service. Atlanta.

Vernal Pool Tadpole Shrimp

Lepidurus packardi

Status	Endangered
Listed	September 19, 1994
Family	Triopsidae (Freshwater tadpole shrimp)
Description	Large shield-like carapace that covers most of the body, and a pair of long cercopods.
Habitat	Vernal pools containing clear to highly turbid water.
Food	Detritus, fairy shrimp, and other invertebrates.
Reproduction	Six clutches of eggs totalling about 860 eggs in the female's lifetime.
Threats	Urban development, agricultural conversion, sterilization by parasites.
Range	California

Description

Lepidurus packardi (vernal pool tadpole shrimp) adults reach a length of 2 in (50 mm). They have about 35 pairs of legs and two long cercopods. This species superficially resembles the ricefield tadpole shrimp (*Triops longicaudatus*). However, Lepidurus possess a flat paddle-shaped supra-anal plate that is entirely lacking in members of the genus *Triops*.

Tadpole shrimp have dorsal compound eyes, a large shield-like carapace that covers most of the body, and a pair of long cercopods at the end of the last abdominal segment.

Behavior

Tadpole shrimp climb or scramble over objects, as well as plow along in bottom sediments. Their diet consists of organic detritus and living organisms, such as fairy shrimp and other invertebrates. The females deposit their eggs on vegetation and other objects on the bottom. Vernal pool tadpole shrimp populations pass the dry summer months as diapaused eggs in pool sediments. Some of the eggs hatch as the vernal pools are filled with rainwater in the fall and winter of subsequent seasons.

The life history of the vernal pool tadpole shrimp is linked to the phenology of the vernal pool habitat. After winter rainwater fills the pools, the populations are reestablished from diapaused eggs that lie dormant in the dry pool sediments. Eggs found in one pool are hatched within three weeks of inundation and mature to sexually reproductive adults in another three to four weeks, although one scientist reported sexually mature adults occurred in another pool three to four weeks after the pools had been filled. A female surviving to large size may lay up to six clutches of eggs, totaling about 861 eggs in her lifetime. The eggs are sticky and readily adhere to plant matter and sediment particles. A portion of the eggs hatch immediately and the rest enter diapause and remain in the soil to hatch during later rainy seasons. The vernal pool tadpole shrimp matures slowly and is a long-lived species. Adults are often present and reproductive until the pools dry up in the spring.

Habitat

The vernal pool tadpole shrimp inhabits vernal pools containing clear to highly turbid water, ranging in size from 54 sq ft (5 sq m) in the Mather Air

Tadpole Shrimp, photograph by Larry Serpa. Reproduced by permission.

Force Base area of Sacramento County, to the 89-acre (36-hectare) Olcott Lake at Jepson Prairie. The pools at Jepson Prairie and Vina Plains have a very low conductivity, TDS, and alkalinity. These pools are located most commonly in grass bottomed swales of grasslands in old alluvial soils underlain by hardpan or in mud-bottomed pools containing highly turbid water.

Distribution

The vernal pool tadpole shrimp is known from 18 populations in the Central Valley, ranging from east of Redding in Shasta County south through the Central Valley to the San Luis National Wildlife Refuge in Merced County, and from a single vernal pool complex located on the San Francisco Bay National Wildlife Refuge in the City of Fremont, Alameda County. Fourteen of the 18 known populations of the vernal pool tadpole shrimp are imperiled, one of which is comprised of less than five pools. The report listed 3,092 "discrete locations"

that contained 345 records of the vernal pool tadpole shrimp.

Threats

Urban development and agricultural conversion imperil populations of the vernal pool tadpole shrimp in the San Joaquin valley. At least five pool complexes in the Central Valley of California that were known to contain suitable habitat for the vernal pool tadpole shrimp were eliminated by urban development in the late 1980s.

A 275-acre (111-hectare) site containing vernal pool and swale habitat for the vernal pool tadpole shrimp in the Jepson Prairie area in Solano County was destroyed by discing in October 1992.

Almond and fruit orchards in Stanislaus, Madera, and Fresno Counties continue to be planted in habitat suitable for the vernal pool tadpole shrimp.

In Solano County, an off-road vehicle park adjacent to the Jepson Prairie Reserve owned by the Nature Conservancy could adversely affect populations of the vernal tadpole shrimp.

A 370-acre (150-hectare) area around the Redding Municipal Airport lost 62% of its vernal pools during the period from 1952 to 1992, and 37% of the pools remaining are degraded. The vernal pool tadpole shrimp has been observed in these pools. Continued residential development and growing Eucalyptus farming around the airport imperils the pools that remain.

In the Chico area, certain areas inhabited by the vernal pool tadpole shrimp recently were ditched and drained, and there are four new proposed developments for this area.

Because of rapid urbanization, several highway projects are proposed that may affect the vernal pool tadpole shrimp. Vernal pools containing this invertebrate in the Sacramento area, in Solano County, and Butte County may be damaged by highway widening and improvements.

The modification of vernal pool areas to create artificial reservoirs, such as the Modesto Reservoir and Turlock Lake in Stanislaus County, have led to the extirpation of the vernal pool tadpole shrimp population that was known to occur in the vernal pools where these reservoirs now lie.

The U.S. Army Corps of Engineers has proposed the Merced County Streams project that would facilitate urban development in many areas that provide suitable habitat for the vernal pool tadpole shrimp.

Introduction of the bullfrog (*Rana catesbeiana*) to areas inhabited by the vernal pool tadpole shrimp appears to increase the threat of predation facing this crustacean. These amphibians are voracious predators on many species of native and exotic animals. Large numbers of vernal pool tadpole shrimp were found in stomach content analysis of bullfrogs captured in vernal pools in the Chico area. Although bullfrogs are unable to establish permanent breeding populations in vernal pools, dispersing immature males take up residence in these areas during the rainy season. A number of bullfrogs were observed at Jepson Prairie during the winter of 1992/1993.

Vernal pool tadpole shrimp were found to have been parasitized by flukes (Trematoda) of an unde-

termined species at the Vina Plains, Tehama County. The gonads of both sexes were greatly reduced in size and their body cavities were filled with many young flukes (metacercariae). Parasitic castration appears to be the major limiting factor affecting reproduction of the vernal pool tadpole shrimp at the Vina Plains. The range and extent of this parasite is unknown.

Conservation and Recovery

Some critical habitats of the vernal pool tadpole shrimp are in the San Luis National Wildlife Refuge, the San Francisco Bay National Wildlife Refuge, and in the privately owned Pacific Commons Project site adjacent to the Don Edwards San Francisco Bay National Wildlife Refuge. These habitats are being conserved. Other critical habitats are privately owned and imperiled by development and other threats. These critical habitats should be protected. This could be done by acquiring the habitats and establishing ecological reserves, or by negotiating conservation easements with the landowners. The populations of the vernal pool tadpole shrimp should be monitored, and studies made of its habitat needs.

Contacts

U. S. Fish and Wildlife Service
Sacramento Fish and Wildlife Office
Federal Building
2800 Cottage Way, Room W-2605
Telephone: (916) 414-6600
Fax: (916) 460-4619

U. S. Fish and Wildlife Service
Regional Office, Division of Endangered Species
Eastside Federal Building
911 N. E. 11th Ave.
Portland, Oregon 97232-4181
(503) 231-6121
http://pacific.fws.gov/

Reference

Goettle, B. 1997. "A "Living Fossil" in the San Francisco Bay Area?" U.S. Fish and Wildlife Service, http://www.r1.fws.gov/sfbnwr/tadpole.html

Insects

Hine's Emerald Dragonfly

Somatochlora hineana

Status	Endangered
Listed	January 26, 1995
Family	Corduliidae
Description	Large dragonfly with a yellow labrum, metallic green frons, and black leg segments.
Habitat	Bogs and a dredged channel of a small stream in heavy swamp woods.
Food	Unknown.
Reproduction	Unknown.
Threats	Habitat destruction.
Range	Illinois, Ohio, Wisconsin

Description

This is a fairly large dragonfly with a yellow labrum (upper part of the mouth), metallic green frons (front of the head capsule), and black leg segments. On its dark thorax (body segment between head and abdomen) are two yellow stripes, the second slightly wider and shorter than the first. The species is also known as Ohio emerald dragonfly.

Behavior

Information regarding the diet and reproductive biology of this species is unavailable.

Habitat

Most of the known specimens were found in bogs, but some were found along a dredged channel of a small stream flowing through heavy swamp woods. Breeding places were in wilder districts where original conditions had not been disturbed.

Distribution

The Hine's emerald dragonfly has been found primarily in Logan, Lucas, and Williams Counties in northwest Ohio and in northwest Indiana's Lake County. Specimens have not been collected at those locations since 1953, however, and the species was thought to be extinct until recently, when a population was discovered at a site in Wisconsin.

The largest number of specimens were collected from Oak Openings State Park at the western end of Lake Erie in Lucas County, near the urban and heavily industrialized Toledo area. Because of the habitat requirements of this species, its survival in that area is questionable. It has not been found in Logan County since 1930, in spite of intensive collecting of similar species. A single, probably stray, male was recorded from Gary, Indiana, but it is doubtful if a viable population was ever present there, since the area is heavily polluted from steel mills and associated industries.

Threats

Habitat destruction is the principal cause of the decline in this species' population.

Conservation and Recovery

An intensive search should be made for any remaining populations in Ohio and Indiana, especially in Lucas County, where the creation of Oak Openings State Park has provided incidental habi-

Illinois State Museum

tat protection. If a population is found there, efforts could be made to maintain the relatively undisturbed conditions in the park. The Wisconsin population is jeopardized by the proposed construction of a garbage compacting and hauling facility near its habitat. Efforts should be made to ensure that the habitat of this and any other surviving populations be protected.

Contact

U. S. Fish and Wildlife Service
Regional Office, Division of Endangered Species
1 Federal Drive
BHW Federal Building
Fort Snelling, Minnesota 55111
Telephone: (612) 713-5360
http://midwest.fws.gov/

Reference

U. S. Fish and Wildlife Service. 13 July 1999. "Availability of a Draft Recovery Plan for the Hine's Emerald Dragonfly (*Somatochlora hineana*) for Review and Comment." *Federal Register* 64 (133): 37806.

Zayante Band-winged Grasshopper

Trimerotropis infantilis

Status	Endangered
Listed	January 24, 1997
Family	Acrididae
Description	Body and forewings are pale gray to light brown with dark crossbanding on the forewings; hind wings are pale yellow with a faint thin band.
Habitat	Open sandy areas with sparse low annual and perennial herbs on high ridges with sparse ponderosa pine.
Food	Unknown.
Reproduction	Unknown.
Threats	Habitat destruction through sand mining and urban development; habitat loss and alteration due to recreational activities and agriculture.
Range	California

Description

The Zayante band-winged grasshopper, *Trimerotropis infantilis*, was first described in 1984 from a sand parkland area near Mount Hermon in the Santa Cruz Mountains, Santa Cruz County, California. The body and forewings are pale gray to light brown with dark crossbanding on the forewings. The basal area of the hind wings is pale yellow with a faint thin band. The hind tibiae (lower legs) are blue gray and the eye is banded. It is one of the smallest species in the genus. Males range in length from 0.5-0.6 in (1.3-1.5 cm); females are larger, ranging in length from 0.7-0.8 in (1.8-2.0 cm).

The Zayante band-winged grasshopper is one of 56 species in the genus *Trimerotropis*. This species is similar in appearance to *T. occulans* and *T. koebelei;* neither of these species is known to the Zayante sand hills region. *T. thalassica* and *T. pallidipennis pallidipennis* have been caught nearby but are not considered sympatric.

Behavior

The flight season of the Zayante band-winged grasshopper extends from late May through August with peak activity during July and August. Specimens have been collected as late as November 1. When flushed, individuals generally fly 3-7 ft (91.4-213.3 cm), stridulating (producing a buzzing sound) in flight. Band-winged grasshoppers often alight on bare ground, and they are conspicuous in flight because of the color of the hind wings and the crackling sound made by the wings. No additional information on the life cycle of this species is available.

Habitat

The habitat of the Zayante band-winged grasshopper was originally described as sandy substrate sparsely covered with lotus and grasses at the base of pines. Subsequent reports describe the habitat as open sandy areas with sparse low annual and perennial herbs on high ridges with sparse ponderosa pine. Such descriptions are consistent with those of sand parkland. Surveys also report that the Zayante band-winged grasshopper co-occurs with *Erysimum teretifolium* (Ben Lomond wallflower), a federally endangered plant. The significance of such an association is unknown.

Distribution

The Zayante band-winged grasshopper is narrowly restricted to sand parkland habitat found on ridges and hills within the Zayante sand hills ecosystem. The species was described from specimens collected in 1977 on sparsely vegetated sandy soil above the Olympia sand quarry. Earlier specimens were labeled only "Santa Cruz Mts., no date;" "Alma, 1928;" "Felton, 1959;" and "Santa Cruz, 1941." Because no specific location or habitat descriptions accompanied the original historic specimens, they were not considered in the assessment of current range and status of the species. The "Alma 1928" record may suggest distributional outliers, but no subsequent collections have been recorded to substantiate the current existence of such a population. Furthermore, the town of Alma has been inundated by a reservoir, and the cited specimens cannot be located in the listed depository for verification.

Between 1989 and 1994, Zayante band-winged grasshoppers were found at 10 of 39 sites sampled during two independent regional surveys. All 10 collection locations were on Zayante series soils. The habitat at these sites was consistently described as sparsely vegetated sandy substrate or sand parkland. The association and restriction of the Zayante band-winged grasshopper to sand parkland was further corroborated by an overlay of collection locations on maps delineating sand parkland habitat. All 10 collection locations fell within seven discrete areas of sand parkland habitat.

Threats

The Zayante band-winged grasshopper is primarily threatened by habitat destruction through sand mining and urban development. Other lesser sources of habitat loss and alteration are recreational activities and agriculture.

The vast majority of habitat loss can be attributed to sand mining and urban development; over 60% of historic sand parkland is estimated to have been lost through and altered by the above human activities. Only 49 acres (19.6 hectares) of sand park-

land habitat are publicly owned: 3 acres (1.2 hectares) of high quality and 6 acres (2.4 hectares) of low quality habitat are protected within the Quail Hollow Ranch, owned by the County of Santa Cruz; 20 acres (8.0 hectares) of low quality sand parkland are protected in the Bonny Doon Ecological Preserve, managed by the California Department of Fish and Game; and approximately 20 acres (8.0 hectares) of low quality habitat occur in Henry Cowell Redwoods State Park. The Zayante band-winged grasshopper does not occur in the Bonny Doon Ecological Preserve or Henry Cowell Redwoods State Park. The remaining 143 acres (57.2 hectares) of sand parkland are privately owned and at risk of loss to sand mining and urban development. Nine of the 10 Zayante band-winged grasshopper collection sites are adjacent to areas used for sand mining, and these insects are susceptible to the same elimination through crushing and exposure as the Mount Hermon June beetle. One site where Zayante band-winged grasshoppers were previously collected is now a parking lot. Two known locations of Zayante band-winged grasshoppers are adjacent to residential, commercial, and public developments.

Collection of the Zayante band-winged grasshopper has occurred during surveys for this and other invertebrate species, but overutilization by collection is not a current threat.

One Zayante band-winged grasshopper specimen was observed to be parasitized by a tachinid fly. However, the significance of parasitization on populations of this species is unknown.

Pesticides could pose a threat to the Zayante band-winged grasshopper. Pesticide application is expected at existing and planned golf courses and may also occur on a limited basis at vineyards in the area. Local landowners may use pesticides to control targeted invertebrate species around homes and businesses. These pesticides may drift and kill nontargeted species such as the Zayante band-winged grasshopper.

Conservation and Recovery

The seven discrete areas of sand parkland containing the 10 currently known collection sites have been secured through fee-title acquisition, conservation easements, or habitat conservation plans for Graniterock Quarry, Kaiser Sand and Gravel Felton Plant, and the County of Santa Cruz. A management plan for Quail Hollow County Park has been developed and is being implemented, and the population numbers are stable or increasing.

Contact

Regional Office of Endangered Species
U. S. Fish and Wildlife Service
Regional Office, Division of Endangered Species
Eastside Federal Complex
911 N. E. 11th Ave.
Portland, Oregon 97232-4181
Telephone: (503) 231-6121
http://pacific.fws.gov/

Reference

U. S. Fish and Wildlife Service. 1998. "Recovery Plan for Insect and Plant Taxa from the Santa Cruz Mountains in California." U.S. Fish and Wildlife Service, Portland.

Ash Meadows Naucorid

Ambrysus amargosus

Status	Threatened
Listed	May 20, 1985
Family	Naucoridae (Naucorid)
Description	Small, dark-colored, flat-backed aquatic insect.
Habitat	Spring outflows.
Food	Plant matter, detritus, insects.
Reproduction	Early spring and summer; eggs adhere to substrate during incubation.
Threats	Limited range, water diversion.
Range	Nevada

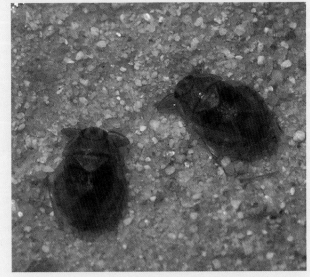

Ash Meadows Naucorid, photograph by Dan A. Polhemus. Reproduced by permission.

Description

The Ash Meadows naucorid, *Ambrysus amargosus*, is a small, dark-colored aquatic insect of the family Naucoridae, order Hemiptera. It is 0.2 in (0.5 cm) in length and superficially resembles a common brown water bug with a flat back and oval carapace.

Behavior

This species lives its complete life cycle in an aquatic habitat. It feeds on plant matter. All life stages feed on small aquatic insect larvae and other benthic arthropods, including spiders, centipedes, and millipedes.

When submerged, it breathes from air stored under its wings.

Although little is known about its life history or habitat requirements, food for closely related naucorids includes aquatic insect larvae that are preyed upon while the bug swims over and through the substrate. Reproduction occurs during early spring

and summer. Female naucorid bugs deposit demersal eggs that adhere to the substrate during incubation.

Habitat

The Ash Meadows naucorid has been found only in a single warm spring and associated outflow streams with rock and gravel substrates. This aquatic insect is known to occupy an extremely restricted habitat where flowing water passes over rock and pebble substrates at Point of Rocks Springs.

Distribution

There is no evidence that this species ever occurred in other springs or streams of the Ash Meadows region in Nevada. Most Ash Meadows springs are cold, while this species requires thermal waters. Channelization of spring flows for irrigation and other purposes has restricted the original habitat.

This naucorid is found only at Point of Rocks Springs and its outflow streams in east-central Ash Meadows. During the late 1970s a developer dammed the Point of Rocks Springs outflow to supply a planned residential and resort community of 55,000. Although this project was eventually abandoned, the natural streams inhabited by the naucorid were lost, and the species is now restricted to several narrow artificial channels less than 33 ft (10 m) long. Approximately 10 acres (4 hectares) at Point of Rocks Springs are designated critical habitat for the species. There is no current population estimate.

Threats

The small size and vulnerability of its habitats makes the naucorid highly susceptible to extirpation. One threat to the naucorid's survival is potential groundwater depletion, which would decrease spring flows. In 1982, it was found that users were certified to consume more water per year than the Ash Meadows aquifer actually discharged. If users drew the maximum amount of water allowed, the habitats supporting the Ash Meadows flora and fauna would be destroyed. Subsequently, the courts acted to limit the amount of groundwater that could be pumped from the aquifer.

Conservation and Recovery

The remaining habitat of the Ash Meadows naucorid falls within the Ash Meadows Wildlife Refuge. About 10 acres (4 hectares) has been designated as critical habitat for the species, including Point of Rocks Springs and its immediate outflows. The federally listed Ash Meadows Amargosa pupfish (*Cyprinodon nevadensis mionectes*) shares the same spring outflow area with the naucorid.

Contact

U. S. Fish and Wildlife Service
Regional Office, Division of Endangered Species
Eastside Federal Complex
911 N. E. 11th Ave.
Portland, Oregon 97232-4181
Telephone: (503) 231-6121
http://pacific.fws.gov/

References

La Rivers, I. 1953. "New *Gelastocorid* and *Naucorid* Records and Miscellaneous Notes with a Description of the New Species, *Ambrysus amargosus* (Hemiptera: Naucoridae)." *The Wasmann Journal of Biology* 11: 83-96.

U. S. Fish and Wildlife Service. 1985. "Determination of Threatened Status with Critical Habitat for Six Plants and One Insect in Ash Meadows, Nevada and California; and Endangered Status with Critical Habitat for One Plant in Ash Meadows." *Federal Register* 50 (97): 20777-20794.

Northeastern Beach Tiger Beetle

Cicindela dorsalis dorsalis

Status	Threatened
Listed	August 7, 1990
Family	Cicindelidae (Tiger beetle)
Description	A ground-dwelling beetle.
Habitat	Sandy, sparsely vegetated beaches.
Food	A predator of other invertebrates; also feeds on carrion.
Reproduction	Lays internally fertilized eggs, and has a life cycle that spans two years.
Threats	Habitat destruction by residential and commercial development, and ongoing damage by trampling, erosion control, and insecticide spraying.
Range	Connecticut, Maryland, Massachusetts, New Jersey, Rhode Island, Virginia

U.S. Fish and Wildlife Service, Gene Nieminen.

Description

The northeastern beach tiger beetle is a small, handsome, sand-colored beetle. Its wing covers (or elytra) are colored whitish to light-tan, and are usually marked with fine dark lines. The head and thorax are colored bronze-green. The body length ranges from 0.5 to 0.6 in (13 to 16 mm). It has long, sickle-like mandibles (mouthparts), which are used to grasp its invertebrate prey. The larvae are also predatory and similarly equipped. It takes two years for the larva to develop into an adult.

Behavior

The adult northeastern beach tiger beetle overwinters in a burrow it digs in the sand. It emerges in June and is active through August to early September. This beetle relies on the sun to regulate its body temperature, and spends the early morning and late afternoon basking. It burrows into the sand at night for protection and to conserve energy. The northeastern beach tiger beetle is largely a scav-enger, feeding on dead crabs and fish, but will also prey on live amphipods or small flies.

Habitat

The northeastern beach tiger beetle inhabits sparsely vegetated, finely sandy, coastal beaches.

Distribution

The northeastern beach tiger beetle occurs in the northeastern United States, and has been reported from Connecticut, Massachusetts, Maryland, New Jersey, New York, Pennsylvania, Rhode Island, and Virginia. The U. S. Fish and Wildlife Service (FWS) considers this species Threatened in Connecticut, Maryland, Massachusetts, New Jersey, Rhode Island, and Virginia.

Threats

The northeastern beach tiger beetle has declined greatly in range and abundance due to the destruction of much of its original habitat, mostly through its conversion into land-uses for residential, commercial, and industrial purposes. Habitat damage has also been caused by trampling by people and all-terrain vehicles, the construction of erosion-control structures, the spraying of insecticides to control mosquitoes, and other disturbances. The decline of the northeastern beach tiger beetle has been especially severe in northern parts of its range; it no longer occurs north of Virginia. The largest remaining populations, albeit in declining numbers, occur on the shores of the Chesapeake Bay in Maryland and Virginia. More than 50 sites still occur in the Chesapeake Bay area, of which about half have more than 100 adults, and 16 have more than 500 adults.

Conservation and Recovery

Numerous habitats of the northeastern beach tiger beetle have been conserved in parks and other kinds of protected areas. However, there is still ongoing habitat damage through trampling and other human activities. It is essential that the critical habitats of this rare beetle are better protected from these and other ongoing stresses, or the populations will probably become extirpated. The FWS has been introducing the northeastern tiger beetle to suitable beach habitat in the Gateway National Recreation Area in New Jersey, a state where the species had been extirpated. If the habitat is suitably protected, this program could probably be expanded to increase the range and abundance of the northeastern beach tiger beetle.

Contact

U. S. Fish and Wildlife Service
Regional Office, Division of Endangered Species
300 Westgate Center Dr.
Hadley, Massachusetts 01035-9589
Telephone: (413) 253-8200
Fax: (413) 253-8308
http://www.northeast.fws.gov/

Endangered Species Unit
New York State Department of Environmental
Conservation
108 Game Farm Road
Delmar, New York 12054

References

New York State Department of Environmental Conservation. 1998. Northeastern Beach Tiger Beetle Fact Sheet. http://www.dec.state.ny.us/website/dfwmr/wildlife/endspec/nbtbfs.html

Luebke, J. I. and D. R. Beatty. 1987. "Natural history and population decline of the coastal tiger beetle. *Cicindela dorsalis dorsalis* Say (Coleoptera: Cicindelidae)." *Virginia Journal of Science* 38(4):293-303.

Puritan Tiger Beetle

Cicindela puritana

Status	Threatened
Listed	August 7, 1990
Family	Cicindelidae (Tiger beetle)
Description	Brownish bronze above and metallic blue below, marginal white bands on wingcovers.
Habitat	Beaches and adjacent cliffs.
Food	Small invertebrates.
Reproduction	Larva with three stages.
Threats	Habitat disruption by humans.
Range	Connecticut, Maryland, Massachusetts, New Hampshire, Vermont

Description

The Puritan tiger beetle measures about 0.5 in (1.2 cm) in length. It is brownish bronze above with a metallic blue underside. The wing covers (elytrons) are marked with narrow marginal and transverse white bands.

In the past it has been considered a subspecies of *Cicindela cuprascens* and of *C. macra*. It was again recognized as a separate species in 1967.

Behavior

Both adult and larval tiger beetles prey on small arthropods. The adults grasp their prey with their mandables in a "tiger-like" manner. The larvae, which live in ground burrows, attach themselves near the entrance with abdominal hooks and extend quickly to capture passing prey.

Adult Puritan tiger beetles appear in mid-June, with numbers peaking in early July and declining by late July. After mating, females move from beaches to nearby cliffs where they deposit their eggs. The newly hatched larvae dig burrows in the cliffs, where they pass through three larval stages (instars). Recent studies indicate that they do not metamorphose into adults until the second year.

Habitat

The Puritan tiger beetle inhabits beach areas with adjacent sand or clay cliffs. Adult beetles feed and mate along the beach and use the sparsely vegetated cliff areas for depositing eggs. Larvae inhabit the cliff sites, moving to the beach as adults.

Distribution

The Puritan tiger beetle was once known from scattered locations along the Connecticut River in Vermont, New Hampshire, Massachusetts, and Connecticut. It has also been found along the Chesapeake Bay in Calvert County, Maryland, and along a short stretch of the Sassafras River in Kent and Cecil counties on Maryland's Eastern Shore.

Most New England collections date from the early 1900s, and until recently it was believed that the beetle had been extirpated from that region. However, recently two new populations have been discovered.

The Puritan tiger beetle survives at two locations in New England and two locations around the Chesapeake Bay in Maryland. In 1986 a small population of fewer than 100 adult beetles was discovered in Hampshire County, Massachusetts, on a small island in the Connecticut River, and on a nearby sandy beach. In 1989 a larger population was found near Cromwell in Middlesex County, Connecticut. This site is unusual since there are no adjacent cliffs or clay banks, and the larvae burrow in the ground.

Five large populations of more than 600 adults and four small populations of fewer than 100 are scattered along 26 miles of the Chesapeake Bay in Clavert County, Maryland. The Sassafras County populations, which were only discovered in 1989, occur on a 1.5-mi (2.4-km) section of the Sassafras River. These consist of fewer than four medium-sized populations of from 100 to 500 adults.

Threats

Decline of the Puritan tiger beetle has been caused by degradation of its beach and cliff habitat, natural and man-made flooding, urbanization, and cliff stabilization projects. A recent study of the beetle's historic collection sites along the Connecticut River determined that 23 percent have been flooded by dams, 38 percent heavily urbanized, and eight percent altered by stabilization projects. It is believed that severe flooding in New England during the 1920s and 1930s contributed to the loss of Puritan tiger beetles in that region.

The only remaining Massachusetts population is threatened by human recreational use. From May through September the beach is heavily used by power boats, motorcycles, and all-terrain vehicles. In Maryland, the principal threat to beetle populations is cliff stabilization projects. Continued breakdown of the cliffs is necessary to provide the exposed areas needed by the larvae. Stabilized cliffs are often quickly overgrown by vegetation.

Conservation and Recovery

The Puritan tiger beetle is somewhat protected by Maryland's critical areas legislation, enacted to help reverse the degradation of the Chesapeake Bay ecosystem. Critical areas, according to this legislation, are those within 1,000 feet of the bay or its tributaries. Development of these areas is curtailed and often prohibited when a state-designated threatened species is present. In addition, four of the Maryland sites are designated "Natural Heritage Areas," giving them further protection from disturbance. Without this strong state protection, the Fish and Wildlife Service would have classified the Puritan tiger beetle as Endangered rather than Threatened.

Collectors pose an additional threat to this beetle species. Tiger beetles are without doubt the most intensely collected of any insect genus. Although collection is not considered a factor in the beetle's decline, the harmful effects are magnified when the species' population is low.

Contacts

Regional Office of Endangered Species
U.S. Fish and Wildlife Service
300 Westgate Center Dr.
Hadley, Massachusetts 01035
http://northeast.fws.gov/

Chesapeake Bay Ecological Services Field Office
177 Admiral Cochrane Dr.
Annapolis, Maryland 21401-7307
Telephone: (410) 573-4500
Fax: (410) 263-2608

References

Boyd, H. P. 1978. "The Tiger Beetles (Coleoptera: Cicindelidae) of New Jersey, with Special Reference to their Ecological Relationships." _Transactions of the American Entomological Society_ 104:191-242.

Knisley, C. B. 1987. "Final Report: Status Survey of Two Candidate Tiger Beetles, _Cicindela puritana_ G. Horn and _C. dorsalis_ Say." U.S. Fish and Wildlife Service, Newton Corner, Massachusetts.

Knisley, C. B., and J. M. Hill. 1990. "Studies of Two Endangered Tiger Beetles, *Cicindela dorsalis dorsalis* and *Cicindela puritana* in Maryland, 1989." Maryland Natural Heritage Program, Annapolis.

Nothnagel, P. 1987. *"Cicindela puritana*—The Puritan Tiger Beetle: Its Current Status in Massachu-setts." Massachusetts Natural Heritage Program, Boston.

___. 1989. "Current Status of the Puritan Tiger Bee-tle *(Cicindela puritana)* in Connecticut." Eastern Heritage Task Force, The Nature Conservancy, Boston.

Delta Green Ground Beetle

Elaphrus viridis

Status	Threatened
Listed	August 8, 1980
Family	Carabidae (Ground beetle)
Description	Dull golden above, metallic green beneath.
Habitat	Bare, sparsely vegetated ground along the edges of vernal pools.
Food	Springtails.
Reproduction	One generation per year.
Threats	Loss of seasonal wetlands.
Range	California

Delta Green Ground Beetle, photograph by Larry Serpa. Reproduced by permission.

Description

The delta green ground beetle, *Elaphrus viridis*, is about 0.25 in (6 mm) long when mature. It is golden or bronze above and metallic green beneath. This beetle resembles a tiger beetle with its relatively large abdomen, smaller but distinct thorax and head, and long slender legs. It is smaller than the tiger beetle and has spotlike depressions on its leathery outer wings. Its antennae are short and blunt.

Behavior

In general, the genus *Elaphrus* is associated with temperate wetland habitats. Many specific details of the life history of the delta green ground beetle are unknown. The primary food source is thought to be springtails (flealike insects of the order Collembola). The delta green ground beetle is active during the warmest and sunniest part of the day from early February to mid-May. The nocturnal larvae are

found in greater concentrations and inhabit damper areas than adults. This species produces one generation per year. Both male and female may mate several times in their lifetimes. Females deposit eggs during winter and early spring after a delayed period of development during which the adults are inactive and metabolism is reduced.

Habitat

Adult beetles inhabit the grassy edges of vernal pools that are filled by winter rains but dry up by late summer. Typically, the pools are small depressions within generally level terrain. Water inundates the area long enough to inhibit development of typical grassland vegetation. The climate is Mediterranean, with cool rainy winters and warm, dry summers. The beetle requires sparsely vegetated ground to utilize its concealing markings and keen vision.

Distribution

Although this beetle was first described in 1878, its range remained a mystery until 1974 when a student from the University of California discovered a population at the Jepson Prairie in Solano County. The species was originally widespread in the once numerous vernal pools of central California.

The delta green ground beetle is known to inhabit two sites in Solano County, California, south of Dixon at Olcott Lake. A portion of the habitat falls within the Jepson Prairie Preserve, which is owned and managed jointly by the Nature Conservancy and the University of California, Davis. Between 1974 and 1985, only 75 individuals were observed at the preserve.

Threats

Many vernal pools have disappeared from the California landscape because of the increased human control of natural water flows. Rivers have been dammed and channeled for irrigation, and wetlands have been drained or filled for cropland. Only a few seasonal pools remain intact. Plowing and water pumping have already caused remaining pools to shrink or dry up earlier in the summer, a change in timing that has a critical impact on the life cycle of dependent insects. In 1980 plowing and grading damaged one inhabited pool, and further disturbance would probably eliminate the beetle from this site.

Conservation and Recovery

The Jepson Prairie Preserve already provides some protection for the delta green ground beetle, and critical habitat was designated to include both known population sites. Recovery will focus on limiting further habitat disturbance and translocating the beetle to other suitable sites within its range. A portion of Olcott Lake outside the preserve has been identified as a potential reintroduction site.

The recovery plan also calls for investigating the mortality factors, biological requirements, and population dynamics associated with the species; and the effects of grazing and prescribed burning on the habitat.

Contact

U. S. Fish and Wildlife Service
Regional Office, Division of Endangered Species
Eastside Federal Complex
911 N. E. 11th Ave.
Portland, Oregon 97232-4181
Telephone: (503) 231-6121
http://pacific.fws.gov/

References

Holland, R. F., and F. T. Griggs. 1976. "A Unique Habitat: California's Vernal Pools." *Fremontia* 4: 3-6.

U. S. Fish and Wildlife Service. 1985. "Delta Green Ground Beetle and Solano Grass Recovery Plan." U. S. Fish and Wildlife Service, Portland, Oregon.

Tooth Cave Ground Beetle

Rhadine persephone

Status	Endangered
Listed	September 16, 1988
Family	Carabidae (Ground beetle)
Description	Tiny reddish brown beetle with rudimentary eyes.
Habitat	Cave dwelling.
Food	Cave cricket eggs.
Reproduction	Not specifically known, but likely has a complex life cycle of egg, several larval stages, pupa, and adult.
Threats	Residential development.
Range	Texas

Tooth Cave Ground Beetle, photograph. U. S. Fish and Wildlife Service. Reproduced by permission.

Description

A moderately robust and convex beetle, the reddish brown Tooth Cave ground beetle, *Rhadine persephone*, attains a maximum length of only 0.35 in (8 mm). This cave-adapted species has only rudimentary eyes.

Behavior

The Tooth Cave ground beetle is suspected to feed on cave cricket eggs. The beetle's reproductive biology is unknown.

Habitat

The Tooth Cave ground beetle is endemic to two caves in the Edwards Limestone formation. Tooth Cave is up to 100 ft (30 m) in length and contains a greater diversity of fauna than any other cave in Texas. Over 48 species have been identified, and other highly adaptive cave fauna no doubt remain to be discovered.

The other known habitat of this beetle is Kretschmarr Cave, which is about 50 ft (15 m) deep. Fauna present in Kretschmarr Cave include the blind millipede *Cambala speobia* and several species of beetles. An associated insect, the Kretschmarr Cave mold beetle (*Texamaurops reddelli*), is also federally listed as Endangered.

Distribution

This species is a highly localized example of the fauna endemic to caves in the Edwards Limestone formation in Travis County, Texas.

The Tooth Cave ground beetle, first discovered in 1965, is only known from Tooth and Kretschmarr caves. Exact population figures are not known. Few individuals of this species have ever been collected, and although its habitat area is large in comparison to its body size, the total population is probably small.

Threats

The only two caves inhabited by the Tooth Cave ground beetle are close to a road leading to residential and industrial areas, and are vulnerable to further development as well as spills of hydrocarbons and other potentially degrading chemicals. Without safeguards, these caves could collapse, become filled, or have their groundwater hydrology changed through a modification of either surface or underground drainage. The shallow caves are also easily accessible, which means they could be invaded by non-native invertebrate predators or competitors, such as alien sowbugs, cockroaches, or fire ants.

Conservation and Recovery

Because the region surrounding Austin also supports the black-capped vireo (*Vireo atricapillus*), the Tooth Cave ground beetle and other karst insects are included in the 1991 U. S. Fish and Wildlife Service Recovery Plan for the vireo.

Contact

U. S. Fish and Wildlife Service
Regional Office, Division of Endangered Species
P.O. Box 1306
Albuquerque, New Mexico 87103-1306
Telephone: (505) 248-6911
Fax: (505) 248-6915
http://southwest.fws.gov/

References

Barr, T. C., Jr. 1974. "Revision of *Rhadine* LeConte (Coleoptera, Carabidae); Vol I. The Subterranean Group." *American Museum Novitates* 2359.

Reddell, R. R. 1984. "Report on the Caves and Cave Fauna of the Parke, Travis County, Texas." Unpublished Report to the Texas System of Natural Laboratories.

U. S. Fish and Wildlife Service. 1988. "Determination of Five Texas Cave Invertebrates to Be Endangered Species." *Federal Register* 53: 36029-36033.

U. S. Fish and Wildlife Service. 1994. "Recovery Plan for Endangered Karst Invertebrates in Travis and William Counties, Texas." U. S. Fish and Wildlife Service, Albuquerque, New Mexico.

Hungerford's Crawling Water Beetle

Brychius hungerfordi

Status	Endangered
Listed	March 7, 1994
Family	Halipilidae (Water beetle)
Description	Small, distinctive, yellowish brown beetle.
Habitat	Cool riffles of clean streams with an inorganic substrate.
Food	Herbivorous.
Reproduction	Larvae probably go through three instar phases and pupate in the moist soil above the water line.
Threats	Modification of habitat due to human activity; over-collecting; limited numbers.
Range	Michigan; Ontario, Canada

Description

Hungerford's crawling water beetle is a small (0.2 in or 4.2 mm), distinctive, yellowish brown beetle with irregular dark markings and longitudinal stripes over the elytra, each of which is comprised of a series of fine, closely-spaced and darkly-pigmented punctures. Males tend to be smaller than females.

In Spangler's (1954) original study, specimens ranged from 0.15 in (3.7 mm) in length and 0.07 in (1.9 mm) in width (a male) to 0.17 in (4.35 mm) in length and 0.09 in (2.25 mm) in width (a female). Males are characterized by thickened tarsal segments of the front legs with small tufts of hair on the first three segments. This species can be differentiated from all other Halipilidae in Michigan by the shape of its pronotum (dorsal plate of the thorax), the sides of which are nearly parallel for the basal two-thirds and are widened mid-laterally.

Behavior

Hungerford's crawling water beetle is thought to live longer than one year and to overwinter as larvae in the dense aquatic vegetation at the stream's edge. As with other Halipilidae, larvae probably go through three instar phases and pupate in the moist soil above the water line. Adults and larvae are seldom captured together, and they appear to inhabit different microhabitats in the stream. Adults are more apt to be found in stronger currents, foraging for algae on gravel and stone.

Compared to other Halipilidae, the adults are strong swimmers, and they obtain oxygen by swimming to the surface or crawling to the water line at the edge of the stream. Larvae obtain oxygen directly from the water and are found in association with dense mats of vegetation which offer protection and foraging. The growth form of this vegetative cover may be more important than the plant composition. Both adults and larvae are herbivorous but little is known about their specific dietary requirements or feeding adaptations. However, it is likely that they scrape food material from rocks by grasping with their tarsal claws and scraping with their distally flattened and singled notched mandibles which are slightly medially-cupped. This speculation is based on observations of the beetles

Hungerford's Crawling Water Beetle, photograph. U. S. Fish and Wildlife Service. Reproduced by permission.

crawling from rock to rock stopping occasionally to grip a rock for varying lengths of time.

There is no evidence that this species has a dispersal flight. No adults have been found at black-light stations, and the adults seem unusually reluctant to fly. It is possible that if this species disperses by flying, it is during a very brief period of time in the spring. The primary mode of dispersal appears to be movement within the stream.

Habitat

The east branch of the Maple River, which is the site of the largest population of Hungerford's crawling water beetle, is a small stream surrounded by forest with a partially-open canopy so sunlight reaches the water. The stream is cool (59-68°F, or 15-20°C) with a relatively fast-flowing current and a substrate of limestone gravel and rock. The forest is intact, the beaver populations are healthy, and their dams function to stabilize water levels so the riffles below the dams remain predictable from year to year.

Distribution

Although streams in the Great Lakes states, especially Michigan, Wisconsin and Minnesota, have been extensively surveyed during the past 30 years, no additional populations of Hungerford's crawling water beetle have been discovered. The survey resulted in the discovery of the only known population in Canada.

The largest population presently occurs in the East Branch of the Maple River in a pristine portion of stream on the boundary of the University of Michigan Biological Station. Two smaller populations are known from the East Branch of the Black River, Montmorency County, Michigan; and the North Saugeen River at Scone, Bruce County, Ontario.

Threats

Because adult beetles must swim to the surface for air, they are vulnerable to predation by fish, tadpoles, and other aquatic insects. The warmer summer water temperatures force the trout population to deeper waters in Lake Kathleen, giving the beetles an opportunity to repopulate.

It appears that human activity in or near the habitat may be speeding up the loss of the species. The removal of existing beaver dams upstream poses a significant threat to the beetle: the downstream side of the beaver dams serve as a riffle and aeration site because they retain sediments and organic material, raise water temperature, and modify nutrient cycling, decomposition dynamics, and riparian zone structure and composition.

Potential threats that may result in modification of the species' habitat include certain fish management activities, such as removal or introduction of fish; stream-side logging and heavy siltation resulting from logging, impoundment, bank stabilization with structures that create an artificial shoreline; stream pollution; and general stream degradation. In Michigan, one site has already been impounded by a dam, and the Ontario site has been impounded upstream.

Given the rate of recreational development and the demands for fish, wildlife, and forest management in northern Michigan, unknown populations of Hungerford's crawling water beetle could be easily extirpated before they are discovered, increasing the need to protect existing populations. Because only three populations of this species are known to exist, loss of even a few individuals could severely affect the continued existence of the species.

Although current scientific research has mostly involved capture and release rather than collecting, the species will continue to draw scientific interest and collection should be regulated. Because of the species' rarity, there is the possibility that amateur scientific collections could occur.

Because all three known populations occur immediately downstream from a roadway, accidental events such as a chemical spill, or the cumulative effects of road salt runoff, pose a threat.

Because of its limited numbers, the beetle faces reduced reproductive vigor and the possibility of stochastic extinction.

Conservation and Recovery

At the present time recovery efforts related to these problems are restricted to legal instruments already in force. The Endangered Species Act requires Federal agencies to evaluate their actions with respect to any listed species. The act also prohibits any imports or exports of listed species, or to offer them for sale. Laws also prohibit any malicious damage or removal of species from their habitat. In the case of this species, the Fish and Wildlife Service has not recommended designating Critical Habitat because of the potential of increased pressure put on the species by vandals or hikers.

The most important regulatory control for protecting this species is the issuance of permits that would modify the beetle's habitat.

Contacts

U. S. Fish and Wildlife Service
Regional Office
Federal Building
Ft. Snelling
Twin Cities, Minnesota 55111
http://midwest.fws.gov/

East Lansing Ecological Services Field Office
2651 Coolidge Rd.
East Lansing, Michigan 48823-6316
Telephone: (517) 351-2555
Fax: (517) 351-1443

References

U. S. Fish and Wildlife Service. 7 March 1994 "Endangered and Threatened Wildlife and Plants; Determination of Endangered Status for Hungerford's Crawling Water Beetle." *Federal Register* 59 (44): 10580-10584.

American Burying Beetle

Nicrophorus americanus

Status	Endangered
Listed	July 13, 1989
Family	Silphidae (Carrion beetle)
Description	Large, shiny black beetle with distinctive orange and red markings.
Habitat	Virgin woodlands, maritime scrub, and grasslands.
Food	Carrion.
Reproduction	Eggs are laid on carrion; larvae emerge as adults after about 50 days.
Threats	Low numbers.
Range	Arkansas, Massachusetts, Michigan, Nebraska, Ohio, Oklahoma, Rhode Island, South Dakota

American Burying Beetle, photograph. U. S. Fish and Wildlife Service. Reproduced by permission.

Description

Also known as the giant carrion beetle, the shiny black American burying beetle, *Nicrophorus americanus*, is identified by two pairs of scalloped red spots on the wing covers (elytra), red antenna stems with orange clubs, and a large orange-red pronotal disk (segment behind the head). It is the largest member of its genus, measuring 1-1.4 in (2.5-3.6 cm).

Behavior

A nocturnal beetle, it is attracted to carrion by smell. A number of beetles fight among themselves over a carcass until one pair—usually the largest male and female—takes possession. They then bury it, constructing a brooding chamber at the same time. The female lays eggs on the carrion, and both parents remain with the eggs until they hatch to tend the larvae. In general, the species exhibits one of the highest levels of parental care of any beetle in the insect order Coleoptera. It seems larvae cannot survive without parental care, although, it is unclear as to why. Brood sizes vary from three to 31, and a positive correlation between carrion weight and number of larvae has been observed. Larvae emerge as adults after about 50 days, and parents and young disperse. Adults burrow in the soil to overwinter. Occasionally, burying beetles capture live insects.

Habitat

Scientists speculate that the American burying beetle prefers mature, virgin forests, but its present New England habitat includes maritime scrub thickets, coastal grasslands, and pasture. The availability of deep humus and top soils suitable for burying carrion is essential. Further research is needed to clarify habitat requirements.

Distribution

This species was once found in 32 states and three Canadian provinces. Its range extended from Nova Scotia and Quebec south to Florida, and west to Texas and the Great Plains.

Since 1970, the range of the species has been documented from only six states including the extant population on Block Island in Rhode Island and occurrences in Oklahoma. More surveys are needed to determine whether populations exist in Kentucky, Arkansas, Missouri, and Nebraska. There is a single 1972 record from Ontario. The extant populations are located on private lands, with the exception of the Cherokee/Muskogee County population, which occurs on a jointly managed state wildlife management area and National Guard installation.

The American burying beetle is currently known to occur in Rhode Island, Oklahoma, Arkansas, and in Nebraska, where six American burying beetles were discovered on the Valentine National Wildlife Refuge in the summer of 1992.

The 1992 discovery indicated that a viable population of the beetles may exist on the refuge. Valentine National Wildlife Refuge is completely outside the previously known Nebraska range of American burying beetles; this was only the third collection of the rare beetle in Nebraska since 1970. Only 11 beetles have been collected in Nebraska since the 1880s.

A remnant population also may exist in Iowa. Wildlife officials have intentionally left the location of the New England population vague to deter collectors. Although no population estimate has been attempted, the species is considered to have experienced one of the most disastrous declines ever recorded for an insect species.

Threats

The cause of the precipitous decline of the range of the American burying beetle is unknown, although contamination by dichlorodiphenyltrichloroethane (DDT) and other pesticides is one possibility. In addition, the black lights on "bug-zappers" are thought to attract and electrocute males. Because they participate in brood-rearing, burying beetle males are not considered surplus population, unlike those of many other beetle species. Although scientists fully expect to discover remnant populations in other states, the status of the species is considered critical.

Conservation and Recovery

In 1991, a pilot effort began to reintroduce this Endangered insect at historical habitat on Penikese Island, Massachusetts. Lab-reared beetles have been released over a period of several years, and trapping confirmed that some of the release stock has reproduced. In the summer of 1994, the U. S. Fish and Wildlife Service (FWS) secured protection for habitat on Block Island, Rhode Island, which is being managed as part of the Ninigret National Wildlife Refuge. One of the purposes of the new unit is to provide protection for the only known natural population of the American burying beetle in the eastern United States.

Effective captive breeding programs also are under way. In the 1992, the FWS reported that the Cincinnati Zoo Insectarium had successfully raised more than 300 larvae from 13 pairs of this Endangered insect that were on loan there. Re-pairings are being conducted to maximize the reproductive output of the short-lived adult beetles.

In 1995, the FWS and Oklahoma Biological Survey hosted the first rangewide recovery coordination meeting for the insect. FWS Region 5 has lead responsibility for recovery of the American burying beetle, although, adding to the challenge of coordinating protection and recovery efforts, all states in which the beetle is known to survive fall within different FWS administrative regions.

More than 40 participants attended the two-day meeting, including representatives of all five involved FWS regions, agency and university researchers from several states, federal agencies such as the Forest Service and Department of Defense, and large landowners such as the Weyerhauser Company. They discussed a wide variety of research and management issues. Although many questions remain about why the beetle disappeared from most of its range and what can be done to reverse the decline, substantial progress toward a better understanding of this unique creature is being achieved.

Contacts

Regional Office of Endangered Species
U.S. Fish and Wildlife Service
P.O. Box 1306
Albuquerque, New Mexico 87103
http://southwest.fws.gov/

Regional Office of Endangered Species
U.S. Fish and Wildlife Service
Federal Building
Ft. Snelling
Twin Cities, Minnesota 55111
http://midwest.fws.gov/

Regional Office of Endangered Species
U.S. Fish and Wildlife Service
1875 Century Blvd., Suite 200
Atlanta, Georgia 30345
http://southeast.fws.gov/

Regional Office of Endangered Species
U.S. Fish and Wildlife Service
300 Westgate Center Dr.
Hadley, Massachusetts 01035
http://northeast.fws.gov/

Regional Office of Endangered Species
U.S. Fish and Wildlife Service
P. O. Box 25486
Denver Federal Center
Denver, Colorado 80225
http://www.r6.fws.gov/

References

Anderson, R. S. 1982. "On the Decreasing Abundance of *Nicrophorus americanus* in Eastern North America." *Coleoptera Bulletin* 36(2):362-365.

Kozol, A. J., *et al.* 1987. "Distribution and Natural History of the American Burying Beetle." Report. Eastern Heritage Task Force of The Nature Conservancy.

Schweitzer, D. F., and L. L. Master. 1987. "American Burying Beetle: Results of a Global Status Survey." Report. U.S. Fish and Wildlife Service, Newton Corner, Massachusetts.

U. S. Fish and Wildlife Service. 1991. "American Burying Beetle (Nicrophorus americanus) Recovery Plan." Newton Corner, Massachusetts.

Coffin Cave Mold Beetle

Batrisodes texanus

Status	Endangered
Listed	September 16, 1988
Family	Pselaphidae (Mold beetle)
Description	Small, long-legged eyeless beetle with no metathoracic wings and a smooth, curved flat head.
Habitat	Limestone caves, sinkholes, and other subterranean voids.
Food	Eggs, feces, nymphs and dead body parts.
Reproduction	Unknown.
Threats	Land development, pollution, and fire ants.
Range	Texas

Description

The Coffin Cave mold beetle is a small, long-legged eyeless beetle with short elytra leaving five abdominal tergites which are exposed. It has no metathoracic wings. The body length of this species is measured at 0.10-0.11 in (2.6-2.88 mm). The males possess a vague groove across the head anterior to the antennal bases. The lateral sides of the head are smooth, curved and flat. A few granules are observed where one might think the eyes should be.

Behavior

Sexual dimorphism is observed in that the female lacks the transverse impression anterior to the antennal bases. The tenth antennal segment is somewhat wider and longer than the ninth. In males the tenth antennal segment is twice as wide as the ninth.

The Coffin Cave mold beetle is a troglobite. A troglobite is a species which spends its entire life in openings underground usually with small or absent eyes, attenuated appendages, and other adaptations to its subsurface dwelling.

Habitat

This species spends its entire life underground. It is endemic to the karst (limestone) formations. These formations include caves, sinkholes, and other subterranean voids. It is dependent on outside moisture and nutrient inputs generated from the subsurface. This species inhabits areas of the cave where temperature and humidity are constant.

The surface vegetation ranges from pasture land to mature oak-juniper woodland.

Karst is formed by the slow dissolution of calcium carbonate from limestone bedrock by mildly acidic ground water. This process results in subterranean voids resembling a honeycomb. The water enters the subsurface through cracks, crevices, and other openings, dissolving soluble beds of rock.

Nutrients to this ecosystem are provided from the outside surface washed in. These nutritional sources include plant material, feces, eggs, and carrion. Cave crickets are believed to provide an important component to the nutritional balance of this cave ecosystem. These crickets introduce nutrients through eggs, feces, nymphs, and dead body parts on which many invertebrates are known to feed.

Coffin Cave Mold Beetle, photograph by Alan Eaton. University of New Hampshire. Reproduced by permission.

Distribution

As this species was not described until 1992, its past distribution is not known. This species occurs in two caves in the North Williamson County karst fauna region and three caves in the Georgetown karst fauna region in Williamson County, Texas.

Threats

The primary threat to the Coffin Cave mold beetle is habitat loss due to urban development activities. Continued urban expansion such as residential subdivisions, schools, golf courses, roads, commercial and industrial facilities, etc. poses a threat in the form of cave filling or collapse, water diversion, vegetation/fauna alteration, and increased pollution.

Some caves have already been filled as a result of road construction and building site preparation. Development directly above caves could result in the collapse of cave ceilings.

Ranchers may have also filled some caves. Justification is placed in reducing hiding places for predators of cattle and goats as well as preventing these animals from falling into the formations.

Troglobites rely upon and in fact require a controlled environment of high humidity and constant temperature. If water drainage paths are altered, this balance is no longer on an even keel. Water diversion away from the caves could lead to the direct mortality of this species. Increased water infiltration could lead to flooding and loss of air space.

As the karst ecosystem relies on the infiltration of nutrients from the surface, a fluctuation in the vegetation or fauna would alter nutrient supplies. During development, native vegetation may be replaced with non-native species, as well as cause the introduction of exotic animal species, such as fire ants. An overall nutrient depletion would result.

The removal of vegetation could also lead to temperature fluctuations, a change in moisture regime and potential for contamination and increased sedimentation from soil erosion.

Conservation and Recovery

A Recovery Plan was published for the Coffin Cave mold beetle in 1994. The conservation of this rare insect requires the strict protection of its cave habitat from disturbances and other changes associated with residential, agricultural, or commercial development. Other necessary actions include studies to monitor the abundance of the Coffin Cave mold beetle and research into its biology and habitat needs. There should also be a public education campaign to develop a broad base of support for the protection of rare cave habitats.

Contact

U.S. Fish and Wildlife Service
Regional Office, Division of Endangered Species
P. O. Box 1306
Albuquerque, New Mexico 87103
Telephone: (505) 766-2321
Fax: (505) 766-8063
www://southwest.fws.gov/

References

U.S. Fish and Wildlife Service. 1993. "Endangered and Threatened Wildlife and Plants; Coffin Cave Mold Beetle (*Batrisodes texanus*) and the Bone Cave Harvestman (*Texella reyesi*) Determined to Be Endangered." *Federal Register* 58(158): 43818-43819.

U.S. Fish and Wildlife Service. 1994. Recovery Plan for Endangered Karst Invertebrates in Travis and Williamson Counties, Texas. Albuquerque, New Mexico.

Kretschmarr Cave Mold Beetle

Texamaurops reddelli

Status	Endangered
Listed	September 16, 1988
Family	Pselaphidae (Mold beetle)
Description	Dark, short-winged, eyeless beetle with elongated legs.
Habitat	Caves.
Food	Fungus.
Reproduction	Not specifically known, but likely has a complex life cycle of egg, several larval stages, pupa, and adult.
Threats	Residential development.
Range	Texas

Description

The tiny Kretschmarr Cave mold beetle, *Texamaurops reddelli*, is less than 0.15 in (3 mm) in length. Eyeless, its reddish-brown body is sparsely and weakly dotted with small pits; it has short wings and elongated legs. According to James Reddell, who first collected this beetle in 1963, it is the most highly cave-adapted species of its family in Texas and among the more unusual species of cave-dwelling beetles in the United States.

Behavior

It is believed that this species is omnivorous but depends on fungus for the bulk of its diet. Little is known about its reproductive biology.

Habitat

The mold beetle inhabits four small, dry, and shallow caves that occur as isolated islands in the Edwards Limestone formation. The largest cave has about 200 ft (61 m) of passage; the other three are much smaller.

Distribution

This species is an example of the highly localized fauna of the caves in the Edwards Limestone formation, Texas. It occurs nowhere else.

This mold beetle is known from Kretschmarr, Amber, Tooth, and Coffin Caves in Travis and Williamson counties. Recent attempts to locate Coffin Cave have been unsuccessful because residential development in the area has destroyed landmarks and collapsed or concealed the entrance. The size of the Kretschmarr Cave mold beetle population is not known.

Threats

The four caves that this species inhabits are close to a road leading to residential and industrial areas. Without safeguards, these caves could collapse or become filled. Any alteration of drainage affects the species as it is dependent on groundwater. The relative accessibility of the shallow caves leaves them especially vulnerable to invasion by introduced invertebrate predators or competitors such as sowbugs, cockroaches, and fire ants.

Conservation and Recovery

The Krestschmarr Cave mold beetle has a Recovery Priority rating of 1C, a Fish and Wildlife Service designation indicating a high degree of threat, but also a high potential for recovery. Conservation of this species requires that its cave habitat be protected from residential development and other threatening activities. It is especially necessary to protect the access sites to the caves, as well as the

Kretschmarr Cave Mold Beetle, photograph. U. S. Fish and Wildlife Service. Reproduced by permission.

local watershed from which its groundwater flow originates. Such protection requires the acquisition of private land supporting the access points and watershed and designation of the areas as an ecological reserve, or the negotiation of conservation easements with the landowners. Management must include the control of incompatible practices that could degrade the cave habitat, such as infilling, and activities that carry a risk of causing spills of pesticides, hydrocarbons, nutrients, or other toxic or degrading chemicals. The populations of the Kretschmarr Cave mold beetle should be monitored in its known habitats, and research undertaken into its little-known biology and habitat needs.

Contact

U. S. Fish and Wildlife Service
Regional Office, Division of Endangered Species
P.O. Box 1306
Albuquerque, New Mexico 87103-1306
Telephone: (505) 248-6911
Fax: (505) 248-6915
http://southwest.fws.gov/

References

Barr, T. C., and H. R. Steeves, Jr. 1963. "*Texamaurops*, A New Genus of Pselaphids from Caves in Central Texas (Coleoptera: Pselaphidae)." *The Coleopterists' Bulletin* 17:117-120.

Mitchell, R. W. 1968. "Food and Feeding Habits of the Troglobitic Carabid Beetle *Rhadine subterranean*." *International Journal of Speleology* 3:249-270.

Reddell, J. R. 1984. "Report on the Caves and Cave Fauna of the Parke, Travis County, Texas." Unpublished Report to the Texas System of Natural Laboratories.

U. S. Fish and Wildlife Service. 1988. "Determination of Five Texas Cave Invertebrates to Be Endangered Species." *Federal Register* 53: 36029-36033.

U. S. Fish and Wildlife Service. 1994. "Recovery Plan for Endangered Karst Invertebrates in Travis and William Counties, Texas." U. S. Fish and Wildlife Service, Albuquerque, New Mexico.

Comal Springs Dryopid Beetle

Stygoparnus comalensis

Status	Endangered
Listed	December 12, 1997
Family	Dryopidae
Description	Weakly pigmented, translucent, thin-skinned, subterranean aquatic beetle with vestigial eyes.
Habitat	Air-filled voids inside spring orifices.
Food	Likely a predator of other invertebrates
Reproduction	Has a complex life cycle of eggs, larvae, and adult.
Threats	Decrease in water quantity and quality; groundwater pollution.
Range	Texas

Description

The Comal Springs dryopid beetle, *Stygoparnus comalensis,* a recently discovered species, was first collected in 1987 and described as a new genus and species in 1992. This species is the first subterranean aquatic member of the beetle family Dryopidae to be discovered.

Adult Comal Springs dryopid beetles are about 0.12 in (3 mm) long. They are weakly pigmented, translucent, thin-skinned, and have vestigial eyes. Most of the specimens have been taken from drift nets or from inside the spring orifices, with collections taking place from April through August.

Behavior

The Comal Springs dryopid beetle is a subterranean, blind, flightless, aquatic insect. Its food is unknown, but it is probably a predator of other aquatic invertebrates.

Habitat

Although the larvae of the Comal Springs dryopid beetle have been collected in drift nets positioned over the spring openings, they are presumed to be associated with air-filled voids inside the spring orifices since all other known dryopid beetle

larvae are terrestrial. Unlike Peck's cave amphipod, the Comal Springs dryopid beetle does not swim, and it may have a smaller range within the aquifer.

Distribution

Collection records for the Comal Springs dryopid beetle are primarily from spring run 2 at Comal Springs, but they have also been collected from runs 3 and 4 at Comal and from Fern Bank Springs about 20 miles to the northeast in Hays County.

Threats

The primary threat to the Comal Springs dryopid beetle is a decrease in water quantity and quality as a result of water withdrawal throughout the San Antonio segment of the Edwards Aquifer. Groundwater pollution from human activities also threatens to seriously degrade the water quality of its habitat. This species is especially vulnerable to cessation of spring flow.

Conservation and Recovery

The Comal Springs dryopid beetle is only known from Comal Springs and Fern Bank Springs. The rare beetle will only survive if its critical habitat at these springs is protected, and the essential hydrological and water-quality characteristics are conserved. The primary threat is associated with the withdrawal of water from the San Antonio segment of the Edwards Aquifer, so it is crucial that this hydrological use is limited to an intensity that does not degrade the critical habitat. The acceptable rate of water use by humans will have to be determined, and will have to account for the effects of periodic drought on groundwater recharge. It will also be necessary to control the risks of local spills of pesticides, hydrocarbon fuels, fertilizers, and other chemicals, any of which could seriously degrade groundwater and damage habitat. The populations of the Comal Springs dryopid beetle will have to be monitored, and research undertaken into its basic biology and habitat needs.

Contacts

U. S. Fish and Wildlife Service
Regional Office, Division of Endangered Species
P.O. Box 1306
Albuquerque, New Mexico 87103-1306
Telephone: (505) 248-6911
Fax: (505) 248-6915
http://southwest.fws.gov/

U. S. Fish and Wildlife Service
Ecological Services Field Office
10711 Burnet Road, Suite 200
Austin, Texas, 78758
Telephone: (512) 490-0057
Fax: (512) 490-0974
http://ifw2es.fws.gov/AustinTexas/

Reference

U. S. Fish and Wildlife Service. 18 December 1997. "Endangered and Threatened Wildlife and Plants: Final Rule To List Three Aquatic Invertebrates in Comal and Hays Counties, TX, as Endangered." *Federal Register* 62 (243):66295-66304.

Comal Springs Riffle Beetle

Heterelmis comalensis

Status	Endangered
Listed	December 18, 1997
Family	Elmidae
Description	Aquatic, surface-dwelling beetle.
Habitat	Gravel substrate and shallow riffles in spring runs.
Food	Likely a predator of other invertebrates.
Reproduction	Has a complex life cycle of eggs, larvae, pupa, and adult.
Threats	Decrease in water quantity and quality; groundwater pollution.
Range	Texas

Description

The *Heterelmis comalensis* (Comal Springs riffle beetle) is an aquatic, surface-dwelling species in the family Elmidae known from Comal Springs and San Marcos Springs. It was first collected in 1976 and was described in 1988. The closest relative of *H. comalensis* appears to be *H. glabra*, a species that occurs farther to the west in the Big Bend region. Adult Comal Springs riffle beetles are about 0.12 in (3 mm) long, with females slightly larger than males. The Comal Springs riffle beetle is not a subterranean species. Some riffle beetle species can fly, but the hind wings of *H. comalensis* are short and almost certainly non-functional, making the species incapable of this mode of dispersal. Larvae have been collected with adults in the gravel substrate of the spring headwaters and not on submerged wood as is typical of most *Heterelmis* species.

Behavior

The Comal Springs riffle beetle forages in aquatic gravel, and is flightless. Its food is unknown, but it is probably a predator of other invertebrates.

Habitat

It occurs in the gravel substrate and shallow riffles in spring runs. Usual water depth in this occu-

pied habitat is 1-4 in (2.5-10 cm), although the beetle may also occur in slightly deeper areas within the spring runs.

Distribution

Populations are reported to reach their greatest densities from February to April. The Comal Springs riffle beetle has been collected from spring runs at Comal Springs in Landa Park and a single specimen was collected from San Marcos Springs 20 mi (32 km) to the northeast.

Threats

The primary threat to the Comal Springs riffle beetle is a decrease in water quantity and quality as a result of water withdrawal throughout the San Antonio segment of the Edwards (Balcones Fault Zone) Aquifer. Groundwater pollution from human activities threatens to seriously degrade the water quality of its habitat as well.

Conservation and Recovery

The Comal Springs riffle beetle is only known from Comal Springs and San Marcos Springs. The rare beetle will only survive if its critical habitat at these springs is protected, and the essential hydrological and water-quality characteristics are conserved. The primary threat is associated with the withdrawal of water from the San Antonio segment of the Edwards Aquifer, so it is crucial that this hydrological use is limited to an intensity that does not degrade the critical habitat. The acceptable rate of water use by humans will have to be determined, and will have to account for the effects of periodic drought on groundwater recharge. It will also be necessary to control the risks of local spills of pesticides, hydrocarbon fuels, fertilizers, and other chemicals, any of which could seriously degrade groundwater and damage habitat. The populations of the Comal Springs riffle beetle will have to be monitored, and research undertaken into its basic biology and habitat needs.

Contacts

U. S. Fish and Wildlife Service
Ecological Services Field Office
Harland Bank Building
10711 Burnet Road, Suite 200
Austin, Texas, 78758-4460.
Telephone: (512) 490-0057

U. S. Fish and Wildlife Service
Regional Office, Division of Endangered Species
P.O. Box 1306
Albuquerque, New Mexico 87103-1306
Telephone: (505) 248-6911
Fax: (505) 248-6915
http://southwest.fws.gov/

Reference

U.S. Fish and Wildlife Service. 18 December 1997. "Endangered and Threatened Wildlife and Plants: Final Rule To List Three Aquatic Invertebrates in Comal and Hays Counties, TX, as Endangered." *Federal Register* 62(243):66295-66304.

Mount Hermon June Beetle

Polyphylla barbata

Status	Endangered
Listed	January 24, 1997
Family	Scarabaeidae (Scarab beetle)
Description	Small scarab beetle with a black head; dark blackish-brown, thick, leathery forewings clothed with scattered long brown hair; and a striped body.
Habitat	Ponderosa pine-chaparral with sandy soil and open, sparsely vegetated areas.
Food	Roots of monkeyflower, oak, fern, grass, and pine.
Reproduction	Females lay eggs at the bottom of their burrows and die soon after.
Threats	Destruction of habitat from sand mining and urban development; predation by birds.
Range	California

Description

The Mount Hermon June beetle was first described in 1938, with the name coming from the place it was discovered in Santa Cruz County, California. The adult male is a cryptic small scarab beetle with a black head, dark blackish-brown elytra (thick leathery forewings) clothed with scattered long brown hair, and a striped body. Elytral vittae (stripes) are broken, often reduced to discontinuous clumps of scales, but still form identifiable lines. Females are larger, with a black head, chestnut-colored clypeus (plate on lower part of face) and elytra, and golden hairs on the head, thorax, and legs. The single adult female described was 0.87 by 0.43 in (2.2 by 1.1 cm), while the holotype male was 0.79 by 0.39 in (2 by 1 cm).

The Mount Hermon June beetle is one of 28 species of *Polyphylla* in North America north of Mexico, and one of 15 species of the diffracta complex within the genus *Polyphylla*. The status of *P. barbata* as a full species was supported in 1940 and again in 1988; several nomenclatural adjustments were made to the genus *Polyphylla* in the late twentieth century but *P. barbata* was retained. Other wide-ranging species of *Polyphylla* that occur in the Ben Lomond-Mount Hermon-Scotts Valley area are *P. crinita*, *P. nigra*, and *P. decemlineata*. The Mount Hermon June beetle is distinguished from other species of *Polyphylla* by the presence of relatively dense, long, erect hairs scattered randomly over the elytra and short erect hairs on the pygidium (abdominal segment).

Behavior

Like other *Polyphylla* species, the Mount Hermon June beetle is believed to require about two to three years to mature from an egg through the adult form. The rate of growth of laboratory-reared larvae, however, suggests that the Mount Hermon June beetle may complete its life cycle within one year. Most of the life cycle is spent in larval stages. The larvae are subterranean and feed on plant roots. While *Polyphylla* larvae are generally considered to be grass and pine root feeders, the Mount Hermon June beetle also may feed on the roots of monkeyflower, oak, fern, and other plants found in the Zayante sand hills ecosystem.

Mount Hermon June beetles emerge during summer as imagos (adult forms) to reproduce. Males are strong fliers, emerging from their burrows to fly low to the ground in search of females. Females are thought to be fossorial, remaining just below the surface in burrows, as they cannot fly due to their large body size. Like other *Polyphylla* species, males are believed to locate females by tracking female pheromone signals; such a mechanism would ensure reproductive success within the limited period for mating. The flight season generally extends from mid-June to late July. The flight time of males appears restricted to evening, being observed only between 8:45 and 9:30 P.M.; flights may occur later during the later part of the flight season.

The small mouthparts and limited flight period of Mount Hermon June beetles suggest that adults of this species do not feed. Adults of the related *P. decemlineata* are known to feed on the leaves of trees. At the end of the flight period each evening, males burrow back into the soil, emerging repeatedly on subsequent evenings to search for mates until their nutrient reserves expire. Females are believed to lay eggs at the bottom of their burrows and die a short time later. The life cycle continues as newly hatched larvae tunnel from the burrow in search of roots.

Habitat

Habitat of the Mount Hermon June beetle is described as ponderosa pine-chaparral with sandy soil and open, sparsely vegetated areas. Mount Hermon June beetles also may occur in more vegetated areas of chaparral. Common vegetation found in these open areas includes bracken fern (*Pteridium aquilinum*), monkeyflower (*Diplacus* sp.; *Mimulus* sp.), grasses, and small annual forbs. While not always present, silver-leafed manzanita seems to be a good indicator of suitable habitat. All of these descriptions are consistent with those of Zayante sand hills habitat.

Distribution

Most *Polyphylla* species have narrow distributions. Of 28 North American species, 20 have restricted ranges; 15 of these are endemic to isolated sand deposits. The restricted distributions of these species are likely due to various factors including substrate and food preferences, edaphic tolerances, and the low mobility of fossorial larvae and females. Most *Polyphylla* species seem to prefer sand and grass or sand, grass, and conifer associations

similar to those found in the Zayante sand hills ecosystem.

The range of the Mount Hermon June beetle is restricted to the Zayante sand hills habitat of the Ben Lomond-Mount Hermon-Scotts Valley area. Specimens were known historically only from sand hills at the type locality of Mount Hermon in Santa Cruz County, California. A single historic specimen collected in 1968 and labeled only "Santa Cruz" has been reported. This is not helpful in extending the historic range of the beetle because of its nonspecific location label.

Between 1989 and 1994, Mount Hermon June beetles were collected at 28 of 43 sites surveyed. Records include results of a regional survey and incidental collections. Twenty-six of the 28 collection locations were on mapped Zayante soils in the primary cluster of the Ben Lomond-Mount Hermon-Scotts Valley area. The other two collection records were within the same area, in proximity to mapped Zayante soils. All sites were similarly characterized by sparsely vegetated sandy substrate with silver-leafed manzanita or ponderosa pine. Mount Hermon June beetles were not found either in surveys of suitable Zayante sand hills habitat outside the Ben Lomond-Mount Hermon-Scotts Valley area nor at locations with habitat uncharacteristic of the Zayante sand hills ecosystem.

Threats

The Mount Hermon June beetle is primarily threatened by habitat destruction in the Ben Lomond-Mount Hermon-Scotts Valley area through sand mining and urban development. Excavation and construction activities that crush or expose fossorial larvae and females result in individual mortalities and the elimination of reproductive populations. The clearing of native Zayante sand hills vegetation and the cultivating of non-native plant species in landscaping also may adversely affect the Mount Hermon June beetle by eliminating food plants and disrupting the soil. Lesser sources of habitat loss and alteration are recreational activities and agriculture.

Sand mining and urban development have been the agents for most of the more than 40% of historic Zayante sand hills habitat lost or altered. This habitat once covered an estimated 6,265 acres (2,535 hectares); now only 3,608 acres (1,460 hectares) remain in a natural state. Portions of the Zayante sand hills ecosystem are protected under public ownership only at the Quail Hollow Ranch, owned by the County of Santa Cruz; Bonny Doon Ecological Preserve, managed by the California Department of Fish and Game; and Henry Cowell Redwoods State Park. The Mount Hermon June beetle, however, is not known to occur in either the Bonny Doon Ecological Preserve or Henry Cowell Redwoods State Park. The majority of Zayante sand hills habitat is on privately owned properties—no federal land is located in the region—and is susceptible to continued sand mining and urban development. Seventeen of the 28 Mount Hermon June beetle collection locations are adjacent to areas used for sand mining. Recent expansion of juvenile hall facilities near Mount Hermon eliminated portions of an area known to support Mount Hermon June beetles. Fourteen collection sites for Mount Hermon June beetles are adjacent to residential, commercial, and public developments.

Amateur collecting for the Mount Hermon June beetle occurs on a limited basis during the narrow flight periods of the species; th interest of collectors, however, may increase as these insects become even more difficult to find.

Mount Hermon June beetles may be preyed upon by some bird species, although the early evening flight time of this insect is thought to reflect an evolutionary adaptation for predator avoidance, coinciding with the cessation of bird activity. Based upon laboratory observations, larvae may be susceptible to fungal infestations if soil conditions are too moist. The significance of these mortality sources is unknown.

Because the Mount Hermon June beetle is fossorial, airborne pesticides would not likely reach and affect the species, but the application of soil permeant pesticides could pose a threat. During the flight season males of this species also may be subject to mortality from attraction to electric "bug zappers." The significance of such mortality is unknown, however.

Conservation and Recovery

The 28 known sites have been secured through fee-title acquisition, conservation easements, or habitat conservation plans for the Granite Rock Quarry, Kaiser Sand and Gravel's Felton Plant, the County of Santa Cruz, and the City of Scotts Valley. A management plan for Quail Hollow County Park has been developed and is being implemented, and the population numbers are stable or increasing.

Contact

U. S. Fish and Wildlife Service
Regional Office, Division of Endangered Species
Eastside Federal Complex
911 N. E. 11th Ave.
Portland, Oregon 97232-4181
Telephone: (503) 231-6121
http://pacific.fws.gov/

Reference

U. S. Fish and Wildlife Service. 1998. "Recovery Plan for Insect and Plant Taxa from the Santa Cruz Mountains in California." U. S. Fish and Wildlife Service, Portland, Oregon. 83 pp.

Valley Elderberry Longhorn Beetle

Elaphrus viridis

Status	Threatened
Listed	August 8, 1980
Family	Cerambycidae (Longhorn beetle)
Description	Brightly colored beetle with elongated cylindrical body.
Habitat	Elderberry thickets in moist riparian woodlands.
Host Plant	Elderberry.
Reproduction	Deposits eggs in cracks of the elderberry host.
Threats	Agricultural development, levee construction, maintenance activities.
Range	California

Description

The valley elderberry longhorn beetle, *Elaphrus viridis*, is a member of the family Cerambycidae (subfamily Lepturinae) that is distinguished by a cylindrical body as long as 2 in (5 cm). Males of the species exhibit several patterns of coloration: dark metallic green above with a bright reddish orange border; four oblong metallic green spots on the outer wings (elytra); or gradations. Males possess longer, more robust antennae than females. Females are larger than males. This beetle is similar in appearance to the California elderberry longhorn beetle (*Desmocerus californicus californicus*). The valley elderberry longhorn beetle has also been classified as *D. c. dimorphus.*

Behavior

About 400 species of longhorn beetles are found in California; all are herbivorous and are frequently associated with a particular plant host. The valley elderberry longhorn beetle is associated with three species of elderberry (*Sambucus*). It deposits eggs in cracks and crevices of the bark of living elderberry bushes; the eggs hatch soon after. The larvae bore into the pith of larger stems and roots and, when

ready to pupate, open holes through the bark. The life cycle probably encompasses two years. Adults emerge about the same time the elderberry blooms—as early as mid-March—and may live until mid-June.

Habitat

The valley elderberry longhorn beetle inhabits elderberry thickets in moist oak woodlands along the banks of streams and rivers. The host plant sometimes suffers from fungus attack at the emergence holes bored by the beetle, weakening or killing the plant.

Distribution

This beetle is endemic to the banks of the Sacramento, American, and San Joaquin Rivers and their tributaries in the Central Valley of California. The beetle's major population center is along the American River.

Remnant populations of this longhorn beetle are found in the few stands of natural riverside (riparian) woodlands that remain in the Central Valley. As of 1988, the beetle was known from 10 localities in five counties: Merced, Sacramento, San Joaquin, Stanislaus, and Yolo. Sacramento County supports the largest concentrations of the beetle.

Populations are found along the American River bordering the American River Parkway; the Merced River in the McConnell State Recreation Area; Putah Creek in Solano Creek Park; and the Stanislaus River. A 1987 survey found beetle emergence holes in elderberry bushes along the Feather, Cosumnes, and upper Sacramento Rivers.

Threats

The primary threat to the valley elderberry long-horn beetle is continued loss of habitat. Riparian woodlands have largely diminished due to agricultural conversion, levee construction, and stream channelization. Elderberry bushes were destroyed during maintenance on the American River Flood Control Project in 1985, but the California Department of Water Resources agreed to replant bushes and prevent future disturbance. In 1987, however, personnel from the state reclamation district mowed the habitat along the east levee of the American River, claiming that all wild growth, without exception, must be removed. This decision was contested by the U. S. Fish and Wildlife Service (FWS).

Conservation and Recovery

In 1986, 430 acres (174 hectares) were purchased by Sacramento County along the American River Parkway. The county plans to maintain this land as a habitat for the beetle and to reclaim portions that were previously used for other purposes.

As part of a mitigation agreement, FWS and state botanists have transplanted elderberry bushes infested with beetle larvae to new locations. At one transplant site near Sacramento, beetles were seen to emerge from transplanted trees in April 1988. A second site near Sacramento's main landfill was destroyed by leaking contaminants. Remnants of riparian woodlands within the historic range of the valley elderberry longhorn beetle are being surveyed to identify other potential transplant sites.

Contact

U. S. Fish and Wildlife Service
Regional Office, Division of Endangered Species
Eastside Federal Complex
911 N. E. 11th Ave.
Portland, Oregon 97232-4181
Telephone: (503) 231-6121
http://pacific.fws.gov/

References

Barr, C. B. 1991. "The Distribution, Habitat, and Status of the Valley Elderberry Longhorn Beetle *Desmocerus californicus dimorphus* Fisher (Coleoptera: Cerambycidae)." U. S. Fish and Wildlife Service, Sacramento.

Eng, L. L. 1984. "Rare, Threatened, and Endangered Invertebrates in Californian Riparian Systems." In *California Riparian Systems: Ecology, Conservation, and Productive Management,* edited by R. E. Warner and K. M. Hendrix. University of California Press, Berkeley.

Sands, A. 1982. "The Value of Riparian Habitat." *Fremontia* 10: 3-7.

U. S. Fish and Wildlife Service. 1984. "Valley Elderberry Longhorn Beetle Recovery Plan." U. S. Fish and Wildlife Service, Portland, Oregon.

Delhi Sands Flower-loving Fly

Rhaphiomidas terminatus abdominalis

Status	Endangered
Listed	September 23, 1993
Family	Apioceridae (Orthorrhaphous Dipteran Insect)
Description	Fly with an orange-brown elongated body and dark brown oval spots on its ventral surface.
Habitat	Sandy, fine soils within or adjacent to consolidated dunes.
Food	Flower nectar.
Reproduction	Eggs are deposited in sand and metamorphosis takes a year.
Threats	Conversion of habitat to agricultural use and commercial sites.
Range	California

Description

The *Rhaphiomidas terminatus abdominalis* (Delhi Sands flower-loving fly) has an elongated body with a long tubular proboscis, which is used to extract nectar from flowers. This fly is about 1 in (2.5 cm) long, orange-brown in color, and has dark brown oval spots on the upper surface of the abdomen.

Behavior

The life history of this fly is not well known, but is probably similar to that of other members of this genus. These flies inhabit arid or semi-arid regions, and may occur in sparsely vegetated sand dune habitats. Adults take nectar from flowers by means of an elongate proboscis. The preference of the species for sparsely vegetated areas may be related to the insect's behavior of flying low, usually less than 3 ft (1 m) above the ground. The vegetation may aid in the selection of egg-laying sites.

Mating behavior has not been observed in the wild, although it is known that eggs are deposited in sand. In captivity a female produced over 50 eggs within a 10 day period. Larval development takes place in the sand and metamorphosis probably takes a full year.

This species is a strong flier and, like a hummingbird, is capable of stationary, hovering flight. The Delhi Sands flower-loving fly probably makes a single annual flight period during August and September. A skewed ratio of males to females (about 2:1) suggests that, as with many other insects, males are more active, spending much of their time flying and investigating vegetation or the sand surface for resting females. The single annual flight suggests that development to metamorphosis takes a full year. Pupas work their way to the surface prior to emergence as adults.

Habitat

The habitat of this fly is sandy, fine soils within or adjacent to consolidated dunes. These soil types are generally called "Delhi" fine sand. Delhi soils cover about 40 sq mi (103 sq km) in several irregular patches, extending from the cities of Colton to Ontario and Chino in northwestern Riverside and southwestern San Bernardino Counties. Much of the area of Delhi soils has been used for agricul-

Delhi Sands Flower-loving Fly, photograph by Greg Ballmer. Reproduced by permission.

ture, chiefly grapes and citrus, since the 1800s. More recently, this area has been used for dairies, housing tracts, and industrial sites. Dominant vegetation includes wild buckwheat, croton, and telegraph weed.

Distribution

Based on this species' present distribution, it is thought that it once occurred throughout much of the entire area (40 sq mi [103 sq km]) of the Delhi fine sand soil.

This fly occurs in San Bernardino and Riverside Counties, California. Documented distribution of this insect extends from the eastern margin of the Delhi fine sand formation in Colton to near its western limit in Mira Loma.

The Delhi Sands flower-loving fly currently occurs at five locations in southern California: four in southwestern San Bernardino County, and one in Riverside County, just south of the San

Bernardino County line. All known colonies occur on privately owned land within an 8 mi (13 km) radius circle.

Threats

The major threats to the Delhi Sands flower-loving fly are habitat loss and degradation. Historic and recent agricultural, residential, and commercial development have significantly reduced suitable habitat. Most of the former habitat was destroyed by agricultural development in the 1800s, and the remaining suitable habitat continues to be destroyed by the construction of homes and businesses, and their associated roads and infrastructure. Soil disturbances are being caused by grading, plowing, discing to remove vegetation for fire control, and off-road vehicle use. The use of off-road vehicles may also contribute to the loss of native vegetation and subsequent invasion of weedy, nonnative species. Illegal dumping of abandoned automobiles and other trash has also contributed to habitat degradation.

The Delhi Sands flower-loving fly will not return to previously farmed areas. Agricultural fields may return or be restored to suitable habitat over time; however, the potential of this species to re-colonize degraded sites is unknown, although this behavior may be pivotal to its recovery.

The use of pesticides in agricultural areas and their persistence in the soil may have harmful effects on this species. Furthermore, the level of disturbance at a given site may favor exotic over native vegetation, which may preclude use by the fly.

Although flies in general are not especially popular with collectors, the Delhi Sands flower-loving fly is prized because of its unusual size, coloration, and rarity. A dedicated collector could readily eliminate this species, given its small isolated populations. Even scientific collecting, or repeated handling and marking, particularly of the females, could eliminate populations through loss of genetic variability. Collection of females dispersing from a colony could also reduce the probability that new colonies will be established.

Conservation and Recovery

The Fish and Wildlife Service published a Recovery Plan for the Delhi Sands flower-loving fly in 1997. Eight populations of this endangered insect are located in protected areas. However, most critical habitats are on private land and are at risk from development and other threatening activities, including the habitat of the largest known population. Conservation of the Delhi Sands flower-loving fly requires that these critical habitats be protected. This can be accomplished by acquiring the land and designating ecological reserves, or by negotiating conservation easements with the owners. The populations of the Delhi Sands flower-loving fly should be monitored, and research undertaken into its biology, habitat needs, and beneficial management practices. The Fish and Wildlife Service intends to implement a program of habitat improvement and captive-breeding and release, which will enhance the recovery of the rare insect.

Contact

U. S. Fish and Wildlife Service
Regional Office, Division of Endangered Species
Eastside Federal Building
911 N. E. 11th Ave.
Portland, Oregon 97232-4181
Telephone: (503) 231-6121
http://pacific.fws.gov/

References

U.S. Fish and Wildlife Service. 23 September 1993. "Endangered and Threatened Wildlife and Plants; Determination of Endangered Status for the Delhi Sands Flower-loving Fly." *Federal Register* 58(183): 49881-49887.

U.S. Fish and Wildlife Service. 1997. "Delhi Sands flower-loving fly (*Rhaphiomidas terminatus abdominalis*) Recovery Plan." U.S. Fish and Wildlife Service, Portland, OR.

Pawnee Montane Skipper

Hesperia leonardus montana

Status	Threatened
Listed	September 25, 1987
Family	Hesperiidae (Silver-spotted skipper)
Description	Small, brownish yellow butterfly.
Habitat	Mountain pine woods.
Host Plant	Blue grama grass.
Reproduction	Deposits single eggs directly on the leaves of blue grama grass.
Threats	Limited numbers.
Range	Colorado

Pawnee Montane Skipper, photograph. (c) Paul and Evi Nature Photography. Reproduced by permission.

Description

The adult Pawnee montane skipper, *Hesperia leonardus montana*, is a brownish yellow butterfly with a wingspan of slightly more than 1 in (2.5 cm). Distinct, yellowish spots occur near the outer margins of the upper surface of the wings; there are one to four tan or off-white spots on the lower (ventral) surface. Ventral spots are larger on the hindwings and are generally whiter in females.

Behavior

Pawnee montane skipper females deposit single eggs directly on leaves of blue grama grass (*Bouteloua gracilis*), the only known larval host plant. Larvae overwinter; pupation lasts 13-23 days. Adult males emerge in late July, followed by females up to ten days later. Adults feed principally on the nectar of the prairie gayfeather. The musk thistle is also an important nectar source. Adults live until the first strong frost.

Habitat

The Pawnee montane skipper inhabits a rugged mountainous region of plateaus cut by deep canyons and narrow river valleys. The skipper is found in dry, open, ponderosa pine forests on outcrops of Pikes Peak granite where soils are thin, unstable, and susceptible to water erosion. Slopes are moderately steep with a south, west, or east aspect. The understory is very sparse, generally with less than 30% ground cover.

Blue grama grass occurs in clumps across the hot, open slopes inhabited by skippers but actually covers only about 5% of the surface area. Prairie gayfeather occurs in patches throughout the ponderosa pine woodlands.

Distribution

The Pawnee montane skipper is endemic to habitat associated with the Pike's Peak granite formation in the South Platte river drainage of Colorado, and has probably always had a very limited range.

This species is found in four Colorado counties directly southwest of Denver: Teller, Park, Jefferson, and Douglas. Within these counties, the skipper is restricted to the South Platte River drainage in a band roughly 25 mi (40 km) long and 5 mi (8 km) wide. A three-year study of pawnee populations conducted by the Denver Water Department as part of the study to construct dams, concluded in 1986, estimated the population at 85,000-116,000 individuals.

Threats

Sections of the current range are managed by the Forest Service, the Bureau of Land Management, Denver Water Department, county governments, and private landowners. Currently, the skipper's limited numbers threaten its survival more than do environmental factors. If, however, plans to construct the Two Forks Dam on the South Platte River are implemented, a portion of the butterfly's habitat would be eliminated. Residential development of the area would probably accelerate if the reservoir were built.

Insecticides aimed at controlling the mountain pine beetle and the spruce bud worm would also eradicate the butterfly population if allowed to be applied near the habitat.

The prairie gayfeather, which provides nectar for adult skippers, appears to grow in areas subject to occasional fire or logging, and the skipper does not recolonize these areas for several years after such disturbances.

Conservation and Recovery

Government lands within the butterfly's range are already managed to conserve the species. Control of logging leases and burning may allow the skipper to expand to additional sites.

Contact

U.S. Fish and Wildlife Service
Regional Office, Division of Endangered Species
P.O. Box 25486
Denver Federal Center
Denver, Colorado 80225
http://www.r6.fws.gov/

References

ERT Company. 1986. "1986 Pawnee Montane Skipper Field Studies." Prepared for the Denver Water Department, Denver.

Scott, J. A., and R. E. Stanford. 1982. "Geographic Variation and Ecology of *Hesperia leonardus* (Hesperiidae)." *Journal of Research on the Lepidoptera* 20 (1): 18-35.

U.S. Fish and Wildlife Service. 25 September 1987. "Determination to List the Pawnee montane skipper, *Hesperia leonardus montana*, as a Threatened Species." *Federal Register* 52 (186): 36176-36180.

Laguna Mountains Skipper

Pyrgus ruralis lagunae

Status	Endangered
Listed	January 16, 1997
Family	Hesperiidae
Description	A small butterfly with extensive white wing markings.
Habitat	In meadows, under pines, and on granite.
Food	Flower nectar.
Reproduction	Produces two generations per year.
Threats	Loss and degradation and fragmentation of habitat due to grazing, urban development, and fire management practices; over-collection and other human disturbance; naturally occurring events such as fire or weather extremes.
Range	California

Laguna Mountains Skipper, photograph by Jack N. Levy. Reproduced by permission.

Description

The *Pyrgus ruralis lagunae*, (Laguna Mountains skipper) is a small butterfly in the skipper family (Hesperiidae). It has a wingspan of about 1 in (2.5 cm) and is distinguished from the rural skipper *(P. ruralis ruralis)* by extensive white wing markings that give adults, particularly males, an overall appearance of white rather than mostly black, and by the banding patterns on the hind wings. The Laguna Mountains skipper is found in montane meadow habitats.

The Laguna Mountains skipper is one of two recognized subspecies of the rural skipper, *P. ruralis lagunae*, based upon population isolation and color differentiation. The Laguna Mountains skipper is restricted to the Laguna Mountains and Mount Palomar in San Diego County. The other subspecies of the rural skipper (*P. ruralis ruralis*) ranges from the mountains of British Columbia and Alberta, Canada, south to the coast ranges and Sierra Nevada of central California, as well as Nevada, Utah, and northern Colorado and has darker wings than the Laguna Mountains skipper.

Three other species in the genus *Pyrgus* occur in San Diego County: the common checkered skipper (*P. communis*), the small checkered skipper (*P. scriptura*), and the western checkered skipper (*P. albescens*). The Laguna Mountains skipper can be distinguished from all three of these species by the whitish appearance of the adults and the use of a single larval host plant, *Horkelia clevelandii*, Cleveland's horkelia, in the rose family. In addition, the western checkered skipper and southern California populations of the small checkered skipper are restricted to desert areas.

Behavior

The Laguna Mountains skipper apparently produces two generations per year. The adult flight season occurs from April to May with a second smaller flight in late June to late July. The Laguna Mountains skipper may have evolved a unique mechanism for coping with the low daytime temperatures it encounters during its spring flight, which is unusually early for butterflies in the Laguna Mountains. It is assumed that the life history of the Laguna Mountains skipper is similar to that of *Pyrgus ruralis ruralis*, which maintains a state of suspended activity as a full grown larva and lives 10-20 days in the adult stage.

Adults of the species feed on flower nectar.

Habitat

Cleveland's horkelia, the larval host plant of the Laguna Mountains skipper, occurs in meadows, under pines, and on granite in the Laguna, Cuyamaca, Palomar, and San Jacinto Mountains of southwestern California and northwestern Baja California, Mexico, from 4,000-8,000 ft (1,200-2,400 m) in elevation. Although the distribution of a butterfly is primarily defined by the presence of its larval host plant, the butterfly may be further restricted by other physiological or ecological constraints. The Laguna Mountains skipper is currently found in a few open meadows of yellow pine forest between 4,000-6,000 ft (1,200-1,800) in elevation.

Distribution

Historically, this skipper may have occurred throughout the higher elevations of San Diego County. There were at least six populations of this taxon in the Laguna Mountains in the 1950s and 1960s; however, current information indicates only one extant population. Until its rediscovery in 1983 and subsequent sightings in 1986 and 1995, this skipper had not been seen in the Laguna Mountains since 1972.

Historically, the Mount Palomar populations were small compared to the populations in the Laguna Mountains. Only five specimens have been collected from Mount Palomar in this century. Prior to specimens collected in 1991 and the additional populations found in 1994, the last known sightings from Mount Palomar were from 1980 and, prior to that, from 1939.

The Laguna Mountains skipper population in the Laguna Mountains in San Diego County was not seen during a relatively extensive survey in 1994 but was seen in 1995. Prior to that observation, it was last seen in the Laguna Mountains in 1986 occupy-

ing a small area along a fence in a U.S. Forest Service campground. The Laguna Mountains population was estimated to consist of fewer than 100 individuals. The Laguna Mountains skipper is currently found at four sites in the Mount Palomar region of San Diego County. The largest of the Mount Palomar populations is estimated to comprise 240 individuals.

Threats

The Laguna Mountain skipper is threatened by loss and degradation and fragmentation of habitat due to grazing, urban development, and fire management practices; over-collection and other human disturbance; and naturally occurring events such as fire or weather extremes.

If there were greater numbers of individuals and more populations, the Laguna Mountains skipper might be able to tolerate certain levels and timing of livestock grazing. However, given the low numbers of this butterfly, any impacts to its habitat would be significant. The grizzled skipper (*Pyrgus malvae*) in England is able to tolerate grazing at a highly managed level. The rare Dakota skipper (*Hesperia dacotae*) is sensitive to even light grazing. Some species of butterflies have habitat requirements that need a managed grazing scheme whereas others have habitat that recovers with reduced grazing. However, previous studies indicate that the use of grazing as a management tool for butterflies must be done carefully and at low intensities. A grazing plan for management of the Laguna Mountains skipper has yet to be developed.

Conservation and Recovery

Some protection is afforded to the Laguna Mountains skipper on U.S. Forest Service land. Considering the small population size and extremely limited distribution of the Laguna Mountains skipper, this protection is insufficient to conserve the butterfly.

Fire may be a necessary component for the maintenance of Laguna Mountains skipper habitat. The diversity of montane meadow habitats may be fire-dependent, including the skipper's larval host plant. Historically, the skipper may have experienced local extirpations and recolonizations following local fire events. However, the present discontinuity and low population numbers would not enable the Laguna Mountains skipper to tolerate local extirpations due to fire.

Contact

U. S. Fish and Wildlife Service
Regional Office, Division of Endangered Species
Eastside Federal Building
911 N. E. 11th Ave.
Portland, Oregon 97232-4181
Telephone: (503) 231-6121
http://pacific.fws.gov/

References

Levy, J. N. 1994. "Status of the Laguna Mountains Skipper Butterfly (*Pyrgus ruralis lagunae* J. Scott).

Biological Survey and Analysis prepared for the Forest Service, United States Department of Agriculture.

Northern Prairie Wildlife Research Center. "Butterflies of Montana." http://www.npwrc.usgs.gov/resource/distr/lepid/bflyusa/mt/659.htm (29 June 2000).

Scott, J. A. 1986. *The Butterflies of North America*. Stanford University Press, Stanford, California.

Schaus Swallowtail Butterfly

Heraclides aristodemus ponceanus

Status	Endangered
Listed	April 28, 1976
Family	Papilionidae (Swallowtail butterfly)
Description	Large, dark brown with a tail bordered in yellow.
Habitat	Hammock vegetation.
Host Plant	Torchwood, wild lime.
Reproduction	Deposits single eggs on the leaves of host plants.
Threats	Habitat destruction; loss of larval food plant.
Range	Florida

Description

Also known as the Keys swallowtail butterfly, Schaus swallowtail, *Heraclides aristodemus ponceanus*, is a large (4-5 in or 10-13 cm), dark brown butterfly with dull yellow markings. Its dark tail is bordered in yellow. The black antennae have yellow knobs and black tips. It is easily confused with the giant swallowtail (*H. cresphontes cramer*), which is found in portions of the same habitat. The giant swallowtail is larger than the Schaus and has deeper coloration—bright yellow on coal black.

The Schaus swallowtail is considered one of five subspecies of *H. aristodemus*, a species endemic to the Antilles that tends to vary in appearance according to geographical region. Some taxonomists believe that the Schaus swallowtail is a distinct species. It has also been scientifically classified as *Papilio aristodemus ponceanus* or *P. ponceana*.

Behavior

The Schaus swallowtail emerges from its chrysalis in May and June and feeds on the nectar of guava, cheese shrub, and wild coffee blossoms. It perches on the torchwood plant to bask in the sun. The male is territorial and patrols by circling slowly around intruding males. Schaus swallowtails do not migrate as a group, although individuals sometimes fly across the open water between islands. Adults live about two weeks.

During courtship, the male hovers above and behind the female, who is positioned on the ground with flattened, vibrating wings and a raised abdomen. After fertilization, the female deposits single eggs on the leaves of torchwood and wild lime, the larval host plants. The larvae hatch after three to five days and go through four successive molts. The caterpillar feeds on tender, new growth. After about 20 days, the caterpillar attaches itself to a branch and weaves a thick chrysalis, which can remain dormant for one or two years before the adult butterfly emerges.

Habitat

The Schaus swallowtail lives on hardwood hammocks, which are areas of mature hardwood forest with deep, humus-rich soil typically found in subtropical regions of the southern United States.

Distribution

In the past, this swallowtail was found in Florida from the South Miami area (Dade County) to the Lower Matecumbe Key (Monroe County). The last known mainland specimen was collected at Coconut Grove in 1924.

Schaus Swallowtail Butterfly, photograph by George Krizek. U.S. Fish and Wildlife Service. Reproduced by permission.

The Schaus swallowtail now occurs only in the Florida Keys (Monroe County) and is most numerous where host plants are abundant. The population at Elliot Key in 1986 was estimated at between 750 and 1,000, with smaller colonies inhabiting several neighboring islands.

Although Hurricane Andrew devastated the butterfly's stronghold, Biscayne National Park, in 1992, the population increased two years later to more than 600 individuals. In the 1990s, major releases of captive-bred butterflies have greatly increased the recovery potential for the species. In April 1995, researchers released 760 captive-bred pupae at six publicly owned sites on Key Largo and one site in Miami, Florida. The purpose of these releases was to supplement the sparse numbers of individuals remaining on Key Largo and to reestablish the subspecies in the Miami area, where it was originally described. In a cooperative effort between the U. S. Fish and Wildlife Service (FWS) and the University of Florida at Gainesville, more than 250 Schaus

swallowtail butterflies were released May 13, 1996 on the 400-acre (162-hectare) Deering Estate at Cutler, south of Miami. Another 550 butterflies were released at the same location a month later.

Threats

With the urbanization of south Florida, the Schaus swallowtail lost much of its original habitat and suffered the effects of pesticide use. During the 1970s it was found only in Key Biscayne National Park and on north Key Largo. It was declared Threatened in 1976 but because of a decline in numbers was reclassified as Endangered in 1984.

Conservation and Recovery

The Florida Park Service and the FWS now protect much of northern Key Largo. Under the FWS Coastal Ecosystem Restoration program, state and federal biologists are planting hardwood hammock species to reconnect fragmented habitats for the butterfly and other listed species endemic to Key Largo. Aerial application of mosquito insecticide, which could harm the Schaus swallowtail, has been discontinued over these conservation lands in the last few years. Additionally, an agreement was reached with the Monroe County Mosquito Control District in early 1995 to discontinue ground spraying of mosquito insecticide in important Schaus swallowtail habitat during the butterfly's breeding season. In another significant action, the Florida Keys Electric Cooperative has agreed to enhance and preserve tropical hardwood hammocks important to Schaus swallowtail recovery within a 15-mi (24-km) powerline easement on Key Largo.

With habitat protection in place, the focus of the recovery effort has shifted to the butterfly itself, with the highly successful Schaus swallowtail captive breeding program, which became very successful. The FWS recovery team recommended reestablishing colonies elsewhere within the historic range; in an attempt to achieve this goal, 800 swallowtails were released in 1996 at the Deering Estate south of Miami, a property owned by the State of Florida and Dade County, which includes the largest original tropical hardwood hammock and pine rockland ecosystem in the mainland United States.

The outlook is encouraging for the survival of the Schaus swallowtail on Key Largo and the islands that make up the Biscayne National Park. Habitats within the park are well-managed, and larval host plants are abundant. Successful control of pesticide spraying within the swallowtail's range has reduced one of its greatest immediate threats. Since 1980 the FWS has been acquiring lands on north Key Largo for the Crocodile Lake National Wildlife Refuge—an area within the historic range of the butterfly. These land acquisitions, combined with the recent species reintroduction efforts, may afford the swallowtail an opportunity to increase its numbers in an expanded habitat.

Contact

Regional Office of Endangered Species
U.S. Fish and Wildlife Service
1875 Century Blvd., Suite 200
Atlanta, Georgia 30345
http://southeast.fws.gov/

References

Brown, C. H. 1976. "A Colony of *Papilio aristodemus ponceanus* in the Upper Florida Keys." *Journal of the Georgia Entomological Society* 11:117-118.

Covell, C. V. 1976. "The Schaus Swallowtail: Threatened Species." *Insect World Digest* 3:21-26.

General Accounting Office. 1988. "Endangered Species: Management Improvements Could Enhance Recovery Program." General Accounting Office, Washington, D.C.

U.S. Fish and Wildlife Service. 1982. "Schaus Swallowtail Butterfly Recovery Plan." U.S. Fish and Wildlife Service.

Lange's Metalmark Butterfly

Apodemia mormo langei

Status	Endangered
Listed	June 1, 1976
Family	Lycaenidae (Gossamer-winged butterfly)
Description	Orange, brightly patterned butterfly with white and black markings.
Habitat	Sand dunes.
Host Plant	Buckwheat.
Reproduction	Produces one brood in a season.
Threats	Competition with introduced plants, land clearing.
Range	California

Photo Researchers Inc., Wm. Munoz

Description

Lange's metalmark butterfly, *Apodemia mormo langei,* is a bright reddish-orange butterfly, brightly patterned above with four black-bordered, pearl-white squares on the front wings. Back wings have large white squares and polygons. The wingspan is 0.8-1.25 in (2-3 cm).

Behavior

The swift-flying Lange's metalmark butterfly produces one brood in a season. Adults emerge in early August and can be observed until mid- or late September. Numbers peak two or three weeks after the earliest date of eclosion, the emergence of the butterfly from the pupal case. The peak in male emergence is generally earlier than that of females.

Egg laying occurs throughout the adult flight period. The gray eggs are laid on the lower half of the larval food plant, a subspecies of naked buckwheat, *Eriogonum nudum* var. *auriculatum.* Eggs are placed on the stem axils on the less pubescent surface of the withered foliage. They often are deposited in clusters of two or four but may infrequently be laid singly. The eggs remain attached and dormant until the rainy season, at which time the larvae hatch and crawl to the base of the plant where they overwinter and feed if new foliage is available. The larvae are nocturnal feeders and they begin to feed on new plant growth in late fall or early winter. Pupation occurs in mid-summer in the litter at the base of the buckwheat.

Adults of both sexes are perchers and are capable of long movements between observed perches. The majority of males move less than 100 ft (30 m) while females may travel up to 1,200 ft (360 m). Both sexes prefer buckwheat flowers as perches and as a nectar source. Female butterflies visit a greater variety of secondary nectar sources than do males, which tend to perch or aggregate more than females. The greater vagility of the females is thought to result from their search for suitable egg-laying sites and secondary nectar sources. Usually neither sex, however, moves very far from the buckwheat plants. Nevertheless, females tend to move more frequently between clumps while the less-mobile males remain within a single clump of buckwheat for various periods of time.

It was previously thought that adult females lived nine days or less while males presumably were even shorter lived. Both sexes, however, live approximately one week.

Habitat

This butterfly inhabits stabilized sand dunes along the San Joaquin River. Its primary host plant is a subspecies of naked buckwheat (*Eriogonum nudum* var. *auriculatum*). It depends on host plants for breeding but feeds on the nectar of other wildflowers, if buckwheat is not available.

Distribution

Lange's metalmark is endemic to the Antioch Dunes, which are situated at the confluence of the San Joaquin and Sacramento rivers east of the City of Antioch in Contra Costa County, California. By the late twentieth century, the range of this subspecies had been reduced to about 15 acres (6 hectares). Annual surveys during peak breeding season produced counts of 150 butterflies in 1986, 140 in 1987, and 500 in 1988. The total population is extrapolated from these counts and is thought to average about 400.

The U. S. Fish and Wildlife Service (FWS) acquired approximately 70 acres (28 hectares) of the Antioch Dunes, including a portion of the Lange's metalmark's range, adding it as a satellite to the San Francisco Bay National Wildlife Refuge complex.

Threats

The primary factors limiting the size of the butterfly populations are the availability of nectar sources for adults, adequate host plants for egg laying, and sufficient food for larvae. Losses of these habitat components because of human activity in the area have severely reduced population levels. (The buckwheat also serves as a primary nectar and pollen source for many of the sand-nesting bees and

wasps present on the dunes.) Invasion by exotic plant species evidently has reduced the potential for reestablishment of such native plants as the buckwheat. Unless the exotic plants are eliminated or reduced to some degree, they will continue to limit the reestablishment of native vegetation. Moreover, additional losses of buckwheat caused by discing for fuelbreaks probably will result in further reductions in the numbers of butterflies. Although most disced and mined areas may eventually support *Eriogonum,* these areas recover slowly. Possibly other natural mortality factors exist that are not known or understood.

A devastating wildfire in 1976 near the Pacific Gas & Electric east tower destroyed most of the butterfly larvae present and much of the buckwheat stand. By the 1990s, the *Eriogonum* had largely regained its former numbers, although the size and shrubbiness of the plants apparently was still not yet sufficient to support a self-sustaining colony. Butterflies have been observed at the site of the wildfire since 1977, but these appear to be immigrants.

In the 1980s Antioch Dunes began to feel the negative effects of increased recreational use. Visitors severely trampled and littered the fragile dunes habitat. The *coup de grace* was applied by the unexpected visit of "Humphrey the Humpback Whale." When this whale—ironically an endangered species, itself—was stranded for a time in the Sacramento River, the highly publicized rescue attempt brought large crowds to the refuge, causing severe damage to plant life. As a result, the FWS closed the Antioch Dunes National Wildlife Refuge to unescorted groups in 1988 and 1989.

Conservation and Recovery

Captive breeding of this butterfly and cultivation of its host plant—along with the removal of introduced plants—may be necessary for its recovery. FWS personnel have discussed importing sand to restore the dunes area. A local utility operating a right-of-way adjacent to the refuge funded buckwheat planting and habitat restoration both on its land and within the refuge.

A public awareness program to provide informational brochures and place interpretive signs has been implemented to alert visitors to the fragility of the dunes habitat.

Contact

U. S. Fish and Wildlife Service
Regional Office, Division of Endangered Species
Eastside Federal Complex
911 N. E. 11th Ave.
Portland, Oregon 97232-4181
Telephone: (503) 231-6121
http://pacific.fws.gov/

References

Arnold, R. A. 1983. "Ecological Studies on Six Endangered Butterflies (Lepidoptera: Lycaenidae): Island Biogeography, Patch Dynamics, and the Design of Habitat Preserves." *University of California Publications in Entomology* 99: 1-161.

Arnold, R. A. 1978. "Survey and Status of Six Endangered California Butterflies." Report. California Department of Fish and Game, Sacramento.

San Bruno Elfin Butterfly

Callophrys mossii bayensis

San Bruno Elfin Butterfly, photograph by George Krizek. U.S. Fish and Wildlife Service. Reproduced by permission.

Status	Endangered
Listed	June 1, 1976
Family	Lycaenidae (Gossamer-winged butterfly)
Description	Small, brown-winged butterfly with gray undersides.
Habitat	Grasslands and coastal scrub.
Host Plant	Liveforever.
Reproduction	One brood per generation.
Threats	Urbanization
Range	California

Description

The San Bruno elfin, *Callophrys mossii bayensis* , is a diminutive butterfly with brown upperside front wings, and undersides that are patterned with gray or dark brown. The head, crown, and front have reddish-brown scaling; the eyes are hairy and bordered with white scales; the labial palpi have mixed black and white scales. The thorax and abdomen are hairy, and concolorus with the dorsal wing surface. The hind wings are without tails.

Behavior

The San Bruno elfin produces one brood per generation. Adults emerge from pupae late February to mid-April, with a peak in late March. Males and females are able to mate soon after emergence. When a male encounters a receptive female, he releases a phermone that may lead to mating. Both sexes may mate more than once. The female deposits several dozen eggs per day for the duration of her lifetime (about one week) on the foliage of the larval host plant. The larvae hatch in five to seven days. By the time the host plant blooms, third instar (stage) larvae crawl up the flowering stalks and feed on the flowerheads. Third and fourth instar larvae are tended by ants. The larvae secrete a honeydew substance, which the ants take in exchange for protecting the larvae from predators. Pupation occurs around the base of the host plant and lasts from June until the following March. While larvae are associated exclusively with the liveforever host, adults consume nectar from the limited number of available inflorescences of other species during the early spring flight period. Males also perch on surrounding vegetation to facilitate mating. However, mating itself occurs on or immediately around liveforever (*Sedum spathulifolium*), and females deposit eggs only on liveforever leaves.

Habitat

San Bruno elfin butterflies are found in a mountainous area with a grassy ground cover. The mountain side supports scattered patches of coastal scrub and woodlands and is crossed by several intermittent streams. The San Bruno elfin butterfly's larval host plants are liveforever (*S. spathulifolium*) and stonecrop. Liveforever tend to occur in shallow soils, particularly on weathered, rocky substrates where chaparral cover is reduced. The cover and shelter requirements of the butterfly are supplied by the succulent leaves of the liveforever where early instar larvae bore, on the flowers where later instar larvae feed, and among the detritus at the base of the plant where pupation occurs.

Distribution

The historic range of this butterfly probably encompassed hilltops and ridges from northern San Mateo County, California, to the San Francisco Peninsula and northward into Marin County.

San Bruno Mountain, the major population site for the San Bruno elfin butterfly, is immediately south of the city of San Francisco in San Mateo County and is the northernmost extension of the Santa Cruz Mountains. The habitat is bordered by South San Francisco on the south, Brisbane on the east, Colma on the southwest, and Daly City on the north. The mountain encompasses about 3,620 acres (1,465 hectares), about half of which is owned by the San Mateo County Parks and Recreation Department. Smaller parcels are owned by the California State Parks Foundation and by Visitacion Associates, a development company.

Additional, small populations of San Bruno elfin butterfly occur at Milagra Ridge, southwest of San Bruno Mountain adjacent to the city of Pacifica, and further south at Montara Mountain, Whiting Ridge, and Peak Mountain, adjacent to the city of Montara. No recent population figures are available, although quarrying recently wiped out a major population.

Threats

Continuing urbanization in the San Francisco Bay area threatens to reduce the San Bruno elfin butterfly's aleady limited habitat. A major portion of its remaining habitat has been under private ownership since the late 1800s. The habitat has been disturbed by road and utility-line construction, rock and sand quarrying, livestock grazing, invasion of exotic species, and water diversion.

Grazing and frequent grassfires have encouraged the growth of many introduced plants in the grasslands and reduced the coastal scrub. The permit for the existing rock quarry expired during the mid-1990s and was closed at that time subject to renewal.

The host plant of the San Bruno elfin butterfly is a persistent perennial but its rate of increase is slow. Furthermore, it only attains a competitive advantage over other plants under restricted environmental conditions that depend upon rocky outcrops and steep, extremely weathered slopes on nutrient-poor substrates. Natural disasters, such as landslides and wildfires help Sedrum and create the potential for new habitat for both the plant and the butterfly.

Conservation and Recovery

In the early 1980s a Habitat Conservation Plan was developed to allow private and public development on the mountain while minimizing the adverse effects on endangered species. The plan's goal is the long-term preservation of all rare species within the area. In the meantime, the U. S. Fish and Wildlife Service Recovery Plan recommends a program to minimize the use of herbicides and other toxic substances, to remove non-native plants, and to reestablish native plants, especially the host plant of the San Bruno elfin butterfly.

Contact

Regional Office of Endangered Species
U.S. Fish and Wildlife Service
911 N.E. 11th Ave.
Portland, Oregon 97232
http://pacific.fws.gov/

References

Arnold, R. A. 1983. "Ecological Studies of Six Endangered Butterflies (Lepidoptera: Lycaenidae): Island Biogeography, Patch Dynamics, and the Design of Habitat Preserves." *University of California Publications in Entomology* 99:1-161.

San Bruno Mountain Habitat Conservation Plan Steering Committee. 1982. "San Bruno Mountain Area Habitat Conservation Plan." San Mateo County Planning Division, Redwood City, California.

U.S. Fish and Wildlife Service. 1984. "Recovery Plan for the San Bruno Elfin and Mission Blue Butterflies." U.S. Fish and Wildlife Service, Portland.

El Segundo Blue Butterfly

Euphilotes battoides allyni

Status	Endangered
Listed	June 1, 1976
Family	Lycaenidae (Gossamer-winged butterfly)
Description	Small bright blue butterfly with black margins on the underwings.
Habitat	Coastal sand dunes.
Food	Wild buckwheat.
Reproduction	One brood per generation.
Threats	Urbanization.
Range	California

El Segundo Blue Butterfly, photograph by Richard A. Arnold. Reproduced by permission.

Description

The El Segundo blue butterfly is 0.8-1 in (20-25 mm) long. Males are bright blue above with black margins on their hindwings; females are dark brown above. Both sexes are light grayish below with black squares or spots and an orange band, bordered on both sides by a row of black dots. Formerly classified as *Shijimiaeoides battoides allyni,* this species is difficult to distinguish from other members of its genus.

Behavior

The El Segundo blue butterfly undergoes complete metamorphosis (egg, larva, pupa, and adult). The life span of this animal is about one year. Some pupae may remain in diapause for two or more years. The adults are active from mid-June to early September; the exact timing depending on the weather. The onset of flight is closely synchronized to the beginning of the flowering cycle of coast buckwheat, the food plant.

Upon emerging from their pupae, the female El Segundo blue butterflies fly to the flower heads of the food plant where they mate with males that constantly move from flower head to flower head. The females then immediately begin laying eggs. Laboratory data indicate females produce 15-20 eggs per day, but must continuously feed on nectar and pollen to maintain egg production. Although field data indicate females at the Chevron site in El Segundo live an average of four days in nature in captivity, females live two weeks and produce up to 120 eggs. Eggs hatch within three to five days. The discrepancy between longevity of adults in the field, 2.3-7.3 days and the laboratory, 16 day average, is most likely due to predation by crab and lynx spiders. These spiders were found at a frequency of about one per 200 flowerheads. One capture of a male El Segundo blue butterfly was observed during 15 person-hours of direct observations of flowerheads.

The larvae of the El Segundo blue butterfly undergo four instars before they pupate, a process that takes 18-25 days. The larvae maintain a symbiotic relationship with ants. The larvae develop glands and reversible tubes that produce a sweet secretion by the third instar, and are thereafter tended by various species of ants. The ants may protect the caterpillars from parasites and/or small predators. Mature larvae are highly polymorphic varying in color from almost pure white or pure dull yellow to strikingly marked individuals with a dull red-to-maroon background broken by a series of yellow or white dashes or chevrons. Larvae remain concealed within the flowerhead when feeding, the color pattern adding to their crypsis. The preferred part of the flowerhead are young seeds, which are consumed preferentially to other flowerparts. The latter are closely webbed together by the caterpillars giving the illusion of an intact flowerhead. One larva requires two or three flowerheads to complete development. By late September, the flowerheads have generally senesced and the larvae have pupated underground or in the leaf litter at the base of the food plants.

The egg population of the El Segundo blue butterfly is chiefly regulated by a parasitic wasp *Trichogramma*, which also attacks the eggs of the gray hairstreak butterfly and at least two species of micro-lepidopterous moths that also feed on buckwheat flowerheads.

Habitat

The El Segundo blue butterfly is only known from the El Segundo sand dunes. This habitat is a biologically sensitive and a unique environment, and is inhabited by a number of plant and animal species of special concern. The El Segundo sand dunes are the largest coastal sand dune system between the mouth of the Santa Maria River in Santa Barbara County and Ensenada in Mexico. The vegetation has been defined as the Sand verbena-beach bursage series in Sawyer and Keeler-Wolf. Native plants on the El Segundo sand dunes include coast buckwheat, dunes golden bush, dunes wall flower, dunes sun-cup, dunes burr-bush, and California croton.

It has an exclusive host relationship with wild buckwheat (*Eriogonum parvifolium*), whose flowers provide a food source for the larvae and nectar for the adults. Habitat requirements for *E. parvifolium* include shifting, wind blown sand dunes. Plants supporting the highest concentration of larvae and adult butterflies are found in swales and on wind

protected dune crests, which indicates that the slope and nature of the dunes are key environmental factors for the butterfly.

Distribution

Historically, this butterfly ranged throughout the El Segundo sand hills in Los Angeles County, California until as recently as several decades ago. Its habitat range has been reduced by development to two habitat patches in a 2-acre (0.81-hectare) preserve controlled by Chevron Oil near the Los Angeles airport. Prior to Chevron's agreeing to protect this area, it was greatly modified so that only a 500-foot wide corridor remained along the boundary of the dunes. However, wild buckwheat appears to be well-adapted to shifting sand dunes, and it and iceplant restabilized in the remaining habitat. Because the wild buckwheat population is limited by the size of the habitat, the butterfly population is proportionately limited as well.

The El Segundo blue butterfly is now found only on remnants of the dune ecosystem, limited to a few acres of an oil refinery near El Segundo and to a larger area at the west end of the Los Angeles International Airport. Estimates of the number of individuals in these two ranges from 100-1,000 in any given year, equally divided with males and females. The population seems relatively stabile, but the limited number of hosts plants means that the butterfly population can never increase substantially within this restricted range.

Threats

All of the known populations of the El Segundo blue butterfly are under threat from various sources. Iceplant and other invasive exotic plants have degraded the sand dune habitat at the west side of the Ballona Wetlands. Non-native plants continue to invade the Airport Dunes. The small size and relatively low diversity of native plants threatens the butterfly at the Chevron reserve in El Segundo. Habitat destruction and invasive exotic plants pose a significant threat to the population at Malaga Cove.

The El Segundo dunes were undisturbed until the Spanish land grants development in the 1840s. Farming was then established on the coastal prairie to the east of the dunes, but generally started farther inland, probably because of agricultural unsuitability of the poorly drained sandstone soil near the backdune. The dunes themselves were undisturbed until the late 1880s when the cities from Redondo Beach to Venice were established, however, urban development was limited. Prior to that time, virtually the entire El Segundo dunes were in a pristine condition.

The city of Redondo Beach separated the main dunes from south Redondo Beach and the Malaga Cove extensions, and development of Venice eliminated the dunes north of the mouth of Ballona Creek. Conversion of the central part of the dunes was slower. Construction of the Chevron oil refinery in 1911 separated the dunes into two fragments. The southern fragment was gradually converted to homes starting at the beginning of the twentieth century and rapidly accelerated in the late 1940s. The natural habitat values in these areas were totally destroyed by the 1970s.

The Airport Dunes, the largest block of remaining natural habitat for the butterfly and other native species, was significantly reduced in quality and quantity between 1938 and 1992. However, the most substantive changes have taken place during the past 25 years. This has been as a result of the realignment of Pershing Drive, construction of Imperial Highway, moving sand to build a hill, and fragmentation and scraping of the coastal prairie. The habitat degradation resulted in extinction or extirpation of many native species and the invasion of the site by exotic plants and animals.

In 1928, the grid of streets on the Airport Dunes was constructed, but development was minimal following the 1929 stock market crash. Significant development did not take place until after the Second World War, with virtually the entire dunes built upon between 1946 and 1965. Nearly all of this area was privately owned. Construction of the Hyperion Sewage Treatment Plant and the Scattergood electrical plant in the 1940s, along with dense housing on the present Airport Dunes, reduced the northern fragment to about 80 acres of coastal sand dune habitat by 1960. The 1.6-acre (0.65-hectare) Chevron butterfly sanctuary site was isolated by residential development in the 1950s.

The most important events affecting the recent biological history of the Airport Dunes was the purchase and clearing of residences from nearly 200 acres between 1966 and 1972, which had resulted in the major contraction of native plants and animals in this area. A major adverse impact resulted from construction of the very high-frequency omni direction radio.

The Los Angeles Department of Airports currently is proposing to expand the Los Angeles International Airport (LAX). One alternative of the LAX 2015 Expansion Master Plan involves a physical intrusion onto the Dunes of graded areas associated with the end of a runway.

Of the 20 species of native terrestrial mammals recorded in 1938-40, most of which were present in 1975, only three are extant today. In their place are the introduced Norwegian rat, red fox, and opossum. Of 31 species of butterfly breeding on the site, seven have been extirpated. Of 18 species of reptiles and amphibians, seven have been extirpated and all five scrub dependent birds have disappeared from the Airport Dunes.

Ecosystem disturbance as a result of changes in the mammalian community has been profound as both rabbits and mice influence the differential reproductive efficiency of herbaceous plant species. The absence of mammalian foraging probably relaxed substantial pressure on seed banks, particularly European weeds. Loss of small mammals is linked to the introduction of the red fox, which themselves now have such limited food resources that they are driven to feeding on garbage, lizards, and even large insects.

During the late 1980s, off-road vehicles trespassed on the Airport Dunes, resulting in damage to El Segundo blue butterfly habitat and the native plant nursery. Areas containing sensitive cryptogamic crusts located on the backdunes at the Airport Dunes were badly damaged by human foot traffic in 1997. Cryptogamic crusts are formed in soils by blue green algae, lichens, mosses, fungi, and bacteria. They increase the ability of the soil to hold moisture, decrease its susceptibility to erosion, and apparently have higher levels of native versus exotic plant species.

Conservation and Recovery

The Los Angeles Airport has agreed to manage its dunes in cooperation with the Fish and Wildlife Service to benefit the El Segundo blue butterfly. The Chevron Corporation established a fenced sanctuary for the El Segundo blue butterfly on the grounds of its USA Refinery in 1983 and is currently managing the habitat for the butterfly's protection.

The Recovery Plan recommends the following steps:

1. Manage the habitat at the airport by removing exotic plants, implementing erosion control, establishing additional buckwheat populations, and controlling human access to the habitat.

2. Establish and protect a Dune Preserve Area at the airport, at a potential golf course habitat, and at the runway light area. Establishing these areas as suitable habitat includes removing exotic vegetation (the iceplant) and man-made structures and debris; planting native dune species; and introducing captive-bred blue butterflies.

3. Study the species life history and ecology to assess the loss from predation, parasitism, disease, and the effect of pollution created by the refinery, airport traffic, and use of herbicides and insecticides in the residential community; also study the propagation requirements and population genetics and incorporate that data into the recovery plan.

Contact

Regional Office of Endangered Species
U.S. Fish and Wildlife Service
911 NE 11th Avenue
Portland, Oregon 97232
http://pacific.fws.gov/

References

Arnold, R. A., and A. E. Goins. 1987. "Habitat Enhancement Techniques for the El Segundo Blue Butterfly: An Urban Endangered Species." In Adam and Leedy, eds., *Integrating Man and Nature in the Metropolitan Environment.* National Institute for Urban Wildlife, Columbia, Maryland.

U.S. Fish and Wildlife Service. 1978. "Sensitive Wildlife Information System-El Segundo Blue Butterfly." Report. U.S. Fish and Wildlife Service, Washington, D.C.

U.S. Fish and Wildlife Service. 1986. "Recovery Plan for the El Segundo Blue Butterfly." USFWS, Portland. 87pp.

U.S. Fish and Wildlife Service. 1998. "Recovery Plan for the El Segundo Blue Butterfly." USFWS, Portland. 78pp.

Smith's Blue Butterfly

Euphilotes enoptes smithi

Status	Endangered
Listed	June 1, 1976
Family	Lycaenidae (Gossamer-winged butterfly)
Description	Small butterfly; males are bright blue above, females are brown.
Habitat	Coastal sand dunes.
Host Plant	Buckwheat.
Reproduction	Females deposit eggs on buckwheat flowers.
Threats	Habitat loss and disturbance.
Range	California

Smith's Blue Butterfly, photograph by B. "Moose" Peterson/WRP. Reproduced by permission.

Description

Smith's blue butterfly, *Euphilotes enoptes smithi*, is slightly less than 1 in (2.5 cm) across. The male's upper wings are a lustrous blue with wide black borders; females are brown above with a band of red-orange marks across the hind wings. Both sexes have prominent checkered fringes on the fore and hind wings. Smith's blue butterfly can be distinguished from other subspecies by a light undersurface ground color and prominent overlying black markings with a faint black terminal line. Smith's blue was formerly classified as *Shijimiaeoides enoptes smithi*.

Behavior

Adult butterflies feed, rest, sun, and mate on several species of buckwheat (*Eriogonum*), never straying far from host plants. Males perch on flowers, sometimes seeming to watch for approaching females to court. Females deposit eggs individually on buckwheat flowers. Larvae hatch four to eight days later and go through five instars (intermediate stages) before pupating in flower heads or in the sand and litter at the base of the plants.

Pupation occurs between mid-August and early September, and pupae hang in place until adults emerge the following year. Males tend to emerge first; females follow about a week later, at which time courtship and copulation occur. The adult flight period from mid-June to early September corresponds with the blooming of the buckwheat plants. Each adult lives for only about one week, but individual emergences are staggered over the extended flight period.

Habitat

Smith's blue butterfly is found on coastal and inland sand dunes, which support buckwheat and associated species, such as Ben Lomond wallflower, California poppy, bicolor lupine, and ponderosa pine. The butterfly is also found on cliffside coastal sage scrub and serpentine grassland, where dominant grasses are intermixed with buckwheat and other forbs.

Distribution

The Smith's blue butterfly is an endemic California subspecies, found primarily along the coast from the mouth of the Salinas River to Del Rey Creek.

The current distribution of Smith's blue butterfly includes coastal portions of Monterey County. Although there is no current population estimate, the butterfly is now considered more abundant than at the time of federal listing due to the discovery of several new populations.

Threats

The Smith's blue butterfly's coastal habitat has suffered a number of disturbances. Dunes are threatened by proposed housing developments, road construction, beach recreation, and off-road vehicles. Some dunes have been invaded by the non-native iceplant and Holland dunegrass, which displace buckwheat. Sand dunes at Fort Ord have been damaged by military activities, and large dunes in the Seaside-Marina dune system have been destroyed by sand mining. Sand mining is also occurring in the Del Monte Forest.

Conservation and Recovery

In 1986 the Marina city council prepared a habitat conservation plan for the coastal dunes that lie between Fort Ord and the Salinas River in Monterey County. In 1977 the Army established a butterfly preserve at Fort Ord, and the Youth Conservation Corps has removed non-native plants and attempted to reestablish native plants there.

In 1987 Smith's blue butterfly was confirmed in remnant habitat at Sand City in Monterey County. Some of this dune area has been zoned for housing development, but the city agreed to complete a conservation plan before work proceeded.

Contact

Regional Office of Endangered Species
U.S. Fish and Wildlife Service
911 N.E. 11th Ave.
Portland, Oregon 97232
http://pacific.fws.gov/

References

Arnold, R. A. 1983. "Ecological Studies on Six Endangered Butterflies (Lepidoptera: Lycaenidae): Island Biogeography, Patch Dynamics, and the Design of Habitat Preserves." *University of California Publications in Entomology* 99:1-161.

Langston, R. L. 1963. "*Philotes* of Central Coastal California." *Journal of the Lepidopterists' Society* 17:210-223.

U.S. Fish and Wildlife Service. 1984. "Smith's Blue Butterfly Recovery Plan." U.S. Fish and Wildlife Service, Portland.

Palos Verdes Blue Butterfly

Glaucopsyche lygdamus palosverdesensis

Status	Endangered
Listed	July 2, 1980
Family	Lycaenidae (Gossamer-winged butterfly)
Description	Small, silvery blue with narrow black wing margins.
Habitat	Cool, fog-shrouded slopes.
Host Plant	Locoweed, rattlepod, and deerweed.
Reproduction	Adults emerge during February and March.
Threats	Urbanization, low numbers.
Range	California

Silvery Blue Butterfly (*Glaucopsyche lygdamus*), photograph by Richard A. Arnold. Reproduced by permission.

Description

The Palos Verdes blue butterfly, *Glaucopsyche lygdamus palosverdesensis*, is a small lycaenid butterfly with a wingspan of about 1 in (25 mm). It belongs to a species commonly called the "silvery blue butterfly" because of its color. Both sexes are pale gray to dark brownish-gray below, with narrow black margins in the male and diffuse wide dark margins in the female. The Palos Verdes blue is similar in appearance to the common blue and the Reakirt's blue.

Behavior

Until the 1994 discovery of a new population of Palos Verdes blue butterflies, entomologists believed the insect used rattlepod (*Astragalus trichopodus* var. *lonchus*) exclusively as the larval host plant during reproduction. Females have since been found to deposit their eggs on the flowers and fruits of deerweed (*Lotus scoparius*) as well. Caterpillars (larvae) hatch from eggs in seven to 10 days and be-

gin feeding on the host plant. Near the end of their larval stage, Palos Verdes blue caterpillars may be tended by ants. The larvae of other *G. lygdamus* subspecies secrete a sugary substance that is eaten by the ants. In return, the ants may protect the caterpillars from predators and parasitoids. Adults emerge during February and March and live for an average of only four days.

Habitat

The Palos Verdes blue's larval host plant, the locoweed, grows on well-drained clay or gravelly soils and is frequently found on rocky slopes, especially along the coast.

Distribution

This species is restricted to the cool, fog-shrouded, seaward side of the Palos Verdes Hills in Los Angeles County, California. The foodplant occurs as far north as Santa Barbara. Until 1994, the species was known to exist only in a single population, which occupied a large vacant lot near the intersection of Los Verdes Drive and Hawthorne Boulevard in Los Angeles. This site was subsequently cleared for a housing development. Several smaller colonies were discovered nearby, but the status of the species was in doubt, and some experts feared it was already extinct. However, on March 10, 1994, U.S. Fish and Wildlife Service (FWS) biologist Dr. Rudi Mattoni rediscovered the Palos Verdes blue butterfly on the grounds of a Department of Defense facility in San Pedro, California, while conducting a survey for ground-dwelling insects. Following the butterfly's rediscovery, FWS entomologists made several additional butterfly sightings outside the Defense facility. The population is estimated to number 200 butterflies.

Threats

Urbanization has been the main cause of decline of the Palos Verdes blue butterfly. The city and suburbs of Los Angeles have expanded to encompass the butterfly's entire historic range. Weed control practices have all but eliminated the locoweed in and around the city. At remnant habitat sites, the Palos Verdes blue must compete with the more common Western tailed blue butterfly, which also feeds on the locoweed.

Conservation and Recovery

The three small habitat areas on the Palos Verdes Peninsula, where the butterfly was last seen before the 1994 sighting at the Department of Defense facility, have been designated as Critical Habitat: Agua Amarga Canyon; Frank Hesse Park; and a section along Palos Verdes Drive in the city of Rancho Palos Verdes.

The Palos Verdes blue population rediscovered by Dr. Mattoni was located in an area proposed for a pipeline project. The coastal California gnatcatcher (*Polioptila californica californica*), a threatened bird, also occurs in this region. The Department of De-

fense currently is working with FWS biologists to develop strategies to conserve both the Palos Verdes blue butterfly and the coastal California gnatcatcher. In addition, Chevron has provided funding for Dr. Mattoni to sample vegetation in the pipeline area in order to determine its suitability for recolonization by these unique species.

Contact

Regional Office of Endangered Species
U.S. Fish and Wildlife Service
911 N.E. 11th Ave.
Portland, Oregon 97232
http://pacific.fws.gov/

References

Arnold, R. A. 1980. "Status of Proposed Threatened or Endangered California Lepidoptera." Contract Report to California Department of Fish and Game, Sacramento.

Arnold, R. A. 1987. "Decline of the Endangered Palos Verdes Blue Butterfly in California." *Biological Conservation* 40(1987):203-217

Mattoni, R. H. T. 1994. "Current Status of the Palos Verdes Blue Butterfly at the U. S. Navy Fuel Storage Reserve, San Pedro, California." Agresearch Inc. report prepared for Chevron Oil.

Mattoni, R. H. T. 1993. "The Palos Verdes blue, *Glaucopsyche lygdamus palosverdesensis* Perkins and Emmel." Occasional Paper of the IUCN Species Survival Commission. No. 8.

Perkins, E. M., and J. F. Emmel. 1977. "A New Subspecies of *Glaucopsyche lygdamus* from California." Proceedings of the Entomological Society, Washington 79:408-471.

U.S. Fish and Wildlife Service. 1984. "The Palos Verdes Blue Butterfly Recovery Plan." U.S. Fish and Wildlife Service, Portland.

Fender's Blue Butterfly

Icaricia icarioides fenderi

Status	Endangered
Listed	January 25, 2000
Family	Lycaenidae (Gossamer-winged butterfly)
Description	A small butterfly.
Habitat	Native prairie.
Food	Feeds only on lupines.
Reproduction	Lays internally fertilized eggs, which develop into larvae with 5 instars, then a pupal stage, followed by metamorphosis into the adult.
Threats	Habitat loss.
Range	Oregon

Common Blue Butterfly (*Icaricia icarioides*), Patti Murray

Description

Fender's blue butterfly is one of about 12 subspecies of the Boisduval's blue butterfly (*Icaricia icarioides*), a widespread species of western North America. Fender's blue butterfly is a relatively small species, with a wingspan of about 1.0 in (2.5 cm). The upper wings of the males are colored a brilliant blue, with black borders and basal areas. The upper wings of the females are colored brown. The undersides of the wings of both sexes are creamy tan, with black spots surrounded with a fine halo of white. Male Fender's blue butterflies have relatively small white spots on the undersides of the wings; this is a distinguishing characteristic of the subspecies.

Behavior

Adult Fender's blue butterflies lay their eggs on species of lupines (*Lupinus* spp.), which are the food plant of the caterpillars during May and June. Of the 32 sites where Fender's blue butterfly is known

to occur, Kincaid's lupine (*Lupinus sulphureus kincaidii*) co-occurs as the larval host plant at 27 of the sites. Other species of lupines are secondary host plants at these and other sites. Newly hatched larvae feed for a short time, reaching their second instar in the early summer, at which point they enter an extended diapause (a state of suspended activity) and eventually overwinter in leaf litter. They become active again when the weather warms sufficiently in the following spring, around March or April. Once the winter diapause is broken, the larvae feed and grow through three to four additional instars, enter the pupal stage, and emerge as adult butterflies in April and May. Overall, a Fender's blue butterfly may complete its life cycle in one year, although this can extend over two calendar years. The larvae of other species of Boisduval's blue butterflies are known to have specialized glands that secrete a sweet solution, which is sought by certain ant species who actively protect the caterpillars from predators and parasites. This mutualism is likely to also occur between ants and larvae of

Fender's blue butterfly, although it has not been specifically observed by field biologists.

Habitat

Fender's blue butterfly inhabits native, dry, upland prairie habitat. The dominant plant species are red fescue (*Festuca rubra*) and/or Idaho fescue (*Festuca idahoensis*), with indicator species including Tolmie's mariposa (*Calochortus tolmiei*), Hooker's catchfly (*Silene hookeri*), strawberry (*Fragaria virginiana*), rose check-mallow (*Sidalcea virgata*), and common lomatium (*Lomatium* spp.).

Distribution

Fender's blue butterfly is a locally evolved (or endemic) subspecies that is only known from the Willamette Valley of Oregon. This is a 130-mi (209-km) long and 20-40 mi (32-64 km) wide alluvial floodplain with an overall northward gradient.

Threats

The indigenous Kalapooya Indians cleared and burned land used for food gathering and hunting in the Willamette Valley. This activity resulted in the maintenance of extensive areas of grassland in a region capable of supporting forest (a habitat inhospitable to the Fender's blue butterfly). After the beginning of the European settlement in 1848, the amount of burning decreased greatly because settlers suppressed large-scale wildfires. This resulted in the change from predominantly open, park-like communities of the valley basin into dense oak and conifer forests, or into scrub lands following logging. Even more important in terms of ecological change was the rapid conversion of most of the bottomland area of the valley into agricultural land-uses. These various changes resulted in an enormous decrease in the amount of habitat available to support Fender's blue butterfly, and a precipitous decrease in its population (and also those of some associated endemic species). In large part, uncultivated fencerows and intervening strips of land along agricultural fields and roadsides served as the only refugia from these forces of ecological change. In the early 1990s, only about 988 acres (400 hectares) of native upland prairie remained in the Willamette Valley, representing only 0.1% of the former area of this ecosystem type. Within this remnant prairie habitat, Fender's blue butterfly occupies about 32 sites totaling 408 acres (165 hectares).

Ongoing threats to the rare butterfly include habitat loss or damage from a wide variety of causes, such as urbanization, agricultural activities (including insecticide spraying), forestry practices, and roadside maintenance (including herbicide spraying). Collecting for the commercial trade in butterflies is also a hazard at some sites.

Conservation and Recovery

Fender's blue butterfly receives no protection under the Oregon Endangered Species Act, which does not include invertebrate animals in the definition of "wildlife." This means that some commercial collecting of the endangered butterfly continues to occur. Conservation of Fender's blue butterfly requires that this collecting be stopped. In addition, most of the surviving habitat occurs on privately owned land. It is crucial that this habitat be protected, which can be done by acquiring the land and establishing ecological reserves, or by negotiating conservation easements or other suitable land-management agreements with the landowners. The U. S. Fish and Wildlife Service has plans to begin to undertake such conservation activities, beginning in the year 2000. Because of the extremely small area of surviving native prairie in the Willamette Valley, it would be prudent to undertake an action in ecological restoration to increase the cover of this community type. This would benefit Fender's blue butterfly as well as other threatened co-occurring species.

Contacts

U. S. Fish and Wildlife Service
Regional Office, Division of Endangered Species
Eastside Federal Complex
911 N. E. 11th Ave.
Portland, Oregon 97232-4181
(503) 231-6121
http://pacific.fws.gov/

U. S. Fish and Wildlife Service
Oregon State Office
2600 SE 98th Ave, Suite 100
Portland, Oregon 97266
Telephone: (503) 231-6179
Fax: (503) 231-6195

Reference

U.S. Fish and Wildlife Service. 2000. Endangered and Threatened Wildlife and Plants; Endangered Status for *Erigeron decumbens* var. *decumbens* (Willamette Daisy) and Fender's Blue Butterfly (*Icaricia icarioides fenderi*) and Threatened Status for *Lupinus sulphureus* ssp. *kincaidii* (Kincaid's Lupine). http://www.epa.gov/fedrgstr/ EPA-SPECIES/2000/January/Day-25/e1561. htm

Mission Blue Butterfly

Icaricia icarioides missionensis

Status	Endangered
Listed	June 1, 1976
Family	Lycaenidae (Gossamer-winged butterfly)
Description	Small butterfly; male is silver-blue to violet-blue above, female is completely brown.
Habitat	Grasslands and coastal scrub.
Host Plant	Lupine.
Reproduction	Single egg is deposited on the host plant.
Threats	Habitat loss, encroachment of non-native vegetation.
Range	California

Mission Blue Butterfly, photograph by Richard A. Arnold. Reproduced by permission.

Description

The mission blue butterfly, *Icaricia icarioides missionensis*, measures about 1-1.4 in (2.5-3.5 cm) across the wingtips. The male is silver-blue to violet-blue above, with dark wing margins; the female is completely brown above or with blue restricted to wing bases. Beneath, both sexes are silver-gray or brownish with black spots on the front wing. This species has also been referred to as *Plebejus icarioides missionensis*.

Behavior

Adults begin to emerge from pupae in late March and fly until mid-June. They have an average life span of 10 days. Females are fertile throughout their life, depositing single eggs on the leaves, stems, flowers, and seedpods of the host plant, one of several species of lupine. Eggs hatch in four to seven days, but the larvae overwinter in leaf litter at the base of the host plants. In spring, the larvae resume feeding, then pupate. Parasitic wasps attack and lay their eggs inside the mission blue's larvae, but often the larvae are tended by ants, which provide some protection from wasp parasites and other predators. In exchange, the larvae secrete honeydew for the ants.

Habitat

The mission blue inhabits grasslands and coastal scrub. It is also found along the borders of dunes or tidal marshes. Spring and summer climate is relatively cool, windy, and cloudy. Maximum summer temperatures average less than 70°F (21°C). Winter temperatures seldom fall below freezing (32°F, or 0°C). Three perennial lupine species serve as larval host plants (*Lupinus albifrons*, *L. formosus*, and *L. variicolor*).

Distribution

The mission blue butterfly is endemic to the San Francisco peninsula and Marin County, California. This subspecies was first collected in 1937 on Twin

Peaks in the Mission District of San Francisco. Except for small colonies in the Mission District of San Francisco and at Fort Baker in Marin County, other colonies of mission blue butterflies were known to occur on about 1,500 acres (600 hectares) of grassland at San Bruno Mountain south of San Francisco. Several populations were recently discovered in northern and central San Mateo County.

Threats

Loss of habitat to urban San Francisco and related residential development is the major cause for the decline of the mission blue butterfly. Its habitat has also suffered from industrial and agricultural development, quarrying, and the encroachment of non-native plant species that crowd out the lupine host plants. The Fort Baker colony near the north end of the Golden Gate Bridge is afforded protection by the Golden Gate National Recreation Area.

Conservation and Recovery

The Mission blue butterfly's host plants grow in a plant community that depends on periodic disturbances, such as rock slides, mud slides, and fires, to establish seedlings. Preserving the mission blue butterfly will require maintaining sufficient tracts of lupine, which, in turn, depends on sustaining the natural succession of vegetation by inducing periodic disturbance.

A development company, Visitacion Associates, donated 298 acres (121 hectares) of habitat on San Bruno Mountain to the San Mateo County Parks and Recreation Department. The San Bruno Mountain Habitat Conservation Plan has been developed to maintain several hundred acres of open habitat while allowing residential development to continue in other parts of the historic habitat area. The long-term outlook for the mission blue is guardedly optimistic.

Contact

U. S. Fish and Wildlife Service
Regional Office, Division of Endangered Species
Eastside Federal Complex
911 N. E. 11th Ave.
Portland, Oregon 97232-4181
Telephone: (503) 231-6121
http://pacific.fws.gov/

References

Arnold, R. A. 1983. "Ecological Studies of Six Endangered Butterflies (Lepidoptera: Lycaenidae): Island Biogeography, Patch Dynamics, and Design of Habitat Preserves." *University of California Publications in Entomology* 99: 1-161.

Arnold, R. A. 1987. "The Mission Blue Butterfly." In *Audubon Wildlife Report 1987.* National Audubon Society, San Diego.

McClintock, E., W. Knight, and N. Fahy. 1968. "A Flora of the San Bruno Mountains, San Mateo County, California." *Proceedings of the California Academy of Science* 32: 587-677.

San Bruno Mountain Habitat Conservation Plan Steering Committee. 1982. "San Bruno Mountain Area Habitat Conservation Plan." San Mateo County Planning Department, Redwood City, Calif.

U.S. Fish and Wildlife Service. 1984. "Recovery Plan for the San Bruno Elfin and Mission Blue Butterflies." U. S. Fish and Wildlife Service, Portland, Oregon.

Lotis Blue Butterfly

Lycaeides argyrognomon lotis

Status	Endangered
Listed	June 1, 1976
Family	Lycaenidae (Gossamer-winged butterfly)
Description	Small butterfly; males are violet-blue, females brown.
Habitat	Wet meadows and sphagnum-willow bogs.
Host plant	Coast trefoil.
Reproduction	Females lay eggs during the adult flight season (mid-April to early June).
Threats	Habitat destruction.
Range	California

Description

The lotis blue butterfly, *Lycaeides argyrognomon lotis* has a wingspan of 0.6-1.3 in (1.5-3.3 cm). The upper wing surfaces are a deep violet-blue in the male with a black border and fringe of white scales along the outer wing margins. In the female, the upper wing surface is brown, sometimes bluish-brown, with a wavy band of orange on both forewings and hindwings. The lotis blue is one of 12 subspecies of *L. argyrognomon* in North America.

Behavior

The life history of the lotis blue butterfly is not well studied, but some information can be extrapolated from closely related species. The larval host plant is most likely the coast trefoil (*Lotus formosissimus*). Females lay eggs on the host plants during the adult flight season from mid-April to early June, and newly hatched larvae begin feeding immediately on leaves, flowers, and seedpods. Larval diapause (the resting stage during larval development) is broken sometime during the following spring, and larvae complete their development four to six weeks later. The pupal stage probably lasts no more than a few weeks.

Habitat

The lotis blue butterfly is found in wet meadows or poorly drained sphagnum-willow bogs, where soils are waterlogged and highly acidic. This habitat has a dense undergrowth of shrubs, including California huckleberry, western Labrador tea, salal, wax myrtle, California rose-bay, western hemlock, and Sitka spruce.

Distribution

The lotis blue butterfly appears to be a naturally rare insect with low population densities. In the past, it was found at seven coastal localities in Mendocino, northern Sonoma, and possibly northern Marin Counties in California. A site near Point Arena (Mendocino County) has not been populated by the butterfly since the 1940s. The limited number of specimens in museum collections and limited field observations make any assessment of the historic range of this butterfly difficult.

Since 1977, the lotis blue butterfly has been found only at a single 5-acre (2-hectare) site north of the town of Mendocino. Between 1977 and 1981 only 16 adult specimens were seen in 42 days of field searching at the site. This may make the lotis blue the rarest butterfly in the continental United States. Nat-

Lotis Blue Butterfly, photograph by Richard A. Arnold. Reproduced by permission.

ural factors and human intrusion may have played a role in the lotis blue's scarcity.

Threats

Because of its low numbers and limited distribution, the lotis blue butterfly is extremely vulnerable to further loss of habitat, and a number of potential threats exist, such as logging, peat mining, power line corridor maintenance, herbicide and pesticide application, and alterations of water regimes.

Fire suppression may affect distribution and abundance of the host plants. Drought during 1976 and 1977 caused the sphagnum bog to dry out, and no lotis blue butterflies were observed in 1977.

Conservation and Recovery

The only known population site is on private land. The U. S. Fish and Wildlife Service has attempted to negotiate a conservation agreement with the landowner to arrange maintenance of vegeta-

tion at the site to limit the use of pesticides and herbicides. If the extant population is ever deemed large enough, several adults may be removed to other breeding locations within the historic range. Captive breeding may also be considered.

Contact

U. S. Fish and Wildlife Service
Regional Office, Division of Endangered Species
Eastside Federal Complex
911 N. E. 11th Ave.
Portland, Oregon 97232-4181
Telephone: (503) 231-6121
http://pacific.fws.gov/

References

Arnold, R. A. 1983. "Ecological Studies on Six Endangered Butterflies (Lepidoptera: Lycaenidae): Island Biogeography, Patch Dynamics, and the Design of Habitat Preserves." *University of California Publications in Entomology* 99: 1-161.

Arnold, R. A. 1981. "A Review of Endangered Species Legislation in the USA, and Preliminary Research on Six Endangered California Butterflies." *Beihefte zu den Veröffentlichungen fuer Naturschutz und Landschaftspflege in Baden-Württemburg* 21: 79-96.

Arnold, R. A. 1978. "Survey and Status of Six Endangered Butterflies in California." Report. California Department of Fish and Game, Sacramento.

Tilden, J. W. 1965. *Butterflies of the San Francisco Bay Region.* University of California Press, Berkeley.

U. S. Fish and Wildlife Service. 1985. "Recovery Plan for the Lotis Blue Butterfly." U. S. Fish and Wildlife Service, Portland, Oregon.

Karner Blue Butterfly

Lycaeides melissa samuelis

Status	Endangered
Listed	December 14, 1992
Family	Lycaenidae (Gossamer-winged butterfly)
Description	Small, silvery-blue (males) or grayish brown and orange (females) butterfly.
Habitat	Sandplains with grassy openings within dry pine/scrub oak barrens.
Host Plant	Wild lupine.
Reproduction	Usually has two broods each year.
Threats	Silviculture, urbanization.
Range	Illinois, Indiana, Michigan, Minnesota, New Hampshire, New York, Ohio, Wisconsin

Karner Blue Butterfly, photograph. U. S. Fish and Wildlife Service. Reproduced by permission.

Description

The Karner blue butterfly has a wingspan of 0.87-1.26 in (2.2-3.2 cm). The dorsal side of the male is silvery blue or dark blue with narrow black margins. The females are grayish brown dorsally, with irregular bands of orange inside the narrow black border on the upper wings. Both sexes are slate grey on the ventral side with the orange bands showing more regularity, and black spots circled with white.

Behavior

This butterfly usually has two broods each year. Eggs that have overwintered from the previous year hatch in April. The larvae feed on wild lupine leaves and mature rapidly. Near the end of May, they pupate and adult butterflies emerge very late in May in most years. The adults are typically in flight for the first 10-15 days of June, when the wild lupine is in bloom. Females lay eggs on or near the wild lupine plants. The eggs hatch in about one week and the larvae feed for about three weeks. Then they pupate, and the second brood adults appear in the second or third week of July. This time, the eggs are laid among plant litter or on grass blades at the base of the lupines, or on lupine pods or stems. By early August, no adults remain, and these eggs do not hatch until the following spring.

The Karner blue butterfly frequently occurs with other rare butterfly species such as the Persius duskywing (*Erynnis persius*) and the frosted elfin (*Incisalia irus*).

The presence of wild lupine is essential to the occurrence and survival of this species. Unaltered by humans, a pine-barren ecosystem is likely to be a mosaic of interspersed woody vegetation, such as pitch pine and scrub oak and more open areas characterized by wild lupine, grasses, and other plants such as spreading dogbane (*Apocynum androsaemifolium*) and New Jersey tea (*Ceanothus americanus*) which serve as nectar for adult butterflies.

Habitat

The habitat of the Karner blue butterfly is characterized by the presence of wild lupine, a member of the pea family. Wild lupine is the only known larval food plant for this butterfly and is, therefore, closely tied to the butterfly's ecology and distribution. In eastern New York and New Hampshire, the habitat typically includes sandplain communities, and grassy openings within very dry, sandy pitch pine/scrub oak barrens. In the Midwest, the habitat is also dry and sandy, including oak savanna and jack pine areas, and dune/sandplain communities. It is believed that this species originally occurred as shifting clusters of populations, or metapopulations, across a vast fire-swept landscape covering thousands of acres. While the fires resulted in localized extirpation, post-fire vegetational succession promoted colonization and rapid population buildups. Periodic disturbance is necessary to maintain openings in the canopy for wild lupine to thrive. A variety of other understory plants associated with the habitat serve as nectar sources for the adult butterflies.

Distribution

The distribution of this species is very discontinuous, and generally follows the northern limits of wild lupine. Eight major population clusters of the butterfly were known historically from portions of Wisconsin, Michigan, Minnesota, Indiana, Illinois, Ohio, Massachusetts, New Hampshire, Pennsylvania, New York, and Ontario. Over the past 100 years, this species' numbers have apparently declined rangewide by 99% or more. More than 90% of the decline occurred in the last 10-15 years. It is now extirpated from Massachusetts, Pennsylvania, and Ohio.

The New York Natural Heritage Program maintains a state list of approximately 50 individual Karner blue butterfly sites, comprising about 10 site-clusters, all found in the area known as the Albany Pine Bush and at scattered locations extending about 40 mi (64 km) to the north. Once the site of a massive Karner blue butterfly population, Albany Pine Bush is the locality from which the butterfly was first described. There are also unverified records of this species in Manhattan and Brooklyn from the mid-1800s. A decline of 85-98% in the Albany Pine Bush over the past decade has been noted, exclusive of one site that has remained stable. The decline in population has been described as dropping from numbers of around 80,000 in 1979, to around 1,000 in 1987, to 100-200 in 1990. North of the Albany Pine Bush, one disturbed site located at an airport has persisted with numbers estimated around 14,000 in 1990. This population is several times larger than all the other New York sites combined. The majority of extant Karner blue butterfly sites in New York are in municipal and private ownership. Other landowners include a State Park, The Nature Conservancy, and Saratoga County.

In New Hampshire, the Concord Pine Barrens along the Merrimack River support the only remaining occurrence of this species in New England. The sole population is extremely low in numbers and occurs on a privately owned, 2-3-acre (0.81-1.21-hectare) site within a power line right-of-way bordering an industrial park, and on the grounds of a nearby airport. The results of 1990 surveys reported by The Nature Conservancy showed a decline in the population size from an estimated 2,000-3,000 individuals in 1983 to an estimated 250-400 individuals in 1990. During that survey, the species was not found at two other sites in the Concord Pine Barrens where it had been documented in 1983.

In Wisconsin, 33 of 36 historical occurrence sites were surveyed during 1990. Survey results revealed that the species was found at only 11 of the 33 historical sites visited. Although 23 previously unknown populations were discovered, the numbers of Karner blue butterfly observed were very small at most sites. Only three sites had 50 or more individuals observed, with none greater than 100. At least half of Wisconsin's populations are small, isolated, and cannot be considered secure or viable in the long term. However, a very good number of quite sizeable populations occur on publicly owned properties offering good opportunities for long-term protection and management. Over three-fourths of the Wisconsin sites are on publicly administered lands, including Necedah National Wildlife Refuge, Department of Defense, Wisconsin Department of Natural Resources, and County Forest.

The Karner blue butterfly has declined throughout its range in Michigan. It still occurs in six of seven counties from which it was known historically, but the existing populations are greatly reduced and have become highly fragmented within expanses of suitable habitat.

Surveys in Indiana in 1990 yielded the following results: this species was reconfirmed at one known site, and was rediscovered on three of seven historical sites. Searches at 27 sites identified as potentially suitable for the species yielded six new locations for the species. However, all extant sites in Indiana are in two population clusters within two counties. Six sites are located on Indiana Dunes National Lakeshore, and other landowners include a county park and recreational department, a school district, and The Nature Conservancy.

During the 1990 surveys of 50 potentially suitable sites in Minnesota, the Karner blue butterfly was located in two areas. Both sites are on a State Wildlife Management Area, in the vicinity of one of the historical locations. Studies conducted in 1991 revealed three new sites within 0.5-3 mi (0.8-4.8 km) of the sites surveyed in 1990. Low numbers of individuals were observed at all five sites, with none greater than 14.

This species was presumed extirpated from Illinois until the species was relocated there in August 1992. A total of seven butterflies, including five males and two females, were reported from a lupine site in the northern part of the state.

Threats

Throughout its range, changes in the habitat occupied by this species resulting from silviculture, urbanization, and the declining frequency of wildfires are largely the reasons for its decline. Modification and fragmentation of remaining areas are continuing threats to the survival of this butterfly. In addition to direct destruction of suitable habitat, urbanization has led to fire suppression on interspersed habitat; in the absence of fire, vegetational succession has made this habitat unsuitable.

Although in the past there have been large scientific collections of the Karner blue butterfly, they are not believed to be a significant factor in the decline of this species. However, any future take could potentially damage recovery efforts.

Disease and predation have not been documented as factors in the decline of this species.

As the continued survival of this species is dependent on the presence of wild lupine, any actions or lack thereof, that affect populations of wild lupine will affect Karner blue butterfly populations.

With small, isolated, and declining populations, this butterfly is particularly vulnerable to extinction.

Extreme isolation will prevent the influx of new genetic material, leading to highly inbred populations that have low viability and/or fecundity.

Vegetation control measures implemented during the fall of 1990 at the Concord site opened habitat for the butterfly's obligate food source, wild lupine, and seeds collected have been planted in several test plots. If these plantings are successful, the butterfly population should increase.

Conservation and Recovery

In March of 1991, the U. S. Fish and Wildlife Service (FWS) and conservation groups persuaded the New Hampshire Department of Environmental Services to deny the city of Concord's application to spread municipal sludge over 200 acres of remnant pine barren habitat at the city airport.

FWS's New England Field Office, the State of New Hampshire, and The Nature Conservancy continue to work with the city of Concord to set aside pine barren preserves for the butterfly and other rare species.

Contacts

U.S. Fish and Wildlife Service
Regional Office
Federal Building
Fort Snelling
Twin Cities, Minnesota 55111
http://midwest.fws.gov/

U.S. Fish and Wildlife Service
Regional Office
300 Westgate Center Dr.
Hadley, Massachusetts 01035
http://northeast.fws.gov

New England Ecological Services Field Office
22 Bridge St., Suite 1
Concord, New Hampshire 03301-4986
Telephone: (603) 225-1411
Fax: (603) 225-1467

Massachusetts Natural Heritage and Endangered Species Program
Division of Fisheries and Wildlife
Route 135
Westborough, Massachusetts 01581
Telephone: (508) 792-7270, extension 200
Fax: (508) 792-7275

References

Schweitzer, D. F., 1989. "Fact sheet for the Karner Blue Butterfly with special reference to New York." The Nature Conservancy, internal document, 7 pp.

U.S. Fish and Wildlife Service 14 December 1992. *Federal Register.* Rules and regulations. 57 (240): 59236-59243.

Uncompahgre Fritillary Butterfly

Boloria acrocnema

Status	Endangered
Listed	June 24, 1991
Family	Nymphalidae (Brush-footed butterfly)
Description	Small, rusty brown butterfly, with upper wings crisscrossed in black.
Habitat	Patches of snow willow on cool, wet mountain slopes.
Host Plant	Snow willow.
Reproduction	Females lay eggs on the host plant.
Threats	Collectors.
Range	Colorado

Uncompahgre Butterfly, photograph. (c) Paul and Evi Nature Photography. Reproduced by permission.

Description

The Uncompahgre fritillary is a small butterfly with a 1-in (2.5-cm) wingspan. The upper wings are rusty brown, crisscrossed with black bars. The forewing is light ocher below, and the hind wing has a jagged white bar separating the crimson-brown inner half from the purple-gray outer half. Females are generally lighter above than males. The body has a rusty brown thorax and a brownish-black abdomen. The species is considered by some to be *Boloria improba* ssp. *acrocnema,* a subspecies of the dingy arctic fritillary. It has also been classified as *Clossiana acrocnema.*

Behavior

Adults feed on a variety of alpine flowers. Females lay eggs on snow willow (*Salix reticulata* ssp. *nivalis*), which is the larval food plant.

Researchers believe that the Uncompahgre fritillary has a biennial life cycle. Eggs laid in the sum-

mer become caterpillars the following summer and mature into adult butterflies during the third summer. There are thus separate even- and odd-year populations within the same habitat area.

This butterfly is relatively sedentary and a weak flyer that stays close to the ground, making it an easy target for collectors.

Habitat

The Uncompahgre fritillary inhabits cool, moist mountain slopes above 13,200 ft (4,020 m). It is always associated with patches of snow willow, which provide larval food and cover.

Distribution

This species has the smallest range of any North American butterfly. It was discovered on Uncompahgre Peak in Hinsdale County, Colorado, in 1978. Another site was discovered in 1982 on land managed by the U. S. Bureau of Land Management

(BLM). In 1988 a few individuals were captured at two additional sites. The total known range includes the San Juan Mountains and southern Sawatch Range in Gunnison, Hinsdale, and possibly Chaffee Counties in southwestern Colorado.

Since this species was discovered only recently, its current range is the same as its historic range, and it is not known whether the species was formerly more widespread. The original Uncompahgre Peak population is in the Big Blue Wilderness in the Uncompahgre National Forest. The second population is in a wilderness study area administered by the BLM. The two additional sites where some individuals were found in 1988 require more study to determine whether they support viable populations. Reports that four additional colonies have been discovered are as yet unconfirmed.

Surveys conducted in the 1970s and 1980s indicated that populations at the major colonies were on the decline. The even-year brood at Uncompahgre Peak had declined from about 800 in 1978 to about 200 in 1988. The population at the BLM site had declined from more than 1,000 in 1984 to about 500 in 1988. The odd-year brood at Uncompahgre Peak, which had been documented in the past, may be extinct, and the status of the odd-year brood at the BLM site was unclear. The U. S. Fish and Wildlife Service estimated the total population to be about 1,000.

Threats

The overwhelming threat to the Uncompahgre fritillary is butterfly collectors. As one of the few North American species discovered in the twentieth century, it is in great demand by collectors, and individual specimens are often sold for more than US$100. Although collecting has been banned by the U. S. Forest Service (USFS) in the Uncompahgre Peak area, some collection apparently continues. There has been no ban on collecting at the BLM site. Now that the Uncompahgre fritillary has been listed as endangered, collecting the species is illegal and can be prosecuted by federal authorities.

The small size of the known population and the need for a cool, wet habitat also threaten the long-term viability of the Uncompahgre fritillary. Besides the pressures of collecting, the species is vulnerable to such unpredictable natural events as prolonged drought or climatic change.

Conservation and Recovery

In 1984 the USFS and the BLM came to an agreement on conservation of the Uncompahgre fritillary. Besides banning collecting on USFS land, trails near the BLM site were rerouted to reduce recreational traffic in the habitat area.

Contact

U. S. Fish and Wildlife Service
Regional Office, Division of Endangered Species
P.O. Box 25486
Denver Federal Center
Denver, Colorado 80225
http://www.r6.fws.gov/

References

Brussard, P. F., and H. Britten. 1989. "Final Report on the Uncompahgre Fritillary (*Boloria acrocnema*)." Report prepared for the U. S. Forest Service, U. S. Bureau of Land Management, and U. S. Fish and Wildlife Service. Montana State University, Bozeman.

Gall, L. E. 1984. "Population Structure and Recommendations for Conservation of the Narrowly Endemic Alpine Butterfly, *Boloria acrocnema* (Lepidoptera: Nymphalidae). *Biological Conservation* 28: 111-138.

U. S. Forest Service and U. S. Bureau of Land Management. 1984. "Interagency Agreement and Species Management Perspective for Mt. Uncompahgre Fritillary Butterfly (*Boloria acrocnema*)." U. S. Forest Service and U. S. Bureau of Land Management, Gunnison, Colorado.

Bay Checkerspot Butterfly

Euphydryas editha bayensis

Status	Threatened
Listed	September 18, 1987
Family	Nymphalidae (Brush-footed butterfly)
Description	Medium-sized butterfly with bright red and yellow spots on the upper forewing.
Habitat	Grasslands associated with outcrops of serpentine.
Food	Feeds on plantain, owl's clover.
Reproduction	Complex life cycle of egg, larvae, pupa, adult.
Threats	Urbanization, drought, overgrazing, fire.
Range	California

Description

The bay checkerspot, *Euphydryas editha bayensis*, is a medium-sized butterfly with a wingspan of 1.5-2.25 in (4-5.6 cm). The upper forewing surfaces have bright red-and-yellow spots and black bands along the veins. Its appearance is more decidedly checkered than other subspecies of *Euphydryas editha*. It is darker than *E. e. luestherae* and lacks a dark red outer-wing band. It has brighter red-and-yellow coloration than *E. e. insularis*.

Behavior

The bay checkerspot lays eggs only on certain host plants, the most important of which is the annual, dwarf plantain (*Plantago erecta*); the owl's clover (*Orthocarpus densiflorus*) is a secondary host. The host plants germinate from early October to late December, and senesce from early April to mid-May. Most of the active parts of the life cycle of the rare butterfly also occur during this time. The bay checkerspot reproduces once and dies in a single year. Adults emerge from pupae in early spring, and feed on the nectar of various species of plants. They mate and lay eggs during a flight season that typically lasts for four to six weeks in the period between late February to early May. Male bay checkerspots typically emerge from their pupae four to eight days

before females, and find and mate with most females soon after they emerge. Males can mate multiple times, but most females are believed to mate only once. However, they are capable of re-mating four to seven days after the first copulation, and some females have been found to carry more than one spermatophore. The average life span for adults of both sexes is about 10 days, but individuals have lived for more than three weeks. Eggs are typically laid in March and April. Females lay up to five egg masses of 5 to 250 eggs each, which they deposit near the base of dwarf plantain, or less often, purple owl's clover. The lifetime production of eggs produced by female bay checkerspots is 250-1,000.

Natural recolonization of sites from which the bay checkerspot has been extirpated is rare. In 21 years of studying marked populations less than 4 mi (6 km) apart, only a single individual was observed to translocate to another colony. As the number of suitable habitat "islands" of the bay checkerspot decreases because of habitat loss, the average distance between sites increases, making recolonization an even less likely event.

Habitat

The host plants only grow in sites with serpentine-influenced soil. The bay checkerspot thrives

Bay Checkerspot Butterfly, photograph by Richard A. Arnold. Reproduced by permission.

only on serpentine outcrops larger than about 800 acres (325 hectares), a size that allows the population to survive the severe population fluctuations that occur during periods of drought. Smaller outcrops support satellite populations that may thrive in years of favorable climate. However, the bay checkerspot can easily become extirpated in small habitats, which must then be recolonized from a larger, surviving habitat nearby.

Distribution

The bay checkerspot ranges around and south of the San Francisco Bay in Alameda, Contra Costa, San Francisco, San Mateo, and Santa Clara Counties, California. In historical times, this area probably supported the bay checkerspot in four large serpentine habitats and dozens of smaller ones. The total historical area of suitable serpentine habitat was about 12,000 acres (4,900 hectares), but it is much less today. There are five core areas: one on the San Francisco peninsula in San Mateo County,

and four on Coyote Ridge in Santa Clara County. These core areas plus smaller satellite habitats comprise two metapopulations, of which that in Santa Clara County is considered to have the greatest chance of long-term survival. At least 26 satellite colonies have been documented, but many have been lost to drought, overgrazing, or urbanization.

Threats

The bay checkerspot is threatened by habitat destruction or degradation caused by urban development, highway construction, drought, fire, livestock grazing, and invasive non-native plants (such as eucalyptus trees). When its host plants are removed or replaced by other species, the bay checkerspot cannot survive. Its largest serpentine outcrop occurs near Morgan Hill (Santa Clara County) in a narrow band extending 16 mi (26 km) from Heller Canyon to Anderson Lake. Two large outcrops in San Mateo County were fragmented by the construction of Interstate Highway 280. A population historically known from San Leandro (Alameda County) is now extirpated. A small population on San Bruno Mountain has not been observed since a 1986 wildfire.

The largest surviving population of bay checkerspot is at Morgan Hill, but the best-studied colony is at Stanford University's Jasper Ridge Biological Preserve east of Searsville Reservoir. The drought of 1976 and 1977, combined with overgrazing, greatly reduced the Jasper Ridge population. The second largest population, located in San Mateo County, is threatened by the proposed addition of a golf course and recreation area to Edgewood Park. If implemented, this construction would eliminate 65% of the remaining habitat and decimate a population that had already declined catastrophically (from 100,000 in 1981 to only about 1,000 in 1987) because of urbanization and adverse weather conditions. A larger population in Redwood City was fragmented by urbanization and reduced to satellite status. A colony near Mt. Diablo (Contra Costa County) was thought to have become extirpated during a severe drought, but bay checkerspots were found there again in 1988.

Conservation and Recovery

Much of the habitat of the bay checkerspot is on privately owned land. A conservation agreement was negotiated between the U. S. Fish and Wildlife Service (FWS) and a corporate landowner, Waste Management Inc., to protect 30% of the Morgan Hill site. The FWS believes that this conservation agreement will decrease the overall threat to the species, even though it was linked to the destruction of 10% of the critical habitat during the construction of a landfill. Waste Management Inc.

agreed to support conservation activities at the site for 10 years. As a result of this conservation action, the FWS downlisted the bay checkerspot from Endangered to Threatened. The populations of the bay checkerspot should be monitored, and, if necessary, extirpated populations should be reestablished by transplantation from surviving populations. Research is needed into the biology and habitat needs of the butterfly, to provide insight into management practices to maintain or enhance its habitat. Prescribed fire, for example, appears to be useful in reducing the abundance of non-native shrubs and trees.

Contact

Regional Office of Endangered Species
U. S. Fish and Wildlife Service
Regional Office, Division of Endangered Species
911 N. E. 11th Ave.
Portland, Oregon 97232-4181
Telephone: (503) 231-6121
http://pacific.fws.gov/

References

Ehrlich, P. R., et al. 1975. "Checkerspot Butterflies: A Historical Perspective." *Science* 188:221-228.

Murphy, D. D., and P. R. Ehrlich. 1980. "Two California Checkerspot Butterfly Subspecies: One New, One on the Verge of Extinction." *Journal of the Lepidopterists' Society* 34:316-320.

U. S. Fish and Wildlife Service. 1987. "Determination of the Bay Checkerspot Butterfly, *Euphydryas editha bayensis*, to Be a Threatened Species." *Federal Register* 52(181): 35366-35378.

Quino Checkerspot Butterfly

Euphydryas editha quino

Status	Endangered
Listed	January 16, 1997
Family	Nymphalidae (Brush-footed butterfly)
Description	A small butterfly checkered with brown, reddish, and yellowish spots.
Habitat	Open grassland and sunny openings within chaparral and coastal sage shrubland.
Food	Larvae feed on dwarf plantain and owl's-clover; adults feed on nectar.
Reproduction	Has a complex life cycle of egg, several larval stages, pupa, and adult.
Threats	Habitat degradation by livestock grazing and invasive non-native plants, and to a lesser degree urban development.
Range	California

Quino Checkerspot Butterfly, photograph. E/D Productions. Reproduced by permission.

Description

The quino checkerspot, *Euphydryas (=Occidryas) editha quino*, is a small member of the brush-footed butterfly family Nymphalidae. It has about a 1 in (2.5 cm) wingspan and is checkered with dark brown, reddish, and yellowish spots. It is one of 12 recognized subspecies of *E. editha* (editha checkerspot). The quino checkerspot can be distinguished from other subspecies of *E. editha* in that the quino checkerspot tends to be larger with redder wings, and the light spots on the wings tend to be fewer and more discrete. This taxon also looks similar to two other species of butterfly that occur within its range. The Chalcedon checkerspot (*E. chalcedona*) is yellower and slightly larger, with sharper forewings, than the quino checkerspot. Gabb's checkerspot (*Chlosyne gabbii*) is smaller than the quino checkerspot and has orange rather than red markings.

Adult quino checkerspot butterflies live from four to eight weeks. The flight season occurs from mid-January to late April and peaks between March and April. The eggs hatch in about 10 days and the larvae begin to feed immediately. Fourth instar (development stage) larvae enter an obligatory diapause as summer approaches and their larval food plant dries up. Extended periods of diapause may occur during times of drought. Post-diapause larvae develop through four more instars and then pupate to emerge as adults in the early spring.

Behavior

The primary larval food of the quino checkerspot is dwarf plantain (*Plantago erecta*). Secondary foods are *P. ovata* and *Castilleja exserta*. The butterfly often basks in the winter sun.

Habitat

The quino checkerspot is restricted to open grassland and sunny openings within chaparral and coastal sage shrubland habitats of the interior foothills of southwestern California and northwestern Baja California, Mexico. Like the Laguna Mountains skipper, its distribution is defined primarily by that of its larval host plants. These plants grow in or near meadows, vernal pools, and lake margins, and spread to upland shrub communities of sparse chaparral and coastal sage scrub. This butterfly is generally found at sites where high densities of the host plants occur and at a variety of elevations from about sea level to about 3,000 ft (914 m). Within these areas, the quino checkerspot may be preferentially selecting sites where exposure to winter sun is greatest. These habitats, like the quino checkerspot, were once common along coastal bluffs, mesas, and inland foothills.

Distribution

The quino checkerspot may have been one of the most abundant butterflies in San Diego, Orange, and western Riverside counties during the early part of the twentieth century. The original range of the quino checkerspot extended as far south as Valle de la Trinidad in northwestern Baja California, Mexico and as far north as Point Dume in Los Angeles County. Currently, only seven or eight populations are known within the United States (the lack of an exact count is due to uncertainty as to whether sightings of very small numbers of butterflies in two areas represent one or two populations). All known extant populations in the United States occur in southwestern Riverside and north-central San Diego counties. One population near Upper Otay Lake in San Diego County was last seen in 1990. In 1996, a very small group of quino checkerspots was sighted on Otay Mesa, but because of the very limited amount of available host plant, this occurrence was not expected to persist beyond 1996. At least one population exists in Mexico, in the Sierra Juarez near Tecate. Although no estimates of population sizes for the quino checkerspot are currently available, all but three populations are known to comprise fewer than five individuals.

Threats

Fifty to 75% of the known range of the quino checkerspot has been lost since 1900 due to habitat degradation or destruction. Sunny openings within chaparral and coastal sage scrub occupied by the quino checkerspot have been degraded by grazing and, to a lesser degree, destroyed by urban development. The primary larval food plant, *Plantago erecta,* can be displaced by exotic plants that invade once the ground is disturbed by discing, grading, and/or grazing. The host plant then recolonizes in sites where grasses do not grow well, like cattle trails and road edges, where quino checkerspot larvae are subject to trampling. The encroachment of urban development in rural Riverside County potentially threatens two of the largest populations of quino checkerspot. This area is growing rapidly and is projected to be fully developed within the decade. One population is in an area that is included in a local community plan that provides for subdivision of parcels into 20-acre (8.1-hectare) lots. Another population is on the site of an approved preliminary map for a housing development. The loss of these two populations is likely to preclude survival and recovery of the taxon.

The quino checkerspot population in southern San Diego County may be threatened by a proposed urban development project on Otay Mesa. The preferred alternative for the Otay Ranch New Town Plan (the largest planned community in the southwestern U. S.) would result in the loss of 14,000 acres (5,665 hectares) of upland shrub communities, or about 52% of the extent of the plant communities within the project area. The effects of this project on the recently observed quino checkerspot population on Otay Mesa are not known at this time but are likely to be significant.

Additional development is expected to further reduce and degrade habitat of the quino checkerspot through construction of homes and roads, and increases in fire frequencies, unauthorized trash dumping, and the distribution and abundance of exotic plants . An existing recreational vehicle park and marina in the vicinity of quino checkerspot habitat attracts unauthorized use of off-road vehicles within natural habitat areas. Off-road vehicles increase erosion and fire hazards and destroy habitat by creating trails. Evidence of off-road vehicle use is apparent at one of the quino checkerspot localities, where a recently created dirt road bisects the center of the habitat. Quino checkerspot habitat at this locality has also been disced in part; these disturbed areas no longer support this taxon, while the surrounding undisturbed areas do.

There is evidence that predation is a threat to the quino checkerspot. Preliminary studies indicate that predation has contributed to the decline of the quino checkerspot at sites where habitat has been invaded by non-native plant species, which may also harbor predatory arthropods. Sites within historical quino checkerspot habitat that have been heavily invaded by Mediterranean plant species also have high sowbug (*Armadillidium* sp. and *Porcellio* sp.) and earwig (*Euborellia annulipes* and *Forficula auricularia*) densities. Sowbugs and earwigs prey upon butterfly eggs. These predators are absent from natural sites currently occupied by the quino checkerspot. Argentine ants are also a potential predator that co-occur with earwigs and sowbugs. The number of these introduced predators is expected to increase with the spread of development because these exotics thrive in irrigated horticultural environments which may be adjacent to natural quino checkerspot habitat.

The quino checkerspot is somewhat adapted to unpredictable weather patterns but requires sufficient patches of suitable habitat to respond to this environmental variability. The quino checkerspot's dispersal capabilities vary considerably depending upon rainfall patterns and the resulting availability of adult nectar sources and larval food plants. For example, in 1984 a San Diego County population of the quino checkerspot exhibited an increase in numbers as a result of favorable weather. The greater number of larvae defoliated the larval food plants. This central core area was left without sufficient egg-laying sites for females, and adults dispersed greater distances in search of additional suitable habitat. Ideally these dispersing adults would have found marginally suitable areas and, in subsequent generations, would have returned to a central core area. In this case, the mass dispersal failed to restore populations in previously occupied habitat, and the butterflies have not recolonized the original site.

Conservation and Recovery

No specific regulations protect the quino checkerspot in Mexico. However, all hunting and export of wildlife in Mexico is prohibited, except under permit. Little is known of the status of the isolated populations in Mexico and any protection afforded to these populations does not insure the survival of the taxon.

The quino checkerspot may be provided some protection to one population by its occurrence, in part, on Bureau of Land Management land in Riverside County. However, this Federal land is currently subject to off-road vehicle activity.

Contacts

U. S. Fish and Wildlife Service
Regional Office, Division of Endangered Species
Eastside Federal Complex
911 N. E. 11th Ave.
Portland, Oregon 97232-4181
Telephone: (503) 231-6121
http://pacific.fws.gov/

U. S. Fish and Wildlife Service
Carlsbad Field Office
2730 Loker Avenue West
Carlsbad, California, 92008-6603
Telephone: (760) 431-9440
Fax: (760) 431-9624

Reference

U. S. Fish and Wildlife Service. 16 January 1997. "Endangered and Threatened Wildlife and Plants: Determination of Endangered Status for the Laguna Mountains Skipper and Quino Checkerspot Butterfly." *Federal Register* 62 (11): 2313-2322.

Saint Francis' Satyr Butterfly

Neonympha mitchellii francisci

Status	Endangered
Listed	January 26, 1995
Family	Nymphalidae (Brush-footed butterfly)
Description	Fairly small, dark brown butterfly with conspicuous dark maroon "eyespots" on the the wings.
Habitat	Wide, wet meadows dominated by sedges.
Food	Graminoids (seeds, grasses, grains).
Reproduction	Two adult flights or generations per year.
Threats	Overcollecting.
Range	North Carolina

Saint Francis' Satyr Butterfly, photograph by Steve Hall. Reproduced by permission.

Description

Saint Francis' satyr is a fairly small, dark brown butterfly with a wingspan of 1.3-1.7 in (33-44 mm). Saint Francis' satyr and Mitchell's satyr (*Neonympha mitchellii mitchellii*), the northern subspecies, which was classified as endangered on May 20, 1992, are nearly identical in size and show only a slight degree of sexual size dimorphism. Like most species in the wood nymph group, Saint Francis' satyr has conspicuous "eyespots" on the lower surfaces of the wings. These eyespots are dark maroon brown in the center, reflecting a silver cast in certain lights. The border of these dark eyespots is straw yellow in color, with an outermost border of dark brown. The eyespots are usually round to slightly oval and are well- developed on the fore wings as well as on the hind wing. The spots are accented by two bright orange bands along the posterior wing edges and two darker brown bands across the central portion of each wing. Saint Francis' satyr, like its subspecies, can be distinguished from its North American con-gener, *N. areolata*, by the latter's well-marked eyespots on the upper wing surfaces and brighter orange bands on the hind wing, as well as by its lighter coloration and stronger flight.

Behavior

The annual life cycle of Saint Francis' satyr, unlike Mitchell's satyr, is bivoltine, having two adult flights or generations per year. Larval host plants are believed to be graminoids associated with grasses, sedges, and rushes. Little else is known about the life history of this butterfly.

Habitat

The habitat occupied by this satyr consists primarily of wide, wet meadows dominated by sedges and other wetland graminoids. In North Carolina sandhills, such meadows are often relics of beaver activity. Unlike the habitat of Mitchell's satyr, the North Carolina species' habitat cannot be properly called a fen because the waters of this sandhills region are extremely poor in organic nutrients. The boggy areas of the sandhills are quite acidic as well as ephemeral, succeeding either to procosin or swamp forest if not kept open by frequent beaver activity. Under the natural regime of frequent forest fires ignited by summer thunderstorms, the sandhills were once covered with a much more open type of woodland, dominated by longleaf pine, wiregrass, and other fire-tolerant species. The type of forest that currently exists along the creek inhabited by Saint Francis' satyr can grow up only under a long period of fire suppression. The dominance on this site of loblolly pine is due primarily to past forestry management practices and not any form of natural succession.

Distribution

Saint Francis' satyr is extremely restricted geographically, and Mitchell's satyr has been eliminated from approximately half of its range in North Carolina. Extensive searches have been made of suitable habitat in North Carolina and South Carolina, but no other populations have been found. The current narrow distribution could be the result of the enormous environmental changes that have occurred in the southern coastal plains within the last 100 years. Only the discovery of additional populations or fossil remains can clarify this situation. Steve Hall (1993) states that "in order for *francisci* to have survived over the past 10,000 years, there must surely have been more populations and greater numbers of individuals than apparently now exist." Reductions in *francisci*'s range would have accompanied the extensive loss of wetland habitats in the coastal plain.

Saint Francis's satyr is now known to exist in only a single population fragmented into less than six small colonies that occupy a total area no larger than a few square miles. In 1989 Parshall and Kral estimated that the single known population produced less than 100 individuals a year, but by 1991 the species appeared to be extinct.

Threats

The enormous changes in the southern coastal plain during the past 100 years have severely altered the butterfly's habitat. The boggy areas of the sandhills are quite acidic as well as ephemeral, succeeding either to procosin or swamp forest if not kept

open by frequent beaver activity. Beavers had been virtually eliminated from North Carolina by the turn of the century, and although beaver reintroduction began in 1939, it took several decades before they again became an agent for creation of the sage meadow habitats favored by Saint Francis' satyr.

In Steve Hall's 1993 study, he states that "as the landscape mosaic of open woodlands and wetlands of the coastal plain declined through the past two centuries, the range of *francisci* must have become increasingly fragmented. Although the isolated populations may have persisted as long as suitable habitat remained, the structure of their meta populations would have been destroyed" and they would have had less access to new habitats because the absence of forest fires would have allowed the forest to become denser.

Saint Francis' satyr is highly prized by collectors, including commercial collectors who often systematically collect every individual available. Several populations are known to have been obliterated by collectors, and others are known to be extremely vulnerable to this threat. The single known population was so hard hit by collectors in the three years following its initial discovery that it was believed to have been collected to extinction. Collectors reportedly visited the known site every day throughout the flight periods, taking every adult they saw. North Carolina law does not protect insects from collection, and the Department of Defense has no regulations restricting collection of military land.

Because the range and numbers of Saint Francis' satyr are so small, the species is threatened by catastrophic climatic events, inbreeding, disease and parasitism. Part of the occupied area is adjacent to regularly traveled roads, where there is the threat of toxic spills onto the species' wetland habitat.

Other potential threats include pest control programs for mosquitoes and gypsy moths, and beaver control.

Conservation and Recovery

Current military use of the species' habitat is favorable; the frequent fires caused by shelling are undoubtedly a reason why the species survives on military lands and not on surrounding private lands. Department of Defense personnel are aware of the species' plight and have been cooperative in protection efforts. Troop movements have been directed away from areas where the satyr occurs.

The U.S. Fish and Wildlife Service determined that to designate critical habitat would further expose the butterfly to collectors. Because the current habitat is on military land, no further protection is needed beyond that stipulated by the Endangered Species Act.

Contacts

U.S. Fish and Wildlife Service
Regional Office of Endangered Species
1875 Century Blvd., Suite 200
Atlanta, Georgia 30345
Telephone: (404) 679-4159
Fax: (404) 679-1111
http://southeast.fws.gov

Asheville Ecological Services Field Office
160 Zillicoa St.
Asheville, North Carolina 28801-1082
Telephone: (828) 258-3939
Fax: (828) 258-5330

References

U.S. Fish and Wildlife Service. 18 April 1994. "Emergency Rule to List the Saint Francis Satyr as Endangered." *Federal Register* 59(74): 18324-18327.

U. S. Fish and Wildlife Service. 26 January 1995. "Saint Francis' Satyr and Hine's Emerald Dragonfly; Final Rules." *Federal Register* 60(17): 5263-5267.

Mitchell's Satyr Butterfly

Neonympha mitchellii mitchellii

Status	Endangered
Listed	May 20, 1992
Family	Nymphalidae (Brush-footed butterfly)
Description	Brown butterfly, with yellow-ringed, black and silver eyespots.
Habitat	Wetland fens.
Host Plants	Sedges.
Reproduction	Females lay eggs in early- to mid-July.
Threats	Collectors, conversion of wetland habitat.
Range	Indiana, Michigan, Ohio

Mitchell's Satyr Butterfly, photograph by Larry West. U. S. Fish and Wildlife Service. Reproduced by permission.

Description

Mitchell's satyr is a medium-sized butterfly of the Satyridae subfamily of the Nymphalidae family. It has a wingspan of 1.5-1.7 in (3.8-4.4 cm) and is rich brown overall. The lower surfaces of all four wings show a series of yellow-ringed, black, circular eyespots with silvery centers. There are two orange bands across the posterior wing edges and lighter orange bands across the wing centers. The species has also been known by the names *Cissia mitchellii* and *Euptychia mitchellii*.

Behavior

The host plant for Mitchell's satyr is believed to be a sedge, possibly more than one species. Adults are active during a brief two- to three-week period in the summer. In early- to mid-July females lay eggs, which hatch in seven to 11 days. The larvae overwinter on sedge leaves and emerge the following May to continue their growth and pupation. The species has a single, short flight period each summer, which lasts about a week for the individual butterfly, and for about three weeks for the local population (late June through mid-July). Mitchell's satyr is relatively sedentary and has a slow, low-level flight pattern.

Habitat

This butterfly is restricted to wetland habitats known as prairie fens, which are characterized by calcareous soils fed by carbonate-rich water from seeps and springs. This uncommon habitat, which is often part of larger wetland complexes, is characterized by tamarak (*Larix laricina*), poison sumac (*Toxicodendron vernix*), dogwood (*Cornus* spp.), and a ground cover of sedges (*Carex* spp.), shrubby cinquefoil (*Potentilla fruticosa*), and other prairie species.

Distribution

Mitchell's satyr was first described in 1889 from specimens collected in Cass County, Michigan. It has been known from about 30 locations in four states. Its historic range included southern Michigan, northeastern Indiana, and northwestern Ohio. In addition several separate populations were known from New Jersey.

It is believed that Mitchell's satyr survives at only 15 sites in nine counties in southwestern Michigan and northeastern Indiana. Intensive surveys of historical sites and suitable habitat were conducted between 1985 and 1990. No populations were found in Ohio, and a population found in New Jersey was eliminated by collectors soon after the area was surveyed.

The U. S. Fish and Wildlife Service (FWS) considers the species Endangered in Indiana, Michigan, and Ohio.

Threats

The main threats to surviving populations of Mitchell's satyr are collectors and the conversion of the butterfly's unique wetland fen habitat. One Michigan site has been destroyed by urban development, and several other sites in Michigan and Ohio have been converted to agricultural use.

Collectors, however, are the greatest immediate threat to the species. Mitchell's satyr is considered a prize specimen by many butterfly collectors and it is clear that collectors have been responsible for the loss of a number of populations, including two in New Jersey. Several Michigan sites are under strong collecting pressure. About one-third of the surviving populations are extremely vulnerable to local extinction through collection, and all known sites are susceptible to this danger.

Conservation and Recovery

Because of the continuing threat from collectors and the fact that half of the known populations had vanished in a period of five years, on June 25, 1991, the FWS listed Mitchell's satyr as endangered on an emergency basis. This gave the species protection under the Endangered Species Act during its 1991 flight period, and, it was hoped, eased the pressure from collectors. Mitchell's satyr received long-term protection as an endangered species on May 20, 1992.

Contact

U. S. Fish and Wildlife Service
Regional Office, Division of Endangered Species
1 Federal Drive
BHW Federal Building
Fort Snelling, Minnesota 55111
Telephone: (612) 713-5360
http://midwest.fws.gov/

References

Martin, M. L. 1987. "Mitchell's Satyr (*Neonympha mitchellii*) in Indiana." Michigan Natural Features Inventory, Lansing.

McAlpine, W. S., S. P. Hubbell, and T. E. Pliske. 1960. "The Distribution, Habits, and Life History of *Euptychia mitchellii* (Satyridae)." *Journal of the Lepidopterist Society* 14 (4): 209-225.

Callippe Silverspot Butterfly

Speyeria callippe callippe

Status	Endangered
Listed	December 5, 1997
Family	Nymphalidae (Brush-footed butterfly)
Description	Medium-sized butterfly; upper wings are brown with extensive black spots; wing undersides are brown, orange-brown, and tan with black lines and distinctive black and bright silver spots.
Habitat	Native grassland and associated habitats.
Food	Johnny jump-up (*Viola pedunculata*).
Reproduction	Lays eggs on the dry remains of the larvae food plant, Johnny jump-up, or on the surrounding debris.
Threats	Urban development.
Range	California

Description

The callippe silverspot butterfly, *Speyeria callippe callippe,* a member of the brush-footed butterfly family (Nymphalidae), is a medium-sized butterfly with a wingspan of approximately 2.2 in (5.5 cm). The upper wings are brown with extensive black spots and lines, while the basal areas are extremely melanic (dark-colored). Wing undersides are brown, orange-brown, and tan with black lines and distinctive black and bright silver spots. Basal areas of the wings and body are densely pubescent (hairy). The discal area on the upper hind wings of the callippe silverspot butterfly is a darker, more extensive yellow than on the related Lilian's silverspot butterfly (*S. c. liliana*). The callippe silverspot butterfly is larger and has a darker ground color with more melanic areas on the basal areas of the wings than the related Comstock's silverspot butterfly (*S. c. comstocki*).

S. c. callippe was first described by J. A. Boisduval in 1852 from specimens collected by Pierre Lorquin in San Francisco during the month of June.

Taxonomic studies were conducted in 1983 and 1985 on the subspecies of *S. callippe* using wing characters. He concluded that the species consisted of three subspecies rather than the widely recognized and accepted 16 subspecies; based on his studies, the range of *S. c. callippe* would extend from Oregon to southern California and east into the Great Basin. A comprehensive analysis of this species in 1986 found that the original classification remains more appropriate and that the subspecies *callippe* is restricted to the San Francisco Bay region. The U. S. Fish and Wildlife Service recognizes the conclusions of Hammond and the distribution of the callippe silverspot butterfly as described by Sterling Mattoon in 1992.

Behavior

Female callippe silverspot butterflies lay their eggs on the dry remains of the larvae food plant, Johnny jump-up (*Viola pedunculata*), or on the surrounding debris. Within about one week of hatching the larvae eat their egg shells. The caterpillars wander a short distance and spin a silk pad upon

Callippe Silverspot Butterfly, photograph by Richard A. Arnold. Reproduced by permission.

which they pass the summer and winter. The larvae are dark-colored with many branching sharp spines on their backs. The caterpillars immediately seek out the food plant upon termination of their diapause in the spring. In May, after having gone through five instars, each larva forms a pupa within a chamber of leaves drawn together with silk. Adults emerge within about two weeks and live for approximately three weeks. Depending upon environmental conditions, the flight period of this single-brooded butterfly ranges from mid May to late July. The adults exhibit hill-topping behavior, a phenomenon in which males and virgin or multiple-mated females seek a topographic summit on which to mate.

Habitat

The callippe silverspot butterfly is found in native grassland and associated habitats.

Distribution

The callippe silverspot butterfly is known from 14 historic populations in the San Francisco bay re-

gion. The historic range of this butterfly includes the inner Coast Ranges on the eastern shore of San Francisco bay from northwestern Contra Costa County south to the Castro Valley area in Alameda County. On the west side of the bay, it ranged from San Francisco south to the vicinity of La Honda in San Mateo County. Five colonies, including the one located at Twin Peaks in San Francisco have been extirpated for a variety of reasons. Extant colonies are currently known only from private land on San Bruno Mountain in San Mateo County and a city park in Alameda County.

Threats

The callippe silverspot butterfly, once fairly widespread in the San Francisco Bay area, has lost at least five populations to urban development and other causes. Only two locations are still extant of the 14 known historical sites in San Mateo, Alameda, Sonoma, and Solano counties. One of the current populations of this butterfly is located in a city park in Alameda County. This colony is small and likely to be imperiled by anthropogenic and natural causes. The population at San Bruno Mountain in San Mateo County is largely protected against further loss of habitat, which will remain undeveloped in perpetuity by virtue of the San Bruno Mountain HCP. However, overcollection of specimens by lepidopterists at San Bruno Mountain and at sites where hybrids can be found in Solano County continues to pose a threat. An additional threat to this callippe silverspot butterfly population is the high level of dust from quarry operations in the vicinity. The adult and early stages of the taxon may be prone to injury and mortality from dust because their spiracles, the apparatus of respiration, are easily clogged.

Conservation and Recovery

One of the two known extant populations of the callippe silverspot butterfly is protected by the San Bruno Mountain Habitat Conservation Program (HCP). In 1982, an incidental take permit was issued to the cities of Brisbane, Daly City, South San Francisco, and the County of San Mateo, for the endangered mission blue butterfly, San Bruno elfin butterfly, and San Francisco garter snake. The permit allowed for the loss of animals and habitat through urban development of approximately 850 acres (340 hectares) of San Bruno Mountain. The HCP permanently protects about 2,752 acres (1,100.8 hectares)

of natural habitat at this site. Ninety-two percent of the habitat for this silverspot is protected at the site through the mechanisms of landowner obligations for land dedications, open space set-asides, mitigation measures, and habitat enhancement; implement annual monitoring of its population; and adaptive management to conserve the species. No specific provisions are, however, included in the HCP to protect the callippe silverspot butterfly from poachers. Habitat for the other known population is partially protected in a city park in Alameda County.

Contact

U. S. Fish and Wildlife Service
Regional Office, Division of Endangered Species
Eastside Federal Complex
911 N. E. 11th Ave.
Portland, Oregon 97232-4181
Telephone: (503) 231-6121
http://pacific.fws.gov/

Reference

U. S. Fish and Wildlife Service. 5 December 1997. "Determination of Endangered Status for the Callippe Silverspot Butterfly and the Behren's Silverspot Butterfly and Threatened Status for the Alameda Whipsnake." *Federal Register* 62 (234): 64306-64320.

Behren's Silverspot Butterfly

Speyeria zerene behrensii

Status	Endangered
Listed	December 5, 1997
Family	Nymphalidae (Brush-footed butterfly)
Description	A medium-sized, brownish butterfly.
Habitat	Coastal terrace prairie.
Food	Larvae eat a species of violet; adults feed on nectar.
Reproduction	Has a complex life cycle of egg, several larval stages, pupa, and adult.
Threats	Habitat destruction by residential development, and degradation by livestock grazing.
Range	California

Behren's Silverspot Butterfly, photograph. E/D Productions. Reproduced by permission.

Description

Behren's silverspot butterfly, *Speyeria zerene behrensii*, is also a member of the brush-footed butterfly family (Nymphalidae). It was first described by William H. Edwards in 1869 from an adult male collected by an unknown lepidopterist in Mendocino, California. It is a medium-sized butterfly with a wingspan of approximately 2.2 in (5.5 cm). The upper surfaces are golden brown with numerous black spots and lines. Wing undersides are brown, orange-brown, and tan with black lines and distinctive silver and black spots. Basal areas of the wings and body are densely pubescent. Behren's silverspot butterfly is similar in appearance to two other subspecies of *S. zerene*. The Oregon silverspot butterfly (*S. zerene hippolyta*), federally listed as threatened, has lighter basal suffusion on the upper sides of the wings than Behren's silverspot butterfly. The endangered Myrtle's silverspot butterfly (*S. zerene myrtleae*), another related taxon, is larger in size and also lighter in color than *S. zerene behrensii*.

Behavior

The life history of Behren's silverspot butterfly is similar to the callippe silverspot butterfly. The females lay their eggs in the debris and dried stems of the larval foodplant, violet (*Viola adunca*). Upon hatching, the caterpillars wander a short distance and spin a silk pad upon which they pass the fall and winter. The larvae are dark-colored with many branching, sharp spines on their backs. The caterpillars immediately seek out the foodplant upon termination of their diapause in the spring. They pass through five instars before forming a pupa within a chamber of leaves that they draw together with silk. The adults emerge in about two weeks and live for approximately three weeks. Depending upon environmental conditions, the flight period of this single-brooded butterfly ranges from July to August. Adult males patrol open areas in search of newly emerged females.

Habitat

Behren's silverspot butterfly inhabits coastal terrace prairie habitat.

Distribution

The historic range of Behren's silverspot butterfly extends from the mouth of the Russian River in Sonoma County northward along the immediate coast to southern Mendocino County in the vicinity of Point Arena. Six historic populations are known from coastal terrace prairie and associated habitats. The single extant population is located on private land near Point Arena in Mendocino County. No specimens have been observed at the sites of the other historically known colonies since 1987.

Threats

Behren's silverspot butterfly has been extirpated from five of its six historical locations, one of which was eliminated by a housing development. This species is currently known from a single locality near Point Arena in Mendocino County which is subject to grazing by livestock. Although no development plans have been proposed for this site, urban development is occurring in the vicinity.

Conservation and Recovery

The greatest need for conservation of the Behren's silverspot is to protect its last remnant of critical habitat in Mendocino County. This site is privately owned, and should be protected by acquiring the land and designating an ecological reserve, or by negotiating a conservation easement. The critical habitat must be protected against degrading ac-tivities, such as trampling by off-road vehicles, equestrians, and pedestrians. The butterfly itself must be protected against collecting for sale in the commercial trade in lepidopteran specimens, or by amateur collectors. The population of the Behren's silverspot should be monitored, and research undertaken into its biology and habitat needs, including management practices needed to maintain its habitat in good condition (such as prescribed burning). Planning should be undertaken towards the establishment of additional populations of this rare butterfly.

Contacts

U. S. Fish and Wildlife Service
Regional Office, Division of Endangered Species
Eastside Federal Complex
911 N. E. 11th Ave.
Portland, Oregon 97232-4181
Telephone: (503) 231-6121
http://pacific.fws.gov/

Sacramento Fish and Wildlife Office
2800 Cottage Way, Room W-2605
Sacramento, California, 95825-1846
Telephone: 916-414-6600
Fax: 916-460-4619

Reference

U. S. Fish and Wildlife Service. 5 December 1997. "Endangered and Threatened Wildlife and Plants: Determination of Endangered Status for the Callippe Silverspot Butterfly and the Behren's Silverspot Butterfly and Threatened Status for the Alameda Whipsnake." *Federal Register* 62 (234): 64306-64320.

Oregon Silverspot Butterfly

Speyeria zerene hippolyta

Status	Threatened
Listed	July 2, 1980
Family	Nymphalidae (Brush-footed butterfly)
Description	Orange and brown butterfly with silver spots on the forewings.
Habitat	Coastal salt spray meadows.
Host Plant	Western blue violet.
Reproduction	Females deposit 200 or more eggs in vegetation near host plant.
Threats	Residential and recreational development, suppression of fire.
Range	California, Oregon

Description

The Oregon silverspot butterfly, *Speyeria zerene hippolyta*, is a medium-sized orange and brown butterfly with black veins and spots on the hind wings, and a yellowish band and bright metallic silver spots on the forewings. It has a forewing length of about 1.1 in (2.9 cm); females are typically slightly larger than males.

The species *S. zerene* consists of 15 subspecies, divided into five major groups. The Oregon silverspot belongs to the *bremnerii* group consisting of five subspecies. Compared to its relatives, the Oregon silverspot is slightly smaller and darker at the base of the wings—these are adaptive traits derived from its persistently windy and foggy environment.

Behavior

Adult butterflies emerge from early July to early September. Mating occurs during adult flights, and females deposit 200 or more eggs in the vegetation near the violet host plant in late August or early September. Eggs hatch in about 16 days, and the larvae seek out suitable places for overwintering. In spring, the larvae feed on violet leaves for two months, then enter pupation for two or three weeks. Some adults emerge during periods of sunny, relatively calm weather.

Habitat

This subspecies is found only in the salt spray meadows along the Pacific Coast of Washington and Oregon. The climate is characterized by mild temperatures, heavy rainfall, and fog. The most important feature of the habitat is the presence of the western blue violet (*Viola adunca*), the larval host plant.

Distribution

The Oregon silverspot was historically found in 17 different locations between Rock Creek and Big Creek, about 15 mi (24 km) north of Florence along the central Oregon Coast, and in the vicinity of Westport, south of Grays Harbor, Washington, which is the northern extent of the range.

By 1980, when it was listed by the U. S. Fish and Wildlife Service (FWS) as a threatened species, the silverspot was known from only one site, which was located on the Siuslaw National Forest along the central Oregon Coast. Since then, the species has been found at six other small sites on federal, state, and private land. The butterfly is not abundant anywhere, and in a typical year there are fewer than 4,000 individuals distributed along 350 mi (560 km) of coastline.

The FWS considers the species Threatened in California and Oregon.

Oregon Silverspot Butterfly, photograph by Richard A. Arnold. Reproduced by permission.

Threats

The main threats to this butterfly are increased housing development and recreational use of the coast. Natural fire patterns have been suppressed, allowing non-native plants to intrude and change the mix of plants in the habitat. There have also been rapid successional changes in the native plant community.

Conservation and Recovery

Critical habitat was designated for an area in Lane County, Oregon, where a healthy population of the butterfly exists. In 1983, the Siuslaw National Forest, in consultation with the FWS, began to restore about 100 acres (40 hectares) of meadow habitat. Efforts included burning, introducing violet seeds and plants, mowing grass thatch, and removing invading trees and shrubs by machine or hand. A cautious approach was used. Treatments were confined to small plots outside of prime habitat where there was little risk of killing butterfly larvae.

Mowing several times a year (every fourth or fifth year), particularly after the initial surge of growth in late spring or early summer, reduces grass thatch and often produces spectacular stands of blooming blue violets. Removing scattered stands of invading woody plants and maintaining shelter areas in the forest fringe has been relatively easy, and has opened up more areas for mowing. As of 1994, burning was restricted largely to removing mowing residue and to clearing steep slopes where mowing was impossible.

Although efforts have not always been successful, results so far have exceeded expectations. Adult silverspots heavily use many of the renovated areas, and by 1994, three populations were reasonably secure within the Siuslaw National Forest. A fourth, introduced population had maintained itself at a low level for four years. Overall, it seems that the species is on the way to recovery in Oregon.

Contact

U. S. Fish and Wildlife Service
Regional Office, Division of Endangered Species
Eastside Federal Complex
911 N. E. 11th Ave.
Portland, Oregon 97232-4181
Telephone: (503) 231-6121
http://pacific.fws.gov/

References

Arnold, R. A. 1988. "Ecological and Behavioral Studies on the Threatened Oregon Silverspot Butterfly." Report. U. S. Fish and Wildlife Service, Olympia, Wash.

Hammond, Paul C., et al. 1980. "Ecological Investigation Report: Oregon Silverspot Butterfly (*Speyeria zerene hippolyta*) Mt. Hebo Supplement." U. S. Forest Service.

Howe, W. H. 1975. *The Butterflies of North America.* Doubleday, Garden City, N.Y.

U. S. Fish and Wildlife Service. 1982. "The Oregon Silverspot Butterfly Recovery Plan." U. S. Fish and Wildlife Service, Portland, Oregon.

Myrtle's Silverspot Butterfly

Speyeria zerene myrtleae

Gary M. Fellers

Status	Endangered
Listed	June 22, 1992
Family	Nymphalidae (Brush-footed butterfly)
Description	Medium-sized butterfly with golden brown upper wings with black spots and lines.
Habitat	Coastal dunes, coastal prairie, and coastal scrub communities.
Host Plant	Western dog violet.
Reproduction	Females lay single eggs.
Threats	Overcollection, grazing disturbance, non-native plants.
Range	California

Description

Myrtle's silverspot, *Speyeria zerene myrtleae,* is a medium-sized butterfly with a wingspan of 2.1-2.3 in (5.3-5.8 cm). The upper surfaces of the wings are golden brown and possess many black spots and lines. The undersides are brown to orange-brown matriculated with tan and black lines and conspicuous silver and black spots. The basal areas of the wings and body are densely pubescent.

Overall, Myrtle's silverspot is similar in size and appearance to Behren's silverspot, but can be distinguished by the center of the underside of the hind wing, which is reddish-brown with yellowish-green overscaling, and a bright yellow submarginal band.

Behavior

During the summer flight season, female Myrtle's silverspot butterflies lay their eggs singly on or near dried leaves and stems of violets. Eggs of the closely related Oregon silverspot butterfly (*S. z. hippolyta*) are milky white at first, then gradually change to pale yellow, then to brownish-grey or pinkish-bronze with pearly longitudinal lines. About five days before hatching, the head capsule can be seen as a dark purple tip, with the remainder of the egg lightening to white or gray.

Within a few weeks after the eggs are laid, the larvae or caterpillars emerge. These caterpillars, which are less than 0.2 in (5 mm) long, crawl a short distance into the surrounding foliage or litter, and spin a silk pad on which they spend the fall and winter. The fall and winter period of inactivity is a physiological resting state called diapause, during which no feeding occurs. The larvae may be able to extend their diapause for more than one year. Upon termination of diapause in the spring, the caterpillar finds a nearby violet and begins feeding. Feeding is difficult to observe, and apparently occurs at dusk and possibly at night. The larval feeding stage lasts about seven to 10 weeks, after which the larvae form their pupal chamber out of leaves spun together with silk.

The adult butterfly emerges from the pupa after about two weeks. Emergence typically occurs from mid-June to mid-July. The timing of adult emergence is probably related to photoperiod and to weather, especially temperature and sunlight, which may result in annual differences in the timing of peak emergence of as much as a few weeks. Although Myrtle's silverspot adults live for only about two to five weeks, because of individual variation in emergence time, the species has a two- to three-month flight period, ranging from mid-June to early October. Adult activity is closely tied to weather conditions: the butterflies are active during calm weather and inactive during windy periods.

Both sexes are good flyers and can trave miles in search of nectar, mates, or violets; if, however, all these resources are available in topographically restricted valleys or basins that are sheltered from strong winds, most movements are short. Males emerge earlier than females and patrol widely for females, a behavior that may tend to bias survey counts in the males' favor. In related species, both sexes produce pheromones that apparently function in mate-finding and courtship. Males of most *Speyeria* species transfer a mating plug at the end of copulation, and most females therefore mate only once.

Little is known about impacts of disease, parasitism, or predation on Myrtle's silverspots. About 40% of 11 Oregon silverspot eggs observed in the field died before hatching, due to predation or disease. The larvae have spines and an eversible (can be protruded) ventral scent gland, similar to structures that in other species are used to ward off predators. Silverspot larvae may be vulnerable to predation by ants, ground beetles, spiders, and shrews.

Adult feeding on nectar is very important to the reproduction of the Myrtle's silverspot. In a related species, *S. mormonia*, a strong correlation exists between the amount of nectar consumed by female butterflies and the number of eggs they produce. Males of Myrtle's silverspot also feed on nectar, possibly to fuel their patrolling and mating activities. Ideally, a spectrum of plants that flower across the flight season of the butterfly is used.

Populations of *Speyeria* butterflies are known to exhibit large fluctuations in numbers of individuals, appearing at times to be virtually on the brink of extinction, and then rebounding to substantially higher numbers the following year. Such wide population fluctuations—changing by a factor of 10 or more in a single year—are typical of insects with little overlap among generations, and of annual plants, and stand in contrast to most vertebrate populations. High and variablemortality during the immature life stages, and corresponding high fecundity to counterbalance the high mortality, are characteristic of these butterflies. The annual variability of California climate, even at the relatively moderate, maritime-influenced locations inhabited by the Myrtle's silverspot, contribute to extreme population fluctuations through effects on development, mortality, and fecundity, either directly or mediated through effects on host plant growth and survival. Myrtle's silverspot butterfly occurs in separate populations whose long-term persistence may depend upon intercolony movement. Habitat degradation resulting in the loss of intervening populations, larval food plants, and adult nectar sources may make movements between populations more difficult.

Habitat

Myrtle's silverspot inhabits coastal dunes, coastal prairie, and coastal scrub at elevations ranging from sea level to 1,000 ft (300 m), and as far as 3 mi (4.8 km) inland. The adult butterflies prefer areas protected from onshore winds, but can be observed in exposed areas when winds are calm. Temperatures in this region are moderated by fog, which keeps summers relatively cool and winters relatively warm compared to inland habitats. The fog also provides moisture to vegetation, in addition to the ample winter rains.

Critical factors in the distribution of the Myrtle's silverspot include presence of the presumed larval host plant, *Viola adunca* (western dog violet), and availability of nectar sources for adults. Although alternate larval host plants have neither been confirmed nor ruled out for the Myrtle's silverspot, other subspecies of *S. zerene* and other species of *Speyeria* can feed on more than one species in the genus *Viola*. Seeds of *Viola* are often dispersed by ants. Violets sometimes bear self-pollinating flowers, and are also cross-pollinated by insects. Selection of habitat for oviposition (egg laying) has been observed in the Oregon silverspot. Gravid (fertilized egg-bearing) females were attracted to areas of low vegetation height (15 in [38 cm] or less), where they would sometimes perform a searching flight characterized by low hovering or dipping. Females flew past areas with deep thatch (covered by plant litter). They were more likely to land and perform a walking search and more likely to lay eggs in areas with higher violet density and cover. Other, unknown factors, however, must also affect the selection of oviposition sites, since some portions of the study sites with low vegetation height and high violet cover were used less frequently than expected. It has been therefore suggested that managing for violet density alone would not necessarily enhance silvrspot oviposition.

Much of the coastal prairie in this species' range has been grazed for more than a century, and is now characterized by a mixture of non-native annuals and forbs and native prairie plants. In the upland grasslands, this butterfly has been observed obtaining nectar from non-native species such as bull thistle and rarely Italian thistle. In dune scrub habitat, these butterflies seek nectar from several native species such as gum plant, western pennyroyal, yellow sand verbena, seaside daisy, and mule ears. Other flowers might serve as good nectar sources for the opportunistic adults, such as brownie thistle and groundsel. Myrtle's silverspot does not use the flowers of the invasive non-native iceplant or sea fig for nectar.

Distribution

Myrtle's silverspot occupies the southernmost range of all the coastal *S. zerene* silverspot butterflies. It was recorded from coastal San Mateo County as far south as Pescadero in 1950, north to the vicinity of Black Point in northern Sonoma County. There were only 10 specimens collected south of the Golden Gate, and by the late 1970s, populations of Myrtle's silverspot south of the Golden Gate Bridge were believed to be extinct and extant populations were known only from Marin County at the Point Reyes National Seashore. In 1990, an additional population was discovered at a site in coastal Marin County, near Estero de San Antonio, on property proposed for golf resort and residential development. This discovery led to more surveys of the current and historical range of Myrtle's silverspot butterfly. The proposal for the golf course was withdrawn and later replaced with a proposal for low-density residential development and open space at the same site. At the private site in coastal Marin, the number of Myrtle's silverspots was estimated to be between 2,500 and 5,000 adults in 1991. Two apparently separate populations in Point Reyes National Seashore were estimated at less than 5,000 individuals and several hundred individuals, re-

spectively, in 1993. As of the late 1990s, this butterfly was known from three occurrences, with a probable total of less than 10,000 individuals. Population sizes can be expected to fluctuate drastically.

Threats

The coastal San Mateo population was last documented at Pescadero in 1950, and was probably extirpated by loss of habitat to urbanization, agriculture, and invasion of non-native plants. Historical occurrences at Valley Ford and Bloomfield may have been extirpated by farming and grazing pressures and by invasion of non-native plants.

Overcollection is a threat to Myrtle's silverspot. Specimens of Myrtle's silverspot butterfly are known to have been illegally collected in Point Reyes National Seashore. Although collectors generally do not adversely affect the healthy, well-dispersed populations of many butterfly species, a number of rare species, highly valued by collectors, are vulnerable to extirpation from collecting. Collection of females dispersing from a colony also can reduce the probability that new colonies will be founded. Butterfly collectors pose a threat because they may be unable to recognize when they are depleting colonies below the thresholds of survival and recovery, especially when they lack appropriate biological training or they visit the area for only a short time.

Inadequate nectar resources appear to be an ongoing problem for several Myrtle's silverspot populations. Butterflies without adequate nearby nectar plants may be forced to expend time and energy reserves searching for nectaring areas, reducing the number of fertilized eggs laid, and at the same time exposing them to predation, winds, and road mortality. Overgrazing of properties within the range of Myrtle's silverspot may have reduced the abundance of native nectar sources, and could be contributing to the regional decline of this species. The reduction in native nectar sources may have been offset, at least partially, by the silverspot's use of non-native thistles as nectar sources. Prolonged, intensive grazing disturbance reduces the vigor of native plant species and disturbs the site, allowing the establishment of invasive non-native weedy plant species. One such weed is the invasive, non-native iceplant, a competitive threatto several native plant species that provide this butterfly with nectar. This plant and other non-native grasses and forbs have undoubtedly displaced larval and adult food plants of the silverspot and contributed to the overall degradation of habitat quality.

Conservation and Recovery

Substantial areas of habitat and potential habitat for Myrtle's silverspot have been conferred a degree of long-term protection at Point Reyes National Seashore. The national seashore has conducted or commissioned a number of studies of the status and biology of the butterfly, and the recent management plan for the Tule Elk Range in Point Reyes National Seashore contains provisions to assess elk grazing effects on butterfly habitat.

The recovery strategy for the Myrtle's silverspot butterfly includes the following measures: (1) protect habitat where remaining populations occur; (2) identify and establish vegetation management that benefits the native ecosystem of larval host plants and adult nectar sources; (3) reintroduce populations of the butterfly to prioritized areas; (4) control illegal collecting; (5) conduct or fund research to identify critical recovery needs or actions; and (6) monitor existing populations and survey historic and unsurveyed locations.

Habitat protection is essential to the recovery of Myrtle's silverspot butterfly. Two populations of the Myrtle's silverspot are protected at Point Reyes National Seashore, but this national seashore does not yet have a management plan for the butterfly. Under the agreement that established Point Reyes National Seashore, much of its area is leased for grazing, mostly by cattle.

More needs to be known about vegetation management practices that would benefit the Myrtle's silverspot. While heavy grazing is thought to have adverse impacts on nectar plants for the butterfly, and possibly also on the larval host plant *Viola*, complete absence of grazing may also have adverse effects. Heavy growth of non-native grasses and other plants and accumulation of dead plant litter on top of the ground can result in overgrowth or shading of *Viola*. Little is known about how to balance these factors in California coastal prairie or dune scrub. Fire is another vegetation management tool that needs further investigaion. A study of Midwestern tallgrass prairie found that populations of three *Speyeria* species were all immediately reduced by fire, but that over the longer term two species benefited or were unaffected, while the third was depressed.

Myrtle's silverspot lives in an ecosystem that has been greatly changed, perhaps forever, by introduced plants, and certain non-native plants have now taken over vital roles in the butterfly's life cycle. In particular, bull thistle (*Cirsium vulgare*) is an important nectar resource, especially in the late season, and should not be eradicated in the absence of a comparable replacement.

Reintroduction of populations is likely to be a useful tool to increase the number of Myrtle's silverspot individuals and populations, and thus reduce extinction risk. Reestablishing Myrtle's silverspot populations should be done in its historic range, on protected public lands and private lands with the full permission and cooperation of the landowners.

One high-priority area of potentially suitable but apparently unoccupied habitat exists around and south of Dillon Beach, extending to south of Tom's Point. Much of this area overlaps or adjoins areas targeted for plant recovery actions. Protecting this habitat, restoring habitat if needed, and reintroducing the Myrtle's silverspot butterfly is the highest priority. Captive rearing of Myrtle's silverspots to produce large numbers for reintroductions may be appropriate.

Contact

U. S. Fish and Wildlife Service
Regional Office, Division of Endangered Species
Eastside Federal Complex
911 N. E. 11th Ave.
Portland, Oregon 97232-4181
Telephone: (503) 231-6121
http://pacific.fws.gov/

References

Hammond, P. C., and D. V. McCorkle. 1983. "The Decline and Extinction of *Speyeria* Populations Resulting from Human Environmental Disturbances (Nymphalidae: Argynninae)." *Journal of Research on the Lepidoptera* 22 (3): 217-224.

Launer, A. E., et al. 1994. "The Endangered Myrtle's Silverspot Butterfly: Present Status and Initial Conservation Planning." *Journal of Research on the Lepidoptera* 31 (1-2): 132-146.

U. S. Fish and Wildlife Service. 22 June 1992. "Six Plants and Myrtle's Silverspot Butterfly from Coastal Dunes in Northern and Central California Determined to Be Endangere

Kern Primrose Sphinx Moth

Euproserpinus euterpe

© David Liebman.

Status	Threatened
Listed	April 8, 1980
Family	Sphingidae (Sphinx moth)
Description	Thick-bodied with white hind wings and dark margins.
Habitat	Sandy washes and alluvial soils.
Host Plant	Evening primrose
Reproduction	Two or three eggs deposited on the underside of evening primrose.
Threats	Collectors; egg laying on unsuitable plants.
Range	California

Description

The thick-bodied Kern primrose sphinx moth, *Euproserpinus euterpe*, is one of three species of the genus *Euproserpinus*. It has white hind wings with dark margins, white underwings, and abruptly hooked antennae. It can be distinguished from the similar phaeton sphinx moth by a marginal band on the hind wing that bows inward rather than running straight along the wing.

Behavior

The flight period of the Kern primrose sphinx moth extends from late February to early April. Adults emerge from pupae in the morning, expand their wings, and fly by midmorning. In the early part of the day, the moth basks on bare patches of soil, dirt roads, or ground squirrel and gopher mounds to warm its flight muscles. Individuals live for one or two weeks.

Mating usually occurs before noon. The female then flies low to the ground and deposits one or two eggs on the underside of the primrose (*Camissonia contorta epilobioides*), the moth's only larval host plant. The larvae develop in the spring, pupate in the soil, and remain inactive until the following spring when they emerge as adults. Some remain in the pupal stage for several years.

Habitat

The Kern primrose moth is found in Walker Basin, an area 4,851 ft (1,470 m) above sea level surrounded by the Greenhorn and Piute Mountains, which are over 6,600 ft (2,000 m) in elevation. The dominant plants on the sandy alluvial soils are filaree, baby blue-eyes, rabbit brush, gold fields, and brome grass. Juniper, oak, rabbitbrush, sagebrush, and pine dominate the surrounding mountain slopes. Winter rains in the basin end by mid-April, and summers are dry and hot.

From the moth's perspective, the most important plant in the habitat is the evening primrose, which grows in dry, disturbed areas, along sandy washes, or adjacent to fallow fields. The plant germinates in February and March, grows quickly, and by mid-June has set seed and dried out.

Distribution

The Kern primrose sphinx moth is endemic to the Walker Basin in Kern County, California. It is considered the rarest sphinx moth in North America. It was thought extinct until rediscovered in 1974 in a barley field on a privately owned cattle ranch in the Walker Basin. The site remains its only known locality. Field surveys from 1975 to 1979 yielded very low numbers, but in 1979 the population increased dramatically, probably as a result of several years of inactive pupae emerging in response to favorable climatic conditions. In the spring of 1990, the U.S. Fish and Wildlife Service field station in Sacramento, California reported that an adult female moth was observed in eastern Kern County, California. The species had not been observed in the wild for several years. A male may also have been present, but the entomologist was unable to get close enough to make a positive identification.

Threats

Land use practices have posed a major threat to the population. The site was repeatedly plowed, disced, and planted from 1962 until the drought of 1975. Since then, cattle have grazed the site, a use that does not seem harmful to the moth or its larval food plant.

A more serious threat to this sphinx moth is the filaree (*Erodium cicutarium*), a plant introduced centuries ago by Spanish explorers. The filaree is widely distributed throughout the area, and egg-laying females often mistake it for the evening primrose. Eggs deposited on filaree hatch, but larvae cannot digest the plant and do not survive. This rare sphinx moth also suffers at the hands of collectors who often take the slower-flying females. Federal law now prohibits taking specimens for sale to collectors.

Conservation and Recovery

Although the habitat site is on privately owned land, a 1983 survey of the Walker Basin found the site to support more potential habitat than previously believed. At least three additional colonies need to be established to prevent extinction. Developing propagation techniques, however, may take several years.

Contact

U. S. Fish and Wildlife Service
Regional Office, Division of Endangered Species
Eastside Federal Complex
911 N. E. 11th Ave.
Portland, Oregon 97232-4181
Telephone: (503) 231-6121
http://pacific.fws.gov/

References

Tuskes, P. M. and J. F. Emmel. 1981. "The Life History and Behavior of *Euproserpinus euterpe* (Sphingidae)." *Journal of the Lepidopterists' Society* 35: 27-33.

U.S. Fish and Wildlife Service. 1984. "The Kern Primrose Sphinx Moth Recovery Plan." U.S. Fish and Wildlife Service, Portland.

Blackburn's Sphinx Moth

Manduca blackburni

Larva of Blackburn's sphinx moth, photograph by Arthur C. Medeiros. Reproduced by permission.

Status	Endangered
Listed	February 1, 2000
Family	Sphingidae (Sphinx moth)
Description	A large tropical moth.
Habitat	Native forest and other areas with plants in the tomato family.
Food	Feeds on plants in the tomato family.
Reproduction	Lays eggs, which hatch into larvae, which grow through several stages, then become pupae, which metamorphose into adult moths.
Threats	Habitat destruction, predation by introduced insects, and collecting of specimens.
Range	Hawaii

Description

The Blackburn's sphinx moth is Hawaii's largest native insect, with a wingspan of up to 5 in (12 cm). It has long, narrow forewings and a thick, spindle-shaped body tapered at both ends. It is grayish brown in color, with black bands across the top margins of the hind wings, and five orange spots along each side of the abdomen. The larva is a large "hornworm" caterpillar, with a spine-like process on the upper surface of the eighth abdominal segment. The caterpillars can be either bright green or grayish. Both color forms have scattered white speckles on the back, a horizontal white stripe on the side, and diagonal stripes on the sides of segments four to seven.

Behavior

Larvae of the Blackburn's sphinx moth feed on plants in the tomato family (Solanaceae). Native host plants are popolo shrubs in the genus *Solanum*

and the tree 'aiea (*Nothocestrum latifolium*). Now, however, the most important food plants are non-native species such as tobacco (*Nicotiana tabacum*), tree-tobacco (*Nicotiana glauca*), eggplant (*Solanum melongena*), and tomato (*Lycopersicon esculentum*). Development from egg to adult can occur in as few as 56 days, but pupae can also remain in a torpid condition in the soil for up to a year.

Habitat

The Blackburn's sphinx moth occurs in coastal, lowland, and dryland forest habitats in areas receiving less than about 50 in (120 cm) of annual rainfall. It has been collected from sea level to 2,500 ft (760 m).

Distribution

The Blackburn's sphinx moth has been recorded from the islands of Kahoolawe, Kauai, Oahu,

Molokai, Maui, and Hawaii. It appears to have historically been most common on Maui.

Threats

Once relatively common, the Blackburn's sphinx moth has declined due to the clearing of its natural forest habitat through conversion into agricultural, commercial, and residential land-uses. Much habitat damage has also been caused by introduced mammalian herbivores, such as cows and goats. These damages have caused the loss of the native food plants of the Blackburn's sphinx moth. Very few specimens of the rare moth were seen after about 1940, and it was considered extinct. In 1984, however, a single population was discovered on Maui, in habitat located on private and State lands, including a natural reserve, areas used by the Hawaii National Guard for training, or land administered by the Department of Hawaiian Homelands. Subsequent monitoring continued to find small numbers of the rare moth on Maui. In 1997, another population of Blackburn's sphinx moth was discovered on the State-owned island of Kahoolawe. Subsequent surveys indicated a relatively large population, with animals discovered on about half of the plants of tree tobacco searched. In 1998, two small populations of unknown size were discovered on State land on the island of Hawaii. Because of its rarity, the Blackburn's sphinx moth is valuable in the commercial lepidopteran trade, and this may pose a risk to the species. It is also thought to be severely threatened by predation by introduced insects, such as the big-headed ant (*Pheidole megacephala*). This may, in fact, may be the most serious ongoing threat to the survival of the Blackburn's sphinx moth and many other native insects of the Hawaiian Islands.

Conservation and Recovery

Listing of the Blackburn's sphinx moth as an endangered species has resulted in it becoming a protected species, and also encourages conservation by State government agencies on state-owned land. The most crucial conservation needs of this endangered moth are to preserve the remnants of its native-forest habitat, and to find ways of reducing the effects on predation by introduced ants and other insects.

Contacts

U. S. Fish and Wildlife Service
Regional Office, Division of Endangered Species
Eastside Federal Complex
911 N. E. 11th Ave.
Portland, Oregon 97232-4181
(503) 231-6121
http://pacific.fws.gov/

U. S. Fish and Wildlife Service, Pacific Islands Ecoregion
300 Ala Moana Boulevard, Room 3-122
P.O. Box 50088
Honolulu, Hawaii 96850
Telephone: (808) 541-2749
Fax: (808) 541-2756

Reference

U. S. Fish and Wildlife Service. 1 February 2000. "Endangered and Threatened Wildlife and Plants: Determination of Endangered Status for Blackburn's Sphinx Moth from the Hawaiian Islands." *Federal Register* 65 (21): 4770-4779.

Lichens

Florida Perforate Cladonia

Cladonia perforata

Status	Endangered
Listed	April 27, 1993
Family	Cladoniaceae (Reindeer lichen)
Description	Lichen with dense groupings with spore-producing branches.
Habitat	Scrub, high pine, dry upland communities in central Florida and in the coastal scrub of the northwestern part of the state.
Threats	Habitat conversion to citrus groves, pasture, and urban developments.
Range	Florida

Description

The Cladoniaceae is represented in Florida by the two large, widespread, and closely related genera, *Cladonia* and *Cladina*. This conspicuous and diverse group is one of the most important in the Florida lichen flora, represented by a total of 33 species, three of which are endemic to the state. *Cladonia perforata* var. *C. perforata* is a member of the family Cladoniaceae, commonly called the reindeer lichens. Unlike the more common and widely-distributed species of the Cladoniaceae it occurs with, *C. perforata* is restricted to the high, well-drained sands of rosemary scrub in Florida. *C. perforata* was listed as endangered because of the significant loss of scrub habitat in Florida. This species is known to occur on 27 sites in Florida; all but four sites are in the South Florida ecosystem. Twelve of the 27 sites are protected, and others are proposed for acquisition in the future.

Florida perforate cladonia, *C. perforata*, is easily recognized in the field by the conspicuous holes or perforations below each dichotomous branch point and its wide, smooth, yellowish gray-green branches. Unlike other fruticose lichens whose branches develop from the primary or vegetative body, the branches of members of *Cladonia* and *Cladina* are developmentally derived from spore-producing structures called apothecia, present as colored, expanded tips of fertile branches. These specialized, hollow branches are called podetia and are structurally characteristic of this group. *C. perforata* differs in color, shape, and texture, in addition to having specific habitat requirements. *C. perforata* has rather wide, pale yellowish gray-green podetia, punctuated in the axils by 0.04-0.06 in (1-1.5 mm) perforations. The branching pattern is complex and consists of roughly subequal dichotomies near the tips and, more commonly, sympodia (unequal branchings with the smaller branch deflected to one side) below, resulting in a more-or-less compressed tuft. Its outer surface is mostly uniformly smooth. Individual podetia are typically 1.6-2.4 in (4-6 cm) long, although specimens of up to 3.1 in (8 cm) across and several inches high have been observed. No primary thallus is known. The oldest parts of the podetia degenerate, leaving no means of determining ages. No studies of growth rates in *C. perforata* have been completed. In boreal areas, growth studies of *Cladonia* species suggest that one branching occurs each year; however, in more tropical areas, more than one branching per year may be possible.

Reproduction in the Cladoniaceae is typically by means of sexually-produced spores or dispersal of vegetative fragments, either by soredia (microscopic clumps of algal cells surrounded by fungal threads

that emerge from the lichen surface as a powder) or simple fragmentation. However, neither spore-producing structures nor soredia are known from *C. perforata*. Presumably, the main form of reproduction is by vegetative fragmentation.

C. uncialis is a closely related and similar looking species; its podetia are wide and perforate, though not at every dichotomy, and are glossy with greenish areolae. The other fruticose, terrestrial species of *Cladonia* and *Cladina* that commonly co-occur with *C. perforata* can easily be distinguished from it. Although *C. leporina* may sometimes have small perforations in the podetia and is occasionally confused with *C. perforata*, *C. leporina* is a darker yellow green color, has narrower podetia with rough surfaces and can often be found with conspicuous red apothecia. *Cladina pachycladodes* is similar in color to *C. perforata* but is more of a light bluish gray color and has finer branches, drooping at the tips. *Cladina subsetacea*, *Cladina evansii*, and *Cladina subtenuis* all have much narrower, filiform podetia, usually less than

0.04 in (1 mm) wide, compared to 0.2 in (4 mm) for *C. perforata*.

Habitat

Several of the fruticose, terrestrial *Cladonia* and *Cladina* species form a conspicuous and characteristic part of Florida's white sand scrub communities. Typical habitat for *C. perforata* is found on the high sand dune ridges of Florida's peninsula, including the Atlantic coastal and the Lake Wales ridges. In these areas Florida perforate cladonia is restricted to the highest, xeric white sands in sand pine scrub, typically in the rosemary phase. Such rosemary scrubs, frequently referred to as "rosemary balds," are particularly well-drained and structurally open. Specific aspects of Florida perforate cladonia microhabitat require further investigation and, presently, can only be roughly generalized with the following associated plant species: scrub oaks, which are clumped and scattered throughout; sand pine, which dominates the tree layer, although the canopy may be sparse or absent; and Florida rosemary, which dominates the shrub layer. Florida perforate cladonia typically occurs in open patches of sand between shrubs in areas with sparse or no herbaceous cover.

In Highlands and Polk counties on the Lake Wales ridge, Florida perforate cladonia occurs at relatively higher elevations than surrounding areas, on excessively well-drained, nutrient-poor, white sands. A small site in xeric scrubby flatwoods on Lake Wales ridge (formerly Lake Arbuckle) was discovered in 1997. Other Lake Wales ridge sites are on open rosemary scrubs or under dense sand pine in rosemary scrub. In the coastal scrubs of Jonathan Dickinson State Park in Martin County, Florida perforate cladonia is reported from open areas in oak-dominated sand pine scrub and scrubby flatwoods. The Okaloosa County sites are on undifferentiated coastal beach sands in white-sand scrub.

Florida perforate cladonia occurs most commonly with Florida rosemary and sand pine, typically in patches of bare sand with other *Cladonia* and *Cladina* species, sometimes forming mixed-species tangled clumps. It can, however, occasionally occur in dense, long-unburned sand pine scrub on a mat of pine needles. However, Florida perforate cladonia decreases in dominance in sites that have gone unburned for more than 20 years. This decrease in dominance on unburned sites may be a result of a combination of factors that influence microhabitat, such as decreased insulation or increased litter accumulation.

Distribution

In northern biomes such as boreal forests and the tundra, members of *Cladonia* and *Cladina* form continuous mats which cover the ground and provide important forage for caribou and reindeer. In temperate and subtropical regions, open rock outcrops or patches of bare ground or sand provide habitat for reindeer lichens. Florida scrub, which is characterized in part by long-lived, open patches of sand, supports a relatively rich assemblage of these terrestrial lichens. Up to eight species of reindeer lichens commonly occur in Florida scrub. Florida perforate cladonia is the most unique member of the scrub lichen community, by virtue of its restricted and unusual disjunct distribution and overall global rarity.

In 1991, the Florida Natural Areas Inventory surveyed 111 sites throughout central and coastal Florida to determine the status of Florida perforate cladonia. A total of only 12 sites were located, six of which were at Archbold Biological Station. Two additional sites were later located at Archbold Biological Station. With one Eglin Air Force Base site in Okaloosa County, and several other more recently discovered south-central and coastal Florida locations, a total of 25 sites for Florida perforate cladonia are currently known from four disjunct geographic regions. The farthest and most disjunct region, supporting the only remaining north Florida site, is defined by Santa Rosa Island in Okaloosa County. This region is about 400 mi (644 km) north of the next closest region. Central Florida's Lake Wales ridge supports the bulk of the known sites. South-coastal Martin and Palm Beach Counties support three sites, and southwest Florida's Manatee County has one disjunct site for this lichen. The east side of Santa Rosa Island in Escambia County also supports a population.

The current patchy distribution of Florida perforate cladonia may reflect all or only part of its historic range, represented by the fragmented scrubs on high white-sand ridges of central Florida.

Threats

The loss of scrub habitat is the primary threat to Florida perforate cladonia. Less than 15% of the historic distribution of scrub habitat remained as of 1992, and land conversion to citrus and residential development continues to diminish scrub habitat almost daily. As with all species restricted to the developable upland landscape, including species of the scrubs of the Lake Wales ridge, nearby parallel central ridges, and the Atlantic Coastal ridge, habitat loss is the most critical concern.

In addition to habitat loss, Florida perforate cladonia is also threatened by trampling, off-road vehicles, hurricane washover, and improper land management. Twelve of the 27 known sites for Florida perforate cladonia occur on dedicated conservation lands and are protected. In Highlands County, eight sites are protected on Archbold Biological Station and one site is protected at the Lake Apthorpe Preserve. In Polk County, two sites occur on the Lake Wales Ridge SF. In Martin County, one site occurs at Jonathan Dickinson SP Other protected areas include two sites at the Jupiter Inlet tract, owned and managed by the Bureau of Land Management in Martin County, the one north Florida site in Okaloosa County on Eglin Air Force Base. The Okaloosa County site occurs on a beach with restricted vehicular access, but completely open to foot traffic. In addition to the already-protected sites for Florida perforate cladonia, the Trout Lake site in Polk County is proposed for inclusion in the state's Preservation 2000 program. Other potential sites for protection include several privately held properties in Highlands County.

A low proportion of all known sites supports large areas of Florida perforate cladonia. At only two of the Archbold Biological Station sites is this lichen very abundant, making up the dominant ground cover in most of the site with densely crowded and overlapping thalli. Abundant stands are also reported from the site at Jonathan Dickinson State Park and from the east end of Santa Rosa Island.

Despite the conservation status of these sites, populations of this lichen may be extremely limited in areal extent and, therefore, subject to significant losses from local events. For example, two Okaloosa County sites supported only small fragments of Florida perforate cladonia prior to Hurricane Opal, which severely impacted Santa Rosa Island in October of 1995. One estimate suggested that more than half of the potential habitat of Florida perforate cladonia at that site was negatively affected by the storm, with large areas swept clean of all ground lichens or inundated with salt water. Only a few fragments of the lichen were relocated after the storm. At Archbold Biological Station, Florida perforate cladonia occurs on eight of more than 100 discrete, available habitat patches (rosemary balds). Five of these eight sites were partially burned in a prescribed fire in 1993, but in each, the lichen persisted in unburned patches, although almost certainly in lower numbers.

Throughout its distribution, Florida perforate cladonia is considered as rare. It has a limited areal extent and its management is further complicated by its limited reproduction and dispersal capability.

Conservation and Recovery

Florida scrub has historically experienced variable fire frequencies and patchy high-intensity fires. Scrub plant communities are therefore fire adapted, and recover relatively quickly. In sand pine and rosemary scrub, however, recovery of dominant species is slower than in oak-dominated scrubs, and open spaces between shrubs persist longer. In fire-maintained systems, low-fuel, bare sand patches may serve as refugia from fire for Florida perforate cladonia and other lichen species that cannot survive fire. These refugia provide a local source for recolonization and population recovery. Land managers should avoid complete burns in large areas supporting Florida perforate cladonia. Such fires likely reduce the possibility of recolonization from unburned patches within sites or from nearby sites. Additionally, complete lack of fire is also detrimental to the species. Fire suppression creates closed canopies and causes microsite characteristics to change. Management recommendations for Florida perforate cladonia should provide for fire return intervals long enough to restore vigorous lichen growth and to allow regeneration of mature shrub layers, since reburning rosemary scrub too frequently can deplete its soil seed banks. More frequent burns in adjacent habitats may serve to occasionally burn small areas of rosemary and reduce fuels enough to prevent large, complete fires. Spatially patchy fires leave unburned areas within a burned matrix from which species of Cladonia may recolonize, and without which Florida perforate cladonia may be threatened with local extinctions. Patchy burns in rosemary scrub at Archbold Biological Station and the Lake Apthorpe Preserve may be successful in promoting the persistence of this species, creating or re-opening new bare sand patches adjacent to occupied, unburned areas.

Management of Florida perforate cladonia should include protection of all sites from vehicle or heavy foot traffic and promoting fire management planning at sites where fire is an important part of that site's ecology. Unpredictable events, like hurricanes and wildfires, are best mediated by having a large number of protected sites, which provide local sources for natural recolonization and population recovery. It may be possible to reintroduce Florida perforate cladonia into severely damaged sites, if impacts have been so severe that the nearby natural population has not been able to recolonize the site.

Contacts

U.S. Fish and Wildlife Service
Regional Office, Division of Endangered Species
1875 Century Blvd., Suite 200
Atlanta, Georgia 30345
http://southeast.fws.gov

Ecological Services Field Office
6620 Southpoint Drive, Suite 310
South Jacksonville, Florida 32216-0912
Phone: (904) 232-2580
Fax: (904) 232-2404

Reference

U.S. Fish and Wildlife Service. 27 April 1993. "Endangered and Threatened Wildlife and Plants; Endangered or Threatened Status for Seven Central Florida Plants." *Federal Register* 58 (79): 25746-25755.

Rock Gnome Lichen

Gymnoderma lineare

Status	Endangered
Listed	January 18, 1995
Family	Cladoniaceae
Description	Lichen with blue-gray terminal portions of lobes and shiny white on the lower surface.
Habitat	Igneous, metamorphic, and metasedimentary rocks; warm and moderately wet summers, moderately cold and moderately dry winters, and a short freeze-free period.
Threats	Highway construction, recreation, balsam wooly adelgid, air pollution.
Range	Georgia, North Carolina, South Carolina, Tennessee

Description

Rock gnome lichen, *Gymnoderma lineare*, occurs in rather dense colonies of narrow straps or small scales, called squamules. The only similar lichens are the squamulose species of the genus *Cladonia*. Rock gnome lichen has terminal portions of the strap-like individual lobes that are blue-gray on the upper surface and generally shiny white on the lower surface; near the base they grade to black. In rock gnome lichen, the sparingly branched squamules are dark greenish mineral grey on the lower surface, becoming white to brownish toward the tips, tapering to the blackened base. The squamules are nearly parallel to the rock surface, but the tips curl away from the rock, approaching or reaching a perpendicular orientation to the rock surface. The fruiting bodies (apothecia) are borne at the tips of the squamules and are black. The apothecia are borne singly or in clusters, usually at the tips of the squamules but occasionally along the sides; these have been found from July through September. The apothecia are cylindrical in shape and radial in symmetry. The primary means of propagation of this lichen appears to be asexual, with colonies spreading by clones.

G. lineare is the only member of its genus occurring in North America; the other two species occur in the mountains of Japan and Eastern Asia, including the Himalayas.

Habitat

The rocks on which this lichen grows are of several types, including igneous, metamorphic, and metasedimentary rocks such as quartz diorite, garnet-rich biotite, muscovite and quartz schist, quartz phyllite, metagraywacke, metaconglomerate, and metarkoses containing feldspar and chlorite, amphibole, hornblende, and feldspar gneiss. The general area has warm and moderately wet summers, moderately cold and moderately dry winters, and a short freeze-free period. Annual rainfall at four occupied sites has ranged from 41 to 102 in (104.1 to 259.1 cm), with snowfall ranging from 4 to 101 in (10.1 to 256.5 cm). Average winter temperatures range from 5° to 48°F (–15° to 8.9°C), and average summer temperatures range from 49° to 73°F (9.4° to 22.8°C).

Rock gnome lichen is primarily limited to vertical rock faces where seepage water from forest soils above flows at very wet times. It appears that the species needs a moderate amount of light but that it cannot tolerate high-intensity solar radiation. It does well on moist, generally open, sites with

Rock Gnome Lichen, photograph by Nora Murdock, U. S. Fish & Wildlife Service. Reproduced by permission.

northern exposures, but needs at least partial canopy coverage where the aspect is southern or western. It is almost always found growing with the moss *Andreaea* and/or *Grimmia* in these vertical intermittent seeps. This association makes it rather easy to search for, due to the distinctive reddish brown color of *Andreaea* that can be observed from a considerable distance. Most populations occur above 5,000 ft (1524 m) in elevation. Common associates of this species include the endangered *Geum radiatum* and *Houstonia purpurea* ssp. *montana*. The high-elevation coniferous forests adjacent to the rock outcrops and cliffs most often occupied by the species are dominated by red spruce (*Picea rubens*) and a species of concern, Fraser fir (*Abies fraseri*), with northern hardwoods such as sugar maple (*Acer saccharum*), yellow birch (*Betula alleghaniensis*), mountain maple (*A. spicata*), mountain ash (*Sorbus americanus*), and beech (*Fagus grandifolia*) mixed in.

Distribution

Rock gnome lichen is endemic to the southern Appalachian Mountains of North Carolina, South Carolina, Tennessee, and Georgia and occurs only in areas of high humidity, either at high elevations, where it is frequently bathed in fog, or in deep gorges at lower elevations. In Tennessee it is apparently restricted to the Great Smoky Mountains and Roan Mountain.

Only 35 populations of rock gnome lichen are currently known to exist. Five populations are known to have been extirpated. The remaining populations are in Mitchell (two populations), Jackson (five), Yancey (four), Swain (one), Transylvania (four), Buncombe (four), Avery (two), Ashe (two), Haywood (one), and Rutherford (one) Counties, North Carolina; Greenville County (one), South Carolina; Rabun County (one), Georgia; and Sevier (seven) and Carter (part of this one population is on the state line with Mitchell County, North Carolina) Counties, Tennessee.

Threats

Although some populations are declining and vanishing for reasons that are, in many cases, not clearly understood, there are several major threats to the remaining lichen populations. Five historically known populations of this species have been completely extirpated. The reasons for the disappearance of the species at most of these sites are undocumented; however, one is believed to have been destroyed by highway construction. Most of the formerly occupied sites are subjected to heavy recreational use by hikers, climbers, and sightseers. In addition, the coniferous forests, particularly those dominated by Fraser fir at the high-elevation sites, are being decimated by the balsam wooly adelgid, an exotic insect pest, and possibly by air pollution. Widespread mortality of mature fir due to the balsam wooly adelgid has resulted in locally drastic changes in microclimate, including desiccation and increased temperatures.

Numerous lichen species are known to be sensitive to air pollution. Documented declines of lichen species have been recorded in the forests of Europe and nearby large industrial cities around the world. Research indicates that rock gnome lichen colonies in the poorest health have a higher content of sulfur compounds than colonies which appeared to be healthy. Furthermore, the species appears to have specific environmental needs, such as a narrow pH range and sulfur deposits. Initial research indicates there is a high likelihood that current and previous air pollution levels, especially from sulfates, may be contributing to the decline of this species.

Only eight of the remaining 35 populations cover an area larger than 21.5 sq ft (2 sq m). Most are 10.8 sq ft (1 sq m) or less in size. It is unknown what constitutes a genetic individual in this species, and it is possible that each of these small colonies or patches consists of only a single clone. Over the past decade several of the currently extant populations have undergone significant declines, some within as little as one year. Although al but five of the remaining populations are in public ownership, many continue to be affected by collectors, recreational use, and environmental factors. Although no populations are known to have been lost as a result of logging operations, it is interesting to note that most of the remaining stream corridor populations occur in areas of old-growth forest.

Conservation and Recovery

In addition to the efforts taken to conserve habitat sites in the national forests, the U.S. Forest Service, the National Park Service, and the U. S. Fish and Wildlife Service have cooperatively funded investigations of the lichen's response to air pollution at different sites.

Contact

U.S. Fish and Wildlife Service
Regional Office, Division of Endangered Species
1875 Century Blvd., Suite 200
Atlanta, Georgia 30345
http://southeast.fws.gov/

References

U.S. Fish and Wildlife Service. 18 January 1995. "Determination of *Gymnoderma lineare* (Rock Gnome Lichen) to be an Endangered Species." *Federal Register* 60 (11): 3557-3562.

U.S. Fish and Wildlife Service. 1997. "Recovery Plan for Rock Gnome Lichen (*Gymnoderma lineare*) (Evans) Yoshimura and Sharp." Atlanta, Georgia. 30 pp.

Fern Allies

Louisiana Quillwort

Isoetes louisianensis

Status	Endangered
Listed	October 28, 1992
Family	Isoetaceae (Quillwort)
Description	Small, grasslike aquatic herb with rounded, hollow numerous leaves.
Habitat	Small to medium-sized shallow, clear streams through riparian forests.
Threats	Clearcutting of streambank timber, canopy removal.
Range	Louisiana

Louisiana Quillwort, photograph by Julia Larke. Reproduced by permission.

Description

The *Isoetes louisianensis* Louisiana quillwort is a small, grasslike aquatic herb in the quillwort family. Louisiana quillwort is a seedless vascular plant which reproduces by spores and is closely related to ferns. The species' slender quill-like leaves arise from a short fleshy stem or corm that is shallowly rooted in the substrate. The leaves are rounded, hollow and swollen at their base. Leaves are numerous, varying in length from 6-16 in (15-40 cm) depending on water depth. The sporangia, or spore-containing structures, are embedded in the broadened bases of the leaves. The species is heterosporous, producing both megasporangia and microsporangia. The species is characterized by its born-spotted sporangial walls and megaspores with high reticulate ridges producing a spiny effect. Louisiana quillwort has been reported to sporulate twice a year, producing megaspores in the spring and microspores in the fall.

Habitat

This semi-aquatic plant is known from three locations in Louisiana. The streams in which the species is found are typically small to medium sized, shallow and with clear, tannin-colored water, running through narrow riparian forest communities. Preferred substrates are stable mixtures of silt, sand, and gravel. Louisiana quillwort occurs predominately on sand and gravel bars on accreting sides of streams and in moist over-flow channels. The species is found less commonly on low sloping banks near, and occasionally below, the low water level. Individuals are regularly inundated as much as 20 in (50 cm) of water following rains, and may be inundated for long periods in wet seasons. Corm depth has been found as great as 1.2 in (3 cm), indicating a tolerance for some deposition of materials. The species may be found singly or in numbers of several hundred.

Distribution

Louisiana quillwort is known to exist in three locations in Washington and St. Tammany Parishes in Louisiana. The largest two populations contain several hundred individuals each; the smallest contains only four immature individuals. It is possible the species was once more widespread, but there is no concrete evidence to support this. The most extensive population occurs in portions of Thigpen and Clearwater Creeks. Four individuals are known from the Mill Creek area. A population in the Little Bogue Falaya Creek contains several hundred individuals.

Threats

The primary threats to Louisiana quillwort are activities that would affect the hydrology or stability of the streams in which it occurs. The species has been eliminated from one location by construction activities and canopy removal. It has been affected in another portion of this area by changes in vegetation composition due to clearcutting of streambank timber and flow diversion.

All known stream habitat supporting this species is associated with a well-developed stream canopy. Canopy removal alters the light regime under which the species is currently known to exist. Some streambank timber harvest have occurred at various locations along all streams supporting Louisiana quillwort. It is believed that these harvests have adversely affected the species. Streambank timber removal can also lead to an increase in surface runoff and contribute to stream erosion and/or siltation.

Sand and gravel mining along the species' range is affecting the hydrology, water quality, and substrate stability of that area. Portions of the area have been completely cleared, channelized or rerouted by sand and gravel mining activities. Headwaters into one area have been ditched to direct surface drainage away from the mining operation. Excessive algal growth and sediment pollution has occurred due to this alteration of the hydrologic regime. All of these factors threaten the existence of this species.

Conservation and Recovery

The recovery efforts of Louisiana quillwort include the following. Further searches for undiscovered individuals in similar habitats need to be conducted. Studies into the reproductive cycle and specific habitat requirements could lead to a better understanding of the species. This information could be used to develop a cultivation and seed bank program that could be used to reintroduce the species in appropriate habitat. Binding agreements with private landowners or possible land acquisition should be considered to protect the few remaining populations that occur on private land. Timber harvesting throughout the species' range should be carefully monitored to help keep the canopy intact. Further mining permits and water diversions throughout the species' range should be carefully considered so as not to further impact Louisiana quillwort.

Contacts

Louisiana Natural Heritage Program
Louisiana Department of Wildlife and Fisheries
Habitat Section
P.O. Box 98000 (70898)
2000 Quail Drive
Baton Rouge, Louisiana 70808

U. S. Fish and Wildlife Service
Ecological Services Field Office
Brandywine II
825 Kaliste Saloom Road, Suite 102
Lafayette, Louisiana 70508-4231
Telephone: (337) 291-3100
Fax: (337)291-3139

U. S. Fish and Wildlife Service
Regional Office, Division of Endangered Species
1875 Century Blvd., Suite 200
Atlanta, Georgia 30345
http://southeast.fws.gov/

Reference

U.S. Fish and Wildlife Service. 28 October 1992. "Endangered and Threatened Wildlife and Plants: Determination of Endangered Status for the Plant *Isoetes louisianensis* (Louisiana Quillwort)." *Federal Register* 57: 48741-48746.

Black-spored Quillwort

Isoetes melanospora

Status	Endangered
Listed	February 5, 1988
Family	Isoetaceae (Quillwort)
Description	Aquatic plant with short, spiral, chive-like leaves.
Habitat	Seasonal pools on granite outcrops.
Threats	Quarrying, off-road vehicles, recreational use of habitat.
Range	Georgia, South Carolina

Andy Robinson, USFWS

Description

Isoetes melanospora (black-spored quillwort) is an aquatic plant with chive-like leaves, 0.8-2.8 in (2-7 cm) long, that spiral upward from a swollen base, called a corm. The plant puts down many fleshy, branched roots that anchor it to the thin soil. Quillworts, which are related to ferns, do not reproduce by seed but by spores. Reproductive spores develop in nodes formed at the base of the leaves.

The family of quillworts has only a single genus, containing about 70 species. Many have a similar appearance and are best differentiated by spore characteristics. Black-spored quillwort, also called Merlin's grass, occasionally hybridizes with *Isoetes piedmontana*, a more common granite outcrop quillwort.

Habitat

Black-spored quillwort grows in rock- rimmed seasonal pools atop granite outcrops in domed or gently rolling areas known locally as "flatrocks." Most pools are only about 3 ft (1 m) across, with a thin bottom deposit of sand or silt that is low in organic matter. These pools fill up after heavy rains, but evaporate quickly, and are usually completely dry by mid-summer. Black-spored quillwort grows quickly when water is available, frequently in association with amphianthus species, one of which—little amphianthus (*Amphianthus pusillus*)—is federally listed as Endangered.

Distribution

Black-spored quillwort was discovered on Stone Mountain in DeKalb County, Georgia, in 1877. It has subsequently been found at 11 other sites in central Georgia and one site in South Carolina. As of 1993, the species was thought to be extant at only eight locations, all in Georgia (in Butts, DeKalb, Gwinnett, Heard and Rockdale counties). The largest remaining population occurs at Davidson-Arabia Mountain Park in DeKalb County.

Black-spored Quillwort, photograph. U. S. Fish and Wildlife Service. Reproduced by permission.

It is extinct at five historical sites in DeKalb and Newton counties. Due to hybridization, it is considered extinct or essentially so at the sole reported site in South Carolina (in Lancaster County) and at two additional sites in Georgia (Butts and DeKalb counties). Only one site supports more than three inhabited pools. The typical site has one or two pools totaling only a few square meters.

By 1993, two of the eight extant locations (both in DeKalb County) were publicly owned. The type locality, Stone Mountain, lies within the state-owned Georgia Stone Mountain Park.

Threats

Black-spored quillwort is threatened by continuing loss of its habitat. Georgia's "flatrocks" are being quarried at a tremendous pace, making the state the world's largest producer of granite building stone. Over 40% of historic quillwort populations have already been lost to quarrying.

Conservation and Recovery

Georgia law prohibits collection of these plants without a permit and regulates interstate transport, but does not protect the plant against habitat destruction. Recovery strategies include the preservation of some "flatrocks" habitat, which requires bringing suitable outcrops into public ownership or encouraging purchase by private conservation groups. The 1993 Fish and Wildlife Service Recovery Plan for Three Granite Outcrop Plant Species (including the black-spored quillwort) notes that the initial recovery objective for the species is downlisting to Threatened status; delisting (removal from the list altogether) potential could not be determined at the time of the plan's release.

Reclassification to Threatened status will be considered if 10 viable and geographically distinct populations (separate outcrops), each with at least two occupied pools, are protected from any foreseeable threats. To achieve this goal, the plan recommends a variety of actions, including the protection of populations and habitat; the preservation of genetic stock from acutely threatened populations; and the monitoring of populations to determine trends and developing threats. The plan also calls for the reestablishment of populations and the augmentation of extant populations at protected locations, if deemed necessary. Management techniques should also be used to maintain and/or enhance populations, and public education programs should be established to spread the word about the value and fragility of the species and its habitat.

Contact

U. S. Fish and Wildlife Service
Regional Office, Division of Endangered Species
1875 Century Blvd., Suite 200
Atlanta, Georgia 30345
http://southeast.fws.gov/

References

Boom, B. M. 1981. "Intersectional Hybrids in Isoetes." *American Fern Journal* 70:1-4.

Rayner, D. A. 1986. "Granite Flatrock Outcrops in South Carolina." *Bulletin of South Carolina Academy of Science* 43:106-107.

U.S. Fish and Wildlife Service. 1993."Recovery Plan for Three Granite Outcrop Plants Species." U.S. Fish and Wildlife Service, Jackson, Mississippi.

Wharton, C. H. 1978. *The Natural Environments of Georgia*. Georgia Department of Natural Resources, Atlanta.

Mat-forming Quillwort

Isoetes tegetiformans

Status	Endangered
Listed	February 5, 1988
Family	Isoetaceae (Quillwort)
Description	Mat-forming aquatic plant with spiraling leaves.
Habitat	Temporary pools on granite outcrops.
Threats	Quarrying, recreational traffic.
Range	Georgia

Description

Isoetes tegetiformans (mat-forming quillwort) is a low-growing, aquatic plant with short, chive-like leaves, spiraling upward from a bulb-like base, called a corm. Individual plants are connected by a fleshy underground rhizome. The stems rise to form a dense mat on the surface of the water, a habit that distinguishes this quillwort from other members of its genus, such as the Endangered black-spored quillwort (*Isoetes melanospora*).

Quillworts produce spores rather than seeds and are closely related to club mosses and spike mosses. The swollen base of the plant contains both male and female reproductive spores that disperse to produce new plants. The size and shape of the spores, which can only be determined under the microscope, is used to differentiate species. Mat-forming quillwort appears to depend as much on vegetative reproduction from its rhizome as on reproduction by spores.

Habitat

The species is found in the temporary and seasonal pools that dot the gently rolling granite "flatrocks" landscape of the Southeastern Piedmont. Granite outcrop pools typically have bottoms of thin sandy or silty soil containing little organic matter. Pools retain water for several weeks after heavy rains, but usually dry up completely in summer.

Distribution

Mat-forming quillwort is endemic to the flatrocks of central Georgia in the region northeast of Macon and west of Augusta. It was first described in 1978 from material collected at Heggie's Rock Preserve in Columbia County, Georgia.

As of 1993, the species was restricted to four Georgia counties, Columbia, Greene, Hancock and Putnam. Three of the seven extant sites are in Columba County; prior to quarrying activities, it occurred at three additional outcrops in that county. The largest population occurs in Hancock County.

Following its discovery, the U.S. Fish and Wildlife Service (FWS) conducted an extensive search of more than 120 granite outcrop sites in Georgia, locating only ten additional populations of mat-forming quillwort. Since that time, the population sites have dwindled. Most sites consist of one or two pools that support quillwort colonies. Although vegetation at these sites appears dense, pools actually contain few genetically distinct individuals since the plant spreads through its rhizome.

All sites for the mat-forming quillwort were in private ownership as of 1993. The type locality, Heggies Rock, is owned by the Nature Conservancy (TNC) and occupies a single, larger-than-average vernal pool. The population is healthy and shows recovery from past vehicular traffic. The two largest populations (in Greene and Hancock counties) are owned by the Georgia-Pacific Corporation.

Threats

Georgia is the world's largest granite producer. Quarrying of granite outcrops has gone on for two hundred years and will certainly continue, steadily

Mat-forming Quillwort, photograph by Kim D. Coder. Reproduced by permission.

constricting the quillwort's habitat. Granite out-crops of the "flatrocks" are also popular as recreational sites, and many pools with quillwort populations have been damaged by hikers or by off-road vehicles.

Conservation and Recovery

TNC owns and manages Heggie's Rock Preserve in Columbia County, which protects one pool with quillwort populations.

The 1993 FWS Recovery Plan for Three Granite Outcrop Plant Species (including the mat-forming quillwort) notes that the initial recovery objective for the species is downlisting to Threatened status; whether de-listing (removal from the list altogether) is possible could not be determined at the time of the Recovery Plan's release.

Reclassification to Threatened status will be considered if ten viable and geographically distinct populations (separate outcrops), each with at least

two occupied pools, are protected from any foreseeable threats. To achieve this goal, the plan recommends a variety of actions, including the protection of populations and habitat; the preservation of genetic stock from acutely threatened populations; and the monitoring of populations to determine trends and developing threats. The plan also calls for the reestablishment of populations and the augmentation of extant populations at protected locations, if deemed necessary. Management techniques should also be used to maintain and/or enhance populations, and public education programs should be established to spread the word about the value and fragility of the species and its habitat.

Contact

U. S. Fish and Wildlife Service
Regional Office, Division of Endangered Species
1875 Century Blvd., Suite 200
Atlanta, Georgia 30345
http://southeast.fws.gov/

References

Boom, B. M. 1982. "A Synopsis of *Isoetes* in the Southeastern United States." *Castanea* 47:38-59.

Matthews, J. F., and W. H. Murdy. 1969. "A Study *Isoetes* Common to the Granite Outcrops of the Southeastern Piedmont, United States." *Botanical Gazette* 130:53-61.

Rury, P. M. 1978. "A New and Unique Mat-Forming Merlin's Grass (*Isoetes*) from Georgia." *American Fern Journal* 68:99-108.

Rury, P. M. 1985. "New Locations for *Isoetes tegetiformans* in Georgia." *American Fern Journal* 75:102-104.

U.S. Fish and Wildlife Service. 1993."Recovery Plan for Three Granite Outcrop Plants Species." U.S. Fish and Wildlife Service, Jackson, Mississippi.

Wawa'iole

Huperzia mannii

Status	Endangered
Listed	May 15, 1992
Family	Lycopodiaceae (Clubmoss)
Description	Clustered red stems with leaves arranged in three rows, and bracted fruit bearing spikes; grows with another plant for support.
Habitat	Grows on plants such as 'ohi'a or Acacia koa in mesic to wet montane 'ohi'a/koa forests.
Threats	Habitat destruction by feral pigs; competing plant species.
Range	Hawaii

Description

Wawa'iole (*Huperzia mannii*) is a pendent epiphyte of the clubmoss family (Lycopodiaceae) with clustered red stems 1.6-3.9 in (4-9.8 cm) long and 0.04 in (1 mm) thick. The leaves, arranged in three rows on the stem, are pointed, flat, and lanceolate. Fruiting spikes branch four to six times and are 7-9 in (17.5-22.5 cm) long and 0.4-0.6 in (1-1.5 cm) wide. The spikes possess 0.04 in (1 mm) long bracts arranged in two to four ranks that function to conceal spore capsules.

Habitat

H. mannii typically grows on plants such as 'ohi'a or Acacia koa in mesic to wet montane 'ohi'a/koa forests on Maui and the island of Hawaii. Associated plant species include pilo, 'olapa, kawa'u, and kolea. Additional associates on the island of Hawaii are mamane and kaluaha.

Distribution

Historically, *Huperzia mannii* was known from Walakoali on Kauai, Haelaau and Hanaula on West Maui, and Hawaii Island. The first collection of this very slender species was made on Maui before 1868.

The majority of remaining *Huperzia mannii* is believed to occur on East Maui, where it was first recorded in 1976 in the Healani region in the Kipahulu Forest Reserve at about 4,200 ft (1,260 m) elevation. A 1982 estimate of the Healani population was 50 individuals in the two colonies

Two populations *of Huperzia mannii* are currently known from the Kahikinui Forest Reserve on East Maui. Six individuals growing on the trunks of two *Acacia Koa* trees were discovered in 1981 within the Reserve in Manawainui Gulch at 5,300 ft (1,590 m) elevation. Art Medeiros and Mahealam Kaiaokamalie, discoverers of the second Reserve population in 1995, observed seven individuals growing on the trunks of *Acacia koa* trees in an unnamed gulch west of Manawamui Gulch at 4,880 ft (1,460 m) elevation.

A fourth East Maui population was discovered in 1992 at 2,000-2,500 ft (600-750 m) elevation on the southern rim of Kipahulu Valley, at a site referred to locally as "Cable Ridge." This occurrence is partially within Haleakala National Park, but it also extends onto adjacent state and private land. "Cable Ridge" has easily the largest population of the species, with several hundred individuals growin on an area of about 650 acres (1,625 hectares). At least a few individuals of *Huperzia mannii* occur in a fifth population at Lihau and Puu-kukui on West Maui. It is also sparingly present in a sixth population on state and private land at Laupahoehoe Natural Area Reserve on the island of Hawaii. The to-

Wawa'iole, photograph by Steve Perlman. Reproduced by permission.

tal number of extant individuals was thought to be fewer than 300 in 1995.

Threats

The major threats to *Huperzia mannii* are habitat degradation caused by pig and cattle predation and trampling; competition for space, light, water, and nutrients by naturalized exotic species, especially prickly Florida blackberry; and the small number of remaining individuals.

Conservation and Recovery

An exclosure was constructed in 1990, using barbed-wire and woven-wire, to protect the Manawainui Gulch population of *Huperzia mannii* in the Kahikinui Forest Reserve, as well as associated species. This fence construction was a cooperative effort between the Native Hawaiian Plant Society and the Maui Division of Forestry and Wildlife. Living Indigenous Forest Ecosystems has fenced the second Kahikinui population of *Huperzia mannii* The

"Cable Ridge" population of *Huperzia mannii* is easily the largest, far exceeding the combined number of individuals of all other known populations. Because of the size of this population of *Huperzia mannii* and the quality of surrounding habitat, protection of this population is the most important step for the long-term conservation of the species. Protection involves construction of a woven-wire exclosure and elimination of feral pigs that are now common and destructive in the area. Control of aggressive alien species like the tree fern *Cyathea cooperi*, which is common and invasive in lower elevation areas of the "Cable Ridge" population, may be necessary in some parts of this occurrence.

The two colonies are currently unprotected from feral goats and pigs. Continued degradation of this site will cause the loss of native tree species and conversion to alien grasslands. Without protection, the continued loss of *Acacia koa* and *Dodonaea viscosa* trees, which host *Huperzia mannii* at this site, will cause decline and eventual extirpation of these populations. Protection by woven-wire fence exclosures in this area has demonstrated potential for increasing cover and density of native tree species.

Contact

U. S. Fish and Wildlife Service
Office of the Regional Director
Eastside Federal Complex
911 N.E. 11th Ave.
Portland, Oregon 97232-4181
Telephone: (503) 231-6118
Fax: (503) 231-2122
http://pacific.fws.gov/

Reference

U.S. Fish and Wildlife Service. 1997. "Recovery Plan for the Maui Plant Cluster." U.S. Fish and Wildlife Service, Portland, Oregon.

Wawae'iole

Phlegmariurus nutans

Status	Endangered
Listed	March 28, 1994
Family	Lycopodiaceae (Clubmoss)
Description	Erect or pendulous plant with stiff, flat, leathery leaves, and branches that end in thick, fruiting spikes.
Habitat	Tree trunks, usually on open ridges and slopes in 'ohi'a-dominated wet forests and occasionally mesic forests.
Threats	Competition from alien plants; stochastic extinction due to limited numbers.
Range	Hawaii

Description

Phlegmariurus nutans (Wawae'iole) is an erect or pendulous herbaceous epiphyte (plant growing above ground on other plants) of the clubmoss family. Its stiff and light green branches, 10-16 in (25-40 cm) long and about 0.2 in (0.5 cm) thick, are covered with stiff, flat, leathery leaves; these overlap at acute angles and are 0.5-0.6 in (1.2-1.5 cm) long and about 0.1 in (2.5 mm) wide. The leaves are arranged in six rows and arise directly from the branches. The branches end in thick, 2.8-5.1 in (7-13 cm) long fruiting spikes that are unbranched or branched once or twice and taper toward a downward-curving tip. Densely layered bracts on the fruiting spikes are between 0.1 and 0.2 in (2.5 and 5 mm) long and conceal the spore capsules.

This species is distinguished from others of the genus in Hawaii by its epiphytic habit, simple or forking fruit spikes, and larger, stiffer leaves. *P. nutans* has been observed fertile, with spores, in May and December. The species has also been classified as *Lycopodium nutans*.

Habitat

P. nutans grows on tree trunks, usually on open ridges and slopes in 'ohi'a-dominated wet forests and occasionally mesic forests at elevations between 2,000 and 3,500 ft (610 and 1,070 m). The vegetation in those areas usually includes kanawao, uluhe, 'uki, hame, kopiko, kokio, and kokeo.

Distribution

Historically, *P. nutans* was known from the island of Kauai and from scattered locations in the Koolau Mountains of Oahu bounded by Kaluanui Valley to the north, Paalaa to the west, and Mount Tantalus to the south. This species is now known from only two sites within its historic range on Oahu—Kaluanui Valley and along Waikane-Schofield Trail.

One population, located on state land, was described as scarce when last observed in 1965. The other population, located about 5 mi (8 km) away on the boundary of the Ewa Forest reserve and Schofield Military Barracks Reserve, grew in several places in this area at the time of its collection in 1961. Two individuals of this population were observed in 1993 by Joel Lau. The entire species totals less than 50 known individuals. The populations at Kaukonahua Ridge, Kaukonahua Gulch, and along Waikane-Schofield Trail on Oahu contained just four individuals in 1997.

Threats

The primary threat to *P. nutans* is stochastic extinction and reduced reproductive vigor due to the

Wawae'iole, photograph by Ken Wood. Reproduced by permission.

small number of remaining individuals and their limited distribution. It is also threatened by extinction due to random natural events. An additional threat is competition from noxious alien plants, especially Koster's curse and strawberry guava.

Conservation and Recovery

Propagation of *P. nutans* was unsuccessfully attempted at the National Tropical Botanical Garden.

Contact

U. S. Fish and Wildlife Service
Regional Office, Division of Endangered Species
Eastside Federal Complex
911 N. E. 11th Ave.
Portland, Oregon 97232-4181
(503) 231-6121
http://pacific.fws.gov/

Reference

U.S. Fish and Wildlife Service. 1998. Recovery Plan for Oahu Plants. U.S. Fish and Wildlife Service, Portland, Oregon. 207 pp., plus appendices.

True Ferns

Adiantum vivesii

No Common Name

Status	Endangered
Listed	July 9, 1993
Family	Adiantaceae (Maidenhair fern)
Description	Colonial fern with creeping rhizomes, erect-spreading fronds, and lustrous purple-black stalks.
Habitat	Deeply shaded hollow at the base of north-facing limestone cliffs at a lower to middle elevation of about 820 ft (250 m).
Threats	Limited range.
Range	Puerto Rico

Description

Adiantum vivesii (maidenhair) is a gregarious colonial fern with creeping nodose and rhizomes about 0.1 in (2.5-3.0 mm) thick. The fronds are distichous (in two vertical rows) and erect-spreading, approximately 0.2 in (0.5 cm) apart and 18-28 in (45-71 cm) long. The stipes or stalks are lustrous purple-black, 10-18 in (25-46 cm) long, irregularly branched, and have hairlike scales. The frond's blades are broad and irregular, 8-11 in (20-28 cm) long, and 9-14 in (23-35 cm) broad. The rachises and costae are more densely covered with hairlike scales than the stipes. The blades have two or three alternative or sometimes subopposite pinnae, the terminal one being larger. These are lance-oblong, 5-8 in (13-20 cm) long, and 1.4-2 in (3.5-5 cm) broad.

The terminal pinna may be up to 2.8 in (7 cm) broad, stalked, and is often somewhat inequilateral. Each pinna has 10-13 pairs of alternate, narrowly oblong-falcate pinnules, which are unequally cuneate at the base. The outer sterile margins of the pinna are irregularly serrulate and the tissue is dull green on both sides. Five elliptic to linear sori (reproductive bodies) are borne along the basal half of the acroscopic margin, and they are close or contiguous but distinct. The indusioid is gray-brown and turgid, with an erose margin.

Habitat

This species occurs in a deeply shaded hollow at the base of north-facing limestone cliffs at a lower to middle elevation of approximately 820 ft (250 m).

Distribution

A. vivesii species is only known from a single colony of an estimated 1,000 plants, or growing apices, at Barrio San Antonio in the municipality of Quebradillas, Puerto Rico.

Threats

A. vivesii occurs on privately owned land and is known from only a single locality. Clearing or development of this area would result in elimination of the species. Also, this species could be an attractive item for collectors.

Conservation and Recovery

Because *A. vivesii* occurs on privately owned land and is known from only a single locality, clearing or development of this area would result in the elimination of the only known population.

Research is needed to determine this species' life history and ecological requirements and to develop and refine propagation and transplant techniques.

Surveys are needed to determine if other populations exist and to locate potential transplant sites.

Contacts

U. S. Fish and Wildlife Service
Regional Office, Division of Endangered Species
1875 Century Blvd., Suite 200
Atlanta, Georgia 30345
(404) 679-4000
http://southeast.fws.gov/

Boquerón Ecological Services Field Office
Boquerón, Puerto Rico 00622-0491
Telephone: (787) 851-7297
Fax: (787) 851-7440

References

Mickel, J. T. 1979. *How to Know the Ferns and Fern Allies.* William C. Brown Publishing, Dubuque, Iowa.

U. S. Fish and Wildlife Service. 9 June 1993. "Endangered and Threatened Wildlife and Plants: Determination of Endangered Status for Four Endemic Puerto Rican Ferns." *Federal Register* 58 (109): 32308-32311.

Pteris lidgatei

No Common Name

Status	Endangered
Listed	September 26, 1994
Family	Adiantaceae (Maidenhair fern)
Description	Frond is oblong-deltoid to broadly ovate-deltoid, thick, brittle, and dark gray-green.
Habitat	Stream banks and next to waterfalls with mosses and other species of ferns.
Threats	The alien plant Koster's curse; habitat destruction by feral pigs; stochastic extinction.
Range	Hawaii

Pteris lidgatei, photograph by Ken Wood. Reproduced by permission.

Description

Cheilanthes lidgatei was described in 1883 on the basis of a specimen collected on Oahu. The genus *Schizostege* was erected in 1888 for this anomalous species. In 1897, it was placed in the genus Pteris by H. Christ, resulting in the currently accepted combination *Pteris lidgatei*. *P. lidgatei*, a member of the maidenhair fern family (Adiantaceae), is a coarse herb 1.6-3.3 ft (0.5-1 m) in height. It has a horizontal rhizome that is 0.6 in (1.5 cm) thick and at least 3.9 in (10 cm) long at maturity. The fronds, including the leafstalks, are 24-37 in (61-94 cm) long and 8-18 in (20-45 cm) wide. The leafy portion of the frond is oblong-deltoid to broadly ovate-deltoid, thick, brittle, and dark gray-green. The sori are apparently marginal in position, either fused into long linear sori or more typically separated into distinct shorter sori with intermediate conditions being common. *P. lidgatei* can be distinguished from other species of *Pteris* in the Hawaiian Islands by the texture of its fronds and the tendency of the sori along the leaf margins to be broken into short segments instead of being fused into continuous marginal sori.

Habitat

P. lidgatei is found in lowland wet forest at elevations ranging from 1,750-3,000 ft (533-914 m). It is generally found on streambanks and next to waterfalls with mosses and other species of ferns. 'Ohi'a is the dominant native overstory tree species.

Distribution

P. lidgatei had historical occurrences at Olokui on Molokai and Waihee on West Maui. The species also occurred at four locations in the Koolau Mountains of Oahu: Waiahole, Lulumahu Stream, Kaluanui, and Wailupe. Seven populations of about 33 individuals were known in 1995. *P. lidgatei* is reported from Oahu at Kawaiiki Stream, North Waimano Gulch, Kawainui Drainage, and South Kaukonahua Gulch. Respective populations of 12 and eight plants were discovered on West Maui in 1994 at Kauaula Valley and Kahakuloa Stream. The extant populations of *P. lidgatei* are on Federal, state, and private land. Three of the Oahu populations are located on lands under the jurisdiction of the U.S. Army.

Threats

The primary threats to *P. lidgatei* are the alien plant Koster's curse, habitat destruction by feral pigs, and stochastic extinction.

Conservation and Recovery

Feral pig control efforts by The Nature Conservancy of Hawaii at Kapunakea Preserve have helped keep pigs from spreading into the Kauaula Valley population of *P. lidgatei* on Maui. The Army has prepared Endangered Species Management Plans for Oahu Training Areas; these plans highlight specific threats to endangered plants and recommend actions to promote recovery. The U.S. Fish and Wildlife Service is studying the environmental effects of establishing a National Wildlife Refuge in the Koolau Mountains. The priority recovery actions for this fern are control of feral ungulates and alien weeds. Although this species is presently very rare, the number of known plants is expected to rise slowly as botanists become more familiar with the plant and its preferred habitat. Additional populations should be carefully documented as they are discovered so that important habitat can be protected. The Koolau Mountains and West Maui Mountains should be targeted for protection.

Contact

U. S. Fish and Wildlife Service
Regional Office, Division of Endangered Species
Eastside Federal Building
911 N. E. 11th Ave.
Portland, Oregon 97232-4181
Telephone: (503) 231-6121
http://pacific.fws.gov/

Reference

U.S. Fish and Wildlife Service. 1998. "Recovery Plan for Four Species of Hawaiian Ferns." U.S. Fish and Wildlife Service, Portland, Oregon.

Asplenium fragile var. insulare

No Common Name

Status	Endangered
Listed	September 26, 1994
Family	Aspleniaceae (Spleenwort)
Description	Fronds are thin-textured, bright green, long and narrow.
Habitat	Lava tubes, pits, deep cracks, and lava tree molds.
Threats	Feral sheep and goats.
Range	Hawaii

Asplenium fragile, photograph by Robert Shaw. Reproduced by permission.

Description

Asplenium fragile var. *insulare* is a fern of the spleenwort family (Aspleniaceae) with a short suberect stem. The leaf stalks are 2-6 in (5-15 cm) long. The main axis of the frond is dull gray or brown, with two greenish ridges. The long and narrow fronds are thin-textured, bright green, 9-16 in (23-41 cm) long, 0.8 in (2 cm) wide above the middle, and pinnate with 20-30 pinnae or leaflets on each side. The pinnae are rhomboidal, 0.3 in (7 mm) wide, and notched into two to five blunt lobes on the side towards the tip of the frond. The sori (spore-producing bodies) are close to the main vein of the pinna, with one to two on the lower side and two to four on the upper side. The Hawaiian fern species most similar to *A. fragile* var. *insulare* is *A. macraei*. The two can be distinguished by a number of characteristics, including the size and shape of the pinnae and the number of sori per pinna.

The Hawaiian plants now referred to as *A. fragile* var. *insulare* were considered by William Hillebrand in 1888 to be conspecific with *A. fragile* from Central and South America. The Hawaiian plants were subsequently treated as a distinct endemic species, *A. rhomboideum*. However, that species is now considered native to the New World and not present in Hawaii. The name *A. fragile* var. *insulare* was published in 1947, as the Hawaiian plants were considered distinct at the varietal level from the extra-Hawaiian plants. Reproductive cycles, longevity, specific environmental requirements, and limiting factors are unknown.

Habitat

This fern is found on the island of Hawaii in *Metrosideros* (ohia) dry montane forest, *Dodonaea* (aalii) dry montane shrubland, *Myoporum/Sophora* (naio/mamane) dry montane forest, *Ohia/Acacia* (koa) forest as well as subalpine dry forest and shrubland. *A. fragile* var. *insulare* grows almost exclusively in lava tubes, pits, deep cracks, and lava tree molds, with at least a moderate soil or ash accumulation, associated with mosses and liverworts. This fern has been found growing infrequently on the interface between younger lava flows and much older pahoehoe lava or ash deposits. The population recently found on Maui is growing in montane wet 'ohi'a forest in a rocky gulch with other species of ferns. Although this plant is found in habitats with three different moisture regimes, the microhabitat for *A. fragile* var. *insulare* is fairly consistent. The fern generally occurs in areas that are moist and dark; its relatively specialized habitat requirements may account for its apparently patchy distribution.

Distribution

A. fragile var. *insulare* was known historically from East Maui, where it was recorded from the north slope of Haleakala and Kanahau Hill. On the island of Hawaii, this fern was found historically below Kalaieha, Laumaia, Keanakolu, and Umikoa on Mauna Kea; Puuwaawaa on Hualalai; west of Keawewai, above Kipuka Ahiu on Mauna Loa; and near Hilo.

This species has eight extant populations on the island of Hawaii at elevations between 5,250 and 7,800 ft (1,600 and 2,400 m); a ninth occurrence was recently reported from East Maui, in Hanawi Natural Area Reserve. The current populations on Hawaii are located at Puu Huluhulu, Pohakuloa Training Area (nine subpopulations), Kulani Correctional Facility, Keauhou, the Mauna Loa Strip Road in Hawaii Volcanoes National Park, Kapapala Forest Reserve, Kau Forest Reserve, and the summit area of Hualalai. The largest population of this fern occurs at Pohakuloa Training Area; the latest monitoring in 1995 put total numbers at about 200 plants, a slight reduction in numbers from 1992. The nine known populations on Federal, state, and private land totaled approximately 278 plants in 1995.

Threats

The primary threats to *A. fragile* var. *insulare* are feral sheep and goats. Large numbers of feral goats are present on the island of Hawaii within Pohakuloa Training Area in the saddle between Mauna Loa and Mauna Kea, where they threaten this fern through both direct browsing on the plants and habitat degradation. Predation by feral goats and sheep has been reported for *A. fragile* var. *insulare* at Pohakuloa Training Area. Because no colonies have been decimated by the animals, it appears that goats do not seek out this fern. However, further predation may occur if their preferred forage is not available. Predation by feral goats is a potential threat to the other two sizable known populations of this fern at Keauhou and Kulani because goats can feed on the ferns at the entrance to lava tubes. At the Hawaii Volcanoes National Park fences are being used to protect the Mauna Loa strip population from eradication by the feral goats.

At least one population at Pohakuloa Training Area is threatened by military operations and fires resulting from these operations; construction needed for military activities could also affect populations at this installation. Another threat to *A. fragile* var. *insulare* at Pohakuloa Training Area is the alien plant fountain grass.

Populations of *A. fragile* var. *insulare* are threatened by the bulldozing of jeep roads and filling in of lava tubes. Also of concern is the small number of existing individuals, a situation that makes stochastic extinction through natural events a very real possibility. Even random fluctuations in numbers of individuals or a small increase in plant mortality could extirpate this species.

Conservation and Recovery

The Army has prepared a Preliminary Endangered Species Management Plan for Pohakuloa Training Area. The Army is also presently consulting with the U.S. Fish and Wildlife Service (FWS) under section 7 of the Endangered Species Act, and negotiations are underway to control threats and promote the recovery of endangered species at Pohakuloa Training Area. The FWS has a cooperative agreement for the management of Kilauea and Kulani forests with Kamehameha Schools/Bishop Estate, Hawaii Department of Land and Natural Resources, Hawaii Department of Public Safety/Corrections Division, and the National Park Service. One portion of Kulani Forest with a population of *A. fragile* var. *insulare* has been fenced and the ungulates removed.

The most important recovery action for this fern is to protect high elevation lava tubes, a process that will need to include removal of hoofed mammals. The areas that are most important for protection include Pohakuloa Training Area, Keahou and Kulani Forests and portions of Kapapaia and Kan Forest Reserves. A portion of Kapapaia and Kan Forest Reserves important for protection of *A. fragile* var. *insulare* and other native plants has been proposed but not yet officially recommended as a potential Natural Area Reserve (Waihaka Natural Area Reserve). The establishment of such a preserve at Waihaka and protection for *A. fragile* var. *insulare* habitat are much-needed recovery actions for this species.

The Army should implement actions proposed in their Preliminary Endangered Species Management Plan for Pohakuloa Training Area. These actions include controlling feral animals, minimizing the impact of training activities, monitoring of known populations, and controlling fires and fountain grass.

Surveys to locate and map additional populations are also important to the recovery of this fern. For example, many areas at Pohakuloa Training Area have not been surveyed for biological re-

sources, so the current level of survey coverage should be considered incomplete. *A. fragile* var. *insulare* has a very scattered distribution, and surveys will help determine the best areas for habitat protection. Optimal survey areas can be determined by considering the age of the substrate and the vegetation type.

Contact

U. S. Fish and Wildlife Service
Regional Office, Division of Endangered Species
Eastside Federal Building
911 N. E. 11th Ave.
Portland, Oregon 97232-4181
Telephone: (503) 231-6121
http://pacific.fws.gov/

Reference

U. S. Fish and Wildlife Service. 10 April 1998. "Recovery Plan for Four Species of Hawaiian Ferns." U. S. Fish and Wildlife Service. Portland, Oregon.

American Hart's-tongue Fern

Asplenium scolopendrium var. americanum

Status	Threatened
Listed	July 14, 1989
Family	Aspleniaceae (Spleenwort)
Description	Fern with evergreen, strap-shaped fronds.
Habitat	Cool limestone sinkholes in mature hardwood forests.
Threats	Quarrying, logging, recreation, residential development.
Range	Alabama, Michigan, New York, Tennessee; Ontario, Canada

American Hart's-tongue Fern, photograph. U. S. Fish and Wildlife Service. Reproduced by permission.

Description

American hart's-tongue fern, *Asplenium scolopendrium* var. *americanum*, has evergreen, strap-shaped fronds, growing up to 17 in (42 cm) long. Fronds, which have lobed (auriculate) bases, arise in clusters from an underground rhizome. Petioles (leaf stalks) are covered with cinnamon-colored scales.

Habitat

This rare fern species is typically found in close association with outcrops of dolomitic limestone in soils that are high in magnesium. It requires cool temperatures, high humidity, moist soil, and the deep shade provided by a mature forest canopy or overhanging rock cliffs. In the southern portion of its range, where the climate would otherwise be too warm, it is found only in pit cave entrances, which are relatively cool and shaded.

Distribution

American hart's-tongue fern is found in small, very isolated populations in a range that extends from southern Ontario, Canada, south from the Great Lakes region to northern Alabama. This disjunct pattern of distribution implies that the fern was once more abundant under the cooler climatic conditions that prevailed at the end of the last major glaciation.

Populations of this fern are known to exist in 21 locations in the United States—two in Alabama, one in Tennessee, six in Michigan, and 12 in New York. The species also grows in southern Ontario, Canada. It is most abundant in Canada, which supports the bulk of the known world population.

The Alabama populations are situated in Jackson and Morgan counties, both located in limestone sinkholes. The Jackson County site is managed as a satellite of the Wheeler National Wildlife Refuge, but the population there had dwindled by 1990 to four (in 1979, 20 plants had been observed at that site). The Morgan County population is healthier, but its numbers saw a similar decline over the same period, dropping from some 97 plants in 1981 to only 39 plants in 1990. That population is on privately owned land.

The single Tennessee population, in Marion County, Tennessee, on land leased by The Nature Conservancy, originally supported 200 plants, but by 1980, the site supported only 17 plants, and by 1991, the plant was nearly extirpated altogether, with only one or two individuals surviving.

Four populations, comprising fewer than 500 plants, are recognized by the Michigan Natural Features Inventory in that state, all in Mackinac County. Two population sites are owned by the Michigan Nature Association and have been described as healthy and vigorous. One population falls within the Hiawatha National Forest and is managed by the Forest Service. The fourth population is on privately owned land and currently receives no protection.

The New York Natural Heritage Program identifies nine populations in that state, all within a limited area of Madison and Onondago counties. One Madison County population of about 350 plants is found within a state park, while two others, totaling fewer than 100 plants, occur on private property. Two large populations, with a combined total of more than 2,500 plants, occur within a state park in Onondago County. Four smaller populations are found on private land nearby and are considered extremely vulnerable. Several historically known populations from this county were lost in the 1930s, primarily to quarrying.

Several vigorous and healthy Canadian populations are found in Bruce County, Ontario, while the four neighboring counties (Peel, Halton, Dufferin, and Simcoe) support smaller, peripheral colonies. Although abundant in Ontario when compared with U.S. populations, hart's-tongue fern remains an extremely rare plant in Canada.

Threats

Because of its occurrence in restricted localities in the United States and its minimal numbers, American hart's-tongue fern is threatened by any number of actions that disturb or alter its specialized habitat. Plants have been lost due to logging, quarrying, residential development, and recreational pursuits (hikers who leave trails and stumble into the habitat have accidentally trampled the plant). Canadian populations also are threatened by lumbering and quarrying, and by development of land for ski resorts or for country estates.

Insect infestations are another natural danger to the plant. A 1985 infestation of leaf miners destroyed the leaves on the trees above one of the Michigan population sites. The resulting loss of shade desiccated many of the ferns growing on the forest floor. Such insect infestations, which temporarily remove the leaves of the canopy or result in long-term damage to the trees found there, remain a potential threat to the species.

Conservation and Recovery

The 1993 recovery plan for the American hart's-tongue fern states that the recovery goal is delisting, which will be considered when there are at least 15 self-sustaining populations in the United States that are protected to such a degree that the species no longer qualifies for protection under the Endangered Species Act. The plan calls for a number of actions, including the protection of known populations; the completion of needed biological studies; and the implementation of habitat management (if needed); the protection of genetic material and the re-establishment of populations (if necessary). The plan also calls for enforcement as well as the development of educational programs and the monitoring of the recovery process. The plan projected a recovery date of 1999, assuming the availability of funds for needed recovery activities.

Contacts

U. S. Fish and Wildlife Service
Regional Office of Endangered Species
Federal Building
Ft. Snelling
Twin Cities, Minnesota 55111
http://midwest.fws.gov/

U. S. Fish and Wildlife Service
Regional Office of Endangered Species
1875 Century Blvd., Suite 200
Atlanta, Georgia 30345
http://southeast.fws.gov/

U. S. Fish and Wildlife Service
Regional Office of Endangered Species
300 Westgate Center Dr.
Hadley, Massachusetts 01035
http://northeast.fws.gov/

References

Cinquemani, D. M., et al. 1988. "Periodic Censuses of *Phyllitis scolopendrium* var. *americana* in Central New York State." *American Fern Journal* 78(2):37-43.

Lellinger, D. B. 1985. *A Field Manual of the Ferns and Fern-Allies of the United States and Canada*. Smithsonian Institution Press, Washington, D.C.

U.S. Fish and Wildlife Service. 1993. "American Hart's-tongue Fern Recovery Plan." U.S. Fish and Wildlife Service. Washington, D.C.

Asplenium-leaved Diellia

Diellia erecta

Status	Endangered
Listed	November 10, 1994
Family	Aspleniaceae (Spleenwort)
Description	Fern that grows in tufts of three to nine lance-shaped fronds; frond stalks are reddish-brown to black.
Habitat	*Diospyros sandwicensis* (lama) / 'ohi'a lowland mesic forest.
Threats	Habitat degradation by pigs, goats, and cattle; competition with alien plant species; stochastic extinction due to the small number of existing individuals.
Range	Hawaii

Description

Diellia erecta, a member of the spleenwort family, is a fern that grows in tufts of three to nine lance-shaped fronds (large divided leaves), each 8-28 in (20.3-71.1 cm) long. The fronds emerge from a 0.4-1-in-long (1-2.5-cm-long) rhizome covered with brown to dark gray scales. The frond stalks are reddish-brown to black, smooth and glossy, 0.8-8.3 in (2-21.1 cm) long, and have a few stiff scales at their bases. Each frond has 15-50 lance-shaped pinnae (leaflets) arranged oppositely along the midrib. The pinnae are usually 0.8-1.6 in (2-4.1 cm) long and 0.2-0.3 in (5.1-7.6 mm) wide. Ten to 20 sori (spore-filled clusters), which may be separate or fused, are borne on each margin of the pinna. Each sorus is covered by a protective membrane that falls short of the edge of the frond and runs parallel to the edge of each pinna. This species differs from other members of the genus in having brown or dark gray scales usually more than 0.8 in (2 cm) in length, fused or separate sori along both margins, shiny black midribs that have a hardened surface, and veins that do not usually encircle the sori.

D. erecta was described by William Dunlop Brackenridge in 1854 based on a specimen collected during the Wilkes Expedition 14 years earlier. Current authorities consider *D. erecta* to be a species with no subspecific designations.

Habitat

D. erecta is found in *Diospyros sandwicensis* (lama)/'ohi'a lowland mesic forests 700-5,200 ft (213.4-1,585 m) in elevation. Other associated plant species include *Dodonaea viscosa* ('a'ali'i), *Dryopteris unidentata*, *Pleomele auwahiensis* (halapepe), *Syzygium sandwicensis* ('ohi'a ha), and *Wikstroemia* sp. ('akia).

Distribution

D. erecta was known historically from the Kokee area on Kauai; the Koolau Mountains on Oahu; Kahuaawi Gulch, Puu Kolekole, Pukoo, Pelekunu Valley, and Kaunakakai Gulch on Molokai; Mahana Valley and Hauola Gulch on Lanai; scattered locations on Maui; and various locations on the Big Island of Hawaii.

The species is currently known from Molokai, Maui, and Hawaii, with a statewide total of six to seven populations that contained approximately 34-36 individuals in 1997.

Asplenium-leaved Diellia, photograph by Steve Perlman. Reproduced by permission.

Threats

The major threats to *D. erecta* are (1) habitat degradation by pigs, goats, and cattle; (2) competition with alien plant species; and (3) stochastic extinction due to the small number of existing individuals.

Feral pigs are a major threat on the island of Hawaii to populations of *D. erecta* in the regions of Manuka and Honomalino in the South Kona District, and their activities also threaten one population of this species on Molokai.

Goats threaten two populations of *D. erecta* in Halawa Valley and Puu Kolekole on Molokai. On both East and West Maui, populations of *D. erecta* continue to be threatened by habitat damage caused by grazing cattle.

D. erecta is not known to be unpalatable to cattle, deer, and goats; as such, predation is a probable threat to this plant at sites where these animals have been reported.

One population of *D. erecta* at Halawa Valley on Molokai has been damaged by Christmas berry. Christmas berry is spreading on East Maui in Iao Valley and on the south slope of Haleakala Volcano, proving in both places to be one of the primary alien plant threats to the populations of *D. erecta* there. On the island of Hawaii, Christmas berry continues to threaten at least two populations of this species in the regions of Manuka and Honomalino in the South Kona District.

Strawberry guava is beginning to invade the habitat of populations of *D. erecta* on East Maui and on Molokai. At least one Molokai population of *D. erecta* is being negatively affected by molasses grass. Molasses grass is spreading quickly throughout the dry regions of West Maui, threatening two populations of the species there.

Conservation and Recovery

Living Indigenous Forest Ecosystems, a community-based nonprofit corporation, manages conservation lands at Kahikinui Forest Reserve; in July 1997 it fenced a portion of the forest reserve that harbors a population of *D. erecta*. Follow-up monitoring will be conducted annually or biannually. It is expected that this action will enhance conservation of the *D. erecta* plants growing there.

A fence that was built in the 1980s protects the population of *D. erecta* in the Manawainui Plant Sanctuary. The Native Hawaiian Plant Society conducts periodic weeding at this site.

An unspecified number of spores are in storage at the National Tropical Botanical Gardens.

Contacts

U. S. Fish and Wildlife Service
Regional Office, Division of Endangered Species
Eastside Federal Complex
911 N. E. 11th Ave.
Portland, Oregon 97232-4181
Telephone: (503) 231-6121
http://pacific.fws.gov/

Pacific Remote Islands Ecological Services Field Office
300 Ala Moana Blvd., Room 3-122
P.O. Box 50088
Honolulu, Hawaii 96850
Telephone: (808) 541-1201
Fax: (808) 541-1216

Reference

U. S. Fish and Wildlife Service. 10 November 1994. "Endangered Status for 12 Plants from the Hawaiian Islands." *Federal Register* 59 (217): 56333-56351.

Diellia falcata

No Common Name

Status	Endangered
Listed	October 29, 1991
Family	Aspleniaceae (Spleenwort)
Description	Terrestrial fern with sickle-shaped or tri-angular leaflets.
Habitat	Dry lowland forest.
Threats	Feral animals, alien plant species, wildfires.
Range	Hawaii

Description

Diellia falcata is a terrestrial fern that grows from an underground stem (rhizome) 0.4-2 in (1-5.1 cm) long. The fronds are 8-40 in (20.3-101.3 cm) tall and have dark brown to pale tan stalks. There are 12-45 undivided leaflets (pinnae) on each side of the stem axis. The lower leaflets are rounded; farther up the frond they become larger and are sickle-shaped or triangular. The fruitdots or sori, which are the fern's spore-bearing bodies, appear as short lines on the underside of the leaflet margins. *D. falcata* hybridizes with *D. unisora*. It has been observed with fronds bearing sori year round. This species has also been known as *Schizoloma falcata*, *Lindsaea falcata*, and *D. erecta* var. *falcata*.

Habitat

D. falcata is a terrestrial fern that typically grows in deep shade or open understory in dryland forest at an elevation of 1,280-2,700 ft (390.1-823 m). Associated plants include aulu, lama, and alaa.

Distribution

D. falcata had historical occurrences on Oahu from Maxfini Gulch to Palehua Iki that spanned almost the entire length of the Waianae Mountains and from Kaipapau Valley to Aiea Gulch in the Koolau Mountains . This species remains in the Waianae Mountains on federal, state, and private land at locations ranging from Manini Gulch to Puu Hapapa, Makua Valley, and Makaha-Waianai Kai Ridge. The 22 known populations, found within an area of about 2 by 11 mi (3.2 by 17.7 km), contained an estimated 5,540-6,540 individuals in 1997. Fourteen populations each number between 40 and 2,000 individuals; however, the eight populations at Nanakuli-Lualualei Ridge, Makaleha Valley, Puu Kumakalii, Mohiakea Gulch, Pualii Gulch, Puu Kaiwi, Palikea Gulch, and Ekahanui Gulch each number fewer than ten individuals. Recent field observations indicate that this plant may be more locally common than previous records suggest.

Threats

The major threats to *D. falcata* are habitat degradation by feral goats, pigs, and cattle; competition from the alien plants Christmas berry, huehue haole, Koster's curse, molasses grass, strawberry guava, and *Blechnum occidentale*; and fire. The two-spotted leafhopper is also a potential threat.

Fire is a threat to *D. falcata* populations near the U. S. Army's Makua Military Reservation and Schofield Barracks. Within a 14-month period from 1989 to 1990, ten fires resulted from weapons practice on the reservation. In order to minimize damage from fires, the army constructed firebreaks between the target areas and the surrounding forest.

Diellia falcata, photograph by Robert J. Gustafson. Reproduced by permission.

Conservation and Recovery

The army adopted a fire management plan that includes realigning targets and establishing firebreaks at Makua Military Reservation, which may aid in protecting *D. falcata* from the threat of fire. Additionally, the army protected individuals in Kahanahaiki Gulch from pigs with a fenced enclosure.

Fencing and removal of feral pigs in the Pahole drainage was completed by the Division of Forestry and Wildlife in July 1997. Weeding of strawberry guava, Christmas berry, and Koster's curse continues into the twenty-first century in the surrounding areas. Individuals of this plant in the Palawai Gulch are protected from hoofed mammals by a fenced enclosure that the Nature Conservancy of Hawaii constructed in 1998.

Specific efforts should be made, wherever feasible, to immediately fence, weed, and otherwise protect the eight populations (cited in the Distribution section above) that have only a few remaining individuals. A commitment should be developed for long-term stewardship and conservation of these areas once they have been enclosed.

Contacts

U. S. Fish and Wildlife Service
Regional Office of Endangered Species
Eastside Federal Complex
911 N. E. 11th Ave.
Portland, Oregon 97232-4181
(503) 231-6121
http://pacific.fws.gov/

U. S. Fish and Wildlife Service
300 Ala Moana Blvd., Rm. 6307
P.O. Box 50167
Honolulu, Hawaii 96850

References

Cuddihy, L. W., and C. P. Stone. 1990. *Alteration of Native Hawaiian Vegetation: Effects of Humans, Their Activities and Introductions.* Cooperative National Park Resources Study Unit, University of Hawaii Press, Honolulu.

Culliney, J. L. 1988. *Islands in a Far Sea: Nature and Man in Hawaii.* Sierra Club Books, San Francisco.

Stone, C. P., and J. M. Scott, eds. 1985. *Hawaii's Terrestrial Ecosystems: Preservation and Management.* Cooperative National Park Resources Study Unit, University of Hawaii Press, Honolulu.

Wagner, W. L., D. R. Herbst, and S. H. Sohmer. 1990. *Manual of the Flowering Plants of Hawaii.* University of Hawaii Press and Bishop Museum Press, Honolulu.

Diellia pallida

No Common Name

Status	Endangered
Listed	February 25, 1994
Family	Aspleniaceae (Spleenwort)
Description	Tufts of three to four light green, lance-shaped dark purple to brownish grey fronds with short black hairs on the underside.
Habitat	Bare soil on steep, rocky dry slopes of lowland mesic forests.
Threats	Goats, pigs, deer, alien plants, fire, limited numbers.
Range	Hawaii

Diellia pallida, photograph. National Tropical Botanical Garden. Reproduced by permission.

Description

Diellia pallida is a plant in the spleenwort family that grows in tufts of three to four light green, lance-shaped fronds along with a few persistent dead ones. The midrib of the frond ranges from dark purple to brownish grey in color and has a dull sheen. Scales on the midrib are brown, grey or black, about 0.1 in (2.5 mm) long, and rather inconspicuous. The fronds, measuring 12-22 in (30-60 cm) in length and 2-5 in (5-12 cm) in width, have short black hairs on the underside. Each frond has approximately 20-40 pinnae (divisions or leaflets). The largest pinnae are in the middle section of the frond, while the lower section has triangular, somewhat reduced pinnae, with the lowermost pair of pinnae raised above the plane of the others. The groups of spore-producing bodies known as sori are encircled by a prominent vein and frequently fused along an extended line. This species differs from others of this endemic Hawaiian genus by the color and sheen of the midrib, the presence and color of scales on the midrib, and the frequent fusion of sori.

Habitat

Diellia pallida grows in bare soil on dry, rocky, and steep slopes of lowland mesic forests at elevations of 1,700-2,300 ft (520-700 m).

Distribution

Diella pallida was known historically from Halemanu on Kauai. This species, unobserved since 1949, was collected again in 1987 from Kuia Natural Area Reserve.

The three current populations of 23 total plants occur over a 3 by 7 mi (5 by 11 km) area of state-owned land at Mahanaloa Valley and Makaha Valley within Kuia National Area Reserve and Koaie Canyon; a count in 1994 found 10 and 12 individuals, respectively, in the first two locations and only one plant at Koaie Canyon. Eight of the plants in the Makaha Valley population were juveniles.

Threats

Competition with alien plants, especially lantana and Chinaberry, constitutes the major threat to this species. St. Augustine grass, basketgrass, and other fast-growing weeds degrade *D. pallida* habitat. Feral goats trample *D. pallida* individuals and cause soil erosion by their relentless browsing in and around the plants. Other threats include habitat degradation by mules and deer, fire, over-collecting for scientific purposes, and reduced reproductive vigor.

Conservation and Recovery

The only two known populations of the *Diella pallida* are on state land on Kauai, within the Kuia Natural Area Reserve and in Koaie Canyon. These populations must be strictly protected. They should be fenced to exclude introduced mammalian herbivores, particularly goats. The abundance of threatening non-native plants, especially lantana and Chinaberry, should be aggressively reduced in the habitat of the endangered fern. Its populations should be monitored, and research undertaken into its biology and habitat needs. Work should be undertaken on the propagation of *Diella pallida* in captivity, with the long-term goal of outplanting to supplement the perilously small wild population.

Contacts

U.S. Fish and Wildlife Service
Pacific Islands Ecoregion
300 Ala Moana Boulevard, Room 3-122
P.O. Box 50088
Honolulu, Hawaii, 96850.
Telephone: (808) 541-3441
Fax: (808) 541-3470

U. S. Fish and Wildlife Service
Regional Office, Division of Endangered Species
Eastside Federal Building
911 N. E. 11th Ave.
Portland, Oregon 97232-4181
Telephone: (503) 231-6121
http://pacific.fws.gov/

Reference

U.S. Fish and Wildlife Service. 25 February 1994. "Endangered and Threatened Wildlife and Plants; Determination of Endangered or Threatened Status for 24 Plants from the Island of Kauai, Hawaii." *Federal Register 59.*

Diellia unisora

No Common Name

Status	Endangered
Listed	June 27, 1994
Family	Aspleniaceae (Spleenwort)
Description	Earth-growing fern with black, shiny frond stalks.
Habitat	Deep shade or open understory in dryland forest.
Threats	Competition from alien plants; habitat destruction by people; fire; limited numbers.
Range	Hawaii

Diellia unisora, photograph by John Obata. Reproduced by permission.

Description

Diellia unisora, a member of the spleenwort family (Aspleniaceae), grows from a slender erect rhizome or underground stem 0.2-1.2 in (0.5-3 cm) tall that is covered with the bases of the leaf stalks and a few small black scales. Stalks of the fronds are black and shiny, and are 0.8-2 in (2-5 cm) long. The fronds are linear, 3-12 in (3-30 cm) tall by 0.2-1.2 in (0.5-3 cm) wide, with 20-35 pinnae (leaflets) per side, and gradually narrowing towards the apex. The pinnae are usually strongly asymmetrical, unequally triangular, with mostly entire (smooth) margins. There usually is a single marginal sorus (the spore-producing body) running along the upper margin of the underside of the pinna. This species is distinguished from others in the genus by a rhizome completely covered by the persisting bases of the leaf stalks and a few very small scales, by sori mostly confined to the upper pinna margins, and by delicate fonds gradually and symmetrically narrowing toward the apex.

Habitat

Diellia unisora is a terrestrial fern that typically grows in deep shade or open understory in dryland forest at an elevation of 1,750-2,500 ft (533-762 m).

Associated plant species include strawberry guava, Christmas berry, 'ohi'a, and a mixture of alien and native grasses, forbs, and shrubs.

Distribution

Diellia unisora was known historically on Oahu from steep, grassy, and rocky slopes on the western side of the Waianae Mountains. Four populations were extant in 1997; scattered over a distance of 2 mi (3.2 km) on state and private land in the southern Waianae Mountains, they contained approximately 700 individuals. The South Ekahanui Gulch occurrence had six plants, Palawai Gulch had 90, Palikea had four, and the Pualii-Napepeiauolelo Ridge had 600.

Threats

The major threats to *Diellia unisora* are competition from the alien plants Christmas berry, molasses grass, huehue haole, strawberry guava, and *Blechnum occidentale*; habitat degradation by feral pigs; potential plant damage from the two-spotted leafhopper, and a risk of extinction from naturally occurring events or reduced reproductive vigor due to the small number of remaining individuals.

Conservation and Recovery

The only three known populations of the *Diellia unisora* are on Lualualei Naval Reservation (Department of Defense) and on privately owned land. Both of these habitats must be protected. The privately owned habitat should be acquired and designated as an ecological reserve, or conservation easements negotiated. In addition, the critical habitat of the rare fern should be fenced to exclude mammalian herbivores, particularly goats. The abundance of threatening non-native plants, especially Christmas berry, huehue haole, and strawberry guava, should be aggressively reduced in the habitat of the endangered fern. Its populations should be monitored, and research undertaken into its biology and habitat needs. Work should be undertaken on the propagation of *Diella unisora* in captivity, with the long-term goal of out-planting to supplement the perilously small wild population.

Contact

U.S. Fish and Wildlife Service
Regional Office of Endangered Species
Eastside Federal Complex
911 N. E. 11th Ave.
Portland, Oregon 97232-4181
Telephone: (503) 231-6121
http://pacific.fws.gov/

Reference

U.S. Fish and Wildlife Service. 27 June 1994. "Endangered Status for Three Plants from the Waianae Mountains, Island of Oahu, HI." *Federal Register* 59: 32933-32939.

Elfin Tree Fern

Cyathea dryopteroides

Status	Endangered
Listed	June 16, 1987
Family	Cytheaceae (Fern)
Description	Dwarf tree fern with bipinnate fronds.
Habitat	Tropical, high altitude, dwarf forests.
Threats	Deforestation, road construction.
Range	Puerto Rico

Description

Tree ferns are a tropical species, typically formed of a woody, trunklike stem crowned with a number of large, divided fronds. Elfin tree fern, *Cyathea dryopteroides,* is a small or dwarf tree fern reaching 24 in (61 cm) in height and approximately 1 in (2.5 cm) in diameter. The fronds are bipinnate, nearly hairless, tapered at both ends, and reach 36 in (91.4 cm) in length and 10 in (25.4 cm) in width. The sori are located dorsally and are enclosed in a cup-shaped indusium.

Fertile fronds have frequently been observed on elfin tree fern at both known sites. The presence of healthy, vigorous plants in all stages of development suggests that successful reproduction and establishment occurs regularly.

Elfin tree fern has also been known as *Alsophila dryopteroides.*

Habitat

This tree fern grows at the highest elevations in Puerto Rico, where temperatures as low as 39.2°F (4°C) have been recorded. Vegetation in these areas is variously termed elfin, dwarf, or cloud forest, and is similar to that found in other tropical montane habitats. Elfin tree fern is generally a component of the ground cover beneath stands of sierra palm.

Distribution

The species is endemic to the Cordillera Central region of Puerto Rico. It is presently known from populations on two peaks that are 12 mi (19.3 km) apart—Monte Guilarte and Monte Jayuya. A 1987 census counted ten trees at Monte Guilarte and 60 trees at Monte Jayuya. Both sites are within the Commonwealth Forest System.

Threats

Habitat acreage has steadily declined over past decades because of deforestation and selective cutting. Logging leases on state lands have encouraged harvesting of mature forests, and replanting has changed the composition of the plant community to the detriment of native plants. In recent years, the increasing construction communications facilities and access roads on the highest peaks have disturbed montane forests. Although the Commonwealth of Puerto Rico owns Monte Guilarte and Monte Jayuya, both have been leased to communications companies. Recently, a large number of tree fern plants were destroyed when satellite dish and control facilities were built on Monte Jayuya.

Construction of a highway through the Toro Negro Forest destroyed a number of elfin tree ferns. Many remaining plants are close to the road and are damaged by maintenance work. Commercial collecting could also become a threat, as considerable unregulated trade in similar species already takes place. Because of this possibility, the U. S. Fish and Wildlife Service declined to designate critical habitat for the species, since that would require publishing detailed location maps.

The small and limited populations limit the gene pool and the genetic viability for reproduction, and encourage stochastic extirpation.

Elfin tree fern is an attractive plant and may have ornamental value. Considerable commercial trade in ferns currently exists, and collecting may be a threat or potential threat to this species.

Conservation and Recovery

Although the Commonwealth of Puerto Rico has adopted a regulation that recognizes and provides protection for rare plants, elfin tree fern is not yet on the Puerto Rico list. It is, however, listed in the Convention on International Trade in Endangered Species of Wild Fauna and Flora (CITES) as a species to be monitored.

The elfin tree fern's federal listing as an endangered species will protect the plant from the disruptive actions of federal agencies. This is expected to restrict federal funding for additional highway construction and to limit army maneuvers that are regularly conducted in the area.

Contact

U.S. Fish and Wildlife Service
Regional Office, Division of Endangered Species
1875 Century Blvd., Suite 200
Atlanta, Georgia 30345
http://southeast.fws.gov

References

Howard, R. A. 1968. "The Ecology of an Elfin Forest in Puerto Rico." *Journal of Arnold Arboretum*, no. 49: 381-418.

Proctor, G. R. 1986. *Ferns of Puerto Rico and the Virgin Islands.* New York Botanical Garden, New York.

Pauoa

Ctenitis squamigera

Status	Endangered
Listed	September 26, 1994
Family	Dryopteridaceae (Wood fern)
Description	Dense covering of tan-colored scales on its fronds.
Habitat	Forest understory at elevations of 1,250-3,000 ft (381-914 m).
Threats	Habitat degradation by feral pigs, goats, and axis deer; competition with alien plants.
Range	Hawaii

Description

The pauoa, *Ctenitis squamigera*, a member of the wood fern family (Dryopteridaceae), has a rhizome 0.2-0.4 in (1-2 cm) thick. This horizontal stem creeps above the ground and is densely covered with scales similar to those on the lower part of the leaf stalk. The leaf stalks are 8-24 in (20.3-50.8 cm) long and densely clothed with tan-colored scales up to 0.7 in (1.8 cm) long and 0.04 in (0.1 cm) wide. The leafy part of the frond is deltoid to ovate-oblong, dark green, thin, and twice-pinnate to thrice pinnatifid (leaflet sections). The sori, tan-colored when mature, are in a single row one-third of the distance from the margin to the midrib of the ultimate segments. The indusium is whitish before wrinkling, thin, suborbicular with a narrow sinus extending about half way, and glabrous except for a circular margin that is ciliolate with simple several-celled glandular and nonglandular hairs arising directly from the margin or from the deltoid base.

C. squamigera can be readily distinguished from other Hawaiian species of *Ctenitis* by the dense covering of tan-colored scales on its fronds.

Habitat

This species is found in the forest understory at elevations of 1,250-3,000 ft (381-914.4 m), in *Ohial*

Diospyros (lama) mesic forest and diverse mesic forest. Associated native plants include *Myrsine* (kolea), *Psychotria* (kopiko), and *Xylosma hawaiiense* (maua).

Distribution

C. squamigera had historical occurrences from above Waimea on Kauai; Kaluanui, southeast of Kahana Bay, Pauoa, Nuuanu, Niu, and Wailupe in the Koolau Mountains of Oahu; Mt. Kaala Natural Area Reserve and Schofield Barracks in the Waianae Mountains of Oahu; at Kalnaaha Valley on Molokai; in the mountains near Koele on Lanai; in the Honokohau Drainage on West Maui; at Manawainui Stream on East Maui; and at "Kalua" on the island of Hawaii. The ten populations that have been observed within the last 20 years occur on Oahu in the Waianae Mountains, Lanai, East and West Maui, and Molokai. The Waianae Mountain populations are in Makaleha Valley, Kaawa Gulch, Maku Valley, and Waianae Kai Forest Reserve. *C. squamigera* occurs on Lanai in the Waiapaa-Kapohaku area on the leeward side of the island and at Lopa Gulch and Waiopa Gulch on the windward side. The West Maui populations are in Iao Valley and Kapunakea Preserve. The Molokai population is in Wawaia Gulch. The ten populations on Federal, state, and private land totaled approximately 100 individuals in 1995.

Pauao, photograph by Steve Perlman. Reproduced by permission.

Threats

The primary threats to *C. squamigera* are habitat degradation by feral pigs, goats, and axis deer; competition with alien plants, especially strawberry guava and Christmas berry; fire; and stochastic extinction due to the small number of existing populations and individuals. Habitat degradation caused by axis deer is now considered a major threat to the forests of Lanai. All three of the Lanai populations of *C. squamigera* are negatively affected to some extent by axis deer.

Conservation and Recovery

The U. S. Army has prepared Endangered Species Management Plans for training areas on the island of Oahu, highlighting specific threats to endangered plants and recommending actions to promote recovery.

On Lanai, building exclosures around some of the most intact portions of native forest in conjunc-

tion with hunting would provide good protection for endangered species, including *C. squamigera*.

Oahu populations of *C. squamigera* would benefit from the proposed expansion of the Mt. Kaala Natural Area Reserve to include Waianae-Kai Forest Reserve and Makaleha Valley Forest Reserve.

Contact

U.S. Fish and Wildlife Service
Regional Office, Division of Endangered Species
Eastside Federal Complex
911 N.E. 11th Ave.
Portland, Oregon 97232-4181
(503) 231-6121
http://pacific.fws.gov/

Reference

U.S. Fish and Wildlife Service. 1998. "Recovery Plan for Four Species of Hawaiian Ferns." U.S. Fish and Wildlife Service, Portland, Oregon. 78 pp.

Diplazium molokaiense

No Common Name

Status	Endangered
Listed	September 26, 1994
Family	Dryopteridaceae (Wood fern)
Description	Leaf stalks are 6-8 in (15-20 cm) long and green or straw-colored.
Habitat	Lowland to montane habitat at 2,800-5,500 ft (853-1,676 m).
Threats	Habitat degradation by feral goats, cattle, and pigs; competition with alien plants; and stochastic (random) extinction.
Range	Hawaii

Diplazium molokaiense, photograph by Ken Wood. Reproduced by permission.

Description

Diplazium molokaiense, a member of the wood fern family (Dryopteridaceae), has a short prostrate rhizome. The green or straw-colored leaf stalks are 6-8 in (15.2-20.3 cm) long. The thin-textured and ovate-oblong frond is 6-20 in (15.2-50.8 cm) long, 4-6 in (10.2-15.2 cm) wide, truncate at the base, and pinnate with a pinnatifid apex. The sori are 0.3-0.5 in (0.8-1.3 cm) long and lie alongside the side veins of the pinnae. *D. molokaiense* can be distinguished from other species of *Diplazium* in the Hawaiian Islands by venation pattern, the length and arrangement of the sori, frond shape, and the degree of dissection of the frond.

Habitat

Recently known populations of *D. molokaiense* were observed at elevations between 2,800 and 5,500 ft (853.4 and 1,676.4 m) in lowland to montane habitat, including montane mesic 'Ohi'a/Koa forest.

Distribution

D. molokaiense was found historically at Kaholu-amano on Kauai; Makaleha and Schofield Barracks on Oahu; Kalae, Kaluaaha, Mapulehu, and the Wailau Trail on Molokai; Mahana Valley and Kaiholena on Lanai; Ainahou Valley and Maliko Gulch on East Maui; and Wailuku Valley and Waikapu on West Maui. However, during the last two decades of the twentieth century, only one population of one individual was recorded; occuring on East Maui at Waiopai Gulch on Department of Hawaiian Home Lands property. A population of ferns on the Makawao side of East Maui may belong to this species, but the population's identity needs to be confirmed.

Threats

The primary threats to *D. molokaiense* are habitat degradation by feral goats, cattle, and pigs; competition with alien plants; and stochastic extinction. On Maui, large populations of feral goats persist on the south slope of Haleakala outside of Haleakala National Park, where they threaten the population of *D. molokaiense* at Waiopai. The habitat of this fern has been reduced to small remnants of its former territory by goat activities. Cattle ranching was once the primary economic activity on the west and southwest slopes of East Maui, where the population of *D. molokaiense* can be found. Although this area is no longer actively ranched, feral cattle threaten this species. Axis deer are also moving into the area.

Conservation and Recovery

The Living Indigenous Forest Ecosystems organization is working to restore the native vegetation of Kahikinui Forest and at the turn of the twenty-first century began fencing a portion of the forest reserve. Although the Waiopai Gulch population of *D. molokaiense* is not within the section of forest being fenced, forest management work in the area should benefit the habitat of this fern. The priority recovery actions for this plant are fencing and removal of hoofed mammals from its habitat, control of competing alien plant species, cultivated propagation, and protection and enhancement of the wild population. Surveys are also needed to locate new populations of this fern and determine the status of occurrences that have not been seen since the late 1970s. The exclosure built by Living Indigenous Forest Ecosysems at Kahikinui Forest might be a good location for establishing new populations of *D. molokaiense*.

Contact

U. S. Fish and Wildlife Service
Regional Office of Endangered Species
Eastside Federal Complex
911 N. E. 11th Ave.
Portland, Oregon 97232-4181
(503) 231-6121
http://pacific.fws.gov/

Reference

U. S. Fish and Wildlife Service. 1998. "Recovery Plan for Four Species of Hawaiian Ferns." U. S. Fish and Wildlife Service, Portland, Oregon.

Aleutian Shield Fern

Polystichum aleuticum

Aleutian Shield-fern, photograph by Gerald F. Tande. U. S. Fish and Wildlife Service. Reproduced by permission.

Status	Endangered
Listed	February 17, 1988
Family	Dryopteridaceae (Wood fern)
Description	Low-growing, tufted fern.
Habitat	Rock outcrops on treeless, alpine talus slopes.
Threats	Extremely limited numbers, grazing animals.
Range	Alaska

Description

Aleutian shield fern, *Polystichum aleuticum*, perhaps the rarest fern in North America, is a low-growing, tufted fern, only about 6 in (15 cm) tall. It sprouts from a stout, dark brown rhizome covered with brown scales and numerous chestnut-brown stubs of former frond bases. The fronds are featherlike (simple pinnate) with spiny-toothed segments (pinnae) and distinctive chestnut-brown stalks (stipes). It is readily distinguishable from all other ferns in the Aleutian Islands and has no close relatives in either North America or northern Asia.

Habitat

The surviving population of Aleutian shield fern grows on a north-facing rock outcrop at an elevation of 1,936 ft (590 m). The alpine talus slopes of the site are treeless and covered with hardy, low-growing herbs and prostrate shrubs.

Distribution

Aleutian shield fern was first collected in 1932 from Atka Island. The two documented populations in the Aleutian Islands provide insufficient information to project an historic range for the species. It is possible that the fern is a relict species that was more prominent thousands of years ago when the Aleutians formed a land bridge between Asia and North America.

Today, the Aleutian shield fern is known from Atka and Adak Islands, two islands of the Andreanof island group in the Aleutians. Surveys so far have failed to relocate the Atka population first described in 1932.

In 1975, botanist D. K. Smith discovered a population of 15 plants on Mt. Reed, Adak Island, about 100 mi (160 km) west of Atka. When Smith revisited the site in 1987, he found only seven plants. The 1992 Recovery Plan, from the U.S. Fish and Wildlife

Service (FWS), noted population numbers of approximately 112 individuals, all on Adak Island. According to a 1989 survey, the majority of the plants (98) are within a 6,400 ft (600 m) area on the northeast arm of the mountain, with the remaining 14 plants growing in a 400 ft (40 m) area to the north.

Threats

Although the fern has long been extremely rare, grazing reindeer and caribou have taken a toll of plant life in the area and have probably cropped back the fern as well. The alpine habitat is also very unstable, suffering from wind erosion and soil movements caused by freezing and thawing. These ground events can kill plants by pushing roots out of the soil.

Conservation and Recovery

The Mt. Reed site on Adak Island lies partially within the Adak Naval Air Station and partially within the Alaska Maritime National Wildlife Refuge. The Navy has cooperated fully with the FWS's efforts to locate and conserve the plant. Atka Island is owned in part by the Atxam Native Corporation; another section is administered as a national wildlife refuge.

The listing proposal suggested several immediate steps to save the fern. These include surveying for additional plants, fencing as protection from grazing animals, and cultivating a nursery stock for reintroduction efforts. Botanists have distributed a drawing and description to Naval personnel and other interested parties to aid the search for additional plants. Recovery of the Aleutian shield fern will depend much on finding new and viable populations.

Propagation efforts are at last paying off. In 1990, researchers at the University of Alaska in Fairbanks were successfully produced the first sporophyte (i.e., the spore-producing phase of a plant) of the Aleutian shield fern. Two previous attempts to propagate the plant in vitro were unsuccessful.

The 1992 Recovery Plan noted that, pending additional information, downlisting could be considered only with the discovery of significant new populations. Other downlisting criteria include the maintenance of a greenhouse population of at least 1,000 mature sporophytes, and the storage of genetic material in a germplasm repository. The extant population must also be protected from disturbance by humans and introduced ungulate. To achieve the downlisting goal, the recovery plan recommends the population protection and habitat management; biological research of the species; and searches for additional populations.

Recovery efforts in the summer of 1995 involved the collection of fronds from wild populations for cultivation by the New York Botanical Garden and the Royal Botanical Garden (Kew) Gardens in Kew, England. Spores were also supplied to the Cincinnati Zoo Plant Conservation Program, where they will be deposited into a permanent germplasm repository.

Reclassification of the species to Threatened status may be appropriate if significant new wild populations are discovered, but it is unlikely that this rare endemic could be delisted in the foreseeable future.

Contact

Regional Office of Endangered Species
U.S. Fish and Wildlife Service
1011 E. Tudor Rd.
Anchorage, Alaska 99503
http://alaska.fws.gov/

References

Christensen, C. 1938. "On *Polystichum aleuticum* C. Chr., a New North American Species." *American Fern Journal* 28:111-112.

Smith, D., 1987. "*Polystichum aleuticum* Chr. on Adak Island, Alaska, a Second Locality for the Species." *American Fern Journal* 75:2

U.S. Fish and Wildlife Service. 1992. "Aleutian Shield Fern Recovery Plan." U.S. Fish and Wildlife Service, Anchorage.

Polystichum calderonense

No Common Name

Status	Endangered
Listed	June 9, 1993
Family	Dryopteridaceae (Wood fern)
Description	Evergreen terrestrial fern with a curved-ascending rhizome; shining black scales; and erect, spreading fronds.
Habitat	Moist, shaded, noncalcareous ledges on mountain tops.
Threats	Indiscriminate cutting, fires, collecting.
Range	Puerto Rico

Description

Polystichum calderonense is an evergreen terrestrial fern. It has a curved-ascending, 0.3 in (7 mm) thick rhizome that is clothed at the apex with lanceolate to oblong, curved, shining black, marginate scales up to 0.4 in (10 mm) long. Its fronds are erect to spreading and may reach 23.5 in (60 cm) in length. The twice-pinnate blades are lanceolate, 10-15.5 in (25-40 cm) long, 2.5-5.5 in (6-14 cm) wide, and narrowed and truncate at the apex. Blades terminate in a scaly proliferous bud that is somewhat narrowed toward the base. This species has 30-36 pairs of oblique, short-stalked pinnae. It has a characteristic 1.5-2.8 in (4-7 cm) long and 0.4-0.5 in (0.9-1.3 cm) wide middle pinnae, with eight to ten pairs of free pinnules. The tissue is dark green, rigid, and opaque. One to five sori are found dorsally on the veins of each pinnule, but are not clearly arranged in rows. The sori are covered by a light brown, deciduous, thin indusium.

Habitat

The plants grow on moist, shaded, noncalcareous ledges on mountain tops at elevations of 3,280-3,770 ft (1,000-1,150 m).

Distribution

P. calderonense was described in 1985 from specimens collected from the summit of La Silla de Calderon, Monte Guilarte Commonwealth Forest, in the municipality of Adjuntas, Puerto Rico. A second population was found in 1987 on Cerrote de Peñuelas, in the municipality of Peñuelas, Puerto Rico. Fifty-seven individual plants are known from the two localities: 45 (including juveniles) on La Silla de Calderon and 12 on Cerrote Peñuelas.

Threats

Both known populations of *P. calderonense* are vulnerable to indiscriminate cutting or fires. In Peñuelas, the plants are on private lands that may be affected by industrial or residential development Although *P. calderonense* occurs within the Guilarte Commonwealth Forest, this population may be affected by forest management practices.

Habitat modification, including indirect effects that alter the microclimatic conditions, may dramatically affect this species. These populations are vulnerable to damage caused by hurricanes.

Collecting for private collections could present a problem, especially after the publicity generated following this species' listing.

Conservation and Recovery

Research is needed to determine this species' life history and ecological requirements and to develop and refine propagation and transplant techniques.

Polystichum calderonense, photograph by Eugenio Santiago. Reproduced by permission.

Surveys are needed to determine if other populations exist and to locate potential transplant sites.

Contacts

U. S. Fish and Wildlife Service
Regional Office, Division of Endangered Species
1875 Century Blvd., Suite 200
Atlanta, Georgia 30345
http://southeast.fws.gov/

U. S. Fish and Wildlife Service
Boquerón Ecological Services Field Office
P. O. Box 491
Boquerón, Puerto Rico 00622-0491
Telephone: (787) 851-7297
Fax: (787) 851-7440

Reference

U. S. Fish and Wildlife Service. 9 June 1993. "Determination of Endangered or Threatened Status for Four Endemic Puerto Rican Ferns." *Federal Register* 58 (109): 32308-32311.

Tectaria estremerana

No Common Name

Status	Endangered
Listed	June 9, 1993
Family	Dryopteridaceae (Wood fern)
Description	Fern with a woody, erect rhizome that bears a dense tuft of erect, brown, glabrous, narrow scales and orange-brown stipes covered with pale jointed hairs.
Habitat	Moist shaded humus on and among limestone boulders on a wooded rocky hillside.
Threats	Limited population size and limited distribution.
Range	Puerto Rico

Tectaria estremerana, photograph by Susan Silander. Reproduced by permission.

Description

Tectaria estremerana has a woody, erect, 0.4-0.6 in (1.0-1.5 cm) thick rhizome. The rhizome's apex bears a dense tuft of erect, brown, glabrous, narrowly deltate-attenuate scales about 0.6 in (1.5 cm) long and 0.02-0.03 in (0.05-0.08 cm) wide at the base. This fern has several loosely fasciculate, 25.6-31.5 in (65-80 cm) long fronds. The light orange-brown stipes are shorter or nearly as long as the blades and are covered with pale jointed hairs. Scales up to 0.47 in (1.2 cm) long clothe the base. The blades are oblong-ovate, 13.8-16.1 in (35-41 cm) long, 7.9-9.8 in (20-25 cm) broad below the middle, and acuminate at the pinnatifid apex. The rachis, the costae, and the costules are softly puberulous with articulate hairs on both sides. This fern has three to four pairs of free pinnae, and has several distal divisions which are more or less adnate. The basal pair of pinnae is deltate-oblong, strongly unequilateral, 4.7-5.1 in (12-13 cm) long, coarsely lobate or subpinnatifid. The lobes are 0.3-0.5 in (0.9-1.3 cm) broad except for the larger basal basiocopic ones. Its tissue is firmly

herbaceous and glabrous, but the margins are ciliate. The sori are located nearer to the midvein than the margin of the pinna-lobes.

Habitat

This species is found in moist shaded humus on and among limestone boulders on a wooded rocky hillside at an elevation of 820.2-984.2 ft (250-300 m).

Distribution

T. estremerana was described in 1984 from specimens collected at Barrio Esperanza, Arecibo, in the vicinity of the Arecibo Radio Telescope. This fern is known only from this site, where a total of 23 individual plants were found.

Threats

The site of this population is about 656 ft (200 m) south of the Arecibo Radio Telescope, and any expansion or development of the facilities may adversely affect the habitat of this endemic fern.

Conservation and Recovery

The one known population of *T. estremerana* is located about 656 ft (200 m) south of the Arecibo Radio Telescope, and any expansion or development of the facilities may adversely affect the habitat of this endemic fern.

Habitat modification, including indirect effects that alter the microclimatic conditions, may dramatically affect this species. These populations are vulnerable to damage caused by hurricanes.

Collecting for private collections could present a problem, especially after the publicity generated following this species' listing.

Research is needed to determine this species' life history and ecological requirements and to develop and refine propagation and transplant techniques. Surveys are needed to determine if other populations exist and to locate potential transplant sites.

Contacts

U.S. Fish and Wildlife Service
Regional Office, Division of Endangered Species
1875 Century Blvd., Suite 200
Atlanta, Georgia 30345
http://southeast.fws.gov/

Caribbean Field Office
Ecological Services Field Office
P.O. Box 491
Boquerón, Puerto Rico 00622
Telephone: (809) 851-7297
Fax: (809) 851-7440

Reference

U.S. Fish and Wildlife Service. 9 June 1993. "Endangered and Threatened Wildlife and Plants; Determination of Endangered or Threatened Status for Four Endemic Puerto Rican Ferns." *Federal Register* 58 (109): 32308-32311.

Pendant Kihi Fern

Adenophorus periens

Status	Endangered
Listed	November 10, 1994
Family	Grammitidaceae (Grammitis)
Description	Small, pendant, epiphytic fern.
Habitat	'Ohi'a/hapu'u lowland wet forest.
Threats	Habitat degradation by pigs; competition with alien plant species; habitat destruction by fires.
Range	Hawaii

Pendant Kihi Fern, photograph. National Tropical Botanical Garden. Reproduced by permission.

Description

The pendant kihi fern (*Adenophorus periens*), a member of the grammitis family, is a small, pendant, epiphytic fern. The rhizome is covered with dark and stiff scales 0.8-1.6 in (2-4.1 cm) long. Its yellowish-green fronds are usually 4-16 in (10.2-40.6 cm) long and covered with hairs. The fronds have slightly hairy stalks less than 0.4 in (1 cm) long. Each frond is comprised of oblong or narrowly triangular pinnae (divisions or leaflets) 0.2-0.6 in (5.1-15.2 mm) long with margins that are smooth or toothed and lined with sparse hairs. The pinnae are situated perpendicular to the axis of the midrib, with each pinna twisted such that its upper surface faces upward. Groups of spore-producing bodies called sori, in this case round, usually develop in the central portion of the fertile frond, forming two regular rows on each pinna. This species differs from other species in this endemic Hawaiian genus by (1) having hairs along the pinna margins, (2) having pinnae at right angles to the midrib axis, (3) the different placement of the sori, and (4) the degree of dissection of each pinna.

A. periens was first collected by Captain Fredrick William Beechey in the 1820s or 1830s. It was not formally described until 1974, when L. Earl Bishop published the name *A. periens*. Prior to its description, the names *Polypodium adenophorus* and *A. pinnatifidus* had been erroneously applied to the species represented by Beechey's specimen.

The breeding system of *A. periens* is unknown, although very likely outbreeding is the predominant mode of reproduction. Spores are dispersed by wind, possibly by water, and perhaps on the feet of birds or insects. Spores lack a thick resistant coat, which may indicate their longevity is brief, probably measured in days at most. Due to the weak differences between the seasons, there seems to be no evidence of seasonality in growth or reproduction. *A. periens* appears to be susceptible to volcanic emissions and consequent acid precipitation.

Habitat

A. periens is found in 'ohi'a/hapu'u lowland wet forest at elevations of 1,540-4,140 ft (469.4-1,261.9 m). It is found in habitats of well-developed, closed canopy that provide deep shade and high humidity. Associated species include kanawao ke'oke'o, 'olapa, uluhe, 'ie'ie, and kopiko.

Distribution

A. periens was known historically from Halemanu on Kauai, the Koolau Mountains of Oahu, the summit of Lanai, Kula Pipeline on East Maui, and Hilo and Waimea on the island of Hawaii. The species is now known from several locations on three islands. On Kauai, one population occurs at the boundary of Hono O Na Pali Natural Area Reserve and Na Pali Coast State Park on state land, one occurs at Waioli on state land, and four are clustered on private land in the Wahiawa area over a distance of 0.8 sq mi (2.1 sq km). There is a single Molokai population of three plants on private land at Kamakou Preserve. On the Big Island of Hawaii, four populations are found at Olaa Tract, Kane Nui o Hamo Crater, Kahaualea Natural Area Reserve, and 1.5 mi (2.4 km) northwest of Puu Kauka on private, state, and federal land. The status of the population at Kane Nui o Hamo is uncertain due to recent volcanic eruptions and drought. The 13-18 extant populations totaled approximately 1,295-1,330 individuals in 1997, of which 79-83 were on

Kaui, six were on Molokai, and 1,215-1,241 were on Hawaii Island.

Threats

The primary threats to *A. periens* are (1) habitat degradation by pigs; (2) competition for light, space, nutrients, and water with alien plant species, among them strawberry guava, Koster's curse, yellow Himalayan raspberry, prickly Florida blackberry, and banana poke vine; and (3) habitat destruction by fires.

An *A. periens* population in Kahaualea Natural Area Reserve on the island of Hawaii is jeopardized by fire. Tephra fallout and lava flows from Kilauea Volcano have affected the Natural Area Reserve over the past several years. Wildfires ignited by volcanic activity have destroyed some of the reserve's mesic and wet forests. While 65,000-100,000 plants were reported from this area in 1988, no plants were found during a 1993 survey. These plants may have been killed by either sulphyr dioxide fumes from Puu Oo or by several periods of drought. Tephra fallout and noxious volcanic gasses have also caused extensive damage to surrounding native forests. Such catastrophic natural events threaten to destroy the region's largest population of *A. periens*.

Conservation and Recovery

Spores were collected in 1996 from an individual on Molokai for cultivated propagation at the University of Hawaii's Lyon Arboretum; however, germination was not successful. An unknown number of spores are in storage at the National Tropical Botanical Garden.

In order to reduce the risk of extirpation of populations of *A. periens* in volcanically active areas, a volcanic hazard contingency plan should be developed for these plants. During some future volcanic event it may be necessary to rescue these populations if habitat becomes threatened by fire, tephra fallout, or lava flows.

Contacts

U. S. Fish and Wildlife Service
Regional Office, Division of Endangered Species
Eastside Federal Complex
911 N.E. 11th Ave.
Portland, Oregon 97232-4181
Telephone: (503) 231-6121
http://pacific.fws.gov/

Pacific Remote Islands Ecological Services Field
Office
300 Ala Moana Blvd., Room 3-122
P.O. Box 50088
Honolulu, Hawaii 96850
Telephone: (808) 541-1201
Fax: (808) 541-1216

Reference

U.S. Fish and Wildlife Service. 10 November 1994.
"Endangered Status for 12 Plants from the
Hawaiian Islands." *Federal Register* 59 (217):
56333-56351.

Elaphoglossum serpens

No Common Name

Status	Endangered
Listed	June 9, 1993
Family	Lomariopsidaceae (Vine fern)
Description	Fern with a wide-creeping thick rhizome; apex and nodes have lustrous reddish-brown sales.
Habitat	Mossy trunks of trees found in a patch of a montane dwarf forest.
Threats	Construction of a communication facility; collecting; hurricanes.
Range	Puerto Rico

Description

Elaphoglossum serpens is an epiphytic fern with a wide-creeping, 0.06-0.08 in (1.5-2 mm) thick rhizome. The apex and nodes bear lustrous reddish-brown scales with ciliate margins that are lanceolate to attenuate and 0.12-0.16 in (3-4 mm) long. This species has only a few distant and erect fronds. Sterile fronds are 2.75-7.5 in (7-19 cm) long. The stipes, from 1.4 to 4.3 in (3.5 to 11 cm) in length, are usually as long or longer than the blades. The blades are ovate, 1.4-3.15 in (3.5-8 cm) long and 0.8-1.4 in (2-3.5 cm) broad, obtuse at the apex, and cuneate at the base. The veins are free, reaching the margins of the blades. The coriaceous tissue is opaque with only scattered scales on the abaxial side. The fertile fronds are 3.3-7 in (8.5-18 cm) long. In contrast to the sterile fronds, the stipes are about three times longer than the blades. The blades are lanceolate to elliptic-oblong with rounded or blunt apex, 1-1.8 in (2.5-4.5 cm) long and 0.4-0.6 in (1-1.5 cm) broad.

Habitat

At present, 22 plants are known from the summit area, all occurring on the mossy trunks of only six trees. These trees are found in a patch of a montane dwarf forest at an elevation of about 4,265 ft (1,300 m). This patch of forest is all that has survived the encroachment of telecommunication towers and was seriously damaged in 1989 by Hurricane Hugo.

Distribution

E. serpens was described in 1947 from specimens on tree trunks at Monte Jayuya, but the fern is now extirpated from this site due to construction of a communication facility. Specimans were found later on the summit of Cerro Punta. Most of these plants were also destroyed with the construction of telecommunications towers.

Threats

The construction of communications facilities at Monte Jayuya destroyed the only other known population of *E. serpens*. The encroachment of similar other facilities have threatened the population at Cerro Punta. This species is in serious danger of extinction.

The most important factor affecting *E. serpens* is its limited distribution. The patch of forest where *E. serpens* is found was seriously damaged in 1989 by Hurricane Hugo.

Conservation and Recovery

The type specimen's site locality was destroyed during the construction of a communication facility. A second population was found at a later date; most of these plants were also destroyed by the construction of telecommunications towers. Future maintenance activities or expansion of the facilities would likely jeopardize the rest of this population. The remainder of this population (22 plants) was seriously damaged in 1989 by Hurricane Hugo.

Collecting for private collections could present a problem, especially after the publicity generated following this species' listing. Research is needed to determine this species' life history and ecological requirements and to develop and refine propagation and transplant techniques. Surveys are needed to determine if other populations exist and to locate potential transplant sites.

Contacts

U. S. Fish and Wildlife Service
Regional Office, Division of Endangered Species
1875 Century Blvd., Suite 200
Atlanta, Georgia 30345
http://southeast.fws.gov/

Caribbean Field Office
Ecological Services Field Office
P.O. Box 491
Boquerón, Puerto Rico 00622
Telephone: (809) 851-7297
Fax: (809) 851-7440

Reference

U. S. Fish and Wildlife Service. 9 June 1993. "Endangered and Threatened Wildlife and Plants; Determination of Endangered Status for Four Endemic Puerto Rican Ferns." *Federal Register*, 58 (109): 32308-32311.

'Ihi'Ihi

Marsilea villosa

Status	Endangered
Listed	June 22, 1992
Family	Marsileaceae (Pepperwort)
Description	Semiaquatic to aquatic fern similar to a four-leaved clover.
Habitat	Ponds and areas which will support its semiaquatic/aquatic habit.
Threats	Habitat degradation and/or predation by wild, feral, or domestic animals.
Range	Hawaii

'Ihi'Ihi, photograph by Derral Herbst. Reproduced by permission.

Description

'Ihi'Ihi (*Marsilea villosa*), a semiaquatic to aquatic fern of the pepperwort family similar to a four-leaved clover, is 2-9.9 in (5-25.2 cm) in height. The plant has four leaflets at the tip of the stem, while the leaves are in pairs and bear a small, hard spore case on a short stalk at its base when fertile. All parts of this plant may be covered with a rust-colored pubescence.

Habitat

M. villosa is an aquatic to semiaquatic fern that grows in small shallow depressions on level or gently sloping terrain. It requires periodic flooding to complete its life cycle. The spore cases normally are produced as the habitat begins to dry up and do not ripen unless the plant is drought stressed. When sufficient water is present, the plant reproduces vegetatively with young plants being produced on creeping rhizomes. The fern's habitat is dynamic, and may shrink or swell from year to year depending upon rainfall and other factors.

Distribution

M. villosa was first collected in the Nuuanu Valley on Oahu and then later at Mokio and Moomomi on Molokai. The three remaining populations are at Koko Head and the Lualualei Naval Reservation on Oahu and near Laau on Molokai. The largest site is in the Lualualei Valley, where clumps of this plant are scattered among kiawe trees in an area of approximately 6 acres (2.4 hectares). The Koko Head population covers about 0.5 acres (0.2 hectares), but comprises the largest number of individual plants. The population on Molokai measures roughly 7 ft by 25 ft (2.1 m by 7.6 m).

Threats

The plant fauna of Oahu and Molokai, like all of the Hawaii Islands, has currently fallen vulnerable to habitat degradation and probable predation by wild, feral, and domestic goats, pigs, and cattle; competition for space, light, water, and nutrients by naturalized, exotic species; habitat loss due to fires; human recreational activities; and military exercises. The most immediate threats to *M. villosa* are competition from exotic vegetation, habitat degradation by off-road vehicles, and cattle. Off-road vehicles not only damage or destroy plants, but also disturb the soil, an action that promotes the invasion of competing exotic plant species.

Conservation and Recovery

The *M. villosa* population at Koko Head has been partially fenced through a management agreement between the city and county and the Nature Conservancy of Hawaii to prevent damage and habitat degradation by off-road vehicles.

Contact

U.S. Fish and Wildlife Service
Regional Office, Division of Endangered Species
Eastside Federal Complex
911 N.E. 11th Ave.
Portland, Oregon 97232-4181
(503) 231-6121
http://pacific.fws.gov/

Reference

U.S. Fish and Wildlife Service. 1996. "*Marsilea villosa* Recovery Plan." U.S. Fish and Wildlife Service, Portland, Oregon. 55 pp.

Thelypteris inabonensis

No Common Name

Status	Endangered
Listed	July 2, 1993
Family	Thelypteridaceae (Marsh fern)
Description	A ground fern.
Habitat	Montane tropical rainforest.
Threats	Habitat loss by forestry or hurricanes, and collecting for horticultural use.
Range	Puerto Rico

Thelypteris inabonensis, photograph by George Proctor. Reproduced by permission.

Description

Thelypteris inabonensis is a terrestrial fern with an erect, slender rhizome, about 0.2 in (0.5 cm) in diameter, covered at its apex with numerous dark, lustrous-brown, densely hairy scales. The fronds are erect, arching, and up to 24 in (60 cm) long. The blade is narrowly elliptic, and up to 21 in (55 cm) long. The blade consists of 25-30 pairs of pinnae (lobes of the frond), rounded at their apex, and with up to seven pairs of simple veins. The leaf tissue has many short, erect, acicular (needle-like) hairs and lacks glands. The sori (spore-bearing structures) are small, with a densely long-ciliate indusium (a covering tissue), and are located dorsally on the veins. The stipes (or stalks of the fronds) are 2-4 in (5-10 cm) long, covered with grayish, acicular hairs, and with numerous spreading scales similar to those of the rhizome. This species differs from all other Puerto Rican thelypterid ferns in having scales and acicular hairs on the rachis.

Habitat

T. inabonensis occurs in montane tropical rainforest, where it grows in deeply shaded conditions in a humus-rich forest floor. It grows in moist, mossy forest dominated by sierra palm (*Prestoea montana*). It occurs at elevations of 3,670-4,100 ft (1,120-1,250 m), near the summit of Cerro Rosa.

Distribution

T. inabonensis is a locally evolved (or endemic) species that is only known from two sites in Puerto Rico: in Toro Negro Commonwealth Forest in the municipality of Ponce, and near the summit of Cerro Rosa in the municipality of Ciales.

Threats

The total known population of the rare fern consists of only about 46 plants. The habitat in Toro

Negro Commonwealth Forest supports 34 plants, and that in Cerro Rosa 12 plants. *T. inabonensis* is a beautiful fern, and is potentially threatened by collecting for sale in the horticultural trade in rare plants. The plant is also potentially threatened by forest management activities. Because of its tiny population and restricted range, the fern is also extremely vulnerable to the devastation of its habitat by a hurricane.

Conservation and Recovery

The critical habitat of *T. inabonensis* is located within the Toro Negro Commonwealth Forest, which is managed by the Commonwealth Department of Natural Resources, Government of Puerto Rico. Apart from strict protection from any collection of specimens, the most important action needed to conserve the rare fern is to preserve its critical habitat. Provisions for its protection must be incorporated into the management plan for Toro Negro Commonwealth Forest. In addition, research should be conducted on its biology and habitat requirements, to provide knowledge for its management.

Contacts

U. S. Fish and Wildlife Service
Regional Office, Division of Endangered Species
1875 Century Blvd., Suite 200
Atlanta, Georgia 30345
http://southeast.fws.gov/

U. S. Fish and Wildlife Service
Boquerón Ecological Services Field Office
P. O. Box 491
Boquerón, Puerto Rico 00622-0491
Telephone: (787) 851-7297
Fax: (787) 851-7440

References

U. S. Fish and Wildlife Service. 2 July 1993. "Endangered and Threatened Wildlife and Plants: Determination of Endangered Status for Three Endemic Puerto Rican Ferns." *Federal Register* 58(126):35887-35891.

U. S. Fish and Wildlife Service. June, 1994. "U.S. Fish and Wildlife Service, Division of Endangered Species, Species Account: Three Endemic Puerto Rican Ferns." *U. S. Fish and Wildlife Service, Endangered Species Program.* (http://endangered.fws.gov/i/s/sas0f.html). (July 6, 2000).

Alabama Streak-sorus Fern

Thelypteris pilosa var. *alabamensis*

Status	Threatened
Listed	July 8, 1992
Family	Thelypteridaceae (Marsh fern)
Description	Small, evergreen fern with clustered fronds.
Habitat	Crevices or rough rock surfaces of Pottsville sandstone.
Threats	Road or dam construction, limited population.
Range	Alabama

Alabama Streak-sorus Fern, photograph by A. Murray Evans. Reproduced by permission.

Description

The Alabama streak-sorus fern is a small evergreen with linear-lanceolate fronds 4-8 in (10.2-20.3 cm) long. The fronds appear clustered, arising from short, slender rhizomes covered with reddish-brown scales. The stipe portion of the frond (petiole) is slender, erect to ascending, 0.4-1 in (1.-2.5 cm) long, and covered with long hairs. The blade is typically 1-4 in (2.5-10.2 cm) long, and divided once into many ovate to suborbicular leaf segments (pinnae). The sori (groups of spore-producing reproductive structures) occur on the underside of the blades and are linear in shape. This is the only southeastern species of *Thelypteris* which lacks indusia (a thin membrane covering the sori).

Habitat

The species takes root in crevices or on rough rock surfaces of Pottsville sandstone along the Black Warrior River in Alabama. Plants typically occur on "ceilings" of sandstone overhangs (rockhouses), on ledges beneath overhangs, and on exposed cliff faces. These bluffs and overhangs are usually directly above the stream; however, some are located a short distance away from the river. Locations vary in slope aspect and shade coverage, from completely shaded to partially sunny on exposed bluff faces. The sites are kept moist by natural water seepage over the sandstone from up-slope runoff. Water vapor from the stream increases the humidity for those sites directly above the water or nearby.

The species grows among various bryophytes and is often associated with climbing hydrangea (*Decumaria barbara*), *Thalictrum clavatum*, *Heuchera parviflora*, and the ferns *Osmunda cinnamonea*, *O. regailis*, and, most notably, the Appalachian bristle fern (*Trichomanes boschianum*).

Distribution

The species' known range is confined to an approximately 3.25 mi (5.2 km) stretch along the Black Warrior River in Winston County, Alabama. Past distribution is thought to have been in this same general area.

Presently in this area, 15 separate localities have been documented. All sites are within the boundaries of the Bankhead National Forest and the majority occur on U.S. Forest Service land. Several localities are on private inholdings.

Threats

The type locality, which is approximately 5 mi (8 km) downstream of extant populations, was destroyed in 1960. The cliffs where the plants grew were leveled when a new bridge was constructed. The area was subsequently flooded with the completion of Lewis Smith Dam several miles downstream. The impoundment inundated suitable habitat, and perhaps plants, upstream and downstream of the type locality. Currently, plants are located on both sides of a highway bridge upstream of the reservoir's influence. Plants may have been destroyed by this bridge construction. Future road or dam construction along the upper reaches of the river poses a potential threat to extant populations.

Logging of woodlands above the occupied sites could adversely affect the microhabitat needed by the species. The species is dependent on up-slope runoff and seepage to maintain the substrate moisture. Heavy timbering or clear-cutting could alter the area's hydrology by interrupting this natural seepage. Additionally, the loss of the canopy would increase ambient light and lower the humidity. Thus, timber removal would dehydrate the habitat and such could be detrimental to this species.

Overhangs or rockhouses are habitat for about 50% of the known populations. These areas are frequented by hikers, fishermen, and campers and are subject to vandalism. Two of the larger populations occur in rockhouses which are often used by humans, as evidenced by numerous footprints, abundant litter, and old campfires. Intentional or incidental damage caused by hikers and campers, in addition to the heat and smoke from campfires, threatens these populations.

Over-collecting for any purpose would adversely impact this species due to its rarity and the small number of individuals at several sites. The species' limited distribution makes it vulnerable to collectors and vandals.

No species-specific diseases or predators have been identified. However, disease or predation could have a serious adverse impact on the small and fragmented populations.

The greatest threat to this species is its extreme vulnerability due to its limited range and small number of plants at many of the sites. A single natural or anthropogenic disturbance could seriously reduce the population size and affect the species' viability. Catastrophic flooding through the narrow gorge could possibly scour all the occupied sites to such a degree that the size of the population would be significantly reduced. Sites near the water have few individuals (one to three plants), probably because of scouring from seasonal (as opposed to catastrophic) flooding. Severe drought would decrease the substrate moisture and be detrimental to this species. A local drought in 1990 appeared to kill individual plants at several localities.

As a natural erosional process, sandstone overhangs and bluffs periodically erode small and large sections. A site could be completely eliminated (including one with a large number of plants) if one such incident occurred.

Conservation and Recovery

Federal involvement is expected to include the Environmental Protection Agency in consideration of the Clean Water Act's provision for pesticides registration, and waste management actions. The U.S. Army Corps of Engineers will include this species in project planning and operation and during the permit review process. The Federal Highway Administration will consider impacts of bridge and road construction at points where known habitat is crossed. Urban development within the drainage basin may involve the Farmers Home Administration and their loan programs.

Contacts

Regional Office of Endangered Species
U.S. Fish and Wildlife Service
1875 Century Blvd., Suite 200
Atlanta, Georgia 30345
http://southeast.fws.gov/

Daphne Ecological Services Field Office
P. O. Box 1190
Daphne, Alabama 36526-1190
Phone: (334) 441-5181
Fax: (334) 441-6222

Reference

U.S. Fish and Wildlife Service. 8 July 1992 "Endangered and Threatened Wildlife and Plants; Threatened Status for the Plant *Thelypteris pilosa* var. *alabamensis* (Alabama Streak-sorus fern)." *Federal Register.* 57(131): 30164-30168.

Thelypteris verecunda

No Common Name

Status	Endangered
Listed	July 2, 1993
Family	Thelypteridaceae (Marsh fern)
Description	A ground fern.
Habitat	Moist, shaded limestone ledges in tropical forest.
Threats	Habitat loss by development or hurricanes, and collecting for horticultural use.
Range	Puerto Rico

Thelypteris verecunda, photograph by George Proctor. Reproduced by permission.

Description

Thelypteris verecunda is a terrestrial fern with creeping rhizomes, about 0.07-0.11 in (2-3 mm) thick. The apex of the rhizome bears brown scales, about 0.04 in (1 mm) long. The fronds are of two types (dimorphic), one of which produces spores, while the other functions only in photosynthesis. The fronds have numerous star-shaped (or stellate) hairs, and many much longer, simple hairs. The stipes (or stalks of the fronds) are 0.4-0.6 in (1.0-1.5 cm) long and 0.02 in (0.4-0.5 mm) thick. The sterile blades are 1.0-1.6 in (2.5-4.0 cm) long and 0.6-0.8 in

(1.5-2.0 cm) wide, and rounded at the broadly-lobed tip. The fertile (spore-bearing) fronds are 5-6 in (13-15 cm) long and 0.5-0.7 in (1.2-1.8 cm) wide, with 15 to 20 pairs of rounded-oblong to oval, non-dissected pinnae (or lobes). The spore-bearing structures (or sori) are small and erect, have a minute indusium (a covering tissue), and bear a tuft of long, white, simple hairs.

Habitat

T. verecunda is found at moist shaded limestone ledges at elevations of about 690 ft (200 m).

The broader ecosystem type is montane tropical rainforest.

Distribution

T. verecunda is a locally evolved (or endemic) species that is only known from three localities in Puerto Rico: Barrio Charcus in the municipality of Quebradillas, Barrio Bayaney in Hatillo, and Barrio Cidral in the municipality of San Sebastian.

Threats

The total known population of *T. verecunda* consists of only about 22 plants. The habitat in Barrio Bayaney consists on only about 20 plants, while those in Quebradillas and San Sebastian have only one known individual. All of the habitat of the rare fern is privately owned, and is therefore threatened by clearing and other disturbances. Because of its extreme rarity, this fern might also be an attractive item for illegal collecting for sale in the horticultural trade. Because of its tiny population and restricted range, the fern is also extremely vulnerable to the devastation of its habitat by a hurricane.

Conservation and Recovery

The critical habitat of *T. verecunda* is entirely located on private land. This habitat should be protected by acquisition and the establishment of ecological reserves, or by the negotiation of conservation easements. The rare fern must also be strictly protected from any collection of specimens. In addition, research should be conducted on its biology and habitat requirements, to provide knowledge for its management.

Contacts

U. S. Fish and Wildlife Service
Regional Office, Division of Endangered Species
1875 Century Blvd., Suite 200
Atlanta, Georgia 30345
http://southeast.fws.gov/

U. S. Fish and Wildlife Service
Boquerón Ecological Services Field Office
P.O. Box 491
Boquerón, Puerto Rico 00622-0491
Telephone: (787) 851-7297
Fax: (787) 851-7440

References

U. S. Fish and Wildlife Service. 2 July 1993. "Endangered and Threatened Wildlife and Plants: Determination of Endangered Status for Three Endemic Puerto Rican Ferns." *Federal Register* 58(126):35887-35891.

U. S. Fish and Wildlife Service. June 1994. "U. S. Fish and Wildlife Service, Division of Endangered Species, Species Account: Three Endemic Puerto Rican Ferns." *U. S. Fish and Wildlife Service, Endangered Species Program.* (http://endangered.fws.gov/i/s/sas0f.html). Date Accessed: July 6, 2000.

Thelypteris yaucoensis

No Common Name

Status	Endangered
Listed	July 2, 1993
Family	Thelypteridaceae (Marsh fern)
Description	A ground fern.
Habitat	Steep, shaded, rocky banks and ledges at high elevations in cloud forest.
Threats	Habitat loss by development or hurricanes, and collecting for horticultural use.
Range	Puerto Rico

Thelypteris yaucoensis, photograph by Eugenio Santiago. Reproduced by permission.

Description

Thelypteris yaucoensis is a terrestrial fern with erect rhizomes, 0.02 in (0.5 mm) thick, and covered at the apex with a tuft of brown, 0.2-0.3 in (5-8 mm) long scales. There are few fronds, which are 17-20 in (44-52 cm) long, and are lustrous, light-brown, hairless, and born on a stipe (stem) 7-9 in (18-22 cm) long. The blade of the frond is oblong, 10-13 in (25-31 cm) long, 4-6 in (10-14 cm) wide, and has 13-15 pairs of alternate pinnae (or lobes). The spore-producing structures (or sori) have minute forked and three-branched hairs, and have a small covering tissue (or indusium).

Habitat

T. yaucoensis is found in humid tropical cloud-forest on steep, shaded, rocky banks and ledges at high elevations (2,800-3,900 ft; 850-1,200 m).

Distribution

T. yaucoensis is a locally evolved (or endemic) species that is only known from three localities in Puerto Rico: from Barrio Rubias in the municipality of Yauco, Los Tres Picahos in Barrio Toro Negro in Ciales, and the summit area of Pico Rodadero, Barrio Sierra Alta in the municipality of Yauco.

Threats

The total known population of *T. yaucoensis* consists of only about 65 plants. All of the habitat of the rare fern is privately owned, and is therefore threatened by clearing and other disturbances. Because of its extreme rarity, this fern might be an attractive item for illegal collecting for sale in the horticultural trade. Due to its tiny population and restricted range, this fern is also extremely vulnerable to the devastation of its habitat by a hurricane.

Conservation and Recovery

The critical habitat of *T. yaucoensis* is entirely located on private land. This habitat should be protected by acquisition and the establishment of ecological reserves, or by the negotiation of conservation easements. The rare fern must also be strictly protected from any collection of specimens. In addition, research should be conducted on its biology and habitat requirements, to provide knowledge for its management.

Contacts

U. S. Fish and Wildlife Service
Regional Office, Division of Endangered Species
1875 Century Blvd., Suite 200
Atlanta, Georgia 30345
http://southeast.fws.gov/

U. S. Fish and Wildlife Service
Boquerón Ecological Services Field Office
P. O. Box 491
Boquerón, Puerto Rico 00622-0491
Telephone: (787) 851-7297
Fax: (787) 851-7440

References

U. S. Fish and Wildlife Service. 2 July 1993. "Endangered and Threatened Wildlife and Plants: Determination of Endangered Status for Three Endemic Puerto Rican Ferns." *Federal Register* 58(126):35887-35891.

U. S. Fish and Wildlife Service. 1994. "U. S. Fish and Wildlife Service, Division of Endangered Species, Species Accounts: Three Endemic Puerto Rican Ferns." *U. S. Fish and Wildlife Service Endangered Species Program.* (http://endangered.fws.gov/i/s/sas0f.html). Date Accessed: July 5, 2000.

Conifers

Santa Cruz Cypress

Cupressus abramsiana

Status	Endangered
Listed	January 8, 1987
Family	Cupressaceae (Cypress)
Description	Densely branched pyramid-shaped evergreen tree.
Habitat	Redwood and mixed evergreen forest with sandstone or granite soils.
Threats	Development, logging, suppression of fire.
Range	California

Description

Santa Cruz cypress, *Cupressus abramsiana*, is a densely branched evergreen tree, reaching a mature height of about 34 ft (10 m) and developing a compact, symmetrical pyramid shape. Mature trees have light green, scale-like foliage and fibrous, gray bark. Trees produce numerous, tiny female cones, no larger than a walnut, near the tips of growing branches. These cones, which are firmly attached to the branch, remain closed and retain their seeds until the tree or supporting branch dies, generally as a result of fire. The late-opening (serotinous) cones enable cypresses to drop abundant quantities of seed to the ground after a fire.

The species grows vigorously under favorable conditions for several decades; an 18-year old tree was estimated at 20 ft (6.1 m) in height, although many trees may grow much more slowly due to competition or poor soil conditions. The champion tree, cut down by vandals in 1983, was estimated to be 98 years old when killed. The tree is considered intermediate in size and other characteristics between Gowen (*C. goveniana*) and Sargent cypress (*C. sargentii*).

Habitat

Santa Cruz cypress has historically been located in patches within coastal chaparral and mixed evergreen forests on sandy or gravelly, well-drained soils. The habitat consists of thickets of low shrubs, called chaparral, within a larger context of redwood and mixed evergreens. Cypress groves are found in soils derived from Eocene or Lower Miocene sandstone. The Mediterranean climate consists of cool, wet winters; hot, dry summers; and little coastal fog. Habitat elevations range from 1,020 to 2,550 ft (300 to 750 m).

Periodically, wild fires burn across the habitat, a historic cycle that has shaped the reproductive strategy of Santa Cruz cypress. Because individual trees fail to sprout again from fire-charred trunks, the species depends upon seed stored in its cones for regeneration. If a grove burns too frequently trees fail to reach seed-bearing age; conversely, the prolonged absence of fire (200 years or more) allows other tree species to replace Santa Cruz cypress as stands die off from old-age.

Distribution

The Santa Cruz Cypress was first collected in 1881 on top of Ben Lomond Mountain within the Santa Cruz Mountains (Santa Cruz County), California. The species is endemic to Santa Cruz and San Mateo counties, California. The Santa Cruz cypress is restricted to five populations totaling approximately 5,100 individuals in Santa Cruz and San Mateo counties, California, including four small groves in Santa Cruz County and a single grove on Butano Ridge in San Mateo County. The Santa Cruz County groves are located mostly on private land near Bonny Doon, Eagle Rock, Braken Brae Creek, and

Santa Cruz Cypress, photograph by Brett Hall. Reproduced by permission.

between Majors and Laguna creeks. A significant portion of the Butano Ridge stand falls within Pescadero Creek County Park, which is under the jurisdiction of the San Mateo County Department of Parks and Recreation.

Threats

Groves of Santa Cruz cypress have been affected by past construction (Bracken Brae and Majors Creek), logging (Butano Ridge and Eagle Rock), vandalism, fire, and a proposed vineyard development (Bonny Doon). The largest tree at the Bonny Doon site was cut down in 1986.

Proposed oil and gas exploration threatens the northernmost Butano Ridge grove. Since the grove is on federal land managed by the Bureau of Land Management any drilling activities will be closely monitored to protect the trees.

Introduced exotic cypresses, such as Monterey (*C. macrocarpa*) and Arizona smooth cypress (*C. glabra*) have been cultivated on tree farms on Ben

Lomond Mountain and could easily hybridize with the native strands of *C. abramsiana*, threatening the genetic integrity of the species.

Conservation and Recovery

Limited protection of Santa Cruz cypress is provided by the state of California, which requires landowners, after being alerted that a state-listed plant grows on their property, to notify the state in advance of land-use changes to allow for salvaging the plant. The state also provides funding for research and land acquisition.

In 1997, a draft recovery plan was announced to provide a framework for the recovery of the Santa Cruz cypress so that protection by the Endangered Species Act is no longer necessary. To accomplish this objective, needed tasks include: protection from incompatible land uses (i.e., timber harvest, agriculture, developments, recreation), implementation of resource management plans that would manage for long-term viability of the populations (i.e.,

Brett Hall, California Native Plant Society

mimic natural fire regime, address genetic introgression, and control insect infestations), and further research into the biology of the species and the threats facing it.

Contact

U. S. Fish and Wildlife Service
Regional Office, Division of Endangered Species
Eastside Federal Complex
911 N.E. 11th Ave.
Portland, Oregon 97232-4181
(503) 231-6121
http://pacific.fws.gov/

References

Bartel, J. A., and M. D. Knudsen. 1982. "Status Review of the Santa Cruz Cypress." U.S. Fish and Wildlife Service, Sacramento.

Libby, J. 1979. "*Cupressus abramsiana* Goes to Court" *Fremontia* 7(3):15.

Young, P. G. 1977. "Rare Plant Status Report, *Cupressus abramsiana.*" C. B. Wolf. California Native Plant Society.

Gowen Cypress

Cupressus goveniana ssp. *goveniana*

Status	Threatened
Listed	August 12, 1998
Family	Cupressaceae (Cypress)
Description	A small coniferous tree or shrub with scale-like light green foliage.
Habitat	Coastal pine forest with poorly drained, acidic soil.
Threats	Habitat destruction by residential and commercial development, as well as habitat change by alien plants and fire suppression.
Range	California

Gowen Cypress, photograph by A. Hiss, CNPS. Reproduced by permission.

Description

Cupressus goveniana ssp. *goveniana* (Gowen cypress) is a small coniferous tree or shrub in the cypress (Cupressaceae) family. Most of the ten taxa in the genus *Cupressus* found in California currently have relatively small ranges. Of the three coastal cypresses, native stands of *C. macrocarpa* (Monterey cypress) and *C. goveniana* ssp. *goveniana* are both restricted to the Monterey Peninsula and Point Lobos in Monterey County. *C. goveniana* ssp. *goveniana* generally reaches a height between 17-23 ft (5-7 m) though Griffin noted one individual that was 33 ft (10 m) high at Huckleberry Hill. The sparsely branched tree forms a short, broad crown with a spread of 7-13 ft (2-4 m). The bark is smooth brown to gray, then becomes rough and fibrous on old trees. The scale-like foliage is a light rich green, with leaves 0.04-0.08 in (1-2 mm). The female cones are subglobose (nearly spherical), 0.4-0.5 in (1-1.3 cm) long, and produce 90-110 seeds. The cones, which typically mature in two years, remain closed for many years while attached to the tree. Seeds can be released upon mechanical removal from the tree or, more typically, upon death of the tree or supporting branch. *C. goveniana* ssp. *goveniana* is distinguished from its close relative *C. goveniana* ssp. *pigmaea* by its much taller stature, the lack of a long, whip-like terminal shoot, and light to yellow-green rather than dark dull green foliage. Gowen cypress is a closed-cone cypress, a member of a fire-adapted family that possesses cones which, after seed has matured, remain sealed and attached to the trees, typically until heat from fires breaks the cones' resinous seal and allows the once-hidden seeds to escape.

C. goveniana ssp. *goveniana* was first collected by Karl Hartweg from Huckleberry Hill on the Monterey Peninsula in 1846. The plant was described as *C. goveniana* by British horticulturalist George Gordon in 1849, who named it after fellow horticulturalist James R. Gowen. Sargent described the tree in 1896 as being widely distributed "from the plains of Mendocino County to the mountains of San Diego County," including taxa now recognized as distinct in his definition of *C. goveniana*. John G. Lemmon published the name *C. goveniana* var. *pigmaea* in 1895 to refer to the stands found on the "White Plains" of Mendocino County, also referred to as pygmy cypress or Mendocino cypress. As a result of this segregation, the material from the Monterey area would be treated as *C. goveniana* var. *goveniana*. The taxon is currently treated as *C. goveniana* ssp. *goveniana*.

Habitat

Gowen cypress is associated with Monterey Pine (*Pinus radiata*), *Pinus muricata*, and several taxa in the heath family (*Ericaceae*)—*Vaccinium, Gaultheria, Arctostaphylos*—on poorly drained and acidic soils. This taxon also needs adequate sunlight and bare mineral soils for seedling establishment; in areas with herbaceous cover seedling mortality is higher due to fungal infections.

Distribution

Only two natural stands of Gowen cypress are known to exist, although individuals can be found locally in cultivation. The largest stand, referred to here as the Del Monte Forest stand, is near Huckleberry Hill on the western side of the Monterey Peninsula. This stand covers approximately 100 acres (40 hectares), with individuals scattered within 0.6 mi (1 km) of the main stand. It was reported in 1948 that patches of crowded, poorly developed individuals, referred to as "canes," were cut for posts, making it difficult to determine the original extent of the grove. At least three fires have burned portions of the Del Monte Forest stand in the last 100 years. A large fire burned most of the stand in 1901. The northern portion of the stand apparently burned in 1959. The most recent fire burned the south central portion of the population in 1987. In each case, regeneration of Gowen cypress has occurred. The Del Monte Forest stand is on lands owned by the Pebble Beach Company and the Del Monte Forest Foundation (DMFF). Originally established as the Del Monte Foundation in 1961 by the Pebble Beach Company, its purpose is to acquire, accept, maintain, and manage lands in the Del Monte Forest which are dedicated to open space and greenbelt. A large portion of the Del Monte Forest stand is within a 84-acre (34-hectare) area designated as the Samuel F. B. Morse

Botanical Reserve in the 1960s and donated to DMFF in 1976. Development of the Poppy Hills Golf Course in the early 1980s removed 840 trees of Gowen cypress outside of the reserve and surrounded other small patches with fairways. The majority of the remaining portion of this stand is on lands owned by Pebble Beach Company that are designated as "forested open space" in the Huckleberry Hill Open Space area, through a conservation easement held by the DMFF. Scattered groups of trees that radiate out from this stand are located on Pebble Beach Company lands within their most recently proposed residential developmens. A second smaller stand of Gowen cypress 40-80 acres (16-32 hectares) in size occurs 6 mi (10 km) to the south at Point Lobos State Reserve near Gibson Creek on a 150-acre (60-hectare) parcel acquired by the California Department of Parks and Recreation (CDPR) in 1962. The very western edge of the stand is on lands recently purchased by the Big Sur Land Trust from a private owner. This parcel was to be transferred to the CDPR in 1997.

In this stand, Gowen cypress is associated with *Pinus radiata* and chaparral species. Due to the physical inaccessibility of the Point Lobos stand and the Reserve's mandate to protect sensitive plant taxa, the Point Lobos stand exhibits fewer signs of human disturbance than the Del Monte Forest stand.

Threats

Gowen cypress is considered threatened rather than endangered because one of two populations, the Gibson Creek stand managed by the California Department of Parks and Recreation, has not been significantly affected by human activities. This long-lived taxon also appears able to withstand several decades without fire as long as sufficient habitat is maintained. This species is threatened by habitat alteration due to the influence of continued urban development in Pebble Beach and to the disruption of natural fire cycles that are likely to result from fire suppression activities. In addition, stands of *C. goveniana* var. *goveniana* at both locations have been invaded by aggressive alien species, including *Cortaderia jubata* (pampasgrass), *Genista monspessulana* (French broom), and *Erechtites spp.* (fireweeds). Invasion of alien plants alters the composition of the plant community and may adversely affect Gowen cypress. Despite measures taken to protect the *Cupressus goveniana* ssp. *goveniana* stand at the Del Monte Forest, the opportunities for maintaining a viable long-term population of this taxon may be compromised by the site's proximity to urbanization. Gowen cypress is adapted to regenerate after fires. While some regeneration following mechanical clearing has occurred along a fire road, periodic fire is the most effective and efficient method of promoting forest regeneration. Fire opens cones that otherwise remain sealed on the trees, and it creates conditions appropriate for seedling establishment. The lands on which most of the cypress grows are included in the Morse Botanical Reserve and will not therefore be developed. Unfortunately, the periodic fires that create conditions necessary for regeneration of the grove, are less likely to occur as residential development encroaches on the Reserve and the Huckleberry Hill Open Space area. This residential development that is occurring on all sides of the stand impede the continuation of vital ecosystem processes, especially the periodic fires so essential for stand regeneration.

Prescribed burning has not been tried at the Pt. Lobos Ranch occurrence, in part due to the risks to surrounding privately owned lands.

Gowen cypress is restricted to only two sites in western Monterey County. The occurrence on the Monterey Peninsula is located in the Morse Botanical Reserve and the Huckleberry Hill Open Space area. As development has surrounded this location, the edges and outlying stands of this occurrence have been eliminated or diminished. For example, portions of this occurrence were lost during construction of the Poppy Hills golf course in the 1980s. Trees planted as mitigation for that loss and a small stand of naturally occurring *C. goveniana* ssp. *goveniana* and *Pinus muricata* were left in a 19.5-acre (8-hectare) habitat patch of Monterey pine forest and chaparral, bounded by golf green. As proposed for the most recent subdivision and development, this site would be converted to a 21-lot residential area, eliminating most of the naturally occurring cypress and leaving the remaining cypress in a portion of 7 acres (3 hectares) of Forested Open Space bounded by roads, a golf green and houses. At least three of the subdivisions proposed for development by the Pebble Beach Company are within 984 ft (300 m) of the Gowen cypress stands in the Morse Reserve, and one proposed residential development abuts the Reserve's southwest corner. The proximity of these residential areas substantially diminishes the opportunity

to use prescribed fire as a management tool within the reserve. In addition, due to concern about potential wildfire, 12-ft (4-m) wide fire roads have been maintained throughout the Reserve and Huckleberry Hill Open Space, removing individual *Cupressus* trees and causing erosion in some places. These fire roads provide a suitable path for alien plants to enter and spread through the stands. An extensive stand of *Genista monspessulana* has been mapped adjacent to the grove of Gowen cypress at Pt. Lobos Reserve, where it may interferes with stand regeneration in the future. The Pebble Beach Company has an on-going eradication program for *Cortaderia jubata* and *G. monspessulana* in the Huckleberry Hill area adjacent to stands of this taxon. However, numerous fire roads provide open habitat for these invasive taxa and it is unlikely that they will ever be completely eradicated from the area. There is some concern among biologists that the establishment of *Pinus radiata* seedlings after the 1987 fire has been so vigorous that this taxon may be expanding its range at the expense of *C. goveniana* ssp. *goveniana*. This view is by no means universally accepted. Other scientsists feel that this pine's preference for richer soils than those that support Gowen cypress would prevent long-term establishment of pines in Gowen cypress habitat.

Conservation and Recovery

One of the two natural habitats of the Gowen cypress, the Gibson Creek stand managed by the CDPR, has not been significantly affected by human activities and is being maintained in a natural condition. The Del Monte Forest stand is on lands owned by the private Pebble Beach Company and the DMFF, and is being managed as the Samuel F.B. Morse Botanical Reserve. However, trees outside of the designated reserve are threatened by development activities. In addition, the conserved habitat must be managed properly, particularly with regards to the fire regime and actions to control invasive non-native plants. The Gowen cypress is also grown in cultivation, although this does not diminish the importance of preserving the rare plant in its wild habitat. The populations of the Gowen cypress should be monitored, and research undertaken into its biology and habitat needs, with the aim of developing management practices appropriate to maintaining or enhancing its habitat.

Contacts

U.S. Fish and Wildlife Service
Ventura Fish and Wildlife Office
2493 Portola Road, Suite B
Ventura, California 93003-7726
Telephone: (805) 644-1766

U. S. Fish and Wildlife Service
Regional Office, Division of Endangered Species
Eastside Federal Building
911 N. E. 11th Ave.
Portland, Oregon 97232-4181
Telephone: (503) 231-6121
http://pacific.fws.gov/

Reference

U.S. Fish and Wildlife Service. 12 August 1998. "Endangered and Threatened Wildlife and Plants; Final Rule Listing Five Plants From Monterey County, CA, as Endangered or Threatened." *Federal Register* 63(155): 43100-43116.

Pinabete

Abies guatemalensis

Status	Threatened
Listed	November 8, 1979
Family	Pinaceae
Description	An evergreen, coniferous tree.
Habitat	Montane forest.
Threats	Excessive harvesting and habitat conversion.
Range	El Salvador, Guatemala, Honduras, Mexico

Description

The pinabete, also known as the Guatemalan fir, is a densely foliated conifer tree, with short, flat leaves and upright cones. The seeds are shed from October to January. Because of the high humidity of its habitat, its branches and bark are densely covered with epiphytic mosses and lichens.

Habitat

The pinabete occurs in humid cloud-forest at elevations above about 8,000 ft (2,440 m) in mountainous regions.

Distribution

The pinabete is a locally distributed (or endemic) species that only occurs in a relatively small area of El Salvador, Honduras, Guatemala, and southern Mexico.

Threats

The pinabete has suffered from excessive harvesting as a source of timber, charcoal, and firewood, and for commercial sale as Christmas trees.

The pinabete is a slow-growing tree, and its stands are easily depleted by excessive harvesting.

Conservation and Recovery

The pinabete is a protected species over much of its range, but the laws are not well-enforced and illegal harvesting still occurs. In some areas, local people value the pinabete extremely highly, because its intact forests are crucial in providing good supplies of clean water from mountain streams, and also for cultural reasons. Some villages have organized tree-guarding patrols, particularly around Christmas-time, to protect their pinabete stands from tree poachers. It occurs in several protected areas, including the Sierra Gorda Biosphere Reserve, Mexico, and Celaque National Park, Honduras.

Contact

Instituto Nacional de Ecología
Av. Revolución, 1425
Col. Campestre, C.P. 01040, Mexico, D.F.
http://www.ine.gob.mx/

Reference

Vidakovic, Mirko. 1991. *Conifers: Morphology & Variation*. Oxford University Press, Inc. New York.

Florida Torreya

Torreya taxifolia

Status	Endangered
Listed	January 23, 1984
Family	Taxaceae (Yew)
Description	Cone-shaped evergreen tree.
Habitat	River bluffs and ravines.
Threats	Residential development, fungal disease.
Range	Florida, Georgia

Description

Florida torreya, *Torreya taxifolia*, is a cone-shaped evergreen conifer that reaches a mature height of 59 ft (18 m). It has whorled branches and stiff needles that emit a pungent, resinous odor when crushed. One common name for this tree is stinking cedar. Dark green, fleshy seeds mature from midsummer to autumn. Pollen cones and ovules grow on separate trees, which reach sexual maturity after about 16 years. Wood from this species has been used in the past for fence posts, shingles, and firewood.

Habitat

Florida torreya is native to the bluffs and ravines of the Apalachicola River Valley. This diverse ecosystem is the only deep river system with headwaters in the southern Appalachian Mountains. When glaciers receded at the end of the last period of glaciation, the bluffs and ravines of this river system maintained cool moist conditions while the surrounding area became drier and warmer. Because of this unique and isolated environment, the torreya and other endemics have attracted the attention of scientists and local plant enthusiasts.

Distribution

Florida torreya was more widespread in the last glacial epoch when the cool, moist conditions in which it thrives were common. Today, it grows in the ravines along the eastern side of the Apalachi-

cola River from Lake Seminole in Georgia to Bristol in Liberty County, Florida. The single Georgia population, on the margins of Lake Seminole, consisted of 27 trees in 1981 and is entirely on public land administered by the U. S. Army Corps of Engineers. A single tree also exists in North Carolina, and is considered the largest and least disease-riddled of the species, perhaps because no other Florida torreyas are nearby.

Florida populations occur on state, city, and privately owned lands. Torreya State Park was established to protect Florida torreya and other endemic species. A city park in Chattahoochee also provides some protected habitat for this species. An isolated population occurs on the margin of Dog Pond which lies to the west of the Apalachicola River.

Threats

The most immediate threat facing Florida torreya is disease. The natural population has been drastically reduced since 1963 by a fungal disease that causes severe defoliation and necrosis of the needles and stems. Trees resprout from the roots but then die before reaching reproductive age. Recent application of fungicides has shown promise for stemming the disease, and cultivated, uninfected specimens from botanical gardens can provide seeds and material for future reintroduction. Extensive research is needed to control disease and develop disease-resistant populations.

Other threats appear momentarily to be in abeyance. In the past, housing developments de-

Florida Torreya, photograph. U. S. Fish and Wildlife Service. Reproduced by permission.

stroyed large tracts of torreya habitat, but the steepness of the bluffs and ravines precludes further development in the remaining habitat. Dams and reservoirs along the Apalachicola may have taken a toll of trees in the past. A water impoundment project planned near Blountstown, however, is not expected to harm the torreya.

Conservation and Recovery

In 1994, biologists from the North Carolina Arboretum and the U. S. Fish and Wildlife Service Asheville Office collected cuttings and a seedling from the largest surviving Florida torreya tree. This tree, planted on a North Carolina farm in the 1800s, is well outside the species' native range in the Florida panhandle and in Decatur County, Georgia. Though all of these wild populations have been decimated by a fungal disease, the North Carolina tree is one of the few remaining disease-free specimens. Although there are no other specimens within several hundred miles or kilometers, the North Carolina tree has produced

fertile seeds at least once, and seedlings are now growing around it. The seedling collected from this tree was planted in a disease-free environment on the Arboretum grounds. The cuttings will be rooted and cultivated at the Arboretum to preserve the tree's genetic material.

Contact

Regional Office of Endangered Species
U.S. Fish and Wildlife Service
1875 Century Blvd., Suite 200
Atlanta, Georgia 30345
http://southeast.fws.gov/

References

Alfieri, S. A., Jr., A. P. Martinez, and C. Wehlburg. 1967. "Stem and Needle Blight of Florida Torreya." *Proceedings of the Florida State Horticultural Society* 80:428-431.

Butler, W. 1981. "Status of the Florida Torreya in Georgia." Report. The Georgia Protected Plants/Natural Areas Program, Atlanta.

Godfrey, R. K., and H. Kurz. 1982. "The Florida Torreya Destined for Extinction." *Science* 138:900-901.

U. S. Fish and Wildlife Service. 1986. "Florida Torreya Recovery Plan." U.S. Fish and Wildlife Service, Atlanta.

Dicots

Cooley's Water-willow

Justicia cooleyi

B. Hansen

Status	Endangered
Listed	July 27, 1989
Family	Acanthaceae (Acanthus)
Description	Perennial herb with lipped, lavender-rose flowers.
Habitat	Moist sand to clay soils in hardwood forests.
Threats	Quarrying, agricultural and residential development.
Range	Florida

Description

Cooley's water-willow, *Justicia cooleyi*, is a rhizomatous perennial herb with upright stems that grow about 16 in (40 cm) tall. The lavender-rose flowers, which resemble small snapdragons, appear from August to December on forked, zigzag branches. The petals are fused into a two-lipped corolla. The slightly longer lower lip is mottled lavender and white; the upper lip is bright lavender-rose.

Habitat

The species grows in a single Florida county, where it is found on moist, sand to clay soils in hardwood forests (hammocks), often on limestone substrate. These forests include such trees as southern magnolia, black gum, sweet gum, live oak, pignut hickory, cabbage palm, and yaupon holly. The understory is mostly ferns, woodland grasses, and sedge.

Cooley's water-willow is only found on a portion of the Brooksville Ridge, an unusual region of the Florida peninsula noted for its extensive limestone outcrops and sinkholes. Surface streams are few, and most drainage is to ponds, prairies and sinkholes. Some of the other rare Florida endemics occurring there are the federally Endangered Brooksville bellflower (*Canpanula robinsiae*) and two terrestrial nodding-cap orchids (*Triphora latifolia* and *T. craigheadii*), which are candidates for federal listing.

Distribution

Cooley's water-willow was first collected in 1924 in a hardwood forest near Mascotte in Lake County. Until recently it was only found in Hernando County, Florida; one population was discovered in the early 1990s in Sumter County, Florida.

The species is known to survive at ten sites, nine in northern Hernando County and one in Sumter Count, Florida. Along with the Brooksville bellflower, it occurs on federal property at an Agriculture Department research station. Other populations on public lands include those at the Chinsegut

Nature Center, managed by the Florida Game and Fresh Water Fish Commission; along a state highway right-of-way; and at a Soil Conservation Service plant materials center. The Nature Conservancy also manages a preserve for Cooley's water-willow.

Threats

Nine of the ten known Cooley's water-willow populations are found in one of the fastest growing counties in the nation. From 1980 to 1986 Hernando County grew by 74.8%; the U.S. Census Bureau dubbed it the nation's fastest growing county. Figures from the 1990 Census confirmed that the trend continues; the proposed Suncoast Corridor toll road, part of a Tampa-Jacksonville corridor, would pass near Brooksville and encourage further population growth in the county. This rapid development has brought about greatly increased conversion of hardwood forest habitat to agricultural use, quarries, and residential housing.

Conservation and Recovery

A number of the known populations of Cooley's water-willow are on protected federal and state lands. The agricultural research station, which conducts beef cattle research, has not harmed the plant with its pasture management. The U. S. Fish and Wildlife Service (FWS) will continue to monitor the station's pasture management and consult on any proposal to clear additional forest.

Managers of all state and federal land with Cooley's water-willow populations have been notified of its presence. In addition, The Nature Conservancy operates a private landholder notification program for this and other rare Florida plants.

The 1994 recovery plan from the FWS, which describes necessary efforts to restore both the Cooley's water-willow and the Brooksville Bellflower, notes that the primary objective for the plan is the eventual delisting of both species. The plan notes, however, that there is a fundamental lack of basic biological (i.e., distributional, ecological, reproductive, and systemic) knowledge about these species, which makes it difficult to set criteria to determine the time-frame or ultimate likelihood of delisting. Still, the plan states that delisting of both species

should become feasible as habitat is protected and new populations are (re)established.

According to the 1994 plan, plausible criteria for recovery might include securing at least 15 viable and self-sustaining populations of Cooley's water-willow, totaling at least 10,000 individuals. The major recovery actions outlined in the plan include the development of management and protection criteria for populations on current managed areas; the acquisition of additional habitat, or protection of habitat through conservation easements and/or regulation; the completion of additional surveys to locate new populations; the augmentation of existing cultivated populations, including the establishment of a germ plasm bank; and the development of plans for possible (re)introduction of plants into sustainable habitat.

Contact

Regional Office of Endangered Species
U.S. Fish and Wildlife Service
1875 Century Blvd., Suite 200
Atlanta, Georgia 30345
http://southeast.fws.gov/

References

Monachino, J. and E. E. Leonard. 1959. "A New Species of *Justicia* from Florida." *Rhodora* 61:183-187.

Muller, J. W., *et al.* In Press. "Summary Report on the Vascular Plants, Animals, and Natural Communities Endemic to Florida." Technical Report. Florida Game and Fresh Water Fish Commission, Tallahassee.

U.S. Fish and Wildlife Service. 1994 "Recovery Plan for Brooksville Bellflower and Cooley's Water-Willow." U.S. Fish and Wildlife Service, Atlanta.

White, W. A. 1970. "The Geomorphology of the Florida Peninsula." *Geological Bulletin* No. 51. Florida Department of Natural Resources, Bureau of Geology, Tallahassee.

Wunderlin, R. P. *Guide to the Vascular Plants of Central Florida.* University Presses of Florida, Gainesville.

Achyranthes mutica

No Common Name

Status	Endangered
Listed	October 10, 1996
Family	Amaranthaceae (Amaranth)
Description	Many-branched shrub with stalkless flowers.
Habitat	Lowland dry forest.
Threats	Habitat degradation and destruction by cattle and feral goats, competition with alien plant species, naturally occurring events.
Range	Hawaii

Description

Achyranthes mutica is a many-branched shrub of the amaranth family (Amaranthaceae) with stems ranging from 12 to 24 in (30.5 to 60.9 cm) in length. The opposite leaves, usually 1.3-1.6 in (3.3-4.1 cm) long and 0.6-0.8 in (1.5-2.0 cm) wide, are inversely egg-shaped to elliptic or inversely lance-shaped. The stalkless flowers are arranged in spikes, 0.2-0.6 in (5.1-15.2 mm) long, directly attached to the main flower axis. The apetalous flowers are perfect (containing both female and male parts). The sepals are of unequal length, sharply pointed at the tips, and range from 0.1 to 0.2 in (0.25 to 0.51 cm) long. This species is distinguished from others in the genus by the shape and size of the sepals and by the short and congested characteristics of the spike. *A. mutica* was first described by Asa Gray in 1867 from a specimen collected on Kauai between 1851-55 by Ezechiel Jules Remy, a French naturalist and ethnologist. *A. nelsonii* is considered to be synonymous with *A. mutica* by the authors of the current treatment of Hawaiian members of the family.

Habitat

A. mutica plants grow at elevations of approximately 3,030 ft (923.5 m) in *Acacia koaia* (koai'a) lowland dry forest. *Dodonaea viscosa* ('a'ali'i), *Myoporum sandwicense* (naio), *Nestegis sandwicensis* (olopua), *Osteomeles anthyllidifolia* ('ulei), and *Sophora chrysophylla* (mamane) accompany *A. mutica*.

Distribution

A. mutica was known historically from three collections from Kauai and Hawaii, at opposite ends of the main archipelago. This species is known today only on private land on Hawaii Island from the Keawewai Stream area, the south slope of Puu Loa in the Kohala Mountains, and Lanikepu Gulch. These populations harbored from 30 to 50 plants in 1997.

Threats

The primary threats to *A. mutica* are habitat degradation and destruction by cattle and feral goats, competition with alien plant species, and a risk of extinction from naturally occurring events like landslides and hurricanes. This taxon may experience reduced reproductive vigor due to the small number of existing individuals left in the populations. Cattle, deer, and goat predation is a possible threat for this plant. The only known population of *A. mutica* in the Keawewai Stream area on the island of Hawaii is presently threatened by goats and cattle-ranching activities.

Collecting for scientific or horticultural purposes and visits by individuals avid to see rare plants are potential threats to *A. mutica*. *A. mutica* is threatened by common guava, *Ageratina riparia*, Kikuyu grass, hairy horseweed, and panini.

Achyranthes mutica, photograph by Ken Wood. Reproduced by permission.

Conservation and Recovery

A. mutica has been successfully propagated at the National Tropical Botanic Gardens where, in 1997, more than 500 seeds were in storage and about 20 plants were in cultivation. A fence constructed by one landowner proved successful in protecting one plant from grazing cattle in an area called Kalopi. The construction of additional exclosures is recommended to reduce the impact from domestic cattle and feral goats. Removal of cattle to locations away from the preferred habitat of *A. mutica* is recommended, as are various methods of feral goat removal. The implementation of such goat removal measures has proven successful elsewhere in the state.

Contact

U. S. Fish and Wildlife Service
Regional Office, Division of Endangered Species
Eastside Federal Complex
911 N. E. 11th Ave.
Portland, Oregon 97232-4181
Telephone: (503) 231-6121
http://pacific.fws.gov/

Reference

U. S. Fish and Wildlife Service. 10 October 1996. "Determination of Endangered or Threatened Status for Fourteen Plant Taxa From the Hawaiian Islands." *Federal Register* 61 (198): 53108-53124.

Round-leaved Chaff-flower

Achyranthes splendens var. *rotundata*

Status	Endangered
Listed	March 26, 1986
Family	Amaranthaceae (Amaranth)
Description	Bushy shrub; leaves covered with silvery hairs.
Habitat	Semi-arid coastal lowlands.
Threats	Shoreline development, competition with introduced plants.
Range	Hawaii

Round-leaved Chaff-flower, photograph by Derral Herbst. Reproduced by permission.

Description

The shrub *Achyranthes splendens* var. *rotundata* grows to a mature height of about 6.5 ft (2 m). It is compact and many-branched. Abundant light green leaves are covered with a silvery down. The plant produces small, inconspicuous flowers that have prominent floral bracts (small leaves at the base of the flower). These leaves were used by native Hawaiians to make their traditional leis.

Habitat

A. splendens var. *rotundata* grows in the arid and semi-arid coastal lowlands of the island of Oahu, Hawaii. It requires sandy soils and full sunlight; it does not tolerate shade.

Distribution

In the 1970s, *A. splendens* var. *rotundata* was considered fairly abundant on the island of Oahu in the seaward portions of the Ewa Coral Plain from Barbers Point north to Kaena Point. Specimens collected from two now-extinct populations on Lanai and Molokai islands may be identical with *A. splendens* var. *rotundata*. If proven correct, this would expand the species' historic range to encompass these islands.

In a short time, *Achyranthes splendens* var. *rotundata* has declined to two fragmented populations, grouped at separate ends of the historic range on Oahu. As of 1986, one population on the military reserve at Kaena Point consisted of only two plants. A second population at Barbers Point consisted of about 400 plants divided into four subgroups. About half of the known surviving plants are located on lands owned by the federal government and managed by the Coast Guard and the Navy. Two smaller colonies are on private lands. Between 1981 and 1986 the number of *Achyranthes* plants decreased precipitously from 2,000 to an estimated 400 plants. Most of one subpopulation near Barbers Point lighthouse was destroyed by industrial development in 1981. A large colony on federal land was bulldozed inadvertently in 1984. A private estate supported nearly 1,600 plants before being developed for an industrial park in 1985, and by 1986 only about 10% of the plants at this site survived.

Threats

Most of the historic range of *A. splendens* var. *rotundata* has already been developed for industry, agriculture, housing, or recreation, and the remaining shoreline also faces strong developmental pressures. In addition, introduced plants have made strong inroads into the habitat. One Barbers Point colony is threatened by the parasitic vine, *Cassytha*

filiformis, which forms a dense canopy that smothers all other vegetation. At Kaena Point, an introduced species of Leucaena has spread aggressively. On the Ewa Plains at Barbers Point, thickets of an exotic *Pluchea* are in direct competition with surviving *A. splendens* var. *rotundata* shrubs.

Conservation and Recovery

Since the present populations are exposed to human disturbance, the U.S. Fish and Wildlife Service Recovery Plan has relocated plants to more protected sites and is rehabilitating habitat by controlling exotic plants. Sixty plants were relocated in 1985 from Barbers Point to a protected site. The historic range on Oahu and potential habitat on the islands of Lanai and Molokai will be surveyed in an attempt to locate additional plants or populations.

Contact

U.S. Fish and Wildlife Service
Regional Office, Division of Endangered Species
Eastside Federal Complex
911 N.E. 11th Ave.
Portland, Oregon 97232-4181
(503) 231-6121
http://pacific.fws.gov/

References

Nagata, K. M. 1981. "Status Report on *Achyranthes splendens* var. *rotundata*." Contract Report #14-16-001-79096. U.S. Fish and Wildlife Service, Honolulu, Hawaii.

St. John, H. 1979. "Monograph of the Hawaiian Species of *Achyranthes* (Amaranthaceae): Hawaiian Plant Studies 56." *Pacific Science* 33(4): 333-350.

Amaranthus brownii

No Common Name

Status	Endangered
Listed	August 21, 1996
Family	Amaranthaceae (Amaranth)
Description	Annual herb with leafy upright or ascending stems and slightly hairy, alternate leaves.
Habitat	Rocky outcrops in fully exposed locations.
Threats	Non-native plants, substrate changes, stochastic extinction.
Range	Hawaii

Description

Amaranthus brownii, an annual herb of the amaranth family (Amaranthaceae), has leafy upright or ascending stems that are 1-3 ft (0.3-0.9 m) long. The alternate leaves, 1.6-2.8 in (4-7 cm) long and 0.06-0.16 in (0.1-0.14 cm) wide, are long, narrow, slightly hairy, and more or less folded in half lengthwise. Flowers are either male or female, and flowers of both sexes are found on the same plant. The green flowers are subtended by two oval, bristle-tipped bracts about 0.04 in (1 mm) long and 0.03 in (0.7 mm) wide. Each flower has three bristle-tipped sepals. These are lance-shaped and 0.05 in (1 mm) long by 0.03 in (0.7 mm) wide in male flowers. Female flowers have spatula-shaped sepals that are about 0.03 in (0.7 mm) long by 0.01 in (0.2 mm) wide. Male flowers have three stamens; female flowers have two stigmas. The flattened oval fruit, approximately 0.03 in (0.7 mm) long and 0.02 in (0.5 mm) wide, does not split open at maturity to reveal its one lens-shaped, reddish black seed. This species can be distinguished from other Hawaiian members of the genus by its spineless leaf axils, its linear leaves, and the aforementioned fruit that does not split open at maturity.

A. brownii is an herbaceous annual with a growing season that extends from December to June or July. Plants in an early stage of flowering have been observed in February, and seed from dead plants have been collected during June. Phenology may vary somewhat from year to year, depending on rainfall and climatic factors. The means of pollination are unknown.

A. brownii was first collected by Edward L. Caum during the Tanager Expedition in 1923. Erling Christophersen and Caum named it in honor of Dr. F. B. H. Brown eight years later.

Habitat

A. brownii typically grows on rocky outcrops in fully exposed locations at elevations between 100 and 800 ft (30 and 244 m). Associated species include 'aheahea, kakonakona, and kupala.

Distribution

A. brownii is the rarest native plant on Nihoa. When it was first collected in 1923, it was considered most common on the ridge leading to Miller's Peak, although also abundant on the ridges to the east. The two groupings of colonies known in recent years, separated by a distance of 0.25 mi (0.4 km), contained a total of approximately 35 individuals in 1983—23 plants at Miller's Peak and about 12 plants in three small colonies in Middle Valley. No plants have been seen at either location since 1983, even though U. S. Fish and Wildlife Service (FWS) staff have surveyed for them annually. However, none of the surveys since 1983 have been done during the winter, when these annuals are easiest to find and identify. It will be necessary to conduct winter surveys in order to get an accurate population count and collect seeds or cuttings to establish cultivated populations.

Individuals of *A. brownii* are difficult to distinguish from other desiccated herbaceous or seedling plants during the dry summer months, when surveys are conducted. The unusually dry conditions of the past several years are another probable factor for this species not being reported.

December through March is the normal growing season for *A. brownii,* but the seas are too rough during these months to permit landing on Nihoa by survey personnel. The FWS continues to attempt winter surveys of Nihoa with veteran field botanist Steve Perlman of the Hawaii Plant Conservation Center, who believes that the species is likely present during the wetter winter months.

Threats

Pigweed, an invasive alien species, is widespread on Nihoa and grows in habitat similar to *A. brownii.*

Because it grows on rocky outcrops, *A. brownii* is more likely to be affected by substrate changes. Due to the small numbers of populations and individuals and its limited distribution, this species is threatened by extinction from naturally occurring events and through reduced reproductive vigor. This species may have experienced a reduction in total numbers due to disturbances resulting from Polynesian settlement of Nihoa.

The very limited range and small populations of *A. brownii* greatly increase the potential for extinction from stochastic events. *A. brownii* has only four colonies and is believed to number fewer than 40 individuals. The limited gene pool of these species may severely depress its reproductive vigor.

Conservation and Recovery

A. brownii seeds have been collected for cultivation, but resulting germination and survival rates were very low. This may indicate a reduction in the reproductive vigor of the species. There are no known plants or seeds in any botanical collection.

Immediate recovery actions should include a winter expedition to monitor and map remaining populations and to collect seeds and cuttings to establish cultivated populations. Micropropagation techniques developed at the Lyon Arboretum in Honolulu offer probably the best prospect for culturing sufficient material to establish protected off-site populations that can later be used to reestablish *A. brownii* in the wild.

Increasing the numbers of plants and locations of this species on Nihoa will be critical to its ultimate survival and recovery. Considerable work will need to be done to identify, prepare, protect, and monitor sites for establishing new wild populations, particularly if the sites are outside of the historic range. Necker Island should be considered since it is adjacent to Nihoa, has similar habitat, and is protected as a FWS refuge. Kilauea Point and Midway Atoll National Wildlife Refuges should also be assessed for suitability since they are protected areas, have plant nursery facilities, and have a full time staff.

Contacts

U. S. Fish and Wildlife Service
Regional Office, Division of Endangered Species
Eastside Federal Complex
911 N. E. 11th Ave.
Portland, Oregon 97232-4181
(503) 231-6121
http://pacific.fws.gov/

U. S. Fish and Wildlife Service
Pacific Islands Ecoregion
Pacific Islands Fish and Wildlife Office
300 Ala Moana Boulevard, Room 3-122
Box 50088
Honolulu, Hawaii, 96850
Telephone: (808) 541-3441
Fax: (808) 541-3470

Reference

U.S. Fish and Wildlife Service. 21 August 1996. "Endangered and Threatened Wildlife and Plants: Endangered Status for Three Plants From the Island of Nihoa, Hawaii." *Federal Register* 61 (163): 43178-43184.

Seabeach Amaranth

Amaranthus pumilus

Status	Threatened
Listed	April 7, 1993
Family	Amaranthaceae (Amaranth)
Description	A low-growing, annual plant.
Habitat	Sandy open areas on barrier beaches.
Threats	Beach stabilization projects, trampling by off-road vehicles and pedestrians, and extreme storm surges and weather events.
Range	Maryland, New York, North Carolina, South Carolina

Description

The seabeach amaranth is an annual plant. It has fleshy, pinkish-red stems with small, rounded, green leaves 0.5-1.0 in (1.3-2.5 cm) in diameter. Its leaves are clustered toward the tip of the stem, are normally a spinach-green color, and have a small notch at the otherwise rounded tip. The flowers and fruits are inconspicuous, and are borne in clusters along the stem. Germination occurs over April to July, and full-grown, well-branched plants can reach a foot (30 cm) in diameter and consist of five to 20 branches. Some plants may exceed 3 ft (1 m) in diameter, and have more than 100 branches.

Habitat

The seabeach amaranth occurs on barrier-island beaches and sandy inlets. It occurs in overwash flats at the accreting end of barrier islands, as well as in lower foredunes and upper strands of non-eroding beaches. It also occurs in blowouts and other disturbed, sandy areas. The seabeach amaranth is intolerant of competition, and becomes eliminated in well-vegetated sites.

Distribution

The seabeach amaranth is native to the U. S. Atlantic coast. It has been reported from Delaware, Massachusetts, Maryland, North Carolina, New Jersey, New York, Rhode Island, South Carolina, and Virginia.

Threats

The seabeach amaranth is threatened by habitat destruction and degradation by beach stabilization structures, the use of off-road vehicles, predation by herbivorous insects and feral mammals, and storm-related erosion and tidal inundation. In the mid-1990s, about 55 populations of the seabeach amaranth survived. Of these, 13 populations were in New York, 34 in North Carolina, and eight in South Carolina. Overall, the rare plant has been eliminated from about two-thirds of its historic range.

Conservation and Recovery

Most of the largest remaining populations of the seabeach amaranth are located on publicly owned land, including Cape Hatteras and Cape Lookout National Seashores. At these sites, the rare plant is being protected from beach armoring, a management practice that has been the single most serious threat to the survival of the seabeach amaranth. In addition, off-road vehicle traffic has been routed around areas where the rare plant is growing on Park Service lands. The collection and storage of seeds and other plant material has begun in cooperation with the Center for Plant Conservation and its member gardens. Other surviving populations of the seabeach amaranth are on different kinds of public lands, but they are not well protected from the threats that face almost all populations. Con-

Seabeach Amaranth, photograph. U. S. Fish and Wildlife Service. Reproduced by permission.

servation of the seabeach amaranth requires the monitoring of its known populations and surveys to discover additional ones, research on the biology and habitat needs of the species, and the establishment of new populations in suitable habitat and the enhancement of depleted ones.

Contacts

U. S. Fish and Wildlife Service
Regional Office, Division of Endangered Species
1875 Century Blvd., Suite 200
Atlanta, Georgia 30345
http://southeast.fws.gov/

U. S. Fish and Wildlife Service
Regional Office, Division of Endangered Species
300 Westgate Center Dr.
Hadley, Massachusetts 01035-9589
Telephone: (413) 253-8200
Fax: (413) 253-8308
http://www.northeast.fws.gov/

U. S. Fish and Wildlife Service,
Asheville Ecological Services Field Office
160 Zillicoa Street
Asheville, North Carolina 28801-1082
Telephone: (828) 258-3939
Fax: (828) 258-5330

References

U. S. Fish and Wildlife Service. 7 April 1993. "Endangered and Threatened Wildlife and Plants: *Amaranthus pumilus* Determined to be Threatened." *Federal Register* 58(65):18035-18042.

U. S. Fish and Wildlife Service. August 1993. "U. S. Fish and Wildlife Service, Division of Endangered Species, Species Accounts: Seabeach Amaranth (*Amaranthus pumilus*)." *U. S. Fish and Wildlife Service Endangered Species Program.* (http://endangered.fws.gov/i/q/saq9z.html). Date Accessed: July 6, 2000.

Kulu'i

Nototrichium humile

Status	Endangered
Listed	October 29, 1991
Family	Amaranthaceae (Amaranth)
Description	Branched, hairy shrub with opposite leaves and a slender flower spike at the stem ends.
Habitat	Gulches, steep slopes, and cliff faces in open dry forest.
Threats	Feral pigs, goats, and cattle; alien plant species.
Range	Hawaii

Description

Nototrichium humile (also called kulu'i) is a branched, upright to trailing shrub of the amaranth family with stems up to 5 ft (1.5 m) long. The stems and leaves are covered with short hairs. The opposite, oblong leaves are 1.2-3.5 in (3-8.9 cm) long. Stalkless flowers appear on a slender spike 1.2-5.5 in (3-14 cm) long at the stem ends. Plants have been observed flowering after heavy rain, but flowering is generally heaviest in the spring and summer. Fruits mature a few weeks after flowering. The species has also been known as *Psilotrichum humile*.

Habitat

N. humile is found on and at the base of rock cliffs and talus slopes in areas that do not receive full sun all day. It typically grows at an elevation of 200-2,300 ft (61-701 m) on cliff faces, gulches, or steep slopes in remnants of open dry forests often dominated by aulu or lama. Associated species include alahee, 'ohia' ha, *Reynoldsia sandwicensis* (ohe), *Pleomele* sp. (halapepe), *Myrsine lanaiensis* (kolea), and papala kepau.

Distribution

N. humile had historical occurrences on Oahu (along the entire length of the Waianae Mountains) and on East Maui. The species is still extant on Oahu from Kaluakaulla Gulch, along Makua-Keaau Ridge to Makaha-Waianae Kal Ridge and Nanakuli, where it occurs on federal, state and private lands. It is also extant in Maui's Lualailua Hills on private land. Fourteen of the 15 known populations grow within an area of about 3 by 11 mi (4.8 by 17.7 km) in the Waianae Mountains; the other population is the poorly documented Maui occurrence at Lualualei. The combined total of all the occurrences was estimated at 1,489-1,519 individuals in 1997. The six populations at Lualualei—Mikilua and Pahoa subdistricts, Palehua, Kealia, Kipuna Gulch, and Waianae Kai—all numbered fewer than 12 individuals.

Threats

On both Oahu and East Maui, the major threats to *N. humile* are habitat degradation by feral goats, pigs, and cattle; military activities; competition from the alien plants Christmas berry, koa haole, molasses grass, and strawberry guava; and fire.

Conservation and Recovery

One *N. humile* individual has been outplanted by the Nature Conservancy of Hawaii in a fenced enclosure in Honolulu Preserve; as of November 1997, this plant was in good condition. There are two col-

Kulu'i, photograph. Reproduced by permission. (Robert J. Gustafson)

lections at the Pahole mid-elevation Nike site. Approximately ten of the wild individuals are within the boundaries of a large fenced enclosure at Kahanahaiki Gulch. General weeding efforts within this area may benefit the species. The National Tropical Botanical Garden has collected *N. humile* seed, and the species is being propagated at the Waimea Arboretum. The populations that have only a few remaining individuals should be immediately fenced, weeded, and otherwise protected. Once these areas have been enclosed, commitments should be developed for their long-term stewardship and conservation. A coordinated fire protection plan for endangered plant species on state forest reserves (Waianae Kal) and federal lands (Lualualei Naval Reservation) needs to be developed and implemented.

Contacts

U. S. Fish and Wildlife Service
Regional Office, Division of Endangered Species
Eastside Federal Complex
911 N. E. 11th Ave.
Portland, Oregon 97232-4181
(503) 231-6121
http://pacific.fws.gov/

Pacific Remote Islands Ecological Services Field Office
300 Ala Moana Blvd., Room 3-122
P. O. Box 50088
Honolulu, Hawaii 96850
Telephone: (808) 541-1201
Fax: (808) 541-1216

References

Cuddihy, L. W., and C. P. Stone. 1990. *Alteration of Native Hawaiian Vegetation: Effects of Humans, Their Activities, and Introductions.* Cooperative National Park Resources Study Unit, University of Hawaii Press, Honolulu.

Culliney, J. L. 1988. *Islands in a Far Sea: Nature and Man in Hawaii.* Sierra Club Books, San Francisco.

Stone, C. P., and J. M. Scott, eds. 1985. *Hawaii's Terrestrial Ecosystems: Preservation and Management.* Cooperative National Park Resources Study Unit, University of Hawaii Press, Honolulu.

Wagner, W. L., D. R. Herbst, and S. H. Sohmer. 1990. *Manual of the Flowering Plants of Hawaii.* University of Hawaii Press and Bishop Museum Press, Honolulu.

Michaux's Sumac

Rhus michauxii

Status	Endangered
Listed	September 28, 1989
Family	Anacardiaceae
Description	Low-growing shrub with compound leaves and clusters of greenish yellow to white flowers.
Habitat	Disturbed areas with sandy or rocky soil.
Threats	Succession, loss of habitat, low numbers.
Range	Georgia, North Carolina, South Carolina, Virginia

Michaux's Sumac, photograph. U. S. Fish and Wildlife Service. Reproduced by permission.

Description

Michaux's sumac, *Rhus michauxii,* or false poison sumac, is a densely hairy shrub with erect stems which are 1-3 ft (30.5-91.4 cm) in height. The shrub's compound leaves are narrowly winged at their base, dull on their tops, and veiny and slightly hairy on their bottoms. Each leaf is finely toothed on its edges. Flowers are greenish yellow to white and are four to five parted. Each plant is unisexual. With a male plant the flowers and fruits are solitary, with a female plant all flowers are grouped in three- to five-stalked clusters. The plant flowers from April to June. The fruit, a dull red drupe, is produced in October and November.

Habitat

Michaux's sumac grows in sandy or rocky open woods. Apparently, this plant survives best in areas where some form of disturbance has provided an open area. Eleven of the plant's 16 remaining populations are on highway rights-of-way, roadsides, or on the edges of artificially maintained clearings. Two other populations are in areas with periodic fires, and two more populations exist on sites undergoing natural succession. One population is situated in a natural opening on the rim of a Carolina bay.

Distribution

Until recently, surviving populations of Michaux's sumac were known only from North Carolina and one site in Georgia. Not even historical records existed for this plant in Virginia. But a recent discovery at Fort Pickett, an army base in Virginia, located what is now the species' largest known population, containing over 21,000 plants. Of the 15 existing populations in North Carolina, nine have less than 100 plants each, and three of these have less than one dozen plants each.

Threats

Perhaps the most crucial factor endangering this species is its low reproductive capacity. Only two of the plant's 16 remaining populations have both male and female plants. The apparent low genetic variability of the species, caused by geographic isolation, complicates this situation. Because of the clonal nature of this species and the scarcity of populations containing both male and female plants, the remaining populations may actually consist of only about two dozen genetic individuals. Hybridization of this plant with smooth sumac (*R. copallina*) and dwarf sumac (*R. glabra*) is another threat to the plant's genetic integrity. In at least two historic sites of Michaux's sumac, hybrid plants (apparently crosses between *R. glabra* and *R. michauxii*) have been found.

Michaux's sumac is threatened by the conversion of native habitat for agriculture and forestry, residential and commercial development, and the suppression of wildfires. Intolerant of shade, the plant can be overtaken by vegetative succession. It prefers open habitat maintained by fire or mowing. Several populations are along roadsides, where they are vulnerable to highway widening and herbicide application. Two of the plant's historic populations were destroyed by development—one by the construction of a water tower, and one by the conversion of the site to a pine plantation.

Conservation and Recovery

The plant is shade-intolerant, and some form of disturbance such as burning is necessary to control the growth of woody species around its habitat.

Timber harvesting and road construction or maintenance should be carefully conducted to preserve this plant's habitat. Prescribed burning is being conducted at the North Carolina Sandhills Game Lands which has the largest population (137 plants).

Genetic analysis work is being done through a cooperative effort between the University of Georgia, the North Carolina Nature Conservancy, and the U.S. Fish and Wildlife Service's Asheville, North Carolina, Field Office. Researchers from the University of Georgia analyze tissue samples collected from the remaining North Carolina and Georgia populations for their genotypes. If possible, male or female plants may be reintroduced into unisex populations of compatible genotypes. The first reintroduction attempt, conducted in Georgia in cooperation with the Georgia Heritage Inventory and Woodlanders, a commercial nursery specializing in native plants, is doing well with good survival of transplanted material.

As part of the recovery effort for Michaux's sumac, the North Carolina office of The Nature Conservancy collected leaf tissue for genetic analysis and demographic data from the 21 locations of this endangered plant that remain in the sandhills and coastal plains of North Carolina and Georgia. The results of this research will be used to plan the reintroduction of Michaux's sumac into its former range and to complement single-sex populations of the deciduous, rhizomatous shrub. Populations are extremely small, and most are made up of only one sex. When the species was listed in 1989, only seven of the then-known 16 populations were comprised of 100 or more plants, and only two included representatives of both sexes.

Very few of the previously known populations produce fruit. In contrast, the Fort Pickett population is prolific. The army is taking advantage of the situation by promoting the recovery of Michaux's sumac with vigor. Recovery activities planned or under way include additional surveys, habitat protection, and genetic studies to determine if hybridization occurs between *R. michauxii* and the common smooth sumac (*R. glabra*). A global positioning system is being used to record species locations into a geographic information system. Graduate studies are planned to determine levels and viability of seed germination, and the feasibility of propagating and transplanting Michaux's sumac to establish or augment populations. The army also plans to set up and monitor prescribed burning plots to determine the best habitat management strategy for this species.

The first reintroduction of Michaux's sumac is doing well. The Georgia Heritage Inventory and Woodlanders (an Aiken, South Carolina, commercial nursery that specializes in native plants) cooperated in the transplant effort.

Contacts

U.S. Fish and Wildlife Service
Regional Office, Division of Endangered Species
1875 Century Blvd., Suite 200
Atlanta, Georgia 30345
http://southeast.fws.gov/

U.S. Fish and Wildlife Service
Regional Office, Division of Endangered Species
300 Westgate Center Dr.
Hadley, Massachusetts 01035-9589
Telephone: (413) 253-8200
Fax: (413) 253-8300
http://www.northeast.fws.gov/

U.S. Fish and Wildlife Service
330 Ridgefield Court
Asheville, North Carolina 28806
Telephone: (704) 665-1195

Reference

U.S. Fish and Wildlife Service. 28 September 1989. "Endangered and Threatened Wildlife and Plants: Determination of Endangered Status for *Rhus michauxii.*" *Federal Register* 54 (187): 39853-39857.

Four-petal Pawpaw

Asimina tetramera

Status	Endangered
Listed	September 26, 1986
Family	Annonaceae (Custard-apple)
Description	Tall, woody shrub with large untoothed leaves, pink to maroon flowers, and a pale yellow fruit.
Habitat	Sand pine scrub.
Threats	Urbanization, fire suppression.
Range	Florida

Four-petal Pawpaw, photograph by Jonathon A. Shaw. Reproduced by permission.

Description

Four-petal pawpaw, *Asimina tetramera*, is a large woody shrub, formed of one or several upright stems, 3.3-10 ft (1-3 m) tall, with large toothless leaves. Flowers have four sepals and six pink or maroon petals (two sets of three each); fruits are pale yellow. Flowering occurs primarily from May to August and sporadically in other months. The fruiting period is from about May to September. The flowers give off a fetid odor.

Habitat

Four-petal pawpaw's habitat is the sand pine scrub that grows along old dune ridges. The plant is well-adapted to the occasional severe fires and hurricanes that visit its habitat, because new sprouts grow readily from the roots. Without fire and hurricanes, four-petal pawpaw is eventually shaded out by evergreen oaks and sand pines.

Distribution

The plant was first discovered in 1924 at Rio, Florida, just north of Stuart. Historically, four-petaled pawpaw grew throughout the scrub sand pine dunes along the Atlantic coast of Florida, stretching from the coast inland in Martin and northern Palm Beach counties.

Much of the original pine scrub habitat of four-petal pawpaw has undergone urban development, and the species is now restricted to small remnant patches of scrub throughout its range. About 100 plants grow in Jonathan Dickinson State Park. In 1985, several dozen plants were surveyed in the Hobe Sound National Wildlife Refuge. Sixty plants grow on several acres that serve as a biological preserve on the grounds of an office building in Palm Beach County.

Other remaining four-petal pawpaw plants are mostly on private lands, scattered along U.S. Highway 1 in northern Palm Beach County, where urban development is proceeding at a break-neck pace. Already one-third of about 100 plants surveyed in June 1985 in Palm Beach and Martin counties outside of parks or preserves have been lost to residential development. Estimated population numbers in the primary sites are: Jonathan Dickinson State Park - 100; private grounds of an office building in Palm Beach County - 60; and a Palm Beach County park - 40. A total of about 500 plants are known to exist in the wild

Threats

Where scrub vegetation survives, four-petal pawpaw may die out because brush fires have been controlled. When there is no fire, scrub oaks or sand pines eventually overtop and shade out the pawpaw. Both Jonathan Dickinson State Park and Hobe Sound National Wildlife Refuge have a program for prescribed burning of vegetation. Tracts of scrub on private land may have to be renewed by other methods, such as cutting. Most of the original sand pine scrub habitat is now urbanized, and the species is essentially confined to remnant areas of scrub vegetation in scattered sites.

Conservation and Recovery

The prescribed fire management plan at the Hobe Sound National Wildlife Refuge should help these plants survive there, but there is little hope for plants on private land, unless landowners can be convinced of the value of preserving sand pine scrub habitat.

The plant is protected in Jonathan Dickinson State Park except for small areas that are used for military communication facilities, which could be altered in the future. Four-petal pawpaw may also occur in areas on or near the Hobe Sound National Wildlife Refuge where the U. S. Army Corps of Engineers holds easements for disposal of dredge spoils from the Intracoastal Waterway. The plants which occur in a Palm Beach County park are threatened by the development of recreational facilities and by illegal dumping.

While resprouting from the roots is characteristic of the species, reproduction from seeds appears to be limited. The large seeds of four-petal pawpaw have oily endosperm and apparently a limited period of viability. Seed collected from fresh, ripe, fruit planted immediately germinated well, but older seeds did not germinate. Cultivated seedlings, grown for four years, have grown slowly, with most growth concentrated in the root system which is sensitive to transplanting disturbance. This indicates that the shrub has a limited reproductive capacity, that long-term germplasm storage may be impractical, and it appears that this shrub's reproductive capacity in the wild is very limited. The species is also so limited in distribution and population size that any indiscriminate scientific or other collecting would pose a threat to its existence. Florida law does regulate taking, transport, and sale of the plants, but it does not provide habitat protection. Moyroud and Susan Wallace of Bok Tower Gardens have successfully germinated seeds and grown young plants in a garden setting.

Contacts

Regional Office of Endangered Species
U. S. Fish and Wildlife Service
1875 Century Blvd., Suite 200
Atlanta, Georgia 30345
http://southeast.fws.gov/

Jacksonville Ecological Services Field Office
6620 Southpoint Dr. S., Suite 310
Jacksonville, Florida 32216-0958
Telephone: (904)232-2580
Fax: (904) 232-2404

References

Austin, D.F., and B.E. Tatje. 1979. *Asimina tetramera*, pp. 5-6. In D.B. Ward, ed. *Rare and Endangered Biota of Florida;* Vol. 5, Plants. University Presses of Florida, Gainesville.

Austin, D. F., B. E. Tatje, and C. E. Nauman. 1980 "Status Report on *Asimina tetramera*." U.S. Fish and Wildlife Service, Atlanta.

Kral, R. 1983. "*Asimina tetramera*." In Report on Some Rare, Threatened, or Endangered Forest-Related Vascular Plants of the South. U.S. Department of Agriculture Forest Service, Washington, D.C.

U.S. Fish and Wildlife Service. 1988. Recovery Plan for Three Florida Pawpaws. U.S. Fish and Wildlife Service, Atlanta, Georgia. 20 pp.

U.S. Fish and Wildlife Service. 1986. Endangered and Threatened Wildlife and Plants: Endangered Status for Three Florida Shrubs. *Federal Register* 51(187):34415-34420.

Wilbur, R. 1970. "Taxonomic and Nomenclatural Observations on the Eastern North American Genus *Asimina* (Annonaceae)." *Journal of the Elisha Mitchell Scientific Society* 86:88-95.

Wunderlin, R. P., D. Richardson, and B. Hansen. 1980. "Status Report on *Asimina rugelii*." Report. U.S. Fish and Wildlife Service, Atlanta.

Beautiful Pawpaw

Deeringothamnus pulchellus

Status	Endangered
Listed	September 26, 1986
Family	Annonaceae (Custard-apple)
Description	A low shrub.
Habitat	Coastal pine flatwoods.
Threats	Habitat destruction through conversion into residential, commercial, and agricultural land-uses, coupled with habitat degradation caused by trampling and fire control.
Range	Florida

Steve Shirah

Description

The beautiful pawpaw, also known as the white squirrel-banana, is a low-growing shrub with stems 4-8 in (10-20 cm) tall and a stout taproot. The stems are annual or biennial in longevity. The leaves are arranged in alternate fashion along the stem. The leaves are leathery in texture and are seasonally deciduous (i.e., they are shed in the autumn). The leaves are 1.6-2.8 in (4-7 cm) long, oblong to oblong-ovate in shape, with a smooth margin. The pleasantly scented flowers are solitary in the leaf axils,

and have linear, creamy-white petals that become recurved as the flower develops. The fruits are cylindrical berries, 1-3 in (3-6 cm) long, with pulpy flesh, and colored yellow-green when ripe. The seeds are about the shape and size of a bean. The plant resprouts from the roots if the top is destroyed by fire or mowing.

The species is adapted to periodic disturbance by wildfire or windstorms. Flowering tends to occur only after fire or mowing promotes new growth of the plant. The flowers are insect-pollinated, and the fruits are distributed by animals and gravity.

Habitat

The beautiful pawpaw grows in poorly drained flatwoods in sandy soils, in stands dominated by slash pine (*Pinus elliotii*) and saw palmetto (*Serenoa repens*). The beautiful pawpaw requires periodic disturbance of its habitat, although this must not be so severe as to kill the perennating roots of the plant.

Distribution

The beautiful pawpaw is only known from northern Lee County (on Pine Island), southern Charlotte County, and Orange County, all in southwestern Florida.

Threats

The beautiful pawpaw has declined greatly in range and abundance. Some of its former populations have been extirpated, especially in the Fort Myers urban area. It is endangered mostly because of the destruction of its habitat for residential, commercial, and agricultural development. Moreover, the best surviving populations are located in areas near Fort Myers which have a high potential for real estate development. The plant has also been affected by trash dumping and damage caused by all-terrain vehicles. Because of its restricted distribution and small population size, the beautiful pawpaw is vulnerable to adverse effects from indiscriminate collecting, or from catastrophic weather events, such as a hurricane. The prevention of wildfire is also detrimental to its habitat quality.

Conservation and Recovery

Because it is an endangered species, the beautiful pawpaw is protected by Florida law from any harvesting, transport, or sale. However, there is no specific protection of the critical habitat of the rare plant, which is vulnerable to residential, commercial, and agricultural development. The most important requirement for conservation of the beautiful pawpaw is to protect the remaining plants and their critical habitat from destruction by development. This could be done by acquiring the habitat and designating it as an ecological reserve, or by negotiating conservation easements with private landowners. In addition, the conserved habitat must be managed through periodic light disturbance, by prescribed burning or mowing, to maintain its suitability for the endangered plant.

Contacts

U. S. Fish and Wildlife Service
Regional Office, Division of Endangered Species
1875 Century Blvd., Suite 200
Atlanta, Georgia 30345
http://southeast.fws.gov/

U. S. Fish and Wildlife Service
3100 University Boulevard, South, Suite 120
Jacksonville, Florida 32216
(904) 791-2580

References

U. S. Fish and Wildlife Service. 1991. Beautiful pawpaw (*Deeringothamnus pulchellus*). http://endangered.fws.gov/i/q/saq3s.html

U. S. Fish and Wildlife Service. 26 September 1986. "Endangered and Threatened Wildlife and Plants: Endangered Status for Three Florida Plants." *Federal Register* 51(187):34415-34420.

Rugel's Pawpaw

Deeringothamnus rugelii

Status	Endangered
Listed	September 26, 1986
Family	Annonaceae (Custard-apple)
Description	A low shrub.
Habitat	Coastal pine flatwoods.
Threats	Habitat destruction through conversion into residential, commercial, and agricultural land-uses, coupled with habitat degradation caused by trampling and fire suppression.
Range	Florida

Rugel's Pawpaw, photograph by Walter K. Taylor and Steve Shirah. Reproduced by permission.

Description

The Rugel's pawpaw is a low-growing shrub with a stout taproot. The pleasantly scented flowers are solitary in the leaf axils, and have straight, oblong, canary-yellow petals. The ripe fruits are cylindrical, yellow-green berries with pulpy flesh, 1-3 in (3-6 cm) long. The seeds are about the size and shape of a bean. The stems are annual or biennial in longevity, and generally 4 -8 in (10-20 cm) tall. The leaves are leathery in texture and are seasonally deciduous (i.e., they are shed in the autumn).

The Rugel's pawpaw is adapted to periodic disturbance by wildfire or windstorms. It resprouts from the roots if the top is destroyed by fire or mowing. Flowering tends to occur only after fire or mowing results in new shoot growth. The flowers are insect pollinated, and the fruits are distributed by animals and gravity.

Habitat

The Rugel's pawpaw grows in poorly drained, slash pine (*Pinus elliotii*) and saw palmetto (*Serenoa repens*) flatwoods in sandy soils. It requires periodic disturbance of its habitat, although this must not be so severe as to kill the perennating roots of the plant.

Distribution

The Rugel's pawpaw is an endemic species that is only known from the vicinity of New Smyrna Beach in Volusia County, Florida.

Threats

The Rugel's pawpaw occurs in only two populations located about 12 mi (19 km) southwest of Lake Ashby, and seven others about 5 mi (8 km) to the west within an area of about 3 sq mi (7.7 sq km). The historical range is thought to be similar to the present one, but there are fewer populations now due to habitat loss through residential and commercial development. In the early 1980s, there were nine known populations containing a total of fewer than 500 plants. Most of the populations were on private land, although two occurred along a State road right-of-way. Most of the surviving habitat is used for cattle grazing, and conversion to residential or commercial land-use is an ongoing, severe threat. In addition, fire suppression allows other vegetation to develop a thick canopy, which eventually would result in the local demise of the Rugel's pawpaw. The rare plant has also been affected by trash dumping and damage caused by all-terrain vehicles. Because of its restricted distribution and small population size, it is vulnerable to adverse effects from indiscriminate collecting, and from natural catastrophes such as a hurricane.

Conservation and Recovery

Because it is an endangered species, the Rugel's pawpaw is protected by Florida law from any harvesting, transport, or sale. However, the law does not provide specific protection for the critical habitat of the rare plant, which is vulnerable to residential and commercial development. The most important requirement for conservation of the Rugel's pawpaw is to protect the remaining plants and their habitat from destruction by development. This can be done by acquiring the land and setting up ecological reserves, or by negotiating conservation easements with the private landowners. In addition, the conserved habitat must be managed through periodic light disturbance by prescribed burning or mowing, to maintain its suitability for the endangered plant.

Walter K. Taylor

Contacts

U. S. Fish and Wildlife Service
Regional Office, Division of Endangered Species
1875 Century Blvd., Suite 200
Atlanta, Georgia 30345
http://southeast.fws.gov/

U. S. Fish and Wildlife Service
6620 Southpoint Drive South, Suite 310
Jacksonville, Florida 32216-0958
Telephone: (904) 232-2580
Fax: (904) 232-2404

References

U. S. Fish and Wildlife Service. February 1991. "U. S. Fish and Wildlife Service Division of Endangered Species, Species Accounts: Rugel's Pawpaw (*Deeringothamnus rugelii*)." *U. S. Fish and Wildlife Service Endangered Species Program.* (http://endangered.fws.gov/i/q/saq3t.html). Date Accessed: July 6, 2000.

U. S. Fish and Wildlife Service. 26 September 1986. "Endangered and Threatened Wildlife and Plants: Endangered Status for Three Florida Plants." *Federal Register* 51(187):34415-34420.

Kearney's Blue-star

Amsonia kearneyana

Status	Endangered
Listed	January 19, 1989
Family	Apocynaceae (Dogbane)
Description	Multi-stemmed perennial with alternate, hairy, lance-shaped leaves and terminal clusters of white flowers.
Habitat	Alluvial, rocky, semidesert soil.
Threats	Livestock grazing, low reproduction.
Range	Arizona

Kearney's Blue-star, photograph. U. S. Fish and Wildlife Service. Reproduced by permission.

Description

Kearney's blue-star, *Amsonia kearneyana*, is a herbaceous perennial which grows to a height of 16-32 in (40-60 cm). Up to 50 erect stems arise from a thick, woody root, giving mature plants a hemispherical appearance. The alternate leaves are hairy and lance-shaped. Pale blue to white flowers appear in terminal clusters in April or May.

The species was first collected in 1926 and was long considered a sterile hybrid. In 1982 it was recognized as a valid taxon, based on distinctive morphological characteristics and the viability of more than 50% of seed.

Habitat

Kearney's blue-star grows in alluvial deposits of small boulders or cobbles that line a dry, semidesert wash. Associated plants are net-leaf hackberry, Arizona walnut, Mexican blue oak, and catclaw acacia.

Distribution

The species is known only from a single population in a canyon on the western slopes of the Baboquivari Mountains in Pima County, Arizona. The canyon is on the Tohono O'odham (formerly Papago) Indian Reservation. When surveyed in 1982, the entire population consisted of 25 plants. By 1988 the species had declined to only eight plants. A glimmer of hope remains however: After transplanting, the Arizona-Sonora Desert Museum propagated seedlings from seed and the new plants are being carefully monitored.

Threats

The principal threats to Kearney's blue-star are habitat degradation caused by livestock grazing and the apparent failure of remaining plants to successfully reproduce. Although livestock do not feed on the plant, overgrazing causes a decline in plant species diversity which may be accompanied by a reduction in pollinators. Overgrazing also increases the potential for soil erosion and flooding, a possible catastrophe for a species of such limited numbers and distribution.

There are troubling signs that the species may not be capable of sustaining a naturally reproducing population. Of the 25 plants found in 1982 only one was a seedling. In 1986 mature plants had only a few developing fruits, and those contained an unusually small number of developing seeds. The cause of this reproductive failure is not known, but possible explanations include extremes of temperature and soil moisture, absence of pollinators, and destruction of seedlings by livestock. Insects are also a possible cause of seed destruction. Stinkbugs (*Chlorochroa ligata*), known to destroy the seeds of the related *A. grandiflora*, occur with the range of Kearney's blue-star.

Conservation and Recovery

The Bureau of Indian Affairs (BIA) is responsible for issuing grazing permits on tribal lands. The U. S. Fish and Wildlife Service (FWS) is currently working with the BIA and the Tohono O'odham Nation to secure protection and a management plan for this extremely Endangered species.

Hopes of preserving the species lie in horticultural science; the Sonoran Desert Museum in Tucson has seeded transplanted individuals, and it is hoped that lasting new populations can be grown from these rare seeds. The 1992 FWS Recovery Plan for the species has as its primary objective the maintenance of enough viable populations in a natural habitat to ensure that the species is safe from extinction. The species will be considered for reclassification from endangered to threatened when ten geographically distinct, self-sustaining, natural populations are protected in Arizona. These ten populations must represent the geographic range of the species.

The recovery plan outlines main actions for saving the species, including identifying and protecting natural and introduced populations; assessing the status of natural, reintroduced, and *ex situ* populations; researching and observing the populations to describe the species' habitat requirements, and modify management as appropriate; surveying for new populations; establishing a sufficient number of reintroduced populations to meet the downlisting criteria; establishing an ex situ conservation program; and information and education programs to inform the public about the importance of preserving and protecting this rare plant.

Contact

Regional Office of Endangered Species
U.S. Fish and Wildlife Service
P.O. Box 1306
Albuquerque, New Mexico 87103
http://southwest.fws.gov/

References

McLaughlin, S. P. 1982. "A Revision of the Southwestern Species of *Amsonia* (Apocynaceae)." *Annals of the Missouri Botanical Garden*. 69(2):336-350.

Phillips, B. G. and N. Brian. 1982. "Status Report on *Amsonia kearneyana*." U.S. Fish and Wildlife Service. Albuquerque, New Mexico.

Turner, R. M. and D. E. Brown. 1982. "Sonoran Desert Scrub." In D. E. Brown, ed., "Biotic Communities of the American Southwest-United States and Mexico." *Desert Plants* 4:181-221.

U.S. Fish and Wildlife Service. 1992. "Kearney's Blue Star (*Amsonia kearneyana*) Recovery Plan." U.S. Fish and Wildlife Service, Albuquerque.

Jones Cycladenia

Cycladenia humilis var. *jonesii*

Status	Threatened
Listed	May 5, 1986
Family	Apocynaceae (Dogbane)
Description	Perennial herb with bright green leaves and rosy flowers.
Habitat	Semi-arid scrub.
Threats	Off-road vehicles.
Range	Arizona, Utah

Description

Jones cycladenia, *Cycladenia humilis* var. *jonesii*, is an herbaceous perennial. Dark green leaves, broadly ovate and cupped, occur in pairs, clustered toward the base. The plants put up a single, erect flowerstalk, up to 6 in (15 cm) tall, bearing many pink or rose-colored, trumpet-shaped flowers, resembling small morning glories. It grows in colonies of stems and new runners are sent out from a deep rhizome.

Habitat

Jones cycladenia survives in badland habitats in semi-arid central Utah, usually on the steep slopes of hills or mesas. It grows in fine textured soils derived from sandstone at elevations of 4,500-5,600 ft (1,400-1,700 m). Surrounding vegetation is sparse, desert scrub. This plant community typically occurs along the lower edge of higher elevation pinyon pine and juniper forests. Associated plants are Mormon tea, shrubby wild-buckwheat, and a perennial sunray (*Enceliopsis nudicaulis*). A subspecies of this last plant found in Nevada, the Ash Meadows sunray (*E. n. corrugata*), is federally listed as endangered.

The Canyonlands section of Utah has more endemic plants—about 70—than any other part of the state. More than a dozen other Canyonlands species are candidates for listing under the Endangered Species Act.

Distribution

Jones cycladenia is the only member of its genus occurring in the intermountain West. Because it is found in three isolated areas more than 100 mi (160.9 km) apart and the nearest related species are in California, Jones cycladenia is believed to be a relict (survival) species from the Tertiary period.

The species was collected and described in 1882 from Pipe Spring (Mohave County), Arizona, but that population, if it still exists, has not been relocated.

Jones cycladenia is currently found in three Utah counties—Emery, Garfield, and Grand. After being considered extinct for a number of years, the plant was rediscovered in 1979 in the San Rafael Desert (east of the San Rafael Swell and south of Interstate 70 in Emery County). One site, with some 2,000 plants, was situated on public land managed by the Bureau of Land Management (BLM); a second site supported about 500 plants on state land.

In 1984 a population was located in the Purple Hills within the Circle Cliffs area of the Glen Canyon National Recreation Area (Garfield County), about 90 mi (144.8 km) south of the San Rafael Swell population. In 1985, about 1,000 plants were located in Castle Valley (Emery County) on BLM land, and another 1,000 plants were found to the northeast along Onion Creek below Fisher Mesa. A recent U. S. Fish and Wildlife Service (FWS) survey discovered a large population of perhaps 5,000 plants in Grand County.

Jones Cycladenia, photograph by Marv Poulson. Reproduced by permission.

As of 1987 the total number of known stems was more than 10,500. Since many of the mature stems are clones of the same plant connected by underground rhizomes, the actual number of plants is hard to determine.

Threats

The arid climate and harsh soils constitute a fragile ecosystem, which is easily degraded and slow to recover from disturbance. Oil and gas leases have been issued near all known population sites, and there has been active exploratory drilling adjacent to the Castle Valley site. Off-road vehicles at Castle Valley and Fisher Mesa have destroyed numerous plants. Sites in the Purple Hills lie within the uranium-bearing Chinle formation, and the area is open to mining claims. Annual exploration and assessment work, required to maintain a valid claim, causes continual disturbance of the habitat.

Conservation and Recovery

Because of this species' threatened status, a review is now required for activities on federal land that might affect populations. Although mineral leases and exploration permits are typically considered on a case-by-case basis, the FWS is working with the BLM to redesign land use policies in the region. If left alone, the plant has a good chance of stabilizing its population and surviving.

Contacts

Regional Office of Endangered Species
U.S. Fish and Wildlife Service
P. O. Box 1306
Albuquerque, New Mexico 87103
http://southwest.fws.gov/

Regional Office of Endangered Species
U.S. Fish and Wildlife Service
P.O. Box 25486
Denver Federal Center
Denver, Colorado 80225
http://www.r6.fws.gov/

References

Holmgren, N. H. 1984. "Cycladenia." In A. Cronquist et al, eds., *Intermountain Flora*, Vol. 4. New York Botanical Garden, Bronx.

U.S. Fish and Wildlife Service. 1986. "Rule to Determine *Cycladenia humilis* var. *jonesii* (Jones cycladenia) to be a Threatened Species." *Federal Register* 53: 16526-16530.

Welsh, S. L. 1970. "New and Unusual Plants from Utah." *Great Basin Naturalist* 30:16-32.

Welsh, S. L. 1984. "Flora of the Glen Canyon National Recreation Area." Report. Glen Canyon National Recreation Area Research Management Team, Page, Arizona.

Welsh, S. L., N. D. Atwood, and J. L. Reveal. 1975. "Endangered, Threatened, Extinct, Endemic, and Rare or Restricted Utah Vascular Plants." *Great Basin Naturalist* 35:327-376.

Holei

Ochrosia kilaueaensis

Status	Endangered
Listed	March 4, 1994
Family	Apocynaceae (Dogbane)
Description	Hairless tree with milky sap, lance- or ellipse-shaped toothless leaves arranged three or four per node, and open clusters of numerous, trumpet-shaped greenish-white flowers.
Habitat	Koa- and 'ohi'a- or lama-dominated montane mesic forests.
Threats	Competition from alien plants; browsing by feral goats; fire; limited numbers.
Range	Hawaii

Description

Holei (*Ochrosia kilaueaensis*) is a hairless tree, 49-59 ft (14.9-18 m) tall, with milky sap. The lance- or ellipse-shaped toothless leaves are arranged three or four per node, are 2.4-7.5 in (6.1-19.1 cm) wide, and have veins arising at nearly right angles to the midrib. Open clusters of numerous flowers have main stalks 1.8-2.5 in (4.6-6.4 cm) long. Each flower has a five-lobed calyx about 0.4 in (1 cm) long and a trumpet-shaped greenish-white corolla with a tube 0.3-0.4 in (7.6-10.2 mm) long and lobes 0.5-0.6 in (1.3-1.5 cm) long. The fruit is a drupe thought to be yellowish-brown at maturity, 1.8-1.9 in (4.6-4.8 cm) long, and 0.9-1.1 in (2.3-2.5 cm) wide. The species is distinguished from other Hawaiian species of the genus by the greater height of mature trees, the open flower clusters, the long flower stalks, and the larger calyx and lobes of the corolla.

Habitat

Holei typically grows in koa- and 'ohi'a- or lama-dominated montane mesic forests at elevations of 2,200-4,000 ft (670.6-1,219.2 m). Associated species include 'aiea, kauila, and kopiko.

Distribution

Historically, this species has been collected on the northern slope of Hualalai and on the eastern slope of Mauna Loa. There may be an extant population located at Puu Waawaa on state land. The population was last collected by Q. Tomich on an unknown date, and the last known observation of the population was in the 1940s, so it may be extinct. The population in Hawaii Volcanoes National Park has not been observed since 1927, although the kipuka was intensively surveyed in 1992.

Threats

O. kilaueaensis has several major threats to its survivability, provided that the taxon remains extant. Feral goats browse and trample the native vegetation, disturbing substrate and understory and providing ample sites for weedy adventives such as *Pennisetum setaceum* (fountain grass). Competition from alien species is a major source of concern for this rare taxon. And drying stands of grass provide an excellent source for fire. In addition, predation of fruits by black rats is a potential problem.

Provided that this taxon persists, human impacts continue to be a serious threat to the species' survival. If this exceedingly rare taxon is extant, the extremely limited number of individuals reduces reproductive rates and increases the probability of extirpation by random events.

Conservation and Recovery

A thorough survey of the area where the last known *O. kilaueaensis* occurred is necessary. If the species is found, genetic material for maintenance of *ex situ* stock should be collected, the existing population protected, and eventual outplanting of propagated material in protected areas within its historic range pursued.

Contacts

U. S. Fish and Wildlife Service
Regional Office, Division of Endangered Species
Eastside Federal Complex
911 N. E. 11th Ave.
Portland, Oregon 97232-4181
(503) 231-6121
http://pacific.fws.gov/

Pacific Remote Islands Ecological Services Field Office
300 Ala Moana Blvd., Room 3-122
P. O. Box 50088
Honolulu, Hawaii 96850
Telephone: (808) 541-1201
Fax: (808) 541-1216

Reference

U. S. Fish and Wildlife Service. 4 March 1994. "Endangered and Threatened Wildlife and Plants; Determination of Endangered or Threatened Status for 21 Plants from the Island of Hawaii, State of Hawaii." *Federal Register* 59 (43): 10305-10325.

Kaulu

Pteralyxia kauaiensis

Status	Endangered
Listed	February 25, 1994
Family	Apocynaceae (Dogbane)
Description	Small tree with dark green egg-shaped leaves and pale yellow trumpet-shaped flowers.
Habitat	Sides of gulches in diverse lowland mesic forests and in lowland wet forests.
Threats	Habitat destruction by feral goats, pigs, and possibly rats; competition with introduced plants.
Range	Hawaii

Description

Kaulu (*Pteralyxia kauaiensis*) is a small tree in the dogbane family (Apocynaceae) that grows to a height of 10-26 ft (3-7.9 m). The leaves are dark green and shiny on the upper surfaces but pale and dull on the lower surfaces. They are generally egg-shaped and usually 4.3-8.7 in (10.9-22.1 cm) long and 1.6-2.6 in (4.1-6.6 cm) wide. The pale yellow flowers are trumpet-shaped, 0.3-0.5 in (7.6-12.7 mm) long, with each of the five lobes 0.1-0.2 in (2.5-5.1 mm) long. The paired fruits, of which usually only one matures, are drupelike, bright red, and fleshy.

The woody endocarp that encloses the single seed has two prominent central wings and two reduced lateral wings. This species differs from the only other member of this endemic Hawaiian genus in having reduced lateral wings on the seed.

Habitat

P. kauaiensis typically grows on the sides of gulches in diverse lowland mesic forests and sometimes in lowland wet forests at elevations of 820-2,000 ft (250-610 m). Associated vegetation includes hame, lama, lantana, 'oki'a, and 'ala'a.

Distribution

P. kauaiensis was known historically from the Wahiawa Mountains in the southern portion of Kauai.

This species is now known from the following scattered locations on private and state land on Kauai at elevations of 820-2,000 ft (250-610 m): Mahanaloa-Kuia Valley in Kuia Natural Area Reserve; Haeleele Valley; Na Pali Coast State Park; Limahuli Valley; the Koaie branch of Waimea Canyon; Haupu Range; Wailua River; and Moloaa Forest Reserve. There is also an undocumented sighting of one individual at Makaleha, above the town of Kapaa, making a total of nine known populations with an estimated 500-1,000 individuals.

Threats

The major threats to *P. kauaiensis* are habitat destruction by feral animals and competition with introduced plants. Animals affecting the survival of this species include feral goats, pigs, and possibly rats, which may eat the fruits. Fire and overcollecting for scientific purposes could threaten some populations. Introduced plants competing with this species include common guava, daisy fleabane, kukui, lantana, strawberry guava, and ti.

Kaulu, photograph by Robert J. Gustafson. Reproduced by permission.

Conservation and Recovery

National Tropical Botanical Garden holds seeds in storage but has been unable to successfully propagate *P. kauaiensis.*

Contacts

U. S. Fish and Wildlife Service
Regional Office, Division of Endangered Species
Eastside Federal Complex
911 N. E. 11th Ave.
Portland, Oregon 97232-4181
(503) 231-6121
http://pacific.fws.gov/

Pacific Remote Islands Ecological Services Field Office
300 Ala Moana Blvd., Room 3-122
P.O. Box 50088
Honolulu, Hawaii 96850
Telephone: (808) 541-1201
Fax: (808) 541-1216

Reference

U. S. Fish and Wildlife Service. 25 February 1994. "Endangered and Threatened Wildlife and Plants; Determination of Endangered or Threatened Status for 24 Plants from the Island of Kauai, HI." *Federal Register* 59 (38): 9304-9329.

Cook's Holly

Ilex cookii

Status	Endangered
Listed	June 16, 1987
Family	Aquifoliaceae (Holly)
Description	Dwarf evergreen shrub with white flowers.
Habitat	Elfin, montane forests at high elevations.
Threats	Deforestation, construction of roads and communications facilities.
Range	Puerto Rico

Description

Cook's holly, *Ilex cookii*, is an evergreen shrub or small shrub reaching eight feet in height. The leaves are alternate, simple, thin but leathery, glabrous, and entire. They are from 0.75-1.75 in (1.9-4.4 cm) long and 0.37-0.87 in (0.9-2.2 cm) wide and reach an abrupt point at the apex. The upper surface is dark shiny green and the lower a pale green with microscopic black dots.

Cook's holly is dioecious: male and female flowers are borne on different plants. Female flowers are minute and white. Fruits are a drupe. Male flowers have not been observed. Pollination is probably effected by insects or wind, although the pollination biology of this species has not been studied. Male flowers and ripe fruit have never been observed and at present only one mature individual is known. The remaining plants are small, both sprouts or seedlings, suggesting that root sprouting or resprouting may occur and that viable seed is occasionally produced.

Habitat

The habitat of Cook's holly is elfin, montane forests at high elevations.

Distribution

Cook's holly is found near the summits of Cerro Punta and Monte Jayuya, both within the Toro Negro Commonwealth Forest. By the turn of the twenty-first century it had not been reported from other sites. At the Cerro Punta location, there were only one mature individual and four sprouts of Cook's holly. At the Monte Jayuya location, the largest population consisted of about 30 sprouts or seedlings that were scattered along the ridgetops. The elevation at these sites ranged from 3,900-4,260 ft (1,188.7-1,298.4 m).

Threats

A serious threat to the dioecious species is the effect population numbers may have on successful reproduction. Only one mature individual is known to exist, and neither male flowers nor mature fruit of this species have ever been reported. Regular pollination and viable seed production may rarely occur and recruitment may be too low to maintain or increase population numbers. Therefore, unless there are sufficient numbers of undiscovered plants, the species could eventually become extinct.

Conservation and Recovery

The successful introduction of Cook's holly is dependent on the propagation of both male and female plants and on the production of viable seed.

Contact

U. S. Fish and Wildlife Service
Regional Office, Division of Endangered Species
Eastside Federal Complex
1875 Century Blvd., Suite 200
Atlanta, Georgia 30345
http://southeast.fws.gov/

References

Ayensu, E. S., and R. A. DeFilipps. 1978. *Endangered and Threatened Plants of the Unites States.* Smithsonian Institution and World Wildlife Fund, Washington, D. C.

Howard, R. A. 1968. "The Ecology of an Elfin Forest in Puerto Rico." *Journal of Arnold Arboretum* 49 (4): 381-418.

Proctor, G. R. 1986. *Ferns of Puerto Rico and the Virgin Islands.* New York Botanical Garden, Bronx.

Ilex sintenisii

No Common Name

Status	Endangered
Listed	April 22, 1992
Family	Aquifoliaceae (Holly)
Description	Shrub or small tree, up to 14.7 ft (4.5 m) in height.
Habitat	Elevations above 2,461 ft (750 m) on windward, ridge, and leeward areas of the mountain tops.
Threats	Establishment and maintenance of plantations, selective cutting, trail and road construction and maintenance, shelter construction, construction of facilities, natural catastrophes.
Range	Puerto Rico

Description

Ilex sintenisii is a shrub or small tree which may reach 14.7 ft (4.5 m) in height and 3 in (7.6 cm) in diameter. Leaves are alternate, glabrous, obovate to elliptic, coriaceous, 0.4-1 in (1-2.5 cm) long and 0.25-0.75 in (0.6-1.9 cm) wide, and notched at the apex with the edges turned under. The bark is gray, smooth, and usually covered with mosses and liverworts. The flowers are white, axillary on pedicels, 0.2-0.4 in (0.4-1 cm) long, and four- to five-parted. The fruits are drupes which are green when immature.

Habitat

The dwarf or elfin forest is found at elevations above 2,461 ft (750 m) on windward, ridge, and leeward areas of the mountain tops. The dwarf forest covers only approximately 556 acres (225 hectares) or 2% of the Caribbean National Forest. Roots of plants in the dwarf forest are found in the soil profile and immediately above, appressed to trunks and hanging freely in the air. The forest is composed of dense stands of short, small diameter, gnarled trees and shrubs. The plants and the forest floor are covered with mosses and epiphytes. This vegetation is exposed to winds and usually shrouded with clouds. The three most common plants are *Pilea krugii*, *Wallenia yunquensis*, and *Calycogonium squamulosum*.

Distribution

I. sintenisii was first discovered by Paul Sintenis in the upper elevations of the Luquillo Mountains. This Puerto Rican endemic is found only in the Luquillo Mountains where it is restricted to the dwarf or elfin forest. A total of 150 individuals in three populations have been reported.

Threats

Forest management practices such as the establishment and maintenance of plantations, selective cutting, trail and road construction and maintenance, and shelter construction may affect the species. The destruction of the dwarf or elfin forests for the construction and/or expansion of communication facilities by the U.S. Navy and private entities continues to be a problem. In addition, the extreme rarity of the species makes it vulnerable to natural catastrophes, such as the passage of Hurricane Hugo in 1989.

Conservation and Recovery

Protection of *I. sintenisii* should be incorporated into management plans for the Caribbean National Forest. Propagation for the establishment of new populations or the enhancement of existing ones should be considered a priority recovery mechanism.

Contacts

U.S. Fish and Wildlife Service
Regional Office, Division of Endangered Species
1875 Century Blvd., Suite 200
Atlanta, Georgia 30345
http://southeast.fws.gov/

Caribbean Field Office
U.S. Fish and Wildlife Service
Box 491
Boquerón, Puerto Rico 00622
Telephone: (809) 851-7297

References

Brown, S., A. E. Lugo, S. Silander, and L. Liegel. 1983. Research history and opportunities in the Luquillo Experimental Forest. General Technical Report SO-44. U.S. Department of Agriculture, Forest Service, Southern Forest Experiment Station, New Orleans, Louisiana. 128 pp.

Little, E. L., Jr., R. O. Woodbury, and F. H. Wadsworth. 1974. *Trees of Puerto Rico and the Virgin Islands.* Second Volume. Agriculture Handbook No. 449. U.S. Department of Agriculture, Forest Service, Washington, D.C. 1024 pp.

U.S. Fish and Wildlife Service. 1991. "Endangered and Threatened Wildlife and Plants; Determination of Endangered Status for Five Puerto Rican Trees." *Federal Register* 57 (78): 14782-14785.

Munroidendron racemosum

No Common Name

Status	Endangered
Listed	February 25, 1994
Family	Araliaceae (Ginseng)
Description	Medium-size tree with a straight, gray trunk and spreading branches; elliptical leaves; and pale yellow flowers.
Habitat	Steep exposed cliffs or ridge slopes in coastal to lowland mesic forests.
Threats	Competition from alien plants, feral goats, insects, over-collecting, limited numbers.
Range	Hawaii

Munroidendron racemosum, photograph by Robert J. Gustafson. Reproduced by permission.

Description

Munroidendron racemosum is a tree in the ginseng family (Araliaceae). It grows to about 23 ft (7 m) and has a straight gray trunk crowned with spreading branches. The leaves are 6-12 in (15-30.5) long and comprise five to nine oval or elliptical leaflets with clasping leaf stalks. Each leaflet is 3-7 in (8-17 cm) long and usually 1.6-3.9 in (4-10 cm) wide. About 250 pale yellow flowers are borne along a stout hanging stalk 10-24 in (25.4-61 cm) long. Each flower has five or six lance-shaped petals 0.3-0.4 in (long, emerging from a cup-shaped or ellipsoid calyx tube). Both the lower surface of the petals and the calyx tube are covered with whitish scaly hairs. The fruit is an egg-shaped drupe 0.3-0.5 in (0.8-1.3 cm) long and nearly as wide, situated atop a flat, dark red disk (stylopodium). This species is the only member of a genus endemic to Hawaii, differing from other closely related Hawaiian genera of the family primarily in its distinct flower clusters and corolla.

Some reproduction is occurring, with flowering and fruiting occurring throughout the year. Self-pollination is assumed to occur due to viable seed produced by isolated individuals. Pollinators have not been observed, but insect pollination is likely. Dispersal mechanisms are unknown.

Habitat

Most *M. racemosum* populations are found on steep exposed cliffs and ridge slopes in coastal to lowland mesic forests. A few populations are found in mesic hala forests, lantana-dominated shrubland, or *Eragrotis* grasslands. Associated plants include common guava (*Psidium guajava)*, kopiko (*Psychotria* spp.), kukui (*Aleurites moluccana)*, and lama.

Distribution

M. racemosum has historical occurrences at scattered locations throughout the island of Kauai. Fifteen populations are now found at elevations of 390-1,310 ft (119-400 m) on private and state land along the Na Pali Coast within the Na Pali Coast State Park and Hono O Na Pali Natural Area Reserve, in the Poomau and Koaie branches of Waimea Canyon, in the Haupu Range area, and on Nounou Mountain.

Although populations are widely distributed, most of them number only one or two individuals. The largest population has fewer than 50 individuals. There are only an estimated 200 *M. racemosum* trees left.

Threats

Competition with introduced plants is the major threat to *M. racemosum*. Kukui and ti plants, introduced by Polynesian immigrants to the Hawaiian Islands, compete with this species for space in the forests of Kauai. Other introduced plants threatening *M. racemosum* habitat include chinaberry (*Melia azedarach)*, common guava, firetree (*Myrcia faya)*, koa haole (*Leucaena leucocephala)*, lantana (*Lantana camara)* and Sacramento burr. Several animal species also pose threats to *M. racemosum*. Feral goats degrade the habitat, and cattle were formerly present in areas where the trees grow. Predation of the trees' fruits by rats is probable. An introduced insect of the longhorned beetle family, which killed a mature cultivated tree, has the potential of affecting wild trees. In addition, because each population of this species contains only one or a few trees, the species is threatened by humans through overcollecting for scientific or horticultural purposes. These practices could lead to stochastic extinction, and reduced reproductive vigor. Fire also endangers *M. racemosum*.

Conservation and Recovery

M. racemosum has been successfully propagated and cultivated by Lyon Arboretum, the National Tropical Botanical Garden, and Waimea Arboretum. In 1995, Lyon Arboretum had seed in the tissue culture lab and five plants on arboretum grounds. The National Tropical Botanical Garden, as of the same year, was holding seeds in storage and had plants growing in their garden. Waimea Arboretum was maintaining three plants at this time.

The Division of Forestry and Wildlife has outplanted about 400 individuals at Kauhao Ridge and other populations at Haeleele Ridge in Puu Ka Pele Forest Reserve.

Contacts

Pacific Joint Venture
300 Ala Moana Boulevard, Room 3-122
P.O. Box 50167
Honolulu, Hawaii 96850-0056
(808) 541-2749

U.S. Fish and Wildlife Service
Regional Office, Division of Endangered Species
Eastside Federal Complex
911 N.E. 11th Ave.
Portland, Oregon 97232-4181
(503) 231-6121
http://pacific.fws.gov/

Reference

U.S. Fish and Wildlife Service. 25 February 1994. "Endangered and Threatened Wildlife and Plant; Determination of Endangered or Threatened Status for 24 Plants from Island of Kauai, HI." *Federal Register* 59 (38): 9304-9329.

ʻOheʻohe

Tetraplasandra gymnocarpa

Status	Endangered
Listed	March 28, 1994
Family	Araliaceae (Ginseng)
Description	Tree is hairless or with fuzzy, short-lived hairs and flowers clustered in threes in an umbrella-shaped arrangement.
Habitat	Windswept summit ridges or in gullies in wet or sometimes mesic forests.
Threats	Competition from alien plants; habitat destruction by feral pigs; limited numbers.
Range	Hawaii

Description

ʻOheʻohe (*Tetraplasandra gymnocarpa*) is a tree in the ginseng family. It is either hairless or with fuzzy and short-lived hairs on the young leaves and flower clusters, and grows to a height of 8-33 ft (2.4-10 m). The leaves, 12-22 in (30.5-56 cm) long, have 7-21 leathery, oval to elliptic leaflets per leaf. Each leaflet, 2.8-7.1 in (7.1-18 cm) long and 1.2-3.1 in (3-7.9 cm) wide, is folded upward along the midveins. The flowers are usually arranged in threes or in an umbrella-shaped arrangement. Petals are 0.2-0.3 in (0.5-0.8 cm) long and usually number five to six per flower, with an equal number of stamens. The ovary, which usually has three to four sections, is atop the receptacle (base of the flower) in a superior position, due to the expansion of the ovary disk (outgrowth of the receptacle) and the reduction of the hypanthium (basal portion of the flower). Fruits are purplish, oval or top-shaded drupes, 0.2-0.5 in (0.5-1.3 cm) long, that enclose a papery endocarp and single seed. This species was observed in flower and fruit in November 1991 and in fruit in May and September 1991.

T. gymnocarpa is distinguished from all other species in the genus in that its ovary appears fully superior.

Habitat

T. gymnocarpa is typically found on windswept summit ridges or in gullies in wet or sometimes mesic forests between elevations of 820-2,790 ft (250-850.4 m). Associated plants include ʻohiʻa (*Metrosideros collina*), olapa, uluhe (*Dicranopteris linearis*), kopiko (*Psychotria* spp.), kamakahala (*Labordia* spp.) and kolea.

Distribution

T. gymnocarpa was historically known from Punahuu, Waikakalaua Gulch, Mount Olympus, and the region between Niu and Wailupe, all in the Koolau Mountains of Oahu.

Seventeen populations are now scattered along summit ridges of the Koolau Mountains over a distance of 28 mi (45 km); from the region of Paumalu at the northern extreme to Kuliouou and Waimanalo at the southeasternmost point. One population in the Waianae Mountains, located on Palikea Ridge on the border of federal and private land, was last visited in 1954, and it is not known if it still exists. Most populations contained between one and six individuals in 1997, although the total for all occurrences was estimated at fewer than 200 plants.

'Ohe'Ohe, photograph by John Obata. Reproduced by permission.

Threats

The primary threats to *T. gymnocarpa* are competition with the aggressive exotic Koster's curse (*Clidemia hirta*), habitat destruction by feral pigs, and reduced reproductive vigor due to the limited gene pool.

Conservation and Recovery

The National Tropical Botanical Garden has attempted propagation of *T. gymnocarpa* seeds with no germination success. To prevent extinction of this species, propagation materials should be collected immediately from remaining populations.

Contacts

Pacific Joint Venture
300 Ala Moana Blvd., Rm. 3-122
Honolulu, Hawaii 96850-0056
Phone: (808) 541-2749
Fax: (808) 541-2756

U.S. Fish and Wildlife Service
Regional Office, Division of Endangered Species
Eastside Federal Complex
911 N.E. 11th Avenue
Portland, Oregon 97232-4181
Phone: (503) 231-6121
http://pacific.fws.gov/

Reference

U.S. Fish and Wildlife Service. 28 March 1994. "Endangered and Threatened Wildlife and Plants; Determination of Endangered or Threatened Status for 11 Plants Species from the Koolau Mountain Range, Island of Oahu, HI." *Federal Register* 59 (59): 14482-14492.

Dwarf-flowered Heartleaf

Hexastylis naniflora

Status	Threatened
Listed	April 14, 1989
Family	Aristolochiaceae (Birthwort)
Description	Low-growing herb, with heart-shaped, evergreen leaves and small beige or brown flowers.
Habitat	Bogs and marshes in mixed hardwood forests.
Threats	Road construction, agricultural and residential development.
Range	North Carolina, South Carolina

Dwarf-flowered Heartleaf, photograph by Robert R. Currie, USFWS. Reproduced by permission.

Description

Dwarf-flowered heartleaf is a low-growing herbaceous plant, rarely exceeding 6 in (15 cm) in height. The evergreen, heart-shaped leaves, dark green and leathery, are supported by slender petioles (leaf stalks), rising from a rhizome. Inconspicuous, beige or dark brown flowers are jug-shaped and bloom at the base of the leaf petioles. Flowers occur from mid-March to early June and the fruit matures from mid-May to early July. The plant may be distinguished from close relatives by its small flowers and distinctive habitat.

Habitat

This species grows in narrow ravines or along the base of bluffs and hillsides that overlook bogs, marshes and small streams. It is restricted to moist, acidic soils and prefers partial sunlight. Habitat areas are typically heavily forested with mature stands of mixed hardwoods.

Distribution

Dwarf-flowered heartleaf is known from an eight-county area in the upper Piedmont of North Carolina and adjacent portions of South Carolina.

Eleven populations of heartleaf are currently known from five North Carolina counties—Cleveland, Catawba, Burke, Rutherford, and Lincoln.

Three Cleveland County sites support about 400 plants that are threatened by timbering or conversion of the habitat to pasture. A healthy population of more than 1,000 plants occurs at one site in Catawba County that is protected by Natural Areas Registry Program of the North Carolina Natural Heritage Program. Burke County harbors three populations in marginal habitat, totaling fewer than 1,000 plants. The site of the largest Rutherford County population, numbering more than 1,000 plants, is a registered natural area, but two smaller sites nearby are threatened by road construction. Of three populations that had been documented from

Lincoln County, two were recently lost to logging and agricultural development, while the third population survives as a remnant of about 160 plants.

Currently, this species is known from 12 populations in three South Carolina counties—Cherokee, Greenville, and Spartanburg. One small population of about 150 plants survives in Cherokee County in habitat that has recently been degraded by road construction. Conversion of woodlands to pasture, logging, and urban expansion have limited the extent of all eight population sites in Greenville County. Numbers in these populations have declined to fewer than 800 plants. The largest population in Spartanburg, once numbering 4,000 plants, declined by nearly 65% when part of its habitat was flooded by a newly constructed reservoir. Two remnant populations have nearly been eliminated by construction of an interstate highway.

Threats

Although surviving populations of dwarf-flowered heartleaf are geographically dispersed, all are threatened by similar factors. In the past, bottomland timber was clear-cut, and bogs and marshes were drained to create pasture for livestock, decreasing the amount of available habitat. Many bogs at the sources of streams have been dammed to create ponds for watering livestock. Conversion of habitat for agricultural uses continues. More recently, land has been cleared to support residential development, particularly near the city of Greenville, South Carolina. Associated construction of new reservoirs to supply the expanding human population and of new roads to handle the increased flow of traffic have claimed large tracts of former heartleaf habitat.

Conservation and Recovery

At some population sites, hardwood stands have grown so dense as to restrict sunlight, reducing the vigor of plants. Where these sites can be accessed, selective logging would improve light penetration. Only four populations are currently protected. The state natural heritage programs (under the direction of the Nature Conservancy) and the city of Spartanburg, South Carolina, are cooperating with the U. S. Fish and Wildlife Service to plan recovery for dwarf-flowered heartleaf.

Contact

Regional Office of Endangered Species
U.S. Fish and Wildlife Service
1875 Century Blvd., Suite 200
Atlanta, Georgia 30345
http://southeast.fws.gov/

References

Gaddy, L. L. 1980. "Status Report on *Hexastylis naniflora* Blomquist." Report. U.S. Fish and Wildlife Service, Atlanta.

Gaddy, L. L. 1981. "The Status of *Hexastylis naniflora* Blomquist in North Carolina." Report. Plant Conservation Program, North Carolina Department of Agriculture, Raleigh.

U.S. Fish and Wildlife Service. 1989. "Determination of Threatened Status of *Hexastylis naniflora* (Dwarf-flowered heartleaf)." *Federal Register* 54 (71): 14964-14967.

Mead's Milkweed

Asclepias meadii

Status	Threatened
Listed	September 1, 1988
Family	Asclepiadaceae (Milkweed)
Description	Perennial unbranched herb with broad, ovate leaves and umbels of cream-colored flowers.
Habitat	Deep, unplowed prairie loam.
Threats	Urban development, agricultural expansion.
Range	Illinois, Indiana, Iowa, Kansas, Missouri, Wisconsin

Mead's Milkweed, photograph by Don Kurz. Reproduced by permission.

Description

Mead's milkweed, *Asclepias meadii*, is a perennial herb that puts up a single, unbranched stalk, 8-16 in (20-40 cm) tall. The stalk is hairless but has a white sheen caused by a waxy covering. The broad, ovate leaves, up to 3 in (7.5 cm) long, are opposite. Six to 15 cream-colored flowers are grouped into a flat-topped cluster (umbel) at the ends of the stems. Blooming is in late May and early June. Fruit pods appear in June and gradually grow to full maturity in October. Mature pods eventually split and disperse hundreds of hairy seeds that are carried by the wind.

Habitat

Mead's milkweed is found on virgin prairie as a solitary plant or in small colonies. Populations, rarely numbering more than 20 plants, are found on unplowed bluestem prairie in Missouri consisting of deep, silty loams. It is found in similar habitat in the other states of its range.

Distribution

The species was formerly widespread over much of the native tallgrass prairie region of the Midwest, which included portions of Illinois, Indiana, Iowa,

Kansas, Missouri, and Wisconsin. Mead's milkweed is thought to have disappeared from Indiana and Wisconsin.

When the species was federally listed, 81 sites were known from 23 counties within Illinois, Iowa, Kansas, and Missouri. Although seemingly widespread, the number of plants at each site are few, and the overall range has shrunk dramatically. The plant's former range of seven Illinois counties has now decreased to three sites in Ford and Saline Counties. Formerly found in 11 Missouri counties, it now occurs in seven, mainly in the southwestern quadrant of the state (Barton, Benton, Dade, Pettis, Polk, St. Clair, and Vernon Counties). Two of the largest populations, numbering more than 800 plants at each site (1988) are near Lawrence, Kansas. Once known from five Iowa counties, only two small populations remain in Adair and Warren Counties. A 1991 theft of an entire population of six individuals in Shawnee National Forest in Illinois offered renewed evidence of the dangers of publicizing, or even acknowledging, the wilderness locations of endangered species. Following the theft, the known populations were reduced to 80.

Fortunately, in the spring of 1996, two new populations of Mead's milkweed were discovered on rhyolite glades in southcentral Missouri. One small population is on Wildcat Mountain in Taum Sauk State Park. A much larger population was found on Profit Mountain within the Missouri Department of Conservation's Ketcherside Mountain Conservation Area.

Threats

The type of virgin prairie preferred by Mead's milkweed and other Midwestern endemics has become increasingly rare in recent years. Most deep-loamed soils have been farmed at one time or another. Hay meadows have gradually been converted to grain crops. Remaining hay meadows are mowed two or three times a year before stray milkweed plants have a chance to set seed.

If there was any question about the dangers of illegal collecting, they were answered, bitterly, in June, 1991, when an entire population of six plants was snatched from a remote location of the Shawnee National Forest in Illinois. Concentrated within a half-acre site, the plants were either carefully dug up or cut off with a razor blade. Monitoring the pop-

ulation weekly, botanists at the National Forest contacted the Fish and Wildlife Service's Division of Law Enforcement in the Twin Cities within two hours of discovering that the plants were gone. The population consisted of both wild specimens and young, introduced stock recently planted in a joint effort to reestablish Mead's milkweed in its historic range. One of only six places where the threatened species was known to exist east of the Mississippi River, Shawnee National Forest was considered the premier site for reintroducing the plant into its native habitat.

Currently, remnants of virgin prairie are succumbing to urban commercial and residential expansion. Several of the largest populations near Lawrence, Kansas are in areas that are virtually certain to be developed for housing within the next few years. None of the known populations are considered secure.

Conservation and Recovery

The key to the survival of the Mead's milkweed is the protection of the remnants of its critical prairie habitat. Some habitats are being conserved, including areas in Taum Sauk State Park and Ketcherside Mountain Conservation Area in Missouri, and in the Shawnee National Forest in Illinois. However, most critical habitats are on private land and are potentially threatened by various human activities, especially agricultural conversion. These habitats should be protected by acquiring the land and designating ecological reserves, or by negotiating conservation easements with the owners. The populations of the Mead's milkweed should be monitored, and research undertaken into its biology, habitat needs, and beneficial management practices. The rare plant should be propagated in captivity to provide stock for out-planting to increase the size of existing populations and to establish new ones in suitable prairie habitat.

Contact

U.S. Fish and Wildlife Service
Division of Endangered Species
Administration Office
Federal Building
1 Federal Drive
Fort Snelling, Minnesota 55111-4056
Telephone: (612) 713-5360
Fax: (612) 713-5292

References

Alverson, W. S. 1981. "Status Report on *Asclepias meadii*." Wisconsin Department of Natural Resources, Madison.

Bacone, J. A., T. J. Crovello and L. A. Hauser. 1981. "Status Report on *Asclepias meadii*." Indiana Department of Conservation, Indianapolis.

Betz, R. F. and J. E. Hohn. 1978. "Status Report for *Asclepias meadii*." Contract Report to U.S. Fish and Wildlife Service, Twin Cities, Minnesota.

Welsh's Milkweed

Asclepias welshii

Status	Threatened
Listed	October 28, 1987
Family	Asclepiadaceae (Milkweed)
Description	Herbaceous perennial with oval leaves and cream-colored flowers.
Habitat	Stabilized sand dunes.
Threats	Off-road vehicles.
Range	Arizona, Utah

Description

Welsh's milkweed, *Asclepias welshii*, is a perennial herb, 10-40 in (24-100 cm) tall, growing from a thickened rhizome. It bears large oval leaves and cream-colored flowers tinged with rose in the center. The flowers grow spherically in groups of 30 and are about 2.75 in (7 cm) in diameter. Welsh's milkweed reproduces both sexually and asexually, flowering May to June. Fruit and seed dispersal occurs from July to September.

Habitat

Welsh's milkweed grows on stabilized sand dunes associated with sagebrush, juniper, and ponderosa pine communities at 5,570-6,230 ft (1,700-1,900 m) elevation, or in sheltered pockets on the leeward slopes of actively drifting dunes. The plant grows in four situations: amongst other vegetation, on exposed shale, on fine grain exposed geological rock types, or in finer grained developed soils. It grows quickly enough to keep ahead of the moving sand dune as it drifts toward the location of the plant.

Distribution

The first plants were collected on the Coral Pink Sand Dunes in Kane County, Utah, in 1979. The plant is endemic to this region of south-central Utah.

Welsh's milkweed is found in only two places in Kane County: the Coral Pink Sand Dunes and 8 mi (13 km) to the northeast in the Sand Hills. In the Coral Pink Sand Dunes about 6,000 plants are scattered across a dune environment administered by the Bureau of Land Management. Perhaps 4,000 more plants grow on adjacent state lands that are part of the Coral Pink Sand Dunes State Park. An estimated 500 plants occur in the Sand Hills area.

Threats

Dunes plants are very sensitive to disturbance and may take years to recover from an environmental disruption. The major populations of Welsh's milkweed grow in the Coral Pink Sand Dunes, an area heavily used by off-road vehicles. These vehicles disturb or destroy plant life and destabilize the fragile dunes ecology. Some of the area has been leased for oil and gas exploration, but the exploration leases stipulate "no surface occupancy," which excludes drilling in the dune areas. Because most plants are growing on government land, management strategies will exclude off-road vehicles from the habitat areas and maintain restrictions on surface occupancy.

Conservation and Recovery

The state of Utah opposed listing Welsh's milkweed because officials thought that a declaration of critical habitat would restrict off-road vehicle recreation, one of the reasons for which the Coral Pink Sand Dunes State Park was established and funded. A local off-road vehicle association, however, agreed to cooperate with the Fish and Wildlife Service (FWS) and has set up an educational program for its membership. The FWS does not anticipate listing to have a direct impact on state park activities.

Critical Habitat was designated to include 4,000 acres of sand dune habitat in the Coral Pink Sand Dunes and the Sand Hills area.

Contacts

U.S. Fish and Wildlife Service
Division of Endangered Species
P.O. Box 1306
Albuquerque, New Mexico 87103
http://southwest.fws.gov/

U.S. Fish and Wildlife Service
Division of Endangered Species
Denver Federal Center
P.O. Box 25486
Denver, Colorado 80225
http://www.r6.fws.gov/

References

Holmgren, N. H., and P. K. Holmgren. 1979. "A New Species of *Asclepias* (Asclepiadaceae) from Utah." *Brittonia* 31(1):110-114.

Luckenback, R. A., and R. B. Bury. 1983. "Effects of Off-Road Vehicles on the Biota of the Algondones Dunes, Imperial County, California." *Journal of Applied Ecology* 20:265-286.

U.S. Fish and Wildlife Service. 1987. "Final Rule Determining Welsh's milkweed, *Asclepias welshii* to Be a Threatened Species with Critical Habitat." *Federal Register* 52(208): 41435-41441.

U.S. Fish and Wildlife Service. 1991." Welsh's milkweed, *Asclepias welshii*, Recovery Plan." USFWS, Denver. 29 pp.

Nevin's Barberry

Berberis nevinii

Status	Endangered
Listed	October 13, 1998
Family	Berberidaceae (Barberry)
Description	An evergreen shrub.
Habitat	Chaparral and alluvial scrub in foothills.
Threats	Habitat destruction by urbanization, and degradation by off-road vehicles and other disturbances.
Range	California

Nevin's Barberry, photograph by Steve Junak. Reproduced by permission.

Description

Berberis nevinii (Nevin's barberry), a member of the barberry family (Berberidaceae), was described by Asa Gray (1895) based on a collection made by Joseph Nevin in 1892 on the east side of the San Fernando Valley near Los Angeles. *Berberis nevinii* has been treated as *Mahonia nevinii* and *Odostemon nevinii*. Recent authorities follow Gray's treatment.

Berberis nevinii is a rhizomatous evergreen shrub 3-12 ft (1-4 m) tall. The pinnately compound leaves (featherlike arrangement of the leaflets) are gray-green with serrate, spine-tipped margins. The flowers, clustered in loose racemes, have six yellow petals arranged in two series. The berries are juicy, yellowish to red, less than 0.3 in (6-8 mm) long with brownish seeds. This species flowers from March through April. *Berberis nevinii* is distinguished from other members of the genus by its nearly flat, narrow, serrate, pinnately veined leaves, few flowered racemes, and reddish fruits.

Habitat

The Nevin's barberry occurs in restricted and localized populations from the interior foothills of San Diego County and northwestern Baja California, Mexico. It occurs in chaparral and alluvial scrub associated with rocky slopes and sediments and sandy washes. It is found in two habitat types: gravelly wash margins in alluvial scrub, and on coarse soils in chaparral, typically between 900 and 2,000 ft (275-610 m) in elevation.

Chaparral habitats of the interior foothill region of southern California are dense shrub associations of moderate height dominated by chamise, California lilac, red berry, manzanita, California scrub oak, sugar bush, laurel sumac, toyon, California buckwheat, and black sage. Chaparral plant communities are adapted to nutrient poor soils, cool wet winters, and hot dry summers.

Distribution

One of the two largest known populations of *B. nevinii* occurs near Vail Lake in southwestern Riverside County. The other large population of *B. nevinii* is in San Francisquito Canyon on the Angeles National Forest in Los Angeles County. The majority of *B. nevinii* plants found outside the Vail Lake and Angeles National Forest sites occur as isolated populations in San Bernardino and Los Angeles Counties.

Historically, the range of this species probably consisted of fewer than 30 scattered occurrences. At least seven populations have been extirpated, probably due to factors associated with urbanization. The species' native range currently extends from the foothills of the San Gabriel Mountains of Los Angeles County to near the foothills of the Peninsular Ranges of southwestern Riverside County. The total number of individuals is reportedly fewer than 1,000, but may be fewer than 500. The largest remaining cluster of native populations, which collectively contain about 200 individuals, occurs in Riverside County in the Vail Lake/Oak Mountain area. Most of these populations are on private lands in the Vail Lake region, although a few individuals occur on Bureau of Land Management lands north of Vail Lake and in the Cleveland National Forest southeast of Vail Lake. In Los Angeles County, another population of 130-250 individuals occurs on an alluvial terrace and on steep slopes in San Francisquito Canyon, Angeles National Forest. Another site was recently discovered on the Angeles National Forest. Two other native populations are small, with fewer than 10 individuals, and occur on private lands.

The range of *Berberis nevinii* has been extensively surveyed, and additional populations are not likely to occur in the Vail Lake area. Searches for *B. nevinii*, based on Boyd's habitat parameters, revealed no additional plants in the San Bernardino National Forest.

Threats

This species is imperiled by various activities, including urbanization and off-road vehicle use, that result in habitat modification, destruction, degradation, and fragmentation. The specific soil and/or hydrological requirements of this plant species naturally limit their distribution to clay soils formed from gabbro and alluvial or sedimentary based substrates (sandy washes and terraces) within the chap-

Steve Junak

arral or scrub plant communities. Most of the alluvial scrub habitat in the San Fernando and San Gabriel valleys has been eliminated by urban development, road widening, flood control measures, or habitat degradation from extensive recreational use. Urban development and mining have generally impacted these habitat types more directly than other activities within the chaparral community, the terrain being more accessible than the typically rugged, steep, boulder-covered terrain of the surrounding chaparral.

Populations of *Berberis nevinii* occurring in alluvial scrub habitats of Los Angeles County have been heavily impacted. A note on a specimen of *B. nevinii* collected in 1932 stated that there were only about 100 plants known, all east of San Fernando Road, and that their numbers were likely to decrease. Urbanization and brush fires are causes of the hastened rate of extinction of this species in the area near San Fernando (Los Angeles County). Several sites apparently containing *B. nevinii* in this area have been destroyed by the extensive urbanization of the eastern San Fernando Valley. A new occurrence of a single plant was found in 1998 in a canyon on the south slope of the San Gabriel Mountains. The occurrence, of questionable origin because it was near an old nursery, consisted of a single plant on a parcel with an approved tentative tract map; this site was recently cleared.

The majority of the 16 native occurrences for *Berberis nevinii*, which are all located in the vicinity of Vail Lake in western Riverside County, consist of five or fewer plants. Urban development in the Vail Lake area threatens the largest group of occurrences of *B. nevinii*, and most of these occurrences at Vail Lake would likely be eliminated by development. Parcels recently sold at Vail Lake contain about 15 of the 16 occurrences and apparently contain more than 150 of the approximately 200 plants of *B. nevinii* in western Riverside County. An application for a conditional-use permit has been filed for one of the parcels that has both *B. nevinii* and another federally listed plant species, *Dodecahema leptoceras* (slender-horned spineflower). This parcel is also adjacent to a parcel that supports *Ceanothus ophiochilus*.

Conservation and Recovery

The California Fish and Game Commission listed *Berberis nevinii* as endangered. Although state law prohibits taking state-listed plants, these statutes inadequately protect against the taking of such plants through habitat modification or land use change by the landowner.

The U.S. Fish and Wildlife Service is working with Riverside and San Bernardino Counties to create multispecies habitat conservation plans that may benefit *Berberis nevinii*. San Bernardino County and Riverside County have signed planning agreements with local, state and federal agencies including the Fish and Wildlife Service.

Contact

U.S. Fish and Wildlife Service
Loren Hays, Chief Branch of Listing and Recovery
U.S. Fish and Wildlife Service
Carlsbad Field Office
2730 Loker Avenue West
Carlsbad, California 92008-6603
Telephone: (760) 431-9440
Fax: (760) 431-9624

Reference

U.S. Fish and Wildlife Service. October 13, 1998. "Endangered or Threatened Status for Three Plants from the Chaparral and Scrub of Southwestern California." *Federal Register* 63(197): 54956-54971.

Island Barberry

Berberis pinnata ssp. *insularis*

Status	Endangered
Listed	July 31, 1997
Family	Berberidaceae (Barberry)
Description	A low shrub with large leaves that are divided into five to nine glossy green leaflets and has clusters of yellow flowers at its branch tips.
Habitat	Moist, shaded canyons on Santa Cruz Island.
Threats	Habitat destruction and degradation by introduced mammalian herbivores and invasive alien plants.
Range	California

Steve Junak

Description

Berberis pinnata ssp. *insularis* (island barberry) was described in 1952 from a specimen collected 20 years earlier "west of summit of Buena Vista Grade (also known as Centinela Grade), interior of Santa Cruz Island." This taxon was included in the genus *Mahonia* in 1981 because the leaves are compound, in contrast with the simple leaves of *Berberis*. However, in 1982 the argument was made that this one character was insufficient to defend *Mahonia* as a distinct natural group, and many subsequent treatments have included all North American taxa previously referred to *Mahonia* as *Berberis*. This taxon has been treated as *Berberis pinnata* ssp. *insularis* since 1974. *Berberis pinnata* ssp. *insularis* is a perennial shrub in the barberry family (Berberidaceae). The plant has spreading stems that reach 5-25 ft (2-8 m) high, with large leaves divided into five to nine glossy green leaflets. Clusters of yellow flowers at the branch tips develop into blue berries covered with a white bloom (waxy coating). Because new shoots can sprout from underground rhizomes,

many stems may actually represent one genetic clone. Recent research indicates that, although the plant is genetically self-compatible, it requires insect visitation for pollination. Each flower produces from two to three seeds, but in seed germination experiments only eight out of 40 seedlings survived long enough to produce secondary leaves. Observations on the one plant in upper Canada Christy indicated that, of over 100 flowers that were in bud in January 1996, only seven immature fruit had developed by May 1996.

Habitat

Island barberry inhabits moist, shaded canyons on Santa Cruz Island.

Distribution

Documentary evidence indicates that this taxa was quite common on Santa Cruz Island in the 1930s. *Berberis pinnata* ssp. *insularis* is currently known from three small populations on Santa Cruz

Island Barberry, photograph by Steve Junak. Reproduced by permission.

resent one or several clonal individuals. In 1979, a second population near Campo Raton (Canada Cristy) was estimated to be fewer than 10 individuals, but in 1985 only one plant was seen. Habitat for the plant was systematically searched recently in the Campo Raton area and two individuals were located. Both plants were in danger of uprooting from erosion and only one plant flowered but it did not set fruit. The size of the third known population, at Hazard's Canyon, has not been determined due to inaccessibility, but it is estimated that there were between one and seven plants at this location. *Berberis pinnata* ssp. *insularis* can be found in moist, shaded canyons on Santa Cruz Island.

Threats

Berberis pinnata ssp. *insularis* is threatened by soil loss and habitat alteration caused by feral pig rooting. Although ex-situ clones have been established from vegetative cuttings, populations in the field show no signs of successful sexual reproduction. The soil from around the roots of *Berberis pinnata* ssp. *insularis* on Santa Rosa Island is actively eroding. The collection of whole plants or reproductive parts of *Berberis pinnata* ssp. *insularis* could adversely affect the genetic viability and survival of this taxa.

Conservation and Recovery

The island barberry only survives as three tiny populations on Santa Cruz Island. The broader habitat on the island is being conserved in a relatively natural condition in the Channel Islands National Park, and by the Nature Conservancy, a private conservation organization. However, the island barberry and other rare plants are severely threatened by the feeding of sheep and other introduced mammals. The protection of the endangered barberry requires that these herbivores be reduced or eliminated from its habitat. The abundance of invasive alien plants should also be reduced or eliminated, because they are providing intense competition to native species. The populations of the island barberry should be monitored, and research undertaken into its biology and habitat needs, including methods of management that would benefit the endangered plant. A captive-propagation program should be developed, to provide stock for outplanting to supplement the tiny natural population, and to reestablish populations on nearby islands from which the barberry has been extirpated.

Island. Several individuals were found "in Elder canyon that runs from west into Canada de la Casa" on Santa Rosa Island in 1930. No plants have been found on Santa Rosa Island since that time despite government and private surveys between 1993 and 1996. *Berberis pinnata* ssp. *insularis* was collected on West Anacapa Island in 1940, but the plant was not found there again until 1980, when one clone was found in Summit Canyon associated with chaparral species, including poison oak (*Toxicodendron diversilobum*), monkeyflower (*Mimulus aurantiacus*), coyote bush (*Baccharis* sp.), goldenbush (*Hazardia detonsus*), island alum-root (*Heuchera maxima*), and wild cucumber (*Marah macrocarpus*).

A 1994 survey found that the clone had died, and *Berberis pinnata* ssp. *insularis* is therefore believed to be extirpated from Anacapa Island. The three known populations of *Berberis pinnata* ssp. *insularis* occur on Santa Cruz Island. One population on the north slope of Diablo Peak comprises 24 large stems and 75 small stems; this number of stems may rep-

Contacts

U. S. Fish and Wildlife Service
Regional Office, Division of Endangered Species
Eastside Federal Building
911 N. E. 11th Ave.
Portland, Oregon 97232-4181
Telephone: (503) 231-6121
http://pacific.fws.gov/

U.S. Fish and Wildlife Service
Ventura Fish and Wildlife Office
2493 Portola Road, Suite B
Ventura, California 93003-7726
Telephone: (805) 644-1766

Reference

U.S. Fish and Wildlife Service. 31 July 1997. "Endangered and Threatened Wildlife and Plants; Final Rule for 13 Plant Taxa From the Northern Channel Islands, California." *Federal Register* 62(147): 40954-40974.

Truckee Barberry

Berberis sonnei

Status	Endangered
Listed	November 6, 1979
Family	Berberidaceae (Barberry)
Description	Shrub with compound pinnate leaves and yellow flowers.
Habitat	Sandy soil in cool canyon microclimate.
Threats	Low numbers, restricted range.
Range	California

Janus Payne Smith, Jr.

Description

Truckee barberry, *Berberis sonnei*, is one of only two shrubs in the otherwise herbaceous barberry family. Also known as the Truckee berberis, this shrub grows from 8-20 in (20-50 cm) tall and bears compound pinnate leaves that are lustrous green on the upper surface with bristle-tipped teeth on the margin. Yellow flowers bloom from mid-April to late May and emit a carnation-like aroma. Fruits mature and turn a dark blue or purple by late September and contain numerous shiny, light brown seeds.

In spite of the profusion of seeds, most plants reproduce vegetatively from underground shoots.

In early May, new shoots push out of the ground up to 3 ft (1 m) from the nearest parent plant. Simultaneously, an abundance of new leaves appear on old growth. Barberries in the wild are considered evergreen, yet for some unknown reason, cultivated plants lose most of their leaves over winter.

Questions have raised by botanists whether *B. sonnei* is distinct from the barberry species *Berberis repens*. If scientists conclude that Truckee barberry is not a valid taxon, it may result in the delisting of the species. The species has also been described as *Mahonia sonnei*.

Habitat

Surviving plants of the only known population grow along a river bank lined with large granite boulders. Soil is a sandy, silt-loam underlain by gravel. The site is about 6-10 ft (2-3 m) above the summer water level of the river and barely above the level of spring floods.

The habitat elevation is about 5,940 ft (1,800 m) in an exceptionally cold area of California about 10 mi (16 km) east of Donner Pass at the lower end of the valley containing Donner Lake. Cold air flowing down the canyon keeps the temperature low year-round. The average yearly minimum is 21°F (–6°C), and winter lows can plunge below zero.

Distribution

The Truckee barberry is probably endemic to the Truckee River Valley and was once more abundant along that river.

For almost 70 years after Truckee barberry was initially described and classified, it was lost and thought extinct. Unsuccessful searches were made for the plant in the 1930s and 1940s. Before the search was renewed by state botanists in 1973, an illustration of the plant was featured in a local newspaper. A high school student recognized the plant from the picture and led searchers to what is now the only known wild population. This population, on the banks of the Truckee River near the town of Truckee, consists of two colonies. In 1985, one colony contained fewer than ten small plants, the other about 40.

Threats

Truckee barberry has survived considerable stress since the settlement of the area. Early Truckee was a lumbering center, and the area was denuded to furnish timbers for Nevada mines, for railroad ties, and for bridge supports for the transcontinental railroad. Check dams were built on the river to flush logs downstream, which stripped the river banks of much of its natural vegetation, including presumably, the barberry.

The most immediate threats to the plant are its low numbers, restricted distribution, and the difficulty of managing the site, which is privately owned in a populated area. In 1982, one of the two colonies was cut back to the rock wall from which it emerges. It resprouted vigorously, however. Other plants are crowding the current colonies and should be removed.

Conservation and Recovery

Botanists have succeeded in establishing a small, expanding colony of healthy plants that will be used to repopulate known historic sites. An attempt to germinate a very limited number of wild-collected seeds was unsuccessful.

Truckee barberry's hold on survival will remain tenuous until some form of permanent protection is achieved. The California Department of Fish and Game is expected to take the lead on the recovery effort.

Contact

U.S. Fish and Wildlife Service
Division of Endangered Species
Eastside Federal Complex
911 N.E. 11th Avenue
Portland, Oregon 97232
http://pacific.fws.gov/

References

Abrams, L. R. 1934. "The *Berberises* of the Pacific States." *Phytologia* 1:89-94.

Roof, J. B. 1974. "Found Alive: The Truckee Barberry." *Four Seasons* 4(4):1-18.

U.S. Fish and Wildlife Service. 1984. "Recovery Plan for Truckee Barberry." U.S. Fish and Wildlife Service, Portland.

Virginia Round-leaf Birch

Betula uber

Status	Threatened
Listed	April 26, 1978 Endangered
Reclassified	November 16, 1994 Threatened
Family	Betulaceae (Birch)
Description	Smooth-barked, deciduous tree with nearly circular, toothed leaves.
Habitat	Along banks of mountain streams.
Threats	Vandalism, encroaching plants.
Range	Virginia

Virginia Round-leaf Birch, photograph by Peter M. Mazzeo. Reproduced by permission.

Description

The Virginia round-leaf birch, *Betula uber,* is a deciduous tree with dark, smooth bark separated into thin plates. It has hairless twigs and foliage, and nearly circular toothed leaves about 1 in (2.5 cm) long. It grows to about 30 ft (10 m) in height and can live 50 years or more. Seed production is believed to be cyclical, with abundant fruits and seeds appearing every three to four years. Leafing out and flowering of mature trees occurs late April to early May. Fruits are mature by mid-October, and seeds are dispersed in January and February.

Originally listed as Endangered in 1978, the species was reclassified to Threatened status in 1994 thanks to the ongoing success of recovery efforts that established, over a decade-long period, 20 additional populations resulting in a dramatic increase in subadult trees.

Habitat

The Virginia round-leaf birch grows along the banks of a small mountain stream at an elevation of 2,700 ft (821 m). The habitat vegetation is characterized as a highly disturbed second-growth, transitional forest of oak-pine and maple-beech-birch associations. Flood plain species, such as elm and cottonwood may also be present.

The climate is relatively cool and moist with an annual rainfall of 48 in (122 cm). Soils are stony colluvium, strongly acidic and highly permeable. The round-leaf birch depends on some disturbance, such as fire or cutting, to maintain itself, as it cannot compete with more long-lived and shade resistant species. Shade forestalls the establishment of seedlings, believed to germinate in mid-June.

Distribution

This species of birch is considered endemic to mountainous southwestern Virginia. It has existed in the wild for at least 60 years with characteristics passed from parent to offspring without losing integrity. It is related to *Betula lenta* and is similar in nearly all ways except for its round leaves. The birch was originally reported along Dickey Creek, although specimens are not now known from that site. Botanists now believe the original reports of populations there may have been erroneous; the collection is thought to have been confused with the Cressy Creek population.

Virginia round-leaf birch was rediscovered in 1975 along the banks of Cressy Creek near Sugar Grove, Virginia. When first surveyed, the population consisted of 14 adult trees and 26 saplings, but by the fall of 1988, only four adult trees and several seedlings remained. Three of these trees are on private property, while the fourth is on adjacent U.S. Forest Service land. Cultivated stocks of round-leaf birch have been established at Reynolds Research Center in Critz, Virginia, and at the National Arboretum in Washington, D.C.

Thanks to dedicated recovery efforts, however, the species population has increased exponentially in the past 15 years. By 1994, an additional 20 populations had been established, increasing the total subadult population to more than 1,400 trees, and sparking the reclassification of the species from Endangered to Threatened.

Threats

Vandals have repeatedly destroyed trees and seedlings at the Cressy Creek site, presumably because of fear that the federal government will use the trees as a reason to intrude on the rights of local landowners. Competition from encroaching veg-etation has limited the tree's ability to recover from these depredations.

Conservation and Recovery

To encourage natural regeneration, canopy cover was removed in 1981 to expose mineral soils at two sites close to fruiting trees. About 80 seedlings sprouted in 1982. About 50 seedlings died, probably due to encroaching plants or to browsing white-tailed deer and rabbits. Despite close observation, additional seedlings were vandalized in 1983 and 1984, and by 1985 only two of the 80 seedlings remained. In 1984, the Nature Conservancy purchased a 36-acre parcel bordering Cressy Creek, directly adjacent to the wild population. This land was in turn purchased by the U.S. Forest Service in 1986, and has been managed ever since as potential habitat for the tree.

Recovery strategies for the Virginia round-leaf birch have focused on establishing a healthy stock of cultivated saplings and then transplanting trees to new, less exposed locations. In 1984, 480 seedlings were transplanted to Forest Service lands from stock cultivated at the Reynolds Research Center. Five additional sites of 40 trees each were established in 1985 using three-year-old seedlings. By 1994, a total of 20 new populations had been established, increasing total populations to more than 1,400 trees.

The National Arboretum has cultivated a number of round-leaf birches and distributed seedlings to public and private nurseries in the United States, England, Belgium, and West Germany. As the Cressy Creek site is consistently vandalized and transplants on Forest Service property have reportedly suffered from vandalism, botanists have been unwilling to hint at the location of other transplanted trees. The cultivation and transplantation effort has already succeeded in bringing this species back from the edge of extinction, and the marked success of recovery efforts, moving the species from Endangered to Threatened status by 1994, makes it likely that the tree could be delisted altogether in the near future—perhaps even sooner than the target delisting date of 2010 projected in the 1990 Fish and Wildlife Service revised recovery plan update for the species.

The Recovery Plan calls for the species to be delisted after the existence can be documented of ten self-sustaining populations, defined on the basis of having each produced through natural regeneration, 500 to 1,000 individuals standing more than 6 ft (2 m) tall.

Contact

U.S. Fish and Wildlife Service
Division of Endangered Species
300 Westgate Center Drive
Hadley, Massachusetts 01035
http://northeast.fws.gov/

References

Hayden, W. J., and S. M. Hayden. 1984. "Wood Anatomy and Relationships of *Betula uber*." *Castanea* 49:26-30.

Sharik, T. L., and R. H. Ford. 1984. "The Current Status of the Virginia Round-Leaf Birch, *Betula uber* (Ashe) Fernald." Annual Progress Report. U.S. Fish and Wildlife Service, Newton Corner, Massachusetts.

U. S. Fish and Wildlife Service. 1986. "Virginia Round-Leaf Birch Recovery Plan." U.S. Fish and Wildlife Service, Newton Corner, Massachusetts.

U. S. Fish and Wildlife Service. 1990. "Virginia Round-Leaf Birch Revised Recovery Plan Update." U.S. Fish and Wildlife Service, Newton Corner, Massachusetts.

Higuero de Sierra

Crescentia portoricensis

Status	Endangered
Listed	December 4, 1987
Family	Bignoniaceae (Bignonia)
Description	Shrub with vinelike stems, leathery leaves, and bell-shaped yellow flowers.
Habitat	Evergreen, semi-evergreen, and deciduous forests.
Threats	Deforestation, floods, erosion.
Range	Puerto Rico

Higuero de Sierra, photograph. Waimea Arboretum & Botanical Garden. Reproduced by permission.

Description

Higuero de Sierra, *Crescentia portoricensis*, is an evergreen vine-like shrub or small tree growing to a maximum height of 20 ft (6.1 m) and attaining a trunk diameter of 3 in (7.6 cm). Vine-like branches and stems spread onto surrounding foliage. The bark is gray and the branches long and slender. The shiny, oblanceolate to narrowly elliptic leaves are dark green and leathery, usually clustered at the stem nodes. Tubular flowers are pale yellow and irregularly bell-shaped. The two-lobed, tubular calyx is leathery; the corolla is yellowish-white with the petals forming a bell-shaped tube. The fruit is dark green, cylindrical, hard, and dry.

Habitat

Higuero de Sierra is endemic to serpentine soils in evergreen, semi-evergreen, and deciduous forests in the lower Cordillera region of the western mountains of Puerto Rico. The Susua Forest is found within the subtropical moist forest life zone, the most extensive life zone found on the island. The Maricao Forest is found within the subtropical moist and wet forest zones. The majority of the area of these forests is covered by serpentine outcrops interspersed with clay soils. The topography is mountainous in both forests, with steep ravines and intermittent streams.

Higuero de Sierra grows beside streams in silty bottomland and is adapted to moderate levels of flooding. In recent years the severity of floods has increased because of land clearing and deforestation of the drainage basin. Stream banks have been undercut by flood waters, causing collapse with loss of plants.

Distribution

The species was first found in 1913 along the Maricao River in western Puerto Rico. A small population was later found in the Susua area 10 mi (16.1 km) to the southwest. Before 1979 the species was known from two small populations in Maricao Commonwealth Forest and a third in Susua Commonwealth Forest, each comprising six or eight mature trees. Both Maricao Forest sites were recently lost to flash flooding and erosion.

Six populations were discovered in the Maricao River Valley with a total of 36 mature individuals; there are six surviving Susua Commonwealth Forest plants, bringing the total number of known shrubs to 42. No seedlings or other evidence of natural reproduction has been observed at any of the six sites, and botanists assume that flash floods are preventing the establishment of new plants.

Threats

Widespread deforestation during the early part of the century, especially at elevations below 1,550 ft (472.4 m), is mainly responsible for the decline of Higuero de Sierra. Further clear-cutting at higher elevations would increase the force of flooding and erosion-induced landslides in the valleys where shrubs survive. In the Maricao Commonwealth Forest, all populations are threatened by increasing erosion as a result of deforestation and poor management practices upstream. The six known individuals in the Susua Forest population are located close to a heavily traveled access road, and to trails

that make them more accessible. They are also located on a steep stream bank and are threatened by erosion and flash flooding.

Conservation and Recovery

The U. S. Army Corps of Engineers has proposed several flood control projects in the mountains, which could significantly improve survival chances for the Higuero de Sierra at some sites, while inundating other former sites. The Corps will consider the welfare of Higuero de Sierra when designing its projects as is required by provisions of the Endangered Species Act. Dialogue with the U. S. Fish and Wildlife Service on the proposed projects has been initiated.

In 1989 both cuttings and fruits were collected for propagation at the Fairchild Tropical Gardens in Miami. Germination of seeds was successful.

Contacts

U. S. Fish and Wildlife Service
Regional Office, Division of Endangered Species
1875 Century Blvd., Suite 200
Atlanta, Georgia 30345
http://southeast.fws.gov/

U. S. Fish and Wildlife Service
Caribbean Field Office
P.O. Box 491
Boquerón, Puerto Rico 00622

References

U.S. Fish and Wildlife Service. 1987. "Determination of Higuero de Sierra, *Crescentia portoricensis*, to Be an Endangered Species." *Federal Register* 52(233): 46085-46087.

U.S. Fish and Wildlife Service. 1989."Draft Recovery Plan for Higuero de Sierra, *Crescentia portoricensis*. U.S. Fish and Wildlife Service, Atlanta. 32 pp.

Vivaldi, J. L., and R. O. Woodbury. 1981. "Status Report on *Crescentia portoricensis* Britton." Report. U.S. Fish and Wildlife Service, Atlanta.

Large-flowered Fiddleneck

Amsinckia grandiflora

Status	Endangered
Listed	May 8, 1985
Family	Boraginaceae (Borage)
Description	Annual with bright green foliage and red-orange, fiddleneck-shaped flowers.
Habitat	Clay soil on ravine slopes.
Threats	Restricted range, reduced gene pool, poor reproduction.
Range	California

Description

Large-flowered fiddleneck, *Amsinckia grandiflora,* is an annual with bright green foliage covered with coarse, stiff hairs. It produces red-orange flowers arranged in a fiddleneck-shaped flowerhead. The species' reproduction system is considered primitive. Two flower types exist, and it is believed that this leads to decreased fecundity.

Habitat

Large-flowered fiddleneck grows on a steep, grassy, southwest-facing slope of a small ravine with light-textured clay soil.

Distribution

The species has been found only in Alameda, Contra Costa, and San Joaquin Counties in California. Development, animal grazing, and reproductive difficulties have reduced numbers throughout the original range. A single population survives on a 0.5-acre (0.2-hectare) site in southwestern San Joaquin County near Livermore. From 1980-84 the population varied in size from 30-70 individuals. The site is on U.S. Department of Energy property used for the testing of chemical high explosives. While plants do not suffer directly from these activities, the construction of an access road may have altered the natural drainage to the plant's detriment.

Threats

Large-flowered fiddleneck's restricted range and reduced gene pool have resulted in very low reproductive potential. Because the species is a rather unique representative of its genus, it has been collected frequently by botanists and further collection could jeopardize its survival.

Introduced plants and more aggressive *Amsinckia* species have invaded the habitat, displacing large-flowered fiddleneck. Controlled burning has been proposed to reduce competition from these other plants, but it is feared that an improperly supervised burn could eradicate the population. The U.S. Department of Defense and Lawrence Livermore Laboratory have authorized controlled burning and will initiate greater protection for the site, although there are currently no plans to end activity at the weapons test site.

Conservation and Recovery

Merely stabilizing the current population will not constitute recovery for the species, since any number of localized threats could render it extinct. One acre (0.4 hectare) of land surrounding the current population has been designated as critical habitat, and the U.S. Fish and Wildlife Service recommended establishing new colonies within the historic range of the species. Researchers have successfully germinated fiddleneck seeds that had been

Large-flowered Fiddleneck, photograph by Jim A. Bartel, USFWS. Reproduced by permission.

refrigerated, improving the chances that a green-house population can be cultivated.

Botanists have identified 160 acres (64 hectares) in San Joaquin County that would provide suitable habitat for expanding or relocating the large-flowered fiddleneck population. The identified habitat area is privately owned, and until it becomes available, active recovery for the species cannot proceed.

Contact

U.S. Fish and Wildlife Service
Regional Office, Division of Endangered Species
Eastside Federal Building
911 N.E. 11th Ave.
Portland, Oregon 97232-4181
Telephone: (503) 231-6121
http://pacific.fws.gov/

References

Ornduff, R. 1976. "The Reproductive System of *Amsinckia grandiflora*, a Distylous Species." *Systematic Botany* 1: 57-66.

Ray, P. M. and H. F. Chisaki. 1957. "Studies on *Amsinckia*." *American Journal of Botany* 44: 529-544.

Cordia bellonis

No common name

Status	Endangered
Listed	January 10, 1997
Family	Boraginaceae (Borage)
Description	Arching to erect shrub with very slender twigs and short hairs; bears white flowers.
Habitat	Serpentine soils of Maricao and Susua at road edges, river margins, and on steep slopes; and in thickets of vegetation on sunny banks along dirt roads or in open saddles between limestone hills.
Threats	Habitat loss, some forest management practices, and very limited distribution.
Range	Puerto Rico

Description

Cordia bellonis, a plant endemic to the island of Puerto Rico, is found only in the public forests of Maricao, Susua, and Rio Abajo. This species is an arching to erect shrub of about 3.3-6.6 ft (1-2 m) high, having very slender twigs with short hairs. The leaves are alternate, oblong to oblong-lanceolate, 0.79-2.36 in (2-6 cm) long, usually two and a half to three times longer than wide. The corolla is white with four subcylindric lobes. The fruit is a pointed drupe, 0.20 in (5 mm) in length. The white axillary flowers are unisexual, and the plants are dioecious (either male or female).

Habitat

C. bellonis has been found in the serpentine soils of Maricao and Susua at road edges, river margins, and on steep slopes. In the Rio Abajo Forest, the species has been found either growing in thickets of vegetation on sunny banks along dirt roads or in open saddles between limestone hills.

Distribution

C. bellonis was first described in 1899 from specimens collected at "Monte Alegrillo." The name of this location in the municipality of Maricao has disappeared from use but most likely referred to the 2,950-ft (900-m) peak at the extreme head of the Rio Maricao whose situation was developed for the installation of telecommunication towers. *C. bellonis* was also collected in the area known as Indiera Fria and from Monte Cerrote near Adjuntas in 1915.

Later collectors and taxononomists identified its distribution as mountainsides in the vicinity of Maricao and, more generally, the mountain slopes and serpentine hills in northwestern districts of Puerto Rico. A 1991 study reported only four individuals of *C. bellonis* from Cain Alto Ward in the Maricao Commonwealth Forest and a 1993 study reported 87 individuals at 17 localities in three areas in Maricao, with half of these localities consisting of isolated individuals. Thirty-four of these individuals have been eliminated due to roadside clearing and the reconstruction of road PR 362. A small population of five individuals of *C. bellonis* was found for the first time in Susua in 1992. This species was also unknown from the Rio Abajo Commonwealth Forest until it was found in 1994. Approximately 118 individuals were found in 12 localities. Ninety-five (82%) of these individuals were removed for possible future reintroduction because of the construction of the road PR 10.

Threats

Only 81 individuals of *C. bellonis* are known to occur in the wild in Maricao, Susua, and Rio Abajo, and this rarity makes the species vulnerable to the loss of any individual. *C. bellonis* is threatened by habitat loss, some forest management practices, and very limited distribution.

The rareness and restricted distribution of this species make it extremely vulnerable to habitat destruction and modification, as well as extinction from naturally occurring events such as fire. Because the majority of these individuals occur along both sides of two public roads—PR 120 and PR 362—maintenance of road sides, as well as fires and vandalism, have already resulted in substantial plant losses, and they remain ever-present threats for these populations in the future.

Any widening of these highways, installation of water and sewer pipelines, and the installation of power-lines along these roads may adversely affect the species.

As noted above, 95 of 118 individuals known from the Rio Abajo Commonwealth Forest were removed for the construction of a highway. Of the remaining 23 individuals, 13 have been found in an area designated for compensation (mitigation) for the highway and 10 are found in highway rights-of-way.

A 1994 study reported that 14 individuals from Maricao appeared to have been eliminated due to forest-clearing along the roadside. Twenty additional individuals were apparently destroyed the following year by the clearing which took place during the reconstruction of road PR 362 in the Camp Santana area.

The species is also known from a private land-holding where extraction of fill material for the construction of the road will likely result in the loss of these plants.

The dioecious condition of the species means that *C. bellonis* individuals require outcrossing to suc-cessfully reproduce. This manner of producing off-spring limits reproduction when plant numbers are very low and restricted in distrbution. Reproduction occurs with difficulty or not at all if adequate numbers of both male and female plants in a viable population are not present; if individuals are too widely separated reproduction becomes impossible. More than half of the individuals previously known have been lost through forest destruction; in a large number of the localities where the species is found, the shrub occurs only as isolated individuals.

Conservation and Recovery

The Commonwealth of Puerto Rico has adopted a regulation that recognizes and provides protection to certain Commonwealth listed species. *C. bellonis* was not one of these species prior to being listed as a federal endangered species.

Federal listing, by virtue of an existing conservation agreement with the Commonwealth, immediately moved the species to the Commonwealth list. These listings enhance the possibilities of obtaining funding for needed research.

Contacts

U. S. Fish and Wildlife Service
Regional Office, Division of Endangered Species
1875 Century Blvd., Suite 200
Atlanta, Georgia 30345
http://southeast.fws.gov/

U. S. Fish and Wildlife Service
Boquerón Ecological Services Field Office
P. O. Box 491
Boquerón, Puerto Rico 00622-0491
Telephone: (787) 851-7297
Fax: (787) 851-7440

Reference

U. S. Fish and Wildlife Service. 1 October 1999. "Recovery Plan for *Cordia bellonis*." U. S. Fish and Wildlife Service Atlanta, Georgia.

Terlingua Creek Cat's Eye

Cryptantha crassipes

Status	Endangered
Listed	September 30, 1991
Family	Boraginaceae (Borage)
Description	Hairy, whitish perennial with narrow leaves and a terminal cluster of white and yellow flowers.
Habitat	Arid savannah over gypsiferous, chalky shale.
Threats	Residential development, off-road vehicles.
Range	Texas

Terlingua Creek Cat's Eye, photograph by Paul Montgomery. Reproduced by permission.

Description

Terlingua Creek cat's eye is a perennial of the borage family that grows to a height of 24 in (61 cm). It has an overall silvery appearance with a terminal cluster of white and yellow flowers. Slender, erect, hairy stems arise from a mound of leaves at the base. The narrow leaves are whitish and hairy. The flowers have yellow knobs rising above laidback petals. Fruits are egg-shaped, hairy nutlets.

Flowering occurs from late March to early June; fruiting continues through July.

Habitat

This species is found only on rounded hills and gentle slopes over gypsiferous, chalky shale in the Trans-Pecos scrub savannah in Brewster County, Texas. It grows in full sun in the arid climate at elevations between 3,150 and 3,320 ft (960 and 1,011 m).

Associated vegetation includes Havard's buckwheat, perennial spurge, Schott acacia, Mormon tea, and creosote.

Distribution

Terlingua Creek cat's eye was first discovered in the late 1930s in Brewster County and described as a new species in 1939. Since then it has been collected only infrequently and no other locations have been found.

Today only six populations of Terlingua Creek cat's eye are known, all on private land in Brewster County, near Big Bend National Park in southwest Texas. According to a 1987 status survey, these populations range in size from less than a hundred to a few thousand plants. The total species population was about 3,750. All populations appeared to be healthy, but only mature plants were observed; no juvenile or seedling plants were in evidence.

Threats

Because Terlingua Creek cat's eye occurs only on private land, none of the sites are protected. Small tracts of land in Brewster County, including some with populations of Terlingua Creek cat's eye, have been sold by a resort, and development of these tracts may eliminate some populations. It is likely that plants have already been destroyed by a network of roads constructed by the resort owners. The U. S. Fish and Wildlife Service (FWS) has had difficulty contacting the many owners of Terlingua Creek cat's eye sites because most of the small tracts have been sold to out-of-state buyers.

In addition to development, the species is threatened by uncontrolled off-road vehicle use. Several of the hills near the closest town are rutted, and a few sites show evidence of vehicle tracks.

Conservation and Recovery

The FWS published a recovery plan for the Terlingua Creek cat's eye in 1994. All 10 of the known critical habitats are on private land and are threatened by residential development, trampling by off-road vehicles, and other activities. This habitat should be protected by acquiring the land and designating ecological reserves, or by negotiating conservation easements with the landowners. The populations of the Terlingua Creek cat's eye should be monitored, additional ones searched for, and research undertaken into its biology, habitat needs, and beneficial management practices.

Contacts

Regional Office of Endangered Species
U. S. Fish and Wildlife Service
P.O. Box 1306
Albuquerque, New Mexico 87103-1306
Telephone: (505) 248-6911
Fax: (505) 248-6915
http://southwest.fws.gov/

U. S. Fish and Wildlife Service
Corpus Christi Ecological Services Field Office
c/o Texas A & M University at Corpus Christi
6300 Ocean Drive, Campus Box 338
Corpus Christi, Texas 78412-5599
Telephone: (361) 994-9005
Fax: (361) 888-3189

References

Poole, J. M. 1987. "Status Report on *Cryptantha crassipes*." U. S. Fish and Wildlife Service, Albuquerque.

U. S. Fish and Wildlife Service. 1994. Terlingua Creek Cat's-eye (*Cryptantha crassipes*) Recovery Plan. U. S. Fish and Wildlife Service, Austin, Texas.

Rough Popcornflower

Plagiobothrys hirtus

Status	Endangered
Listed	January 25, 2000
Family	Boraginaceae (Borage)
Description	A small, annual or perennial, herbaceous wildflower.
Habitat	Wet meadows
Threats	Overgrazing by livestock, and habitat loss and degradation by agricultural or residential conversion, flooding or draining, and road construction.
Range	Oregon

Don Eastman

Description

The rough popcornflower is an annual herbaceous plant on drier sites, or a perennial herb on wetter sites. It grows as tall as 1-2 ft (30-70 cm) and has a stout stem with coarse, firm, widely spreading hairs on the upper part. The leaves of the main stem are arranged opposite each other in pairs. The inflorescence (floral group) is paired and without bracts (small subtending leaves). The individual flowers are 0.04-0.08 in (1-2 mm) wide and white in color.

Habitat

The rough popcornflower grows in open, seasonal wetlands in poorly-drained clay or silty-clay loam soils. It grows in wet, grassy habitats known as swales, at elevations ranging from 100-890 ft (30-270 m). It appears to be dependent on seasonal flooding and/or fire to maintain its habitat in an open, weakly competitive condition. Annual populations of the rough popcornflower can be quite variable from year to year, depending on environmental conditions, such as the persistence of standing water in the springtime.

Distribution

The rough popcornflower is endemic to the interior valley of the Umpqua River in southwestern Oregon.

Threats

In historical times, the rough popcornflower was probably widespread on the floodplains of the interior valleys of the Umpqua River. However, it was collected only four times between 1887 and 1961, all at sites in Douglas County, Oregon. In fact, it was considered possibly extinct, until it was "rediscovered" in 1983. The principal threats to the rough popcornflower appear to have been grazing by domestic livestock, the draining of wetlands for urban and agricultural uses, flooding of its habitat by the construction of reservoirs, and disturbances associated with road building. In addition, the suppression of wildfires has allowed its habitat to be invaded by more competitive species of woody and herbaceous plants. The rough popcornflower is now limited to 17 isolated patches of habitat in the vicinity of Sutherlin and Yoncalla, Oregon. These habitat patches range in area from 0.1 to 17 acres (0.04-6.9 hectares), with population sizes ranging from 1 to 3,000 plants. The 17 habitat patches are estimated to support a total of about 7,000 plants on a combined area of less than 45 acres (18 hectares). Of the 17 habitat patches, one is 17 acres in area (7 hectares), three are between 5 and 10 acres (2-4 hectares), four are between 1 and 5 acres (0.4-2 hectares), and nine are less than 1 acre (0.4 hectare). The largest known population (3,000 plants) occurs in a habitat patch with an area of 1 acre (4 hectares). Ongoing threats include habitat destruction by conversion to urban or agricultural land-uses, hydrological alterations, fire suppression, livestock grazing, roadside mowing and herbicide spraying, and competition with invasive, non-native plants.

Conservation and Recovery

Three of the occupied habitat patches of the rough popcornflower are owned by the Nature Conservancy and are managed as natural areas. This includes the largest population of the rare plant. The other habitat patches have little or no protective management, and the endangered plant is at great risk of extirpation from development, grazing, farming practices, roadside maintenance, recreational activities, and vandalism. Conservation of the rough popcornflower requires that a larger area of its critical habitat is protected and managed appropriately. This can be done by acquiring private land and setting up ecological reserves, or by negotiating conservation easements with the landowners. The populations of the endangered plant must be monitored in its remaining habitats, and studies made of the environmental factors limiting its spread and abundance.

Contacts

U. S. Fish and Wildlife Service
Regional Office, Division of Endangered Species
Eastside Federal Complex
911 N. E. 11th Ave.
Portland, Oregon 97232-4181
(503) 231-6121
http://pacific.fws.gov/

U. S. Fish and Wildlife Service
Oregon Fish and Wildlife Office
2600 S. E. 98th Ave., Suite 100
Portland, Oregon 97266-1398
Telephone: (503) 231-6179
Fax: (503) 231-6195

Reference

U. S. Fish and Wildlife Service. 25 January 2000. "Endangered and Threatened Wildlife and Plants: Endangered Status for the Plant *Plagiobothrys hirtus* (Rough Popcornflower)." *Federal Register* 65 (16): 3866-3875.

Calistoga Allocarya

Plagiobothrys strictus

Status	Endangered
Listed	October 22, 1997
Family	Boraginaceae (Borage)
Description	An annual, herbaceous wildflower.
Habitat	Pools and swales associated with hot springs and small geysers in grasslands.
Threats	Habitat loss and damage caused by recreational activities, airport maintenance, urbanization, and other disturbances.
Range	California

Description

Calistoga allocarya, *Plagiobothrys strictus* is a small and erect annual herb of the borage family (Boraginaceae) that grows 4-15 in (10-38 cm) tall. The nearly hairless plant has either a single stem or branches from near the base. The linear lower leaves are 1.5-4 in (3.8-10 cm) long. White flowers, small and usually paired, appear in March to April in a slender, unbranched inflorescence. The fruit is an egg-shaped nutlet about 0.6 in (1.5 cm) long, keeled on the back, with wart-like projections without any prickles. *Plagiobothrys greenei*, *P. lithocaryus*, *P. mollis* var. *vestitus*, *P. stipitatus*, and *P. tener* have ranges that overlap with that of *P. strictus* and occur in similar habitats, but they neither resemble *P. strictus* nor have they been found at the known *P. strictus* sites.

Habitat

Calistoga allocarya is found in pools and swales adjacent to and fed by hot springs and small geysers in grasslands at elevations between 300 and 500 ft (91 and 152 m).

Distribution

Three historical populations occurred within a two-mile radius of Calistoga in Napa County, one of which was extirpated by urbanization and agricultural land conversion. One remaining population occurs near a geyser and some undeveloped thermal hot springs, while the other occurs at the Calistoga City Airport.

Threats

Calistoga allocarya is threatened by recreational activities, airport maintenance, urbanization, and destructive random events. Since this species occurs at the same sites as Napa bluegrass, they face nearly identical threats.

One historical occurrence and over 70% of the original habitat of Calistoga allocarya have been extirpated by urbanization and conversion of land to vineyards. The two remaining populations are threatened by urbanization. The Calistoga Airport location had a population of about 5,000 individuals in a 2,000 square foot area in 1994. The number of individuals in this population fluctuates considerably, perhaps due to variations in spring rainfall between years. Airport maintenance and operational activities, including vehicle traffic, parking by vehicles on the plants, grass mowing, and any land use changes, currently threaten this population, and any future development at the site would likely threaten the remaining plants.

Grass mowing is done periodically through the spring and summer to reduce fire and aircraft safety hazards. Airport users include a spray plane ser-

Calistoga Allocarya, photograph by Mark Skinner. Reproduced by permission.

vice, recreational gliders, and associated tow planes. Service vehicles for the planes and the private vehicles of the customers harm this plant there, especially during the spring and summer when airport use increases.

The other population is scattered over a ten-acre area bisected by an asphalt road on private land near Myrtledale Hot Springs in the City of Calistoga. The number of individuals in this population was estimated to be in the hundreds, although it has been impossible to verify current numbers because the landowner has denied access to the site in recent years. The landowner has proposed to build a hospital on this site, but he has been unsuccessful due to the current zoning status of his property. Both populations of Calistoga allocarya depend on moisture from adjacent hot springs or surface runoff; any action that alters the hydrology or flow from these hot springs would be very damaging.

Conservation and Recovery

Both populations of the Calistoga allocarya are on private land, and are threatened by various disturbances associated with human activities. These populations must be protected. This could be done by acquiring the critical habitats and establishing ecological reserves, or by negotiating conservation easements with the private landowners. The Calistoga allocarya should be monitored at its known habitats, and searches made to see if there are any undiscovered populations. Research should be conducted into its biology and habitat needs. Additional populations should be established in suitable habitats.

Contacts

U. S. Fish and Wildlife Service
Regional Office, Division of Endangered Species
Eastside Federal Complex
911 N. E. 11th Ave.
Portland, Oregon 97232-4181
Telephone: (503) 231-6121
http://pacific.fws.gov/

U. S. Fish and Wildlife Service
Sacramento Fish and Wildlife Office
2800 Cottage Way, Room W-2605
Sacramento, California 95825-1846
Telephone: (916) 414-6600
Fax: (916) 460-4619

Reference

U. S. Fish and Wildlife Service. 22 October 1997. "Endangered and Threatened Wildlife and Plants: Determination of Endangered Status for Nine Plants From the Grasslands or Mesic Areas of the Central Coast of California." *Federal Register* 62 (204): 54791-54808.

Vahl's Boxwood

Buxus vahlii

Status	Endangered
Listed	August 13, 1985
Family	Buxaceae (Boxwood)
Description	Large, evergreen shrub with simple and opposite shiny, dark green leaves.
Habitat	Limestone ravines and ledges in semi-evergreen forests.
Threats	Limited numbers, wildfires, commercial development.
Range	Puerto Rico

Vahl's Boxwood, photograph by Eugenio Santiago. Reproduced by permission.

Description

Vahl's boxwood, *Buxus vahlii*, is an evergreen shrub or small tree that can grow up to 15 ft (4.6 m) high. Individual stems extend about 5 in (13 cm) before branching. Twigs show two characteristic grooves below each pair of leaves. Simple, opposite leaves are oblong to obovate, a shiny, dark green color, and up to 1.5 in (3.8 cm) long.

Vahl's boxwood reproduces by seed, which it produces in relatively large quantities. Light green flowers bloom in clusters from December to April. Clusters are often difficult to see because of their small size and location beneath foliage. A solitary female flower blooms at the tip, and several male flowers are borne on the stem just below it. The fruit is a tiny, three-horned capsule.

Habitat

Vahl's boxwood is restricted to limestone ravines and ledges in semi-evergreen forests along the coast

at elevations below 330 ft (100 m). It prefers the heavy shade of the forest canopy and is often situated on steep, east-facing slopes.

The Punta Higuero site (see below) is a ravine located on the eastern end of a nuclear power plant; the Hato Tejas site is on hills surrounded by a large shopping center and industrial activities. Part of the east-facing slope containing this population has been mined for limestone and reduced to a narrow ledge. The Punta Higuero site has shallow, clay soil with an abundance of small limestone rocks over a limestone bedrock. The Hato Tejas ledge, where the boxwood grows, has very shallow, stony soil that is barren and dry.

Distribution

This species was originally thought to occur in St. Croix and on Jamaica, as well as in Puerto Rico, but this no longer appears to be correct. It has not been collected outside of Puerto Rico in recent times and is now considered restricted to the island.

At present, two isolated populations—separated by about 70 mi (110 km) of coastline—survive near Hato Tejas (west of Bayamon) and Punta Higuero (north of Rincon). Cultivated plants exist elsewhere in Puerto Rico.

In 1987, the Hato Tejas site consisted of about 25 healthy shrubs on privately owned land. The site is in a tract of remnant forest within a group of haystack hills—limestone hills with a characteristic haystack shape. The shrubs grow along the edge of an old limestone quarry, surrounded by a large shopping center and several commercial and industrial lots.

The Punta Higuero population was surveyed in 1987 when it consisted of 60 plants, many dwarfed and depleted of chlorophyll by salt spray and high winds. The site is owned by the commonwealth of Puerto Rico but is readily accessible to houses on adjacent private property. Residents keep goats that could seriously harm the boxwood if allowed to escape into the public area.

Threats

Much of the lowland, semi-evergreen forest along the northern coast of Puerto Rico was long ago logged or clear-cut to support agriculture. Once a fairly common constituent of the plant community, Vahl's boxwood has been virtually eliminated by deforestation. Because of current low numbers, fire poses a significant threat to both populations, particularly during the dry season. In spite of harsh conditions at the Punta Higuero site, the boxwood appears to be reproducing well. Surveys have located seedlings and plants of various sizes.

Conservation and Recovery

Because of its beauty and potential for professional cultivation as an ornamental plant, there is a society devoted to Vahl's boxwood cultivation. This society works to preserve the plant and discourages collection from the wild, an act prohibited under commonwealth law. Privately cultivated plants could be used to reestablish populations in the wild. Attempts to propagate the shrub from seed have been largely unsuccessful. Propagation with cuttings tends to be more successful.

The karst region of the coast is rugged enough that unreported populations of Vahl's boxwood might yet exist. Fish and Wildlife Service personnel will conduct surveys of potential habitat along the north coast. The Recovery Plan recommends fencing the Punta Higuero site and devising conservation agreements with private landowners.

Contacts

Regional Office of Endangered Species
U.S. Fish and Wildlife Service
1875 Century Blvd, Ste 200
Atlanta, Georgia 30345
http://southeast.fws.gov/

Caribbean Field Office
U.S. Fish and Wildlife Service
P.O. Box 491
Boquerón, Puerto Rico 00622

References

Little, E. L., R. O. Woodbury, and F. H. Wadsworth. 1974. *Trees of Puerto Rico and the Virgin Islands.* Forest Service Agricultural Handbook No. 449. U.S. Department of Agriculture, Washington, D.C.

Vivaldi, J. L., and R. O. Woodbury. 1981. " *Buxus vahlii baill.*" Status Report Submitted to the U.S. Fish and Wildlife Service, Maygaguez, Puerto Rico.

Tobusch Fishhook Cactus

Ancistrocactus tobuschii

Status	Endangered
Listed	November 7, 1979
Family	Cactaceae (Cactus)
Description	Solitary, top-shaped cactus with yellow-green flowers; each spine cluster has a characteristic fish-hook spine.
Habitat	Limestone gravel along stream banks.
Threats	Residential development, live-stock grazing, collectors.
Range	Texas

Tobusch Fishhook Cactus, photograph by Paul Montgomery. Reproduced by permission.

Description

Tobusch fishhook cactus, *Ancistrocactus tobuschii*, typically grows as a solitary top-shaped (turbinate) stem, up to 5 in (13 cm) tall and about 3.5 in (9 cm) thick. Each spine cluster (areole) consists of seven to nine radial spines and three light yellow central spines. The central spines have red (immature) or gray (mature) tips. One of the three central spines is distinctively hooked. Prominent yellow-green flowers bloom from mid-February to early April. Green fruits mature by the end of May and split open to disgorge about twenty black seeds.

The genus *Ancistrocactus* (derived from Latin for "fishhook") contains four species, three from the Rio Grande River region in southern Texas and Mexico, and one endemic to Mexico. The species has also been known as *Echinocactus tobuschii* and *Mammillaria tobuschii*.

Habitat

The Tobusch cactus is found on the Edwards Plateau of Texas, a region of canyons and arroyos scoured by numerous seasonal creeks and rivers. The soil is derived from limestone and the dominant vegetation is juniper, oak, sycamore, and associated grasses. Livestock have grazed much of the plateau for many years, denuding ground cover and triggering localized erosion.

The Tobusch cactus occurs in gravels and gravelly soils along stream banks subject to periodic flash floods. During spring and fall, storms develop over the mountains of Mexico and stall over the Edwards Plateau, producing heavy downpours and torrential runoff. Although particularly severe floods will destroy plants, the scouring action of moderate flooding appears to benefit the Tobusch cactus by removing competing plants and grasses. Habitat elevation is about 1,600 ft (490 m).

Distribution

The Tobusch fishhook cactus was once more abundant in a five-county range comprising northern Bandera, western Kerr, and most of Kimble, Real, and Uvalde counties. The population at the discovery site near Vanderpool (Bandera County) was eliminated when the ground was cleared in the 1960s.

At the time of federal listing in 1979, fewer than 200 plants were known to survive. Six populations were surveyed in 1985, adding to the population count, but a current estimate of total numbers does not exist.

Several populations grow along the Sabinal River in Bandera County. A small population on the river above Vanderpool, believed extirpated, was rediscovered in 1985. Kimble County populations are northeast of Segovia and near the town of Junction. In Uvalde County, a small population occurs north of the town of Uvalde. In Real County, north of Leakey on the Frio River, a population survives at a site formerly used for grazing. Here, a strong population of seedlings has taken root around mature plants.

Threats

The decline of the Tobusch fishhook cactus was initiated by overgrazing of the habitat by live-stock. Animals trample or browse seedlings, preventing the establishment of new plants. Overgrazing contributes to erosion, which worsens flood damage. U.S. Fish and Wildlife Service (FWS) personnel have successfully negotiated with some private land owners to secure protected fields for the cactus.

While livestock continue to graze several sites, a more immediate threat to surviving plants is the loss of stream bank habitat to residential development. Stream and river front lots in the region are being promoted by real estate developers as sites for summer cottages.

Commercial collectors have also played a significant role in the decline of the species. Collectors return to the same sites year after year to dig up wild plants for sale. The damage they cause is intensified by the low number of surviving plants. The Endangered Species Act cannot protect plants from being collected on private land.

Conservation and Recovery

The primary goal of the FWS Recovery Plan is to establish four secure populations of 3,000 plants each. Reintroduction of the cactus to suitable sites within the historic range is anticipated. If recovery recommendations are actively pursued, this Endangered cactus could be considered for reclassification as Threatened very soon.

Contacts

U.S. Fish and Wildlife Service
Division of Endangered Species
P.O. Box 1306
Albuquerque, New Mexico 87103
http://southwest.fws.gov/

References

Marshall, W. T. 1952. "A New and Interesting Cactus from Texas." *Saguaroland Bulletin* 6(7):78-81.

U.S. Fish and Wildlife Service. 1987. "Tobusch Fishhook Cactus (*Ancistrocactus tobuschii*) Recovery Plan." U.S. Fish and Wildlife Service, Albuquerque.

Weniger, D. 1970. *Cacti of the Southwest.* University of Texas Press, Austin.

Star Cactus

Astrophytum asterias

Status	Endangered
Listed	October 18, 1993
Family	Cactaceae (Cactus)
Description	Small, spineless cactus, brownish or dull green and speckled with tiny white scales; flowers are yellow with orange centers.
Habitat	Sparse, open brushland.
Threats	Collecting; habitat loss due to agricultural development.
Range	Texas

Star Cactus, photograph by Jackie Poole. Reproduced by permission.

Description

The star cactus is a small, spineless cactus. It is disk- or dome-like in shape, 0.7-6 in (2-15 cm) across and up to 2.7 in (7 cm) tall. This species is brownish or dull green and speckled with tiny white scales. Eight triangular sections are a result of vertical grooves dividing the main body. Each section is marked with a central line of circular indentations filled with straw-colored to whitish wooly hairs. The flowers are yellow with orange centers. These flowers are up to 2 in (5 cm) in diameter. The fruits are green to grayish-red, about 0.5 in (1.25 cm) long, oval, and fleshy.

Habitat

The star cactus is associated with low elevations in grasslands and shrublands. The area in which this cactus is found (Rio Grande Plains and Tamaulipan thorn shrub) was originally a subtropical grassland. Due to extensive suppression of fire and overgrazing, much of the area is now invaded with thorny

shrub and tree species. The star cactus is found in sparse, open brushland, most commonly associated with partial shade of other plants or rocks growing on gravelly saline clays of loams overlaying the Tertiary Cathoula and Frio formations.

Distribution

Historically, the star cactus occurred in Cameron, Hidalgo, and Starr counties in Texas, and the adjacent states of Nuevo Leon and Tamaulipas in Mexico.

The star cactus is presently known from one locality in Texas and one in Tamaulipas, Mexico. Only about 2,100 plants are known to exist in the wild. The Nuevo Leon site is believed extirpated due to collecting activities. The Tamaulipas site has been reduced to very few individuals.

Threats

Much of the native habitat of the star cactus has been converted to agriculture or improved pasture.

In the areas where this plant presently occurs, pasture improvement is done through a process of shrub clearing and then planting buffelgrass, *Cenchhrus ciliaris*. Therefore a mosaic of buffelgrass pasture and shrub stands results. It is unlikely that the star cactus would be able to withstand this type of land management. In Mexico, much of the once suitable habitat has been converted to corn fields or orange groves.

This cactus has been a favorite collection among succulent dealers for many years. Despite the fact that this plant is easily propagated, wild specimens are found in the commercial market. In Texas, about 400 wild specimens were found at one nursery.

Conservation and Recovery

As the star cactus is easily grown from seed and has been for many years by the succulent trade, propagation techniques are currently under investigation. Plants have been grown from seed in a greenhouse environment. These plants seems to be consistently hardier and more disease resistant than plants taken from the wild.

Contacts

U.S. Fish and Wildlife Service
Division of Endangered Species
P. O. Box 1306
Albuquerque, New Mexico 87103
http://southwest.fws.gov/

Austin Ecological Services Field Office
Compass Bank Building
10711 Burnet Road, Suite 20
Austin, Texas 78758

Arlington Ecological Services Field Office
Suite 252, 711 Stadium Drive East
Arlington, Texas 76011

Houston Ecological Services Field Office
17629 El Camino Real, Ste 211
Houston, Texas 77058

References

U.S. Fish and Wildlife Service. 18 October 1993 "Endangered and Threatened Wildlife and Plants; Determination of Endangered Status for the Plant *Astrophytum asterias* (Star Cactus)." *Federal Register* 58(199): 53804-53807.

Fragrant Prickly-apple

Cereus eriophorus var. fragrans

Status	Endangered
Listed	November 1, 1985
Family	Cactaceae (Cactus)
Description	Column-shaped cactus with sprawling, cane-like stems.
Habitat	Sand dunes on ocean coast.
Threats	Shoreline development, low numbers, high winds.
Range	Florida

Description

Fragrant prickly-apple, *Cereus eriophorus* var. *fragrans*, is a columnar species of the cactus family. It has cane-like stems, measuring from 3 ft to as much as 16 ft (1-5 m). Stems sprawl over surrounding vegetation as they grow and use these plants for support. The cylindrical, succulent stems measure up to 2 in (5 cm) in diameter and bear numerous spines. The large white or pink flowers, which appear in May, are nocturnal and heavily scented. Orange-red fruits, about 2.5 in (6 cm) in length, grow from May to October.

Habitat

Fragrant prickly-apple is found among sand dunes along the coast. It typically grows a distance back from the water behind sheltering dunes in stabilized sands where other sand-adapted plants have become established.

Distribution

The fragrant prickly-apple was first collected in 1917 from sand dunes south of Ft. Pierce (St. Lucie County) and is considered endemic to Brevard, St. Lucie, and Indian River counties, Florida. A population documented near Malabar (Brevard County) was later extirpated. Two historic sites in Monroe County were recently searched for the plant without success.

Based on recent field surveys by Florida botanists, the only remaining population is found along a short stretch of beach dunes in St. Lucie County. During a 1984 survey, the U. S. Fish and Wildlife Service botanists found plants at only two of three sites that had been documented in 1980. An additional smaller grouping of plants was subsequently discovered nearby. All three groups of plants are within about 328 yd (300 m) of one another and probably constitute the remnant of a single biological population. Altogether, only 14 cacti were located.

Threats

The fragrant prickly-apple has declined significantly because of the residential and commercial development of beachfront property. The few surviving cacti could be severely damaged or eliminated by a single catastrophic event, such as a strong hurricane. Because of its fragile stems, sprawling nature, and dependence on supporting vegetation, fragrant prickly-apple is particularly vulnerable to damage from high winds. Often dune lots are cleared by bulldozing. In many cases, even when cacti were left standing as ornamentals, the removal of the natural buffer of surrounding vegetation resulted in eventual loss of the population.

Many species of cacti are commercially exploited, and it is likely that because of its rarity and beauty, this cactus would be collected if the specific loca-

Andy Robinson

tion of remaining plants became widely known. Some past evidence of collecting has been noted at the St. Lucie County site.

Conservation and Recovery

The Florida Regional Comprehensive Plan sets policy for the protection of endangered species by local governments, requiring counties to examine the impact of zoning changes on rare plant species. This, completed in the late 1980s, helps preserve remaining habitat in St. Lucie County and provides sites where plants can be reintroduced. In the late 1980s, the state also acquired a tract of suitable habitat, containing several prickly-apple plants, for inclusion as a satellite of the Savannas State Reserve.

Contact

Regional Office of Endangered Species
U.S. Fish and Wildlife Service
1875 Century Blvd., Suite 200
Atlanta, Georgia 30345
http://southeast.fws.gov/

References

Austin, D. F. 1984. "Resume of the Florida Taxa of Cereus (Cactaceae)." *Florida Scientist* 47(1):68-72.

Benson, L. 1982. *The Cacti of the U.S. and Canada.* Stanford University Press, Palo Alto.

Small, J. K. 1917. "The Tree Cactus of the Florida Keys." *Journal of the New York Botanical Garden* 18:199-203.

Nellie Cory Cactus

Coryphantha minima

Status	Endangered
Listed	November 7, 1979
Family	Cactaceae (Cactus)
Description	Dwarf cactus with egg-shaped or cylindrical stems and rose-purple flowers.
Habitat	Chihuahuan Desert; desert grassland in gravelly soils.
Threats	Collectors, limited distribution.
Range	Texas

Nellie Cory Cactus, photograph. U. S. Fish and Wildlife Service. Reproduced by permission.

Description

The dwarf Nellie cory cactus, *Coryphantha minima*, grows up to 1.5 in (4 cm) high and 0.8 in (2 cm) in diameter. The stems are simple or branching, and either egg-shaped or cylindrical. The ash gray or pink spines are in clusters (areoles) of about 20. The unique club-shaped spines thicken toward the end then taper abruptly to a point. Rose or purple flowers bloom in May; fruits mature by early June. Heavy rains dislodge the seeds and runoff carries them away from the base of the cactus. Plants are often covered with spikemoss. Information on this plant has also been published under other scientific names: *Coryphanta nellieae*, *Escobaria nellieae*, and *Mammillaria nellieae*.

Habitat

This cactus species grows in Chihuahuan Desert grassland and is restricted to the Caballos Novaculite Formation, a series of rocky outcrops that form low-lying ridges highly resistant to erosion. These ridges support perennial bunch grasses and a wide variety of shrubs and cacti. The Nellie cory cactus is usually found growing among chips of weathered and fractured novaculite (a silica-bearing rock). Habitat elevation is between 3,960 and 4,455 ft (1,200 and 1,350 m); average annual rainfall is about 16 in (41 cm).

Distribution

Nellie cory cactus is endemic to the Chihuahuan Desert of northern Brewster County, Texas, in the Big Bend region. It is believed to have developed within a very limited range. The cactus is found in two separate populations on private land near the town of Marathon in Brewster County. When the recovery plan was issued in 1984, the total population was estimated at about 40,000-80,000 plants. Population densities vary widely, from several hundred plants per square meter to no plants at all in nearby areas. Seedlings were found throughout the population, and their success rate is estimated at fair to good.

Threats

Nellie cory cactus is threatened on several fronts. The major threat is from commercial cactus dealers who collect this highly prized cactus from the wild. Although the dwarf size of the cactus makes it difficult to find, its dense populations are easily located and harvested. Additionally, the low population numbers and extremely restricted distribution worsen the threat. A highway that cuts through the habitat undoubtedly destroyed many individuals and renders the population easily accessible to collectors. Livestock grazing and trampling, modification to the habitat, brush control—through the use of herbicides—to cultivate pastures are potential threats, as are novaculite mining, and highway and fence maintenance.

Conservation and Recovery

As with many other cacti, the major recovery strategy aims at reducing commercial collecting. Because the cactus grows readily in cultivation, botanists will initiate a propagation program to supply the commercial market in sufficient quantities to bring down the high price that wild plants now command, making collection from the wild less profitable. A second part of the strategy is to arrest and prosecute illegal collectors and publicize the fact in trade publications. The plant is protected by the state of Texas.

Contact

U. S. Fish and Wildlife Service
Regional Office, Division of Endangered Species
P.O. Box 1306
Albuquerque, New Mexico 87103-1306
Telephone: (505) 248-6911
Fax: (505) 248-6915
http://southwest.fws.gov/

References

Brown, D. 1982. "Desert Plant-Biotic Communities of the American Southwest—United States and Mexico." Report. University of Arizona, for Boyce Thompson Southwestern Arboretum, Superior, Arizona.

U. S. Fish and Wildlife Service. 1987. "Endangered and Threatened Species of Texas and Oklahoma (with 1988 Addendum)." U. S. Fish and Wildlife Service, Albuquerque.

U. S. Fish and Wildife Service. 1984. "Nellie Cory Cactus Recovery Plan." U. S. Fish and Wildlife Service, Albuquerque.

Weniger, D. 1979. *Cacti of the Southwest.* University of Texas Press, Austin.

Bunched Cory Cactus

Coryphantha ramillosa

Status	Threatened
Listed	November 6, 1979
Family	Cactaceae (Cactus)
Description	Dark green cactus with nearly spherical stems and pink flowers.
Habitat	Chihuahuan Desert; limestone outcroppings.
Threats	Livestock grazing, collectors, low numbers.
Range	Texas; Coahuila, Mexico

Bunched Cory Cactus, photograph. U. S. Fish and Wildlife Service. Reproduced by permission.

Description

Bunched cory cactus, *Coryphantha ramillosa*, grows as a solitary, nearly spherical dark grayish-green stem about 3.5 in (9 cm) in diameter. Spine clusters (areoles) consist of from 9 to 20 gray, dark-tipped radial spines, about 1 in (2.5 cm) long, and four prominent central spines that are mottled brown and spread out in all directions. Budding occurs April to June; the showy flowers are pale pink to rose-purple, about 2 in (5 cm) wide, and appear in the spring. The oval or egg-shaped fruits are covered with tiny hairlike scales that give them a silvery appearance. This monoclinous plant reproduces sexually and is pollinated by solitary bees. The fruits are juicy and dispersal may be enhanced by vertebrates that remove it.

The species has also been known as *Mammillaria ramillosa*.

Habitat

Bunched cory cactus grows in loose limestone on rocky outcroppings on ledges or at the base of cliffs. It is part of the Chihuahuan Desert scrub community in the Big Bend region of Texas. The habitat elevation ranges from 2,500-3,500 ft (762-1,067 m).

Distribution

Bunched cory cactus is endemic to the Chihuahuan Desert, from Brewster and Terrill counties, Texas, southeast to the Mexican state of Coahuila.

Current populations of the bunched cory cactus are in the hills along the Maravillas and Reagan canyons of southeastern Brewster County, and in several smaller canyons farther east in Terrill County. A single, more isolated site was discovered in the Big Bend National Park. There are no current population estimates, but numbers are considered low. The status of the cactus in Mexico is unknown.

Threats

The major threat to the bunched cory cactus is livestock grazing at several of the population sites. Livestock can denude the land of its sparse vegetation, promoting severe erosion. Cattle have also been observed trampling plants, particularly seedlings. This threat is magnified by the limited numbers of the plant.

Bunched cory cactus has suffered somewhat at the hands of collectors, although the relative inaccessibility of much of its habitat offers some protection. Because populations occur mostly on private land, there are no prohibitions against collecting with the landowner's permission. The population in Big Bend National Park is threatened by the increasing popularity of the park as a recreation area, which brings more casual collectors into contact with the plant. The plant is protected by Texas state law.

Conservation and Recovery

The U. S. Fish and Wildlife Service Recovery Plan examines ways to deter illegal collection and restrict undue or unescorted recreational access to remote canyon sites where the cactus is found. An attempt will be made to locate other populations that may exist in isolated canyons. Otherwise, known population sites will be monitored, and more active measures taken to conserve the plant if numbers decline further.

Contact

Regional Office of Endangered Species
U.S. Fish and Wildlife Service
P.O. Box 1306
Albuquerque, New Mexico 87103-1306
(505) 248-6911
Fax: (505) 248-6915
http://southwest.fws.gov/

References

U. S. Fish and Wildlife Service. "Bunched Cory Cactus Recovery Plan." U. S. Fish and Wildlife Service, Albuquerque.

U. S. Fish and Wildlife Service. 1987 "Endangered and Threatened Species of Texas and Oklahoma (with 1988 Addendum)." U.S. Fish and Wildlife Service, Albuquerque.

Weniger, D. 1970. *Cacti of the Southwest*. University of Texas Press, Austin and London.

Cochise Pincushion Cactus

Coryphantha robbinsorum

Status	Threatened
Listed	January 9, 1986
Family	Cactaceae (Cactus)
Description	Unbranched, many-spined cactus with yellowish green, bell-shaped flowers and orange-red fruits.
Habitat	Limestone hills in semidesert grassland.
Threats	Low numbers, grazing animals.
Range	Arizona; Sonora, Mexico

Cochise Pincushion Cactus, photograph. U. S. Fish and Wildlife Service. Reproduced by permission.

Description

Cochise pincushion cactus, *Coryphantha robbinsorum*, is a small, spiny, unbranched cactus that, as its name implies, resembles a founded pincushion. It lacks central spines and typically has 11-17 sharp, radial spines. The flowers, which appear in March and April, are a pale yellow-green with a slight bronze cast. Fruits ripen to orange-red in July and August, but quickly turn a dull red.

Most of the stem is underground, with usually only 0.4 in (1 cm) protruding above ground level. During the spring and fall, when droughts normally occur, the plants shrink. The proportion of plant exposed during drought periods depends on the microsite. Plants growing on bedrock will shrink during droughts but cannot retract into the soil. In microsites with some accumulated soil, the plant surface can be flush with the substrate surface when retracted.

This species has a much lower reproductive potential than other related cacti. Each plant produces an average of three fruits annually, each containing about 20 seeds. A dynamic balance between the disappearance of colonies from localized sites and the emergence of new colonies nearby seems a natural feature of its biology.

The species has been known by two other scientific names: *Cochiseia robbinsorum* Earle, and *Escobaria robbinsorum*.

Habitat

This pincushion cactus grows in semidesert grassland on limestone hills at an elevation of 4,200 ft (1,280 m). Dominant associated species are sandpaper bush, ocotillo, desert spoon, snakeweed, Palmer agave, amole, and prickly pear.

Distribution

The Cochise pincushion cactus is endemic to the Sonoran Desert of southwestern Arizona and Mexico. Reports of populations in neighboring Sonora, Mexico, would suggest that this cactus was once distributed over a wider area. Today, it is found on several isolated hills in Cochise County, Arizona, at sites averaging about 2.5 acres (1 hectare) each. Density of plants on these limestone hills varies greatly. Plants are rare and scattered throughout most of the hilly area but small, isolated clusters of 100-1,000 plants occur sporadically.

All known populations are on privately owned ranchland or public land held in trust and managed by the Arizona State Land Department. A population has been reported in adjacent Sonora, Mexico, but its status is unknown. There are no current population estimates, other than an indication that numbers are low.

Threats

The bulk of the Cochise County population is located on an active cattle ranch. Cattle have been known to graze on and trample this species. Limestone quarrying and oil drilling in the habitat are also potential threats to the cactus. Quarries are currently active in the region, and new areas are slated for mineral development.

Significant climatic changes can also affect the cactus; several researchers involved in the annual U. S. Fish and Wildlife Service (FWS) monitoring project during the late 1980s and early 1990s observed during data collection that many plants appeared stressed, and it was concluded that lower-than-average rainfalls during the winters of 1987 through 1991 were probably responsible for the stress to the plants.

Predation is another threat. Insects, such as cactus specialist moths (which use the plants as larval food, frequently killing the host plant) and large cactus specialist beetles (which always kill the host plant), are a real danger to the cactus. Mammal predators who feed on the cactus include the woodrat and other rodents, rabbits and javelina.

Because of its size, rarity, and beauty, Cochise pincushion cactus is sought by plant collectors. If collectors are patient, however, they will not have to contribute to the species' decline by taking collecting wild plants. The cactus has been successfully propagated in the greenhouse, and seeds as well as cultivated plants will be made commercially available within the next few years.

Conservation and Recovery

The FWS published its recovery plan for the Cochise pincushion cactus in 1993, calling for a number of actions, including the stricter enforcement of laws banning collection and trade. Other recovery efforts deemed necessary to achieve the goal of delisting the species within a decade include the development and implementation of a habitat management plan in cooperation with private and state landowners; the study of population biology to determine the effects of management; protection from loss of individuals and habitat; and the establishment of conservation and research programs. The plan also calls for the definition of range and distribution of Cochise pincushion cactus and biological studies necessary for effective species management.

The 1993 plan notes that recovery of the species will require permanent protection and management of the habitat, trade protection through retention of the species on the Highly Safeguarded Lists of the Arizona Native Plant Law and CITES list following delisting, and demonstration through years of monitoring that viable populations are being maintained.

Contact

Regional Office of Endangered Species
U.S. Fish and Wildlife Service
P.O. Box 1306
Albuquerque, New Mexico 87103
http://southwest.fws.gov/

References

Earle, W. H. 1976. "*Cochiseia* Earle, Genus Novum." *Saguaroland Bulletin* 30:65-66.

Lopresti, V. 1984. "*Coryphantha robbinsorum* in Mexico." *Cactus and Succulent Journal of Mexico* 29:81.

U.S. Fish and Wildlife Service. 1987. "Endangered and Threatened Species of Arizona and New Mexico (with 1988 Addendum)." U.S. Fish and Wildlife Service, Albuquerque.

U.S . Fish and Wildlife Service. 1993. "Chochise Pincushion Cactus Recovery Plan." U.S. Fish and Wildlife Service, Albuquerque.

Zimmerman, A. D. 1978. "The Relationships of *Cochiseia robbinsorum* Earle." *Cactus and Succulent Journal* (U.S.) 50:293-297.

Pima Pineapple Cactus

Coryphantha scheeri var. *robustispina*

Status	Endangered
Listed	September 23, 1993
Family	Cactaceae (Cactus)
Description	Hemispherical cactus with strong, centralized hooked spines, short and light yellow, turning black with age, having yellow flowers.
Habitat	Slopes in semi-desert grassland in shallow to deep soil.
Threats	Alteration of habitat due to recreational activities, agriculture, road construction; illegal collecting.
Range	Arizona; Mexico

Description

The pima pineapple cactus is a hemispherical cactus measuring 4 to 18.4 in (10 to 46 cm) tall and 3 to 7.2 in (7.5 to 18 cm) in diameter. The spine clusters have one centralized spine that is especially strong and usually hooked. The spines are short and light yellow; with age the spines turn black. This plant may be single-stemmed, multi-headed, or in clusters. The clustered appearance is a result of the seeds germinating at the base of a mother plant or when a tubercle of the mother plant roots. The flowers are a silky yellow and appear in July through August. The green fruit is ellipsoidal, succulent and sweet.

Habitat

This cactus grows in alluvial basins or on slopes in semidesert grassland and Sonoran desert-scrub. Soils range from shallow to deep, and silty to rocky. It seems the pima pineapple cactus prefers silty to gravelly deep alluvial soils. This plant occurs most frequently in open areas on flat ridgetops or areas with very little slope at an elevation of 2,296 to 4,593 ft (700 to 1,400 m). Associated vegetation includes white-thorn acacia, creosotebush, velvet mesquite, triangle-leaf bursage, thread snakeweed, chain fruit cholla, *Isocoma tenuisecta*, Lehman's lovegrass, and other cacti species.

Distribution

The pima pineapple cactus is known from Pima and Santa Cruz Counties, Arizona and northern Sonora, Mexico.

The range of this cactus extends from the Baboquivari Mountains east to the western foothills of the Santa Rita Mountains. It is difficult to ascertain the area of potential habitat for this species due to its habitat requirements and the topographic complexity within its range.

The population density is difficult to attain as well because the pima pineapple cactus is difficult to find in the field. Minimum density estimates for areas near the Sierrita Mountains of Arizona range from a low of 0.3 plants per acre (0.12/ha) to 1.3 plants per acre (0.54/ha).

This plant must compete for space, light and nutrients with exotic vegetation. Some plants seem to be damaged by the larval stage of lepidoptera.

Threats

The pima pineapple cactus is currently threatened by many factors including illegal collection, habitat degradation due to recreational activities, habitat destruction by livestock, and habitat loss due to mining, agriculture, road construction, and urbanization.

Pima Pineapple Cactus, photograph. U. S. Fish and Wildlife Service. Reproduced by permission.

It is approximated that about 75% of the pima pineapple cactus's range is threatened by construction associated with growing human populations. Home building, commercial development, road construction and maintenance, and utility corridor construction are only a few of the activities destroying this species's habitat.

Mining activities have resulted in the loss of hundreds of pineapple cacti because they were not salvaged before expansion. Mineral extraction activities such as road access, tailing piles and settling or leaching ponds have also adversely affected this species.

Those areas that are currently undeveloped are utilized for livestock grazing. Over-grazing has most likely resulted in the current alteration of the ecosystem in this area. Erosion; changes in hydrology and microclimate; invasion of exotic vegetation; shifts in density, relative abundance, and vigor of native species; and increases in woody perennials have all been a result of this overgrazing.

This species is also faced with competition from aggressive exotics such as Lehman's lovegrass and Mediterranean grass.

Conservation and Recovery

Conservation of the Pima pineapple cactus requires the protection of its critical habitat, most of which is on privately owned land. These habitats should be protected by acquiring the land and designating ecological reserves, or by negotiating conservation easements with the owners. All critical habitats must be better protected from illegal collecting of plants by amateurs and for commercial trade. The populations of the Pima pineapple cactus should be monitored, and research undertaken into its biology, habitat needs, and beneficial management practices. The rare plant should be propagated in captivity to provide stock for out-planting to increase the size of existing populations and to establish new ones in suitable habitat. Surveys should be made in the Mexican range of the rare plant to determine its status there.

Contacts

U.S. Fish and Wildlife Service
Office of the Regional Director
P.O. Box 1306
500 Gold Avenue SW
Albuquerque, New Mexico 87103-1306
Telephone: (505) 248-6282
Fax: (505) 248-6845

U.S. Fish and Wildlife Service
Division of Endangered Species and Habitat Conservation
2105 Osuna Road NE
Albuquerque, New Mexico 87113-1001
Telephone: (505) 346-2525
E-mail: r2esweb@fws.gov
http://ifws2es.fws.gov/

Reference

U.S. Fish and Wildlife Service. 23 September 1993. "Endangered and Threatened Wildlife and Plants; Determination of Endangered Status for the Plant Pima Pineapple Cactus (*Coryphantha scheeri* var. *robustispina*)." *Federal Register* 58 (183): 49875-49879.

Lee Pincushion Cactus

Coryphantha sneedii var. *leei*

Status	Threatened
Listed	October 25, 1979
Family	Cactaceae (Cactus)
Description	Pincushion cactus, forming tight clumps of club-shaped stems and bearing brownish-pink flowers.
Habitat	Chihuahuan Desert; semi-desert grasslands in hard limestone soils.
Threats	Limited numbers, collectors, grazing deer.
Range	New Mexico

Lee Pincushion Cactus, photograph. U. S. Fish and Wildlife Service. Reproduced by permission.

Description

The Lee pincushion cactus, *Coryphantha sneedii* var. *leei*, forms tight clumps of as many as 100 stubby, club-shaped stems, 0.6-7.5 in (1.5-7.5 cm) tall and 0.4-1.2 in (1-3 cm) in diameter. Stems are densely covered with white spines, giving each plant the appearance of a mass of white-spined balls. Pink-tipped central spines are clustered six to 17 per areole; radial spines are clustered 35-90 per areole.

Ample winter and spring moisture is important for budding, which begins in late March or early April. With favorable weather, flowers are produced in a few weeks and generally last no more than four days. Most Lee cacti bloom only after three or four years. Dull, brownish-pink flowers are about 0.5 in (1.2 cm) long and do not open widely. Fruits form from August to November.

This species is known by two other scientific names: *Escobaria leei* and *Mammillaria leei*.

Habitat

This cactus grows in cracks and crevices of limestone within semi-desert grasslands of the Chihuahuan Desert. It is restricted to north-facing ledges of the Tansil limestone formation. These limestones are generally resistant to erosion and support a sparse covering of low shrubs, perennials, cacti, and herbs. The elevation is between 3,900 and 4,900 ft (1,200 and 1,500 m) and the annual rainfall is about 11.8 in (30 cm).

Distribution

Lee pincushion cactus is probably endemic to the rugged uplands of extreme southeastern New Mexico. It is found at two locations in Carlsbad Caverns National Park (Eddy County), New Mexico. Until 1994, it was known at only one location, which, in the early 1980s, had population estimates of between 1,000 and 2,000 and appeared to have stabilized. A new population of the plant was found in the early 1990s in Carlsbad Caverns National Park. The discovery was made during planning efforts for a prescribed burn.

Threats

This cactus has always been rare and has further declined at the hands of collectors. It is assumed, as well, that browsing deer crop seedlings, limiting plant reproduction.

Conservation and Recovery

Because this cactus's only known natural habitat is within the Carlsbad Caverns National Park, the primary recovery goal is to protect the two known populations from park visitors and from trampling and grazing. Fencing some portions of the habitat may be necessary. Collecting within the park is strictly prohibited, and enforcement has been tightened.

Contact

Regional Office of Endangered Species
U.S. Fish and Wildlife Service
P.O. Box 1306
Albuquerque, New Mexico 87103
http://southwest.fws.gov/

References

Castetter, E. F., and P. Pierce. 1966. "*Escobaria leei* Bodeker Rediscovered in New Mexico." *Madrono* 5:137-140.

Heil, K. D., and S. Brack. 1985. "The Cacti of Carlsbad Caverns National Park."*Cactus and Succulent Journal* (U.S.) 57:127.

U.S. Fish and Wildlife Service. 1986. "Sneed and Lee Pincushion Cacti (*Coryphantha sneedii* var. *sneedii* and *Coryphantha sneedii* var. *leei*) Recovery Plan." U.S. Fish and Wildlife Service, Albuquerque.

U.S. Fish and Wildlife Service. 1987. "Endangered and Threatened Species of Arizona and New Mexico (with 1988 Addendum)." U.S. Fish and Wildlife Service, Albuquerque.

U.S. Fish and Wildlife Service. 1979. "Determination of Lee Pincushion Cacti (*Coryphantha sneedii* var. *leei*) as an Endangered Species." *Federal Register* 44: 61556.

Sneed Pincushion Cactus

Coryphantha sneedii var. *sneedii*

Status	Endangered
Listed	November 7, 1979
Family	Cactaceae (Cactus)
Description	Pincushion cactus with densely clumped cylindrical stems and brownish-pink to pale pink flowers.
Habitat	Chihuahuan Desert; limestone ledges in desert grassland.
Threats	Collectors, loss of habitat.
Range	New Mexico, Texas

Description

The Sneed pincushion cactus, *Coryphantha sneedii* var. *sneedii*, grows in clumps of as many as 100 or more cylindrical or spherical stems, 1-3 in (2.5-7.5 cm) long and 0.4-1.2 in (1-3 cm) in diameter. The central spines, 6-17 per areole, are white, tipped with pink or brown; radial spines, 35-90 per cluster, are white. Spines often grow nearly parallel to the stem.

Sneed cacti flower after about three years, usually in April. The brownish-pink to pale rose flowers, 0.5 in (1.2 cm) wide, open at midday. Fruits develop from August to November and, when ripe, barely project beyond the tips of the spines. Ripe fruits have a prune-like odor and attract rodents, which serve to disperse the seeds.

This species has also been known as *Escobaria sneedii* and *Mammillaria sneedii*.

Habitat

This cactus grows in cracks on cliffs or ledges in semi-desert grasslands of the Chihuahuan Desert. These limestone outcrops support only sparse vegetation, such as low shrubs, some rosette-forming perennials, cacti, and herbs. Habitat elevation is between 3,900- 7,700 ft (1,200-2,350 m); annual rainfall varies from 8-16 in (20-40 cm) per year.

Distribution

Sneed pincushion cactus was once fairly widespread in the Franklin, Guadalupe, and Organ mountains—between Las Cruces and Carlsbad, New Mexico and south into Hudspeth, Culberson, and El Paso counties, Texas. Its range may well have extended into Mexico. It was first collected from Anthony Gap, Texas.

It is still locally abundant in the Franklin Mountains (El Paso County, Texas, and adjacent Dona Ana County, New Mexico), where nine populations are known. There are two smaller populations in the Organ Mountains north of El Paso (Dona Ana County, New Mexico); and nine in the Guadalupe Mountains (Hudspeth and Culberson counties, Texas). Another population was recently discovered at Carlsbad Caverns (Eddy County, New Mexico).

Seven populations are on private lands; other sites are in Lincoln National Forest, Guadalupe Mountains National Park, and Carlsbad Caverns National Park. In 1986, the total population was estimated to be in excess of 10,000 plants.

Threats

Although not showy, some collectors prize the Sneed cactus for its unusual appearance, and it is systematically collected from the wild. Collectors

Sneed Pincushion Cactus, photograph. U. S. Fish and Wildlife Service. Reproduced by permission.

visit privately owned sites on a regular basis. Population sites in the Franklin Mountains are accessible from the roads and, if located by collectors, could be depleted. Access to other localities is more difficult, affording a measure of natural protection.

Conservation and Recovery

Recovery will depend on enforcing existing prohibitions against collection and on increasing the number of plants on protected land. Several sites in the Guadalupe Mountains and Carlsbad Caverns National Park are under federal protection. All populations are covered by the endangered species plant laws of New Mexico and Texas.

To reduce collection pressures, the Fish and Wildlife Service Recovery Plan recommends that the cactus be cultivated and plants made available to the commercial trade. Nearly all cultivated plants produce viable fruit. The Forest Service has provided the New Mexico Nature Conservancy with

nursery stock of Sneed pincushion cacti to transplant on protected land. The plant will be considered for reclassification as Threatened when at least three populations each have been established on the Guadalupe, Franklin, and southern Organ mountains and when the total number of plants on these federally owned sites reaches 20,000.

Contacts

U.S. Fish and Wildlife Service
Division of Endangered Species
P.O. Box 1306
Albuquerque, New Mexico 87103
http://southwest.fws.gov/

References

Benson, L. 1982. *The Cacti of the United States and Canada.* Stanford University Press, Stanford.

Heil, K. D. and S. Brack. 1985. "The Cacti of Carlsbad Caverns National Park." *Cacti and Succulent Journal* 57:127-134.

U.S. Fish and Wildlife Service. 1986. "Sneed and Lee Pincushion Cacti (*Coryphantha sneedii* var. *sneedii* and *Coryphantha sneedii* var. *leei*) Recovery Plan." U.S. Fish and Wildlife Service, Albuquerque.

U.S. Fish and Wildlife Service. 1987. "Endangered and Threatened Species of Arizona and New Mexico (with 1988 Addendum)." U.S. Fish and Wildlife Service, Albuquerque.

Weniger, D. 1970. *Cacti of the Southwest*. University of Texas Press, Austin and London.

Nichol's Turk's Head Cactus

Echinocactus horizonthalonius var. *nicholii*

Status	Endangered
Listed	October 26, 1979
Family	Cactaceae (Cactus)
Description	Eight-ribbed barrel cactus with a single blue-green stem and pink or purplish flowers.
Habitat	Sonoran Desert; in full sun on limestone talus slopes.
Threats	Collectors, quarrying, off-road vehicles.
Range	Arizona; Sonora, Mexico

Nichol's Turk's Head Cactus, photograph. U. S. Fish and Wildlife Service. Reproduced by permission.

Description

Nichol's turk's head cactus, *Echinocactus horizonthalonius* var. *nicholii*, is an eight-ribbed barrel cactus, reaching a maximum height of 20 in (50 cm) and a diameter of 8 in (20 cm). The blue-green stem bears spines on vertical, spiraling ridges. Each spine cluster (areole) contains three central and five radial spines. Bright pink or purplish flowers bloom from April to mid-May. Fruits are covered with white, woolly hairs. The plant always grows as a single stem, but because seedlings often grow around its base, it may appear to have multiple stems.

Population dynamics are slow and the turnover rate is low. The mean age of this cactus is nine and one-half to more than 13 years and maximum age varies from 24-39 years.

Habitat

Nichol's turk's head cactus is found within the Arizona Upland Subdivision of Sonoron Desert scrub at an elevation between 3,281 and 3,829 ft (1,000 and 1,167 m). Preferred sites are in full sun on limestone talus slopes in soils rich in calcium carbonate. Surrounding vegetation is characterized by sparse trees and scattered low shrubs dominated by foothill palo verde, triangle leaf bursage, white ratany, and prickly pear cactus. The semiarid habitat receives less than 13 in (33 cm) of annual rainfall. Freezing temperatures occur only about five nights per winter.

There are differences in fecundity and survival rates for plants in rocky terrace versus alluvial habitats. Populations are denser at the higher sites where there is more moisture and rocks. In the alluvial habitat, plants grow in open, exposed areas containing few plants in the shrub-tree strata. Shaded plants grow, flower, and survive at lower rates than plants in the open. Soil erosion is an important factor; half-buried plants do not grow well and rodents eat plants that have washed out or been injured.

Distribution

Nichol's turk's head cactus is endemic to the Sonoran Desert of southern Arizona and adjacent Mexico. Its estimated potential habitat in the Waterman Mountains is 5,000 acres (2,025 hectares). The Vekol Mountains add another 5,700 acres (2,305 hectares) of suitable habitat.

Populations of the cactus are grouped at two locations in south-central Arizona: the Waterman Mountains (north-central Pima County); and the Vekol Mountains (southwestern Pinal County). One small population has been found in northwestern Mexico in Sierra del Viejo (in the state of Sonora). In 1983, U. S. Bureau of Land Management (BLM) personnel surveyed a population on the north side of Waterman Peak that numbered 1,179 cacti. There are no current population estimates for other sites.

Threats

Nichol's turk's head cactus is threatened primarily by collectors. Between 1982 and 1984, this cactus was advertised for sale in 11 different plant catalogs, two of which specified field-collected plants. At least one nursery is known to collect seeds from the cactus in the wild, a practice that damages the plant and inhibits propagation.

Limestone quarrying eliminated a small population near the Happy Jack Mine in the Waterman Mountains, and roads leading to this quarry cut through several other colonies. Recreational off-road vehicles have damaged habitat and destroyed plants. Hunters sometimes use cacti for target practice.

Conservation and Recovery

This cactus is on the Arizona state protected list (Arizona Native Plant Law), which prohibits collecting except by permit. In 1983 the species was given a CITES (Convention on International Trade in Endangered Species of Wild Fauna and Flora) classification that requires a permit for importing or exporting the cactus. More strict enforcement of the Lacey Act, which makes it illegal to buy or sell any plant taken or possessed in violation of any law, will be needed to deter collectors.

Since many populations of this cactus are on lands managed by the BLM and the Bureau of Indian Affairs (BIA), proper management and regulation of mining operations and claim surveys will do much to preserve remaining Nichol's turk's head cactus populations. The recovery plan recommends that the BLM withdraw all suitable, unclaimed habitat from any future mining activities; consolidate federal agencies that manage the lands; develop off-road vehicle management; and coordinate with the BIA to monitor and manage populations on the Papago Reservation.

Contact

U. S. Fish and Wildlife Service
Regional Office, Division of Endangered Species
P.O. Box 1306
Albuquerque, New Mexico 87103-1306
Telephone: (505) 248-6911
Fax: (505) 248-6915
http://southwest.fws.gov/

References

Benson, L. 1969. *The Cacti of the United States and Canada.* Stanford University Press, Stanford, Calif.

Fuller, D. 1985. "U.S. Cactus and Succulent Business Moves toward Propagation." *Traffic* (U.S.A.) 6 (2): 1-11.

U. S. Fish and Wildlife Service. 1979. "Determination that Nichol's Turk's Head Cactus (*Echinocactus horizonthalonius* var. *nicholii*) Is an Endangered Species." *Federal Register* 44: 61927-61929.

U. S. Fish and Wildlife Service. 1986. "Recovery Plan for the Nichol's Turk's Head Cactus (*Echinocactus horizonthalonius* var. *nicholii*)." U. S. Fish and Wildlife Service, Albuquerque.

Weniger, D. 1970. *Cacti of the Southwest.* University of Texas Press, Austin. Press.

Chisos Mountain Hedgehog Cactus

Echinocereus chisoensis var. *chisoensis*

Status	Endangered
Listed	September 30, 1988
Family	Cactaceae (Cactus)
Description	Green-stemmed cactus with tricolored flowers.
Habitat	Alluvial flats.
Threats	Low numbers, limited distribution, collectors.
Range	Texas

Description

Chisos Mountain hedgehog cactus, *Echinocereus chisoensis* var. *chisoensis*, measures 3-6 in (7.5-15 cm) tall and has deep green or blue-green stems. The spine cluster consists of 12-14 radial spines and one to four white central spines. From March to early June, plants are conspicuous because of showy tricolored flowers. Petals are red at the base, white at mid-length, and fuschia at the tips. Red-tinged, fleshy green fruits, covered with long white wool and bristles, mature between May and August. Each fruit contains 200-250 seeds.

Habitat

Chisos Mountain hedgehog cactus occurs on alluvial flats beside the Rio Grande River and smaller tributaries. It occurs at the base of mountain ridges at elevations of 1,050-2,390 ft (595-717 m). Ground cover in the area is sparse, estimated at 20-30%. The cactus is typically found on bare soil, within spreading clumps of *Opuntia schottii,* or in the shade of other associated plants.

Distribution

This cactus is endemic to flats and lower slopes of the southern Chisos Mountains in the Texas Big Bend Region. Botanists speculate that it was once more widespread in the region, because plants do not now occupy all available habitat within the current range. Surveys of the Mexican states of Chihuahua and Coahuila in 1982 did not locate any plants even though the habitat there is similar.

Only 11 small populations are known, all found within a small area—about 30 sq mi (77.7 sq km)—in the Big Bend National Park in Brewster County. Surveys conducted in 1986 and 1987 produced counts of only 183 plants, even though estimates in the early 1980s suggested a total population of about 1,000. The species 1993 recovery plan estimated that fewer than 1,000 plants remained, though it noted that a recent reconnaissance survey of the park located only a few dozen plants in visits to known sites, leading to the conclusion that the plants are very rare even within all of their known sites. Based on this and other surveys, the recovery plan noted that the plant had suffered a reduction in its geographical area of distribution and in the size and number of its populations. Many of the populations, especially those accessible to roadways, have been noted to be in decline.

Threats

Long-term climatic change—principally the region's desertification beginning some 5,000 years ago—may have contributed to the overall decline of Chisos Mountain hedgehog cactus. In spite of this

Don Kurz

decline, the cactus was still locally abundant in the early twentieth century, until the region was heavily used for cattle grazing. Cattle almost entirely eliminated the plant.

The species is presently threatened by its low numbers and narrow distribution. Plants growing next to a road have shown evidence of being collected casually by park visitors. The cactus is especially vulnerable to collectors during flowering when it is highly visible. During extended dry periods of the late 1980s Big Bend National Park personnel also noted damage to the plants from some kind of mammal predation, probably rodents or jackrabbits. Natural changes in climatic conditions, tending toward dryness, may also be adversely affecting the plant's reproduction. Catastrophic events such as fires, freezes and droughts could have potentially lethal effects on the existing populations, because of the plant's extremely limited distribution.

Conservation and Recovery

With the establishment of the Big Bend National Park, livestock grazing was suspended, and the gradual recovery of overgrazed rangeland may assist the plant's reestablishment. An effort to propagate seedlings for transplanting to suitable sites will figure prominently in recovery of this species. Unfortunately, low population viability may be limiting recovery.

But early cultivation experiments have been effective. In cooperation with the National Park Service, Sul Ross State University and the Chihuahuan Desert Research Institute have experimented with cultivating the cactus from cuttings and seeds, reporting in 1992 that they had grown more than 300 plants, though most were cloned from only a few individuals. This promising cultivation work has shown the potential for establishing a seed bank and cultivated collection. The Center for Plant Conservation (CPC) is also working with the National Seed Storage Laboratory in Fort Collins, Colorado, and the Desert Botanical Garden in Phoenix, to implement cultivation initiatives.

In 1990, the U.S. Fish and Wildlife Service (FWS) gave the species a recovery rating of 9 (on a scale of 1-18, with 1 being given the highest recovery priority). The 9 rating indicates that this is a plant variety with a moderate degree of threat and a high recovery potential.

The 1993 recovery plan for this species, from the FWS, calls for a goal of delisting by 2009. The species will be considered delisted when 50 distinct populations, each consisting of at least 100 reproductive individuals, have been established; and when it can be demonstrated that the populations are demographically stable and reproductively successful over a 10-year monitoring period.

Among the needed actions called for in the plan are the protection of present and newly discovered populations; the establishment of a reserve germ bank/cultivated population; the search for additional populations; and the development of a public education program. The plan also calls for research into successful management and restoration, and the assessment of restoration feasibility and establishment of a pilot reintroduction program.

Contact

Regional Office of Endangered Species
U.S. Fish and Wildlife Service
P.O. Box 1306
Albuquerque, New Mexico 87103
http://southwest.fws.gov/

References

Benson, L. 1982. *The Cacti of the United States and Canada*. Stanford University Press, Stanford, California.

Evans, D. B. 1986. "Survey of Chisos Pitaya *Echinocereus reichenbachii* var. *chisoensis*." Report. U.S. National Park Service, Big Bend National Park, Texas.

Heil, K. D., and E. F. Anderson. 1982. "Status Report on *Echinocereus chisoensis*." U.S. Fish and Wildlife Service, Office of Endangered Species, Albuquerque.

Heil, K. D., S. Brock, and J. M. Porter, 1985, "The Rare and Sensitive Cacti of Big Bend National Park." U.S. National Park Service, Big Bend National Park, Texas.

Taylor, N. P. 1985. *The Genus Echinocereus*. Timber Press, Portland, Oregon.

U.S. Fish and Wildlife Service. 1993. "Chisos Mountain Hedgehog Cactus Recovery Plan." U.S. Fish and Wildlife Service, Albuquerque.

U.S. Fish and Wildlife Service. 1988. "Determination of Threatened Status for *Echinocereus chisoensis* var. *chisoensis*." *Federal Register*. 53(190): 38453-38456.

Kuenzler Hedgehog Cactus

Echinocereus fendleri var. *kuenzleri*

Status	Endangered
Listed	October 26, 1979
Family	Cactaceae (Cactus)
Description	Cone-shaped, single-stemmed or branched cactus, with magenta flowers.
Habitat	Limestone outcrops among pinyon-juniper woodlands.
Threats	Collectors.
Range	New Mexico

Keunzler Hedgehog Cactus, photograph. U. S. Fish and Wildlife Service. Reproduced by permission.

Description

The dark green stems of the Kuenzler hedgehog cactus, *Echinocereus fendleri* var. *kuenzleri*, are short and conically shaped, about 10 in (25 cm) long and about 4 in (10 cm) in diameter. The plant may be single-stemmed or branched; when branched, less than four stems are typically clumped. Stems display up to 12 flabby ribs with prominent tubercles (nodules) from which spine clusters protrude. Straw-colored radial spines, five to seven in number are recurved (bent back towards the stem) and vary in length up to about 1 in (2.5 cm). Central spines are generally lacking.

Bright magenta flowers appear in late May, and the bright red fruit ripens in July. Flowers are about 4 in (10 cm) long. Fruits are spiny and egg-shaped, slightly more than 2 in (5 cm) long; the seeds are black.

This cactus has also been known as *E. kuenzleri*, and *E. hempelli*.

Habitat

Kuenzler hedgehog cactus is primarily found on the lower fringes of pinyon-juniper woodland. The dominant overstory of this habitat is one-seeded juniper (*Juniperus monosperma*). The cactus prefers a southern exposure and grows in cracks on sloping limestone outcrops or in shallow soils on hillsides at elevations from 5,800- 6,400 ft (1,770-1,950 m). When in bloom, it is easily seen from a distance.

Distribution

The Kuenzler hedgehog cactus is endemic to the open, semi-arid woodlands of south-central New Mexico. It is found in northeastern Otero County and adjacent Lincoln and Chaves counties, New Mexico. The total population is less than 500 plants in two small populations in the Rio Hondo and Rio Penasco drainages. Most plants occur on private land, although one small area falls within the Lincoln National Forest. A few scattered plants are also found on the Mescalero Apache Indian Reservation.

Threats

Although its habitat appears to have suffered no human-made modifications, this cactus has been brought to the verge of extinction by collectors. It is not known how many plants have been removed from the wild, but the species was already rare when discovered in 1961. It is habitually taken by collectors despite legal prohibitions.

Conservation and Recovery

This cactus cannot be recovered without reducing collection. Stricter enforcement of regulations may deter casual collectors but may not reduce black market trade. One recovery strategy might be to provide propagated Kuenzler cacti to the commercial market. It is estimated that a domesticated production of 10,000 plants a year over a period of five years would diminish the novelty of owning a Kuenzler cactus to the point that collecting in the wild would cease to be a problem.

Since there are so few wild plants left, the U. S. Fish and Wildlife Service has given a high priority to establishing a large-scale propagation program. However, research efforts have been hindered by the reduced size of the populations. In 1983, The Nature Conservancy leased a parcel of private land, containing the largest remaining population, to serve as a research site. New Mexico state law requires an application to sell collected wild plants and affords limited protection to plants within 1,200 ft (366 m) of any highway, growing on either state or private land.

Contact

Regional Office of Endangered Species
U.S. Fish and Wildlife Service
P.O. Box 1306
Albuquerque, New Mexico 87103
http://southwest.fws.gov/

References

Benson, L. 1982. *The Cacti of the United States and Canada.* Stanford University Press, Stanford.

Castetter, E. F., P. Pierce, and K. H. Schwerin. 1976. "A New Cactus Species and Two New Varieties from New Mexico." *Cactus and Succulent Journal* (U.S.) 48:76-82.

U.S. Fish and Wildlife Service. 1985. "Kuenzler Hedgehog Cactus Recovery Plan." U.S. Fish and Wildlife Service, Albuquerque.

Lloyd's Hedgehog Cactus

Echinocereus lloydii

Status	Endangered
Listed	October 26, 1979
Delisted	June 24, 1999
Family	Cactaceae (Cactus)
Description	Low-growing, columnar cactus, with coral pink or orange flowers and a greenish-orange fruit.
Habitat	Chihuahuan Desert; desert scrub on gravelly slopes.
Threats	Collectors, hybridization.
Range	New Mexico, Texas; Chihuahua, Mexico

Description

Echinocereus lloydii (Lloyd's hedgehog cactus) is a low-growing, columnar cactus with stems up to 12 in (30 cm) tall and 4.5 in (12 cm) in diameter. The greenish bowl of the cactus is ribbed and thickly covered with straight red or pinkish spines, half- hiding the stem surface. Radial spines number from 14 to 17, central spines from four to eight.

Attractive flowers appear in April and May, varying in color from coral pink, to reddish purple, scarlet, or intense orange. Pink tends to predominate as the flower ages. The small, oval fruit is green, tinged with orange. It is protected by white spines, and filled with hard, black seeds, which germinate easily in cultivation.

The taxonomic status of this cactus has been much debated. It has been categorized as a full species, and also as the subspecies *Echinocereus roetteri* var. *lloydii*. More recently, botanists have conducted taxonomic and population studies that show that the Lloyd's hedgehog cactus is a recent hybrid between the Texas rainbow cactus (*Echinocereus dasyacanthus*) and a claret-cup cactus (*Echinocerus coccineus*).

Habitat

Lloyd's hedgehog cactus occurs in the Chihuahuan Desert on mid-elevation mountain slopes in association with desert scrub vegetation. Habitat elevation ranges from 4,600-5,000 ft (1,400- 1,525 m). The cactus prefers rocky soils derived from weathered metamorphic rock.

Distribution

Lloyd's hedgehog cactus occurs in the rugged desert uplands of extreme southern New Mexico and south into western Texas and the state of Chihuahua, Mexico. Although this range appears extensive, this cactus grows under very localized conditions and is quite rare in the wild.

In New Mexico, this cactus is found only in a single scattered population in the Guadalupe Mountains (Otero and Eddy counties). It has been found in Culberson County, Texas, in the Guadalupe Mountains National Park, and has been described from several sites in Pecos and Brewster counties, Texas. In Chihuahua, Mexico, a population has been located near Flores Magon in the Sierra del Nido. There are no current estimates of the populations at these sites.

Threats

Collecting poses the most immediate threat to the survival of the Pecos County, Texas, population, and has probably contributed to a decline at other known sites. Most plants observed in the wild are old; seedlings and smaller plants seem less common

Lloyd's Hedgehog Cactus, photograph by Jackie Poole, USFWS. Reproduced by permission.

and may have been collected. Several sites have been over-grazed by livestock, preventing the establishment of seedlings and limiting reproduction.

Conservation and Recovery

Much of the confusion surrounding the status of Lloyd's hedgehog cactus has been caused by significant "introgression," or genetic hybridization, among several species of cacti occurring in the Chihuahuan Desert. Some biologists believe that continued cross-fertilization with other species of cacti could eventually "hybridize" the Lloyd's hedgehog out of existence. However, other botanists maintain that the Lloyd's hedgehog cactus is itself a hybrid, and that continued protection of this cactus might threaten the genetic purity of its parent species. In 1999, the Fish and Wildlife Service removed the Lloyd's hedgehog cactus from the list of endangered or threatened plants. This was done because of evidence that this cactus is not a distinct species but rather a hybrid that is not evolving independently of its parental species.

Contact

U. S. Fish and Wildlife Service
Regional Office, Division of Endangered Species
P.O. Box 1306
Albuquerque, New Mexico 87103
Telephone: (505) 248-6911
http://southwest.fws.gov/

References

Benson, L. 1982. *The Cacti of the United States and Canada.* Stanford University Press, Stanford.

Heil, K. D., and S. Brack. 1985. "The Rare and Sensitive Cacti of Carlsbad Caverns National Park." National Park Service, Santa Fe.

Heil, K. D., and S. Brack. 1985. "The Rare and Sensitive Cacti of Guadalupe Mountains National Park." National Park Service, Santa Fe.

Powell, A.M., A.D. Zimmerman, and R.A. Hilsenbeck. 1991. "Experimental Documentation of Natural Hybridization in Cactaceae: Origin of

Lloyd's Hedgehog Cactus, *Echinocereus* X *lloydii*." *Plant Systematics and Evolution* 178:107-122.

U. S. Fish and Wildlife Service. 1979. "Determination of Lloyd's Hedgehog Cactus, *Echinocereus lloydii*, as an Endangered Species." *Federal Register* 44: 61786.

U.S. Fish and Wildlife Service. 24 June 1999. "Endangered and Threatened Wildlife and Plants; Final Rule To Remove the Plant *Echinocereus lloydii* (Lloyd's Hedgehog Cactus) From the Federal List of Endangered and Threatened Plants." *Federal Register* 64 (121): 33796-33800.

Zimmerman, A.D. 1993. "Systematics of *Echinocereus* X *roetteri* (Cactaceae), including Lloyd's hedgehog-cactus. In: *Southwestern Rare and Endangered Plants*; Proceedings of the Southwestern Rare and Endangered Plant Conference. Forestry and Resources Conservation Division of the New Mexico Energy, Minerals, and Natural Resources Department." Miscellaneous Publication 2: 270-288.

Black Lace Cactus

Echinocereus reichenbachii var. *albertii*

Status	Endangered
Listed	October 26, 1979
Family	Cactaceae (Cactus)
Description	Low-growing cactus with cylindrical stems and large pink flowers.
Habitat	Mesquite brush along streams in poorly drained soils.
Threats	Agricultural practices, livestock grazing, collectors.
Range	Texas

Charlie McDonald, USFWS

Description

Black lace cactus, *Echinocereus reichenbachii* (=*melanocentrus*) var. *albertii*, grows as a solitary stem or sometimes as a clump of 5 to 12 ribbed, cylindrical stems, each about 6 in (15 cm) tall. Each spine cluster is formed of 14 to 16 radial spines and crowned with a single, purple-tipped central spine. The common name for the species derives from the "lace-like" pattern of the spines over the stem. The pink to rose flowers, about 3 in (7.5 cm) in diameter, are showy and attractive.

Habitat

The black lace cactus prefers poorly drained, sandy soils along stream beds on the Texas coastal plain. It tends to grow in slightly depressed areas that hold standing rainwater. Ground cover consists of mesquite and other scattered shrubs, interspersed with "islands" of hardy grasses and annuals. Colonies of the cactus are found in openings in the mesquite brush or in the midst of broomweed and spiny aster stands with overhanging mesquite.

Distribution

The black lace cactus genus ranges from western Kansas to northern Mexico. The *albertii* variety may once have been more widespread along the south Texas coast, but the exact extent is unknown. The species' discovery site in Jim Wells County, Texas, was nearly destroyed by bulldozing, and only four to 12 cacti remain there. Two populations known from Kleberg County were lost to agricultural use.

The black lace cactus has been found in three south Texas coastal counties: Jim Wells, Kleberg, and Refugio. Jim Wells County supports a population numbering about 16,000 plants. A large part of the Kleberg County population was destroyed by brush clearing sometime before 1986, but an estimated 13,000 cacti remain. The Refugio County population is transected by a road, and suffers from collecting and road maintenance. While it numbers more than 80,000 plants, many were in poor condition as recently as 1986, and the habitat area is currently leased for grazing and oil exploration. The Refugio County population borders the Welder Wildlife Foundation reserve, which works to discourage collecting of the cacti. These localities form a semicircle around two other counties (Nueces and San Patricio) where the cactus has not been discovered.

Threats

Biologists consider habitat loss and degradation the greatest threat to the cactus's survival. Much of the Texas coastal plain is cattle country, and it is common practice in the region to clear brush and undergrowth to plant coastal Bermuda grass for pastureland. This practice has partly or completely eliminated many known populations of the black lace cactus.

Because of the cactus's rarity and showy flowers, collectors also pose a threat. All three known populations are on private lands. Two of the three sites are not well-known and are fairly inaccessible. This gives the species some protection from casual collectors, but not from professionals.

Conservation and Recovery

Landowners need to be informed of the presence and significance of populations and asked to cooperate in recovery efforts. The Texas Nature Conservancy has already begun this dialogue, and one family has agreed to join the Conservancy's Land Steward Society.

The large number of seedlings found at population sites indicate that seeds germinate well in the wild. Seedlings from Jim Wells County have been transplanted to similar habitats, but the long-term fate of such transplants are unknown. Researchers need to know more about the plant's microhabitat requirements before transplantation can be considered as a practical recovery strategy. Propagation studies are currently underway to establish a nursery population.

Cloning is also being explored as a propagation method as a way to supply the commercial market. Tissue culture laboratories at Texas A & M University and the University of Texas have produced clones of a number of cactus species. While suitable for the commercial trade, these clones could not be used for reintroduction because of their lack of genetic diversity.

Contact

Regional Office of Endangered Species
U.S. Fish and Wildlife Service
P.O. Box 1306
Albuquerque, New Mexico 87103
http://southwest.fws.gov/

References

Jones, F. B. 1982. *Flora of the Texas Coastal Bend*. Rob and Bessie Welder Wildlife Foundation, Sinton, Texas.

U.S. Fish and Wildlife Service. 1987. "Black Lace Cactus (*Echinocereus reichenbachii* var. *albertii*) Recovery Plan." U.S. Fish and Wildlife Service, Albuquerque.

Weinger, D. 1984. *Cacti of Texas and Neighboring States: A Field Guide*. University of Texas Press, Austin.

Arizona Hedgehog Cactus

Echinocereus triglochidiatus var. *arizonicus*

Status	Endangered
Listed	October 25, 1979
Family	Cactaceae (Cactus)
Description	Hedgehog cactus with dense clusters of cylindrical stems and bright red flowers.
Habitat	Granite boulder outcrops within woodlands.
Threats	Low numbers, collectors, mining.
Range	Arizona

Arizona Hedgehog Cactus, photograph by Marv Poulson. Reproduced by permission.

Description

From a thickened root, Arizona hedgehog cactus branches into dense clumps of cylindrical to egg-shaped stems, 8.8-16 in (22-40 cm) high. One to three central spines, 0.06 in (1.5 mm) long, and five to 11 shorter radial spines are dark gray, tinged with pink. Flowers, appearing in late April to mid-May, are bright red with greenish midribs. This variety is the most robust of all the red-flowered hedgehog cacti.

This species has also been classified as *Echinocereus arizonicus*.

Habitat

Arizona hedgehog cactus is restricted to granite boulder outcrops in mountain woodlands at 3,800-5,200 ft (1,160-1,585 m) elevation. It prefers open slopes or an open canopy rather than dense shrub overstory typical of chaparral. The hedgehog cactus plants are scattered across open slopes and tend to grow from narrow cracks between boulders, which it requires for stability, in the understory of shrubs. Its plant associates are live oak and manzanita.

Distribution

This species is endemic to the wooded highlands of central Arizona, generally east of Phoenix and north of Tucson.

Once more widespread, this species now occurs at a few locations in the rugged country north of the Gila River near the boundary of Gila and Pinal counties. The density of the populations observed ranged from one to 155 plants per 1,196 sq yd (1,000 sq m); population estimates range from 1,500-14,000 individuals. Without adverse impact from humans, the Arizona hedgehog cactus population appears to be stable. Plants are easy to grow and require only shade and temperatures below 110 degrees F (43.3 degrees C), and so their recovery potential is favorable.

Threats

Collectors are the principal threat to this cactus, and its bright red flowers make it an easy target. Private collectors and commercial dealers are familiar with the location of plants and collect them on a regular basis, even removing plants that have been fenced off for research purposes. Because of the low numbers and extremely restricted range, collectors can deplete a population in a short time.

Populations are also threatened by active copper mining in the vicinity and activities associated with mineral exploration. Roads cut for mining activities also provide access to collectors. Open pit mining is the most destructive to the plants, and if mining activity continues at its present rate, this hedgehog cactus will be placed under greater stress.

Conservation and Recovery

All members of the family Cactaceae are protected under Arizona law, which prohibits their collection from the wild without a permit. Arizona hedgehog cactus is listed as a species of concern by the Convention on International Trade in Endangered Species (CITES), which regulates export of rare plant species.

The Recovery Plan for the Arizona hedgehog cactus calls for studies of the ecology and population biology; comparisons with similar varieties of hedgehog cacti; mapping populations and size; and development of propagation techniques to provide nursery stocks for reintroduction and commercial sale (to reduce collecting).

Contact

Regional Office of Endangered Species
U.S. Fish and Wildlife Service
P.O. Box 1306
Albuquerque, New Mexico 87103
http://southwest.fws.gov/

References

Benson, L. 1982. *The Cacti of the United States and Canada.* Stanford University Press, Stanford.

U.S. Fish and Wildlife Service. 1987. "Endangered and Threatened Species of Arizona and New Mexico (with 1988 Addendum)." U.S. Fish and Wildlife Service, Albuquerque.

Davis' Green Pitaya

Echinocereus viridiflorus var. *davisii*

Status	Endangered
Listed	November 7, 1979
Family	Cactaceae (Cactus)
Description	Dwarf single-stemmed turbinate cactus with yellow-green flowers.
Habitat	Chihuahuan Desert; semi-arid grasslands.
Threats	Collectors, encroaching plants.
Range	Texas

Davis' Green Pitaya, photograph by Don Kurz. Reproduced by permission.

Description

Davis' green pitaya, *Echinocereus viridiflorus* var. *davisii*, is a dwarf cactus, usually growing as a single stem with six to nine ribs. The stem is turbinate to ovate, up to 1 in (2.5 cm) tall and 0.8 in (2 cm) in diameter. Each spine cluster (areole) consists of eight to 11 radial spines, which are white, gray, or gray tipped with red. Typically, each cluster has a single prominent central spine but the number may vary.

Plants mature after three or four years and bloom in late March and early April. The yellow-green flowers are nearly as large as the plant itself. The stubby, green fruit ripens in May. A metallic green sweat bee (Family Halictidae) is believed to be the major pollinator. The bulk of the stem is often underground and can be hidden by other low-growing plants, such as little club moss. Some scientists have referred to this species as *E. davisii*.

Habitat

Davis' green pitaya grows in semi-arid grasslands of the Chihuahuan Desert, an area that receives 16 in (41 cm) annual precipitation. It is restricted to rock crevices along ridgetops composed of outcroppings of the Caballos Novaculite formation. The habitat supports perennial bunch grasses and a wide variety of shrubs and cacti at an elevation of 3,960-4,455 ft (1,200-1,350 m).

Distribution

This cactus is endemic to Brewster County in the Big Bend region of Texas.

A single population of Davis' green pitaya is known from near the town of Marathon in northern Brewster County. This population totaled about 20,000 plants in 1984, a significant increase over previous counts. It is believed this increase was due to favorable weather conditions in 1983.

Threats

Twenty years ago, the green pitaya had nearly been collected to extinction by European, Japanese, and American collectors. Today it is threatened by multiple pressures: collection by both commercial and private collectors, competition for space and moisture, and highway fence construction and maintenance. The destruction and modification of the habitat by overgrazing of livestock, brush control, and herbicide use also impact this species.

Conservation and Recovery

The population site, with the cooperation of the private landowners, has now been securely fenced, which seems to have stopped bulk collecting. Annual monitoring indicates that the number of cacti has stabilized and may be climbing. The cactus has recently reestablished itself at several sites where it had previously been eliminated.

All of the population occurs on private land, and the posting of "No Trespassing" signs discourages collectors. The landowners have also been cooperating to reduce disruption of habitat.

The Recovery Plan recommends studying: the feasibility of reducing collecting by promoting a nursery propagation program, the plant's seed dispersal methods and seedling establishment, and the pollinators.

Contact

Regional Office of Endangered Species
U.S. Fish and Wildlife Service
P.O. Box 1306
Albuquerque, New Mexico 87103
http://southwest.fws.gov/

References

Benson, L. 1982. *The Cacti of the United States and Canada*. Stanford University Press, Stanford.

U.S. Fish and Wildlife Service. 1984. "Davis' Green Pitaya Cactus Recovery Plan." U.S. Fish and Wildlife Service, Albuquerque.

U.S. Fish and Wildlife Service. 1987. "Endangered and Threatened Species of Texas and Oklahoma (with 1988 Addendum)." U.S. Fish and Wildlife Service, Albuquerque.

Lloyd's Mariposa Cactus

Echinomastus mariposensis

Status	Threatened
Listed	November 6, 1979
Family	Cactaceae (Cactus)
Description	Single-stemmed, spherical cactus with pink flowers.
Habitat	Chihuahuan Desert; barren areas along limestone ridges.
Threats	Low numbers, livestock grazing, off-road vehicles.
Range	New Mexico, Texas; Coahuila (probable), Mexico

Lloyd's Maiposa Cactus, photograph by Jackie Poole, USFWS. Reproduced by permission.

Description

Lloyd's mariposa cactus, *Echinomastus mariposensis*, grows as a single spherical or egg-shaped stem, about 3.5 in (9 cm) tall and 2 in (5 cm) in diameter. An immature plant begins with 13 smooth ribs and develops up to 21 wrinkled ribs as the plant matures. Spine clusters (areoles) consist of 26-32 short, off-white radial spines and from two to four tan central spines with blue or brown tips. Funnel-shaped, pinkish flowers, about 1.25 in (3.2 cm) in diameter, bloom in the spring. Yellowish green fruits are spherical or oblong and split open when ripe.

Other scientific appellations have been applied to this cactus, including *Echinocactus mariposensis* and *Neolloydia mariposensis*.

Habitat

A resident of the Chihuahuan Desert, this cactus grows on hills and lower slopes of very rocky, stable limestone gravel mesas in barren areas of thin soils overlaying hot, exposed limestone ridges. The habitat is 2,600-3,800 ft (790-1,160 m) in elevation.

Occurring in full sun in patches of limestone chips, the reflection from the white rocks raises the heat and light radiation to extremes. Rainfall averages 10-14 in (25-36 cm) annually.

Distribution

Lloyd's mariposa cactus is endemic to the Chihuahuan Desert, particularly Brewster and Presidio counties, Texas, and probably to northern Coahuila, Mexico. It has been found in low numbers along the Rio Grande River from Reagan Canyon in the east (Brewster County) to the Bofecillos Mountains in the west (Presidio County). Most populations occur on private land, although some plants are found within the Big Bend National Park. The plant's range almost certainly extends southward into Mexico, but the status of the Mexican population is unknown.

Threats

Lloyd's mariposa cactus declined in the 1940s when mining for mercury ore destroyed large sections of its habitat. Surviving plants are now widely scattered. Many plants have been destroyed or damaged by heavy livestock grazing in the dry, marginal habitat. Livestock-induced erosion has more recently been worsened by the intrusion of off-road vehicles, used as recreation or to develop mineral claims.

The habitat areas near Terlingua and Lajitas, Texas are being developed for resort homes; the populations at Dove Mountain, Reagan Canyon, and Big Canyon are subject to livestock grazing; and the Big Bend National Park population is exposed to camping, hiking, and road maintenance. As a rare show specimen, this cactus is always subject to collection.

Conservation and Recovery

This cactus has been collected in its more accessible locations, but the remoteness of most sites and its scattered distribution give it some protection. Collecting is prohibited within the Big Bend National Park, although enforcement is difficult. The cactus is protected by Texas laws, but there are no effective prohibitions against taking plants from private land with the landowners' permission.

Currently, the population is small but appears stable. The U. S. Fish and Wildlife Service (FWS) personnel will continue to monitor populations on a regular basis but will undertake no active recovery measures unless numbers decline steeply or unless a more immediate threat, such as coal or oil development, appears. The two known populations occur within Big Bend National Park on private lands mostly owned by the Lajita Museum and Desert Garden, which has an active interest in preserving the species.

The FWS recommends studying the soil and water requirements of the species, the role of animals in seed dispersal, habitat factors affecting seed dispersal, pollinators, and population dynamics. With this data, additional habitat areas might be established and populated.

Contact

Regional Office of Endangered Species
U.S. Fish and Wildlife Service
P.O. Box 1306
Albuquerque, New Mexico 87103
http://southwest.fws.gov/

References

Benson, L. 1982. *The Cacti of the United States and Canada*. Stanford University Press, Stanford, California.

U.S. Fish and Wildlife Service. 1987. "Endangered and Threatened Species of Texas and Oklahoma (with 1988 Addendum)." U.S. Fish and Wildlife Service, Albuquerque.

U.S. Fish and Wildlife Service. 1987. "Lloyd's Mariposa Cactus Recovery Plan." U.S. Fish and Wildlife Service, Albuquerque. 35 pp.

Higo Chumbo

Harrisia portoricensis

Status	Threatened
Listed	August 8, 1990
Family	Cactaceae (Cactus)
Description	Slender, spined, columnar cactus with night-blooming greenish white flowers.
Habitat	Dry forests.
Threats	Limited range, feral pigs and goats, development.
Range	Puerto Rico

Robert Ross

Description

A night-flowering cactus, higo chumbo (*Harrisia (=Cereus) portoricensis*) produces funnel-shaped greenish white flowers. The cactus, which can grow up to 6 ft (1.8 m) tall, is slender, usually 3 in (7.6 cm) in diameter, and upright. It generally has no branches. Higo chumbo has eight to eleven ribs that are separated by shallow grooves. Its 1-3-in spines (2.5-7.6-cm spines) appear in groups approximately 0.5-0.75 in (1.3-1.9 cm) apart. These spines are grayish white to brownish in color. The plant's fruit—a round, yellow, spineless berry—is enclosed in a white pulp and is a favorite food of the endangered yellow-shouldered blackbird (*Agelaius xanthomus*).

Habitat

Higo chumbo is common in semi-open, xerophytic forests. The three islands on which the cactus is found (Mona, Monito, and Desecheo) are semiarid, with an average of only 32 in (81.3 cm) of rainfall a year. These islands are composed of carbonate rocks, stratified limestone, dolomite, reef rock, and boulder rubble. Some common associates of higo chumbo are *Metopium toxiferum, Tabebuia heterophylla, Bursera simaruba, Euphorbia petiolaris,* and *Epidendrum brittonianum.*

Distribution

Once occurring on mainland Puerto Rico, the species has not been collected there since 1913 and is considered extirpated. The plant currently is restricted to three islands west of Puerto Rico—Mona, Monito, and Desecheo—and is common in these areas. All of these islands are in the Mona Passage between Puerto Rico and the Dominican Republic.

Threats

Favorable habitat conditions for the species once existed over most of southern and southwestern Puerto Rico. In fact, the Ponce area of Puerto Rico once offered this type location. However, all of these areas have been destroyed or altered by urban, industrial, or agricultural development. Mona Island, which currently supports most of the available habitat, has been proposed for development as a superport, an oil storage facility, and a prison.

Feral pigs are another threat on Mona Island because they uproot the cactus while foraging for edible roots. On both Mona and Desecheo islands, feral goats forage on vegetation. This foraging may indirectly affect higo chumbo by modifying the vegetative composition of its habitat. The cactus moth has caused disease, infestation, and cactus die-offs in the past, but this threat has not been observed recently.

Conservation and Recovery

Mona, Monito, and Desecheo islands are all publicly owned. The government of Puerto Rico, through the Puerto Rico Department of Natural Resources, owns and manages both Mona and Monito islands as wildlife preserves. Public access to Monito Island is restricted, but the public is permitted to visit Mona Island. During the hunting season on Mona Island, public hunting of pigs and goats is allowed. Desecheo is a wildlife refuge managed by the U. S. Fish and Wildlife Service, and public access is restricted.

Contacts

U. S. Fish and Wildlife Service
Regional Office, Division of Endangered Species
1875 Century Blvd., Suite 200
Atlanta, Georgia 30345
(404) 679-4000
http://southeast.fws.gov/

Boquerón Ecological Services Field Office
P.O. Box 491
Boquerón, Puerto Rico 00622-0491
Telephone: (787) 851-7297
Fax: (787) 851-7440

References

Ayensu, E., and R. A. DeFilipps. 1978. *Endangered and Threatened Plants of the United States.* Smithsonian Institution and World Wildlife Fund, Inc., Washington, D. C.

U. S. Fish and Wildlife Service. 8 August 1990. "Determination of Threatened Status for the Plant *Harrisia portoricensis* (Higo chumbo)." *Federal Register* 55 (153).

Leptocereus grantianus

No Common Name

Status	Endangered
Listed	February 26, 1993
Family	Cactaceae (Cactus)
Description	Sprawling, nearly spineless cactus growing 6.6 ft (2 m) in height, with elongated stems that have three to five prominent ribs with broadly scalloped edges.
Habitat	Steep, rocky banks.
Threats	Low numbers; potential habitat destruction.
Range	Puerto Rico

Description

A sprawling or suberect and nearly spineless cactus, *Leptocereus grantianus* may reach up to 6.6 ft (2 m) in height and 1.2-2 in (3-5 cm) in diameter. Its elongated stems have from three to five prominent ribs with broadly scalloped edges. Ribs of young joints are thin, and the small areoles or spine-bearing areas may bear one to three minute spines that are nearly black and disappear as the joints grow older. The flowers are solitary at terminal areoles, 1.2-2.4 in (3-6 cm) long, and nocturnal. The outer perianth segments are linear, green, and tipped by an areole like those of the tube and ovary. The inner perianth segments are numerous, cream-colored, oblong-obovate, obtuse, and about 0.3 in (8 mm) long. The fruit is subglobose to ellipsoid and about 1.6 in (4 cm) in diameter.

Habitat

L. grantianus is located close to the shoreline on the steep and crumbling rocky banks of Culebra Island, a subtropical dry forest life zone. Mean annual rainfall ranges from a minimum of 23.6 in (600 mm) to a maximum of 39.4 in (1,000 mm) in this life zone. The vegetation tends to form a complete ground cover and is almost entirely deciduous on most soils. Leaves of surrounding trees are often small and succulent or coriaceous, and species with thorns and spines are common. Tree heights do not usu-ally exceed 49 ft (15 m) and crowns are typically broad, spreading, and flattened. Fire is common, and successional vegetation is composed mainly of grasses.

Associated species include sea grape (*Coccoloba uvifera*) and almacigo (*Bursera simaruba*).

Distribution

L. grantianus is endemic to the island of Culebra, located just off the northeastern corner of Puerto Rico. Only one population, consisting of approximately 50 individuals, occurs along the rocky coast near Punta Melones.

Threats

Historically, grazing, production of charcoal, deforestation and selective cutting for agriculture, and the cutting of wood for construction materials have affected dry forest vegetation. At the end of the twentieth and the beginning of the twenty-first centuries, the island of Culebra was subject to intense pressure for residential and tourist development. Land adjacent to the population was proposed for the development of a housing project.

The ornamental potential of the species may lead to overcollection in the future. The steep rocky banks along the shoreline of Culebra are unstable; therefore, natural events such as hurricanes might

Leptocereus grantianus, photograph by Susan Silander. Reproduced by permission.

result in the complete elimination of the only known population of *L. grantianus*.

Conservation and Recovery

This population might be given protection through conservation easements or acquisition. Propagation for introduction into protected areas (to establish new populations) should be considered a priority recovery mechanism. Preliminary efforts at propagation indicate that the species roots easily from cuttings.

Contacts

U. S. Fish and Wildlife Service
Regional Office, Division of Endangered Species
1875 Century Blvd., Suite 200
Atlanta, Georgia 30345
(404) 679-4000
http://southeast.fws.gov/

Boquerón Ecological Services Field Office
P.O. Box 491
Boquerón, Puerto Rico 00622-0491
Telephone: (787) 851-7297
Fax: (787) 851-7440

References

Britton, N. 1933. "An undescribed cactus of Culebra Island, Puerto Rico." *Cactus and Succulent Society of America* 5: 469.

Procter, G. R. 1991. "Status report on *Leptocereus grantianus* Britton." In *Puerto Rican Plant Species of Special Concern, Status and Recommendation.* Publicacion Cientifica Miscelanea No. 2. Department of Natural Resources, San Juan.

U. S. Fish and Wildlife Service. 1993. "Determination of endangered status for the plant *Leptocereus grantianus.*" *Federal Register* 58: 11550.

Bakersfield Cactus

Opuntia treleasei

Status	Endangered
Listed	July 19, 1990
Family	Cactaceae (Cactus)
Description	Prickly pear cactus with large magenta flowers and spines arising from areoles.
Habitat	Grasslands, scrub.
Threats	Agricultural and urban development, oil and gas drilling.
Range	California

Description

Like other beavertail cacti, Bakersfield cactus, *Opuntia treleasei,* has fleshy, flattened, green stems (pads) that vary from rounded, heart-shaped, or diamond-shaped to nearly cylindrical. A single plant may consist of hundreds of pads, which originate both at ground level and from the tips of other pads. The number of individuals in a population may be difficult to determine because pads from adjacent plants often overlap. Thus, cactus populations usually are described by the number of clumps (groups of pads that are rooted at the same point) rather than as a number of individuals. Clumps of Bakersfield cactus can grow up to 14 in (35 cm) high and 33 ft (10 m) across. The pads and fruits are dotted with eyespots, which are rounded structures that contain barbed bristles. Tiny leaves are produced on the youngest pads of beavertail cacti but are shed quickly. Bakersfield cactus has showy magenta flowers. The dry fruits are the size and shape of small eggs and may contain grayish-white seeds. Bakersfield cactus is unique among the varieties of *O. basilaris* in that the eyespots contain spines in addition to the bristles. Other features of Bakersfield cactus that differentiate it from related beavertail cacti include the smooth pad surfaces, cylindrical pad bases, nonsunken eyespots, and longer leaves. Bakersfield cactus has also been classified as *O. basilaris* var. *treleasii.*

Habitat

Bakersfield cactus is a perennial. The life span of wild plants has not been determined, but clumps in cultivation survived for 48 years, until extremely wet winter weather caused the pads to rot. Bakersfield cactus typically flowers in May. Reproductive biology of this taxon has not been studied, but certain other *Opuntia* species require cross-pollination for seed-set and many are pollinated by bees. One potential pollinator of Bakersfield cactus is the native solitary bee *Diadasia australis* ssp. *california,* which is known to occur in Kern County and which specializes in collecting pollen from *Opuntia* species. Vegetative reproduction, which is the production of new plants from sources other than seed, is typical in Bakersfield cactus and several related species. Fallen pads root easily if sufficient water is available, but Bakersfield cactus does not survive prolonged inundation. Cactus seeds require warm, wet conditions to germinate, a combination that is extremely rare in the Bakersfield area. Pads may be dispersed by flood waters, but seed dispersal agents are unknown.

Soils supporting Bakersfield cactus typically are sandy, although gravel, cobbles, or boulders also may be present. Known populations occur on floodplains, ridges, bluffs, and rolling hills. Bakersfield cactus is a characteristic species of the Sierra-Tehachapi Saltbush Scrub plant community,

Bakersfield Cactus, photograph by B. "Moose" Peterson/WRP. Reproduced by permission.

but populations near Caliente are in Blue Oak woodland and the Cottonwood Creek population is in riparian woodland. Many Bakersfield cactus sites support a dense growth of red brome and other annual grasses. Sand Ridge is characterized by sparse vegetation and a preponderance of native species such as California filago and yellow pincushion. Historical records indicate that the majority of Bakersfield cactus occurred at elevations of 460-850 ft (140- 260 m). The highest-elevation population is at 1,800 ft (550 m) near Caliente and the lowest remaining is at 396 ft (121 m) at Fuller Acres.

Distribution

Bakersfield cactus is endemic to a limited area of central Kern County in the vicinity of Bakersfield. Approximately one-third of the historical occurrences of Bakersfield cactus have been eliminated, and the remaining populations are highly fragmented. The range was extended to the south, how-

ever, when several occurrences were discovered in the late 1980s in south-central Kern County, just north of Wheeler Ridge.

The total population of Bakersfield cactus was not estimated historically. Historical photographs showing extensive stands of Bakersfield cactus are believed to have been taken southwest of Sand Ridge near the eastern margin of the Kern Lake bed. When the known sites were last inventoried, fewer than 20,000 clumps of Bakersfield cactus were estimated to remain. Only four areas had populations of 1,000 clumps or more: Comanche Point, Kern Bluff, north of Wheeler Ridge, and Sand Ridge. The metapopulations reported to incorporate the greatest morphological diversity included those in the Bena and Caliente Hills, Kern Canyon, and Sand Ridge.

Threats

The primary reason for the decline of Bakersfield cactus was habitat loss. The formerly extensive tracts of Bakersfield cactus near Edison and Lamont were destroyed by the conversion of habitat to row crops and citrus groves; much of the conversion occurred prior to 1931. In the late twentieth century, residential development eliminated numerous occurrences in northeast Bakersfield. Petroleum production has contributed to habitat loss and fragmentation, particularly in the vicinity of Oildale. Populations near Hart Park, the Kern Bluffs, Oildale, Fairfax Road, and parts of Sand Ridge have been degraded by off-road vehicle activity, trash dumping, and sand and gravel mining. Overgrazing may have damaged plants near Hart Park, Mettler, and Caliente, and flooding decimated populations along Caliente Creek and the Kern River. Air pollution is also suspected to have contributed to the decline of Bakersfield cactus.

At the end of the twentieth century, all these causes of decline continued to threaten existing populations. Almost all the known sites were on private land, much of which had commercial value. Residential development constituted the most serious threat. Conversion for either agricultural or residential use was possible, and inundation was a potential intermittent problem for populations in floodplains. The largest concentration of clumps in the Wheeler Ridge metapopulation was situated adjacent to an overflow drain for the Aqueduct, resulting in a risk of flooding if an earthquake occurred anywhere along the drain's length. Even the two protected populations were adjacent to agricultural land and faced impacts from pesticide drift. Both off-road vehicle use and mining continued to degrade the populations mentioned earlier.

Direct competition from introduced, annual grasses is believed to threaten the survival of mature Bakersfield cactus plants and to hinder the establishment of new plants. Indirect effects from exotic grasses also may threaten Bakersfield cactus in several ways. First, the dense herbaceous growth may promote a greater fire frequency and intensity than would have occurred with the sparse native vegetation typical in historical times. Second, dense grass cover may harbor insects that damage cactus. Third, the moist microclimate created by dense herbaceous growth may promote growth of decay organisms and cause pads to rot in years of above-average precipitation.

A lack of genetic diversity may threaten some populations of Bakersfield cactus. Contributing factors to this problem include the small size of many populations, a lack of gene flow between popula-

tions, and infrequent sexual reproduction. Populations low in genetic variation are more vulnerable to diseases and parasites and to chance events, including environmental fluctuations, catastrophes, and genetic drift.

Conservation and Recovery

The Nature Conservancy began preservation efforts for Bakersfield cactus more than 25 years ago by purchasing a portion of Sand Ridge. The Nature Conservancy doubled the size of the Sand Ridge Nature Preserve to 275 acres (110 hectares), and the preserve was transferred to the Center for Natural Lands Management in 1998. Prescribed burns will be used to control exotic grass competition. Several colonies of Bakersfield cactus were acquired for conservation purposes in the late 1990s.

Salvage efforts have been undertaken by local members of the California Native Plant Society, who transplanted Bakersfield cactus clumps from sites slated for destruction to Sand Ridge Nature Preserve and the California Living Museum in Bakersfield. Prior to construction of the East Hills Mall in Bakersfield, a few of the cactus clumps growing on the site were removed, then were replanted in a display bed when the mall was completed. Transplanted individuals have not been monitored at any of the sites to determine survival rates or reproductive success.

Contacts

U. S. Fish and Wildlife Service
Regional Office, Division of Endangered Species
Eastside Federal Complex
911 N. E. 11th Ave.
Portland, Oregon 97232-4181
Telephone: (503) 231-6121
http://pacific.fws.gov/

U. S. Fish and Wildlife Service
Sacramento Fish and Wildlife Office
Federal Building
2800 Cottage Way, Room W-2605
Sacramento, California 95825-1846
Telephone: (916) 414-6600
Fax: (916) 460-4619

References

Benson, L. 1969. *The Native Cacti of California.* Stanford University Press, Palo Alto, Calif.

Heady, H. F. 1977. "Valley Grassland." In *Terrestrial Vegetation of California*, edited by M. G. Barbour and J. Major. Wiley, New York.

Hoover, R. F. 1970. *The Vascular Plants of San Luis Obispo County, California.* University of California Press, Berkeley.

Wester, L. 1981. "Composition of Native Grasslands in the San Joaquin Valley, California." *Madrono* 28: 231-241.

Brady Pincushion Cactus

Pediocactus bradyi

Status	Endangered
Listed	October 26, 1979
Family	Cactaceae (Cactus)
Description	Dwarf cactus with a single, semi-spherical stem and a straw-yellow flower.
Habitat	Navajoan Desert; shale-derived soil.
Threats	Collectors, off-road vehicles, mineral exploration.
Range	Arizona

Brady Pincushion Cactus, photograph by Marv Poulson. Reproduced by permission.

Description

Brady pincushion cactus, *Pediocactus bradyi*, is a dwarf, semi-spherical cactus, typically with a single stem, up to 2.4 in (6 cm) tall and 2 in (5 cm) in diameter. Spines are white or tan and about 0.24 in (6 mm) long. Large straw-yellow flowers bloom in the spring. The green, top-shaped fruit turns brown at maturity. During the dry season, the plants largely retract into the soil.

Two close relatives of the Brady pincushion, Peebles Navajo cactus (*Pediocactus peeblesianus*) and Siler pincushion cactus (*P. sileri*), are federally listed as Endangered.

Habitat

Brady pincushion cactus occurs in the Navajoan Desert plant community on the Colorado Plateau.

It grows where stony rubble overlays soils derived from Moenkopi shale. Ground cover is characterized by scattered, low-growing shrubs, clumps of perennial grasses and seasonal annuals, dominated by shadscale, snakeweed, Mormon tea, and desert trumpet. Habitat elevation is between 3,860 and 4,490 ft (1,176 and 1,368 m).

Distribution

Brady pincushion cactus is a native of the Colorado Plateau north of the Kaibab Plateau. The range extends along the Grand Canyon to the Arizona-Utah boundary. It has been found in Coconino County, Arizona, in an area of about 27 sq mi (70 sq km). The Glen Canyon Dam, completed in 1963, inundated a large area of habitat. Potential habitat in the Marble Canyon area is estimated to be 17,000 acres (6,880 hectares), but only about 20% of this area supports the cactus.

Brady pincushion cactus has been found on both sides of the Colorado River in the area of U.S. Highway 89 near Marble Canyon in northern Coconino County. One population occurs in Glen Canyon National Recreation Area, while other sites are scattered along the river south and west. Many plants are found on Bureau of Land Management (BLM) lands that have been leased for grazing or uranium exploration. The Navajo Indian Reservation east of Marble Canyon supports several groups of plants that fall under the jurisdiction of the Bureau of Indian Affairs. Sites that fall within the Grand Canyon National Park are fully protected by the Park Service.

The total population in 1984 was estimated at about 10,000 plants in a highly localized distribution pattern. The decline in numbers since its discovery in 1958 has been precipitous.

Threats

Brady pincushion cactus is in worldwide demand by collectors of rare cacti. Collectors have decimated populations, particularly where plants are accessible from highways. Even casual collectors seem to easily locate and remove flowering cacti before they can set seed.

Uranium exploration and mining pose a potential threat because much of the habitat lies above a rich, ore-bearing seam. So long as the uranium market remains weak, however, there will be little incentive for mining companies to develop these ores. West of Marble Canyon, off-road vehicle traffic—partly recreational and partly associated with mineral exploration—have torn up large areas of natural vegetation, including several populations of Brady pincushion cactus.

Conservation and Recovery

The U.S. Fish and Wildlife Service and BLM are annually monitoring the size and vigor of the cactus population. Plans for recovery are focusing on developing techniques to propagate the cactus for commercial sale, thereby reducing incentives for collecting wild plants. A greenhouse population would also provide stock for transplanting cacti to other sites within the historic range.

The Plant Resources Institute in Salt Lake City, Utah, has developed a way to propagate several species of *Pediocactus* by transplanting cultivated buds; funding availability will determine the extent to which this program will include the Brady pincushion cactus.

Contact

Regional Office of Endangered Species
U.S. Fish and Wildlife Service
P.O. Box 1306
Albuquerque, New Mexico 87103
http://southwest.fws.gov/

References

Fletcher, R. 1979. "Status Report on *Pediocactus bradyi*." Report to U.S.D.A. Forest Service.

Heil, K., B. Armstrong, and D. Schleser. 1981. "A Review of the Genus *Pediocactus*." *Cactus and Succulent Journal of America* 53:17-39.

U.S. Fish and Wildlife Service. 1985. "Brady Pincushion Cactus Recovery Plan." U.S. Fish and Wildlife Service, Albuquerque.

San Rafael Cactus

Pediocactus despainii

Status	Endangered
Listed	September 16, 1987
Family	Cactaceae (Cactus)
Description	Dwarf cactus with barrel-shaped stems and peach-colored flowers.
Habitat	Colorado Plateau; semi-arid grasslands.
Threats	Collectors, habitat disturbance.
Range	Utah

San Rafael Cactus, photograph by Marv Poulson. Reproduced by permission.

Description

San Rafael cactus, *Pediocactus despainii*, is a dwarf barrel-type cactus with stems up to 2.3 in (6 cm) tall and 4 in (10 cm) wide. Spine clusters (areoles), composed of nine to 13 white, flattened radial spines, partially obscure the stem. Central spines are absent. Flowers, about 1 in (2.5 cm) across, are peach to yellow with a bronze tint.

This cactus is distinguished from other closely related members of its genus by its larger stem size and the bronze tint of its flowers. Buds form in the fall at ground level and overwinter to blossom in spring.

Habitat

San Rafael cactus grows on hills, benches, and flats of the Colorado Plateau's semi-arid grasslands, a savannah-like habitat characterized by scattered junipers, pinyon pines, low shrubs, and hardy herbs.

Distribution

The genus *Pediocactus* comprises eight rare species that are derived from a parent genus that was widely distributed throughout Arizona, Colorado, New Mexico, and Utah, thousands of years ago. Four members of the genus—Brady pincushion cactus (*P. bradyi*), Knowlton cactus (*P. knowltonii*), Peebles Navajo cactus (*P. peeblesianus* var. *peeblesianus*), and Siler pincushion cactus (*P. sileri*)—are federally listed as endangered. The remaining relatives—*P. paradinei*, *P. peeblesianus* var. *fickeiseniae*, and *P. winkleri*—are currently being considered for listing under the Endangered Species Act.

This species has been found in Emery County, Utah, and grows in two populations about 25 mi (40 km) apart. Each population contains 2,000-3,000 individual plants.

Threats

Collectors pose the greatest threat to the San Rafael cactus. Since the plant is very rare, it is eagerly sought by collectors in the United States and abroad. Commercial collectors are known to "make the rounds" of the Four Corners to collect complete sets of *Pediocacti*. This activity is illegal under U. S. and international statutes.

One concentration of San Rafael cacti is adjacent to a popular camping area, which attracts many hikers and recreational off-road vehicles. Many plants there have been trampled underfoot or crushed by vehicles. Although the cactus' stems recede into the ground during the dry season, ground disturbance can destroy the delicate buds that overwinter at the surface, limiting the plant's reproduction.

Conservation and Recovery

Roughly half of the surviving cacti occur on Bureau of Land Management (BLM) lands that have been leased for oil, gas, and mineral exploration. Although these claims are not being actively developed, mineral companies are required to conduct annual assessments of their claims to retain their permits. Assessment activities, including scraping, drilling, and use of explosives, continue to disturb the habitat and destroy plants.

Since this cactus was listed, the BLM has undertaken a review of its process of granting land-use permits where activities may damage cacti populations. Annual surveys of the sites are conducted by U.S. Fish and Wildlife Service botanists.

Contact

U. S. Fish and Wildlife Service
Regional Office, Division of Endangered Species
P. O. Box 25486
Denver Federal Center
Denver, Colorado 80225
http://www.r6.fws.gov/

References

Heil, K., B. Armstrong, and D. Schleser. 1981. "A Review of the Genus *Pediocactus*." *Cactus & Succulent Journal* 53:17-39.

U. S. Fish and Wildlife Service. 1987. "Determination of Endangered Status for *Pediocactus despaini* (San Rafael Cactus)." *Federal Register* 52(179): 34914-34917.

Welsh, S. L., and S. Goodrich. 1980. "Miscellaneous Plant Novelties from Alaska, Nevada, and Utah." *Great Basin Naturalist* 40:78-88.

Knowlton Cactus

Pediocactus knowltonii

Status	Endangered
Listed	October 26, 1979
Family	Cactaceae (Cactus)
Description	Dwarf, globular cactus, lacking central spines; pink flowers.
Habitat	Navajoan Desert; sagebrush and pinyon pine.
Threats	Collectors
Range	Colorado, New Mexico

Knowlton Cactus, photograph by Marv Poulson. Reproduced by permission.

Description

The dwarf Knowlton cactus, *Pediocactus knowltonii*, is a nearly globular cactus with solitary or clustered gray-green stems, from 0.3-1 in (0.5-2.5 cm) tall and from 0.4-1.2 in (1-3 cm) in diameter. Spine clusters (areoles) are characterized by 18-23 radial spines with no central spines.

Most plants bloom at three or four years of age, budding in early April and flowering until early May. Pink flowers open by mid-morning, close in late afternoon, and persist two or three days. Fruits form by early June, and seeds disperse in late June, falling to the base of the parent plant. Rain then carries seeds downslope where they sprout among cobbles or at the base of other plants.

Habitat

Knowlton cactus occurs within the Colorado Plateau Province of the Navajoan Desert and is found along the slopes of the San Juan Mountains.

The cactus is restricted to red-brown clay soils, derived from alluvial deposits that overlie the San Jose Formation. These deposits form rolling, gravelly hills covered with pinyon pine, Rocky Mountain juniper, and sagebrush. The surface is strewn with rocks from pea to cobble-sized. Habitat elevation is between 6,800 and 7,600 ft (2,075 and 2,300 m).

Distribution

This species was once more numerous in northern New Mexico and possibly extended into La Plata County, Colorado. The distribution pattern is highly localized.

The Knowlton cactus survives at a single site of about 11 acres (5 hectares) in San Juan County, New Mexico. This population was estimated to number about 100,000 plants in 1960, but by the mid-1970s, numbers had declined so steeply that many collectors thought the cactus was extinct. By 1987, the population had rebounded slightly to about 7,000 plants and by 1993 to 9,000. The cactus has been recently transplanted to two additional locations.

Threats

Systematic collecting has been the major reason for the decline of this species and continues to threaten its survival. Although the cactus's flowers are small and not showy, collectors prize it for its rarity alone. Many private and commercial collectors know the location of the Knowlton cactus population and have returned on a regular basis to take wild plants, even though greenhouse plants have recently been cultivated.

In 1960, while the nearby Navajo Dam was under construction, well-meaning members of a local cactus society set out to rescue Knowlton's cactus from an expected inundation. This group collected thousands of plants from the population and sought to transplant them, but the transplanted colonies did not survive. As it turned out, the dam reservoir never flooded the site.

In addition to collectors, several natural threats to the cactus have been identified. Many plants have been found with root systems exposed, apparently pushed completely out of the ground by frost heave, and cacti growing on the steep slopes are often undermined by erosion.

Conservation and Recovery

To help preserve the Knowlton cactus, the Public Service Company of New Mexico donated 25 acres (10.1 hectares) containing part of the surviving population to the Nature Conservancy. The organization then erected a strong barbed wire fence to keep out livestock and to deter collectors. Many seedlings have since been observed at this site, offering hope for recovery if the plants are left undisturbed.

In addition, cuttings of the cactus were transplanted to a protected site in 1985 and have shown a 93% survival rate for new seedlings. Half of the surviving plants there are flowering and fruiting. A second site was established by seed in 1987. Botanists will compare data from the two sites to determine which transplantation technique works best in preparation for expanding the reintroduction effort.

Contacts

Regional Office for Endangered Species
U.S. Fish and Wildlife Service
P.O. Box 1306
Albuquerque, New Mexico 87103
http://southwest.fws.gov/

Regional Office for Endangered Species
U.S. Fish and Wildlife Service
P. O. Box 25486
Denver Federal Center
Denver, Colorado 80225
http://www.r6.fws.gov/

References

Backeberg, C. 1982. *The Cacti of the United States and Canada*. Stanford University Press, Stanford.

Knight, P. 1981. "Rare, Threatened, Endangered, and Other Plants of Concern in the BLM Chaco-San Juan Planning Area of Northwestern New Mexico." New Mexico Department of Natural Resources Heritage Program, Santa Fe.

U.S. Fish and Wildlife Service. 1985. "Knowlton Cactus Recovery Plan." U.S. Fish and Wildlife Service, Albuquerque.

U.S. Fish and Wildlife Service. 1987. "Endangered and Threatened Species of Arizona and New Mexico (with 1988 Addendum)." U.S. Fish and Wildlife Service, Albuquerque.

U.S. Fish and Wildlife Service. 1985. "Knowlton Cactus Recovery Plan." Albuquerque. 53 pp.

Peebles Navajo Cactus

Pediocactus peeblesianus var. *peeblesianus*

Status	Endangered
Listed	October 26, 1979
Family	Cactaceae (Cactus)
Description	Small, spherical cactus, with yellowish flowers.
Habitat	Navajoan Desert; gravelly soils on slopes and hilltops.
Threats	Quarrying, residential development, collectors.
Range	Arizona

Description

Peebles Navajo cactus—*Pediocactus peeblesianus* var. *peeblesianus,* also known as the Navajo plains cactus—is small and spherical. It usually grows as a single stem, which is up to 1 in (2.5 cm) tall and 0.75 in (2 cm) in diameter. The four radial spines of each cluster (areole) grow in the form of a twisted cross; central spines are absent. Yellow to yellow-green flowers appear in the spring and are often larger than the stem itself. During dry weather, stems retract into the ground and are difficult to locate. Seedlings germinate August through October and are typically found very close to the base of the parent plant. The genus for this cactus has also been given as *Echinocactus, Navajoa, Toumeya,* and *Utahia.*

Habitat

This cactus grows on sunny slopes and flat hilltops in well-drained, gravelly soils derived from Shinarump conglomerate (Chinle Formation). The preferred soils are found in a strip about 1 mi (1.6 km) wide and 7 mi (11 km) long, running from southeast to northwest across the hills north of Holbrook, Arizona. Habitat elevation is between 5,400 and 5,600 ft (1,645 and 1,710 m).

Surrounding vegetation is open and sparse, consisting of low shrubs, grasses, and annuals of the Navajoan Desert community: snakeweed, shadscale, four-winged saltbush, rabbitbrush, sage-brush, Mormon tea, Galleta, beehive cactus, Whipple devil claw, and Opuntia.

Distribution

Peebles Navajo cactus is found only in Navajo County in the area around Joseph City and Holbrook. In 1987, five known populations were estimated to contain a total of about 1,000 plants. Two populations are on U. S. Bureau of Land Management (BLM) land; the three others are on private land. The welfare of populations on public lands is given a high priority in the most recent BLM management plans.

Threats

Over the years, much of the suitable habitat for this cactus has been destroyed by gravel quarrying, which has worked the seam of gravels the cactus prefers. During the late twentieth century, suburbs of Holbrook have expanded into the surrounding hills. Remaining cactus habitat is considered prime land for residential development.

Illegal collection is a serious threat to this cactus. Because pediocacti are difficult to cultivate, commercial dealers prefer to collect wild plants.

Conservation and Recovery

Peebles cactus is on the Arizona State Protected list as *Toumeya peeblesiana* and cannot be legally col-

Peebles Navajo Cactus, photograph by Marv Poulson. Reproduced by permission.

lected without a permit. In 1983 it was listed as a rare species by the Convention on International Trade in Endangered Species of Wild Fauna and Flora (CITES). Under this treaty, any import or export of the cactus requires a permit. Enforcement of treaty prohibitions, however, is difficult.

Monitoring plots were established in 1980 and are examined yearly to evaluate the growth and reproductive potential of the cacti. An intensive survey, conducted in 1987, noted many seedlings at known sites but found no new populations.

Contact

U. S. Fish and Wildlife Service
Regional Office, Division of Endangered Species
P.O. Box 1306
Albuquerque, New Mexico 87103-1306
Telephone: (505) 248-6911
Fax: (505) 248-6915
http://southwest.fws.gov/

References

Benson, L. 1962. "A Revision and Amplification of *Pediocactus*, III and IV." *Cactus and Succulent Journal of America* 34 (57-61): 163-168.

Heil, K., B. Armstrong, and D. Schleser. 1981. "A Review of the Genus *Pediocactus*." *Cactus and Succulent Journal of America* 53: 17-39.

U. S. Fish and Wildlife Service. 1987. "Endangered and Threatened Species of Arizona and New Mexico (with 1988 Addendum)." U. S. Fish and Wildlife Service, Albuquerque.

U. S. Fish and Wildlife Service. 1984. "Peebles Navajo Cactus (*Pediocactus peeblesianus* (Croizat) L. Benson var. *peeblesianus*) Recovery Plan." U. S. Fish and Wildlife Service, Albuquerque.

Siler Pincushion Cactus

Pediocactus sileri

Status	Endangered
Listed	October 26, 1979
Family	Cactaceae (Cactus)
Description	Spherical cactus with yellowish flowers.
Habitat	Clay soils rich in gypsum and calcium.
Threats	Off-road vehicles; collectors; uranium mining.
Range	Arizona, Utah

Siler Pincushion Cactus, photograph by Marv Poulson. Reproduced by permission.

Description

Siler pincushion cactus (*Pediocactus sileri*) is formed of inconspicuous globular stems, solitary or clustered, up to 4 in (10.2 cm) in diameter. Each spine cluster (areole) contains between three and seven straight or slightly curved central spines about 1 in (2.5 cm) long. These central spines are dark brown and lighten to nearly white with age. Each areole also has 11-16 whitish radial spines, which are slightly shorter than the central spines. Yellowish flowers with maroon veins, about 1 in (2.5 cm) in diameter, appear in spring. Fruits are greenish-yellow and dry out at maturity.

Siler pincushion cactus has also been classified as *Echinocactus sileri* and *Utahia sileri*. This species was originally labeled endangered, not threatened, when it was first listed by the U. S. Fish and Wildlife Service (FWS) in 1979. In December 1993 it was reclassified under the threatened status because of the ongoing success of recovery efforts.

Habitat

Siler pincushion cactus is found on gypsum- and calcium-rich soils derived from the Menkopi formation. These soils are high in soluble salts that, while inimical to many plants, apparently suit this cactus, which does not grow well in other soils. The rolling clay hills where Siler pincushion cactus grows have a barren "badlands" appearance. Elevations are from 2,000-5,400 ft (610-1,646 m). At higher elevations, trees and small shrubs become more abundant.

Distribution

Restricted to a highly specific soil type, Siler pincushion cactus probably never extended much beyond its current range in northwestern Arizona and southwestern Utah.

Siler pincushion cactus is sparsely distributed in a narrow band that extends from southeast of Fredonia (Coconino County) west for about 70 mi (113 km) into north-central Mohave County, Arizona. This range is only about 30 mi (48 km) wide and reaches north, extending slightly into Utah's Washington and Kane Counties. The total population was estimated at about 7,000 individual plants when surveyed in the mid-1980s.

Threats

Siler pincushion cactus was listed as endangered in 1979 because of threats posed by livestock grazing, off-road vehicles, mining, road construction, and illegal collecting. Recovery actions carried out in the 1980s and early 1990s by the Bureau of Land Management included developing a habitat management plan and conducting surveys for other populations. As a result, the status of Siler pincushion has improved, although it is not yet secure enough to remove from protection under the Endangered Species Act. In recognition of the progress made toward full recovery, the FWS reclassified Siler pincushion on December 27, 1993, to the less critical category of threatened.

Gypsum mining in the area was considered a major threat to this cactus when it was first listed. Potential uranium mining, however, now seems a greater danger. By 1990 much of the "Arizona Strip" had been claimed by uranium mining companies, and more than 200 mining plans had been filed—81 within the cactus's habitat. A rise in uranium prices could induce mining companies to develop these claims.

Portions of the habitat have been overgrazed by livestock, contributing to erosion of the slopes. Off-road vehicle disturbance has also increased, particularly near towns. The sparse, rolling hills are attractive sites for off-road recreation, but the vehicles create erosion channels that are destructive to the habitat.

Conservation and Recovery

Cactus collectors pose a continual threat. From 1982 to 1984 Siler pincushion cacti were offered for sale in five plant catalogs, one even specifying "field-collected plants." Attempts are currently under way to develop techniques for nursery propagation of the cactus to supply the commercial trade.

Siler pincushion cactus is listed as a protected plant in Arizona, which prohibits collecting except by permit. It is considered a species of concern by the Convention on International Trade in Endangered Species (CITES). The success of ongoing recovery efforts has conservationists hopeful that Siler pincushion cactus might someday be delisted.

Contacts

U. S. Fish and Wildlife Service
Regional Office, Division of Endangered Species
P. O. Box 1306
Albuquerque, New Mexico 87103-1306
Telephone: (505) 248-6911
Fax: (505) 248-6915
http://southwest.fws.gov/

U. S. Fish and Wildlife Service
Regional Office, Division of Endangered Species
P. O. Box 25486
Denver Federal Center
Denver, Colorado 80225
http://www.r6.fws.gov/

References

Gierisch, R. K. 1981. "Observations and Comments on *Pediocactus sileri* in Arizona and Utah." *Desert Plants* 3: 9-16.

U. S. Fish and Wildlife Service. 1986. "Siler Pincushion Cactus Recovery Plan." U. S. Fish and Wildlife Service, Albuquerque.

U. S. Fish and Wildlife Service. 1987. "Endangered and Threatened Species of Arizona and New Mexico (with 1988 Addendum)." U. S. Fish and Wildlife Service, Albuquerque.

Winkler Cactus

Pediocactus winkleri

Status	Threatened
Listed	August 20, 1998
Family	Cactaceae (Cactus)
Description	Small globular cactus; bears flowers peach-to-pink in color.
Habitat	The tops and sides of rocky hills or benches in saltbush-dominated desert shrub communities.
Threats	Off road vehicular activity, mineral development, road and utility corridor development, and livestock trampling.
Range	Utah

Description

Winkler's cactus, *Pediocactus winkleri* is a small globose (globular) cactus with stems 1 to 2.5 in (2.5 to 6.2 cm) tall and up to 2 in (5 cm) in diameter. It has clusters of 9 to 11 small radial spines with dense fine woolly hairs at their base; erect central spines are lacking. The flowers of this taxon are urn shaped, 0.7 to 1 in (1.7 to 2.5 cm) long and 0.7 to 1.5 in (1.7 to 3.7 cm) diameter, and have a peach-to-pink color. The fruit is barrel shaped, 0.3 to 0.4 in (7.5 mm to 1 cm) high and 0.31 to 0.43 in (7.7 mm to 1.7 cm) wide, dehiscing (process of opening) by a vertical slit along the ovary wall. The seeds are shiny black, 0.12 in (3 mm) long and 0.08 in (2 mm) wide.

Pediocactus winkleri was discovered in the early 1960s and described in the scientific literature in 1979. The plant genus *Pediocactus* contains eight species, of which seven are rare endemics of the Colorado Plateau region of Utah, Colorado, New Mexico, and Arizona.

Habitat

Individual *P. winkleri* plants are usually situated on the tops and sides of rocky hills or benches in *Atriplex* (saltbush)-dominated desert shrub communities. The species grows in alkaline silty loam or clay loam soils derived primarily from the Dakota formation, the Brushy Basin member of the Morri-son formation, and the Emery sandstone member of the Mancos formation.

Distribution

P. winkleri is endemic to lower elevations of the Colorado Plateau in south-central Utah. Three of the four populations of this taxon form a narrow arc extending from near Notom in central Wayne County to the vicinity of Last Chance Creek in southwestern Emery County, Utah. The fourth is a disjunct population occurring near Ferron, Utah, in western Emery County. Most of these populations occur in widely scattered patches 2.4-48 acres (1-19.2 hectares) in size in a range about 36 mi (58 km) long and about (0.76 mi) 480 m wide. About two thirds of the population occurs on lands managed by the Bureau of Land Management east and north of the Capitol Reef National Park boundary. The remainder of the plants are found within the Park.

Based on extrapolations from direct surveys of the four extant populations conducted in the late 1990s, the U.S. Fish and Wildlife Service (FWS) has estimated that *Pediocactus winkleri* numbers about 20,000 plants. This estimate is substantially higher than the one provided in the October 1993 proposal to list *P. winkleri* as endangered; a total of 3,500 plants in six populations was given then, based on a 1984 status report. More intensive and accurate recent surveys have prompted this upward revision Surveys through 1998 have documented about 5,800 individual *P. winkleri* plants, and analysis of survey data collected in 1994, 1996, 1997, and 1998 indicates that the total population for this taxon, based on these numbers and the amount of available habitat, could be reasonably estimated at the 20,000 figure given above.

Other recent developments tend to support this new population estimate.

Since the proposed rule to list the species was published, a survey conducted by the Bureau of Land Management (BLM) discovered an additional population near the town of Ferron in southwest Emery County, Utah. Joint FWS and BLM surveys conducted throughout the entire potential habitat range of *P. winkleri*—silty soils derived from the Dakota, Mancos, and Morrison geologic formations—discovered additional sites within existing population areas. The Park Service reported larger numbers of this cactus within Capitol Reef National Park, as did the BLM from the Last Chance Desert population. FWS biologists visited these sites, reviewed the status of all extant populations of this cactus, and then consolidated the five *P. winkleri* populations in Wayne County into the Notom and Hartnet groups, in an effort to be consistent with the more recently discovered Last Chance and Ferron populations in Emery County. This increased total populaton estimate for Winkler cactus is not so much evidence of reduced threats to the species as it is a function of the increased effort put forth to locate individual plants. Older surveys were conducted by one or two individuals with limited resources, while more recent BLM surveys were conducted by four or more individuals over a period of several weeks.

The range of Winkler cactus converges upon populations of the listed endangered cactus *P. despainii* (San Rafael cactus). *P. despainii* and *P. winkleri* are described as separate species in all taxonomic treatments involving those species in regional floras and in monographs of the genus. Cytotaxonomic research demonstrates that typical *P. winkleri* from the Notom population is genetically different from typical *P. despainii* from the San Rafael Swell. However, the two species are phylogenetically related, and it was suggested by Lass in 1990 that they be treated as varietal subspecies of *P. winkleri*, the earlier of the two species to be described. Occasional plants within the northern portion of the Last Chance popu-

lation bear characteristics intermediate between *P. winkleri* and *P. despainii*. The two species are, however, morphologically distinct and geographically separated. Winkler cactus has uniformly smaller seeds than *P. despainii*.

P. winkleri areoles—the basal structure at the tip of stem tubercles which forms the base from which the spines arise—are wooly with dense villous hairs, while *P. despainii* areoles are naked except for its spines. These facts, established through recent cytotaxonomic research strongly suggest the current taxonomic distinction between the species is accurate. If they later become recognized as subspecies, their designations as threatened and endangered species will still remain valid.

Threats

The small, restricted populations of Winkler cactus make the species highly vulnerable to human-caused habitat disturbances. Off-road vehicular (ORV) activity, mineral development, road and utility corridor development, and livestock trampling have adversely affected this species. *P. winkleri* is especially vulnerable during the spring flowering period, when seasonally moist soils make it susceptible to damage and mortality from surface disturbance of its habitat. The taxon is easily dislodged by domestic livestock and ORV actvity during periods when the soil is wet. ORV use and livestock grazing are most intense during the mild spring season when the species is most vulnerable to habitat disturbance. During periods of drought, these cacti do not protrude above ground level, thus rendering them less susceptible to livestock trampling and damage by ORV activity. However, the species forms flower buds in the autumn that persist over winter. These flowering buds at the ground surface level are very vulnerable to surface disturbance.

A considerable portion of the habitat of this species, as well as individual plants, are being damaged by ORV activity. Occupied Winkler cactus habitat, located at the northern and southern limits of its range on sparsely vegetated slopes in readily accessible areas, is adjacent to heavily used ORV recreational areas, and is being harmed by this activity. Except for habitat within Capitol Reef National Park and the Last Chance population on BLM lands, the remaining habitat of *P. winkleri* is experiencing similar but lesser damaging impacts from ORV activity. Hard-tired ORVs such as motorcycles, four-wheel drive trucks, and other heavy highway vehicles are most damaging to the species. These hard-tired vehicles can cause damage and mortality even when the plant is dormant. Increased erosion as a consequence of ORV damage to the natural desert pavement and cryptogamic crust potentially increases *P. winkleri* exposure to losses from extreme weather events which occur in the area.

Livestock trampling has affected every population of this cactus including those in Capitol Reef National Park (the Park is not closed to livestock grazing). This species is poorly adapted to the impacts of large, sharp-hoofed ungulates, and plants are easily dislodged and killed by domestic livestock herds moving through its habitat. This trampling impact is most damaging during periods when the soil surface is wet. These conditions occur most commonly during mild winter and early spring days when livestock grazing is most intense in the desert range habitat of *P. winkleri*. According to the BLM, livestock use in Winkler cactus habitat has decreased in recent years, but trampling continues to damage some populations. Most of the reduction in livestock grazing within Capitol Reef National Park occurred in its southern portions, out of the range of this cactus. Grazing and trampling impacts are believed to be mostly low-level chronic threats rather than high-level acute threats, affecting no more than one percent of the *P. winkleri* population every year. Individuals lost due to livestock trampling probably could be replaced by natural recruitment from the populations' seed bank. However, cumulative impacts from collecting, localized ORV destruction, and natural losses from disease and parasitism are at sufficient levels in the Notom and Ferron populations that their viability is impaired.

The habitat of Winkler cactus contains oil and gas, bentonite clay, and some uranium ore deposits. The development of these natural resources and the surface disturbances caused by annual mineral assessment work have directly affected the species. Oil and gas field development activities are currently harming the Ferron population. This activity has destroyed individual plants and occupied habitat. Over 80% of the area occupied by the Ferron population is leased for oil and gas, and mining claims cover almost the entire Last Chance Desert population, a portion of which has already been lost to a gas well. A portion of the Hartnet population is also in an oil and gas lease area. The transfer of mining claim patents from the Public domain to private ownership is not affected by the ESA. The recent development of a mine for high quality, cosmetic grade bentonite clay is damaging the Last Chance population by destroying individual plants and occupied habitat.

Winkler cactus is an attractive small cactus, especially when it is in flower. This rare plant, difficult to cultivate in most horticultural settings, has become highly desired in cactus collections and gardens; so much so that both hobby and commercial cactus collectors seek it out. The fact that this species is difficult to maintain in garden settings stimulates a continual demand for replacement plants as cultivated garden and greenhouse plants die. Cactus collectors are active in the Colorado Plateau, going from the habitat of one species of *Pediocactus* to the next to collect a complete set of the genus. A portion of the Notom population of *P. winkleri* has been severely reduced, primarily from losses to plant collectors. Overall the population in the immediate vicinity of monitoring transect periodically inspected by the the FWS declined from 387 individuals in 1994 to 221 in 1997. In addition to the Notom population, the Hartnet and Ferron populations are highly vulnerable to specimen collecting because of their ease of access and their being known to cactus collectors.

There are several other factors and conditions that pose lesser current or potential threats to this taxon. Because of its small size and the shortness of its spines, this species of cactus is less protected from animals than more spiny species. The effects of livestock grazing on desert vegetation may produce indirect impacts on Winkler cactus populations. The desert range of this cactus had very sparse use by large, wild ungulates prior to the introduction of domestic livestock. Livestock grazing has caused changes in the floristic composition of the *P. winkleri* desert ecosystem with the introduction of weeds. These introduced weeds have the potential to outcompete native plants like *P. winkleri* over the long term, eventually reducing or displacing them. This taxon is also susceptible to natural infestations of beetle larvae, an insect known to kill an individual plant within two years of initial infestation. Unauthorized utility and road development in the Notom population area caused individual plant mortality and habitat degradation in 1995; further activities of this kind remain a potential threat to the species. Winkler cactus is restricted to a small geographic area with scattered, isolated occurrences and relatively low population numbers per occurrence, which render this cactus vulnerable to any random natural events.

Prior to federal listing, the inadequacy of existing regulatory mechanisms was itself a threat to this species. Without direct federal protection for *P. winkleri*, the National Park Service and the BLM found it hard to control overcollection of this taxon, one of the activities most deleterious to its long-term prospects for survival. Collection of desirable and small cacti that are widely scattered over remote country is an action very difficult to detect and control, even in Capitol Reef National Park. Federal listing provides greater statutory protection and more stringent penalities for take.

Conservation and Recovery

Winkler cactus occurs on federal lands managed by the Bureau of Land Management and the National Park Service (NPS). Both of these federal agencies are responsible for insuring that all activities and actions on lands that they manage are not likely to jeopardize the continued existence of *P. winkleri*.

Both the BLM and NPS are aware of the threats facing Winkler cactus and are actively involved in the management and monitoring of this listed taxon. BLM has drafted a Conservation Agreement and Strategy with the assistance of the NPS and other partners aimed at reducing and eliminating identified threats to *P. winkleri*. In an effort to eliminate soil compaction and plant destruction, the BLM Draft will restrict ORV use to existing roads and trails through the preparation of a managment plan.

Contact

U.S. Fish and Wildlife Service
Utah Ecological Services Field Office
145 East 1300 South, Suite 404
Salt Lake City, Utah 84115-6110
Telephone: (801) 524-5009
Fax: (801) 524-5021

Reference

U.S. Fish and Wildlife Service. 20 August 1998. "Final Rule To Determine the Plant *Pediocactus winkleri* (Winkler cactus) To Be a Threatened Species." *Federal Register* 63 (161): 44587-44595.

Key Tree-cactus

Pilosocereus robinii

Status	Endangered
Listed	July 19, 1984
Family	Cactaceae (Cactus)
Description	Tall, slender cactus with branched cylindrical stems.
Habitat	Tropical hardwood hammocks.
Threats	Development, collectors, low numbers.
Range	Florida

Andy Robinson

Description

Key tree-cactus, *Pilosocereus robinii*, is the largest of the native Florida cacti. It is characterized by erect, branched stems that can reach a maximum height of 30 ft (10 m). These succulent stems are cylindrical, spiny, and light or bluish-green, measuring up to 4 in (10 cm) in diameter. Attractive flowers vary in color from white to pale green or purple, average 2.5 in (6 cm) across, and open in late afternoon or early evening. The fruit is a dark red berry that measures 2 in (5 cm) in diameter. Key tree-cactus is the only native Florida cactus that stands erect at maturity and is sometimes considered a tree. Plants are either self-pollinated or pollinated by moths.

Habitat

The Key tree-cactus grows in the rocky tropical hammock habitat of the Florida Keys. These hammocks are isolated groups of hardwoods amid freshwater or saltwater wetlands. The upper Keys support high hammocks with tree canopies 100-132 ft (30-40 m) high, dominated by gumbo limbo, pigeon plum, poisonwood, mahogany, and other large trees. The hammocks of the lower and middle Keys have canopies in the 66-79 ft (20-24 m) range, and are sometimes called thorn scrub or thorn forest. Much of the flora of the Florida Keys is derived from tropical species of the West Indies rather than from temperate forms that usually dominate communities of the Florida peninsula.

Key tree-cactus is typically found on Key West oolite (a type of dolomite) and on the limestone soils of Key Largo. The soil layer consists of partially decomposed organic matter resting directly on a porous limestone substrate. This thin organic layer is necessary to support the plantlife of hammocks. Where the tree canopy is closed it forms an insulative environment, moderating weather extremes and reducing the loss of soil moisture.

Distribution

This unique cactus occurs in the Florida Keys, where historically it was known from 11 sites, and in northwestern Cuba from two sites. Plant communities associated with Key tree-cactus have largely disappeared from the Keys and Cuba due to development and urbanization, and the tree-cactus itself is near extinction.

Five Key tree-cactus populations survive in remnant habitat in the Florida Keys. The loss of hammock acreage is estimated at 80-90%. Twelve likely areas within the historical range were searched in June 1979, but the cactus was found in only four. One of these sites, on Layton's Hammock, was visited again in August 1979, and most of the hammock and its vegetation had been bulldozed for residential construction. The plants on this site were presumed eliminated, but several survivors were rediscovered in 1982. A fifth site was discovered on private property in 1982. The largest populations occur in the southeastern corner of Big Pine Key, most of which falls within the boundaries of the National Key Deer Wild Refuge.

In Cuba, housing and resort development have destroyed a large percentage of the species' historic habitat, and it is now considered endangered there by the International Union for the Conservation of Nature and Natural Resources.

Threats

Of the remaining tree-cactus populations in the Keys, three occur on privately-owned lands that are in imminent danger of being developed for housing.

A major problem for the Key tree-cactus is its restrictive habitat requirements. It grows only on lightly shaded upland sites. Rare in the Keys, this habitat type is typically covered by dense growths of tropical hardwoods, which produce too much shade for the tree-cactus. Furthermore, habitat conditions are continually changing in the Keys, and what may be suitable habitat in one year may evolve into less suitable habitat in a short time.

Like many other species of cacti, Key tree-cactus is vulnerable to collectors. Even on public lands, enforcing prohibitions against collecting has been difficult. Evidence of vandalism has been noted from one site, where deep and damaging initials were carved in the trunks of several plants. Natural factors, such as hurricane wind damage, also threaten this species.

Conservation and Recovery

One population occurs on federal land in the National Key Deer Refuge administered by the U.S. Fish and Wildlife Service. The habitat is managed to benefit the cactus. Another population is protected on Florida state lands, but the habitat is not actively managed.

The Recovery Plan recommends rehabilitating all five Key tree-cactus sites by controlling non-native vegetation; restricting agricultural practices; clearing land; application of herbicides; restricting off-road vehicles; and preventing salt water intrusion. The plan also recommends purchasing the habitat site on Big Pine Key.

Contact

Regional Office for Endangered Species
U.S. Fish and Wildlife Service
1875 Century Blvd., Suite 200
Atlanta, Georgia 30345
http://southeast.fws.gov/

References

Austin, D. F. 1980. "Endangered and Threatened Plant Species Survey in Southern Florida and the National Key Deer and Great White Heron Wildlife Refuges, Monroe County, Florida." Report. U.S. Fish and Wildlife Service, Jacksonville.

Little, E. L., Jr. 1975. "Our Rare and Endangered Trees." *American Forests* 81(7):18.

U.S. Fish and Wildlife Service. 1986. "Recovery Plan for the Key Tree-Cactus." U.S. Fish and Wildlife Service, Atlanta.

Ward, D. B. 1979. *Rare and Endangered Biota of Florida; Vol. 5, Plants.* University Presses of Florida, Gainesville.

Uinta Basin Hookless Cactus

Sclerocactus glaucus

Status	Threatened
Listed	October 11, 1979
Family	Cactaceae (Cactus)
Description	Dwarf cactus, usually with a single spherical stem and purplish red flowers.
Habitat	Desert hills and mesas.
Threats	Collectors.
Range	Colorado, Utah

Uinta Basin Hookless Cactus, photograph by Marv Poulson. Reproduced by permission.

Description

A leafless, succulent plant, the stubby Uinta Basin hookless cactus, *Sclerocactus glaucus*, has one or several spherical stems 1.6-2.4 in (4-6 cm) long and about 2 in (5 cm) in diameter, usually with twelve ribs. Spines are dense, relatively long, and overlap to obscure the stem. The central spines are 1 in (2.5 cm) long; the lower central spine is not hooked but sometimes curves. The straight radial spines are white or brown, numbering six to eight spines per cluster, spreading in a circle. The purplish red flower is about 2 in (5 cm) in diameter; the sepals have lavender midribs and pink margins. From a distance, the white and brown spines covering the green ribs give the cactus a gray-green appearance. This color blends with the background rocks, making the cactus hard to locate.

This species of cactus has been known by a confusing variety of scientific names: *Echinocactus glaucus, E. subglaucus, E. whipplei* var. *glaucus, Pediocac-*

tus glaucus, Sclerocactus franklinii, and *S. whipplei* var. *glaucus.*

Habitat

Uinta Basin cactus is found on hills and mesas in or near desert areas of the Colorado Plateau in alluvial soils at 4,600-6,900 ft (1,400-2,100 m) elevation.

Distribution

Uinta Basin hookless cactus is endemic to the semi-arid plateau region of northeastern Utah and northwestern Colorado, west and south of the Uinta Mountains. It is found at only three population centers, two in Colorado and one in Utah. As of 1990, the species had a documented population of about 22,000 individuals. The Uinta Basin of northeastern Utah hosts a major population center with three important population groups, one on alluvial river terraces near the confluence of the Green, White and

Duchesne Rivers, another along the base of the Badlands Cliffs in southeastern Duchesne County, and
a small third population of a morphologically distinct form growing on the clay badlands.

In western Colorado, the cactus occurs in two
major population centers in the upper Colorado and
Gunnison River valleys. One of these is on the
alluvial river terraces of the Gunnison River from
near Delta, Colorado, to southern Mesa County,
Colorado; and the other is on alluvial river terraces of the Colorado River and in the Plateau and
Roan Creek drainages in the vicinity of De Beque,
Colorado.

The majority of the species' range is on federal
land managed by the Bureau of Land Management
(BLM), with important populations on Fish and
Wildlife Service (FWS) lands (at the Ouray National
Wildlife Refuge), Department of Energy lands (at
the Naval Oil Shale Reservoir #2), and on Indian
lands (Ute Tribe, Uintah and Ouray Reservation).
Private land on which the species occurs is primarily near De Beque, Colorado.

Threats

Despite the plant's natural camouflage and scattered distribution, its greatest nemesis is the collector. Because of its rarity and the beauty of its flower,
this cactus is highly prized by both amateur gar-
deners and plant dealers. Botanists have encouraged artificial propagation of the plant for sale to
the commercial market, in order to spare the wild
population.

Much of the habitat area has been targeted for oil
and gold exploration, and the local development of
energy and water resources also threatens the habitat. Since the cactus has been listed as Endangered,
the BLM must now consult with the FWS when activities such as these are planned on federal land.
Such activities must be regulated to benefit the cactus whenever possible or else be prohibited. The
limited grazing allowed in the habitat actually appears to benefit the cactus.

Conservation and Recovery

The objective of the 1990 Uinta Basin Hookless
Cactus Recovery Plan (from the FWS), is to delist
the species as early as the year 2000. To achieve this
goal, the plan calls for inventory of suitable habitat
for additional populations, minimum viable population studies on at least six different populations;
formal land management designations to provide
for long-term, undisturbed habitat, and studies to
determine the taxonomic status of morphologically
distinct populations.

If these actions are taken, the FWS projects that
the species could be delisted, once it can be documented that a total population of 30,000 individuals in six separate populations (of at least 2,000
plants each) exists. Other criteria for delisting include the requirement that these six populations be
at minimum viable population levels, and that four
of these six populations are preserved and protected
on lands with formal management designations to
provide long-term, undisturbed habitat.

Contact

U.S. Fish and Wildlife Service
Division of Endangered Species
Denver Federal Center
P.O. Box 25486
Denver, Colorado 80225
http://www.r6.fws.gov/

References

Benson, L. 1982. *Cacti of the United States and Canada*.
     Stanford University Press, Stanford.

U.S. Fish and Wildlife Service. 1990. "Uinta Basin
     Hookless Cactus Recovery Plan." U.S. Fish and
     Wildlife Service, Denver.

Mesa Verde Cactus

Sclerocactus mesae-verdae

Mesa Verde Cactus, photograph by Marv Poulson. Reproduced by permission.

Status	Threatened
Listed	October 30, 1979
Family	Cactaceae (Cactus)
Description	Spherical-stemmed cactus with single or clustered stems and yellow or greenish flowers.
Habitat	Navajoan Desert; alkaline clay soils on slopes.
Threats	Collectors, off-road vehicles, livestock.
Range	Colorado, New Mexico

Description

Mesa Verde cactus, *Sclerocactus mesae-verdae*, usually grows as a single spherical stem, 1.5-3 in (3.8-7.6 cm) in diameter, but may form clusters of up to 15 stems. Eight to 11 straw-colored or gray spines, 0.25-0.5 in (6.4-12.7 mm) long, form radial clusters, typically without central spines. The color of the cactus allows it to blend into its surroundings.

The plant bears creamy yellow to greenish-white flowers, 0.75 in (1.9 cm) in diameter, from late April to early May. A green fruit forms late in May, browns with age, and splits open at the end of June

to release black seeds. The major pollinator is believed to be a metallic green sweat bee belonging to the family Halictidae. No other pollinators have been observed.

Seedlings have been found at all population sites. Often seeds germinate adjacent to the parent plant. Given the large number of seeds produced per plant and the actual number of seedlings observed, it is apparent that the success rate for these seedlings is very low.

The species is closely related to the Wright fishhook cactus (*S. wrightiae*) and to the Brady pincushion cactus (*Pediocactus bradyi*), both of which are federally listed as endangered. It has also been known by the scientific names *Coloradoa mesae-verdae*, *Echinocactus mesae-verdae*, and *Pediocactus mesae-verdae*.

Habitat

Mesa Verde cactus grows on the Colorado Plateau in the floristic province of the Navajoan Desert. It is generally restricted to the Mancos and Fruitland shale formations—alkaline soils with "shrink-swell" properties that make them harsh sites for plant growth. These clay formations erode easily, forming what are known locally as badlands (low rolling hills with sparse vegetation). This cactus is most frequently found growing at elevations of 5,280-6,600 ft (1,609-2,012 m) on the tops and slopes of hills.

Distribution

Mesa Verde cactus was first discovered near Cortez, Colorado, in 1940 and is considered endemic to the Navajoan Desert of San Juan County, New Mexico, and of Montezuma and possibly Montrose Counties, Colorado.

A major population of the Mesa Verde cactus is located on the Ute Mountain Indian Reservation in Colorado. Other populations have been noted near Waterflow, New Mexico, and at several sites on the Navajo Indian Reservation between Shiprock and Sheep Springs. Indian reservation lands are administered in part by the Bureau of Indian Affairs (BIA).

The total population of the Mesa Verde cactus is 5,000-10,000 plants, but the species is not evenly distributed throughout its range. It grows in dense clusters within certain favorable subhabitats.

Threats

The Mesa Verde cactus, like most other endangered cacti, has suffered at the hands of collectors; very few mature plants can still be found in the wild. Even European and Asian tourists seem to know right where to find the cactus and, along with commercial collectors, are depleting the population, especially during flowering season when the plants are easier to spot. The Mesa Verde cactus is difficult to cultivate, especially in areas of high humidity, because it rots very easily. As many as 90% of the plants collected rot and die within the first year, so collectors are not truly "collecting" the cactus, they are killing it.

Habitat disturbance is also a threat. Oil and gas exploration, livestock trampling, road maintenance, and off-road vehicle use have all taken a toll on the Mesa Verde cactus. Because many cacti grow on the tops and sides of hills, off-road vehicles crush and uproot plants and seedlings when following the high ground.

Conservation and Recovery

Better enforcement of laws and international trade agreements against the collection and trade of endangered species would greatly benefit the Mesa Verde cactus. Monitoring journals and commercial plant catalogs will also help to identify and prosecute violators. At least 70% of the population of the Mesa Verde cactus lies within the Navajo Nation and another 20% within the Ute Mountain Indian Reservation. Recovery efforts will require the cooperation and assistance of both tribal councils and the BIA.

Contacts

U. S. Fish and Wildlife Service
Regional Office, Division of Endangered Species
P. O. Box 1306
Albuquerque, New Mexico 87103-1306
Telephone: (505) 248-6911
Fax: (505) 248-6915
http://southwest.fws.gov/

U. S. Fish and Wildlife Service
Regional Office, Division of Endangered Species
P. O. Box 25486
Denver Federal Center
Denver, Colorado 80225
http://www.r6.fws.gov/

References

U. S. Fish and Wildlife Service. 1984. "Mesa Verde Cactus Recovery Plan." U. S. Fish and Wildlife Service, Albuquerque.

Weniger, D. 1970. *Cacti of the Southwest*. University of Texas Press, Austin/London.

Weniger, D. 1984. *Cacti of Texas and Adjacent States*. University of Texas Press, Austin/London.

Wright Fishhook Cactus

Sclerocactus wrightiae

Status	Endangered
Listed	October 11, 1979
Family	Cactaceae (Cactus)
Description	Single-stemmed, spherical cactus, with a reddish brown flower.
Habitat	Varied soils in semi-arid scrub.
Threats	Collectors, off-road vehicles, mineral exploration.
Range	Utah

Wright Fishhook Cactus, photograph by Marv Poulson. Reproduced by permission.

Description

Wright fishhook cactus, *Sclerocactus wrightiae*, is formed of several unbranched stems, each about 2 to 3 in (5 to 7.5 cm) in diameter with about a dozen ribs. Spine clusters (areoles) have four central spines, the lowest of which is sharply hooked. Eight to 10 radial spines on each areole are white. The fragrant flower has reddish brown, reddish green, or lavender centers with pale pink to white margins. Flowers develop when plants are still quite small, forming on new growth. Blossoms cluster at the top of each barrel. Specific pollinators are not known, but a small beetle has been observed in closed flowers.

Reproduction is primarily by seed. The fruits mature in June, dispersing seeds near the base of the parent plant. As the summer progresses and conditions become drier, the cactus shrinks, becoming almost level with the ground surface.

This cactus has also been known by the scientific name *Pediocactus wrightiae*.

Habitat

Unlike many of Utah's native cacti, which are restricted to a narrow habitat, such as a single geologic subformation or soil type, Wright fishhook cactus is less demanding in its requirements. It can be found in various soils of the Mancos shale formations, ranging from Blue Gate clays to sandy silts or on the fine sands of Ferron and Entrada sandstones. Some sites have well-developed gypsum layers, others have little or no gypsum. Common to most sites is a litter of sandstone or basalt gravels, cobbles, and boulders.

The habitat is semi-arid, with widely spaced shrubs, perennial herbs, bunch grasses, pinyon, and juniper.

Distribution

The historic range of the Wright fishhook cactus extends in an arc from Emery (Emery County),

Utah, through the Goblin Valley region to Hanksville (Wayne County), about 50 mi (80 km) to the southeast. This range lies in the Canyonlands section of the intermountain region, a low-elevation desert trough that curves around the southern end of the San Rafael Swell.

When the species was listed in 1979, it was known from five locations on public lands managed by the Bureau of Land Management (BLM) or on state lands. Later surveys located additional populations in 25 townships in Wayne and Emery Counties. Most of these populations consist of only scattered individuals. Where there is good habitat, populations can be almost continuous, although individual plants are widely dispersed. The populations can be divided into two general areas: the Emery area and the Caineville-Hanksville area. A thorough inventory and population count has not yet been conducted.

Threats

This cactus, like many others, is threatened by illegal collecting. However, because populations are widely dispersed, it is difficult to collect on a commercial scale. Finding the plants over such a large area is more time-consuming than taking a more readily available species, such as the federally listed Uinta Basin hookless cactus (*Sclerocactus glaucus*).

Because the cactus' range lies within an area with known coal resources near Emery, habitat loss to coal mining development is a potential threat. The Environmental Impact Statement produced to support the region's designation as a coal resource area made no mention of the Wright fishhook cactus.

In the Caineville-Hanksville area, off-road vehicle traffic has damaged some plants and contributed to harsh erosion patterns, and cattle have trampled plants at several sites. A proposal to designate the area a "wilderness study area" was dropped because of widespread protest.

Conservation and Recovery

The Fish and Wildlife Service's Recovery Plan for the Wright Fishhook Cactus sets the goal of establishing two separate and self-sustaining populations of 10,000 plants each before the cactus is reclassified from Endangered to Threatened.

Contact

Regional Office of Endangered Species
U.S. Fish and Wildlife Service
Denver Federal Center
P.O. Box 25486
Denver, Colorado 80225
http://www.r6.fws.gov/

References

Anderson, J. 1982. "Travel Report on Cactus Investigations, April 28-30." Report. U.S. Fish and Wildlife Service, Denver.

Heil, K. D. 1979. "Three New Species of Cactaceae from Southeastern Utah." *Cactus and Succulent Journal* 51:25-30.

U.S. Fish and Wildlife Service. 1985. "Wright Fishhook Cactus Recovery Plan." U.S. Fish and Wildlife Service, Denver.

Woodruff, D., and L. Benson. 1976. "Changes in Status in *Sclerocactus*." *Cactus and Succulent Journal* 48:131-134.

'Olulu

Brighamia insignis

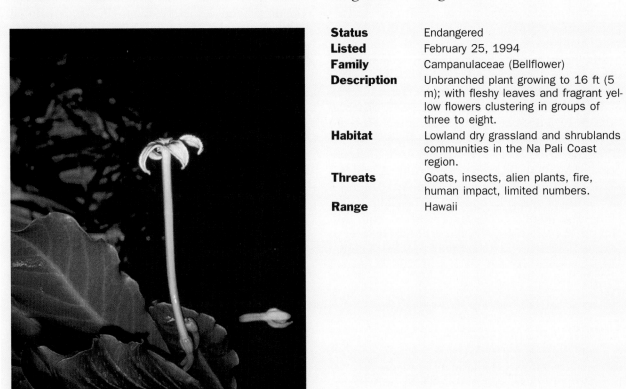

Status	Endangered
Listed	February 25, 1994
Family	Campanulaceae (Bellflower)
Description	Unbranched plant growing to 16 ft (5 m); with fleshy leaves and fragrant yellow flowers clustering in groups of three to eight.
Habitat	Lowland dry grassland and shrublands communities in the Na Pali Coast region.
Threats	Goats, insects, alien plants, fire, human impact, limited numbers.
Range	Hawaii

'Olulu, photograph by Warren L. Wagner. Reproduced by permission.

Description

'Olulu (*Brighamia insignis*) is an unbranched bellflower plant 3-16 ft (1-5 m) tall with a succulent stem that is bulbous at the bottom and tapers toward the top. The fleshy leaves, which measure 5-8 in (13-20 cm) long and 2.5-4.5 in (6-11 cm) wide, are arranged in a compact rosette at the top of the stem. Fragrant yellow flowers cluster in groups of 3-8 in the leaf axils (the point between the leaf and the stem), with each flower on a stalk 0.4-1.2 in (1-3 cm) long. The hypanthium (basal portion of the flower) has ten ribs and is topped with five oval or loosely triangular calyx lobes (partially fused sepals). The yellow petals are fused into a tube 2.8-5.5 in (7.1-14 cm) long, which flares into five elliptical lobes. The fruit is a capsule about 0.5 in (1.3 cm) long, containing numerous seeds.

Habitat

Stream and wave action along the Na Pali Coast have cut deep valleys and eroded the northern coast to form precipitous cliffs as high as 3,000 ft (914 m). *B. insignis* grows predominantly on rocky ledges with little soil or steep sea cliffs in lowland dry grassland and shrubland from sea level to 1,300 ft (396 m) in elevation.

Distribution

B. insignis had historical occurrences at the headland between Hoolulu and Waiahuakua Valleys along the Na Pali Coast on the island of Kauai and at Kaali Spring on the island of Niihau. The five extant populations grow on state and private land and total approximately 60-70 plants. Two populations are found along the Na Pali Coast, although approximately half of the individuals were destroyed in 1992 by Hurricane Iniki. These populations are within 0.4 mi (0.6 km) of each other within or on the boundary of the Hono Na Pali Natural Area Reserve. The most recent observations in 1994 estimated the population at Hoolulu to be 10-20 plants and the population at Waiahuakua to be 30-40 plants. There are also two populations in the Haupu Range within 2.7 mi (4.3 km) of each other. Hurricanes Iwa and Iniki destroyed 10 of the 12 individuals in the Haupu area. Only one plant survived in 1994 at both Mt. Haupu and Niumalu. The status of the small population on privately owned Niihau is not known, although there are reports that it was destroyed when the supporting cliff fell away.

Threats

Feral goats pose the major threat to *B. insignis* by causing defoliation and stem damage, restricting populations to inaccessible cliffs, and probably causing rock slides that degrade the plant's habitat. Alien plants pose another threat, especially introduced grasses such as molasses grass (*Melinis minutiflora*), yellow foxtail (*Setaria gracilis*), and smutgrass (*Sporobolus indicus*), which prevent the establishment of seedlings. Other alien plants that potentially pose a threat are lantana (*Lantana camara*), strawberry guava (*Psidium cattleianum*), common guava (*Psidium guajava*), and Java plum (*Syzygium cumini*).

Hikers transport weed seeds, dislodge rocks and damage plants, to areas where *B. insignis* grows. Wildfire also poses a serious threat. Another problem is that some plants flower but fail to set seed, which may be due to a lack of pollinators or a reduction of genetic viability due to such few individuals. The carmine spider mite, an introduced insect, has been observed to cause leaf loss in both cultivated and wild individuals.

Conservation and Recovery

Current reproduction is not thought to be sufficient to sustain populations, with poor seedling establishment due to competition with alien grasses as the limiting factor. Pollination failure is common, and may be due to a lack of pollinators or a reduction in genetic variability due to the few remaining individuals. The flower structure appears to favor outcrossing. Some vegetative cloning has been observed and flower and leaf size appear to be dependent on moisture availability. Seeds of this species are undoubtedly dispersed by gravity. Although they may be blown for short distances, they are not obviously adapted for wind dispersal, being ovoid to ellipsoid, smooth, and lacking any sort of wing or outgrowth. *B. insignis* has been successfully propagated and then cultivated by Lyon Arboretum, National Tropical Botanical Garden, and Waimea Arboretum. The 1995 holdings at Lyon Arboretum consisted of two plants in the tissue culture lab, 10 plants in the greenhouse, and 18 plants in the nursery. In the same year, National Tropical Botanical Garden had both seeds in storage and plants growing in their garden, while Waimea Arboretum had 14 growing plants.

The Kauai District of Division of Forestry and Wildlife has outplanted 20 individuals of *B. insignis* at Kalepa and Nounou Forest Reserves.

Contacts

Pacific Joint Venture
300 Ala Moana Blvd., Rm. 3-122
Honolulu, Hawaii 96850-0056
Telephone: (808) 541-2749
Fax: (808) 541-2756

U.S. Fish and Wildlife Service
Regional Office, Division of Endangered Species
Eastside Federal Complex
911 N.E. 11th Avenue
Portland, Oregon 97232-4181
Telephone: (503) 231-6121
http://pacific.fws.gov/

Reference

U.S. Fish and Wildlife Service. 25 February 1994. "Endangered and Threatened Wildlife and Plant; Determination of Endangered or Threatened Status for 24 Plants from the Island of Kauai, HI." *Federal Register* 59 (38): 9304-9329.

Pua'ala

Brighamia rockii

Status	Endangered
Listed	October 8, 1992
Family	Campanulaceae (Bellflower)
Description	Bellflower with oval leaves, fragrant flowers clustered in groups of three to eight.
Habitat	Rock crevices on inaccessible steep sea cliffs.
Threats	Habitat disturbance; predation by wild, feral, or domestic animals.
Range	Hawaii

Pua'ala, photograph by Warren L. Wagner. Reproduced by permission.

Description

Pua'ala, *Brighamia rockii*, is a bellflower that grows as an unbranched plant 3.3-16 ft (1-5 m) tall with a thickened succulent stem that tapers from the base. The fleshy, oval leaves are widest at their tips and are arranged in a rosette at the top of the plant. The leaves measure 2.4-8.7 in (6-22 cm) long and 2-6 in (5-15 cm) wide. The fragrant flowers are clustered in groups of three to eight on the leaf axils. Each flower cluster is on a stalk 1.4-3 in (3.5-7.5 cm) long, and individual flowers connect to a stalk 0.2-0.4 in (6-12 mm) long. The 10-ribbed hypanthium is topped by five calyx lobes 0.2-0.5 in (6-13 mm) long.

The petals are fused into a green to yellowish-green tube that flares into five white, elliptic lobes. The capsulelike fruit is 0.5-0.8 in (1.3-2 cm) long and contains numerous seeds. This species is an endemic Hawaiian genus that differs from other *Brighamia* species by the color of its petals, the longer calyx lobes, and the shorter flower stalks.

Habitat

B. rockii grows in rock crevices on inaccessible steep sea cliffs along East Molokai's northern coastline in coastal dry to mesic forests or shrublands at an elevation of sea level to 1,540 ft (470 m).

Associated species include *Canthium odoratum* (alahe'e), *Osteomeles anthyllidifolia* ('ulei), and *Scaevola* (nanpaka).

Distribution

Endemic to the Hawaiian Islands, *B. rockii* once ranged along the northern coast of East Molokai from Kalaupapa to Halawa and may possibly have grown on Lanai and Maui. Its range is now reduced to scattered populations on steep, inaccessible sea cliffs along East Molokai's northern coastline from Anapuhi Beach to Wailau Valley on private land, and on the relatively inaccessible state-owned sea stack of Huelo, east of Anapuhi Beach. The five known populations of *B. rockii* that extend over this 6.5-mi (10.5-km) long stretch total fewer than 200 individuals.

Threats

Habitat damage and possible predation by deer and goats pose serious threats to *B. rockii*. Competition with alien plants is also a threat. Although there is no evidence that rats feed on the fruits, these rodents are also a potential threat, as evidenced by their predation on related Hawaiian genera. Recent observations suggest that low reproductive rates in wild populations could be due to a combination of factors including low production of pollen, low establishment of seedlings, and a lack of pollinators.

Conservation and Recovery

Hand pollinations of *B. rockii* have been conducted, and seeds have been collected and propagated by the National Tropical Botanical Garden. No additional species-specific conservation efforts have been undertaken.

Contacts

U. S. Fish and Wildlife Service
Regional Office, Division of Endangered Species
Eastside Federal Complex
911 N. E. 11th Ave.
Portland, Oregon 97232-4181
Telephone: (503) 231-6121
http://pacific.fws.gov/

U. S. Fish and Wildlife Service
Pacific Remote Islands Ecological Services Field Office
300 Ala Moana Blvd., Room 3-122
P.O. Box 50088
Honolulu, Hawaii 96850-5000
Telephone: (808) 541-1201
Fax: (808) 541-1216
http://www.r1.fws.gov/pacific/

Reference

U. S. Fish and Wildlife Service. 8 October 1992. "Determination of Endangered or Threatened Status for 16 Plants from the Island of Molokai, Hawaii." *Federal Register* 57 (196): 46325-46340.

Brooksville Bellflower

Campanula robinsiae

Status	Endangered
Listed	July 27, 1989
Family	Campanulaceae (Bellflower)
Description	Solitary annual herb with deep purple, bell-shaped flowers.
Habitat	Moist pond margins.
Threats	Residential and agricultural development.
Range	Florida

Nancy Morin

Description

Brooksville bellflower, *Campanula robinsiae*, is a small annual herb that grows up to 6 in (15 cm) tall and bears deep purple, bell-shaped flowers about 2.5 in (1 cm) wide. Leaves are ovate to elliptical and are larger near the base. Many of the flowers are inconspicuous, being closed and self-pollinating. Others are solitary, open and cross-pollinating. The open flowers consist of a sepal 0.04-0.1 in (1-2.5 mm) long and a bell-shaped corolla, about 0.28-0.31 in (7-8 mm) wide. Flowering is in March and April.

The only other bellflower in Florida, *C. floridana*, is widespread, and can be distinguished by its shorter sepals and longer corolla.

This species, which was first described in 1926, was previously considered an introduced Eurasian species. However, it has now been shown to be a native, narrowly endemic species.

Habitat

The Brooksville bellflower was first discovered on the moist north slope of a hill. Field work in the

1980s showed that the species was primarily found on moist ground at the edges of two nearby ponds. Due to its rarity, any habitat alteration, such as unnatural fluctuations in water level or quality, could be disastrous.

Distribution

This bellflower is known only from three sites in Hernando County, north of Tampa, Florida. One site is the discovery site on Chinsegut Hill; two larger sites are at the margins of nearby ponds.

One of the sites in Hernando County is on land owned by the U.S. Department of Agriculture, one is a tract administered by the Florida Game and Fresh Water Fish Commission, and the third population at Lake Lindsey is under private ownership. The ponds that support the main populations are subject to seasonally fluctuating water levels, which determine the plant's year to year abundance.

Threats

The main threat to the species, apart from unintentional mismanagement of known sites, may be from changes in quality or quantity of surrounding watersheds, which may be contaminated by petroleum products, fertilizers, and herbicides. Because it is so small and short-lived, the Brooksville bellflower may be easily overlooked, and for this reason biologists hope that further searches might reveal additional sites harboring the species.

The Hernando County development boom of the 1980s and 1990s (according to the Census Bureau it was the second fastest-growing county in the nation from 1980 to 1986, growing by almost 75 percent) is also cause for concern; further development, such as a planned Tampa-Jacksonville corridor toll road (which would pass west of Brooksville), would only enhance the threat from construction and community growth.

Conservation and Recovery

The main populations of Brooksville bellflower are not apparently in danger of destruction of their habitat. Plants occur on a U.S. Department of Agriculture (USDA) research station and on protected state land, although the recent spread of rapidly proliferating, exotic plant species, especially the skunk vine (*Paederia foetida*) at the USDA tract at Chinsegut Hill, are considered a growing threat.

The 1994 recovery plan from the U. S. Fish and Wildlife Service, which describes necessary efforts to restore both the Brooksville bellflower and the Cooley's water-willow, notes that the primary objective for the plan is the eventual delisting of both species. The plan notes, however, that there is a fundamental lack of basic biological (i.e., distributional, ecological, reproductive, and systemic) knowledge about these species, which makes it difficult to set criteria to determine the time-frame or ultimate likelihood of delisting. Still, the plan states that delisting of both species should become feasible as habitat is protected and new populations are established or old ones reestablished.

According to the 1994 plan, plausible criteria for recovery might include securing at least 10 viable and self-sustaining populations of Brooksville bellflower in pond margin habitats, consisting of approximately 10,000 individuals during prolific years. The major recovery actions outlined in the plan include the development of management and protection criteria for populations on current managed areas; the acquisition of additional habitat, or protection of habitat through conservation easements and/or regulation; the completion of additional surveys to locate new populations; the augmentation of existing cultivated populations, including the establishment of a germ plasm bank; and the development of plans for possible introduction or reintroduction of plants into sustainable habitat.

Contact

Regional Office of Endangered Species
U.S. Fish and Wildlife Service
1875 Century Blvd., Suite 200
Atlanta, Georgia 30345
http://southeast.fws.gov/

References

Shetler, S. G. and N. Morin. 1986. "Seed Morphology in North American Campanulaceae." *Annals of the Missouri Botanical Garden* 73:653-688.

U.S. Fish and Wildlife Service. 1994 "Recovery Plan for Brooksville Bellflower and Cooley's Water-Willow." U.S. Fish and Wildlife Service, Atlanta.

'Oha Wai

Clermontia drepanomorpha

Status	Endangered
Listed	October 10, 1996
Family	Campanulaceae (Bellflower)
Description	Terrestrial branching tree; bears stalked leaves, flowers, and orange berries.
Habitat	Montane wet forests.
Threats	Ditch improvements; competition from alien plant taxa; habitat disturbance by feral pigs; girdling of the stems by rats.
Range	Hawaii

'Oha Wai, photograph by Robert J. Gustafson. Reproduced by permission.

Description

Clermontia drepanomorpha, the 'oha wai, is a member of the bellflower family (Campanulaceae), a terrestrial or epiphytic (not rooted in the soil), branching tree 8.2-23 ft (2.5-7 m) tall. The stalked leaves are 4-11 in (10.2-28 cm) long and 0.6-1.8 in (1.5-4.5 cm) wide. Two to four flowers, each with a stalk 0.8-1.4 in (2-3.5 cm) long, are positioned at the end of a main flower stalk 2-5 in (5-12.7 cm) long. The calyx (fused sepals) and corolla (fused petals) are similar in size and appearance, and each forms a slightly curved, five-lobed tube 1.6-2.2 in (4-5.6 cm) long and 0.6-0.8 in (1.5-2 cm) wide which is blackish purple. The berries are orange and 0.8-1.2 in (1.5-3 cm) in diameter. This species is distinguished from others in this endemic Hawaiian genus by similar sepals and petals, the long drooping inflorescence, and large blackish purple flowers.

Joseph F. Rock (1913) named *C. drepanomorpha* on the basis of specimens collected in the Kohala Mountains of the island of Hawaii in the early 1900s.

This taxonomy was retained in the latest treatment of the genus.

Habitat

This species typically grows in *Metrosideros polymorpha* ('ohi'a), *Cheirodendron trigynum* ('olapa), and *Cibotium glaucum* (hapu'u) dominated montane wet forests, often epiphytically, at elevations between 3,850 and 5,150 ft (1,174 and 1,570 m). Associated taxa include *Carex alligata*, *Melicope clusiifolia* (alani), *Styphelia tameiameiae* (pukiawe), *Astelia menziesii* (pa'iniu), *Rubus hawaiiensis* ('akala), *Cyanea pilosa* (haha), and *Coprosma* sp. (pilo).

Distribution

Historically, *C. drepanomorpha* was known from four populations in the Kohala Mountains on the island of Hawaii. Only 13-20 individuals in two populations, bordering private ranch lands, were known to be extant until recent surveys. In 1995, the U.S. Fish and Wildlife Service contracted with the

National Tropical Botanical Garden (NTBG) to conduct a thorough survey of the Kohala area. Approximately five populations totaling 200 individuals of *C. drepanomorpha* were found within a 5-mi (8-km) state-owned area of the only remaining habitat for the species.

Threats

The major threats to *C. drepanomorpha* are ditch improvements, competition from alien plant taxa, like thimbleberry, habitat disturbance by feral pigs, girdling of the stems by rats, and a risk of extinction from naturally occurring events (such as hurricanes) and/or reduced reproductive vigor due to the small number of existing populations.

Conservation and Recovery

As of May 1998, there are 48 plants at the Volcano Rare Plant Facility. The NTGB has 50 seeds in storage, but the viability is unknown. Lyon Arboretum contains 13 separate tissue culture associations and 90 plants from tissue culture. They also have five greenhouse plants.

Contact

U.S. Fish and Wildlife Service
Regional Office, Division of Endangered Species
Eastside Federal Complex
911 N.E. 11th Ave.
Portland, Oregon 97232-4181
(503) 231-6121
http://pacific.fws.gov/

Reference

U.S. Fish and Wildlife Service. 1998. "Big Island II: Addendum to the Recovery Plan for the Big Island Plant Cluster." U.S. Fish and Wildlife Service, Portland, Oregon. 80 pp. + appendices.

'Oha Wai

Clermontia lindseyana

Status	Endangered
Listed	March 4, 1994
Family	Campanulaceae (Bellflower)
Description	Branched shrub or tree with alternate, stalked, toothed leaves, two whitish to purplish flowers, and orange berries.
Habitat	Koa and 'ohi'a dominated montane mesic forests, often not rooted in soil, at high elevations.
Threats	Competition from alien plants; habitat destruction by cattle, goats and pigs; limited numbers.
Range	Hawaii

Description

This 'oha wai, *Clermontia lindseyana*, is a terrestrial or epiphytic (not rooted in the soil) branched shrub or tree 8.2-20 ft (2.5-6.1 m) tall. The alternate, stalked, toothed leaves are 5-9 in (12.7-22.8 cm) long and 1.5-2.6 in (3.8-6.6 cm) wide. Two flowers, each with a stalk 0.4-1 in (1-2.5 cm) long, are positioned at the end of a main flower stalk 1-1.6 in (2.5-4 cm) long. The calyx (fused sepals) and corolla (fused petals) are similar in size and appearance, and each form a slightly curved, five-lobed tube 2.2-2.6 in (5.6-6.6 cm) long and 0.4-0.7 in (1-1.8 cm) wide, which is greenish-white or purplish on the outside and white or cream-colored on the inside. The berries are orange and 1-1.6 in (2.5-4 cm) in diameter. This species is distinguished from others in this endemic Hawaiian genus by larger leaves and flowers, similar sepals and petals, and spreading floral lobes.

Habitat

This species typically grows in koa and 'ohi'a dominated montane mesic forests, often epiphytically (on other plants) at elevations between 4,000 and 7,050 ft (1,219 and 2,149 m). Associated species include pilo, kawa'u, and kolea.

Distribution

Historically, 'oha wai was known from the island of Maui on the southern slope of Haleakala, and from the island of Hawaii on the eastern slope of Mauna Kea and the eastern, southeastern, and southwestern slopes of Mauna Loa.

Since 1975, 12 populations of *C. lindseyana* have been identified, one on private, nine on state and two on federal land. One of these is on Maui and 11 are on the Big Island (Hawaii). Although the total number of extant individuals on the Big Island is unknown, approximately 86 individuals are thought to persist. The Maui population is located on state-owned land between Wailaulau Gulch and Manawainui Gulch, and estimated to consist of about 330 individuals.

Populations on the Big Island occur in or near Piha, Laupahoehoe, Makahanaloa, Kukuiopae, Puu Oo, Kulani Correctional Facility, Kahikinui, Kulani Boys Home, Kau Forest Reserve, and Hakalau National Wildlife Refuge. Observations indicate that most of the individuals are in excellent vigor.

Threats

Major habitat destruction resulting from ungulates, particularly pigs, is a primary cause of the de-

'Oha Wai *(Clermontia lindseyana)*, photograph by Jack Jeffrey. Reproduced by permission.

cline of this taxon. Roof or black rats may limit fruit production. Loss of pollinators may limit the species' reproductive capability, making recovery difficult or impossible. Natural events such as fire and flooding may severely inhibit the survivability of the taxon.

Small numbers of individuals and the scattered distribution of populations are significant threats, not only because they limit the gene pool and further depress reproductive vigor, but because a single natural or human-induced disturbance may be catastrophic and lead to the extirpation of the taxon. Unwarranted visits could adversely impact the populations.

Conservation and Recovery

The recovery of this and most other Hawaiian species depends on how well management practices can be implemented. The habitat of this and other Hawaiian species has undergone extreme alteration because of past and present land management practices, including deliberately introducing alien animals and plants, and agricultural and recreational development. To understand the recovery problems facing this species, it is necessary to understand the long-term causes of habitat destruction.

Contact

U.S. Fish and Wildlife Service
Regional Office, Division of Endangered Species
Eastside Federal Complex
911 N.E. 11th Ave.
Portland, Oregon 97232-4181
(503) 231-6121
http://pacific.fws.gov/

Reference

U.S. Fish and Wildlife Service. 1996. "Big Island Plant Cluster Recovery Plan." U.S. Fish and Wildlife Service, Portland, Oregon. 202+pp.

'Oha Wai

Clermontia oblongifolia ssp. *brevipes*

Status	Endangered
Listed	October 8, 1992
Family	Campanulaceae (Bellflower)
Description	Terrestrial shrub or tree with short leaves, leaf stalks, and flower stalks.
Habitat	Volcanic soils of coastal plains, upland slopes, mountain ranges, and summits.
Threats	Habitat disturbance and predation by wild, feral, or domestic animals.
Range	Hawaii

'Oha Wai, photograph by Derral Herbst. Reproduced by permission.

Description

'Oha wai (*Clermontia oblongifolia* ssp. *brevipes*) is a shrub or tree of the bellflower family that reaches a height of 6.6-23 ft (2-7 m). The leaves, on petioles (leaf stalks) 0.7-1.2 in (1.8-3 cm) long, are lance-shaped, have thickened, rounded teeth, reach a length of 2.8-4.3 in (7-11 cm), and have a width of 0.8-2 in (2-5 cm). Two or sometimes three flowers are grouped together on a stalk 0.2-0.4 in (0.5-1 cm) long, each flower having a stalk 0.4-1.8 in (1-4.5 cm) long. The flower is 2.4-3.1 in (6-8 cm) long. The calyx (fused sepals) and corolla (fused petals) are similar in size and appearance, and each forms an arched tube, which is greenish-white or purplish on the outside and white or cream-colored on the inside. The nearly spherical, orange fruit is a berry 0.7-1.2 in (1.8-3 cm) long. This species is distinguished from others in the genus by the structure of its calyx and corolla as well as by the lengths of the flower, the floral lobes, and the green hypanthium. This subspecies differs from others of the species by the shape of its leaves and the lengths of its leaves, leaf stalks, and flower stalks.

Habitat

C. oblongifolia ssp. *brevipes* typically grows in shallow soil on gulch slopes in wet 'ohi'a dominated forests at elevations between 3,500-3,900 ft (1066-1189 m) on East Molokai.

Distribution

C. oblongifolia ssp. *brevipes* is known from a single population located in the southeastern part of the Nature Conservancy's Kamakou Preserve on East Molokai. This population, last seen in 1982, is thought to contain fewer than 20 individuals. Another possible population, also from the Kamakou area, has not been seen for more than 40 years and is believed to have been extirpated. Other than this population, the historical range is not known. If the species cannot be found, it may be considered for delisting due to extinction.

Threats

The plant fauna of Molokai has currently fallen vulnerable to habitat degradation and/or predation by wild, feral, or domestic animals (axis deer, goats, pigs, sheep, and cattle); competition for space, light, water, and nutrients by naturalized, exotic species; habitat loss due to fires; predation by rats; human recreational activities; and military exercises.

Overgrazing by axis deer and goats has irreparably damaged much native vegetation of Molokai and Hawaii.

Cattle ranching on Molokai has played a significant role over most of the past 150 years in reducing areas of native vegetation to vast pastures of alien grasses. In 1960 about 61% of Molokai's lands were devoted to grazing, primarily in west and central Molokai. Cattle degrade the habitat by trampling and feeding on vegetation, eventually exposing the ground cover and increasing soil vulnerability to erosion. Red erosional scars resulting from decades of cattle disturbance, exacerbated by other feral ungulate activities, are still evident on West Molokai and the upper elevations of East Molokai. Cattle facilitate the spread of alien grasses and other plants.

Alteration of vegetation limits natural areas. It was here on the upper elevation mesic to wet forests of East Molokai, which the state designated a single protected area: the Molokai Forest Reserve. This reserve accounts for 30% of Molokai land area. Cattle ranching was succeeded in the 1920s by pineapple cultivation. Most of the land used for this agricultural activity had already been altered through the decades of cattle ranching. However, pineapple cultivation contributed to a high degree of erosion until its decline in the 1970s.

Feral pigs are an immediate threat to the habitat of the single remaining population of *C. oblongifolia* ssp. *brevipes*. The limited numbers in this occurrence make the species vulnerable to extinction through a single random natural event. Predation on related species suggests that rats may possibly feed on the fruit or plant parts of *C. oblongifolia* ssp. *brevipes*.

Conservation and Recovery

Currently, conservation efforts regarding *C. oblongifolia* ssp. *brevipes* are limited. The last observed population was found on land now protected by the Nature Conservancy's Kamakou Preserve.

Contacts

U.S. Fish and Wildlife Service
Regional Office, Division of Endangered Species
Eastside Federal Complex
911 N.E. 11th Avenue
Portland, Oregon 97232-4181
Telephone: (503) 231-6121
http://pacific.fws.gov/

Pacific Joint Venture
300 Ala Moana Blvd., Rm. 3-122
Honolulu, Hawaii 96850-0056
Telephone: (808) 541-2749
Fax: (808) 541-2756

Reference

U.S. Fish and Wildlife Service. 8 October 1992. "Endangered and Threatened Wildlife and Plants; Determination of Endangered or Threatened Status for 16 Plants from the Island of Molokai, Hawaii." *Federal Register* 57 (196): 46325-45339.

'Oha Wai

Clermontia oblongifolia ssp. *mauiensis*

Status	Endangered
Listed	May 15, 1992
Family	Campanulaceae (Bellflower)
Description	Shrub or tree whose leaves are oblong with thickened, rounded teeth and two to three flowers that bunch together on a short stalk; the flowers are greenish white or purplish and the fruits are orange.
Habitat	Sides of ridges in 'ohi'a dominated wet forests.
Threats	Habitat destruction by feral animals, competing plant species.
Range	Hawaii

Description

The 'oha wai (*Clermontia oblongifolia* ssp. *mauiensis*) is a shrub or tree in the bellflower family (Campanulaceae) that grows to heights of 6.6-23 ft (2-7 m). The leaves are located on petioles and are 1-4.5 in (2.5-11.5 cm) long. These oblong or elliptic leaves have thickened, rounded teeth and reach a length of 3-7.5 in (7.6-19 cm). This plant produces two or three flowers that are bunched together on a 0.2-1.8 in (0.5-4.5 cm) long stalk. The flower itself is 2.4-3.1 in (6-7.9 cm) long. The calyx and corolla are similar in size and appearance in that each forms an arched tube which is greenish white or purplish on the outside and white or cream-colored on the inside. The orange-colored fruit is a spherical berry. This subspecies is distinguished from other *C. oblongifolia* by its leaf shape; the lengths of its leaves, the leaf stalk, and flower stalk; the shapes of the leaf tip and the flower bud; and the purple or magenta color of the fused stamens.

Habitat

C. oblongifolia ssp. *mauiensis* typically grows on the sides of ridges in 'ohi'a dominated wet forests at an elevation of 2,800-3,000 ft (853-914 m). These wet, montane communities usually occur on steep windward slopes and valley walls. They are often characterized by bogs with thick peat overlaying an impervious clay substrate in which grow hummocks of sedges, grasses, stunted trees, and shrubs. Associated native species include *Coprosma*, *Clermontia*, *Hedyotis*, and *Melicope*.

Distribution

C. oblongifolia ssp. *mauiensis* was known historically from Lanai and Maui. The subspecies *mauiensis* was first collected on Lanai in Mahana valley and Kaiholena Valley. No specimens of the plant have been found on Lanai since 1913. *C. oblongifolia* was collected from East Maui on the windward slopes of Mt. Haleakala along the Kailua ditch trail in the valley of Honomanu at an elevation of 2,800-3,000 ft (853-914 m) in the rainforest. It was found growing in the company of *C. macrocarpa*, *C. kakeana*, the most common species in that locality, and *C. arborescens*. The last collection of this species on East Maui was made in 1927. On West Maui, the ssp. *mauiensis* was collected for the first time in the 1980s. This single individual exists along the trail to Puukukui in the Honokowai section of the West Maui Natural Area Reserve on state land.

In May 1994, Richard Palmer of the University of Hawaii at Manoa collected material possibly referable to *C. oblongifolia* ssp. *mauiensis* at 3,100 ft (945 m) elevation on the lower flume road in Koolau Forest Reserve, northwest Haleakala. Two individuals were observed on jeep road cuts, with *C. arborescens* and *C. kakeana* growing nearby. DNA analysis of these specimens and material from the West Maui *C. oblonglfolia* ssp. *mauiensis* indicates that *C. oblongifolia* and its subspecies may be hybrids of *C. arborescens* and *C. kakeana*. This information has not been confirmed as of the writing of this article. The genus *Clermontia* comprises 22 species, all restricted to the Hawaiian Islands. The specific epithet *oblongifolia* refers to the oblong shape of the leaf blade, while the subspecies epithet *mauiensis* refers to Maui Island, one of its places of occurrence.

In summary, *C. oblongifolia* ssp. *mauiensis* is currently known to exist only on West Maui. Good quality habitat still exists for this species in the windward rainforests of East Maui, and this taxon may still occur there. Because of the degradation of forest in its former habitat on Lanai, this taxon is likely extirpated on that island.

Threats

Many of the native plants of Maui are very vulnerable to habitat degradation caused by the browsing, rooting, and trampling of goats, pigs, sheep, and cattle. These native species are also threatened by competition in their habitats for space, light, water, and nutrients from naturalized alien species; human-ignited fires; recreational activities by tourists and visitors; and military exercises. Any of these threats could extirpate the single remaining *C. oblongifolia* plant, although it is not currently threatened by pig rooting. The complete lack of genetic diversity that exists for this species also means that its reproductive vigor is likely impaired.

Conservation and Recovery

Over the past three years, Maui Land and Pine and the Nature Conservancy of Hawaii have conducted management for the reduction of pigs in Kapunakea Preserve and the Honokowai section of the West Maui Natural Area Reserve where this subspecies still occurs. The combination of fencing, snaring and hunting under this program has reduced pigs to the point where they are no longer a direct threat to the single known individual of *C. oblongifolia* ssp. *mauiensis*, so localized fencing for this individual is no longer necessary.

Germ plasm from *C. oblongifolia* ssp. *mauiensis* is not held in any cultivated collection. Fruits from the East Maui plants were collected, then provided to the Lyon Arboretum. Attempts by Lyon Arboretum to propagate *C. oblongifolia* ssp. *mauiensis* were unsuccessful.

Contacts

U.S. Fish and Wildlife Service
Regional Office, Division of Endangered Species
Eastside Federal Complex
911 N.E. 11th Avenue
Portland, Oregon 97232-4181
Telephone: (503) 231-6121
http://pacific.fws.gov/

Pacific Joint Venture
300 Ala Moana Blvd., Rm 3-122
Honolulu, Hawaii 96850-0056
Telephone: (808) 541-2749
Fax: (808) 541-2756

Reference

U.S. Fish and Wildlife Service. 15 May 1992. "Endangered and Threatened Wildlife and Plants; Determination of Endangered or Threatened Status for 15 Plants from the Island of Maui, Hawaii." *Federal Register* 57 (95): 20772-20787.

'Oha Wai

Clermontia peleana

Status	Endangered
Listed	March 4, 1994
Family	Campanulaceae (Bellflower)
Description	Tall shrub with alternate, stalked, oblong, toothed leaves; and blackish-purple or greenish-white petals.
Habitat	Montane wet forests dominated by koa (*Acacia koa*), 'ohi'a (*Metrosideros collina*) and/or tree ferns.
Threats	Habitat disturbance caused by feral pigs and illegal cultivation of *Cannabis sativa*, roof or black rat damage, flooding, and stochastic extinction.
Range	Hawaii

'Oha Wai, photograph by Robert J. Gustafson. Reproduced by permission.

Description

This 'oha wai, *Clermontia peleana*, of which there are two subspecies, is a shrub or tree 5-20 ft (1.5-6 m) tall, which does not root in soil and grows on the plants 'ohi'a, koa, and ama'u's. The alternate, stalked, oblong or oval toothed leaves reach a length of 3-8 in (7.5-20.3 cm) and a width of 1.2-2 in (3-5 cm). Flowers are single or paired, each on a stalk 1.2-1.8 in (3-4.6 cm) long with a main stalk 0.3-0.7 in (0.8-1.8 cm) long. Five small green calyx lobes top the hypanthium. The blackish-purple (ssp. *peleana*) or greenish-white (ssp. *singuliflora*) petals are 2-2.8 in (5-7 cm) long and 0.3-0.5 in (0.8-1.3 cm) wide. They are fused into a one-lipped, arching tube with five down-curved lobes. Berries of spp. *peleana* are orange and 1-1.2 in (2.5-3 cm) in diameter. Berries of spp. *singuliflora* are unknown. This species is distinguished from others of the genus by its epiphytic growth habit; its small, green calyx lobes; and its one-lipped, blackish-purple or greenish-white corolla.

Habitat

This species typically grows epiphytically in montane wet forests dominated by koa (*Acacia koa*), 'ohi'a (*Metrosideros collina*) and/or tree ferns at elevations between 1,740 and 3,800 ft (530 and

1,158 m). Associated species include 'olapa, kolo-kolo mokihana, and naupaka kuahiwi (*Scaevola gaudichaudii*).

Distribution

Historically, *C. peleana* ssp. *peleana* has been found on the island of Hawaii on the eastern slope of Mauna Loa and the northeastern and southeastern slopes of Mauna Kea.

C. peleana spp. *singuliflora* was formerly found on the island of Hawaii on the northern slope of Mauna Kea and on East Maui on the northwestern slope of Haleakala, but the subspecies has not been seen in either place since the early part of the twentieth century and is believed to be extinct.

Today, this species is known near Waiakaumalo Stream; by the Wailuku River; near Saddle Road; and between the towns of Glenwood and Volcano on the eastern side of the Big Island. The four known populations, which extend over a distance of about 12 by 5 mi (19.3 by 8 km), are located on state and federally-owned land, and contain a total of approximately eight known individuals.

Threats

Major habitat destruction resulting from ungulates, particularly pigs, is a primary cause of the decline of this taxon. Cultivation of *Cannabis sativa* (marijuana) has also disturbed areas which might be suitable habitat for *C. peleana* ssp. *peleana*. Roof or black rats may limit fruit production. Loss of pollinators may limit *C. peleana* ssp. *peleana*'s reproductive capability, making recovery difficult or impossible; however, little information is available regarding the relationship between *C. peleana* ssp. *peleana* and nectar-feeding birds and/or other suitable pollinators. Natural events such as fire and flooding may severely inhibit the survivability of the taxon.

Small numbers of individuals and the scattered distribution of populations are significant threats, not only because they limit the gene pool and further depress reproductive vigor, but also because a single natural or human-induced disturbance may be catastrophic and lead to the extirpation of the taxon. Unwarranted visits by humans could adversely impact the populations.

Conservation and Recovery

Volcano Rare Plant Facility germinated one individual from seed acquired in 1992. The National Tropical Botanical Garden (NTBG) has germinated seeds and propagated the taxon. Lyon Arboretum has been successfully cloning *C. peleana* ssp. *peleana* using leaf tissue and has about 300 plants in the greenhouse. There have been no attempts to outplant the taxon at this point because these clones are not considered representative of the population and thus not useful for conservation purposes.

In order to prevent possible extinction of this taxon, maintenance of *ex situ* (at sites other than the plant's natural location, such as a nursery or arboretum) genetic stock is necessary. The eight known plants should be protected from ungulates, particularly pigs, via fencing or other means. Propagation and outplanting of *ex situ* stock will likely be needed in order to establish a sufficient number of plants for recovery within the taxons's four known locations, and a fifth population will need to be established.

Contacts

Pacific Joint Venture
300 Ala Moana Blvd., Rm. 3-122
Honolulu, Hawaii 96850-0056
Telephone: (808) 541-2749
Fax: (808) 541-2756

U.S. Fish and Wildlife Service
Regional Office, Division of Endangered Species
Eastside Federal Complex
911 N.E. 11th Avenue
Portland, Oregon 97232-4181
Phone: (503) 231-6121
http://pacific.fws.gov/

Reference

U.S. Fish and Wildlife Service. 4 March 1994. "Endangered and Threatened Wildlife and Plants; Determination of Endangered or Threatened Status for 21 Plants from the Island of Hawaii, State of Hawaii." *Federal Register* 59 (43): 10305-10325.

'Oha Wai

Clermontia pyrularia

'Oha Wai *(Clermontia pyrularia)*, photograph by Jack Jeffrey. Reproduced by permission.

Status	Endangered
Listed	March 4, 1994
Family	Campanulaceae (Bellflower)
Description	Terrestrial tree with alternate, toothed leaves; a cluster of up to five white or greenish-white flowers; five small green calyx lobes covered with fine hairs; and ovoid or pear-shaped orange berries.
Habitat	Koa (*Acacia koa*) and/or 'ohi'a (*Metrosideros collina*) dominated montane wet forests and subalpine dry forests.
Threats	Competition from alien plants, limited numbers.
Range	Hawaii

Description

This 'oha wai, *Clermontia pyrularia*, is a terrestrial tree 10-13 ft (3-4 m) tall, has alternate, toothed leaves 5.9-11 in (15-28 cm) long and 1-2 in (2.5-5.1 cm) wide, with winged petioles. A cluster of up to five flowers has a main stalk 1.1-2.4 in (2.8-6.1 cm) long; each flower has a stalk 0.3-0.8 in (0.8-2 cm) long. Five small green calyx lobes top the hypanthium. The white or greenish-white petals are covered with fine hairs, measure 1.6-1.8 in (4-4.6 cm) long, and are fused into a curved two-lipped tube 0.2-0.3 in (0.5-0.8 cm) wide with five spreading lobes. The or-

ange berry is inversely ovoid or pear-shaped. This species is distinguished from others of the genus by its winged petioles; its small, green calyx lobes; its two-lipped flowers with white or greenish-white petals; and the shape of the berry. This species was observed in fruit and flower during December 1978 and November 1957. No other life history information is currently available.

Habitat

This species typically grows in koa and/or 'ohi'a dominated montane wet forests and subalpine dry forests at elevations between 3,000 and 7,000 ft (914 and 2,134 m). Associated species include pilo (*Platydesma* sp.), pukamole (*Lythrum mariturnum*), and 'akala.

Distribution

Historically, 'oha wai has been found only on the island of Hawaii on the northeastern slope of Mauna Kea, the western slope of Mauna Loa, and the saddle area between the two mountains.

Since 1975, two populations have been identified on state and federal lands in north Hilo at elevations of 5,900-6,240 ft (1,798-1,901 m). One population consisted of an individual previously found near Laupahoehoe Natural Area Reserve; the plant is now dead and this population may be extirpated. The second population consists of three plants found on state land at Piha, adjacent to the Hakalau National Wildlife Refuge (NWR). Although this second population also originally consisted of one plant that eventually died, three more plants were recently discovered. In addition, approximately 30 individuals grown from seeds of the original plant were outplanted in two enclosures at Hakalau NWR by refuge staff in December 1990 and June and July 1992.

Threats

Alien grasses, shrubs, and vines, particularly banana poka (*Passiflora mollissima*), negatively impact *C. pyrularia*. The canopy of banana poka is shading out seedlings in Piha and must be controlled. By rooting and trampling native vegetation and eliminating juveniles, pigs also appear to be a major contributor to the taxon's demise. Pigs are attracted by the fruits of *Passiflora mollissima* and the fruits are dispersed in their digestive tracts, hooves, and hair.

Predation on fruits and seeds of *C. pyrularia* by black rats may limit the successful establishment of new plants. Scattered distribution, few populations, and small number of individuals make this taxon highly vulnerable to random events and human impacts, and may also affect reproductive vigor. The plant originally known from Piha rapidly died from unknown causes in 1995. There was no indication of natural reproduction even though viable seeds for the outplants were produced. The general decline of the environment may have eliminated or re-

duced native vectors and thereby precluded or lessened pollination. Other individuals known from the Piha area disappeared a few years ago, probably eaten by cattle. The area is pasture land and is heavily grazed.

Conservation and Recovery

Volcano Rare Plant Facility at the Volcano Agricultural Station has successfully germinated *C. pyrularia* and currently has approximately 50 seedlings growing in the greenhouse. Lyon Arboretum has successfully cloned the taxon and has about 100 seedlings in the greenhouse.

Approximately 30 individuals have been outplanted and are growing in two enclosures at Hakalau NWR. Seeds were acquired from the wild plant at Piha that died in 1989. The individuals grown from seed are healthy and two or three have flowered. There are plans to fence the three remaining wild plants in the near future.

The known remaining individuals should be protected from ungulates and encroachment of alien plants. In order to prevent possible extinction of this taxon, maintenance of *ex situ* genetic stock is necessary. Propagation and outplanting of *ex situ* stock will be needed in order to establish a sufficient number of populations and plants for recovery. Research into the taxon's pollination vectors may be necessary.

Contacts

Pacific Joint Venture
300 Ala Moana Blvd., Rm. 3-122
Honolulu, Hawaii 96850-0056
Phone: (808) 541-2749
Fax: (808) 541-2756

U.S. Fish and Wildlife Service
Regional Office, Division of Endangered Species
Eastside Federal Complex
911 N.E. 11th Avenue
Portland, Oregon 97232-4181
Phone: (503) 231-6121
http://pacific.fws.gov/

Reference

U.S. Fish and Wildlife Service. 4 March 1994. "Endangered and Threatened Wildlife and

Plant; Determination of Endangered or Threatened Status for 21 Plants from the Island of Hawaii, State of Hawaii." *Federal Register* 59 (43): 10305-10325.

ʻOha Wai

Clermontia samuelii

Status	Endangered
Listed	September 3, 1999
Family	Campanulaceae (Bellflower)
Description	A tropical shrub.
Habitat	Humid tropical forest.
Threats	Habitat destruction and degradation caused by introduced mammalian herbivores and invasive plants.
Range	Hawaii

Gerald D. Carr

Description

The ʻoha wai is a shrub growing as tall as 16 ft (5 m). Its leaves are elliptical in shape, with blades 2-4 in (5-10 cm) long and 0.7-1.8 in (1.8-4.5 cm) wide. The upper surfaces of the leaves are dark green, often tinged purplish, and may be sparsely hairy. The lower surfaces are pale green and sparsely to densely hairy. The leaf margins are thickened, with shallow, ascending, rounded teeth. The tip and base of the leaves are typically sharply pointed. The inflorescences (or flowering clusters) bear two to five flowers on a peduncle (supporting stem) that is 0.2-0.7 in (4-18 mm) long. The hypanthium (a cup-like structure at the base of the flower) is widest on the top, 0.3-0.6 in (8-14 mm) long, and 0.2-0.4 in (5-10 mm) wide. The sepals and petals are both colored rose or greenish white to white, and are curved and tubular. The flowers are 1.4-2.2 in (36-55 mm) long and 0.2-0.4 in (5-10 mm) wide. The lobes of the sepals and petals are erect, and extend 0.2-0.5 times beyond the tube. Berries of this species have not yet been observed. The subspecies *hanaensis* is differ-

entiated from *samuelii* by its greenish white to white flowers, longer narrower leaves with the broadest point near the base, and fewer hairs on the lower surface of the leaves.

Habitat

The ʻoha wai occurs in montane wet forest dominated by the ohiʻa (*Metrosideros polymorpha*), with with an understory of hapu u' (*Cibotium* sp.) and other native shrubs. The subspecies *hanaensis* is found at or below an elevation of 3,000 ft (915 m), while *samuelii* occurs between 6,000 and 6,900 feet (1,800 and 2,100 m).

Distribution

The ʻoha wai is a locally evolved (or endemic) species that has been reported from eight locations in East Maui, from Keanae Valley on the windward (northeastern) side to Manawainui on the more leeward (southeastern) side of Haleakala. The Hawaiian archipelago has an extremely large fraction of endemic species; about 89% of the indigenous flowering plants occur nowhere else in the world.

Threats

Threats to *hanaensis* include habitat destruction or degradation caused by introduced feral pigs (*Sus scrofa*) and by competition and habitat change associated with non-native plants, such as glorybush (*Tibouchina herbacea*) and two species of ginger (*Hedychium* spp.). The extremely invasive plants velvet tree (*Miconia calvescens*) and Koster's curse (*Clidemia hirta*) are also a potential threat. The subspecies *samuelii* is also threatened by wild pigs and invasive plants. The 'oha wai is known from several populations on the northeastern side of Haleakala, totaling fewer than 300 individuals. The populations occur on state owned land, within a Natural Area Reserve and a Forest Reserve. The subspecies *hanaensis* is known from several populations on the northeastern side of Haleakala, totaling fewer than 300 individuals. The populations occur on state owned land, within a Natural Area Reserve and a Forest Reserve. The subspecies *samuelii* is known from 5 to 10 populations totaling 50 to 100 individuals, most of which occur on the back walls of Kipahulu Valley, within Haleakala National Park, with two or three others on adjacent state owned land.

Conservation and Recovery

The population of *samuelii* in Haleakala National Park has been enclosed in a fence, and pigs have been eradicated there. The populations occurring on State Forest Reserve or State Natural Area Reserve lands are also being managed to conserve their indigenous ecological values, although pigs have not been eradicated. Actions needed to conserve the 'oha wai include the protection of its known critical habitats, and research into its biology and the deleterious effects of introduced mammalian herbivores and invasive plants, and ways of controlling those biological damages.

Contacts

U. S. Fish and Wildlife Service
Regional Office, Division of Endangered Species
Eastside Federal Complex
911 N. E. 11th Ave.
Portland, Oregon 97232-4181
(503) 231-6121
http://pacific.fws.gov/

U. S. Fish and Wildlife Service
Pacific Islands Ecoregion, Pacific Islands Fish and Wildlife Office
300 Ala Moana Boulevard, Room 3-122
P. O. Box 50088
Honolulu, Hawaii 96850
Telephone: (808) 541-3441
Fax: (808) 541-3470

Reference

U. S. Fish and Wildlife Service. 3 September 1999. "Endangered and Threatened Wildlife and Plants: Final Endangered Status for 10 Plant Taxa From Maui Nui, Hawaii." *Federal Register* 64 (171): 48307-48324.

Haha

Cyanea acuminata

Status	Endangered
Listed	October 10, 1996
Family	Campanulaceae (Bellflower)
Description	Leaves are inversely lance shaped to narrowly egg-shaped or elliptic; the upper leaf surface is green, whereas the lower surface is whitish green; the slightly hardened leaf edges contain small, spreading, pointed teeth.
Habitat	Slopes, ridges, or stream banks in mesic to wet 'ohi'a-uluhe, koa-'ohi'a, or lama-'ohi'a forest.
Threats	Habitat degradation and destruction by feral pigs; potential impacts from military activities; potential predation by rats; competition with noxious alien plants; and risk of extinction from naturally occurring events.
Range	Hawaii

Description

Cyanea acuminata, a member of the bellflower family (Campanulaceae), is an unbranched shrub 1-6.6 ft (0.3-2.0 m) tall. The leaves, 4.3-12.6 in (109.2-320.0 mm) long and 1.2-3.5 in (30.4-88.9 mm) wide, are inversely lance-shaped to narrowly egg-shaped or elliptic. The upper leaf surface is green, whereas the lower surface is whitish green. The slightly hardened leaf edges contain small, spreading, pointed teeth. The leaf stalks are 0.8-4.0 in (20.3-101.6 mm) long. Six to 20 flowers are arranged on a flowering stalk 0.6-2.4 in (15.2-70 mm) long. The calyx lobes, 0.08-0.2 in (2-5 mm) long, are narrowly triangular. The corolla is white and sometimes tinged purplish, 1.2-1.4 in (30.5-35.6 mm) long and 0.1-0.2 in (2.5-5.1 mm) wide. The tubular portion of the flower appears almost erect to slightly curved, while the lobes are one-fourth to one-third as long as the tube and spreading. The yellow-yellowish orange, round berries are approximately 0.2 in (5.1 mm) long. The color of the petals and fruit and length of the calyx lobes, flowering stalk, and leaf stalks distinguish this species from others in this endemic Hawaiian genus. *C. acuminata* has been observed fruiting in February and November. Other published names considered synonymous with *C. acuminata* var. *calycina*, include *C. acuminata forma latifolia*, *C. occultans*, *Delissea acuminata* var. *calycina*, *D. acuminata forma latifolia*, *D. acuminata* var. *latifolia*, *D. occultans*, and *Lobelia acuminata*.

Charles Gaudichaud-Beaupre, while a pharmaceutical botanist on the vessel Uranie, collected a new lobelioid on Oahu, which he later described and named *Delissea acuminata*. Wilhelm Hillebrand transferred this species to the genus *Cyanea* in 1888, resulting in the new combination *Cyanea acuminata*. This is the name accepted in the current treatment of Hawaiian members of the family.

Habitat

C. acuminata typically grows on slopes, ridges, or stream banks from 1,000 to 3,000 ft (304.8 to 914.4 m) in elevation. The plants are found in mesic to wet 'ohi'a-uluhe, koa-'ohi'a, or lama-'ohi'a forest.

Haha *(Cyanea acuminata),* photograph by John Obata. Reproduced by permission.

Distribution

Historically, *C. acuminata* was known from 31 scattered populations in the Koolau Mountains.

The 15 extant populations contained a total of fewer than 100 plants in 1997. These populations occur on private land; City and County of Honolulu land; state land, including land leased by the Department of Defense for the Kawailoa Training Area; and federal land on Schofield Barracks Military Reservation and the Omega Coast Guard Station. Eleven populations each have fewer than 10 individuals, of which seven locations harbor only one or two plants each, and four populations each number from 10-40 individuals.

Threats

The major threats to *C. acuminata* are habitat degradation and destruction by feral pigs; potential impact from military activities; potential predation

by rats; competition with the noxious alien plants Christmasberry, Koster's curse, and Maui pamakani. Additionally, the species faces the risk of extinction from naturally occurring events or through reduced reproductive vigor due to the small number of remaining individuals.

C. acuminata is potentially threatened by feral pig predation because the species is not known to be unpalatable to pigs and they favor plants from the bellflower family for food.

It is possible that rats eat the fruit of *C. acuminata,* a plant with fleshy stems and fruit that grows in areas where rats occur.

The noxious shrub Koster's curse is a threat to this species. Christmasberry grows in dense thickets that threaten *C. acuminata.* The mat-forming weed Maui pamakani also threatens this plant.

Populations of *C. acuminata* that occur on land leased and owned by the U.S. Army face the threat of being damaged through military activity, either by troops in training maneuvers or by the construction, maintenance, and utilization of helicopter landing and drop-off sites.

Conservation and Recovery

This species is being propagated at the Lyon Arboretum, and seeds are in storage at the National Tropical Botanical Garden.

Contact

U. S. Fish and Wildlife Service
Regional Office, Division of Endangered Species
Eastside Federal Complex
911 N. E. 11th Ave.
Portland, Oregon 97232-4181
(503) 231-6121
http://pacific.fws.gov/

Reference

U.S. Fish and Wildlife Service. 1998. *Recovery Plan for Oahu Plants*. U.S. Fish and Wildlife Service, Portland.

Haha

Cyanea asarifolia

Status	Endangered
Listed	February 25, 1994
Family	Campanulaceae (Bellflower)
Description	Sparingly branched shrub with heart-shaped leaves and 30-40 slightly curved white flowers with purple stripes.
Habitat	Pockets of soil on sheer rock cliffs in lowland wet forests.
Threats	Pigs, rats, natural disaster, overcollecting, limited numbers.
Range	Hawaii

Haha *(Cyanea asarifolia)*, photograph. National Tropical Botanical Garden. Reproduced by permission.

Description

This haha (*Cyanea asarifolia*) is a sparingly branched shrub in the bellflower family that grows to a height of 1-3.3 ft (0.3-1.0 m). The heart-shaped leaves are 3.3-4.1 in (8.4-10.4 cm) long and 2.8-3.1 in (7.1-7.9 cm) wide, with leaf stalks 4.7-5.9 in (11.9-15.0 cm) long. Thirty to 40 flowers are clustered on a stalk about 1 in (2.5 cm) long, each having an individual stalk about 0.3 in (7.6 mm) in length. The slightly curved flowers are white with purple stripes, with wide spreading lobes. The five anthers have tufts of white hairs at the tips. The nearly spherical fruit is a dark purple berry. This species is distinguished from others of the genus that grow on Kauai by the shape of the leaf base, the leaf width in proportion to the length, and the presence of a leaf stalk.

Habitat

C. asarifolia grows in pockets of soil on sheer rock cliffs in lowland wet forests at an elevation of approximately 1,080 ft (329 m). Associated plant species include ferns, manono, 'ohi'a, alona, and opuhe.

Distribution

For more than 20 years *C. asarifolia* was known only from a population of five or six plants above the bed of Anahola stream on Kauai. When later attempts to locate the population were unsuccessful, the population was thought to be extirpated. A population of 14 mature plants and five seedlings was discovered in 1991 on state-owned land at the headwaters of the Wailua River in central Kauai.

Threats

C. asarifolia is threatened by stochastic extinction and reduced reproductive vigor due to the small number of existing individuals. Plants in the area in which the only currently known population occurs are vulnerable to occasional hurricanes, natural rockslides, and overcollecting for scientific purposes. Hurricane Iniki heavily damaged the population in 1992, directly or indirectly destroying all but four or five juvenile plants. Plants observed after Hurricane Iniki were frequently damaged by introduced slugs or rodents.

Conservation and Recovery

C. asarifolia has been successfully propagated and then grown in cultivation by National Tropical Botanical Garden; this institution also has seeds in storage. In 1995, Lyon Arboretum had 1,283 plants in the tissue culture lab and three individuals in their certified greenhouse. The Kauai District Division of Forestry and Wildlife has outplanted nine individuals of this species in the "blue hole" area of Mount Waialeale.

Contacts

U. S. Fish and Wildlife Service
Regional Office, Division of Endangered Species
Eastside Federal Complex
911 N. E. 11th Ave.
Portland, Oregon 97232-4181
Telephone: (503) 231-6121
http://pacific.fws.gov/

U.S. Fish and Wildlife Service
300 Ala Moana Boulevard, Room 6307
P.O. Box 50167
Honolulu, Hawaii 96850
Telephone: (808) 541-2749

Reference

U.S. Fish and Wildlife Service. 25 February 1994. "Endangered and Threatened Wildlife and Plant; Determination of Endangered or Threatened Status for 24 Plants from the Island of Kauai, HI." *Federal Register* 59 (38): 9304-9329.

Haha

Cyanea copelandii ssp. *copelandii*

Status	Endangered
Listed	March 4, 1994
Family	Campanulaceae (Bellflower)
Description	Shrub with alternate, stalked, toothed leaves, clusters of five to 12 rose-colored flowers, and dark orange berries.
Habitat	Montane wet forests.
Threats	Limited numbers, feral ungulates, rats, and alteration of habitat.
Range	Hawaii

Joseph Rock

Description

This haha, *Cyanea copelandii* ssp. *copelandii*, is a shrub with a growth habit similar to that of a woody vine. The alternate, stalked, toothed leaves are 7.9-10.6 in (20.1-26.9 cm) long and 1.4-3.3 in (3.6-8.3 cm) wide, and have fine hairs on the lower surface. Five to 12 flowers are clustered on the end of the main stalk 0.8-1.8 in (2.0-4.6 cm) long; each flower has a stalk of 0.2-0.6 in (0.5-1.5 cm) long. The slightly hairy hypanthium (basal portion of the flower) is topped by five small, triangular calyx tubes. Petals, which are yellowish but appear rose-colored be-cause of a covering of dark red hairs, are fused into a curved tube with five spreading lobes; the corolla is 1.5-1.7 in (3.8-4.3 cm) long and about 0.2 in (5.0 mm) wide. Berries are dark orange and measure 0.3-0.6 in (0.7-1.4 cm) long. This subspecies is distinguished from ssp. *haleakalaensis,* the only other subspecies of *C. copelandii,* by its narrower leaves. The species differs from others in this endemic Hawaiian genus by its growth habit and the size, shape, and dark red pubescence of its corolla. This taxon was observed in fruit and flower during December of 1914. No other life history information is currently available.

Habitat

This species often grows not rooted in soil and is typically found in montane wet forests at elevations between 2,200 and 2,900 ft (671 and 884 m). Associated species include tree ferns.

Distribution

This species, which has been collected only twice on the southeastern slope of Mauna Loa near Glenwood, was last seen in 1957. It is difficult to adequately survey the area because of vegetation density and the terrain.

The only known population, located on state land and sighted in 1957, is still considered extant, although it contains an unknown number of individuals.

Threats

C. copelandii ssp. *copelandii* has been particularly impacted by the grazing of feral ungulates. Black rats may also constitute a threat by consuming fruits and seeds, and thereby reducing reproductive and establishment success. The loss of Hawaiian honeycreepers has likely resulted in elimination of the bird pollinator for this plant. Because only one small plant population may exist, reduction in reproductive vigor and susceptibility to random extinction are threats.

The major known threat is stochastic extinction and reduced population vigor within the single population.

Conservation and Recovery

At this time, neither the Volcano Rare Plant Facility nor Lyon Arboretum is attempting to germinate and/or grow individuals from tissue culture. Since the last plant specimen was collected in 1957, the availability of plant materials is the present constraint. If materials are obtained, attempts will be made to grow and outplant individuals.

This taxon should be located in the wild, and seeds and/or tissue collected for propagation and maintenance of *ex situ* genetic stock. Additional populations will need to be established and, along with the extant population, protected from ungulates and other threats.

Contacts

U. S. Fish and Wildlife Service
Regional Office, Division of Endangered Species
Eastside Federal Complex
911 N. E. 11th Ave.
Portland, Oregon 97232-4181
Telephone: (503) 231-6121
http://pacific.fws.gov/

Senior Resident Agent Office
U.S. Fish and Wildlife Service
300 Ala Moana Boulevard, Room 7-235
P.O. Box 50223
Honolulu, Hawaii 96850-5000
Telephone: (808) 541-2681
Fax: (808) 541-3062

Reference

U.S. Fish and Wildlife Service. 4 March 1994. "Endangered and Threatened Wildlife and Plant; Determination of Endangered or Threatened Status for 21 Plants from the Island of Hawaii, State of Hawaii." *Federal Register* 59 (43): 10305-10325.

Haha

Cyanea copelandii ssp. *haleakalaensis*

Robert J. Gustafson

Status	Endangered
Listed	September 3, 1999
Family	Campanulaceae (Bellflower)
Description	A vine-like, tropical shrub.
Habitat	Native tropical forest.
Threats	Habitat destruction, introduced mammalian herbivores, non-native slugs, invasive alien plants.
Range	Hawaii

Description

The haha is a vine-like shrub, growing 1-7 ft (0.3-2 m) tall, with sprawling stems. Its sap, visible when branches are broken, is a tan-colored latex. Stems grow from the base and are unbranched or sparingly branched. The leaves are elliptical, 4-7 in (10-19 cm) long, and 1.4-3.3 in (3.5-8.5 cm) wide. The lower surface of the leaves is hairy, but the upper surface is not. The margin of the leaves is slightly thickened, and has small, widely spaced, sharp teeth. The leaf petiole is 1-4 in (2.5-10 cm) long. The inflorescence contains 5 to 12 flowers, and is supported by a peduncle (stalk) 0.8-1.8 in (20-45 mm) long. The hypanthium (flower base) is oval, wider at the top, 0.2-0.4 in (6-10 mm) long, about 0.2 in (5 mm) wide, and hairy. The corolla (the petals) is yellowish, but appears pale rose in color due to a covering of dark red hairs. The corolla is 1.4-1.6 in (37-42 mm) long and about 0.2 in (5 mm) wide. The corolla tube is gently curved and the lobes spread beyond the tube. The ripe berries are dark-orange in color, oval-shaped, and 0.3-0.6 in (7-15 mm) long.

This subspecies is differentiated from other subspecies of *Cyanea copelandii* by its elliptical, relatively short leaves. It differs from others in the endemic genus *Cyanea* by its vine-like habit and yellowish flowers that appear red due to the covering of hairs.

Habitat

The haha inhabits stream banks and wet scree slopes in montane wet or mesic tropical forest dominated by koa (*Acacia koa*) and/or o'hia (*Metrosideros polymorpha*). It occurs at elevations between 2,400 and 4,400 feet (730-1,340 m).

Distribution

The haha is a locally evolved, or endemic, species that is only known from the island of Maui, Hawaii. The Hawaiian archipelago has an extremely large fraction of endemic species; about 89% of the indigenous flowering plants occur nowhere else in the world. The haha was historically reported from six locations on the windward (northeastern) side of

Haleakala, East Maui, from Waikamoi to the Kipa-hulu Valley.

Threats

The major threats to the haha are habitat degradation and/or destruction by feral pigs, and competition with several species of introduced, invasive plants, such as the shrub strawberry guava (*Psidium cattleianum*), the thimbleberry (*Rubus rosifolius*), and other non-native plants. Introduced rats and slugs are also probably herbivores of this plant. Because of its limited range and small population size, the haha is also potentially threatened by catastrophic events of weather, wildfire, or other disturbances. The haha is now known from only two populations. One population of about 200 individuals is in the Kipahulu Valley within Haleakala National Park, and the other of 35 individuals is on the lower Waikamoi flume, on privately owned land.

Conservation and Recovery

The major surviving population of the haha is located within Haleakala National Park, which is managed to conserve its indigenous biodiversity. The other population is on private land, and is potentially at risk from disturbance or other human actions. Conservation of the endangered haha requires that all its critical habitat be protected and managed to reduce the threats posed by non-native herbivores and competitors. The populations of the haha should be monitored against further change, and research undertaken to develop a better understanding of degrading influences faced by the endangered plant, and ways of mitigating those effects.

Contacts

U. S. Fish and Wildlife Service
Regional Office, Division of Endangered Species
Eastside Federal Complex
911 N. E. 11th Ave.
Portland, Oregon 97232-4181
(503) 231-6121
http://pacific.fws.gov/

U. S. Fish and Wildlife Service
Pacific Islands Ecoregion, Pacific Islands Fish and Wildlife Office
300 Ala Moana Boulevard, Room 3-122
P. O. Box 50088
Honolulu, Hawaii 96850-0056
Telephone: (808) 541-3441
Fax: (808) 541-3470

Reference

U.S. Fish and Wildlife Service. 3 September 1999. "Endangered and Threatened Wildlife and Plants: Final Endangered Status for 10 Plant Taxa From Maui Nui, Hawaii." *Federal Register* 64 (171): 48307-48324.

Cyanea crispa

No Common Name

Status	Endangered
Listed	March 28, 1994
Family	Campanulaceae (Bellflower)
Description	Unbranched shrub with broad, oval, toothed leaves, and clusters of three to eight fuzzy, pale magenta flowers.
Habitat	Steep, open mesic forests to gentle slopes or moist gullies of closed wet forests.
Threats	Habitat alteration and suspected predation by rats, slugs, and feral pigs; competition with noxious alien plants.
Range	Hawaii

Loyal A. Mehrhoff

Description

Cyanea crispa, a member of the bellflower family, is an unbranched shrub with leaves clustered at the ends of succulent stems. The broad oval leaves, 12-30 in (30.5-76.2 cm) long and 3.5-6.3 in (8.9-16 cm) wide, have undulating, smooth or toothed leaf margins. Each leaf is on a stalk 0.3-1.6 in (0.8-4.1 cm) long. Clusters of three to eight fuzzy flowers grow on stalks 0.8-1.2 in (2-3 cm) long, with each flower borne on a stalk 0.4-0.8 in (1-2 cm) long. The oval or oblong calyx lobes often overlap at their bases and are 0.2-0.5 in (0.5-1.3 cm) long. The fused petals, 1.6-2.4 in (4.1-6.1 cm) long and fuzzy, are pale magenta with darker longitudinal stripes. The fruits are spherical berries 0.4 in (1 cm) in diameter that contain many minute, dark seeds. *C. crispa* is distinguished from other species in this endemic Hawaiian genus by its leaf shape, distinct calyx lobes, and the length of the flowers and stalks of flower clusters.

This species was observed in flower in April 1930; in 1998, it was observed fruiting in June and September.

Cyanea crispa, photograph by Loyal A. Mehrhoff. Reproduced by permission.

Habitat

C. crispa is found at elevations between 600 and 2,400 ft (183 and 732 m) in habitats ranging from steep, open mesic forests to gentle slopes or moist gullies of closed wet forests. Associated plants include common *Cyrtandra* species (haiwale), papala kepau, and *Touchardia latifolia* (olona).

Distribution

C. crispa was known historically from scattered locations throughout the upper elevations of the Koolau Mountains of Oahu from Kaipapau Valley in the north to Waialae Iki Ridge in the southeast. The seven extant populations, scattered over a distance of 19 mi (31 km), contained about 40 total individuals in 1996. Twenty-six plants occurred at Hidden Valley, one at Palolo Valley, one at Kapakahi Gulch, one at Pia Valley, five at the Kaipapau-Kawainui summit divide, four at Upper Aina Haina, and only a few at Moanalua Valley. These

populations are on state land, private land leased to the Department of Defense on the Kawailoa Training Area, and normal private land.

Threats

The major threats to *C. crispa* are habitat alteration and suspected predation by rats, slugs, and feral pigs; competition with noxious alien plants like kulmi, Koster's Curse, and strawberry guava; and the risk of extinction through random natural events. Reduced reproductive vigor due to the small number of remaining individuals, their limited gene pool, and their restricted distributions is another significant threat.

Conservation and Recovery

The Division of Forestry and Wildlife has undertaken a pig control program in Hidden Valley; however, a site visit in September of 1997 revealed abundant pig signs, with many individuals of

C. crispa defoliated or dead. This species is being propagated at the Lyon Arboretum and the National Tropical Botanical Garden.

Contacts

U. S. Fish and Wildlife Service
Regional Office, Division of Endangered Species
Eastside Federal Complex
911 N. E. 11th Avenue
Portland, Oregon 97232-4181
503-231-6118
http://pacific.fws.gov/

Pacific Islands Ecological Services Field Office
300 Ala Moana Blvd., Rm. 6307
Honolulu, Hawaii 96850
Telephone: (808) 541-2749
Fax: (808) 541-2756

Reference

U. S. Fish and Wildlife Service. 28 March 1994. "Endangered and Threatened Wildlife and Plants: Endangered Status for 11 Plant Species from the Koolau Mountain Range, Island of Oahu, HI." *Federal Register* 59 (59): 14482-14492.

Haha

Cyanea dunbarii

Status	Endangered
Listed	October 10, 1996
Family	Campanulaceae (Bellflower)
Description	Branched shrub without prickles; bears white and pale lilac flowers.
Habitat	Mesic to wet forest.
Threats	Competition with alien plants.
Range	Hawaii

Haha *(Cyanea dunbarii)*, photograph by Steve Perlman. Reproduced by permission.

Description

Cyanea dunbarii, a member of the bellflower family (Campanulaceae), is a branched shrub 4.9-6.6 ft (1.5-2.0 m) tall. The oval to broadly elliptic leaves are 3.9-8.7 in (9.9-22.1 cm) long and 2.4-5.5 in (6.1-14.0 cm) wide, with irregularly lobed or cleft margins. The flowers are arranged in groupings of six to eight on a stalk that is 1.2-2.8 in (3.1-7.1 cm) long. The white corolla, tinged or striped with pale lilac, is 1.2-1.5 in (3.1-3.8 cm) long. The corolla is slightly curved, with spreading lobes three-fourths as long as the tube. This species is distinguished from others in this endemic Hawaiian genus by the lack of prickles on the stems and the irregularly lobed and cleft leaf margins.

C. dunbarii was observed in flower, with immature fruit, in September.

Habitat

C. dunbarii is found along a stream in mesic to wet *Dicranopteris linearis* (uluhe)—*Metrosideros polymorpha* ('ohi'a) forest on moderate to steep slopes. Associated species include *Perrottetia sandwicensis* (olomea), *Pipturus albidus* (mamaki), *Clermontia kakeana* (haha), *Cheirodendron trigynum* ('olapa), and *Freycinetia arborea* ('ie'ie).

Distribution

C. dunbarii was collected in 1918 at Waihanau Valley and Waialae and was not observed again until 1992 at which time it was found in Mokomoko Gulch. This population had approximately 35-40 mature plants in 1998, 15-20 of which occurred in the Mokomoko streambed and the remaining 20 of which occurred in the next small gulch to the north. All individuals grow at an elevation of 2,250 ft (686 m) on state-owned land within Molokai Forest Reserve.

Threats

The major threat to *C. dunbarii* is competition with the alien plants thimbleberry, *Commelina diffusa*, ginger, and air plant. An almost equally pressing threat to this small remaining population is the risk of sudden extinction from natural events like flooding and landslides or slower extinction through reduced reproductive vigor. Rats are a potential threat since they are known to be in the area and eat stems and fruits of other species of *Cyanea*. Axis deer and pigs are potential threats to this species, since they are known to occur in areas adjacent to the only known population. Axis deer, observed in areas south of the only known population of *C. dunbarii*, now pose a potential threat to this species. If not controlled, habitat degradation by pigs may also become a significant problem to this population. Slugs feed preferentially on plants with fleshy leaves, stems, and fruits, and they are a primary threat to *C. glabra* and *C. kunthiana*.

Collection of even a few whole *C. dunbarii* plants or their reproductive parts could threaten the survival of this species because of its small numbers in one population. Some of the individuals are close to trails or roads and are therefore easily accessible to collectors.

Conservation and Recovery

Cuttings of this species have been collected and propagated by the Lyon Arboretum and the National Tropical Botanical Garden.

Contacts

U. S. Fish and Wildlife Service
Regional Office, Division of Endangered Species
Eastside Federal Complex
911 N. E. 11th Ave.
Portland, Oregon 97232-4181
Telephone: (503) 231-6121
http://pacific.fws.gov/

Senior Resident Agent Office
U.S. Fish and Wildlife Service
300 Ala Moana Boulevard, Room 7-235
P.O. Box 50223
Honolulu, Hawaii 96850-5000
Telephone: (808) 541-2681
Fax: (808) 541-3062

Reference

U.S. Fish and Wildlife Service. 1988. "Molokai II: Addendum to the Recovery Plan for the Molokai Plant Cluster." U.S. Fish and Wildlife Service, Portland.

Haha

Cyanea glabra

Status	Endangered
Listed	September 3, 1999
Family	Campanulaceae (Bellflower)
Description	A tropical shrub.
Habitat	Native tropical forest.
Threats	Habitat destruction, introduced mammalian herbivores, non-native slugs, invasive alien plants.
Range	Hawaii

Description

The haha is a branched shrub. The leaves of juvenile plants are deeply lobed, while those of adult plants are more entire and elliptical. Adult leaves are 9-14 in (23-36 cm) long and 3-5 in (7-12 cm) wide. The upper surface of the leaves is green and hairless, while the lower surface is pale green and hairless to sparsely hairy. The margins of mature leaves are thickened and shallowly toothed to irregularly lobed. The flowers are borne in an inflorescence of six to eight, supported by a peduncle (inflorescence stalk) 0.8-2.2 in (20-55 mm) long. The hypanthium is 0.3-0.4 in long (7-10 mm), up to 0.2 in (5 mm) wide, and widest at the top. The corolla (petals) is white, often with a pale lilac tinge, and is 2-2.4 in (50-60 mm) long and about 0.3 in (8 mm) wide. The tube of the corolla is curved, and the lobes are spreading, up to one-third times as long as the tube, and covered by small, sharp projections. The ripe berries are 0.4-0.6 in (10-15 mm) long, elliptical, and colored yellowish orange. The calyx (sepals) persists on the berry. This species is differentiated from others in this endemic Hawaiian genus by the size of its flowers and the deeply lobed juvenile leaves.

Habitat

The habitat of the haha is wet tropical forest dominated by koa (*Acacia koa*) and/or o'hia (*Metrosideros polymorpha*). It occurs at elevations between 3,200 and 4,400 ft (975 and 1,340 m).

Distribution

The haha is a locally evolved, or endemic species that is only known from the island of Maui, Hawaii. The Hawaiian archipelago has an extremely large fraction of endemic species; about 89% of the indigenous flowering plants occur nowhere else in the world. The haha is historically known from two locations on West Maui and five on Haleakala, East Maui.

Threats

The primary threat to the haha is destructive herbivory by introduced species of slugs. It is also affected by habitat degradation and destruction by feral pigs, flooding, and competition with several introduced species of invasive plants, including the shrub strawberry guava (*Psidium cattleianum*), the Koster's curse (*Clidemia hirta*), and other non-native plants. Introduced rats are also probably herbivores of this plant, as may be the non-native two-spotted leafhopper (*Saphonia rufofascia*). Because of its limited range and small population size, the haha is also potentially threatened by catastrophic events of weather, wildfire, or other disturbances. There are only two surviving populations of the haha. One population consists of only 12 individuals in Kauaula Gulch on West Maui on privately owned land, and another contains a scattered population of about 200 individuals in Kipahulu Valley, within Haleakala National Park.

Conservation and Recovery

The major surviving population of the haha is located within Haleakala National Park, which is managed to conserve its indigenous biodiversity. The other, smaller population is on private land, and is potentially at risk from disturbance or other human actions. Conservation of the endangered haha requires that all of its remaining critical habitat be protected and managed to reduce the threats posed by non-native herbivores and competitors. The populations of the haha should be monitored against further change, and research undertaken to develop a better understanding of degrading influences faced by the endangered plant, and ways of mitigating those effects.

Contacts

U. S. Fish and Wildlife Service
Regional Office, Division of Endangered Species

Eastside Federal Complex
911 N. E. 11th Ave.
Portland, Oregon 97232-4181
(503) 231-6121
http://pacific.fws.gov/

U. S. Fish and Wildlife Service, Pacific Islands
Ecoregion, Pacific Islands Fish and Wildlife Office
300 Ala Moana Boulevard, Room 3-122
P. O. Box 50088
Honolulu, Hawaii 96850
Telephone: (808) 541-3441
Fax: (808) 541-3470

Reference

U.S. Fish and Wildlife Service. 3 September 1999. "Endangered and Threatened Wildlife and Plants: Final Endangered Status for 10 Plant Taxa From Maui Nui, Hawaii." *Federal Register* 64 (171): 48307-48324.

Haha

Cyanea grimesiana ssp. grimesiana

Status	Endangered
Listed	October 10, 1996
Family	Campanulaceae (Bellflower)
Description	Shrub that bears purplish or greenish to yellowish-white flowers.
Habitat	Mesic forest often dominated by 'ohi'a or o'hi'a and koa, or on rocky or steep slopes of stream banks.
Threats	Habitat degradation and destruction caused by feral axis deer, goats, and pigs and competition with various alien plants.
Range	Hawaii

Description

Cyanea grimesiana ssp. *grimesiana*, a member of the bellflower family (Campanulaceae), is a shrub 3.3-10.5 ft (1.0-3.2 m) in height. The leaves are pinnately divided, with nine to 12 segments per side. The leaf blades are 10.6-22.9 in (26.9-58.2 cm) long and 5.5-12.6 in (13.9-32.0 cm) wide across the segments. The inflorescence comprises six to 12 flowers. The calyx lobes, 0.4-2.0 in (1.0-5.1 cm) long and 0.2-0.55 in (0.5-1.4 cm) wide, are egg-shaped to lance-shaped and overlap at the base. The petals, purplish or greenish to yellowish white and often suffused or striped with magenta, are 2-3 in (5.1-7.6 cm) long. The orange berries are 0.7-1.2 in (1.8-3.0 cm) long. This species is distinguished from others in this endemic Hawaiian genus by the pinnately lobed leaf margins and the width of the leaf blades. This subspecies is distinguished from the other two subspecies by the shape and size of the calyx lobes, which overlap at the base.

C. grimesiana ssp. *grimesiana* was collected by Charles Gaudichaud-Beaupre in 1819 on Oahu, while he was pharmaceutical botanist on the vessel *Uranie*. Gaudichaud later described this plant and named it for the French navy's head pharmacist. Other published names considered synonymous with *C. grimesiana* ssp. *grimesiana* include *C. grimesiana* var. *lydgatei*, *C. grimesiana* var. *mauiensis*, *C.* *grimesiana* var. *munroi*, and *C. lobata* var. *hamakuae*. The three currently recognized subspecies are the extinct ssp. *cylindrocalyx*, ssp. *grimesiana*, and the federally endangered ssp. *obatae*.

Habitat

C. grimesiana ssp. *grimesiana* is typically found in mesic forest often dominated by 'ohi'a or o'hi'a and koa, or on rocky or steep slopes of stream banks, at elevations between 1,150 and 3,100 ft (351 and 945 m). Associated plant taxa include *Antidesma* sp. (hame), *Bobea* sp. ('ahakea), *Psychotria* sp. (kopiko), *Xylosma* sp. (maua), and various native and alien ferns.

Distribution

C. grimesiana ssp. *grimesiana* had at least 40 historical populations located in the Waianae and Koolau mountains of Oahu, Wailau Valley, and Puu Kahea on Molokai, central and northern Lanai, and scattered locations on Maui. *C. grimesiana* ssp. *grimesiana* is now known from 14 populations on those four islands. In 1997 the total of all statewide populations consisted of less than 50 individuals.

Oahu populations in 2000 were located in the Waianae and Koolau Mountains. The Waianae Mountains populations were as follows: one popu-

Haha *(Cyanea grimesiana)*, photograph by John Obata. Reproduced by permission.

lation of three individuals from Mt. Kaala Natural Area Reserve; two populations of one individual each from North Haleauau Gulch on the federally owned Schofield Barracks Military Reservation and North Kaluaa Gulch on private land; and possibly three populations of an unknown number of individuals from Pahole Natural Area Reserve on state land. The three tentative populations reported from Pahole were not seen since the late 1970s; surveys conducted during 1996-97 proved unsuccessful in relocating them. The Koolau Mountains populations consisted of four individuals in Kului Gulch and three individuals in Waialae Iki-Kapakahi on state and private land.

Molokai has one population of five individuals on Kukuinui Ridge and another population of two individuals within Olokui Natural Area Reserve, both on state land.

On Lanai, one population of an unknown number of individuals at Kaiholena Gulch and one population of two individuals at Waiakeakua occur on private land.

Maui has two populations on private land of an unknown number of individuals at Iao Valley. A population previously reported in lower Kipahulu Valley within Haleakala National Park was determined to be *C. asplenifolia,* based on updated material on flowering.

Threats

The major threats to *C. grimesiana* ssp. *grimesiana* are habitat degradation and destruction caused by feral axis deer, goats, and pigs and competition with various alien plants. Potential overcollection, trampling by hikers, crushing through military activities, and fire threaten the Palikea population on Oahu. The Oahu populations are also threatened by landslides. Additionally, rats are a potential threat since they are known to eat the fruits and girdle the stems of species in the bellflower family.

Two populations of *C. grimesiana* ssp. *grimesiana* on Oahu are threatened by pigs, and goats threaten the Kukuinui Ridge population on Molokai. Activities of axis deer threaten one of the two popula-tions of *C. grimesiana* ssp. *grimesiana* on Lanai.

Cattle, deer, pig, and goat predation is a possible threat to this species, whose fleshy fruit is also a po-tential food source for hungry rats that occur in ar-eas where this plant grows.

Collecting for scientific or horticultural purposes and visits by individuals avid to see rare plants are potential threats to *C. grimesiana* ssp. *grimesiana,* of which populations are well known and near trails and roads.

Military training exercises, troop ground ma-neuvers, and helicopter landing and drop-off activ-ities on Oahu could trample and flatten individuals of this species that occur on land leased or owned by the Army.

Lantana poses a threat on Kauai to two popula-tions of *C. grimesiana* ssp. *grimesiana.* Strawberry guava, a major invader of forests in the Waianae and Koolau Mountains of Oahu, poses an immedi-ate threat to one population of *C. grimesiana* there. Strawberry guava threatens one of Lanai's popula-tions of this plant. One of the two populations of *C. grimesiana* ssp. *grimesiana* on Lanai is threatened by thimbleberry. Koster's curse poses a serious threat to two populations of this endangered plant in the Waianae Mountains of Oahu and threatens one of the two populations on Molokai.

Erosion, landslides, and rockslides due to natural weathering are particular threats to the Oahu pop-ulations of this plant.

Fire also poses a potential threat to populations of *C. grimesiana* ssp. *grimesiana.*

Conservation and Recovery

The U.S. Army Garrison's five-year Ecosystem Management Plan to protect endangered species, prevent range fires, and minimize soil erosion is ex-pected to enhance conservation of the *C. grimesiana* ssp. *grimesiana* plants growing on the Schofield Barracks Military Reservation.

A long-range management plan has also been drafted for Honouliuli Preserve. It includes actions for alien plant management, ungulate control, fire control, small mammal control, rare species recov-ery, and native habitat restoration. These actions are expected to benefit *C. grimesiana* ssp. *grimesiana* within the preserve.

C. grimesiana ssp. *grimesiana* has been successfully propagated at Lyon Arboretum's micropropagation laboratory and at Division of Forests and Wildlife's Pahole Plant Nursery. More than 1,000 seeds were in storage at the National Tropical Botanic Gardens in 1997.

Contact

U. S. Fish and Wildlife Service
Regional Office, Division of Endangered Species
Eastside Federal Complex
911 N. E. 11th Ave.
Portland, Oregon 97232-4181
Telephone: (503) 231-6121
http://pacific.fws.gov/

Reference

U. S. Fish and Wildlife Service. 10 October 1996. "De-termination of Endangered or Threatened Status for Fourteen Plant Taxa from the Hawaiian Is-lands." *Federal Register* 61 (198): 53108-53124.

Haha

Cyanea grimesiana ssp. *obatae*

Robert J. Gustafson

Status	Endangered
Listed	June 27, 1994
Family	Campanulaceae (Bellflower)
Description	Unbranched shrub with small pickles with petals that are purplish or greenish and often striped with magenta.
Habitat	Steep, moist, shaded slopes in diverse mesic to wet forests.
Threats	Competition from alien plants; habitat destruction by feral pigs; limited numbers.
Range	Hawaii

Description

Cyanea grimesiana ssp. *obatae* is a shrub in the bellflower family, usually unbranched, that grows to a height of 3.3-10.5 ft (1.0-3.2 m). Its leaves, 10.5-23 in (0.3-0.6 m) long by 5.5-12.5 in (14.0-31.8 cm) wide, are deeply cut into nine to 12 lobes per side. The plant usually has small pickles on its stem and leaves. Clusters of six to 12 stalked flowers arise from the leaf axils. Sepals are fused to the ovary, forming a cup 0.3-0.6 in (7.6-15.2 mm) long with small, narrow, triangular lobes at the tips. The petals are purplish or greenish to yellow-white, often washed or striped with magenta, and are about 2-3 in (5.1-7.6 cm) long by 0.2-0.4 in (5.1-10.2 mm) wide. Fruits are elliptical orange berries 0.7-1.2 in (1.8-3.0 cm) long. This species is distinguished from the other two subspecies by its short, narrow calyx lobes that are not fused or overlapping. *C. grimesiana* ssp. *obatae* flowers and fruits year round, depending on rainfall.

Habitat

C. grimesiana ssp. *obatae* typically grows on steep, moist, shaded slopes in diverse mesic to wet forests at an elevation of 1,800-2,200 ft (549-671 m). Associated plants include mamaki, papala kepau, kukui, and various ferns.

Distribution

Historically, *C. grimesiana* ssp. *obatae* was known in the southern Waianae Mountains from Puu Hapapa to Kaaikukai, a distance of about 4 mi (6.4 km).

The three extant populations, 4 mi (6.4 km) apart on Federal and private land, contained 13 individuals in 1997—Kaluaa had four plants, Ekahanui had eight, and North Palawai had one.

Threats

The major threats to *C. grimesiana* ssp. *obatae* are competition from alien plants such as Koster's

Haha *(Cyanea grimesiana)*, photograph by A. Kay Kepler. Reproduced by permission.

curse, kukui, and Christmasberry; habitat degradation by feral pigs; predation of seeds or fruits by introduced slugs and rats; damage to flowers and stems of plants by rats; damage by the two-spotted leafhopper; risk of extinction due to naturally occurring events; and reduced reproductive vigor due to the small number of living individuals.

Conservation and Recovery

The Nature Conservancy of Hawaii fenced the population of eight plants in Ekahanui Gulch and is controlling alien weeds and monitoring this population. Field crews count and map plants and gather basic phenological data.

The Division of Forestry and Wildlife is growing 19 individuals of *C. grimesiana* ssp. *obatae* at the mid-

elevation Nike missile site in the Walanae Mountains, with 10 individuals ready for planting in The Nature Conservancy of Hawaii preserve at Honouliuli. This species is also being successfully propagated at the National Tropical Botanical Garden and the Lyon Arboretum.

The only population that is fenced is Ekahanui Gulch. Efforts should be made to fence and manage the remaining two extant populations at Kaluaa and North Palawai. Subsequent control or removal of pigs from these areas will alleviate their impact on native ecosystems. A commitment should be developed for long-term stewardship and conservation of these areas once they have been enclosed. Specific efforts should be made to immediately weed and protect all extant populations.

The three populations of *C. grimesiana* ssp. *obatae* on Oahu are seriously threatened by rat predation. A rat control plan should be developed and implemented. This should include the use of the currently approved diphacinone bait blocks and ultimately a more broad-scale method such as aerial dispersal of rodenticide.

Contacts

U. S. Fish and Wildlife Service
Regional Office, Division of Endangered Species
Eastside Federal Complex
911 N. E. 11th Ave.
Portland, Oregon 97232-4181
Telephone: (503) 231-6121
http://pacific.fws.gov/

Senior Resident Agent Office
U.S. Fish and Wildlife Service
300 Ala Moana Boulevard, Room 7-235
P.O. Box 50223
Honolulu, Hawaii 96850-5000
Telephone: (808) 541-2681
Fax: (808) 541-3062

Reference

U.S. Fish and Wildlife Service. 27 June 1994. "Endangered and Threatened Wildlife and Plants: Endangered Status for Three Plants from the Waianae Mountains, Island of Oahu, HI." *Federal Register* 59 (122): 32932-32938.

Haha

Cyanea hamatiflora ssp. *carlsonii*

Status	Endangered
Listed	March 4, 1994
Family	Campanulaceae (Bellflower)
Description	Palm-like tree with alternate, stalkless leaves, clusters of five to 10 magenta flowers, and purplish red berries.
Habitat	'Ohi'a-dominated montane wet forests at elevations between 4,000-5,700 ft (1.2-1.7 km).
Threats	Competition from alien plants; habitat destruction by cattle; limited numbers.
Range	Hawaii

Haha *(Cyanea hamatiflora)*, photograph. National Tropical Botanical Garden. Reproduced by permission.

Description

This haha, *Cyanea hamatiflora* ssp. *carlsonii*, a palmlike tree, grows 9.8-26 ft (3.0-7.9 m) tall and has alternate, stalkless leaves 20-31 in (50.8-78.7 cm) long and 3.0-5.5 in (7.6-14.0 cm) wide. Clusters of five to 10 flowers have a main stalk 0.6-1.2 in (1.5-3.0 cm) long; each flower has a stalk 0.2-0.5 in (0.5-1.3 cm) long. The hypanthium is topped with five small, narrow calyx lobes. The magenta petals are fused into a one-lipped tube 2.3-3.1 in (5.8-7.9 cm) long and 0.2-0.4 in (0.5-1.0 cm) wide, with five downcurved lobes. The purplish red berries are topped by the persistent calyx lobes. This subspecies is distinguished from *C. hamatiflora* ssp. *hamatiflora*, the only other subspecies, by its long flower stalks and larger calyx lobes. The species differs from others in the genus by its growth habit, its stalkless leaves, the number of flowers in each cluster, and the size and shape of the corolla and calyx. This taxon was observed in flower during December of 1980 and August of 1995. Seeds were collected by Hawaii Division of Forestry and Wildlife (DOFAW) in October of 1991 and November of 1995. No other life history information is currently available.

Habitat

This species typically grows in 'ohi'a-dominated montane wet forests at elevations between 4,000 and 5,700 ft (1,219 and 1,737 m). Associated species include kawa'u, pilo, and naio.

Distribution

This subspecies is known only to have occurred at two sites on the island of Hawaii, on the western slope of Hualalai and the southwestern slope of Mauna Loa.

The two extant populations, located on private and state land at Honuaulu Forest Reserve and Keokea, are about 28 mi (87 km) apart and contain approximately 14 individuals. Forty-five individuals were outplanted on the Honuaulu Forest Reserve.

Threats

Alien plant invasion represents a serious threat to the long-term survival of *C. hamatiflora* ssp. *carlsonii. Banana poka,* an invasive alien weed, negatively impacts *C. hamatiflora* by competing for nutrients, water, and light. Grazing and trampling by domestic and escaped cattle and rooting by pigs degrade the habitat and open sites conducive for alien plant establishment. Rats and alien birds may eat the juicy fruits, reducing the potential numbers of successive individuals. The small remaining numbers of individuals and their limited and scattered distribution are serious threats because a single natural or human-induced event may have catastrophic effects on the few surviving plants. Seeds collected by DO-FAW in 1991 had little or no insect damage, but seeds collected in 1995 were heavily damaged by an undetermined species of caterpillar. Reproductive vigor may be depressed by a limited gene pool.

Conservation and Recovery

The National Tropical Botanical Garden has propagated this species. Seeds planted at Volcano Rare Plant Facility have not germinated, and seeds acquired by Lyon Arboretum from storage were not viable. Attempts are being made to obtain new seed. In 1993, 22-27 individuals were planted within two exclosures at Honuaulu Forest Reserve. Currently, 21 plants remain alive in the first and 23 in the second. One individual was planted outside the exclosures and is surviving. Three unhealthy plants were planted near Honomalino, but all died. Of several individuals planted at Puu Waawaa, six have survived.

Current populations need to be protected from ungulates, and banana poka and other alien species controlled, to the extent possible, within the taxon's habitat. Propagation and outplanting efforts should be encouraged and continued.

Contacts

U. S. Fish and Wildlife Service
Regional Office, Division of Endangered Species
Eastside Federal Complex
911 N. E. 11th Ave.
Portland, Oregon 97232-4181
Telephone: (503) 231-6121
http://pacific.fws.gov/

Senior Resident Agent Office
U.S. Fish and Wildlife Service
300 Ala Moana Boulevard, Room 7-235
P.O. Box 50223
Honolulu, Hawaii 96850-5000
Telephone: (808) 541-2681
Fax: (808) 541-3062

Reference

U.S. Fish and Wildlife Service. 4 March 1994. "Endangered and Threatened Wildlife and Plant; Determination of Endangered or Threatened Status for 21 Plants from the Island of Hawaii, State of Hawaii." *Federal Register* 59 (43): 10305-10325.

Haha

Cyanea hamatiflora ssp. *hamatiflora*

Status	Endangered
Listed	September 3, 1999
Family	Campanulaceae (Bellflower)
Description	A tropical shrub or small tree.
Habitat	Native tropical wet montane forest.
Threats	Habitat destruction, introduced mammalian herbivores, non-native slugs, and invasive alien plants.
Range	Hawaii

Cyanea hamatiflora, © Bob Butterfield.

Description

The haha is a is a palm-like shrub or small tree that grows as tall as 10-26 ft (3-8 m). Its latex, which is visible when twigs are broken, is tan in color. The leaves are elliptical, with the broadest point near the tip, or they may be narrowly oblong. The leaf blades are 20-30 in (50-80 cm) long, 3-5.5 in (8-14 cm) wide, and have no petiole. The upper surface of the leaf is sparsely hairy to hairless, and the lower surface is hairy along the midrib and veins. The leaf margins are minutely round-toothed. The 5-10 flowered inflorescence is supported by a peduncle (stalk) 0.6-1.2 in (15-30 mm) long. The hypanthium is widest at the top, 0.5-1.2 in (12-30 mm) long, and 0.2-0.5 in (6-12 mm) wide. The corolla is magenta in color, 2-3 in (60-80 mm) long, 0.2-0.4 in (6-11 mm) wide, and hairless. The tube of the corolla is slightly curved, with lobes up to 0.5 times as long as the tube. The corolla lobes all curve downward, making the flower appear one-lipped. The anthers (pollen-bearing structures) are hairless except for the lower two, which have apical tufts of white hair. The ripe fruit is a purplish red berry, 1.2-1.8 in (30-45 mm) long, and 0.8-1.1 in (20-27 mm) wide. The berry is crowned by persistent calyx lobes. This subspecies is differentiated from *Cyanea hamatiflora carlsonii* by its longer calyx lobes and shorter individual flower stalks, and from others in this endemic Hawaiian genus by having fewer flowers per inflorescence and narrower leaves.

Habitat

Typical habitat of the haha is tropical montane wet forest dominated by The o'hia (*Metrosideros polymorpha*). It occurs over an altitudinal range of 3,200-4,920 ft (975-1,500 m).

Distribution

The haha is a locally evolved, or endemic species that is only known from the island of Maui, Hawaii. The Hawaiian archipelago has an extremely large fraction of endemic species; about 89% of the indigenous flowering plants occur nowhere else in the world. The haha was historically known from eight locations on the windward (northeastern) side of Haleakala, on Maui, stretching from Puu o Kakae to Manawainui.

Threats

The major threats to the haha are habitat degradation and destruction caused by feral pigs, landslides, and competition with the alien plant, sticky snakeroot (*Ageratina adenophora*). Introduced rats and slugs are also potential threats, since other Hawaiian members of this family are known to be eaten by these herbivores. Because of its limited range and small population size, the haha is also potentially threatened by catastrophic events of weather, wildfire, or other disturbances. The haha is now known from only two areas. There are five or six populations totaling 50-100 individuals in Kipahulu Valley within Haleakala National Park, and five or six populations totaling 20-25 widely scattered individuals in the Waikamoi-Koolau Gap area on privately owned land.

Conservation and Recovery

One of the surviving population of the haha is located within Haleakala National Park, which is managed to conserve its indigenous biodiversity. The other, smaller population is on private land, and is potentially at risk from disturbance or other human actions. Conservation of the endangered haha requires that all of its remaining critical habitat be protected and managed to reduce the threats posed by non-native herbivores and competitors. The populations of the haha should be monitored against further change, and research undertaken to develop a better understanding of degrading influences faced by the endangered plant, and ways of mitigating those effects.

Contacts

U. S. Fish and Wildlife Service
Regional Office, Division of Endangered Species
Eastside Federal Complex
911 N. E. 11th Ave.
Portland, Oregon 97232-4181
(503) 231-6121
http://pacific.fws.gov/

U. S. Fish and Wildlife Service
Pacific Islands Ecoregion, Pacific Islands Fish and Wildlife Office
300 Ala Moana Boulevard, Room 3-122
P. O. Box 50088
Honolulu, Hawaii 96850
Telephone: (808) 541-3441
Fax: (808) 541-3470

Reference

U. S. Fish and Wildlife Service. 3 September 1999. "Endangered and Threatened Wildlife and Plants: Final Endangered Status for 10 Plant Taxa From Maui Nui, Hawaii." *Federal Register* 64 (171): 48307-48324.

Haha

Cyanea humboldtiana

Status	Endangered
Listed	October 10, 1996
Family	Campanulaceae (Bellflower)
Description	Leaf edges are hardened and have shallow, ascending rounded teeth; five to 12 flowers are arranged on a hairy, downward bending flowering stalk; berries are pale orange.
Habitats	Wet 'ohi'a-uluhe shrubland.
Threats	Habitat degradation by feral pigs, predation by rats; competition from alien plants; human disturbance.
Range	Hawaii

Haha *(Cyanea humboldtiana)*, photograph by Robert J. Gustafson. Reproduced by permission.

Description

Cyanea humboldtiana, a member of the bellflower family, is an unbranched shrub with woody stems 3.2-6.6 ft (1-2 m) tall. The leaves are inversely egg-shaped to broadly elliptic, 7-18 in (17.8-45.7 cm) long and 2.8-6.3 in (7.1-16.0 cm) wide. The leaf edges are hardened and have shallow, ascending rounded teeth. Five to 12 flowers are arranged on a hairy flowering stalk that is downward bending and 3-10 in (7.6-25 cm) long. The dark magenta or white petals are 2.4-3 in (6.1-7.6 cm) long and hairy. The pale orange yellow berries are elliptic to inversely egg-shaped. This species differs from others in this endemic Hawaiian genus by the downward bending flowering stalk and the length of the flowering stalk.

Charles Gaudichaud-Beaupre collected a new lobelioid on Oahu on his third trip to Hawaii while a botanist on the vessel *La Bonite.* He later described the lobelioid and named it *Rollandia humboldtiana.* Other published names considered synonymous with *R. humboldtiana* include *Delissea racemosa, R. humboldtiana forma albida, R. pedunculosa,* and *R. racemosa.* T. G. Lammers, Thomas Givnish, and Kenneth Sytsma merged the endemic Hawaiian genera, *Cyanea* and *Rollandia,* under the former name, publishing the new combination, *C. humboldtiana.* The specific epithet honors the German naturalist and explorer, Baron Alexander von Humboldt.

Habitat

This species is usually found in wet 'ohi'a-uluhe shrubland from 1,800-3,150 ft (549-960 m) in elevation. Associated native plant taxa include ferns, alani, 'uki, kawa'u, and naupaka kuahiwi.

Distribution

C. humboldtiana was known historically from 17 populations in the central portion to the southern end of the Koolau Mountains of Oahu. The three current populations occur on private, state, and federal land on the Omega U.S. Coast Guard Station. There were 125-225 total plants known from these locations in 1997—20 individuals at Konahuanui summit, 100-200 at Moanalua-Kaneohe summit, and less than five at Lulumahu Gulch.

Threats

Habitat degradation and destruction by feral pigs, potential predation by rats, competition with the alien plant Koster's curse, and a risk of extinction from naturally occurring events or through reduced reproductive vigor in very small populations are the major threats to *C. humboldtiana.* The Konahuanui summit population also is threatened by trampling by hikers.

C. humboldtiana is potentially threatened by feral pig predation because the species is not known to be unpalatable to pigs and they favor plants from the bellflower family for food. It is possible that rats eat the fruit of *C. humboldtiana,* a plant with fleshy stems and fruit that grows in areas where rats occur. The noxious shrub Koster's curse is a threat to this endangered species. Overcollection for scientific or horticultural purposes and excessive visits by individuals interested in seeing rare plants in their natural settings could seriously damage *C. humboldtiana,* whose populations are close to trails and roads, thus giving easy access to potential collectors.

C. humboldtiana has populations in recreational areas, near trails, and close to roads, making it very vulnerable to human disturbances.

Conservation and Recovery

This species is being propagated at the Lyon Arboretum.

Contact

U. S. Fish and Wildlife Service
Regional Office, Division of Endangered Species
Eastside Federal Complex
911 N. E. 11th Ave.
Portland, Oregon 97232-4181
Telephone: (503) 231-6121
http://pacific.fws.gov/

Reference

U.S. Fish and Wildlife Service. 1998. "Recovery Plan for Oahu Plants." U.S. Fish and Wildlife Service, Portland.

Haha

Cyanea koolauensis

Status	Endangered
Listed	October 10, 1996
Family	Campanulaceae (Bellflower)
Description	Leaves are linear to narrowly elliptic with a whitish underside.
Habitat	Slopes and ridge crests in wet 'ohi'a-uluhe forest or shrubland.
Threats	Predation by pigs and rats; competition from alien plants; military activities.
Range	Hawaii

Description

Cyanea koolauensis is an unbranched shrub in the bellflower family with woody stems that grow 3.5-5 ft (106.7-152.4 cm) tall. The leaves are linear to narrowly elliptic with a whitish underside, 6.3-14.2 in (16.0-36.0 cm) long and 0.6-1.6 in (1.5-4.0 cm) wide. The leaf edges are hardened with shallow, ascending rounded teeth; leaf stalks are 0.6-1.8 in (1.5-4.6 cm) long. The flowering stalks, 0.6-1.6 in (1.5-4.0 cm) long, are three to six flowered. The hypanthium (basal portion of the flower) is 0.2-0.5 in (0.5-1.3 cm) long. The calyx lobes are fused into a sheath 0.08-0.3 in (2.0-7.6 mm) long. The dark magenta petals are 2.0-3.5 in (5.1-8.9 cm) long. The fruit is a round berry. *C. koolauensis* is distinguished from others in this endemic Hawaiian genus by the leaf shape and width, the whitish green lower leaf surface and, the lengths of the leaf stalks, calyx lobes, and hypanthium. *C. koolauensis* has been observed in flower and fruit during the months of May through August.

C. koolauensis was first described by Wilhelm Hillebrand in 1888 as *Rollandia longiflora* var. *angustifolia* from a specimen he collected on Oahu. Joseph Rock elevated the variety to full species status in 1918 as *Rollandia angustifolia*. In 1993, T. G. Lammers and others published the new name *C. koolauensis* to replace *Rollandia angustifolia* when they merged *Cyanea* and *Rollandia,* as the name *Cyanea angustifolia* had already been used.

Habitat

C. koolauensis usually is found on slopes and ridge crests in wet 'ohi'a-uluhe forest or shrubland at elevations from 1,700-2,660 ft (518-811 m). Associated plant taxa include alani, *Antidesma* sp. (hame), *Diplopterygium pinnatum, Psychotria* sp. (kopiko), and *Scaevola* sp. (naupaka).

Distribution

C. koolauensis was known historically from about 30 populations scattered throughout the Koolau Mountains on Oahu. In 1997, approximately 22 populations of less than 80 plants were known from the Walmea-Malaekahana Ridge to Hawaii Loa Ridge in the Koolau Mountains. These populations occur on City and County of Honolulu land, state land, and private land, including land leased to the Department of Defense for the Kahulm and Kawailoa Training Areas. Only two populations have as at least 10 individuals.

Threats

C. koolauensis is threatened by habitat destruction by feral pigs, potential impacts from military activities, potential predation by rats, competition with the aggressive alien plants Koster's curse and strawberry guava, trampling by hikers, overcollection, and risk of extinction from naturally occurring events or through reduced reproductive vigor due to the small number of remaining individuals.

C. koolauensis is potentially threatened by feral pig predation because the species is not known to be unpalatable to pigs, and they favor plants from the bellflower family for food.

It is possible that rats eat the fruit of *C. koolauensis,* a plant with fleshy stems and fruit that grows in areas where rats occur.

The noxious shrub Koster's curse is a threat to *C. koolauensis,* as are the dense stands of strawberry guava.

Overcollection for scientific or horticultural purposes and excessive visits by individuals interested in seeing rare plants in their natural settings could seriously damage *C. koolauensis,* whose populations are close to trails and roads, thus giving easy access to potential collectors.

Populations of *C. koolauensis* that occur on land leased and owned by the U. S. Army face the threat of being damaged through military activity, either by troops in training maneuvers or by the construction, maintenance, and utilization of helicopter drop-off and landing sites.

C. koolauensis has populations in recreational areas, near trails, and close to roads, making it very vulnerable to human disturbance.

Conservation and Recovery

Enclosures should be constructed around the known populations of *C. koolauensis* to reduce impacts from feral pigs. Subsequent control or removal of pigs from these areas will alleviate their impact on native ecosystems. Additionally, specific efforts should be made to immediately fence off and systematically weed within those populations at Kawailoa Training Area, Poamoho-Helemano Ridge, Hawaiiloa Ridge, and Halawa Ridge Trail that have only a few remaining individuals. In areas where fencing is not feasible, snaring as a means of ungulate control should be implemented. A commitment should be developed for long-term stewardship and conservation of these areas once they have been enclosed.

To prevent extinction of *C. koolauensis,* cultivated propagation should be initiated. Propagation material should be collected immediately from those populations mentioned above that have only have a few remaining individuals.

The threat of rat predation needs to be determined for *C. koolauensis.* If rats are deemed a significant threat, a management plan to control rats should be developed and implemented. This should include the use of the currently approved diphacinone bait blocks and ultimately a more broad-scale method such as aerial dispersal of rodenticide.

Contact

U. S. Fish and Wildlife Service
Regional Office, Division of Endangered Species
Eastside Federal Complex
911 N. E. 11th Ave.
Portland, Oregon 97232-4181
Telephone: (503) 231-6121
http://pacific.fws.gov/

Reference

U.S. Fish and Wildlife Service. 1998. "Recovery Plan for Oahu Plants." U.S. Fish and Wildlife Service, Portland.

Haha

Cyanea lobata

Status	Endangered
Listed	May 15, 1992
Family	Campanulaceae (Bellflower)
Description	Sparsely branched shrub with irregularly lobed leaves and a cluster of flowers having greenish white or purplish petals fused into a curved tube.
Habitat	Steep stream banks in mesic lowland forests.
Threats	Habitat destruction by feral animals; competing plant species.
Range	Hawaii

Joseph E. Rock, Type Specimen in Cornell Herbarium

Description

Cyanea lobata, a shrub in the bellflower family (Campanulaceae) that grows to 4.3-7.5 ft (1.3-2.3 m) in height, has few branches and may be smooth or occasionally rough due to small projections on the stems and lower leaf surfaces. The leaves are 12-20 in (30.5-50.8 cm) long and 4-6 in (10.2-15.2 cm) wide, with 12-25 irregular lobes on each side of the leaf. The flowers of *C. lobata* cluster in groups of five to 12. These flowers have greenish white or purplish petals fused into a curved tube 2.4-2.8 in (6.1-7.1 cm) long and 0.2-0.4 in (0.5-1.0 cm) wide. The yellow berries are spherical.

This species can be relatively long-lived, even though it is a low, soft-wooded shrub. The sole individual of this species known from Lanai was discovered as an adult in 1919 and was still living in 1934.

C. lobata is known to flower from August to February, even in plants as small as 19.7 in (50.0 cm) in height.

Habitat

This species typically grows on steep stream banks in mesic lowland forests at an elevation of

1,800-3,000 ft (549-914 m). The lowland mesic shrub-land and forest habitats on West Maui and other Hawaiian islands occurs mainly at elevations between 100-5,300 ft (305-1,615 m) in areas topographically unsuitable for agriculture. Annual precipitation ranges from less than 40-150 in (101-381 cm). The diverse substrate ranges from shallow rocky soils on steep slopes to deep soils in gulches and erosional plains.

Distribution

Historically, *C. lobata* was known from Lanai and West Maui. *C. lobata* (formerly *C. baldwinii*) was known on Lanai from the single plant referenced above. Although Munro collected a number of specimens of this species, all were from a single plant located at approximately 3,000 ft (914.4 m) elevation at the extreme head of Hookio Gulch, only some 400 ft (121.9 m) below the island's summit on Lanaihale. Despite intensive fieldwork on Lanai in search of this species from 1919 to 1934, Munro found no other individuals of this plant. Munro propagated material of the single known individual, outplanting individuals in the mountains of Lanai at Lanaihale and Waikeakua and in the garden at his residence on Mount Tantalus, Oahu. The original plant and all outplantings of *C. baldwini* on Lanai had perished within 10 years after Munro's exertions. This species has not been collected since on that island.

Wilhelm Hillebrand collected this species on West Maui in the 1870s, where he found *C. lobata* to be distributed in the gulches of Kaanapali, Honokahau, Wailuku. No other collections were made on West Maui for more than a century. *C. lobata* was rediscovered on West Maui in 1982 at 2,000 ft (609.6 m) elevation in Waikapu valley on privately owned land. The single known plant of this species was destroyed in 1990 by a landslide triggered by heavy rains. Based on its fairly extensive historical distribution and the lack of adequate surveys due to the inaccessibility of steep slopes in the West Maui mountains, there is a good chance that *C. lobata* may still be extant.

Threats

Habitat degradation caused by the browsing and trampling of wild, feral, and domestic animals is believed to be the primary cause of the decline of this plant. The next most important threat to the species has been invasive alien plants that have outcompeted it for space, light, water, and nutrients. Fire continues to be a serious threat to any individuals that might survive. The fundamental fact of a very limited distribution is itself a serious threat to the survival of *C. lobata*.

Conservation and Recovery

C. lobata was propagated by Munro in the past, but it is not currently being propagated at any of the collections surveyed by Loyal Mehrhoff.

The best chance for rediscovery of this species is in the mountains of West Maui. Habitat on Lanai is extremely limited. Searches should start in but not be limited to Waikapu valley, where the species was last seen in 1982. The upper Kauaula valley in the western part of West Maui is another area with suitable habitat for this species. The vegetation of steep walls in deep valleys of windward West Maui is largely intact, with little alien plant invasion. There is a very good chance that this species occurs on steep walls of one or more valleys of West Maui, in sites inaccessible by normal means.

West Maui has a number of pig-free reserves that would be good sites for new populations.

Contacts

U. S. Fish and Wildlife Service
Regional Office, Division of Endangered Species
Eastside Federal Complex
911 N. E. 11th Ave.
Portland, Oregon 97232-4181
Telephone: (503) 231-6121
http://pacific.fws.gov/

Pacific Islands Ecological Services Field Office
Room 6307, 300 Ala Moana Blvd.
Honolulu, HI 96850
Phone: 808-541-2749
Fax: 808-541-2756

Reference

U.S. Fish and Wildlife Service. 15 May 1992. "Endangered and Threatened Wildlife and Plants; Determination of Endangered or Threatened Status for 15 Plants from the Island of Maui, Hawaii." *Federal Register* 57 (95): 20772-20787.

Haha

Cyanea longiflora

Status	Endangered
Listed	October 10, 1996
Family	Campanulaceae (Bellflower)
Description	Unbranched shrub with woody stems with five to ten flowers per stalk and pear-shaped berries.
Habitat	Steep slopes or ridge crests in mesic koa-'ohi'a forest in the Waianae Mountains or wet 'ohi'a-uluhe forest in the Koolau Mountains.
Threats	Habitat degradation and destruction by feral pigs, potential impacts from military activities, potential predation by rats, competition with alien plants, and fire.
Range	Hawaii

Description

Cyanea longiflora, a member of the bellflower family, is an unbranched shrub with woody stems 3.5-10 ft (1-3 m) long. The leaves are elliptic or inversely lance-shaped, 12-22 in (30.5-55.8 cm) long and 2.4-4.7 in (6-12 cm) wide. Mature leaves have smooth or hardened leaf edges with shallow, ascending, and rounded teeth. The flowering stalks are five- to ten-flowered and 1.2-2.4 in (3-6 cm) long. The calyx lobes are fused into an irregularly toothed sheath 0.08-0.2 in (0.2-0.5 cm) long. The petals, 2.4-3.5 in (6-9 cm) long, and the hairless staminal column are dark magenta. The berries are almost pear-shaped. *C. longiflora* differs from others in this endemic Hawaiian genus by the fused calyx lobes.

C. longiflora was first collected on Oahu, then named *Rollandia longiflora* by Dr. Heinrich Wawra in 1873. Other names considered synonymous with *Rollandia longiflora* are *R. lanceolata* var. *brevipes* and *R. sessilifolia*.

The new combination *C. longiflora* was published in 1993. The specific epithet refers to the long flowers.

Habitat

C. longiflora usually is found on steep slopes or ridge crests in mesic koa-'ohi'a forest in the Wa-ianae Mountains or wet 'ohi'a-uluhe forest in the Koolau Mountains, usually at elevations between 2,030 and 2,560 ft (619 and 780 m). Associated plant taxa in koa-'ohi'a forest include hame, kopiko, uluhe, *Coprosma* sp. (pilo), and *Syzygium* sp. (ha). In wet 'ohi'a-uluhe forest, associated native taxa include 'akia, alani, *Cibotium* sp. (hapu'u), *Dubautia* sp. (na'ena'e), *Hedyotis* sp., and *Pittosporum* sp. (ho'awa).

Distribution

C. longiflora was known historically on Oahu from five populations in the Waianae Mountains and six populations in the Koolau Mountains. Only five populations of this species are extant: Pahole Gulch, Makaha Valley, and Makaha-Waianae Ridge in the Waianae Mountains, as well as Kawainui Drainage and Opaeula Gulch in the Koolau Mountains. These five populations total between 220 and 300 plants. The Pahole Gulch population contains more than 200 individuals, while the remaining two populations contain fewer than ten individuals. These occurrences are found on City and County of Honolulu land, private land leased by the Department of Defense for the Kawailoa Training Area, and state-owned land that includes territory on Pahole National Area Reserve.

Haha *(Cyanea longiflora)*, photograph by Robert J. Gustafson. Reproduced by permission.

Threats

The major threats to *C. longiflora* are habitat degradation and destruction by feral pigs, potential impacts from military activities, potential predation by rats, competition with the alien plants strawberry guava and prickly Florida blackberry in the Waianae Mountains and Koster's curse in the Koolau Mountains, potential fire, and a risk of extinction from naturally occurring events or through the reduced reproductive vigor so prevalent in very small and widely dispersed populations.

C. longiflora is potentially threatened by feral pig predation because the species is not known to be unpalatable to pigs, who favor plants from the bellflower family for food.

It is possible that rats eat the fruit of *C. longiflora*, a plant with fleshy stems and fruit that grows in areas where rats occur.

The noxious shrub Koster's curse and the noxious weed prickly Florida blackberry are significant threats to *C. longiflora*. Dense stands of strawberry guava also threaten this listed plant.

Populations of *C. longiflora* that occur on land leased and owned by the U. S. Army face the threat of being damaged through military activity, either by troops in training maneuvers or by the construction, maintenance, and utilization of helicopter landing and drop-off sites.

Fire is also a potential threat to *C. longiflora*, which occurs in dry or mesic habitats where seasonal conditions exist for the easy spread of fire.

Conservation and Recovery

Fencing and removal of feral pigs in the Pahole drainage was completed by Division of Forestry and Wildlife in July 1997. Weeding of strawberry guava, Christmas berry, and Koster's curse continues in the surrounding areas. Plants in the Pahole drainage have been measured and mapped, and seeds have been collected from plants outside the fence for nursery cultivation and reintroduction into the fenced areas. This species is also being propagated at the Lyon Arboretum and the National Tropical Botanical Garden.

Contact

U. S. Fish and Wildlife Service
Regional Office, Division of Endangered Species
Eastside Federal Complex
911 N. E. 11th Ave.
Portland, Oregon 97232-4181
(503) 231-6121
http://pacific.fws.gov/

Reference

U. S. Fish and Wildlife Service. 1998. "Recovery Plan for Oahu Plants." U. S. Fish and Wildlife Service, Portland, Oregon. 207 pp., plus appendices.

Cyanea macrostegia ssp. gibsonii

No Common Name

Status	Endangered
Listed	September 20, 1991
Family	Campanulaceae (Bellflower)
Description	A tropical tree with attractive, blue flowers.
Habitat	Tropical rainforest near streams.
Threats	Habitat destruction, feeding by non-native mammalian herbivores, and competition with invasive alien plants.
Range	Hawaii

Description

Cyanea macrostegia ssp. *gibsonii*, a member of the bellflower family (Campanulaceae), is a palm-like tree 3.3-23 ft (1-7 m) tall. The leaves are elliptic or oblong, about 7.9-31.5 in (20-80 cm) long and 2.6-7.9 in (6.6-20 cm) wide; the upper surface is usually smooth, while the lower is covered with fine hairs. The leaf stem is often covered with small prickles throughout its length. The inflorescences are horizontal and clustered among the leaves, each bearing five to 15 curved flowers that are blackish-purple externally and white or pale lilac within. The fruit is a yellowish-orange berry about 0.6-1.2 in (1.5-3 cm) long. The following combination of characters separates this species from the other members of the genus on Lanai: calyx lobes are oblong, narrowly oblong, or ovate in shape; and the calyx and corolla are both more than 0.2 in (0.5 cm) wide. *Cyanea macrostegia* ssp. *gibsonii* was seen flowering in the month of July, but the details of its flowering period are not known.

Habitat

The *Cyanea macrostegia* ssp. *gibsonii* grows in tropical lowland rainforest on moderate to steep grades, usually in lower gulch slopes and the bottom or edges of streambanks. These relatively inaccessible locations offer some protection from introduced mammalian herbivores. Its sites are sunny to shady, mesic to wet, and with clay or other soil substrates. The *Cyanea macrostegia* ssp. *gibsonii* has

been reported from elevations of 2,500-3,180 ft (760-970 m). Associated vegetation includes native ferns, shrubs, trees in wet *Metrosideros* forest or *Diplopteryqium-Metrosideros* shrubland (sometimes with *Dicranopteris*), *Perrottetia*, *Scaevola chamissoniana*, *Pipturus*, *Antidesma*, *Freycinetia*, *Psychotria*, *Cyrtandra*, *Dicranopteris*, *Broussaisia*, *Cheirodendron*, *Clermontia*, *Dubautia*, *Hedyotis*, *Ilex*, *Labordia*, *Melicope*, *Pneumatopteris*, and *Sadleria*, and the alien *Rubus rosifolius*.

Distribution

Cyanea macrostegia ssp. *gibsonii* is historically documented from the summit of Lanaihale and wet forest in the upper parts of the Mahana, Kaiholena, and Maunalei drainages of Lanai at elevations between 2,490-3,180 ft (760- 970 m). In 1989, only a single plant could be found at one site in Kaiholena Valley, and it was being overgrown by kahili ginger. The 1991 survey done by the Hawaii Heritage Program of The Nature Conservancy of Hawaii provided virtually the only information on recently observed populations. Populations of *Cyanea macrostegia* ssp. *gibsonii* occur on Lanai in two gulches in upper Kaiholena Valley, two feeder gulches into Maunalei Valley, and four sites near the Lanaihale summit. In the Maunalei Valley feeder gulches, the 1991 survey located two populations with a total of four mature plants and two juveniles. In the upper Kaiholena Valley, one mature plant and five seedlings were seen in Waialala

Cyanea macrostegia, photograph by Joel Lau. Reproduced by permission.

Gulch, while 10 mature plants were seen in the gulch between Kunoa and Waialala Gulches. The populations near the Lanaihale summit include one population of 34 mature and eight juvenile individuals and three populations with a total of eight mature plants and one juvenile. The known surviving individuals of the species thus comprise eight populations totaling approximately 75-80 plants.

Threats

Deer have not yet fully invaded the current habitat of *Cyanea macrostegia* ssp. *gibsonii*, although they have contributed to the decline of this species both directly through browsing and trampling of plants and indirectly through opening up avenues of invasion in damaged habitat for alien species. Browsing and habitat disturbance by axis deer promise to eliminate if drastic management efforts are not undertaken.

Kahili ginger was observed overgrowing the only plant found at one of the Kaiholena sites in 1989.

Even small pockets of virtually undisturbed forest in the heads of gulches on the upper slopes of Lanaihale are being invaded by strawberry guava, firetree, manuka, sourbush, molasses grass, *Rubus rosifolius,* and *Paspalum conjugatum.*These alien species have become pervasive on adjacent ridges since the forest floor is bombarded by alien propagules, and natural openings, or openings created by habitat disturbance by axis deer, provide ample sites for these aliens to obtain a foothold. Continuing disturbance by axis deer exacerbates the alien plant invasion problem.

The limited local gene pool that is available in a total population of 75-80 individuals in many small occurrences threatens to depress reproductive vigor.

Since native birds may have been the pollinators of *Cyanea macrostegia* ssp. *gibsonii*, their decline is very likely to pose a major, although currently undocumented, threat.

Conservation and Recovery

As of August 1992, the Hawaii Plant Conservation Center had in storage a total of 570 seeds of *Cyanea macrostegia* ssp. *gibsonii* from Lanai.

Contacts

U.S. Fish and Wildlife Service
Pacific Islands Ecoregion
300 Ala Moana Boulevard, Room 3-122
Box 50088, Honolulu, Hawaii, 96850
Telephone: (808) 541-3441
Fax: (808) 541-3470

U. S. Fish and Wildlife Service
Regional Office, Division of Endangered Species
Eastside Federal Building
911 N. E. 11th Ave.
Portland, Oregon 97232-4181
Telephone: (503) 231-6121
http://pacific.fws.gov/

Reference

U.S. Fish and Wildlife Service. 1995. "Lana'i Plant Cluster Recovery Plan: *Abutilon eremitopetalum, Abutilon menziesii, Cyanea macrostegia* ssp. *gibsonii, Cyrtandra munroi, Gannia lanaiensis, Phyllostegia glabra* var. *lanaiensis, Antalum freycinetianum* var. *lanaiense, Tetramolopium remyi,* and *Viola lanaiensis.*" U.S. Fish and Wildlife Service, Portland, OR.

Haha

Cyanea mannii

Status	Endangered
Listed	October 8, 1992
Family	Campanulaceae (Bellflower)
Description	Branched shrub with narrow leaves and smooth green flowers.
Habitat	Sides of deep gulches in 'ohi'a-dominated mesic to wet forests.
Threats	Habitat disturbance; predation by wild, feral, or domestic animals.
Range	Hawaii

Berlin Herbarium

Description

Cyanea mannii is a branched shrub in the bellflower family that grows 5-10 ft (1.5-3 m) in height. The leaves are narrowly elliptic or lance-shaped and have hardened teeth along the leaf margins. Each flower cluster arises from the axil of a leaf on a stalk; these clusters comprise six to 12 flowers, each on a stalk 0.3-0.5 in (7.6-12.7 mm) long. Each flower has a smooth, green hypanthium topped by triangular calyx lobes. The purplish corolla forms a nearly upright tube that ends in five spreading lobes. Berries have not been observed on this haha, but flowering was observed in July. This species is distinguished from the seven other species of the genus on

Molokai by (1) a branched, woody habit; (2) leaves with small, hardened, marginal teeth; and (3) a purplish corolla.

Habitat

C. mannii typically grows on the sides of deep gulches in 'ohi'a-dominated mesic to wet forests at elevations of 3,000-4,000 ft (914-1,219 m) on East Molokai.

Distribution

This species was known only from a historical occurrence at Ka Lae until 1984, when a single plant was discovered by Joan Aidem on privately owned land west of Puu Kolekole on East Molokai. Additional populations have been discovered since then in the east and west forks of Kawela Gulch within Kamakou Preserve on East Molokai; as of 1996 there were nine known populations of fewer than 1,000 total individuals.

Threats

Feral pigs threaten the habitat of *C. mannii*. Rats may feed on the fruit or other parts of the plant, as shown by predation on related species. Because of the small number of remaining individuals, one random naturally occurring event could extirpate a significant proportion of the populations.

Conservation and Recovery

Seeds of *C. mannii* have been collected and propagated by the National Tropical Botanical Garden.

Contacts

U. S. Fish and Wildlife Service
Regional Office, Division of Endangered Species
Eastside Federal Complex
911 N. E. 11th Ave.
Portland, Oregon 97232-4181
(503) 231-6121
http://pacific.fws.gov/

Pacific Remote Islands Ecological Services Field Office
300 Ala Moana Blvd., Room 3-122
P.O. Box 50088
Honolulu, Hawaii 96850
Telephone: (808) 541-1201
Fax: (808) 541-1216

Reference

U.S. Fish and Wildlife Service. 8 October 1992. "Endangered and Threatened Wildlife and Plants; Determination of Endangered or Threatened Status for 16 Plants from the Island of Molokai, Hawaii." *Federal Register* 57 (196): 46325-46340)

Haha

Cyanea mceldowneyi

Status	Endangered
Listed	May 15, 1992
Family	Campanulaceae (Bellflower)
Description	Unbranched shrub with prickly, hardened teeth leaves and a cluster of flowers whose petals are white with purple stripes.
Habitat	Wet montane forests.
Threats	Habitat destruction by feral animals; competing plant species.
Range	Hawaii

Haha *(Cyanea mceldowneyi)*, photograph by Robert J. Gustafson. Reproduced by permission.

Description

This haha, *Cyanea mceldowneyi,* an unbranched shrub in the bellflower family, has leaves 8-14 in (20.3-35.6 cm) long. These leaves have wedge-shaped bases, hardened teeth, and occasionally a few short prickles on the upper surface. Immature leaves are distinguished by their shorter length, rounded bases, hardened marginal teeth, and a greater number of prickles. The flowers of *C. mceldowneyi* are a five-to- seven-member cluster with a 0.6-1.2 in (1.5-3 cm) stalk. Each flower is on a stalk 0.4-0.6 in (1- 1.5 cm) in length. The petals, which are white with purple stripes, are fused into a curved tube that is 1.6 in (4.1 cm) long and 0.3 in (7.6 mm) wide; there are small prickles on the lobes, and berries have not been observed.

Habitat

C. mceldowneyi typically grows in wet montane forests with mixed *Metrosideros* and *Acacia koa* at an elevation of 3,000-4,200 ft (914-1,280 m). Associated native plant species include alani, manono, and 'ohi'a. Associated alien plants include *Ageratina adenophora, Rubus argutus, Setaria palmifolia,* and *Tibouchina herbacea.*

Distribution

Historically, *C. mceldowneyi* was found in rain forests from west of Waikamoi to Honomanu on northwestern Haleakala at 3,030-4,200 ft (924-1,280 m). This species is now known from six populations, ranging from 2,950 to 4,200 ft (899-1,280 m) in elevation, in the vicinity of Waikamoi Drainage on East Maui. All populations occur on private land owned by Alexander & Baldwin, none of which is part of the Nature Conservancy of Hawaii Waikamoi Preserve. Only one population contained more than ten individuals in 1994. Even this relatively large population (more than 100 individuals) represents a population drastically reduced since the late 1970s by feral pig impacts. Feral pig activity is intense in the area, and fresh disturbance of the habitat continues. The status of the Honomanu population is not known.

Threats

C. mceldowneyi is threatened by (1) habitat destruction caused by animal predation and trampling, (2) competition from aggressive alien plants that rob the species of space and nutrients, and (3) habitat loss due to fire, human recreational activities, and military exercises.

Conservation and Recovery

C. mceldowneyi has been successfully propagated by the Lyon Arboretum.

Contacts

U. S. Fish and Wildlife Service
Regional Office, Division of Endangered Species
Eastside Federal Complex
911 N. E. 11th Ave.
Portland, Oregon 97232-4181
(503) 231-6121
http://pacific.fws.gov/

Pacific Remote Islands Ecological Services Field Office
300 Ala Moana Blvd., Room 3-122
P. O. Box 50088
Honolulu, Hawaii 96850
Telephone: (808) 541-1201
Fax: (808) 541-1216

Reference

U. S. Fish and Wildlife Service. 15 May 1992. "Endangered and Threatened Wildlife and Plants; Determination of Endangered or Threatened Status for 15 Plants from the Island of Maui, Hawaii." *Federal Register* 57 (95): 20772-20787.

Haha

Cyanea pinnatifida

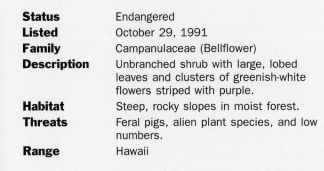

Status	Endangered
Listed	October 29, 1991
Family	Campanulaceae (Bellflower)
Description	Unbranched shrub with large, lobed leaves and clusters of greenish-white flowers striped with purple.
Habitat	Steep, rocky slopes in moist forest.
Threats	Feral pigs, alien plant species, and low numbers.
Range	Hawaii

Haha *(Cyanea pinnatifida)*, photograph. National Tropical Botanical Garden. Reproduced by permission.

Description

Cyanea pinnatifida is an unbranched shrub of the bellflower family that grows 2.6-10 ft (0.8-3 m) tall. The deeply lobed leaves are 10-24 in (24.4-61 cm) long and 6-20 in (15.2-50.8 cm) wide. Greenish-white flowers with purple stripes appear in clusters of eight to 15 at the leaf axils. This species has been observed flowering in August. The fruits have not been described. This species has also been known by the names *Lobelia pinnatifida*, *Rollandia pinnatifida*, *Delissea pinnatifida*, and *C. selachicauda*.

Habitat

C. pinnatifida is found in the Waianae Mountains in diverse moist forest on steep, rocky slopes at elevations of 1,500-1,600 ft (457-488 m). Associated species are mamaki *(Pipturus albidus)* and a variety of ferns.

Distribution

First collected in 1817 from the central Waianae Mountains, *C. pinnatifida* has never been found anywhere else. In 1997 the only known population consisted of one plant on private land in Kaluaa Gulch.

Threats

The greatest threat to *C. pinnatifida* is mortality due to environmental disturbances such as washout and falling rocks and trees. Predation by rats and slugs are also potential threats.

The species is not immediately threatened by alien weeds; weeding of Koster's curse on the steep slope above the plant could be more of a threat than the weeds themselves. The plant is not directly threatened by pigs because of its location on the side of a gulch wall, and fencing is not feasible.

With only a single living representative, *C. pinnatifida* is extremely vulnerable to extinction through an unpredictable natural or human-caused event. Even one instance of collecting or trampling would be disastrous.

Conservation and Recovery

Twenty-five individuals have been cloned by the Division of Forestry and Wildlife at the mid-elevation Nike missile site in the Waianae Mountains. Two individuals were outplanted in a fenced enclosure in Kaluaa Gulch in May 1996 in Honouliuli Preserve and are being monitored. This species is also being propagated at the Lyon Arboretum and the National Tropical Botanical Garden.

Surveys are needed of appropriate habitat in historical locations to determine if any other extant populations of this plant exist.

Potential management actions include weeding of invasive plants and control of feral pigs, slugs, and rats—if and when these threats are serious enough to warrant direct intervention. Once adequate propagated material is available and appropriate fencing, rat control, and weed removal are under way in the area of the remaining plant, this population should be enhanced by outplanting. Establishment of new populations within the historical range of *C. pinnatifida* should be initiated, but only in areas that are managed to minimize the impacts of feral ungulates, rats, and alien plants.

Contacts

U. S. Fish and Wildlife Service
Regional Office, Division of Endangered Species
Eastside Federal Complex
911 N. E. 11th Ave.
Portland, Oregon 97232-4181
(503) 231-6121
http://pacific.fws.gov/

Pacific Remote Islands Ecological Services Field Office
300 Ala Moana Blvd., Room 3-122
P. O. Box 50088
Honolulu, Hawaii 96850
Telephone: (808) 541-1201
Fax: (808) 541-1216

References

Cuddihy, L. W., and C. P. Stone. 1990. *Alteration of Native Hawaiian Vegetation: Effects of Humans, Their Activities and Introductions.* Cooperative National Park Resources Study Unit, University of Hawaii Press, Honolulu.

Stone, C. P., and J. M. Scott, eds. 1985. *Hawaii's Terrestrial Ecosystems: Preservation and Management.* Cooperative National Park Resources Study Unit, University of Hawaii Press, Honolulu.

Haha

Cyanea platyphylla

Steve Perlman

Status	Endangered
Listed	October 10, 1996
Family	Campanulaceae (Bellflower)
Description	Unbranched palm-like shrub, covered with short, sharp, pale spines.
Habitat	Lowland and montane wet forests.
Threats	Pigs, habitat-modifying introduced plant taxa, rats, and volcanic activity.
Range	Hawaii

Description

Cyanea platyphylla, of the bellflower family, is an unbranched palm-like shrub 3-10 ft (0.9-3 m) tall with stems that are covered with short, sharp, pale spines on the upper portions, especially as juveniles. This species has different leaves in the juvenile and adult plants. The juvenile leaves are 4.1-10 in (10.4-25.4 cm) long and 1.6-3 in (4- 7.6 cm) wide, with prickles on leaves and stalks. Adult leaves are 13-34 in (33-86.4 cm) long and 2.8-8.7 in (7.1-22.1 cm) wide, and are only sparsely prickled.

Six to 25 flowers are clustered on the end of a main stalk 8-35 in (20.3-89 cm) long, and each flower has a stalk 0.4-1 in (1-2.5 cm) long. The hypanthium is topped by five small, triangular calyx lobes. Petals, which are white or yellowish white with magenta stripes, are fused into a curved tube with five spreading lobes. The corolla is 1.7-2.1 in (4.3-5.3 cm) long and 0.2 to 0.4 in (0.5-1 cm) wide.

Berries are pale orange, 0.3-0.4 in (0.74-1 cm) long, and 0.2-0.3 in (0.5-0.74 cm) wide. The species differs from others in this endemic Hawaiian genus by its juvenile and adult leaves, precocious flowering, and smaller flowers.

Asa Gray (1861) named *Delissea platyphylla* from a specimen collected by Horace Mann and W.T.

Haha *(Cyanea platyphylla)*, photograph by Steve Perlman. Reproduced by permission.

Brigham in the Puna District of the island of Hawaii. Wilhelm Hillebrand (1888) transferred the species to *Cyanea*, creating *C. platyphylla*. Harold St. John, believing there to be no generic distinction between *Cyanea* and *Delissea*, transferred the species back to the genus Delissea, the older of the two generic names. The current treatment of the family, however, maintains the separation of the two genera. The following taxa have been synonymized with *C. platyphylla*: *C. bryanii*, *C. crispohirta*, *C. fernaldii*, *C. nolimetangere*, *C. pulchra,* and *C. rollandioides*. However, some field biologists argue that *C. fernaldii*, represented by the Laupahoehoe populations, is a distinct entity that should be resurrected as a separate species.

Habitat

C. platyphylla is typically found in Metrosideros polymorpha ('ohi'a)-Acacia koa (koa) Lowland and Montane Wet Forests at elevations between 390 and 3,000 ft (119 and 914 m). Associated taxa include *Ci-*

botium sp. (hapu'u), *Athyrium sandwichianum* (ho'i'o), *Antidesma* sp. (hame), *Clermontia* spp. ('oha wai), *Hedyotis* sp. (pilo), and *Cyrtandra* spp. (ha'iwale).

Distribution

C. platyphylla was historically known from the Kohala Mountains, Laupahoehoe in the Hamakua District, in the mountains above Hilo, Pahoa, Glenwood, Honaunau in South Kona, and the unknown location "Kalanilehua." One population of five mature individuals and two juveniles is known to still exist in Laupahoehoe Natural Area Reserve, which is owned and managed by the State of Hawaii. Approximately four additional populations, totaling 50-100 individuals, were recently rediscovered during surveys by National Tropical Botanical Garden in the Kohala Mountains. Two additional populations in Laupahoehoe Natural Area Reserve (NAR) have not been seen since 1982 and could not be relocated in 1989. The extant Laupahoehoe population has been spot-fenced by the NAR System to protect it from pig depredation.

Threats

The major known threats to *C. platyphylla* are pigs; habitat-modifying introduced plant taxa, including strawberry guava, guava, sweet granadilla, and thimbleberry; rats, which may eat the fruit; and volcanic activity. Another threat is the risk of extinction from naturally occurring events and/or reduced reproductive vigor due to the low numbers of populations and individuals.

Conservation and Recovery

As of May 1998, Volcano Rare Plant Facility has 38 plants, and also donated 12 plants to the Division of Forestry and Wildlife for outplanting in a fenced area in the Waiakea Forest Reserve. The National Tropical Botanical Garden has 18 plants in their nursery and 125 seeds in storage. Propagation by tissue culture has also been attempted. The ex-

tant Laupahoehoe population was fenced by the Division of Forestry and Wildlife in 1966 to protect it from pig depredation; however, this fence was vandalized shortly thereafter. The Institute of Pacific Islands Forestry is working with the University of Hawaii's Cooperative Parks Studies Unit to develop a biocontrol program for strawberry gauva.

Contact

U.S. Fish and Wildlife Service
Regional Office, Division of Endangered Species
Eastside Federal Complex
911 N.E. 11th Ave.
Portland, Oregon 97232-4181
(503) 231-6121
http://pacific.fws.gov/

Reference

U.S. Fish and Wildlife Service. 1998. "Big Island II: Addendum to the Recovery Plan for the Big Island Plant Cluster." U.S. Fish and Wildlife Service, Portland, OR. 80 pp. + appendices.

Haha

Cyanea procera

Status	Endangered
Listed	October 8, 1992
Family	Campanulaceae (Bellflower)
Description	Palmlike, stalkless, flowering tree with berries.
Habitat	Steep rock walls with thin soil on the southwest slope of a narrow gulch.
Threats	Habitat destruction; predation by feral or domestic animals.
Range	Hawaii

Haha (*Cyanea procera*), photograph by Ken Wood. Reproduced by permission.

Description

Cyanea procera is a palmlike tree in the bellflower family. It has both flowers and berries and can grow to a height of 10-30 ft (3-9.1 m). *C. procera*'s stalkless, lanceolate leaves feature tiny hardened teeth along the margins. Each flower cluster has a stalk 1-1.6 in (2.5-4.1 cm) long, and each individual flower has a hypanthium that is topped by shallow triangular calyx lobes. The purplish corolla forms a nearly upright or slightly curved tube; this tube ends in five downwardly curving lobes that make the flower appear one-lipped. The berries are ellipse shaped. This species can be distinguished from other species of the genus and from *C. mannii* by its growth habit, its sessile leaves, and the single-lipped appearance of the corolla.

Habitat

C. procera individuals have been found in wet 'ohi'a-dominated forest at an elevation of 3,480 ft (1,061 m). The growth site is steep rock walls with thin soil on the southwest slope of a narrow gulch on Molokai. Associated plant species are *Asplenium* sp., *Coprosma ochracea* (pilo), *Pipturus albidus,* and *Touchardia latifolia.*

Distribution

C. procera was known from a historical site in the Kamalo region of East Molokai. Another occurrence was discovered in 1987 on private land at Puu O Kaeha. There were three known populations with a total of eight individuals in 1995.

Threats

Goats have been observed in the vicinity of this species. Because only eight plants of *C. procera* are known to exist, the species is especially vulnerable to extinction from landslides and other random natural events. Like other *Cyanea* species and related genera, *C. procera* is threatened by predation by rats. Habitat degradation by feral pigs is also a potential threat.

Conservation and Recovery

The plant fauna of Molokai has currently fallen vulnerable to habitat degradation and/or predation by feral or domestic animals (axis deer, goats, pigs, sheep, and cattle); competition for space, light, water, and nutrients by naturalized, exotic species; habitat loss due to fires; predation by rats; human recreational activities; and injuries caused by military exercises. Overgrazing by axis deer and goats has irreparably damaged much of the native vegetation of Molokai and Hawaii.

Since the mid-1850s cattle ranching on Molokai has played a significant role in reducing areas of native vegetation to vast pastures of alien grasses. In 1960 about 61% of Molokai's lands were devoted to grazing, primarily in the western and central sections of the island. Cattle degrade the habitat by trampling and feeding on vegetation, eventually exposing the ground cover and thereby increasing soil vulnerability to erosion. Red erosional scars resulting from decades of cattle disturbance, exacerbated by other feral ungulate activities, are still evident on West Molokai and the upper elevations of East Molokai. Cattle facilitate the spread of alien grasses and other plants.

Cattle ranching was succeeded in the 1920s by pineapple cultivation. Most of the land used for this agricultural activity had already been altered through the decades of cattle ranching. However, pineapple cultivation contributed to a high degree of erosion until its decline in the 1970s.

To improve the quality of vegetation in these natural areas, the State of Hawaii designated a single protected area—called the Molokai Forest Reserve—along the upper elevation mesic to wet forests of East Molokai. This reserve accounts for 30% of Molokai's land area.

Contacts

U. S. Fish and Wildlife Service
Regional Office, Division of Endangered Species
Eastside Federal Complex
911 N. E. 11th Ave.
Portland, Oregon 97232-4181
(503) 231-6121
http://pacific.fws.gov/

Pacific Remote Islands Ecological Services Field Office
300 Ala Moana Blvd., Room 3-122
P. O. Box 50088
Honolulu, Hawaii 96850
Telephone: (808) 541-1201
Fax: (808) 541-1216

Reference

U.S. Fish and Wildlife Service. 8 October 1992. "Endangered and Threatened Wildlife and Plants; Determination of Endangered or Threatened Status for 16 Plants from the Island of Molokai, Hawaii." *Federal Register* 57 (196): 46325-46340.

Haha

Cyanea recta

Status	Threatened
Listed	October 10, 1996
Family	Campanulaceae (Bellflower)
Description	Unbranched shrub bearing five to seven purple or white and purple striped flowers.
Habitat	Lowland wet or mesic 'ohi'a forest or shrubland.
Threats	Bark removal by rats; habitat degradation by feral pigs; browsing by goats; competition with the alien plant species.
Range	Hawaii

Ken Wood

Description

Cyanea recta, a member of the bellflower family, is an unbranched shrub 3.3-4.9 ft (1-1.5 m) tall. The narrowly elliptic leaves are 4.7-11 in (12-28 cm) long and 0.5-2 in (1.3-5 cm) wide, with minutely toothed margins. The upper surface is green and smooth, while the lower surface is whitish green to pale green, and smooth or hairy. Five to seven flowers are arranged on an inflorescence stalk 3-4 in (7.6-10.2 cm) long, each having an individual stalk 0.2-0.7 in (0.5-1.8 cm) in length. The densely hairy flowers are purple or white with purple longitudinal stripes, 1.2-1.6 in (3-4 cm) long, and 0.1-0.2 in (0.25-0.5 cm) wide, with spreading lobes. The staminal column is smooth or sparsely hairy at the base. The anthers are covered with minute epidermal projections, the lower two with tufts of white hairs at the tip. The fruit is an egg-shaped, purple berry. *C. recta* is distinguished from other species in the genus that grow on Kauai by the following collective characteristics: horizontal or ascending inflorescence, narrowly elliptic leaves, flat leaf margins, and purple berries.

Habitat

C. recta grows in lowland wet or mesic 'ohi'a forest or shrubland, usually in gulches or on slopes at elevations of 1,300-3,070 ft (396-936 m). Associated

Haha *(Cyanea recta)*, photograph by Steve Perlman. Reproduced by permission.

plant species include kopiko, *Antidesma* sp. (hame), *Cheirodendron platyphyllum* (lapalapa), *Cibotium* sp. (hapu'u), and *Diplazium* sp.

Distribution

C. recta was known historically from scattered locations in northeastern and central Kauai, including upper Hanalei Valley, Waioli Valley, Hanapepe Valley, Kalalau cliffs, Wainiha Valley, Makaleha Mountains, Limahuli Valley, Powerline Trail, and the Lehua Makanoe-Alakai area. Six current populations on state and private land total approximately 500-1,500 individuals. More than 150 plants occur in the upper Waioli Valley, several hundred plants in the Wainiha Valley, about 123 in the Makaleha Mountains, fewer than 50 in the Limahuli Valley, a single plant along the Powerline Trail, and an unknown number of plants at the back of Hanalei Valley.

Threats

The major threats to *C. recta* are bark removal by rats; habitat degradation by feral pigs; browsing by goats; and competition with the alien plant species lantana, thimbleberry, Koster's curse, fireweed, and hilo grass.

Although populations of this species are threatened by rat and goat predation, habitat modification by pigs and goats, and competition with alien plant species, the wider distribution of populations through a relatively large area and greater numbers of individual plants reduce the likelihood that this species will become extinct in the near future.

The Makaleha Mountains population of *C. recta* is threatened by feral pigs. Pigs also constitute a potential threat to the Wainiha Valley populations. Habitat degradation reported to occur in areas near these populations, if not controlled, may become a problem for these occurrences.

The Makaleha Mountains population of *C. recta* is threatened by goats. Browsing damage by goats has been verified for *C. recta*.

Rat damage to the stems of species of *Cyanea* has been reported in the Makaleha Mountains, Waioli Valley, and at the base of Mount Waialeale, and this rodent activity poses a threat to the populations of *C. recta* that occur there.

Erosion, landslides, and rock slides—natural events that kill individual plants and destroy habitat—are especially dangerous threats to the two largest populations of *C. recta*.

Conservation and Recovery

The National Tropical Botanical Garden has collected and is storing *C. recta* seeds.

Contact

U.S. Fish and Wildlife Service
Regional Office, Division of Endangered Species
Eastside Federal Complex
911 N.E. 11th Ave.
Portland, Oregon 97232-4181
(503) 231-6121
http://pacific.fws.gov/

Reference

U.S. Fish and Wildlife Service. 1988. "Kauai II: Addendum to the Recovery Plan for the Kauai Plant Cluster." U.S. Fish and Wildlife Service, Portland, Oregon. 84+pp.

Haha

Cyanea remyi

Status	Endangered
Listed	October 10, 1996
Family	Campanulaceae (Bellflower)
Description	Shrub with erect stems, without prickles, dark purple and hairy toward the apex.
Habitat	Lowland wet forest.
Threats	Competition with the alien plant species; habitat degradation by feral pigs; browsing by goats; predation by rats; unidentified slugs that feed on the stems.
Range	Hawaii

David Lorence

Description

Cyanea remyi, a shrub of the bellflower family between 3.3 and 6.6 ft (1 and 2 m) in height, has generally unbranched stems 0.4-1 in (1-2.5 cm) in diameter. The stems are erect, without prickles, dark purple and hairy toward the apex, and brown and hairless below. The leaves are broadly elliptic, egg-shaped, or broadly oblong, and 6-16 in (15.2-40.6 cm) long and 3.7-7.7 in (9.4-19.6 cm) wide. The upper leaf surface is green, glossy, and hairless. The lower leaf surface is whitish green and glossy with scattered short white hairs on the midrib and veins. The leaf margins are hardened and slightly toothed. The inflorescence rises upward, contains six to 13 flowers, and is covered with short white hairs. The dark maroon sepal lobes are triangular or narrowly triangular, spreading or ascending, and 0.2 in (0.5 cm) long and 0.04-0.08 in (0.1-0.2 cm) wide. The tubular flowers, 2 in (5 cm) long, have two lips, are dark purple (shading to purplish white at the apex of the lobes on their inner surface), and are densely covered with short white hairs. The flower tube is curved, 1 in (2.5 cm) long and 0.2 in (0.5 cm) in diameter. The staminal column is slightly protruding. The maroon or dark purple fruit is a round berry, 0.4-0.5 in (1-1.3 cm) in diameter, with orange flesh and small projections on the outer surface. *C. remyi* is distin-

Haha *(Cyanea remyi)*, photograph by Steve Perlman. National Tropical Botanical Garden. Reproduced by permission.

guished from others in the genus that grow on Kauai by its shrubby habit; relatively slender, unarmed stems; smooth or minutely toothed leaves; densely hairy flowers; the shape of the calyx lobes; length of the calyx and corolla, and length of the corolla lobe relative to the floral tube.

The French naturalist and ethnologist Ezechiel Jules Remy first collected *C. remyi* on Kauai or Niihau between 1851 and 1855. The specimen, labeled as an unidentified *Delissea*, languished in the herbarium of the Natural History Museum in Paris until Joseph Rock formally described it in 1917, naming it in honor of the collector.

In the current treatment of the family done in 1990, Lammers surmised, even with the inadequate material available for study at the time, that the species may be synonymous with *C. truncata*. Several recent collections by botanists from National Tropical Botanical Garden have confirmed the distinctness of *C. remyi*.

Habitat

C. remyi is usually found in lowland wet forest at elevations of 1,180-3,060 ft (360-933 m). Associated plant species include hame, kanawao, 'ohi'a, *Freycinetia arborea* ('ie'ie), and *Perrottetia sandwicensis* (olomea).

Distribution

C. remyi was originally known only from Remy's nineteenth century collection. In 1991, after more than 130 years, *C. remyi* was rediscovered in the Blue Hole on Kauai by botanists from National Tropical Botanical Garden. This species is now known from four widely separated locations on state and private land in northeastern and southeastern Kauai: a population of 14 plants in Waioli Valley; several hundred plants at the base of Mount Waialeale; about 140-180 plants in the Wahiawa Mountains, near Hulua; and a population of about 10-50 plants on the summit plateau of the Makaleha Mountains. This species is estimated to have a total population of approximately 500 plants.

Threats

Competition with the alien plant species fireweed, Hilo grass, strawberry guava, thimbleberry, and *Melastoma candidum*; habitat degradation by feral pigs; browsing by goats; predation by rats; unidentified slugs that feed on the stems; and a risk of extinction from naturally occurring events due to the small number of remaining populations are the major threats to *C. remyi*.

The Makaleha Mountains and Wahiawa Mountains populations of *C. remyi* are threatened by feral pigs. The Makaleha Mountains population is threatened by the browsing of goats. Rat damage to the stems of species has been reported in the Makaleha Mountains, Waioli Valley, and at the base of Mount Waialeale. Indiscriminate predation by slugs on plant parts of *C. remyi* has been observed by field botanists. The effect of slugs on the decline of this and related species is unclear, although slugs may pose a threat by feeding on the stems and fruit, thus reducing the vigor of the plants and limiting regeneration.

Fireweed, an annual herb native from Mexico to Brazil and Argentina, threatens the Makaleha Mountains and Wahiawa Mountains populations. *Melastoma candidum* is a noxious weed that threatens the Makaleha Mountains population; strawberry guava is known to pose a direct threat to the Wahiawa Mountains population; the shrub thimbleberry threatens the Wahiawa Mountains and Waioli Valley populations; and the perennial Hilo grass threatens the Makaleha population.

Conservation and Recovery

The National Tropical Botanical Garden held more than 1,000 *C. remyi* seeds in storage in 1997.

Contact

U.S. Fish and Wildlife Service
Regional Office, Division of Endangered Species
Eastside Federal Complex
911 N.E. 11th Ave.
Portland, Oregon 97232-4181
(503) 231-6121
http://pacific.fws.gov/

Reference

U.S. Fish and Wildlife Service. 1988. "Kauai II: Addendum to the Recovery Plan for the Kauai Plant Cluster." U.S. Fish and Wildlife Service, Portland, Oregon. 84+ pp.

Haha

Cyanea shipmannii

Status	Endangered
Listed	March 4, 1994
Family	Campanulaceae (Bellflower)
Description	Shrub with few or no branches; small, sharp projections; wide and deeply cut stalked leaves; and greenish-white flowers that are covered with fine hairs and clustered in groups of 10-15.
Habitat	Koa- and 'ohi'a-dominated montane mesic forests at elevations of 5,400-6,200 ft (1,646-1,890 m).
Threats	Limited numbers.
Range	Hawaii

Haha *(Cyanea shipmannii)*, photograph by Jack Jeffrey. Reproduced by permission.

Description

This haha, *Cyanea shipmannii*, is a shrub with few or no branches. It can grow to be 8-13 ft (2.5- 4 m) tall and features small, sharp projections, especially when young. The plant's alternate stalked leaves are 6.7-12 in (17-30.5 cm) long, 2.8-5.5 in (7.1-14 cm) wide, and deeply cut into 20-30 lobes per leaf. Flowers are covered with fine hairs and are clustered in groups of 10-15; the main stalk is 0.4-1.2 in (1-3 cm) long, and each flower stalk is 0.4-0.6 in (1-1.5 cm) long. The hypanthium is topped with five small calyx lobes. This haha's pale greenish-white petals (1.2-1.4 in [3-3.6 cm] long) are fused into a curved five-lobed tube 0.1-0.2 in (2.5-5.1 mm) wide. The fruit is an ellipsoid berry. *C. shipmannii* is distinguished from others in the genus by 1) its slender stems, 2) its stalked, pinnately lobed leaves, and 3) its smaller flowers.

Habitat

This species typically grows in koa- and 'ohi'a-dominated montane mesic forests at elevations of 5,400-6,200 ft (1,646-1,890 m). Associated species include kawa'u and kolea.

Distribution

C. shipmannii has been known from only one population, located on the island of Hawaii on the eastern slope of Mauna Kea on private land.

When originally discovered, only one mature plant was found. Since 1975 four populations have been identified. The total number of individuals is unknown but estimated at fewer than 10.

Threats

Recent pig rooting of tree ferns and other native taxa was evident at the Upper Waiakea Forest population. Small numbers of extant individuals and localized distribution may result in a limited gene pool and reduced reproductive vigor, as well as vulnerability to extirpation by random events. Small population size probably affects vector and flower relationships, precluding or reducing effective pollination; furthermore, reduction in the number of endemic nectar feeding birds may have disrupted their fundamental role in pollination.

Conservation and Recovery

Seeds have been germinated at Volcano Rare Plant Facility at the Volcano Agricultural Station. About ten plants are growing in the garden and four in the greenhouse. Lyon Arboretum has cloned about 300 individuals from immature seed. An individual found in 1994 by Thane Pratt in a shaded ravine south of Powefi'me Road in the Upper Waiakea Forest Reserve is now protected from feral pigs by a small fence built by the Division of Forestry and Wildlife. The individual appears healthy.

Propagation and maintenance of *ex situ* stock should be continued and current populations protected from pigs and augmented. One new population will need to be established and numbers increased in order to meet recovery criteria.

Contacts

U. S. Fish and Wildlife Service
Regional Office, Division of Endangered Species
Eastside Federal Complex
911 N. E. 11th Ave.
Portland, Oregon 97232-4181
(503) 231-6121
http://pacific.fws.gov/

Pacific Remote Islands Ecological Services Field Office
300 Ala Moana Blvd., Room 3-122
P. O. Box 50088
Honolulu, Hawaii 96850
Telephone: (808) 541-1201
Fax: (808) 541-1216

Reference

U. S. Fish and Wildlife Service. 4 March 1994. "Endangered and Threatened Wildlife and Plants; Determination of Endangered or Threatened Status for 21 Plants from the Island of Hawaii, State of Hawaii." *Federal Register* 59 (43): 10305-10325.

Haha

Cyanea stictophylla

Status	Endangered
Listed	March 4, 1994
Family	Campanulaceae (Bellflower)
Description	Shrub or tree sometimes covered with small sharp projections and yellowish-white or purple flowers.
Habitat	Koa- and 'ohi'a-dominated lowland mesic and wet forests.
Threats	Grazing and trampling by feral cattle, limited numbers.
Range	Hawaii

Jon G. Griffin

Description

Cyanea stictophylla, a type of haha, is a shrub or tree 2-20 ft (0.6-6.1 m) tall, sometimes covered with small sharp projections. The alternate, stalked, oblong, shallowly lobed, and toothed leaves are 3-6 in (7.6-15.2 cm) long and 1.6-3.1 in (4.1-7.9 cm) wide. Clusters of five or six flowers have main flowering stalks 0.4-1.6 in (1-4.1 cm) in length; each flower has a stalk 0.3-0.9 in (7.6-22.9 mm) long. The hypanthium is topped with five calyx lobes 0.1-0.2 in (2.5-5.1 mm) long and 0.04-0.1 in (1-2.5 mm) wide. The yellowish-white or purple petals, 1.4-2 in (3.6-5.1 cm) long, are fused into an arched, five-lobed tube about 0.2 in (5.1 mm) wide. The spherical berries are orange. This species differs from others in the genus by its lobed toothed leaves and its larger flowers with small calyx lobes and deeply lobed corollas.

Habitat

C. stictophylla sometimes grows epiphytically (not rooted in soil) and is found in koa- and 'ohi'a-dominated lowland mesic and wet forests at elevations of 3,500-6,400 ft (1,066.8-1,950.7 m). Associated species include tree ferns, alani, and opuhe.

Haha *(Cyanea stictophylla)*, photograph by Jon G. Giffin. Reproduced by permission.

Distribution

Historically, this species was known only from the island of Hawaii on the western, southern, southeastern, and eastern slopes of Mauna Loa.

In the late 1990s it was known to be extant near Keauhou and in South Kona on private land. The three known populations, which extend over a distance of about 38 by 10 mi (61.2 by 16.1 km), contain a total of approximately 15 individuals. Forty-six outplanted individuals survive on Puu Waawaa and in Kau Forest Reserve.

Threats

The primary reasons for decline of this species are destruction of former habitat by cattle grazing and degradation of current habitat by feral pigs. In addition, the small number of plants and the scattered distribution of populations may limit the gene pool (resulting in decreased reproductive vigor) and make them vulnerable to extirpation by random events.

Conservation and Recovery

The National Tropical Botanical Garden has germinated seeds and propagated the taxon. The single wild individual on Puu Waawaa has been fenced. Seeds from this wild plant were germinated, and approximately 68 individuals were planted in the mid-1990s within a separate enclosure on Puu Waawaa. Of these individuals, about 40 have survived. Seeds from the same wild individual at Puu Waawaa were used to establish six individual plants in an enclosure on the Kau Forest Reserve.

Propagation and maintenance of *ex situ* stock should be encouraged. Current populations should be protected from ungulates and augmented, where possible. At least two new populations will need to be established and numbers increased to meet recovery criteria.

Contacts

U.S. Fish and Wildlife Service
Regional Office, Division of Endangered Species
Eastside Federal Complex
911 N.E. 11th Ave.
Portland, Oregon 97232-4181
Telephone: (503) 231-6121
http://pacific.fws.gov/

Pacific Remote Islands Ecological Services Field
Office
300 Ala Moana Blvd., Room 3-122
P.O. Box 50088
Honolulu, Hawaii 96850
Telephone: (808) 541-1201
Fax: (808) 541-1216

References

U.S. Fish and Wildlife Service. 1996. "Big Island Plant Cluster Recovery Plan." U.S. Fish and Wildlife Service, Portland, Oregon. 202 pp.

Haha

Cyanea st.-johnii

Status	Endangered
Listed	October 10, 1996
Family	Campanulaceae (Bellflower)
Description	Unbranched shrub with a woody stem, smoothly toothed, thick leaf edges, and hairless white petals suffused with pale violet in the inner surface.
Habitat	Wet, windswept slopes and ridges in 'ohi'a mixed shrubland or 'ohi'a-uluhe shrubland.
Threats	Habitat degradation by feral pigs and hikers, potential predation by rats, and competition with Koster's curse.
Range	Hawaii

Description

Cyanea st.-johnii (haha) is an unbranched shrub of the bellflower family with a woody stem 12-24 in (30-60 cm) long. The leaves are lance-shaped to inversely lance-shaped, 2.4-5.1 in (6.1-13.0 cm) long, and 0.6-0.8 in (1.5-2.0 cm) wide. The smoothly toothed leaf edges are thickened and curl under. A flowering stalk between 0.2 and 0.6 in (0.8 and 1.5 cm) in length supports 5 to 20 flowers. The white petals, hairless and suffused with pale violet in their inner surfaces, are 1.2-2.4 in. (3.0-6.1 cm) long. *Cyanea st.-johnii* is distinguished from others in its endemic Hawaiian genus by the length of the leaves, the distinctly curled leaf margins, and the petal color. This species has been observed in flower in July through September.

Edward Hosaka, who collected a new lobelioid while hiking in the Koolau Mountains of Oahu, later described and named it *Rollandia st.-johnii* in 1935. *Rollandia st.-johnii* var. *obtusisepala*, named by Wimmer 1953, is not recognized in the most recent treatment of Hawaiian members of the family. Lammers and others published the new name *Cyanea st.-johnii* in 1993 when they merged *Cyanea*

and *Rollandia*. The specific epithet honors the late Harold St. John.

Habitat

Cyanea st.-johnii typically grows on wet, windswept slopes and ridges from 2,260-2,800 ft. (690-850 m) elevation in 'ohi'a mixed shrubland or 'ohi'a-uluhe shrubland. Associated plants include naupaka kuahiwi, uki, kookoolau, kamakahala, naenae, kopiko, hapuu, kanawao, maile, hame, and *Freycinetia arborea* (ieie).

Distribution

Cyanea st.-johnii was known historically from 11 populations in the central and southern Koolau Mountains of Oahu. Six extant populations contained between 40 and 50 total plants in 1997: less than 10 individuals at Waimano Trail summit to Aiea Trail summit, four at the summit ridge crest between Manana and KipaPa trails, 15 between the summit of Aiea and Halawa trails, one at Summit Trail south of Poamoho cabin, six at Wamano ridge between North and North central Waimano and 12 at Wailupe-Waimanalo summit ridge. These popu-

Haha (*Cyanea st.-johnii*), photograph by John Obata. Reproduced by permission.

lations are found on City and County of Honolulu, state, and private, lands.

Threats

Cyanea st.-johnii is threatened by habitat degradation and destruction by feral pigs, potential predation by rats, competition with the noxious alien plant Koster's curse, and risk of extinction from naturally occurring events or through reduced reproductive vigor due to the small number of remaining populations and individuals. The plants between the summit of Aiea and Halawa Trail also are threatened by trampling by hikers.

Cyanea st.-johnii is potentially threatened by feral pig predation; pigs favor plants from the bellflower family for food, and this species is not known to be unpalatable to rodents.

It is possible that rats eat the fruit of *Cyanea st.-johnii*.

The noxious shrub Koster's curse is also a threat to this listed species.

Overcollection for scientific or horticultural purposes and excessive visits by individuals interested in seeing rare plants in their native situations could seriously damage *Cyanea st.-johnii*, whose populations are close to trails and roads and therefore easily accessed by potential collectors.

Cyanea st.-johnii has populations in recreational areas, near trails, and close to roads, making it very vulnerable to general human disturbance.

Conservation and Recovery

A Recovery Plan for the haha and associated species was published by the Fish and Wildlife Service in 1998. It survives in only five known populations, and these must be rigorously protected from environmental threats. Its critical habitat must be managed to reduce the damage caused by pigs and rats. This could be done by enclosing the plants in secure fencing, or by reducing or eliminating the non-native mammals. The abundance of alien invasive plants must also be reduced in the habitat of the haha. Hiking trails must also be located away from the critical habitat of the rare plant. The populations of the haha should be monitored, and research undertaken into its biology and habitat needs, with the aim of developing management practices appropriate to maintaining or enhancing its habitat.

Contacts

U. S. Fish and Wildlife Service
Pacific Island Ecoregion
300 Ala Moana Boulevard, Room 3108
P.O. Box 5088,
Honolulu, Hawaii 96850
Telephone: (808) 541-3441
Fax: (808) 541-3470

U. S. Fish and Wildlife Service
Regional Office, Division of Endangered Species
Eastside Federal Building
911 N. E. 11th Ave.
Portland, Oregon 97232-4181
Telephone: (503) 231-6121
http://pacific.fws.gov/

References

U.S. Fish and Wildlife Service. 10 October 1996. "Endangered and Threatened Wildlife and Plants; Determination of Endangered Status for Twenty-five Plant Species From the Island of Oahu, Hawaii." *Federal Register* 61 (198) 53089-53108.

U.S. Fish and Wildlife Service. 1998. "Recovery Plan for Oahu Plants." U.S. Fish and Wildlife Service, Portland, Oregon.

Cyanea superba

No Common Name

Status	Endangered
Listed	September 11, 1991
Family	Campanulaceae (Bellflower)
Description	Unbranched palm-like tree with a crown of large leaves and clusters of curved, white, tubular flowers.
Habitat	Moist forest understory.
Threats	Low numbers, feral pigs, alien plant species.
Range	Hawaii

Description

Cyanea superba is a palm-like tree of the bellflower family that grows to a height of 20 ft (6.1 m). It is unbranched and crowned with a rosette of large oblanceolate leaves, 20-40 in (50.8-101.6 cm) long. Curved white tubular flowers hang in pendant clusters below the leaves. The flowering season of *C. superba* varies from year to year depending on precipitation; the normal range is from late August to early October. Flowering is generally at, its peak in early to mid-September. Fruits have been known to mature from two to five months, depending on the climatic conditions.

This species has been known by a variety of scientific names, including *Lobelia superba*, *C. regina*, *Delissea regina*, *D. superba*, and *Macrochilus superbus*.

Habitat

C. superba grows in the understory of moist forests on western Oahu in well-drained, rocky soil at elevations between 1,760 and 2,200 ft (536.4 and 670.6 m). Canopy species such as kukui or candlenut (*Aleurites moluccana*) and *Pisonia brunoniana* keep the open understory in shade. The understory is heavily shaded by canopy trees, including ileurites *moluccana* (kukui) and *P. brunoniana* (papala kepan), but remains partially open. The understory is readily invaded by aggressive exotic plants. *C. superba* will not grow in direct sunlight.

Distribution

C. superba ssp. *regina* had an historical presence in the southern Koolau mountains of Oahu, but this variety has not been collected since 1932. *C. superba* ssp. *superba* had an historical occurrence in the gulches of Makaleha on Mt. Kaala in the Waianae Mountains, although there were no documented sightings of the plant after its collection in 1870 until the species was rediscovered in 1971. This sole confirmed population on federal land and within Makua Military Reservation contained only five plants in 1998. A population of fewer than five plants was extirpated during the late 1990s on state land in Pahole Gulch. A third population, previously reported, appears to be based on a misidentification.

Threats

C. superba faces a number of threats. The extremely low number of known plants and their limited distribution makes the species vulnerable to extinction through unpredictable human or natural events. In addition, the species faces habitat degradation from the activities of feral pigs and competition from invasive non-native species. When surveyed in 1990, scientists observed feral pigs and noted the effects of rooting around plants in both populations. The greatest immediate threats to the survival of *C. superba* are the degradation of its habitat due to the introduction of alien plants such

Cyanea superba, photograph. National Tropical Botanical Garden. Reproduced by permission.

as strawberry guava and Christmas berry and predation by rats and slugs. Other major threats is the potential for destruction by wildfires generated in a nearby military firing range. The plants are confined to two small areas of 1,800 and 600 sq ft (167.2 and 55.7 sq m). The restricted range of this species makes it vulnerable to even small and localized environmental disturbances; a single incident could easily eliminate the entire remaining population. The very limited gene pool may also depress reproductive vigor.

Conservation and Recovery

Fencing and removal of feral pigs in the Pahole drainage, where the second population was located, was completed by the Division of Forestry and Wildlife in July 1997. Weeding of strawberry guava, Christmas berry, and Koster's Curse was conducted in the surrounding areas. Forty individuals grown from the Pahole Gulch population of *C. superba* were planted in three different exclosures in Pahole Na-

tional Area Reserve. Seventeen individuals are in the Nike missile mid-elevation.

The army has plans to outplant four individuals in a fenced exclosure in Kahanahaiki on Makua Military Reservation. The wild population on army land is within a fenced exclosure. The army implemented an intensified rat control effort involving diphacinone bait blocks and snap-trapping during the 1997 fruiting season, which ensured production and protection of mature fruit.

This species is also being propagated at the Lyon Arboretum and the National Tropical Botanical Garden.

Contacts

U. S. Fish and Wildlife Service
Regional Office, Division of Endangered Species
Eastside Federal Complex
911 N. E. 11th Avenue
Portland, Oregon 97232-4181
(503) 231-6121
http://pacific.fws.gov/

U. S. Fish and Wildlife Service
300 Ala Moana Blvd., Rm. 6307
P.O. Box 50167
Honolulu, Hawaii 96850

References

Cuddihy, L. W., and C. P. Stone. 1990. *Alteration of Native Hawaiian Vegetation: Effects of Humans, Their Activities and Introductions.* University of Hawaii Cooperative National Park Resources Study Unit, Honolulu.

Culliney, J. L. 1988. *Islands in a Far Sea: Nature and Man in Hawaii.* Sierra Club Books, San Francisco.

Lammers, T. G. 1988. "New Taxa, New Names, and New Combinations in the Hawaiian Lobelioideae (Campanulaceae)." *Systematic Bontany* 13 (4): 496-508.

Lammers, T. G. 1990. "Campanulaceae." In *Manual of the Flowering Plants of Hawai'i,* edited by W. L. Wagner, D. R. Herbst, and S. H. Sohmer. University of Hawaii Press and Bishop Museum Press, Honolulu.

Tomich, P. Q. 1986. *Mammals in Hawai'i,* second edition. Bishop Museum Special Publication 76. Bishop Museum Press, Honolulu.

Haha

Cyanea truncata

Dan Palmer

Status	Endangered
Listed	March 28, 1994
Family	Campanulaceae (Bellflower)
Description	Unbranched or sparsely branched shrub with small sharp prickles, oval leaves, and clusters of eight to 40 white flowers with magenta stripes.
Habitat	Windward slopes in mesic to wet forests.
Threats	Competition from alien plants, habitat destruction by feral pigs, limited numbers.
Range	Hawaii

Description

This haha, *Cyanea truncata,* is an unbranched or sparsely branched shrub covered with small sharp prickles. The oval leaves, which are widest above the middle area, are 8-24 in (20.3-61 cm) long and 4-10 in (10.2-25.4 cm) wide. The leaves are lined with hardened teeth along the margins. The upper surface of the leaf is hairless; the lower surface is hairy, has sparse projections, and is pale green. Clusters of eight to 40 white flowers with magenta stripes are produced on horizontal or hanging stalks 2-12 in (5.1-30.5 cm) long. Each slightly curved flower is 1.3-1.7 in (3.3-4.3 cm) long, about 0.3 in (7.6 mm) wide, and has spreading corolla lobes that are one-

quarter to one-half as long as the flower. The fruits are round orange berries about 0.4 in (1 cm) long that contain many tiny seeds. *C. truncata* is distinguished from other members of this genus by the length of the flower cluster stalk and the size of the flowers and flower lobes.

C. truncata was seen in flower in December 1919 and November 1980, the last time the species was observed before feral pigs extirpated the population.

Habitat

C. truncata typically grows on windward slopes in mesic to wet forests at elevations of 800-1,300 ft (243.8-396.2 m). Associated plants include koki'o ke'oke'o, lama, 'ohi'a, kukui, ha'iwale, ma'aloa, pa-pala kepau, and 'awa.

Distribution

C. truncata was known historically from Punaluu, Waikane, and Waiahole in the northern Koolau Mountains of Oahu. These sites have not been recently surveyed because of their inaccessibility, but it is known that suitable habitat is present. One population of at least two individuals was known to exist in Hidden Valley, a drainage northwest of Kaaawa Valley that terminates at Kaaawa Point in the Koolau Range; however, this occurrence was destroyed by feral pigs.

In 1991 John Obata discovered 20 immature lobeloids growing on private land along a gully floor farther upstream from the site of the destroyed population. This was thought to be the only known population of *C. truncata*. An individual from this sterile population was salvaged from pig-damaged areas in 1991 and flowered in June 1993. However, this individual turned out to be *Rollandia crispa*, not *C. truncata*. A site visit in July 1993 determined that all the plants thought to be *C. truncata* were actually *R. crispa*. No individuals of *C. truncata* were located, though it is possible that juvenile plants could be found in the valley floor. At present, no confirmed population exists, although the species is not considered extinct.

Threats

The major threats to *C. truncata* are 1) habitat degradation and predation by feral pigs, 2) suspected predation by rats and slugs, 3) competition with the invasive plants Koster's curse and strawberry guava, and 4) a risk of extinction due either to random natural episodes or to reduced reproductive vigor. At best, only a tiny number of individuals remain.

Conservation and Recovery

No specific conservation measures have been undertaken for *C. truncata*. Surveys of appropriate habitat in historical locations are needed to determine if any other extant populations of this plant exist. To prevent extinction of this species, cultivated propagation should be initiated immediately if extant individuals are located.

Once adequate propagated material is available and appropriate fencing, rat control, and weed control are under way in the areas of any remaining naturally situated populations, these occurrences should be enhanced by outplanting. Establishment of new populations within the historical range of *C. truncata* should be initiated in areas that are managed to minimize the impacts of feral ungulates, rats, and alien plants.

Contacts

U. S. Fish and Wildlife Service
Regional Office, Division of Endangered Species
Eastside Federal Complex
911 N. E. 11th Ave.
Portland, Oregon 97232-4181
(503) 231-6121
http://pacific.fws.gov/

Pacific Remote Islands Ecological Services Field Office
300 Ala Moana Blvd., Room 3-122
P. O. Box 50088
Honolulu, Hawaii 96850
Telephone: (808) 541-1201
Fax: (808) 541-1216

References

U. S. Fish and Wildlife Service. 28 March 1994. "Endangered and Threatened Wildlife and Plants: Endangered Status for 11 Plant Species from the Koolau Mountain Range, Island of Oahu, HI." *Federal Register* 59:14482-14492.

Cyanea undulata

No Common Name

Status	Endangered
Listed	September 20, 1991
Family	Campanulaceae (Bellflower)
Description	Unbranched shrub with narrowly elliptic leaves and a cluster of curved yellowish flowers.
Habitat	Stream bank.
Threats	Low numbers, alien plant species.
Range	Hawaii

Description

Cyanea undulata, an unbranched or occasionally fork-stemmed shrub or subshrub of the bellflower family, is 1.5-15 ft (0.5-4.5 m) in height with narrowly elliptic leaves 11-17 in (28-43 cm) long and 1-2 in (2.5-5 cm) wide that have wavy margins, smooth upper surfaces, and fine rust-colored hairs covering the lower surfaces. The petiole (leaf stem) may be winged. The inflorescence is unbranched, 3-17 in (7.5-43 cm) long, and bears two to six flowers that are slightly curved, hairy, yellowish or greenish yellow and purplish at their base. Flowering material was collected from April to July. The fruit is an orange berry about 0.7 in (1.7 cm) long. The Hawaiian lobelioid species, including the genus *Cyanea*, are generally believed to have adapted to pollination by native nectarivorous passerine birds, such as the Hawaiian "honeycreepers". The long, tubular, slightly curved flowers of *C. undulata* fit this model, but field observations are lacking. The fleshy orange fruits of this species are adapted for bird dispersal like other species of *Cyanea*.

C. undulata is invariably found in the most pristine, undisturbed, and un-invaded sites, often on shady stream banks or steep to vertical slopes that are prone to erosion or landslides. Flowering occurs during the summer months, although adults do not seem to flower every year. *C. undulata* appears to grow slowly; consequently, it is likely to be damaged by any feral animal disturbance or alien plant invasion of its habitat. Microhabitat conditions for seed germination and growth also may be extremely specific.

Habitat

C. undulata was described from two original collections made in the early 1900s. The type specimen was gathered in 1909 by Forbes in damp woods surrounding the Wahiawa swamp, and a now-lost collection was made in the same area by Lydgate in 1908. This species was collected in 1988 from a single population of three to four plants growing at about 2,300 ft (701 m) elevation along the bank of a tributary of the Wahiawa Stream.

Distribution

Five adult and 23 juvenile plants are known from seven localities in the Wahiawa Drainage. Adults of *C. undulata* generally occur as scattered individuals, although several juveniles occasionally are found growing together. The high juvenile to adult ratio indicates that this species is reproducing, but the low total number suggests that regeneration is extremely slow.

Threats

The main threats to *C. undulata* are the species' extreme low numbers and competition from introduced alien plant species. With only three or four plants constituting the entire species population, *C. undulata* is highly vulnerable to extinction. An un-

Cyanea undulata, photograph. National Tropical Botanical Garden. Reproduced by permission.

predictable human or natural event could easily destroy these plants. Although the Wahiawa drainage has been largely undisturbed, alien plant species are now spreading upstream. Strawberry guava (*Psidium cattleianum*) and melastoma (*Melastoma candidum*) are aggressive species that out-compete native species. They gained a foothold in the basin in 1982 when Typhoon Iwa opened sections of the forest canopy. This invasion is assisted by the actions of feral pigs which transport seed and open additional ground through their rooting. Although there are only slight indications of pig activity in the basin, any increase could quickly help spread invading plants.

Conservation and Recovery

No natural site or cultivated site conservation efforts have been attempted for *C. undulata;* however, certain other species of Hawaiian *Cyanea* have been successfully germinated and grown to seedling stage. The Fish and Wildlife Service published a Recovery Plan for the *C. undulata* in 1994.

Only 28 individuals of this critically endangered plant are known to exist in the wild, all in the Wahlawa drainage. The critical habitat of the *C. undulata* must be protected from disturbances. The habitat must also be managed to reduce the damage caused by introduced mammalian herbivores, invasive alien plants, and other threats. The known individuals of the *C. undulata* must be monitored, and research undertaken into the biology of the species, habitat needs, and management practices to maintain and enhance its populations. The rare plant should be propagated in captivity, to provide stock for out-planting to enhance the tiny wild population.

Contacts

U.S. Fish and Wildlife Service
Pacific Islands Ecoregion
300 Ala Moana Boulevard, Room 3-122
Box 50088, Honolulu, Hawaii, 96850
Telephone: (808) 541-3441
Fax: (808) 541-3470

U. S. Fish and Wildlife Service
Regional Office, Division of Endangered Species
Eastside Federal Building
911 N. E. 11th Ave.
Portland, Oregon 97232-4181
Telephone: (503) 231-6121
http://pacific.fws.gov/

References

Cuddihy, L. W., and C. P. Stone. 1990. *Alteration of Native Hawaiian Vegetation: Effects of Humans, Their Activities and Introductions.* Cooperative National Park Resources Study Unit, University of Hawaii Press, Honolulu.

Culliney, J. L. 1988. *Islands in a Far Sea: Nature and Man in Hawaii.* Sierra Club Books, San Francisco.

Stone, C. P., and J. M. Scott, eds. 1985. *Hawai'i's Terrestrial Ecosystems: Preservation and Management.* Cooperative National Park Resources Study Unit, University of Hawaii Press, Honolulu.

Lammers, T. G. 1990. "Campanlaceae." In *Manual of the Flowering Plants of Hawai'i,* by W. L. Wagner, D. R. Herbst, and S. H. Sohmer. University of Hawaii Press and Bishop Museum Press, Honolulu.

U.S. Fish and Wildlife Service. 1994. "Recovery Plan for the Wahiawa Plant Cluster: *Cyanea undulata, Dubautia pauciflorula, Herperomannia lydgatei, Labordia lydgatei* and *Viola helenae.*" U.S. Fish and Wildlife Service, Portland, Oregon.

Delissea rhytidosperma

No Common Name

Status	Endangered
Listed	February 25, 1994
Family	Campanulaceae (Bellflower)
Description	Branched shrub 1.6-8.2 feet tall, with lance-shaped or elliptic toothed leaves and clusters of 5-12 greenish-white or pale purple flowers.
Habitat	Lowland dry forests.
Threats	Deer, goats, pigs, rats, alien plants, fire, natural disaster, human impact, low populations.
Range	Hawaii

Delissea rhytidosperma, photograph by Thomas Lammers. Reproduced by permission.

Description

Delissea rhytidosperma is a branched shrub of the bellflower family that grows to a height between 1.6-8.2 ft (0.5 and 2.5 m). The lance-shaped or elliptic leaves with toothed margins are 3.1-7.5 in (7.9-19.1 cm) long and 0.8-2.2 in (2-5.6 cm) wide. Clusters of five to 12 flowers are borne on stalks 0.4-0.8 in (1-2 cm) long. Each flower has a stalk 0.3-0.5 in (0.8-1.3 cm) long. The greenish white corolla is 0.6-0.8 in (1.5-2 cm) long. The stamens are hairless, except for a small patch of hair at the base of the anthers. The nearly spherical dark purple fruits are 0.3-0.5 in (0.8-1.3 cm) long and contain numerous white seeds. This species differs from other plants of the genus by the shape, length, and margins of the leaves and by having hairs at the base of the anthers.

Habitat

D. rhytidosperma generally grows in diverse lowland mesic forests or *Acacia koa*-dominated lowland dry forests, characterized by an annual rainfall of 20-80 in (50.8-203.2 cm), which falls between November and March. The terrain is a well drained, highly weathered substrate with a fine textured subsoil rich in aluminum.

Distribution

D. rhytidosperma was known from historical occurrences scattered throughout the island of Kauai. Populations ranged as far north as Wainiha and Limahuli valleys, as far east as Kapaa and Kealia, and as far south as Haupu range between the elevations of 1,000-3,000 ft (304.8-914.4 m).

Only two populations still exist. A population located on state-owned Kuria Natural Area Reserve contains six individuals. It was thought that Hurricane Iniki completely destroyed the population of 20 plants in the Haupu range in 1992, but two years later four plants and nine seedlings were observed.

Threats

Habitat degradation by mule deer, black-tailed deer, feral goats, and feral pigs is the major threat to *D. rhytidosperma*. Other threats are competition with alien plants such as lantana, sweet granadillal, and banana poka; predation by rats; fire; overcollecting for scientific or horticultural purposes; and landslides. With a single extant population of only six individuals, this species is threatened by stochastic extinction or reduced reproductive vigor. Hurricanes pose an additional threat.

Conservation and Recovery

D. rhytidosperma has been successfully propagated and then cultivated by Lyon Arboretum, National Tropical Botanical Garden, and Waimea Arboretum. The holdings at Lyon Arboretum in 1995 consisted of 93 plants in the tissue culture lab and one plant in the certified green house. National Tropical Botanical Garden had both seeds in short-term storage and plants growing in their garden, while Waimea Arboretum had 19 plants and 100 seedlings.

Thomas Lammers

Contacts

U. S. Fish and Wildlife Service
Regional Office, Division of Endangered Species
Eastside Federal Complex
911 N. E. 11th Ave.
Portland, Oregon 97232-4181
(503) 231-6121
http://pacific.fws.gov/

U.S. Fish and Wildlife Service
300 Ala Moana Blvd., Rm. 6307
P.O. Box 50167
Honolulu, Hawaii 96850
(808) 541-2749

Reference

U. S. Fish and Wildlife Service. 25 February 1994. "Endangered and Threatened Wildlife and Plant; Determination of Endangered or Threatened Status for 24 Plants from the Island of Kauai, HI." *Federal Register* 59 (38): 9304-9329.

'Oha

Delissea rivularis

Status	Endangered
Listed	October 10, 1996
Family	Campanulaceae (Bellflower)
Description	Shrub with hairy stems; leaves arranged in a rosette.
Habitat	Near streams on steep slopes in 'ohi'a-'olapa montane wet or mesic forests.
Threats	Competition with the encroaching alien plant prickly Florida blackberry; habitat destruction by feral pigs.
Range	Hawaii

Steve Perlman

Description

Delissea rivularis, also known as 'oha, a shrub with hairy stems in the bellflower family, is unbranched or branched near the base and grows to a height of 13-16 ft (3.9-4.8 m). The leaves are arranged in a rosette at the tips of the stems. The elliptic to lance-shaped leaves are 8-12 in (20.3-30.5 cm) long and 1.2 to 3.2 in (3-8.1 cm) wide, with minutely toothed margins. Both leaf surfaces are covered with hairs. Six to 12 flowers are arranged on an inflorescence stalk 1.6-3.2 in (4-8.1 cm) long, each having an individual stalk 0.4- 0.6 in (1-1.5 cm) in length. The curved and hairy flowers, white with blue longitudinal stripes, are 1.2-1.6 in (3-4 cm) long and have one dorsal knob. The fruit is a spherical, dark purple berry 0.4-0.6 in (1-1.5 cm) in diameter. This species is distinguished from others of the genus by the color, length, and curvature of the corolla; shape of the leaves; and presence of hairs on the stems, leaves, flower clusters, and corolla.

Habitat

D. rivularis is found near streams on steep slopes in 'ohi'a-'olapa montane wet or mesic forests. Associated native species include kanawao, *Athyrium* sp., *Carex* sp., *Coprosma* sp. (pilo), and *Sadleria* sp. ('ama'u).

Distribution

D. rivularis had historical occurrences on Kauai at an unknown location near Waiakealoha waterfall, Waialae Valley, Hanakoa Valley, and Kaholuamano. This species, recently recollected after almost 80 years, is now known only from the upper Hanakoa Valley stream area of northwestern Kauai. This population of 15-20 plants, scattered over an area of more than 1,100 sq ft (102.2 sq m), is on sate land within the Hono O Na Pali Natural Area Reserve at about 3,900 ft (1,188.7 m) in elevation.

Threats

The major threats to *D. rivularis* are competition with the encroaching alien plant prickly Florida blackberry, habitat destruction by feral pigs, and reduced reproductive vigor and a risk of extinction from naturally occurring events due to the small number of remaining individuals in the single remaining population. It is probable that rats eat the fruit. Erosion, landslides, rock slides, and other natural events that kill individual plants and destroy habitat are especially dangerous threats to this species.

Conservation and Recovery

Seeds are being stored at the National Tropical Botanical Garden, and the Lyon Arboretum has propagated stock by tissue culture.

Contact

U.S. Fish and Wildlife Service
Regional Office, Division of Endangered Species
Eastside Federal Complex
911 N.E. 11th Ave.
Portland, Oregon 97232-4181
(503) 231-6121
http://pacific.fws.gov/

Reference

U.S. Fish and Wildlife Service. 1988. "Kauai II: Addendum to the Recovery Plan for the Kauai Plant Cluster." U.S. Fish and Wildlife Service, Portland, Oregon. 84 pp.

'Oha

Delissea subcordata

Status	Endangered
Listed	October 10, 1996
Family	Campanulaceae (Bellflower)
Description	Shrub producing six to 18 greenish white flowers, hairless anthers, and egg-shaped berries.
Habitat	Moderate to steep gulch slopes in mesic native or alien-dominated forests.
Threats	Habitat degradation and direct destruction by pigs and goats; potential impacts from military activities, including road construction and housing projects; potential predation by rats; competition with the alien plants.
Range	Hawaii

M. Chapin, National Tropical Botanical Garden

Description

Delissea subcordata, a variety of 'oha and a member of the bellflower family, is a branched or unbranched shrub 3.5-10 ft (1-3 m) in height. The egg-shaped or oval lance-shaped leaves have heart-shaped bases and blades 4.7-12 in (12-30.5 cm) long and 2.4-6.7 in (6.1-17 cm) wide. The leaf margins have shallow, rounded to sharply pointed teeth. Occasionally the leaf margin may be irregularly cut into narrow and unequal segments with one to six triangular lobes, 0.4-0.7 in (1-1.8 cm) long, toward the leaf base. Six to 18 white or greenish-white flowers are arranged on a flowering stalk 1.6-4 in (4-10.2

cm) long. The calyx lobes are awl-shaped and 0.02-0.04 in (0.05-0.1 cm) long. The curved corolla is 1.8-2.4 in (4.5- 6.1 cm) long and has a knob on the back side. The anthers are hairless, while the fruit is an egg-shaped berry. This species is distinguished from others in this endemic Hawaiian genus by the shape and size of the leaves, the length of the calyx lobes and corolla, and the hairless condition of the anthers.

D. subcordata was first collected on Oahu more than 150 years ago. It was later described and named it for its heart-shaped leaf base. All subsequently named varieties have been considered to be synonymous with *D. subcordata*, including *D. sub-*

cordata var. *kauaiensis*, *D. subcordata* var. *obtusifolia*, *D. subcordata* var. *waialaeensis*, *D. subcordata* var. *waikaneensis*, and *Lobelia subcordata*.

Habitat

D. subcordata typically grows on moderate to steep gulch slopes in mesic native or alien-dominated forests from 1,400 to 2,500 ft (426.7-762 m) elevation. Associated plant taxa include a variety of native trees such as 'ala'a, hame, kukui, 'ohi'a, papala kepau, lama, olopua, and kopiko.

Distribution

Historically, *D. subcordata* was known from 21 scattered populations in the Waianae Mountains and eight populations in the Koolau Mountains of Oahu. A specimen collected in the 1860s and labeled as from the island of Kauai is believed to have been mislabeled. *D. subcordata* is now known only from the Waianae Mountains in nine populations distributed from Kawaiu Gulch in the Kealia land section in the northern Waianae Mountains to the north branch of North Palawai Gulch about 12 mi (19.3 km) to the south. This species occurs on private land at the Nature Conservancy of Hawaii's Honouliuli Preserve, on Federal land at Schofield Barracks Military Reservation and Lualualei Naval Reservation, and on state land at Pahole and Kaala Natural Area Reserves and Makua Military Reservation (a property that is leased to the Federal government). The total number of plants in the nine remaining populations was estimated to be between 70 and 80 in 1997.

Threats

D. subcordata is threatened by habitat degradation and direct destruction by pigs and goats; potential impacts from military activities, including road construction and housing development; potential predation by rats; several noxious plants: the shrub Koster's curse, dense stands of strawberry guava, Christmas berry—which grows in dense, smothering thickets, and lantana—a thicket-forming shrub; potential fire; and a risk of extinction from random natural events or through reduced reproductive vigor due to the small number of remaining individuals.

D. subcordata is directly threatened by feral goat trampling of plants and seedlings, as well as by goat-induced substrate erosion. Feral pig predation is a potential threat to *D. subcordata* because the plant is not known to be unpalatable to pigs and they favor plants from the bellflower family for food. *D. subcordata* is not known to be unpalatable to goats and grows in areas where they have been reported; direct predation is therefore a possible threat. It is possible that rats eat the fruit of *D. subcordata*, a plant with fleshy stems and fruit that grows in areas where rats occur.

Populations of *D. subcordata* that occur on land leased and owned by the U. S. Army face the threat of being damaged through military activity, either by troops in training maneuvers or by the construction, maintenance, and utilization of helicopter landing and drop-off sites. Unintentionally ignited fires from ordnance training practices on military reservations pose a potential threat to *D. subcordata*.

D. subcordata has populations in recreational areas, near trails, and close to roads, making it very vulnerable to human disturbance.

Conservation and Recovery

Four individuals were outplanted in a fenced enclosure in Kaluaa Gulch in Honouliuli Preserve in November 1994. Three survive, with two producing flowers and fruit; however, no recruitment has been observed. The individuals in Palawai Gulch were included in a fenced enclosure that the Nature Conservancy of Hawaii constructed in 1998. Twenty-six individuals growing in the mid-elevation Nike site in the Waianae Mountains were obtained as cuttings from the Nature Conservancy of Hawaii's Honouliuli preserve in 1997. This species is also being successfully propagated at the Lyon Arboretum, the National Tropical Botanical Garden, and the Waimea Arboretum. In addition, seeds are in storage at the National Tropical Botanical Garden.

Contact

U.S. Fish and Wildlife Service
Regional Office, Division of Endangered Species
Eastside Federal Complex
911 N.E. 11th Ave.
Portland, Oregon 97232-4181
(503) 231-6121
http://pacific.fws.gov/

Reference

U.S. Fish and Wildlife Service. 1998. "Recovery Plan for Oahu Plants." U.S. Fish and Wildlife Service, Portland, Oregon. 207 pp., plus appendices.

'Oha

Delissea undulata

Status	Endangered
Listed	October 10, 1996
Family	Campanulaceae (Bellflower)
Description	Unbranched, palm-like, woody-stemmed tree, 6-32 ft (1.8-9.8 m) tall.
Habitat	Dry and mesic forests.
Threats	Degradation of habitat by feral animals.
Range	Hawaii

Description

This 'oha, *Delissea undulata*, is an unbranched, palm-like, woody-stemmed tree, 6-32 ft (1.8-9.8 m) tall. A dense cluster of leaves occurs at the stem tip. Leaf blades are elliptic to narrowly lance-shaped, 2-8 in (5.1-20.3 cm) long, and 1-4 in (2.5-10.2 cm) wide. Leaf edges are wavy or flat and toothed. Leaf stalks are 0.8-5.9 in (2-15 cm) long. Flower clusters are subtended by a main stalk 2-20 in (5-50 cm) long. Each cluster is composed of about five to 20 flowers. The calyx and petals are fused at the base to form an oval tube 1.2-2.7 in (3-6.9 cm) long. Calyx lobes are awl- or triangular-shaped 0.04-0.08 in (0.1-2 mm) long. Petals are green-white and slightly down-curved, 0.6-1 in (1.5-2.5 cm) long. One or two knoblike structures often occur on the back of the flower tube. Fruits are oval or round, purple berries 0.2-0.48 in (.5-1.2 cm) long.

This taxon is distinguished from the other closely related members of the genus by its large flowers and berries and broad leaf bases. Three subspecies, all but the last of which are considered extinct, may be separated on the basis of leaf shape and margin characters: *D. undulata* var. *Kauaiensis* (leaf blades are oval and flat-margined with sharp teeth), *D. undulata* var. *Niihauensis* (leaf blades are heart shaped and flat-margined with shallow, rounded teeth) and *D. undulata* var. *undulata* (leaf blades are elliptic to lance-shaped and wavy-margined with small, sharply pointed teeth.

The remaining wild individual was observed in flower and (immature) fruit in August 1992, and outplanted individuals were observed in flower in July 1995. No other life history information is available.

Habitat

D. undulata occurs in dry and mesic forests at elevations of about 3,300-5,700 ft (1,005.8-1,737.4 m) in open *Sophora chrysophylla* (mamane) and *Metrosiderospolymorpha* (ohia) forest. Taxa that are associated with *D. undulata* also include *Santalurn ellipticum* gaud. (iliahi) and *Acacia koa* (koa). Another endangered taxon, *Nothocestrum brevifiorum*, grows in the area where the single individual was found in 1992.

Distribution

D. undulata spp. *undulata* was observed in the late nineteenth century on southwestern Maui in four valleys and in the early twentieth century on western Hawaii in North and South Kona. It was observed in South Kona at Puu Lehua in 1971, but was later thought to be extirpated. In 1992 a single individual was rediscovered at Puu Waawaa at the edge of a collapsed lava tube in a thin substrate at an elevation of 3,250 ft (990.6 m). Since then, about 50 individuals have been outplanted within three enclosures at Puu Waawaa, Waihou Forest Reserve.

Delissea undulata, photograph by Steve Perlman. Reproduced by permission.

Threats

Damage from feral and domestic animals and the degradation from grazing, browsing, and trampling by cows, sheep, goats, and pigs are threats. Although palatability of the taxon is not documented, lack of seedling establishment and low numbers of individuals suggest that the taxon may be negatively impacted by these animals. Three alien plant taxa pose a threat to *D. undulata*. Two vines—*Passiflora mollissima* and *Senecio mikanioides Otto ex* Walp. (German ivy)—and a noxious grass—*Pennisetum clandestinurn* (kikuyu grass)—compete with *D. undulata* for light, nutrients, and space and therefore limit or preclude reproductive success. Fire is potentially a threat, although fuel loads from *Pennisetum clandestinum* are minimized by heavy grazing by cattle. Predation of the fleshy fruits by black rats and introduced game birds is a threat to *D. undu-lata*. Because only one remaining wild adult plant known, *D. undulata* is threatened by extinction due to random events. For instance, natural changes to the habitat may threaten the preservation of this individual as it grows in a collapsing lava tube. Obviously a limited gene pool exists.

Conservation and Recovery

Seeds were obtained from the Puu Waawaa plant and germinated. Approximately 50 individuals were outplanted within three exclosures at Puu Waawaa, Waihou Forest Reserve.

The propagation and maintenance of *ex situ* genetic stock for this taxon is necessary in order to protect it from the serious threat of extinction by random event. Protection and outplanting efforts should be encouraged and continued.

Contact

U. S. Fish and Wildlife Service
Regional Office of Endangered Species
Eastside Federal Complex
911 N. E. 11th Ave.
Portland, Oregon 97232-4181
(503) 231-6121
http://pacific.fws.gov/

Reference

U. S. Fish and Wildlife Service. 1996. *Big Island Plant Cluster Recovery Plan*. U. S. Fish and Wildlife Service, Portland, Oregon.

Water Howellia

Howellia aquatilis

Steve Shelley

Status	Threatened
Listed	July 14, 1994
Family	Campanulaceae (Bellflower)
Description	Branched water plant with submerged or floating stems having narrow leaves and white flowers.
Habitat	Firm, consolidated clay and organic sediments in shallow water or the edges of deep ponds.
Threats	Loss of wetland habitat due to timber harvesting, livestock grazing, residential development, competition from alien plants.
Range	California, Idaho, Montana, Oregon, Washington

Description

Howellia aquatilis (water howellia), a highly specialized wetlands plant, is a monotypic genus in the bellflower family (Campanulaceae). The plant was first described in 1879, from specimens collected in Multnomah County near Portland, Oregon. Water howellia is as an aquatic annual plant that grows 4-24 in (10-60 cm) in height, and has extensively branched, submerged or floating stems with narrow leaves 0.4-2 in (1-5 cm) in length. Two types of flowers are produced: small, inconspicuous flowers beneath the water's surface, and emergent white flowers 0.08-0.11 in (2-2.7 mm) in length. The plant predominantly self-pollinates with each fruit containing up to five large (0.08-1.6 in; 2-4 mm) brown seeds.

Habitat

Water howellia grows in firm consolidated clay and organic sediments that occur in wetlands associated with ephemeral glacial pothole ponds and former river oxbows. These wetland habitats are filled by spring rains and snowmelt run-off. Depending on temperature and precipitation they may exhibit some drying during the growing season. This plant's micro habitats include shallow water and the edges of deep ponds partially surrounded by deciduous trees.

Howellia reproduces entirely from a seed. Germination only occurs when ponds dry out and the seeds are exposed to air. The size of an annual population varies in abundance depending on the extent of drying in the previous growing season.. Exceedingly wet or dry seasons can have a detrimental effect on plant numbers the following year. The length of time seeds remain viable is unknown. However, seeds that remain in the soil longer than 8 months have shown decreased rates of germination and vigor. Genetic variability in howellia populations is low throughout its range. This suggests that all populations of howellia most likely represent a single, narrowly adapted genotype. This low rate of genetic variability within populations may explain why the species is restricted to a highly specific habitat.

Distribution

Water howellia has been extirpated from more than one-third of its former range including California, Oregon, and some sites in Washington (Mason and Thurston counties) and Idaho (Kootenai County). Populations are extant only in very small areas of Montana, Washington, and Idaho.

Only 79 small populations of this aquatic plant were known to exist when the proposed rule to list the species was published. Subsequent inventories conducted for howellia in Washington state located 28 new sites in Spokane County alone, thus expanding the number of known populations to 107. Nearly all of the remaining populations of howellia are clustered in two main population centers or metapopulations. They occur primarily in groups of closely adjacent ponds, although some ponds within the range of these metapopulations are unoccupied. One metapopulation near Spokane, Washington, consists of 46 individual populations in Spokane County, Washington, and one in Latah County, Idaho. A second metapopulation is found in the drainage of the Swan River in northwestern Montana (Lake and Missoula Counties) where 59 individual populations are found. This total represents a plant presence in only 13.5% of 437 potential habitats that have been surveyed since 1987. In addition to metapopulations, a third site near Vancouver in southwestern Washington (Clark County) contains two small populations in close proximity.

The large fluctuations in annual numbers, the low genetic variability, and habitat specificity indicates that isolated populations of howellia may be vulnerable to extirpation. However, the individual populations within the metapopulations appear interdependent and may act as founders. Most populations are extremely small. The fifty-nine populations found in Montana cover an area of only about 127 acres (51 hectares). Of this area, one population occurs in a 30-acre (12-hectare) pond, one in a 5-acre (2-hectare) pond, one in a 4-acre (1.6-hectare) pond, four in 3 acres (1.2 hectares) of ponds, 24 in ponds of 1-2 acres (0.4-0.8 hectares) in size, and the remaining 28 are in ponds of 1 acre (0.4 ha) or less. The U.S. Forest Service (Forest Service) estimates total area of occupied and suitable unoccupied habitat on Forest Service lands to be less than 200 acres (80 hectares).

Populations of howellia occur both on private and public lands. Of the 59 known populations in Montana, 21 (36%) are found on private lands, 34 (57%) occur on lands administered by the Forest Service, and four (7%) occur on a mixture of private and Forest Service lands. In Washington, 34 of the 47 populations (72%) are found on Service administered lands, 11 (24%) occur on private lands, one (2%) is on State land, and one (2%) is on Bureau of Land Management land. The one population in Idaho occurs solely on private property.

Threats

The major threats to Water howellia are loss of wetland habitat and habitat changes due to timber harvesting, livestock grazing, residential development, and competition by introduced plant species. The genetic similarity between different populations of howellia, its consequent confinement to extremely specific habitats, and its relative inability to adapt to abrupt environmental changes add to the vulnerability of the species.

Howellia populations can be threatened by the environmental effects associated with timber harvesting. The removal of trees from around ponds may increase water temperatures and evaporation, thus increasing wetland drying and influencing plant succession. Increased siltation occurs in wetlands where logging or associated road building and maintenance is conducted, and this action changes bottom substrates and the vegetational composition of the sites. Water howellia occurs most frequently in ponds with firm and consolidated organic clay bottom sediments. It is also found in more open areas within these ponds. An increase in bottom sedimentation and subsequent competition from other vegetation could have an adverse effect on howellia populations. Of the 59 populations of howellia in the Swan Valley, Montana, 22 (37%) occur within areas where logging has taken place around the wetland margins. In Montana, 58% of the populations of howellia occur on Forest Service lands, and an additional 7% occur on lands partially owned by the Forest Service. The Plum Creek Timber Company owns 38% of the private lands in Montana where howellia occurs. Timber harvest has been increasing within the area of the Spokane metapopulation.

Livestock, by their grazing and trampling, can also adversely affect howellia populations due to the disturbance of shorelines and associated vegetation. Trampling of bottom sediments adversely affects the seed bank and the consolidated substrate which appears to be necessary for germination. Additionally, livestock waste increases nutrient loading in wetlands causing a change in the water quality that may alter pond vegetation composition. It is not known how much grazing impact can be tolerated by howellia, although the plant still exists in ponds that have been disturbed by grazing. The plant's ability to withstand grazing is evidently influenced by the timing, magnitude, and duration of grazing. The cumulative impacts of grazing and other human-induced disturbances threaten a number of populations. The California population may have been eliminated by cattle grazing and trampling, and two wetlands on private lands in Montana with populations of howellia have been heavily impacted by domestic livestock, especially horses. In Washington, 23% of the populations occur on private lands, many of which are subject to grazing. Grazing also took place on some of the lands administered by FWS until 1993. In Spokane County, Washington, several of the ponds containing howellia have been significantly altered by past and current grazing practices.

Sites where howellia was historically found in Oregon have been converted to urban areas, and an increase in residential development is occurring in the Spokane metapopulation area. Additionally, the construction of dams along the Columbia and Willamette Rivers has led to a loss of suitable wetland habitats. Many wetlands within the historic range of water howellia have been drained, filled, or excavated for other uses.

Howellia has narrow ecological requirements, and even subtle habitat disturbances that alter the surface or subsurface hydrology of the pond could devastate a population. Activities that affect the ecology of a wetland bottom habitat also may affect wetland succession and the survival of howellia populations.

Howellia does not compete well with other aquatic vegetation and its wetland habitats are being threatened by *Phalaris arundinacea* (reed canary grass), a highly competitive, robust grass that invades wetlands. Howellia has been observed growing amongst reed canary grass stands, but only where these stands are sparse, or in openings entirely free of the grass. Reed canary grass has the potential to extirpate howellia populations due to its ability to rapidly form dense monocultures which cause the decline of nearly all other plants in a wetland. This exotic grass accelerates the rate of wetland succession causing significant changes in substrate and water table levels. Both native and exotic varieties of this grass occur in North America, and it is not known whether the variety occuring in wetlands within the range of howellia is native or exotic. However, due to the pernicious characteristic of the invasions and the lack of historical records of its presence in this region, some ecologists in the Pacific northwest believe this invasive variety of *P. arundinacea* is an exotic form that was introduced by humans. Reed canary grass is considered a major threat to howellia in the state of Washington since it occurs in 83% of the ponds where howellia is present. This exotic grass also threatens the howellia population in Idaho due to its presence in nearby ponds. Reed canary grass has also been found in several Montana ponds occupied by howellia.

Lythrum salicaria (purple loosestrife), another aggressive exotic plant, also poses a threat to howellia because it can out-compete and eliminate other aquatic plants. Purple loosestrife is present in Lake County, Montana, and also in the immediate vicinity of the Spokane howellia metapopulation.

Conservation and Recovery

Some protection already exists for this species since it is contained on the Forest Service's list of sensitive species for the Pacific Northwest region. However, populations that occur on private lands are not legally protected. Federal, state and local agencies have been notified of the localities of howellia, and landowners have been notified of the location and importance of protecting habitat of this species. FWS believes that federal involvement can be effective without the designation of critical habitat.

Contact

U.S. Fish and Wildlife Service
Regional Office, Division of Endangered Species
Eastside Federal Complex
911 N.E. 11th Ave.
Portland, Oregon 97232
(503) 231-6121
http://pacific.fws.gov/

References

U. S. Fish and Wildlife Service. July 14, 1994. "Determination of The Plant Water Howellia (*Howellia aquatilis*), Determined to Be a Threatened Species." *Federal Register* 59(134): 35860-35864.

Lobelia gaudichaudii ssp. *koolauensis*

No Common Name

Status	Endangered
Listed	October 10, 1996
Family	Campanulaceae (Bellflower)
Description	Unbranched, woody shrub with greenish or yellowish white corolla and an egg-shaped fruit capsule.
Habitat	Moderate to steep slopes in 'ohi'a or 'ohi'a-uluhe lowland wet shrublands.
Threats	Habitat destruction from feral pigs, competition from alien plants, rock slides and erosion.
Range	Hawaii

Lobelia gaudichaudii, photograph by Ken Wood. Reproduced by permission.

Description

Lobelia gaudichaudii ssp. *koolauensis*, a member of the bellflower family, is an unbranched, woody shrub 1-3.5 ft (0.3-1 m) in height. The inversely lance-shaped to rectangular leaves are 3-7.5 in (7.6-19 cm) long and 0.5-1.1 in (1.3-2.8 cm) wide. The leaf edges are thickened or curled under, fringed with hairs toward the base, and sharp-pointed at the tip. The flowering stalk is two to six-branched and 16-28 in (40.6-71.1 cm) long. The hairless bracts are lance-shaped to egg-shaped and 0.7-1.3 in (1.8-3.3 cm) long. The calyx lobes are triangular, lance-shaped, or egg-shaped, and 0.4-0.6 in (1-1.5 cm) long.

The greenish or yellowish-white corolla is 2-3 in (5-7.5 cm) long. The tubular portion of the flower is curved, with spreading lobes; the fruit is an egg-shaped capsule. The subspecies *koolauensis* is distinguished by the greenish or yellowish-white petals and the branched flowering stalks. The species is distinguished from others in the genus by the length of the stem, the length and color of the corolla, the leaf width, the length of the floral bracts, and the length of the calyx lobes. A specimen of *L.*

gaudichaudii ssp.*koolauensis* was collected on Oahu in 1937, which was described the following year as a variety of *L. gaudichaudii*, naming it for the Koolau Mountains. The variety was elevated to a subspecies in 1988.

Habitat

L. gaudichaudii ssp. *koolauensis* typically grows on moderate to steep slopes in 'ohi'a or 'ohi'a-uluhe lowland wet shrublands at elevations between 2,100 and 2,400 ft (640 to 731.5 m). Associated plant taxa include alani, ko'oko'lau, naupaka, 'uki, and kanawao.

Distribution

L. gaudichaudii ssp. *koolauensis* was known historically from two populations in the central Koolau Mountains on Oahu; the number of extant populations has now been increased by two as a result of further field research. These four small populations occur on the Manana Ridge system in the central Koolau Mountains on privately owned land and on the Army's Schofield Barracks Training Area in the East Range. An additional population that is suspected to be *L. gaudichaudii* ssp. *koolauensis* occurs on the Kaipapau-Kawainui summit divide on land leased by the Army for Kawailoa Training Area; however, this cannot be confirmed until the individuals flower. The total number of plants was estimated to be fewer than 280 in 1997, thought to be about evenly distributed between the four populations.

Threats

The primary threats to the remaining populations of *L. gaudichaudii* ssp. *koolauensis* are habitat degradation and destruction by feral pigs, competition with the noxious alien plant Koster's curse, trampling by hikers, potential overcollection, landslides, and risk of extinction from naturally occurring events or through reduced reproductive vigor. *L. gaudichaudii* ssp. *koolauensis* is potentially threatened by feral pig predation because the plant is not known to be unpalatable to pigs and they favor plants from the bellflower family for food. It is possible that rats eat the fruit of *L. gaudichaudii* ssp. *koolauensis*, a plant with fleshy stems and fruit that grows in areas where rats occur. The noxious shrub Koster's curse is also a threat to the plant. Overcollection for scientific or horticultural purposes and excessive visits by individuals interested in seeing rare plants in natural settings could seriously damage *L. gaudichaudii* ssp. *koolauensis*, whose populations are close to trails and roads, thus giving easy access to potential collectors.

Erosion, landslides, and rockslides—events caused by natural weathering that often destroy individual plants and damage habitat—potentially threaten some populations of *L. gaudichaudii* ssp. *koolauensis*.

Conservation and Recovery

Seeds of *L. gaudichaudii* ssp. *koolauensis* have been collected by the National Botanical Garden. Enclosures should be constructed around populations of this species to reduce impacts from feral pigs. Subsequent control or removal of pigs from these areas will alleviate their impact on native ecosystems. Where fencing is not feasible due to topography or potential damage to sensitive habitat, snaring should be used as a means of ungulate control.

Contact

U.S. Fish and Wildlife Service
Regional Office, Division of Endangered Species
Eastside Federal Complex
911 N.E. 11th Ave.
Portland, Oregon 97232-4181
(503) 231-6121
http://pacific.fws.gov/

Reference

U.S. Fish and Wildlife Service. 1998. "Recovery Plan for Oahu Plants." U.S. Fish and Wildlife Service, Portland, Oregon. 207 pp., plus appendices.

Lobelia monostachya

No Common Name

Status	Endangered
Listed	October 10, 1996
Family	Campanulaceae (Bellflower)
Description	Prostrate woody shrub with prostrate woody shrub leaves and short pink flowers.
Habitat	Steep, sparsely vegetated cliffs in mesic shrubland.
Threats	Predation by rats, competition with alien plants.
Range	Hawaii

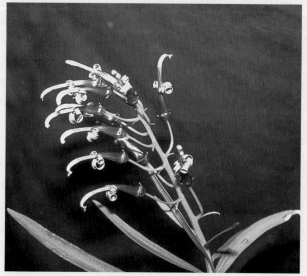

Lobelia monostachya, photograph by John Obata. Reproduced by permission.

Description

Lobelia monostachya, a member of the bellflower family, is a prostrate woody shrub with stems 6-10 in (15.2-25.4 cm) long and leaves 2.8-6 in (7.1-15.2 cm) long and 0.2-0.3 in (0.5-0.75 cm) wide. The flowering stalk is unbranched. The pale magenta corolla is 0.6-0.7 in (1.5-1.8 cm) long and approximately 0.2 in (0.5 cm) wide; the lobes of the corolla overlap spirally. The species is distinguished from others in the genus by the narrow, linear leaves without stalks and the short pink flowers. A new variety of *L. hillebrandii* was described in 1919 from a specimen collected in the 1800s, naming it *L. hillebrandii* var. *monostachya*. This variety was elevated to the species level in 1974 and was transferred to a new genus as *Neowimmeria monostachya*. The species was transferred back to the original genus as *L. monostachya* in 1988.

Habitat

L. monostachya occurs on steep, sparsely vegetated cliffs in mesic shrubland at an elevation of about 950 ft (289.5 m). Associated plant taxa include ahinahina, *Carex meyenii*, moa, and kawelu.

Distribution

L. monostachya, known only from the Koolau Mountains and not seen since its original discovery in the 1800s in Niu Valley and in the 1920s in Manoa Valley, was rediscovered by Joel Lau in 1994 at a previously unknown location in Wailupe Valley on state-owned land. Eight additional plants have since been located in the same area where Lau found his one plant, bringing the 1997 total of known individuals to nine.

Threats

The major threats to *L. monostachya* are predation by rats; competition with the alien plants Christmas berry, Hamakua pamakani, Kalanchoe pinnata (air plant), and molasses grass; and risk of extinction from naturally occurring events or through reduced reproductive vigor due to the low number of individuals in the only known population. *L. mono-stachya* is potentially threatened by feral pig predation because the plant is not known to be unpalatable to pigs, who favor plants from the bellflower family for food. Rat damage has also been observed in the only known population of *L. monostachya*. Christmas berry grows in dense thickets that threaten *L. monostachya*. The mat-forming weed Hamakua pamakani is a threat to this species. Air plant, an herb that occurs mostly in dry to mesic areas on all the main islands except Niihau and Kahoolawe, poses a significant threat to the only population of *L. monostachya*.

Molasses grass also threatens this sole population through the smothering mats it forms and the intense fires it can fuel.

Conservation and Recovery

L. monostachya is being propagated at the Lyon Arboretum. The remaining population needs to be weeded and protected immediately. A management plan to control rats, a potential serious threat to this species, should be developed and implemented. This strategy should include the use of the currently approved Diphacinone bait blocks and then the broader-scale application of rodenticide though aerial dispersal.

Contact

U.S. Fish and Wildlife Service
Regional Office, Division of Endangered Species
Eastside Federal Complex
911 N.E. 11th Ave.
Portland, Oregon 97232-4181
(503) 231-6121
http://pacific.fws.gov/

Reference

U.S. Fish and Wildlife Service. 1998. "Recovery Plan for Oahu Plants." U.S. Fish and Wildlife Service, Portland, Oregon. 207 pp., plus appendices.

Lobelia niihauensis

No Common Name

Status	Endangered
Listed	October 29, 1991
Family	Campanulaceae (Bellflower)
Description	Shrub with terminal rosettes of narrowly elliptic leaves and clusters of magenta flowers.
Habitat	Exposed moist to dry cliffs.
Threats	Feral pigs and goats, alien plant species.
Range	Hawaii

Lobelia niihauensis, photograph by Derral Herbst. National Tropical Botanical Garden. Reproduced by permission.

Description

Lobelia niihauensis is a low, branched shrub of the bellflower family in which each branch ends with a rosette of narrowly elliptic leaves, 3-6 in (7.6-15.2 cm) long. Clusters of magenta flowers appear at the ends of the branches. The fruits are egg-shaped capsules that contain numerous brown seeds. It flowers in late summer and early fall. Fruits mature one month to six weeks later. Plants are long-lived and are known to live as long as 20 years.

The species has been known by a variety of scientific names: *L. niihauensis* var. *forbesii, L. niihauensis* var. *meridiana, L. tortuosa, L. tortuosa* var. *glabrata, L. tortuosa* var. *haupuensis,* and *L. tortuosa* var. *intermedia.*

Habitat

L. niihauensis grows on exposed moist to dry cliffs at elevations between 330 and 2,720 ft (100.5 and 829.1 m) in the Waianae Mountain Range on the western side of the island of Oahu and on the western portion of the island of Kauai. Associated plants include kawelu, kookoolau, *Plectranthus parviflorus*, *Lipochaeta* sp. (nehe), and ahinahina.

Distribution

L. niihauensis, first described in 1931 from a specimen collected on the island of Niihau in 1912, also had historical occurrences on Oahu and western Kauai. The species was known on Oahu from Uluhulu Gulch to Nanakuli Valley in the Walanae mountains. On Kauai, it occurred from Limahnli Valley to near the Hanapepe River, as well as in the east at Nounou Mountain and the Haupu Range. *L. niihauensis* is now known to be extant only on these two islands. On Oahu, this species remains on Kamaileunu Ridge; Mt. Kaala; Kamaileunu; six locations in Waianae Kai; three locations in Makua Military Reservation, Nanakuli, and South Mohiakea Gulch; and six locations in Lualualei Naval Magazine. The 19 Oahu populations growing on federal, state, county, and city lands had a 1997 total of 718-753 individuals. This species is found on Kauai on state and private land in Waimea Canyon, on Polihale Ridge, along the Na Pali Coast, and in the Haupu Range. The 14 Kauai populations had a 1997 total of 960-2900 individuals. The 33 current populations on Oahu and Kauai combined totaled approximately 1,678-3,653 plants in 1997. The populations on Oahu are located within an area of about 85 by 10 mi (136.8 by 16.1 km); the western population on Kauai occurs in an are of 8 by 10 mi (12.8 by 16.1 km) and is about 23 mi (37 km) from the eastern Kauai population. While some populations are not well documented, at least 14 Oahu populations and four Kauai populations contain less than 13 individuals.

Threats

The main threats to *L. niihauensis* are habitat degradation and predation by feral goats, rats, and slugs; fire; military activities; and competition from the alien plant species Christmasberry, koa haole, daisy fleabane, Hamakua pamakani, and molasses grass.

Christmasberry, a tree introduced to Hawaii before 1911, forms dense thickets and may also release chemicals that inhibit the growth of other species. The koa haole tree is able to make its own nitrogen, enabling it to compete with native species adapted

David H. Lorence

to low nitrogen soils. Molasses grass grows in dense mats that smother native vegetation.

In addition, some populations of *L. niihauensis* on Oahu are located near the U.S. Army's Makua Military Reservation and Schofield Barracks. Within a 14-month period from 1989 to 1990, 10 fires resulted from weapons practice on the reservation. In order to minimize damage from fires, the army has constructed firebreaks between the target areas and the surrounding forest.

Conservation and Recovery

The army has adopted a fire management plan that includes realigning targets and establishing firebreaks. Implementation of the plan may aid in protecting this species from fire. Completion of a boundary fence on the south and southeast perimeter of Makua Valley and continued goat control efforts, though limited, should help to protect the Makua-Keaau ridge plant from further goat damage.

This species is being propagated at the Lyon Arboretum and the National Tropical Botanic Garden.

Contacts

U. S. Fish and Wildlife Service
Regional Office, Division of Endangered Species
Eastside Federal Complex
911 N. E. 11th Ave.
Portland, Oregon 97232-4181
Telephone: (503) 231-6121
http://pacific.fws.gov/

Senior Resident Agent Office
U.S. Fish and Wildlife Service
300 Ala Moana Boulevard, Room 7-235
P.O. Box 50223
Honolulu, Hawaii 96850-5000
Telephone: (808) 541-2681
Fax: (808) 541-3062

Reference

Cuddihy, L. W. and C. P. Stone. 1990. *Alteration of Native Hawaiian Vegetation: Effects of Humans, Their Activities and Introductions.* Cooperative National Park Resources Study Unit, University of Hawaii Press, Honolulu.

Lobelia oahuensis

No Common Name

Status	Endangered
Listed	March 28, 1994
Family	Campanulaceae (Bellflower)
Description	Stout, erect, unbranched shrub, with elliptic leaves and 50-200 flowers.
Habitat	Steep slopes along ridgetops; on summit cliffs in cloud-swept wet forests frequently exposed to heavy wind and rain.
Threats	Competition from alien plants.
Range	Hawaii

Lobelia oahuensis, photograph by John Obata. Reproduced by permission.

Description

Lobelia oahuensis is a stout, erect, and unbranched shrub in the bellflower family that reaches a height of 3-10 ft (0.9-3.0 m). The elliptic leaves, 16-24 in (40.6-60.9 cm) long and 1.6-2.4 in (4.1-6.1 cm) wide, are typically stalkless and form a very dense rosette at the end of the stem. The upper surface of the leaves is hairless and the lower surface is covered with rather coarse, grayish or greenish hairs. The inflorescence is branched three to five times from its base, with each erect spike 3-5 ft (0.9-1.5 m) tall and comprised of 50-200 flowers. Each flower measures

1.7-1.8 in (4.3-4.6 cm) long and about 0.2 in (0.5 cm) wide, with a 1.2-in (3.1-cm) long bract just below it. The linear calyx lobes are about 0.6 in (1.5 cm) long and 0.1 in (0.3 cm) wide. The fruits, 0.4-0.7 in (1.1 cm-1.8 cm) long and about 0.4 in (1.1 cm) wide, are hairy, oval capsules that contain numerous brownish seeds. This species was observed in flower during November 1991.

L. oahuensis differs from other members of the genus in having erect stems 3-10 ft (0.9-3.0 m) long, dense rosettes of leaves at the end of stems, lower leaf surfaces covered with coarse grayish or greenish hairs, and flowers 1.7-1.8 in (4.3-4.6 cm) long.

Habitat

L. oahuensis grows on tree trunks on summit cliffs in 'ohi'a-dominated, cloud-swept wet forests or in areas of low shrub cover that are frequently exposed to heavy wind and rain. The 11 populations occur at elevations between 2,800 and 3,500 ft (853.4 and 1,066.8 m). The vegetation in those areas usually includes kanawao, uluhe, 'uki, hame, and kopiko.

Distribution

L. oahuensis had historical occurrences on Oahu from Kahana Ridge, Kipapa Gulch, and the southeastern Koolau Mountains. The species currently grows on steep slopes along Koolau Mountain ridgetops from Waikane and Halawa to Mount Olympus and the summit ridges above Kuliouou and Wainmanalo, a distance of about 17 mi (27.4 km). A single mature individual was discovered in 1995 on the boundary between state land and Schofield Barracks Military Reservation, extending the distribution of this species to the Waianae Mountain Range of Oahu.

The 11 extant populations are located on private and state land and in areas on the boundary of private, state, and Federal land. These occurrences totaled about 110 individuals in 1996. Except for two populations that contained between 30-40 individuals, the remaining nine populations at Mount Olympus, Kohahuanui, Puu o Kona, Aiea-Halawa Valley summit ridge, Kaneohe-Moanalua summit, Kapakahi-Waimanalo summit ridge, Puu Kalerm, Eleao, and Moanalua all contained less than 10 individuals.

Threats

The primary threat to *L. oahuensis* is the noxious alien plant Koster's curse because it effectively competes for water, space, light and nutrients. Additional threats are habitat degradation and predation by feral pigs, predation by rats and slugs, and a risk of extinction from random natural events and reduced reproductive vigor due to the small number of remaining individuals.

Conservation and Recovery

Seeds of *L. oahuensis* have been collected by the National Botanic Garden. It is currently being propagated by the Lyon Arboretum.

Enclosures should be constructed, where practicable, around the known populations of *L. oahuensis* to reduce impacts from feral pigs. Subsequent control or removal of pigs from these areas will alleviate their impact on native ecosystems. Specific efforts should be made, where feasible, to immediately fence, weed, and otherwise protect the nine populations noted above that have only a few remaining individuals. A commitment should be developed for long-term stewardship and conservation of these areas once they have been enclosed. Where fencing is not deemed feasible due to topography or potential damage to sensitive summit habitat, judicious use of snaring should be used as a means of ungulate control.

Populations of *L. oahuensis* are seriously threatened by rat predation. A management plan to control rats should be developed and implemented. This should include the use of the currently approved diphacinone bait blocks and ultimately a more broad-scale method such as aerial dispersal of rodenticide.

Contacts

U. S. Fish and Wildlife Service
Regional Office, Division of Endangered Species
Eastside Federal Complex
911 N. E. 11th Ave.
Portland, Oregon 97232-4181
Telephone: (503) 231-6121
http://pacific.fws.gov/

Senior Resident Agent Office
U.S. Fish and Wildlife Service
300 Ala Moana Boulevard, Room 7-235
P.O. Box 50223
Honolulu, Hawaii 96850-5000
Telephone: (808) 541-2681
Fax: (808) 541-3062

Reference

U.S. Fish and Wildlife Service. 28 March 1994. "Endangered and Threatened Wildlife and Plants: Endangered Status for 11 Plant Species from the Koolau Mountain Range, Island of Oahu, HI." *Federal Register* 59 (59): 14482-14492.

Trematolobelia singularis

No Common Name

Status	Endangered
Listed	October 10, 1996
Family	Campanulaceae (Bellflower)
Description	Unbranched shrub with long and narrow leaves and violet petals.
Habitat	Steep, windswept cliff faces or slopes in 'ohi'a-uluhe lowland wet shrubland.
Threats	Habitat degradation by feral pigs, potential predation by rats, competition with the aggressive alien plant Koster's curse.
Range	Hawaii

Trematolobelia singularis, photograph by Steve Perlman. Reproduced by permission.

Description

Trematolobelia singularis, an unbranched shrub of the bellflower family, has stems 2-5 ft (0.6-1.5 m) long. The long and narrow leaves are 4-7 in (10- 18 cm) long and 0.4-0.7 in (1.0-1.8 cm) wide. The unbranched, erect flowering stalk is 8-16.5 in (20-42 cm) long. The violet petals are about 0.2 in (0.5 cm) long and collectively form a three-lobed tube; the largest lobe is curved downward, while the other two are bent backward, giving the appearance of two lips. The capsules are almost round and contain numerous small, wind-dispersed seeds. This species differs from others of this genus by the unbranched, erect flowering stalk.

Harold St. John described *Trematolobelia singularis* in 1982 from a specimen collected by John Obata in 1974. This species has been maintained in the most recent treatment of this endemic Hawaiian genus. The specific epithet refers to the solitary flowering stalk.

Habitat

T. singularis usually grows at elevations from 2,300-3,150 ft (701-960 m) on steep, windswept cliff faces or slopes in 'ohi'a-uluhe lowland wet shrubland. Associated plant species include 'akia, hapu'u, kanawao, and na'ena'e pua melemele.

Distribution

T. singularis has been reported only from the southern Koolau Mountains. Approximately 165 plants were known in 1997 from three populations found on private, City and County of Honolulu, state, and Federal lands—50 plants occurred at Moanalua-Tripler Ridge summit to Puu Keahiakahoe, 40 at Konahuanui, and 75 at Puu Lanipo.

Threats

The most serious threats to *T. singularis* are habitat degradation by feral pigs, potential predation by rats, competition with the aggressive alien plant Koster's curse, and risk of extinction from random natural events and through reduced reproductive vigor due to the small number of extant populations.

T. singularis is potentially threatened by feral pig predation because the plant is not known to be unpalatable to pigs and they favor plants from the bellflower family for food. It is possible that rats eat the fruit of *T. singularis*.

The noxious shrub Koster's curse is also a threat to this species.

Conservation and Recovery

The known habitat of the *T. singularis* is on land owned by the City and County of Honolulu, the State of Hawaii, and the Federal Government (Omega Coast Guard Station). These publicly owned habitats should be protected from degrading influences, and managed to reduce the impacts of introduced mammalian herbivores and alien plants. Some habitat is on private land, and should also be protected. This could be done by acquiring the habitat and establishing ecological reserves, or by negotiating conservation easements with the landowners. The populations of the *T. singularis* should be monitored, and studies made of its habitat needs.

Contacts

U. S. Fish and Wildlife Service
Pacific Islands Ecoregion
300 Ala Moana Boulevard, Room 3-122
P.O. Box 5088
Honolulu, Hawaii 96850.
Telephone: (808) 541-3441
Fax: (808) 541-3470

U. S. Fish and Wildlife Service
Regional Office, Division of Endangered Species
Eastside Federal Building
911 N. E. 11th Ave.
Portland, Oregon 97232-4181
(503) 231-6121
http://pacific.fws.gov/

Reference

U.S. Fish and Wildlife Service. 10 October 1996. "Endangered and Threatened Wildlife and Plants; Determination of Endangered Status for Twenty-five Plant Species From the Island of Oahu, Hawaii." *Federal Register* 61(198): 53089-53108.